Books by James Thomas Flexner

American Painting

FIRST FLOWERS OF OUR WILDERNESS

THE LIGHT OF DISTANT SKIES

THAT WILDER IMAGE

THE POCKET HISTORY OF AMERICAN PAINTING
(also published as *A Short History of American Painting*)

History and Biography

DOCTORS ON HORSEBACK
Pioneers of American Medicine

STEAMBOATS COME TRUE
(also published as *Inventors in Action*)

THE TRAITOR AND THE SPY
(also published as *The Benedict Arnold Case*)

MOHAWK BARONET
Sir William Johnson of New York

WILLIAM HENRY WELCH AND THE HEROIC AGE OF AMERICAN MEDICINE
(with Simon Flexner)

AMERICA'S OLD MASTERS

JOHN SINGLETON COPLEY

GILBERT STUART

THE WORLD OF WINSLOW HOMER
(with the editors of Time-Life Books)

GEORGE WASHINGTON

I. The Forge of Experience (*1732–1775*)
II. In the American Revolution (*1775–1783*)

GEORGE
WASHINGTON

In the American Revolution

(1775–1783)

G. Washington.

George Washington, portrait engraved in Paris by Prévost, after a drawing by Pierre Eugène du Simitière. Courtesy of the New-York Historical Society.

GEORGE WASHINGTON

in the *American Revolution*

(*1775-1783*)

by JAMES THOMAS FLEXNER

with maps and photographs

LITTLE, BROWN AND COMPANY · BOSTON · TORONTO

COPYRIGHT © 1967, 1968 by JAMES THOMAS FLEXNER
ALL RIGHTS RESERVED. NO PART OF THIS BOOK MAY BE REPRO-
DUCED IN ANY FORM OR BY ANY ELECTRONIC OR MECHANICAL
MEANS INCLUDING INFORMATION STORAGE AND RETRIEVAL SYS-
TEMS WITHOUT PERMISSION IN WRITING FROM THE PUBLISHER,
EXCEPT BY A REVIEWER WHO MAY QUOTE BRIEF PASSAGES IN A
REVIEW.

LIBRARY OF CONGRESS CATALOG CARD NO. 68–11529

THIRD PRINTING

Portions of this book have appeared in slightly different form
in *American Heritage*.

*Published simultaneously in Canada
by Little, Brown & Company (Canada) Limited*

PRINTED IN THE UNITED STATES OF AMERICA

To the memory of my mother
HELEN THOMAS FLEXNER
My first and best teacher of
writing

If historiographers should be hardy enough to fill the page of history with the advantages that have been gained with unequal numbers (on the part of America) in the course of this contest, and attempt to relate the distressing circumstances under which they have been obtained, it is more than probable that posterity will bestow on their labors the epithet and marks of fiction; for it will not be believed that such a force as Great Britain has employed for eight years in this country could be baffled, in their plan of subjugating it, by numbers infinitely less, composed of men oftentimes half starved, always in rags, without pay, and experiencing, at times, every species of distress which human nature is capable of undergoing.

—GEORGE WASHINGTON TO NATHANAEL GREENE
February 6, 1783

Contents

[xi]

CONTENTS

CONTENTS

List of Illustrations

List of Maps

MAPS BY SAMUEL H. BRYANT

[xvii]

GEORGE
WASHINGTON

In the American Revolution

(1775–1783)

Introduction

T HIS volume is dedicated to narrating the wartime deeds and searching out the wartime emotions of the man who came from civilian life during the American Revolution to lead the Continental Army and also the whole nation down the vexed and bloody road to independence. Few stories out of the American past have so often been retold, but that fact has, in itself, augmented the need for a fresh retelling. The minds of generations tend to drone along until an oft-repeated tale becomes a self-perpetuating entity that parallels but hardly touches the truth that first gave it birth. As Biblical scholars had to exorcise centuries of exegesis and saints' tales, so it is necessary, in the pursuit of the true George Washington, to ignore legend and make a new start based on examination of original evidence.

The effort has here been made to achieve a biography not only in the scholarly but in the literary meaning of the term. This is not a history of the period arranged for convenience around George Washington. It is an account of the adventures and emotions of an individual man: how he had a great trust thrust upon him; how he handled himself and what changes experience, grievous or gay, made in his knowledge and his skills and his character, and what effect all this had on the history of the United States and, indeed, the world.

Once it was considered the duty of Washington's biographers to suppress all aspects of his character which someone might find unsuitable, and to fabricate incidents (like the lie about the cherry tree and the young Washington's inability to tell a lie) that were supposed to inculcate, particularly in infantile minds, virtue. Thus one of the greatest men that ever lived was edited down into a prig, frozen into a statue.

The traditional image of Washington presiding, during the Revolution, over a desperate cause with all the calm control of a marble statue is less accurate than would be an opposite vision: Washington plunging wildly from side to side, like an untamed bull in a restricted pen, trying to break down the walls that hem him tight.

The record shows us the Washington concerning whom an intimate friend (Gouverneur Morris) wrote that few men "had to contend with passions so

[3]

violent." His path through the Revolution was studded with mistakes (from which he learned), indiscretions (which he repeated when the strain became again too strong), personal hatreds (few but powerful), boredom, resentments, lies, exaggerated complaints, and a great deal of personal misery. "The poor general," his wife summarized, "was so unhappy that it distressed me exceedingly."

Washington also manifested dedication, idealism, efficiency, sober thought, bursts of genius, and love. It is questionable whether in all American history another man has ever been so greatly loved by his compatriots as was George Washington. And he loved in return, not only the great abstractions—his army, his nation, justice, mankind as a whole— but the individual humans Fate strewed in his path. He wept unashamedly at his own dinner table when he spoke of his affection for the Marquis de Lafayette.[1]

Spanning a major gulf between the past and what was then the un-explored future, Washington could not resemble a block of granite: like a bridge, he was a balance of opposing stresses. Personally gentle, uneasy about witnessing bloodshed except in the excitement of battle, he fought year after year a bloody war. A civilian drawn by crisis from his fields, never truly a soldier, he outlasted three British commanders in chief and defeated them all. A political moderate who believed in complete freedom of intellect, he argued for tolerance as he led a revolution. Washington was an agrarian gentleman, rooted in a society more ancient than that of the New England traders who sometimes regarded him as a political anachronism. However, he proved, at what might well have been the most crucial moment in the entire history of the United States, a defender of republican principles such as the world has rarely if ever otherwise known.

Throughout that era of social upheavals which the American Revolution began and which still continues today, national leader after national leader has descried, dividing before him, alternate roads, one toward more democracy, the other to the establishment of order through the exertion of personal power. From the road to absolutism, there rises the dust of marching crowds: newly crowned kings and emperors, perpetual presidents, Duces, Fuehrers, generalissimos, protectors, party secretaries, dictators of the proletariat: they advance to band music over the prostrate body of political freedom with their bodyguards, their legions, their storm troopers, their people's militia. On the other road we find a solitary figure, in a rusty blue and buff uniform without a single medal to sparkle on his breast, "hastening [as Washington himself exulted] with unspeakable delight to the still and placid walks of domestic life."[2]

Historical imperatives did not force Washington thus to retire or even to pursue the republican way. As the war with England abated and the central government seemed about to fall apart, the horses of absolutism—military coercion of the civil government—were saddled and mounted by leaders as important as Robert Morris and Alexander Hamilton. Had Washington been willing to leap onto the lead horse, which had been subtly prepared for him, America would inevitably have thundered down the road to a new, more bloody civil war. The end might have been a monarchy or a dictatorship or, more probably, a scramble of mutually hostile separate nations—like those of Europe—warring with each other where the United States came to be.

Almost every other world leader when faced with such temptation has succumbed. Why did George Washington stay his hand?

I

The Anvil of Necessity

CHAPTER

1

Dark Dawn of Adventure

ON June 15, 1775, George Washington, Esq., was elected, by the Second Continental Congress meeting in Philadelphia, "to command all the Continental forces raised or to be raised for the defense of American liberty."[1] Members of the Congress thereupon tendered the General a dinner at Peg Mullen's Beefsteak House. Washington saw across the table the familiar face of that lanky young redhead from his native Virginia, Thomas Jefferson, and also the jowled, aged features of Benjamin Franklin, whom he admired but hardly knew. There were other congressmen: Pennsylvania's radical physician Benjamin Rush, with his determined squirrel's face; plump John Langdon from far-off New Hampshire where Washington had never been, and so on to the number of about a score.

When the steaks had been eaten and the table cleared, when the wine bottle had made its circuit, the first toast was, "The Commander in Chief of the American armies!"

"General Washington," so Rush remembered, "rose from his seat and with some confusion thanked the company for the honor they did him. The whole company instantly rose and drank the toast standing. This scene, so unexpected, was a solemn one. A silence followed it, as if every heart was penetrated with the awful but great events which were to follow the use of the sword of liberty which had just been put into General Washington's hands by the unanimous voice of his country."[2]

Rush remembered that Washington responded to the toast with "some confusion." These were, for the new military leader, unhappy days. "I feel," he told the Congress, "great distress." Tears stood in his eyes when he confided to his fellow Virginian Patrick Henry, "Remember, Mr. Henry, what I now tell you. From the day I enter upon the command of the American armies, I date my fall and the ruin of my reputation." He was haunted by a "conviction of my own incapacity and want of experience in the conduct of so momentous a concern."[3]

[9]

Washington postponed notifying his wife, lest she be too upset, and when he finally found the heart to tell her, he begged her not to add to his perturbation with her own. He had done everything in his power, he assured her, to avoid the appointment. "But as it has been a kind of destiny that has thrown me upon this service, I shall hope that my undertaking it is designed to answer some good purpose."[4]

If there ever was a war which the Commander in Chief had wished could have been avoided, this was it. He had retired from his previous service—five years of wilderness fighting during the French and Indian War—with such a distaste for the military life that for the next fifteen years he had not even drilled a militia company.

Although he had early concluded that the relationship between England and her American colonies could not continue forever as overlordship and dependence, Washington had hoped that the matter could be left "to posterity to determine." He foresaw eventual drastic increases in home rule. However, the authorities in London had an exactly opposite view of how the future should go. Deciding that America should pay what they assessed as her fair share of the general expenses of the empire, they attempted to establish a hitherto unenforced principle: the collection on American soil of taxes voted in London.[5]

Since the eighteenth century regarded the power to tax as the power to govern, this encroachment on what Washington called "the liberty which has been derived from our ancestors" seemed to threaten America with "slavery." However, being (as he wrote) "unsuspicious of design and then unwilling to enter into disputes with the mother country," Washington did his best to conclude that the seeming tyranny was a random result of political confusion and incompetence in England. He only sprang into action when successive British acts convinced him that America was being subjected to "a regular plan at the expense of law and justice to overthrow our constitutional rights and liberties."[6]

The controversy had in 1774 reached such a point that the various colonies overcame all precedent and met together. As a representative from Virginia to the First Continental Congress, Washington voted with the majority for a boycott of British trade to go into effect if the oppressive laws were not, as was humbly requested, repealed—and also for an announcement that any attempt by the British to use force would be repelled by force. This concluded, Washington went home.

He was at Mount Vernon when the actual fighting began. The English Parliament had voted various punitive acts against the colony of Massachusetts and had enlarged the garrison of regulars in Boston. The patriots had countered by establishing an arsenal in the nearby town of Concord. On the night of April 18, 1775, the British command sent out a force to capture the arsenal. The result was a burst of true guerrilla warfare. Before the British could fight their way back to Boston past armed farmers crouching behind stone walls, they lost in killed, wounded, and missing over two hundred and fifty out of an expeditionary force of eight hundred. The colonial loss was under one hundred.

A farmers' army quickly encircled Boston to make sure that the British would not march out again. Although this force was recruited primarily from Massachusetts, nearby Connecticut, Rhode Island, and New Hampshire had sent men. New England was fighting, but that was all: only four colonies out of the continental thirteen. However, twelve of the thirteen (Georgia had not yet appeared) were represented at the Second Continental Congress when it met in Philadelphia during May.

Washington was again to be a member of the Virginia delegation. As he got ready to leave his plantation, Mount Vernon, he made no preparations for a prolonged absence. He did, it is true, pack, to wear at the legislative sessions, the buff and blue uniform he had himself designed for the militia of Fairfax County, but—in his conscious mind at least—he intended this merely as a testimony that Virginia was ready (if necessary) to fight. He assumed that if the hostilities expanded he would return home to command (as he had done in the French and Indian War) Virginia's local forces.

Washington found little martial eagerness when he arrived at Philadelphia. In the Congress, at the taverns, and by the firesides, the reigning hope was that "the best of kings," George III, would protect his American colonies from encroachments by Parliament. Although Washington was one of the less sanguine, afraid that only the use of force could make the British see reason, even he could not bring himself to think of the invaders as the army of the English nation. Surely, they represented only the Tory party that was at that moment in power! Like his colleagues, he referred to the occupiers of Boston as the "ministerial army."[7]

Congressional sessions pounded into Washington's blood day after day the realization (it was to be very useful to him later) that this was no such legislature as the Virginia House of Burgesses where he had sat for almost twenty years. It was a meeting ground for separate political entities, whose only official connection was their weakening allegiance to a common king. The various colonies had not only a long history of local rivalry, but divergent economic needs and, indeed, widely contrasting climates. South Carolina and New Hampshire were half again as far apart as England and Italy.

Under these circumstances, a majority vote of the Congress could not commit the minority. Decisions would only stick if all the colonies could be brought to unanimous agreement. This meant that Congress could not lead events. At best, it could only influence reactions to what had already taken place.

War had already taken place in Massachusetts—new-dug graves in bloody soil. The New England delegates pointed out that they could not by themselves for long hold off the might of Great Britain, and it was clear that, should New England be defeated, yokes would be fastened on all the colonies. Sooner or later the Congress would have to bring them all behind New England's army—that is, unless the continent dawdled until it was too late.

New England complained that Congress was moving like molasses, yet sentiment did advance, although with anguished reluctance. An obvious question was: If Congress adopted the army already in New England, who would command it?

On the floor of the house, George Washington sat quietly, rarely rising to speak. His uniform cried out like a bugle call in contrast to the surrounding civilian clothes, but there was nothing flamboyant about the man. He was known to have been slow in accepting the conclusion that armed resistance was necessary.[8]

When, on adjournment, the members rose, Washington stood almost a head taller than those around him. Although his shoulders and chest were narrow, he gave the impression of great physical power. His bones were all large: big hands and feet, heavy thighs, a massive, strongly sculptured head. The painter Gilbert Stuart was to find "features in his face totally different from what I had observed in any other human being. The sockets of the eyes, for instance, were larger than what I had ever met before, and the upper part of the nose broader." He was of a blond cast: his complexion sunburned but without much color, his face slightly marked by smallpox, his eyes gray-blue, his hair a reddish-brown. When he moved, it was, for a heavy man, with surprising grace. He walked out of the congressional chamber with a lithe stride developed on wilderness trails.[9]

If, sometime later, he came riding down a street, the pedestrians were impelled to pause and watch him out of sight. At a time when everyone knew about horses, Washington was, so wrote Jefferson, "the best horseman of his age and the most graceful figure that could be seen on horseback."[10]

Who was this George Washington? No impoverished adventurer—so the word went round—who might be fomenting trouble to put his hands in other people's pockets, but (here rumor greatly exaggerated) the richest man in Virginia. He had had much military experience during the French and Indian War, and was said (again with exaggeration) to have saved, while the British regulars blundered, what was left of Braddock's army after that general's stupendous defeat by the Indian tribes.[11]

The delegates got to know Washington over tavern tables. He was still quiet but always affable, ready to propose a toast, beat time to a song, laugh at a joke, or amuse the company with some shrewd, humorous observation on the way of the world. When serious matters were discussed, he would be grave, think hard, and say little; but sometimes in the end sum up all. Indignation could flood his rugged countenance, and then his eyes, which were not lively in repose, would flash and he would make big gestures with his huge hands. His character seemed a combination of strength and amiability, and he practiced always that courtesy that comes from imaginative sympathy with other men's feelings. Yet those who were long in his presence sensed in his nature a hidden violence that could be attuned to the brutal necessities of war. As Stuart put it, "All his features were indicative of the strongest passions, yet, like Socrates, his judgment and self-command made him appear of a different cast in the eyes of the world. . . . Had he been born in the forests . . . he would have been the fiercest man among the savage tribes."[12]

Should George Washington prove the right man to lead a combined American army, Providence had certainly rooted him in the ideal place. The delegates from elsewhere were afraid that a New England–dominated military force would, after expelling the British, give law to the rest of America; they dreaded substituting King Stork for King Log. To achieve general agreement, the commander appointed by Congress clearly should be from outside New England. The most powerful colony outside New England was Virginia, and Washington was Virginia's favorite officer.[13]

As the direction of congressional thinking became clear, Washington reacted with dismay. He told everyone who hinted the matter to him that the command was "too boundless for my abilities and far, very far beyond my experience." This was annoying when the congressmen so needed reassurance. Yet an America devoid of experts was used to employing semi-amateurs. The conclusion was drawn that in Washington's diffidence there lay safety: he could be counted on to take the best advice and not sacrifice the army to his personal pride or use it to further his personal ambitions.[14]

And so, little by little, in the minds of delegate after delegate the thought of Washington made the horrors looming ahead seem less dark. This development did not escape the short, plump leader of the Massachusetts delegation, that pouter pigeon of a shrewd politician, John Adams. He had read enough history to recognize the dangers to a state of a magnetic leader and he trusted no man not to gobble in all power within reach—but Adams felt himself clever enough to use Washington now and attend to the dangers later. He resolved—or so he remembered—to sweeten for Congress the bitter pill of warfare by overlaying it with the personality of Washington.[15]

The Congress did not specifically vote to carry the continent into war. The decision was sidled into by electing George Washington to assume, in Congress's name, the command of the forces already in battle and what further forces might be raised. The Congress then found the fortitude to resolve that "they will maintain and assist him, and adhere to him, the said

George Washington, Esq., with their lives and fortunes in the same cause."[16] From the moment of election Washington was thus more than a general: he was the standard about which the cause was supposed to rally.

The army Washington was to command did not represent any existing nation. It only represented a loose alliance established by delegates chosen, most of them illegally, from separate colonies in opposition to the legal government of all and in defiance of one of the greatest military powers in the world.

Congress defined Washington's task as "the maintenance and preservation of American liberty." Washington was at that time profoundly convinced, as he was to assert again and again in later years, that this did not imply independence from the British Crown. (The Declaration of Independence lay more than a year in the future.) The object was a "loyal protest" that would make the British overlords return to reason.[17] Beyond that, the cause was shrouded in a conciliatory vagueness that had contributed to the agreement on violent measures. Men of different interests and experience could each make his own interpretation of how far military opposition to Parliament would be carried and what concessions would be required before the sword was again sheathed. Washington does not seem to have thought out the matter (which would in any case much depend on decisions made in London) beyond a general conviction that there was now no turning back until the direction of British policy had been reversed. He clung to the hope—however irrational it may have seemed to him at times— which he wrote to his wife that somehow the issues would be settled in time to let him return to Mount Vernon in the autumn.[18]

Where minds were in so fluid a state, the possibility existed that the very Congress which had commissioned Washington might not persevere. Washington might find himself deserted as he stood on a battlefield holding the bloody sword he had been induced to draw against his king. The penalty then in force for treason was thus described by a sentencing judge to some Irish rebels: "You are to be drawn on hurdles to the place of execution, where you are to be hanged by the neck, but not until you are dead; for, while you are still living your bodies are to be taken down, your bowels torn out and burned before your faces, your heads then cut off, and your bodies divided each into four quarters, and your heads and quarters to be then at the King's disposal; and may the Almighty God have mercy on your souls."* [19]

---

* As it turned out, the penalties for treason were not applied to the American rebel leaders. They were, if captured, merely imprisoned. However, this concession to the segment of British public opinion which sympathized with the Americans was not foreseeable. The British Tory press exulted in the vision of severed American "noddles" decorating "the naked poles on Temple Bar." Washington was to recall that he and his companions had fought "with halters about their necks."[20]

Washington's uniform: dark blue coat with buff facings and plain gilt buttons. No military insignia. Waistcoat, buff with gilt buttons; knee breeches, buff. Courtesy of The Smithsonian Institution.

In his acceptance speech before Congress and the world, Washington made no promises of victory: "Lest some unlucky event should happen, unfavorable to my reputation, I beg it may be remembered, by every gentleman in the room, that I, this day, declare with the utmost sincerity, I do not think myself equal to the command I am honored with."[21]

"It was known," Washington was to state in retrospect, "that . . . the expense in comparison with our circumstances as Colonists must be enormous, the struggle protracted, dubious, and severe. It was known that the resources of Britain were, in a manner, inexhaustible, that her fleets covered the ocean, and that her troops had harvested laurels in every quarter of the globe. Not then organized as a nation, or known as a people upon the earth, we had no preparation. Money, the nerve of war, was wanting. The sword was to be forged on the anvil of necessity."[22]

Washington's previous military experience had taught him that if a command were not accompanied with the means that would enable success, it harvested not honor but abuse. And even the New England delegates did not claim that the force they were handing over to him was an effective army. The commission Congress prepared for their new commander urged him primarily to establish those rudiments of military organization: obedience to orders and strict discipline. The army was admittedly "but little more than a mere chaos."[23]

Although no one knew for sure (the militiamen came uncounted and left as they pleased) there were said to be some eighteen thousand to twenty thousand New Englanders under arms. This was at least fifteen times larger than any force Washington had previously commanded. All his military experience had been on the frontier, where he had had little need for the techniques which hundreds of years of experience on thousands of battle-fields had established as the bases of conventional military science. Yet, having served on two campaigns under well-trained British generals, he had some realization of how important such skills could be in the type of warfare in which he would now have to engage.

Most basic of all Washington's worries was an introspective one: did he actually possess any unusual gifts in the military line? How could he forget that, during the French and Indian War, in the kind of combat for which he was most trained, he had been glorious, if at all, primarily in defeat? Then, the British regulars had, by capturing Fort Duquesne in a manner that had seemed to him impossible, succeeded where he had failed. Now those British regulars were to be his opponents.

To his brother-in-law, Burwell Bassett, Washington wrote, "I can answer but for three things: a firm belief in the justice of our cause, close attention in the prosecution of it, and the strictest integrity. If these cannot supply the place of ability and experience, the cause will suffer, and more than probable my character along with it."[24]

2

A Desperate Search for Advisers

A S he prepared to assume the command he considered so far beyond his abilities, Washington reached out eagerly for all the help he could find. He saw that his commission stated that he was to obey the directions given him by Congress or a committee of Congress. Where another officer might have trembled at being subjected to a committee of legislators, Washington welcomed the sharing of responsibility.[1]

Congress had decided to elect four major generals. The first in order of seniority and thus the second in command was chosen to placate those New Englanders who resented that a "foreigner" from faraway Virginia had been put in charge of their army. Massachusetts was complimented by the appointment of the existing commander outside Boston, Artemas Ward.

Ward had fought one campaign during the French and Indian War which damaged his health. He had turned to storekeeping and the political manipulation that kept him powerful at militia musters. His bearing was more aldermanic than martial; even in Massachusetts the abler patriots doubted his military competence.[2]

By far the most experienced available officer was the transplanted Englishman Charles Lee. Commissioned in the British regular army as a boy, Lee had come to America with his regiment to fight in the French and Indian War—it was then he met Washington—and had gone on to serve with distinction on the Iberian Peninsula. Peace annoyed him: he adventured to Poland, where he became a major general, and accompanied a Russian army against the Turks. Back home in England, Lee wrote radical political pamphlets and insulted George III to his royal face.

In 1773, Lee settled in Virginia. Now, he supported the patriot cause with voice and pen. On military matters, he was particularly vocal; among his more enchanted listeners had been George Washington, who enjoyed his company, lent him money, and put him up at Mount Vernon. It was assumed in England that if true hostilities broke out, Lee would be given the American command. And most Americans in the know would, from a purely military point of view, have preferred him to Washington. However, there was always the possibility that, as an Englishman, Lee might waver in his allegiance to the American cause; and his undoubted brilliance was mingled with extreme eccentricity. He was lank as a scarecrow and almost as ragged. Unwashed and foul-mouthed, boastful but in perpetual need of reassurance, preferring dogs to people, Lee had—although Washington found him amusing—a discouraging resemblance to a wayward, exhibitionist child.[3]

Many hesitated about ranking one so strange even as third in command, but Washington, who considered Lee his warm friend, felt he needed the guidance of so experienced a professional. He said this to Congress and he undoubtedly said it to Lee. For his part, Lee stated that he should "at least" have considered being ranked below Ward the "greatest indignity," which indicated his belief that he had been generous in permitting himself to be subordinate to Washington. Before he accepted his commission, he made a committee of Congress "wait on" him and agree to reimburse any financial losses he might sustain.[4]

The remaining two major general's commissions were given for geographic reasons to Philip Schuyler of New York and Israel Putnam of Connecticut, officers whose experience had been, like Washington's, gained in frontier fighting during the French and Indian War.

Yearning for more professional help, Washington spoke to members of Congress about Horatio Gates. The son of a duke's housekeeper (and presumably the duke), Gates had, like Lee, entered the British army at an early age. He had served with Washington in the Braddock debacle, and later distinguished himself at the capture of Martinique. However, after he had become a major in the British regular army, he found that he could rise no higher; all his undoubted ability could not, in that aristocratic force, counterbalance his seemingly lowly birth. He resigned and, in 1772, came to Virginia at the urging of his fellow veteran George Washington.

Although few members had ever heard of Gates, the Congress indulged Washington by electing the unknown to the top staff post, adjutant general, with the rank of brigadier. One of Washington's brothers thereupon expressed to Gates his relief at hearing that George would have "your greater experience" to "assist him in the arduous business."[5]

Thus, as they entered the American service, both the former British regulars, Gates and Lee, were given reason to conclude that Washington had been elevated over them merely as a native-born figurehead whom they should lead. However, Washington's pleasure that the two veterans would be available to him for consultation included no forebodings.

On June 20, when Washington had been engaged for only five days on harried preparations, Congress resolved, "You are to repair with all expedition to the Colony of Massachusetts Bay, and take charge of the army of the United Colonies."[6]

At the thought of going so much farther from home on so desperate an errand, Washington was flooded with homesickness. It was, he later remembered, "bidding adieu to my family and home, to which I never expected to return if the smiles of heaven should prove unpropitious."[7]

Except in the silences of the wilderness, Washington was unused to being far from familiar places. He had, it is true, moved habitually through northern Virginia and along Maryland's Potomac shore, but almost every elegant driveway he came on there led to the welcoming home of a friend. In the forty-three years of his life, he had only ventured on the ocean when he had taken his dying brother to Barbados on a brief and tragic pilgrimage for health. By land, he had never been south of Virginia, and, apart from his journeys to the two Congresses and his forays in the wilderness, he had been northeast of Maryland only three times: once not beyond Philadelphia, once on to New York, and once all the way to Boston. This last had been his only experience of the New England to which he was now headed: it had happened nineteen years before, he had stayed in Boston only a few days, and his memory of the errand that had taken him there was not now reassuring. He had gone so far in order to protest the pretensions of an officer from another state to command Virginia soldiers. Now, he was going to try, as a Virginian, to command a New England army.

The Yankees, he felt only too strongly, were peculiar people whom he did not understand and who could not be expected to understand him. They were the most aggressive levelers among Americans, the least given to acknowledging rank or obeying authority. How was an outsider to break them to discipline?

Having habitually lived his life surrounded by intimates, Washington felt a deep need for companions who thought as he did. Had there been any suitable men from his Virginia world available at Philadelphia, he would surely have urged them to go along with him as members of his staff. As it was, he reached out with almost anguished urgency to a friend he had made in Philadelphia at the sessions of the two Congresses.

Joseph Reed was somewhat ponderous of body, with a long melancholy face that could relax into poetic sensitivity or tighten with the passionate intolerance of a zealot. Although he was younger than Washington—only thirty-four—his experience was many times wider, and particularly in that now crucial world of politics. Despite his long service in the Virginia Burgesses, Washington had been primarily a neighborhood patriarch. Virginia's capital of Williamsburg being only a village, he had, during all his years before the sessions of the Continental Congresses, spent only a few months in any city. Reed, however, was as familiar with London, where he had studied law and made important connections, as with Philadelphia, where he now successfully practiced. He had been elected president of the Pennsylvania Provincial Congress. Washington listened fascinated as he expounded legal stratagems and parliamentary niceties.

Always impressed by highly educated, articulate, intellectual men, Washington was sure that Reed would be invaluable in helping him deal with the accomplished politicians of mercantile New England. However, Washington had no better appointment to offer the paragon than that of military secretary. He begged Reed to accept, stressing his need. Reed finally agreed to make the sacrifice—but would not promise to stay more than a few months.[8]

Washington's other immediate personal appointment, that of aide-de-camp, went to another Philadelphia member of Congress, Thomas Mifflin. An inheritor of mercantile wealth and skill, Mifflin had deserted the pacifist convictions of his Quaker upbringing to become one of the great orators of the patriot cause. His face had that combination of hauteur and openness which marks the histrionic face at its most impressive: a high brow, brown eyes large and staring, a jutting noble nose, a tense mouth that moved easily with emotion. Washington was not usually drawn to individuals so facile, but the young man—he was thirty-one—was certainly very able, abler than any coadjutor Washington had ever had in his more restricted Virginia career.

On June 23, when he had been Commander in Chief eight days, Washington wrote Martha:

"My Dearest

"As I am within a few minutes of leaving this city, I could not think of departing from it without dropping you a line, especially as I do not know whether it may be in my power to write you again till I get to the camp at Boston. I go fully trusting in that Providence which has been more bountiful to me than I deserve, and in full confidence of a happy meeting with you sometime in the fall. I have no time to add more, as I am surrounded with company to take leave of me. I retain an unalterable affection for you which neither time or distance can change."[9]

Also on June 23, Adams wrote his wife, "I have this morning been out of town to accompany our generals . . . a little way on their journey to the American camp before Boston. The three generals were all mounted on horseback." There was a parade: politicians in carriages, "a large troop of light horse in their uniforms; many officers of militia besides, in theirs; music

Phila. June 23d 1775.

My dearest,

As I am within a few Mi
nutes of leaving this City, I could not
think of departing from it without
dropping you a line; especially as I
do not know whether it may be in
my power to write again till I get to
the Camp at Boston — I go fully trus
ting in that Providence, which has
been more bountiful to me than I de
serve, & in full confidence of a happy
meeting with you sometime in the
Fall — I have not time to add more, as
I am surrounded with Company to
take leave of me — I retain an un
alterable affection for you, which
neither time or distance can change
my best love to Jack & Nelly, & regard
for the rest of the Family concludes
me with the utmost truth & sincerety
Yr entire

Go: Washington

Washington's farewell to his wife on departing for Cambridge to join his
army. Courtesy of the Mount Vernon Ladies' Association of the Union.

playing, etc., etc. Such," Adams continued, "is the pride and pomp of war. I, poor creature, worn out with scribbling for my bread and my liberty, low in spirits and weak in health, must leave others to wear the laurels which I have sown, others to eat the bread which I had earned; a common case."[10]

Washington could not see the eyes of the most influential member of Congress peering from Adams's carriage aglow with envy. And, as he surveyed his companions—Lee, Gates, Schuyler, Reed, and Mifflin—on this journey to the true start of his adventure, he could not know that, before the adventure was over, four out of the five would prove his enemies.

What were Washington's thoughts at this moment of departure he never recorded, but surely, as martial music blared and the procession swung into motion behind him, some elation must have mingled with his often reiterated forebodings. A man who so cherished the confidence of his neighbors could not be indifferent to what he had called "the partiality of Congress [which] has placed me in this distinguished point of view." He could be proud that he was not shirking his duty, was doing what honor demanded of him. He believed that the cause he was preparing to fight for was just, and he was sure that Providence intervened in the affairs of men to support the righteous. He furthermore felt that he was lucky. Maybe he would succeed in serving the cause well. Maybe he would earn not obloquy but that praise and gratitude of his countrymen which he considered "the most valuable and agreeable reward a citizen can receive." As he was to write, "To struggle with misfortune, to combat difficulties with intrepidity and finally surmount the obstacles which oppose us, are stronger proofs of merit and give a fairer title to reputation than the brightest scenes of tranquillity or the sunshine of prosperity could ever have afforded."[11]

CHAPTER

3

Traveler's Dust

THE skies lowered overhead and Washington's mind was haunted, as he rode through New Jersey toward his distant command, by a particularly urgent anxiety. Vague word had come that a battle had just been fought in Massachusetts, but whether it had been a victory or a defeat no one knew. The rumors which met them on the road only indicated that the engagement had been fought on Bunker Hill or Breed's Hill, that it had been bloody, and that the town of Dorchester had been burned.[1]

Washington had sent his own heavy chariot and four-horse team back to Mount Vernon and had bought on the public account a light doctor's phaeton which gave him an alternative to the saddle. It was drawn by two of the five horses he had purchased: a pair of whites. Inaugurating at once the time schedule of all his Revolutionary journeys, he started out at daybreak, and took breakfast after several hours on the road. The cavalcade was large, with aides and servants, and a persevering company of Philadelphia light horse.[2]

During a rainstorm, the three generals could just crowd into the doctor's phaeton. Lee would then dominate the conversation, pouring forth his intentionally bizarre mixture of profanity, radical politics, and military lore. Convinced of Lee's military genius, Washington listened with amusement and respect, but Schuyler certainly found it hard to bear the unrestrained speech of the sloppy and unwashed eccentric.

Like Washington, Schuyler was a large landowner who speculated in wilderness acres and had engaged in forest warfare. However, as the scion of a great New York family, he had never known, as Washington had, what it was to live without wealth and power. He found his social inferiors tolerable only if they kept their lowly distance. And he had the solemnity of a grotesquely ugly man. His tiny eyes were blue-black buttons under his shaggy brows, and his pear-shaped nose was a red blob dominating a florid

[23]

face. His manners and dress were impeccable, and the words that came from his thick lips revealed the hardheaded worldly knowledge of a seasoned handler of great affairs.

As the generals and their aides started to work out intricate interrelationships that were to make history, perpetual movement surged around them. Whenever they passed a farmhouse, the family rushed out to stare and be bowed to; wherever there was a hamlet, the road was blocked by an eager committee; around any curve there might be a troop of local gentlemen, banded together as light horse, anxious to brandish their swords and receive compliments and accompany the party with dusty clanking to the next town. Washington and his companions could never eat by themselves: they were always subject to speeches or toasts that delayed sleep or departure.

The new Commander in Chief could not foresee that this would be his fate whenever he traveled for the rest of his life. But he already handled brilliantly the strangers who flocked around him, leaving behind admirers who considered themselves his personal friends; and already he fretted at being "retarded by necessary attentions to the successive civilities."[3]

He was all eagerness to get to his army, but first he had to pass through New York, and, as he came closer, he learned that chance had staged a situation that might prove only too indicative of sentiment in that colony of undetermined loyalty. The Royal Governor, William Tryon, was due to arrive in the harbor on the same day that Washington and his generals would come into the city from New Jersey. The New York Provincial Congress had in perturbation voted that one militia company should meet the commanders of the revolutionary protest and another the representative of the King, while the residue should hold themselves in readiness "to receive either the general or the Governor Tryon, whichever shall first arrive."[4]

Since Tryon would come with a naval detachment, prudence dictated that Washington's party should not cross the Hudson near the bay. They embarked at Hoboken, intending to land more than a mile above the town (at what is now the Canal Street entrance of the Holland Tunnel).

The view that approached Washington as he crossed the river on that fine spring afternoon was such as usually he found most restful: well-spaced mansions separated by fine trees and fronted with lawns dabbling in a lordly flow. But the lawn at which his boat was aimed was more crowded than a racetrack: bands, uniforms, cavorting horsemen, strutting officers, and in the foreground a little group of soberly dressed citizens who could only be a committee of the Provincial Congress. Anyway, everyone was not off greeting Tryon. (It soon developed that the issue had not been raised, since Tryon had not yet arrived.)

[24]

As Washington stepped from the boat to be followed by Lee, Schuyler, and the others, he noticed eagerness on the part of the committee to get the initial ceremonies over. They almost hurried him into the parlor of Leonard Lispenard's mansion house and, having closed the door, handed him a sealed dispatch. It was from Massachusetts and addressed to the Continental Congress. When Washington hesitated to open it, the committeemen argued that true information of what had happened at Bunker Hill might be of use to his immediate plans. Washington broke the seal.

The dispatch stated that, after the British General Gage had received reinforcements of both horse and foot from Ireland, the Committee of Safety had decided to forestall an attack by sending out twelve hundred men, who began to fortify "a small hill, south of Bunker's Hill." Then the British "marched up to our entrenchments, from which they were twice repulsed, but in the third attack forced them. . . . At this time, the buildings in Charlestown appeared in flames in almost every quarter, kindled by hot balls, and is since laid in ashes. Though this scene was almost horrible and altogether new to most of our men, yet many stood and received wounds by swords and bayonettes before they quitted their lines. At five o'clock the enemy were in full possession of all the posts within the isthmus." The American loss was sixty or seventy killed and missing, "perhaps one hundred" wounded. "The loss of the enemy is doubtless great" although they were said to "exult much in having gained the ground. . . . If any error was committed on our side, it was in taking a post so much exposed."[5]

There were dark faces and sad hearts in Lispenard's parlor at what the dispatch presented as a serious defeat. The Massachusetts authorities went on to say that they had very little gunpowder left. Hurry some! If a commander in chief had been appointed, hurry him!

Washington yearned to get off, but first New York had to be attended to. There was a long dinner at Lispenard's with the usual speeches. Then, at about four in the afternoon, he rode into town as the feature of a parade, amidst what a Loyalist called "the repeated shouts and huzzas of the seditious and rebellious multitude." He dismounted at Hull's Tavern.

He had hardly entered his room when word came that the expected warship had anchored and that the Governor's barge was coming up the bay. Some of the men hovering around Washington looked embarrassed, made excuses, and disappeared to join the staid pacing to the Battery of worthies listed by the Loyalist chronicler: the members of His Majesty's Council, the officials of the state and city government, the Church of England clergy, and "a numerous train of his Majesty's loyal and well-affected subjects."[6]

Had it been necessary to bring the matter home to Washington, there could have been no better object lesson on his fundamental situation. He

[25]

was supposed to be a general, and would presumably serve as one when he got to Massachusetts, but here in New York he was a political symbol. With his sword sheathed, he lodged a few doors away from a leading enemy, and the contest between them was for signs of popular support.

The first returns were favorable to Washington. The Moravian pastor Shewkirk ruled that the general had received "the chief attention," while William Smith, the Tory chief justice, noted that Tryon "appeared grave this evening and said little." However, when the Provincial Congress of New York voted an address to Washington the next day, the whole contest was thrown wide open.[7]

Having balanced assurances of their continued allegiance to George III with congratulations to Washington as the leader of a regrettably necessary protest, the New York Congress reached the heart of their resolution: they expressed the hope that, after "the fondest wish of each American soul, an accommodation with our mother country," had been achieved, Washington would "cheerfully" lay down his arms "and resume the character of our worthiest citizen."[8]

Since the plea struck most sympathetic chords within his own breast, Washington did not need to ponder on his reply. He promised that he and his colleagues would devote themselves equally "to the re-establishment of peace and harmony . . . as to the fatal but necessary operations of war. When we assumed the soldier, we did not lay aside the citizen; and we shall most sincerely rejoice with you in that happy hour when the establishment of American liberty upon the most firm and solid foundations shall enable us to return to our private stations."[9]

By expressing in this widely circulated statement his own feelings, Washington kindled in thousands of hearts a flame of affection for this stranger who had, at this black time, emerged as a crucial determiner of their destinies.

More immediate political problems presented Washington with greater difficulties. Tryon's warship remained in the harbor and might be the harbinger of a force that was on its way to New York. From his city residence, the Governor was rallying the enemies of Congress. Although all this was legal—the harbor was still George III's and the Governor was officially in office—if no preventive steps were taken, the city might be quietly occupied by the enemy. However, any steps that could conceivably be effective would widen the conflict and might therefore alienate that public opinion which was more important than gunpowder to the eventual control of New York.

Twenty-one years before, almost to the day, Washington had been in a similar position in relation to an emerging, undeclared conflict. He had leapt ahead, as if the future were already the present, attacking in the wilderness a French force under Sieur de Jumonville. The French had then claimed that Jumonville had been an ambassador and that he had been assassinated. Washington, who had shed the first blood in what became the French and Indian War on this continent and the Seven Years' War in Europe, was excoriated in France as a murderer and in England as a numskull.

Now, he knew nothing of New York politics, but had at his side in General Schuyler a major New York leader. Furthermore, Schuyler belonged to the extreme conservative wing of the patriot cabal: any acts Schuyler would be willing to initiate would outrage only the most confirmed Tory. And so Washington threw the matter into Schuyler's lap.

He instructed his subordinate to keep "a watchful eye" on Tryon and use his own judgment. If the Governor began arming Tories to fight the will of Congress, it might be necessary to arrest him. This would be "quite a new thing and of exceeding great importance." Therefore, Schuyler should first consult Congress. If, however, Congress were not sitting and Schuyler was convinced that Tryon must be stopped, "I should have no difficulty in ordering of it."

Although he had never seen them, Washington knew that the various established routes between the revolting colonies and Canada (where the Crown was still unchallenged) came into northern New York. The military problems thus raised, plus "the command of all the troops destined for the New York department," Washington also entrusted to Schuyler, who was to follow his "own good sense" and report not only to him but directly to their common superior, Congress.[10]

These orders, the first important ones Washington gave as Commander in Chief, were motivated altogether by expediency and showed no concern with the precedents that might be established. In his need to get off to his major command in Massachusetts, he laid the groundwork for an independent department in the army that was to make him no end of trouble. However, while giving away military power, he expressed willingness to encroach, if necessary, on the civil. Since "the cause" would have no government if Congress was not sitting, he was willing to act for the nonexistent executive, ordering an arrest which could not help having wide political implications.

After only twenty-four hours in New York, Washington posted northeastward. His mind, so he remembered ten years later, was not enough "at ease" for him really to look around him, but his farmer's eye did note "a great deal of delightful country covered with grass (although the season has been dry) in a very different manner to what our lands in Virginia are." Six days brought him, on July 2, to Watertown, the seat of the Massachusetts Congress.[11]

Having enunciated the fulsome felicitations to "Your Excellency" with which Washington was becoming familiar, the Massachusetts Congress apologized for their army. Hurry in raising it and a lack of military experience had left the men, "although naturally brave and of good understanding," with little discipline and hardly any knowledge "of divers things most essential to the preservation of health and even life." Here was a clear mandate to Washington to straighten out a frightening mass of confusions. He was anxious to ride the remaining three miles to Cambridge and get about it.[12]

The day being Sunday, New England's Sabbatarianism made impossible a formal welcome. The Massachusetts politicians may have concluded that this was just as well, since they knew that many of their officers were awaiting with resentment the arrival of the Virginian.

The silences of history are sometimes as eloquent as a cannonade of sources. Practically nothing was recorded of Washington's reception in Cambridge. On that Sunday, he slipped inconspicuously into camp. He must have spent the evening somewhere, and perhaps, as a story has it, he joined a group of officers at a bibulous occasion when "Adjutant Gibbs of Glover's was hoisted (English fashion) chair and all upon the table, and gave the company a rollicking bachelor's song."[13]

We know, from succinct notations in General Ward's orderly book, that the next day the army paraded in Washington's presence, but no description was sent to a newspaper or composed in a diary. Tales of an elaborate ceremony under the "Washington Elm" seem to have been fabricated by writers who cannot bear silences. History was holding her breath, waiting to discover how so strange a phenomenon as a southern commander imported into Massachusetts would work out.[14]

4

A Virginian Among New Englanders

A
T first, Washington was not horrified. He went at cleaning out the
Augean stable of the army with all the energy of a determined Her-
cules. It was only when he feared that he would never be finished
that he succumbed to a frustration which rose to anger, to a discouragement
that sometimes became despair. It was only in anger and despair that he
wrote privately but dispatched indiscreetly letters insulting to the New
Englanders whom it was a major part of his mission to conciliate.

General Washington and General Lee were quartered with their staffs in
the house of Samuel Langdon, the president of Harvard, who patriotically
retired to one room. The new commander received a stream of military
callers, every one "a stranger to me but from character [reputation]."[1] He
surely made a special effort to ingratiate himself with the sharp-nosed, stout,
and deliberately paced Yankee whom he identified as General Ward, his
predecessor and now his second in command. But Ward saw no reason to
countenance, by reciprocal politeness, the interloper whose appointment he
regarded as an insult not only to himself personally but to that only
admirable and virtuous section of the universe, New England.

Washington also distinguished from the mass an elderly weatherbeaten
officer, with a high square forehead, and a chin so shallow that when he
smiled, he looked as if he had no bottom to his face. This was Connecticut's
favorite veteran, Israel Putnam. Washington expressed pleasure in handing
him his commission as fourth major general. Putnam smiled and was
pleased.

As Washington prepared similarly to honor the officers for whom he had
bought commissions as brigadiers, he was warned to proceed with care:
Congress, in making its rulings, had scrambled seniorities. Influential
soldiers who had been demoted or passed over felt outraged and insulted.
Having, during the previous war, experienced in his own breast so much

resentment concerning matters of rank, Washington understood instantly "the apparent danger of throwing the whole army into the utmost disorder." He pushed the commissions back into his pocket.[2]

However, the officers knew what was in the documents, for they had read in the newspapers to whom and in what order Congress had accorded the rank of brigadier. Of the nine designated, three reacted with wrath. Seth Pomeroy had already decamped from the service (and this book). Sixty-year-old Joseph Spencer was outraged; had he not outranked Putnam in the Connecticut service? Most serious was the dissatisfaction of John Thomas, an officer all agreed was valuable. He had been lieutenant general under Ward, and could hardly believe that he now was supposed to serve as a brigadier.

In arguing with Thomas not to precipitate what might be a wave of resignations, Washington described the idealism of the cause as he saw it at this time, before he extended his views beyond the welfare of the United Colonies. The issue was the contention of "a people . . . for life and liberty . . . a defense of all this is dear and valuable in life." Thomas's duty was "to your country, your posterity, and yourself." Paraphrasing the play he had loved since his young manhood, Addison's *Cato,* Washington exhorted, "Surely every post ought to be deemed honorable in which a man can serve his country."[3]

Thomas agreed to return. Unfortunately, so did Spencer, whose services to the cause were to earn him the nickname "Granny."

Of course, Washington began at once exploring around the camp. He was pleased to see that the soldiers looked well fed and still healthy. Their lodgings were visible manifestations of New England individualism. "Every tent," another observer wrote, "is a portraiture of the temper and taste of the persons who encamp in it." The habitations were built of boards or sailcloth, of stones or turf, of brick or brush. "Some are thrown up in a hurry, others curiously wrought with doors and windows, done with wreaths and withes, in the manner of a basket." However, over much of the camp there hung a stench which made it clear that little care had been given to digging privies.[4]

When Washington wished to remonstrate with the officers, he had great difficulty identifying them. They were, he decided, "nearly of the same kidney with the privates." They ate and bunked with their men in complete equality: if one had happened to be a barber in private life, he shaved his soldiers. On being ordered to step forward, they did not take kindly to the Virginian's questions about where, if anywhere, were the company privies.[5]

Resentment of the new Commander in Chief went so far that some sentries refused to let him pass and their officers, when summoned, were deaf to all arguments that this was actually George Washington. The general tried to cope with this problem by buying for three shillings "a ribbon to distinguish myself."[6]

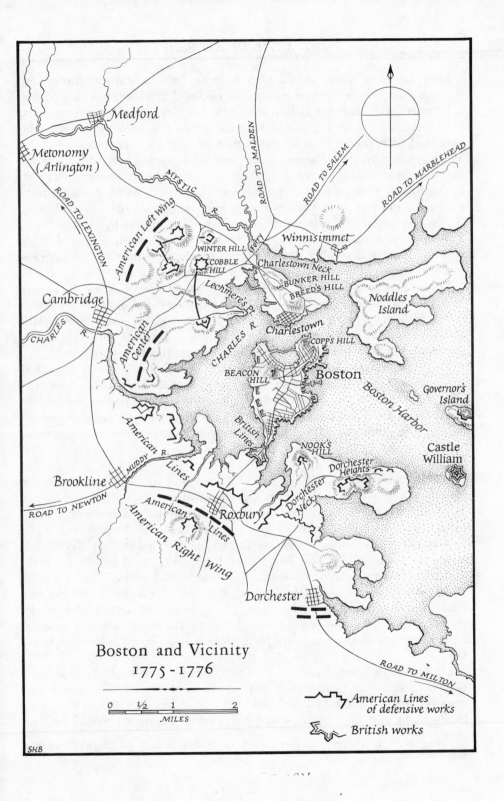

Medford

Metonomy
(Arlington)

ROAD TO LEXINGTON

ROAD TO MALDEN

ROAD TO SALEM

ROAD TO MARBLEHEAD

MYSTIC R.

American Left Wing

WINTER HILL

COBBLE HILL

Winnisimmet

Charlestown Neck

Lechmeres P.

BUNKER HILL

BREED'S HILL

Noddles Island

Cambridge

CHARLES R.

American Center

CHARLES R.

Charlestown

COPP'S HILL

BEACON HILL

Boston

Boston Harbor

Governor's Island

American Lines

British Lines

NOOK'S HILL

Dorchester Heights

Castle William

Brookline

MUDDY R.

American Lines

ROAD TO NEWTON

American Lines

Roxbury

Dorchester Neck

American Right Wing

Dorchester

ROAD TO MILTON

Boston and Vicinity
1775-1776

0   ½   1   2
MILES

⌐╚⌐╚ American Lines
      of defensive works

✶   British works

SHB

From his own camp, Washington rode up hills to stare at the enemy through field glasses. He saw a wide bay enclosed in a shoreline shaped like a battered and indented half-moon. Into this bay jutted two peninsulas, each resembling a fat jug with a long neck. The two necks adhered to the mainland at opposite sides of the half-moon, eight or ten miles apart, so Washington estimated. However, the peninsulas pointed toward each other, and their broad heads almost met, being separated by only a narrow channel.

The British were on the two peninsulas. The largest, which came up from the south, and was more than two miles long, comprised the city of Boston. It was connected to the shore, at the village of Roxbury, by Boston Neck. The other peninsula, coming down from the north with a considerable westerly slant, was smaller and had on its tip the ruined village of Charlestown. Its connection with the mainland was called Charlestown Neck.

Washington was pleased to see that there was no easy way for the enemy to break out at either end by land. The terrain around Boston Neck was rough and easily fortified. Although the British had captured Bunker Hill and Breed's Hill on Charlestown Neck, there were other hills within the American position that could be used to dominate the narrow passage.*

The weakness in the American position showed itself through Washington's glasses as what seemed to be a forest of dead trees rising from the outer harbor. This was a British fleet. Since the patriots had no equivalent naval force, the enemy could use their vessels to land an army anywhere around the perimeter of the bay, or indeed anywhere on the American coast.

Washington's second full day with the army was July 4. What Americans would soon be commemorating on that date was in 1775 unforeseeable, but. Washington had his own anniversary to remember. Twenty-one years before, he had surrendered to his enemies—then the French and their Indians—an indefensible wilderness fort—he had called it Fort Necessity— where his own foolhardiness had placed his bleeding and humiliated little army. The memory served to remind him that he had within himself a wild streak of military rashness. He yearned to prepare for a quick and glorious return to Mount Vernon and civilian life by a sudden assault that would send the ministerial army reeling out of Boston. However, he saw a safer, if slower and less glorious, method for getting himself home before the snow flew.[7]

All that was expected of him, he wrote, was by a tight blockade around Boston to keep the British from any communication with the rest of the country. If they tried to break out, he was to prevent them, first with fortifications and then by harassing any march. The result would be that

---

* Since much of the bay has been filled in, Boston Harbor no longer shows this configuration.

"the whole force of Great Britain . . . can answer no other end than to sink her under the disgrace and weight of the expense." Surely their inability to achieve anything "must totally overthrow the designs of the administration."[8]

Washington resolved to improve the fortifications on the two necks, to keep lookouts around the curving shore, to build barricades at all convenient landing places, and to have ready at Cambridge, which was a mile and a half inland from the center of the bay, a mobile force which would rush to the menaced area at any alarm.

When serving with Braddock and Forbes, Washington had seen enough of professional military engineering to know what the New England army offered him in this line was woefully inadequate. He begged Congress for experts. However, as a Virginia plantation owner, he was habituated to improvisation. He kept the men—even on New England's usually sacrosanct Sabbath—ditching, raising earthen ramparts, and laying felled trees sidewise, their bristling branches sharpened with axe or knife. In directing this labor, he was much assisted by Lee, who called himself a "scamperer general," since he rode around the lines twelve hours a day.[9]

Five years later, Washington wrote the French General Rochambeau, who had just visited Boston: "Perhaps it is to our advantage that you will have found few traces of works hastily thrown up by very inexperienced soldiers, and which, were they standing, would only serve to betray our ignorance of military matters at that time of day." However in 1775, after three weeks of passionate activity, Washington considered the works "so far advanced as to leave us little to apprehend on that score."[10]

On the subject of powder, the news was good. He was assured that there were in the Massachusetts storehouse three hundred and eight barrels, plenty for any immediate emergency.[11] It was not till later that he discovered that this was the total amount received since before Bunker Hill, and that most of it had been expended.

Washington agreed with his top officers that, since their defensive role forced his army to guard many places while the waterborne enemy could suddenly concentrate their men at a single point, the Americans needed twice the enemy's estimated ten thousand to twelve thousand men. He was assured that his army numbered eighteen thousand to twenty thousand, but his informants had to admit that was a guess. His first general orders had required regimental commanders to send in exact returns. Every morning, he was assured (as he wrote) that he would receive the figures "in the evening," and every evening that he would "surely . . . find them in the morning." Finally, he resorted to "threatening means." This produced papers which, "although full of imperfections," were shocking enough: the patriots had only some sixteen thousand men of whom only fourteen thousand—hardly more than the British—were fit for duty. He dispatched official pleas

[33]

for reinforcements, and added privately to his fellow Virginian, Richard Henry Lee, whom he had selected as his confidant in Congress, "I think we are in an extremely dangerous situation!"[12]

By Washington's order, whaleboats kept moving all night off every point where the enemy might try to land; saddled horses were kept tied to trees ready to carry news of a sudden attack to Cambridge; the reserves in that village slept on their guns. Expecting a "visit" from the enemy, preparing for the worst, Washington's Council of War defined a place where the troops, if routed, could reassemble: Welch Mountains behind the Roxbury lines.[13]

The reinforcements he yearned for would only make additional trouble, Washington realized, unless he could enforce hygienic measures and establish that "order, regularity, and discipline without which our numbers would embarrass us, . . . in case of an action."[14]

Washington's solution was to establish an officer corps that would have the authority and the ability to discipline and train the men. This, he believed, could only be achieved by making sharp distinctions, social as well as military, between those in command and those commanded. Although a principle that has down the years been accepted in all effective armies, this ran counter to New England equalitarianism and, indeed, to the then existing democratic organization of the militia in every colony. However, the need had been brought home to Washington during his service in the previous war beside British regulars. And, in any case, distinctions of rank came to him naturally as a scion of semi-aristocratic Virginia. "The person commanded yields but reluctant obedience to those he conceives are undeservedly made his superiors," Washington believed. "Gentlemen of fortune and reputable families generally make the most useful officers." He recommended to Congress that the subalterns' pay be raised so that they could "support the character and appearance of officers," and thus keep that distance from their men which would enable them to exert command. John Adams's reaction was that Southerners disliked New England's equality and that to pay the officers on a much higher scale than the men would be undemocratic. However, Congress as a whole followed the Commander in Chief's lead.[15]

Vigorously, Washington was engaged in weeding. On August 29 he wrote Richard Henry Lee, "I have made a pretty good slam among such kind of officers as the Massachusetts government abound in, since I came to this camp, having broke one colonel and two captains for cowardly behavior in the action on Bunker's Hill, two captains for drawing more provisions and pay than they had men in their company; and one for being absent from his post when the enemy appeared there and burnt a house just by it. Besides these, I have at this time one colonel, one major, one captain, and two subalterns under arrest for trial. In short, I spare none, yet fear it will not all do, as these people seem to be too inattentive to everything but their interest."[16]

The grandfather of Ralph Waldo Emerson, Regimental Chaplain William Emerson, noted, "There is great overturning in the camp as to order and regularity. New lords, new laws. The Generals Washington and Lee are upon the lines every day." Orders were read to the regiments each morning after prayers. "Great distinction is made between officers and soldiers. Everyone is made to know his place and keep it, or be tied up and receive thirty or forty lashes according to his crime. Thousands are at work every day from four till eleven o'clock in the morning. It is surprising how much work has been done."[17]

Before Washington had come on the scene, officers had been "broken"—discharged in disgrace—for military crimes, while soldiers had been whipped or in extreme cases hanged. The new commander merely added clearer rules and stronger enforcement. Soldiers got in trouble if they were found wandering away from camp; sentries were no longer allowed to sleep at their posts or gossip with the enemy. Insubordination became a major offense. On matters less specifically military, Washington followed New England mores, ordering, for instance, attendance at divine service. However, John Adams's wife Abigail noticed a laxness in the "continental connection" toward improving "the morals of our youth. A little less swearing at our New England Puritanism would be full as honorary to our Southern brethren."[18]

On July 25, there appeared in camp the first body of troops from outside New England: a corps of the rifle-wielding frontiersmen whose enlistment the Continental Congress had empowered. They created a sensation because of their strange costumes—white frock-like hunting shirts and round hats; their stature and physical prowess—some had marched six hundred miles from the Virginia frontier in three weeks; their tendency to be forever brawling—they soon started a riot; and, above all, their skill with their peculiar weapons. The guns they carried were much longer than muskets and the insides of the narrow barrels were rifled to send the bullets spinning through the air. It might take the riflemen a long time to shove shot down the muzzles to the firing chambers, but once the shot came out again, they traveled three times as far as musket balls and, instead of moving vaguely, were accurate as arrows. Running at full speed and firing while they ran, the riflemen reputedly could hit a target so small and so distant that a New England farmboy had to stare hard even to see it.

Reinforcements were also coming in from Massachusetts, Connecticut, and Rhode Island. As his ranks filled up, Washington began to wish that the British would come out from their lines and let him get a crack at them. But when on August 2 he sent in a routine request for powder, he changed his mind in a hurry. Someone took a careful look and discovered that the three hundred and eight barrels that Washington had been informed were in the magazine actually numbered thirty-six. Less than nine rounds a man! In moments of great shock Washington was inclined to recede into a deep silence. On hearing the truth about the powder, "for half an hour, he did not utter a word."[19]

Washington was convinced that, if the British realized his situation, they would instantly attack with consequences "terrible even in idea. . . . The existence of the army and salvation of our country" would be at an end. As a first step, he leaked word to the enemy (which their intelligence eagerly gobbled up) that he had eighteen hundred barrels of powder. He started a rumor in his own camp that he was almost embarrassed at having so much, but in his orders forbade random firing on the ground that it elicited "the ridicule of the enemy."[20]

On some plausible pretext, he galloped off to the seat of the Massachusetts Congress, Watertown. He could not know that within a month a member of the Massachusetts Provincial Congress (Dr. Samuel Church) would be caught in treasonable correspondence with the enemy, but he decided that the powder shortage was "a secret of too much consequence" to divulge to anyone but the Speaker. He wrote the patriot authorities in various places that he needed powder because he expected an enemy bombardment he would like to reply to, and even persuaded Rhode Island to send out a secret naval expedition to seize some powder he was told was in a remote part of Bermuda. "Enterprises which appear chimerical," he wrote, often succeeded because common sense does not foresee danger. (However, the British commander in chief, General Thomas Gage, had foreseen and removed the powder.)[21]

Washington saw with assumed casualness to the making and sharpening of spears.[22] He lay awake at night listening for the sound of galloping hoofs, or for that relay of drum signals—first far off and then nearer and nearer—he had established as an alarm.

In letters that came to headquarters, "the word powder," Reed wrote, ". . . sets us all atiptoe." The word appeared with agreeable frequency as the military potential of the colonies had not yet been really tapped. In roughly three weeks, Washington had thirty cartridges a man. He began again to wish they would "come out as soon as they please." But they showed no signs of doing so. The war was going on as a stalemate with no end in sight.[23]

Washington was anything but happy. He wrote Richard Henry Lee that his life had been, since he joined the army, "one continued round of *annoyance* and *fatigue*." Not only was he not defeating the ministerial forces but he felt he was making personal enemies among the patriots. "I expect," he continued to Lee, "by showing so little *countenance* to irregularities and public *abuses, to* render myself very obnoxious to a *greater* part" of the New Englanders with whom he was surrounded.[24]

In his second set of general orders (they were promulgated exactly a year before the Declaration of Independence) Washington had stated, "The Continental Congress having now taken all the troops . . . into their pay and service, they are now the troops of the UNITED PROVINCES of North America, and it is hoped that all distinctions of Colonies will be laid aside." Washington could thus hope, but the ticklishness of his situation as a Virginia commander in New England did not abate. And his own emotions were becoming raw. If ever discretion was called for, it was now. But when Washington sat down to write his friends, his frustration spilled out in angry attacks on New England which mischance—or the indiscretion of the recipients—might well bring under the focus of the wrong—and very angry—eyes. He burst out, for instance, to his cousin and estate manager Lund Washington that the New England officers "are generally speaking the most indifferent kind of people I ever saw. . . . I dare say the men would fight very well if properly officered, although they are an exceeding dirty and nasty people."* And again, this time to Joseph Reed, who had left him more lonely by returning to Philadelphia, "Notwithstanding all the public virtue which is ascribed to these people, there is no nation under the sun (that I ever came across) pay greater adoration to money than they do."[25]

Washington resisted Massachusetts pressure to put a Massachusetts man in charge of the purchase of military supplies. "Between you and I, there is more in this than you can easily imagine," he wrote R. H. Lee when he appointed the Philadelphian Mifflin as quartermaster general. Adams protested on the principle that Congress's delegating of such "important and lucrative" appointments to the Commander in Chief gave Washington too much power—and furthermore, the selection of an outsider was "a great misfortune to our Colony."[26]

To please the New England leader, Washington had appointed Adams's lawyer's clerk, William Tudor, as aide-de-camp. Adams thereupon requested Tudor to report to him what went on at headquarters, and particularly "the name, character, and behavior of every stranger that shall be put into any place in the army." Washington moved Tudor on to the post of judge advocate and showed no passion for replacing him with another New Englander.[27]

---

* Amusingly enough, an unenthusiastic attitude toward New England's military prowess had been sown in Washington's mind nineteen years before by the very man he was now opposing as Commander in Chief. In 1756 his friend Major Thomas Gage, who was serving on the New York border against the French and Indians, had written Colonel Washington that the New Englanders were "the greatest boasters and worst soldiers on the continent. We have enlisted soldiers from all the provinces, but I never saw any in my life as infamously bad."[28]

That Washington's military "family" was largely made up of outlanders enabled the Virginian to give a freer vent to his feelings around head-quarters—and also brought its only continental tone to the army: since the New England governments would only give their own citizens commissions in their regiments, there was no way to employ volunteers—not even, as Washington complained, that dashing New Jersey patrician Aaron Burr—in the regular service.[29]

From Philadelphia came a letter from Reed warning Washington that his strictures on the New Englanders were being bruited around the capital and were making trouble.

Washington replied that Reed could have given no more "convincing proof of your friendship" than by sending this warning. Washington was eager "to make my conduct coincide with the wishes of mankind, as far as I can . . . without departing from that great line of duty which, though hid under a cloud for some time from a peculiarity of circumstances, may nevertheless bear scrutiny. . . . I can bear to hear of imputed or real errors. The man who wishes to stand well in the opinion of others must do this, because he is thereby enabled to correct his faults and remove prejudices which are imbibed against him."

His indiscreet remarks on New England, Washington continued, had been made in "private letters" only. Although he did not ask, he must have wondered how his sentiments had got abroad. He could not know that his intimate correspondent on Congress, R. H. Lee, had formed a close alliance with the Massachusetts Adamses—nor could he foresee how much trouble this situation was going to make him.

Washington promised Reed, "I will endeavor at a reformation." He would make his private letters as circumspect as his public ones.

"I cannot," Washington continued, "charge myself with incivility, or, what in my opinion is tantamount, ceremonious civility, to the gentlemen of this colony." He had often, he admitted, in his concern with immediate problems forgotten "that there is such a body in existence" as the Massachusetts legislature, yet he could not remember that he had—as Reed seems to have charged—actively slighted them. Surely, they did not want him to tell them the secrets of the army or to consult them on details. The problem must be lack of social contact. "How to remedy it, I hardly know, as I am acquainted with few of the members, never go out of my own lines, or see any of them in them." If only he had adhered to his resolution of having every day several local gentlemen to dinner![30]

Had British spies reported in Boston or London that the Virginian Commander in Chief had been caught insulting in his correspondence the proud New Englanders, there would have been much rejoicing. British and American Tories would have reasoned that the unnatural conspiracy of the thirteen long-separate colonies against the rightful King of all was about to

Richard Henry Lee, by Charles Willson Peale. Courtesy of Independence
National Historical Park Collection.

fall apart. And the historian may well ask himself why Washington's indiscretions did not make more immediate trouble.

Since no picture of the new Commander in Chief existed that could have preceded him to Massachusetts, the soldiers had, before they saw him, no idea what he looked like. They were, so the medical officer Dr. James Thacher remembered, "much gratified" by their ability to distinguish at a glance, as he rode by in a group of horsemen, which of the party was the new commander.[31] "Truly noble and majestic, being tall and well proportioned," he looked every inch the conquering warrior. Word, indeed, traveled to London to be published in the *Morning Post and Daily Advertiser* that Washington's "martial dignity" would distinguish him as a soldier among ten thousand men: "Not a king in Europe but would look like a valet de chambre by his side."[32]

Washington possessed to a superlative degree that quality which sociologists call "charisma": personal magnetism that inspires awe, trust, and love. On meeting him, John Adams's wife Abigail quoted to her husband what the Queen of Sheba had said on meeting Solomon, "I thought the half was not told me."[33]

The levelers of New England were impressed despite themselves by the blooded charger Washington rode; by the "rich epaulette" on each shoulder of his blue uniform coat with its buff facings; by the "elegant small sword" that hung from his belt. Gossip was that in Boston the British officers staged plays in which they depicted Washington as their idea of a typical rebel: "dressed in an uncouth style, with a large wig and long rusty sword." It was impossible not to be glad that this was a libel. Even John Adams had written that Washington's acceptance of the Continental command was the more admirable because he was abandoning for hardships so much high-bred ease.[34]

As a Virginia planter to whom receiving wages was alien, as a neighborhood patriarch who felt it his duty to lead and assist at no charge, Washington had obeyed the instincts of his calling and class by refusing to accept any salary as Commander in Chief. He had asked Congress to do no more than reimburse his expenses.[35] Modern levelers have denounced this as an anti-democratic gesture—wasn't Washington trying to make clear that he was richer than other people?—but the eighteenth-century Yankees viewed such a refusal of money with the awe of Don Juan at the continence of St. Anthony. Indeed, nothing that Washington could have done could more successfully have persuaded all America of his altruism. Throughout the war his renunciation of all gain was to protect him from whole arsenals of barbed charges.

For all the complaints of Massachusetts politicians at Washington's acts that went against leveling principles, they knew that he was pulling essential chestnuts out of the fire. An army had to be well commanded; soldiers had to obey; discipline and sanitation had to be imposed. It was nice to soothe your constituents and your own prejudices by objecting, and at the same time have the job done. Furthermore, there was sometimes less democracy in the hearts of the Massachusetts leaders than there was in their larynxes: it was John Adams not George Washington who came out, after the war had been won, for the establishment of American titles.

The New Englanders, whose stony fields had taught them thrift, may well have feared that the rich planter from the south would throw their money around. If so, they were happily disabused. As a young man poorer than his companions, Washington had been forced to consider every penny—and he had remained a compulsive keeper of accounts. The Massachusetts Congress was charmed by the "parsimony" with which he managed the army.[36]

Yankees respected fidelity and labor—and certainly no man was more faithful and worked harder than George Washington. As the youthful commander of Virginia's army during the French and Indian War, Washington had done what seemed not only comfortable but reasonable—stayed behind the lines to attend to supply—and had brought much criticism down on his head.[37] He had learned his lesson so well that he never left his army's encampment except to ride on very occasional urgent business the three miles to the legislature at Watertown. "I pity our good general," wrote James Warren, the president of the Massachusetts Congress, "who has a greater burden on his shoulders and more difficulties to struggle with than I think should fall to the share of so good a man. . . . I see he is fatigued and worried."[38]

Washington yearned in loneliness for Mount Vernon. However, the New England troops were in their own part of the world, serving in knots with their neighbors. That the enemy were bottled up seemed to them the best type of victory short of having the enemy quietly disappear. The artisans and farmboys did not pray for a baptism of blood, while exiled Bostonians feared that an attack on the city would destroy their property, their friends and relations.

The army was stationary in a country full of every necessity. Goods, Washington was later to remember quite ruefully, were then plentiful and cheap. The men got corned beef or pork four times a week, beef twice, and fish once, the helpings of beef being set down as one and a half pounds. Although the local spruce beer depressed British officers, the Yankees relished it: they received a quart a day. That Washington could not secure the ten thousand hunting shirts he wanted for uniforms bothered him more than it did the troops, who did not wish to appear all alike. They saw nothing unmilitary in recognizing the ranks of officers by the colors of the cockades in varieties of civilian hats. And when there was a shortage of tents, sails to drape over ridgepoles could always be secured from seaport towns.[39]

Well housed and fed, living an outdoor life in a climate to which they were accustomed, coming from neighborhoods subject to the same diseases to which they had all established immunity, the troops placed little responsibility on the hospital department. The resemblance was to a huge hunting trip. The participants as a group found the siege of Cambridge an agreeable adventure.

However, the resentments caused by Washington's insults to New England were not forgotten by the Yankees he had most offended. They were to reappear to plague the Commander in Chief at a moment when his leadership no longer seemed indispensable. But for the time being, annoyance had to be suppressed, since, outside the also bickering Congress, Washington remained the most prominent symbol of the united cause.

His indiscretions would probably have made more trouble had more day-to-day unity prevailed. Since all the colonies had prejudices against each other, everyone expected a certain amount of prejudice. Being thrown by their common plight into necessary cooperation, the patriots minimized backsliding, emphasized success.

And over all there brooded a great intangible which no one at that time adequately realized and the importance of which is even today overlooked by historians concerned primarily with pinning down little facts. Environment had already created an American man: Washington's perpetual critic, the New England radical lawyer John Adams, was more like the Virginia planter than either was like prominent Englishmen, be they lord or commoner, Whig or Tory. Both Americans had been shaped by a land devoid of true wealth in the European sense or of (for freemen) true poverty. A land where social class was not an impregnable cliff but sand that shifted. A land where a man could turn his hand without shame to almost any gainful occupation: Adams had started life as a schoolmaster, Washington as a surveyor—trades impossible to English gentlemen.

Neither had ever been to Europe. In Virginia as in New England, the past, so powerful in European thinking, was a dim murmur beside the shouting present. Both Washington and Adams had been profoundly habituated to the pragmatism forced on men and groups of men by problems for which the past offered no workable solutions. Alongside rail fence or in country courthouse, by wilderness stream or in provincial assembly, both men had learned to think things out anew and for themselves. In such fundamental similarity under regional and personal diversity lay—although not clearly seen—the transcendent hope for the American cause.

The great diversity between Washington and Adams was, of course, that the Virginian was an agrarian, the New Englander, although raised on a small farm, essentially a bourgeois. That the United States has become a bourgeois nation has made Adams's ideas seem a more natural approach to the rebellion than Washington's. (Few have ever wondered why Adams revolted against his king, while it is fashionable in some circles to regard Washington's decision as a puzzle.) Actually, Washington was more exclusively shaped by America than was Adams. He relied for knowledge more on direct experience, which was usually native, than on books, which were usually imported. His calling as a planter, particularly as he developed it, depended infinitely less on precedent than Adams's law. And Adams's experience was limited to the well-settled, half-Europeanized American seaboard, while the wilderness, the shaper of so much American originality, had played a major role in shaping Washington. The army at Cambridge could hardly have had a more completely American commander.

This the revolutionary New Englanders sensed, and it made them feel strangely at home with the sometimes angry southerner. The Massachusetts born and bred artilleryman Henry Knox wrote, "General Washington fills his place with vast ease and dignity, and dispenses happiness around him." And President Joseph Warren of the Massachusetts Congress commented: "The General has many difficulties with officers and soldiers. His judgment and firmness I hope will carry him through them. He is certainly the best man for the place he is in, important as it is, that ever lived."[40]

CHAPTER

5

The War of Positions

WASHINGTON'S first large expenditure after his arrival in Cambridge had been $333.33 for someone "to go into the town of Boston to establish secret correspondence."[1] By himself arranging this, and by not noting the spy's name in any record—a record might be captured—he cast himself as his own master of intelligence. He was soon securing good information on whatever could be observed in the streets or overheard in the coffeehouses. Every report indicated that the patriot blockade was very effective. Fresh food had vanished from Boston; the milk cows had been slaughtered for beef since they could not be fed; fuel was so scarce that even the richest inhabitants who had cast their lot with the British were glad to secure horse dung to burn. Washington reasoned that unless the British were planning to use their shipping to sail away to another part of the continent—and his spies reported no preparation for this—or were going to "relinquish the dispute"—which certainly could not be counted upon—they would try to break out of the trap.[2]

Had his spies been able to penetrate the British inner councils, Washington would have been informed that unless some stupidity on his part should present them with a sensational opportunity, the enemy would not attack. Although their commander in chief, General Thomas Gage, had been his friend during the French and Indian War, Washington could not imagine himself into the brain of a British regular.

Washington agreed with the Massachusetts authorities that, since the patriots had not driven the British from Boston or even held the position they had tried to fortify, the Battle of Bunker Hill had been an American defeat. The attitude of the command in Boston was almost exactly opposite. They agreed with the former British regular General Lee, who expressed astonishment that "fifteen hundred, the most disorderly peasantry, without a single officer to command 'em," had been able to commit such execution on

[44]

"3000 very good regular troops, under the command of the very best officer in the British service."[3]

That officer, General William Howe, succeeded Gage as commander in chief during October. Neither he nor his predecessor could forget that the British casualties at Bunker Hill had been a stupendous 1054 out of 2400 engaged.

Add to this inconceivable fiasco an unbelievable development. Britons were being dropped from impossible distances by "shirt-tailed men with damned twisted guns." Since the riflemen concentrated not on the common soldiery but on the high-bred officers, such sharpshooting was basically subversive to the aristocratic way of life. It was a violation of the accepted rules of war—and it was eerie.

A story circulated in the American camp that some newly arrived British officers, walking on now supposedly safe Bunker Hill, were frightened by bullet-like whinings in the air although they heard no shots. They dashed off crying that the rebels were now firing at them with air guns—but it was only New England's redoubtable bugs.[4]

The rebels, Howe complained, were "entrenched upon every advantageous spot" and "though raw as soldiers, are nevertheless accustomed to the use of arms." To drive them by direct assault from their prepared positions would cost unjustifiable losses.[5]

Military historians of the Revolution have long pointed out that the British commanders were urged to shield their men by the fact that replacements would have to travel three thousand miles across the ocean. However, there existed further and more significant pressures toward caution. These were necessary outgrowths of aristocratic institutions; they dominated established military strategy as practiced in Europe as well as America.[6]

The efforts Washington was making to pry officers and soldiers apart until there was an appreciable space between them would have been utterly unnecessary in any European force. The armies of aristocratic states were grounded on prevailing sharp distinctions between the upper classes and ordinary men. The officers were aristocrats. They were supposed to have a sense of personal honor, loyalty to their sovereign, and also a stake in what they were fighting for. The enlisted men were of an entirely different breed. They were not called on for honor or any further loyalty than a primitive allegiance to their regiments. It was considered essential to keep them unconcerned with the issues of the war, since if a man began applying his own judgment to where he directed his sword, he might decide to direct it against his king.

The common soldiers did not even represent the solid part of the lower classes. A king, so Frederick the Great pointed out, should guard "useful,

[45]

hardworking people . . . as the apple of one's eye." Armies were made up of foreigners and derelicts. Often a ruler hired (as George III was to do with the Hessians) altogether foreign legions from princes who made a speciality of such livery service.[7]

Such armies could not possibly be, in the manner of later democratic armies, raised by a draft, nor could a king expect, as Washington did, that men with any other resources would of their own volition enlist in the ranks. Soldiers were hard to come by and they usually had to be bought, which was expensive.* An aristocratic leader could not, like a modern President, send a whole army to its death knowing that he had effective machinery by which it could be replaced.

Visiting royal palaces, with all their ormolu and glitter, the modern observer is likely to conclude that kings were very rich. They were as individuals, but not as heads of governments. The nobility of each nation was restive under even light taxation; there were no industrial establishments to create capital the government could drain; and the poor, however much a monarch sweated them, could give up only pennies. A royal government could totter into bankruptcy while the country's wealth remained largely untapped. Impoverished in comparison to the ruler of a democracy, a king, if he lost one expensive army, often could not afford to buy another.

Add the fact that the common soldiers, who were supposed not ever to think for themselves, had to be trained as you would train a horse or a dog for a circus. That takes time. Making soldiers obey commands without question and face death without motive was achieved partly by brainwashing and partly by terror.

Washington referred to the aristocratic soldier as an "abandoned vagabond to whom all causes and countries are equal and alike indifferent." However, he tried to fill in for his own inexperience by reading the standard imported books,† and on one occasion he quoted to Congress the aristocratic conception that three things kept men regular in action: natural bravery, hope of reward, and fear of punishment. Recruits might have the first two; it was fear of punishment that distinguished the veteran. "A coward," Washington explained, "when taught to believe that if he breaks his ranks and abandons his colors, will be punished with death by his own

---

* In England, colonels were subcontractors who enlisted their regiments, receiving so much per head from the government, and pocketing whatever they could keep from paying out. The conception that officers should recruit their own men carried over into the American army, causing Washington much trouble, since the best recruiter was far from necessarily the best soldier.

† Washington told the French general Chastellux that his favorite military texts were Frederick's *Instructions to his Generals* and Guibert's *Tactics*. However, he recommended to his officers that they should learn "manual exercises, the evolutions and maneuvers of a regiment," and the like, from simpler manuals, particularly Humphrey Bland's *Treatise on Military Discipline*.[8]

party, will take his chance against the enemy." Otherwise, the soldier "acts from present feelings regardless of consequences." In this passage, Washington followed his sources too exactly to mention what was in truth his own greatest reliance—that sense of personal interest, that patriotism, which colored all feelings, and which was available to him as the commander of an anti-aristocratic, people's army.[9]

For aristocratic officers to make the common soldiers into the necessary automatons took a minimum of two years; however hard you beat the bushes, you could not instantly find a new soldier except by buying him ready-made from some other prince.

This being the universal situation, strategy was not established in terms of battles to the death.* It was generally recognized that the outcome of total battles depended, unless the odds were overwhelming on one side, too much on chance to respond to calculation. Neither command could risk all in confidence that its irreplaceable instrument would not be smashed. Battles were avoided by forces notably the weaker, and when engagements did actually take place, they were continued until one side showed a definite advantage, at which the other side withdrew. The object of what has been called the "war of positions" was to gain territory, without seriously engaging your own army, by forcing the enemy to fall back.

This philosophy of warfare placed little emphasis on destroying the enemy once he was doing what you wanted by retiring,† and, indeed, destructive pursuit was dangerous for the victor: not so much because the fleeing enemy might turn like a stag at bay, but because successful mopping-up operations involved spreading the pursuing forces widely over the countryside. It was axiomatic in aristocratic armies that if ordinary soldiers were permitted to get out of formation and away from their officers, they would probably never be seen again. They would desert. This same fear made it extremely difficult for conventional armies to divide into units small enough for guerrilla warfare.

Seeking small successive advantages rather than the annihilation of the enemy, conventional generals maneuvered to control roads, cut supply lines, overrun magazines, and reduce the fortifications the enemy had erected at key positions until at last the victor captured (or grievously menaced) the major seaports and cities without which the enemy's war effort must collapse. In the process, the countryside was devastated as little as possible, since if the victor was going to annex it, he wanted to acquire more than burned cities and disemboweled peasants.

---

* The conception that it was the function of an army to destroy its opponent was first importantly enunciated by Clausewitz in the 1830's.
† That kings did not seek to decimate each other's forces until perhaps neither would have any troops left to fight with, encouraged the custom, which was imported into the American war, of keeping up the numbers on both sides by exchanges of prisoners.

General Howe was an expert practitioner of this kind of warfare. At the moment, he saw nothing to be gained by risking his troops. To enlarge his holdings around Boston would be idiotic since the base was already uncomfortably large for the number of defenders. And to push Washington back into inner Massachusetts—which could be attempted by landing boats on either flank beyond the American fortifications—would gain nothing, as the New England peasants were too hostile to be brought back to their old allegiance, and there were no important cities to take, no vital supply lines to cut.

Agreeing with Howe's judgment of the situation, the ministry in London ordered him to move from Boston to New York or some other city to the southward where the strategic possibilities would be greater and pro-rebel sentiment weaker. Howe lacked shipping to transport his army in one bite, however, and taking two bites would not be safe when so many rebels hovered around. Howe saw no alternative but to sit still until succor came from across the ocean.

CHAPTER

6

The Spreading Blaze

A S the stalemate dragged on from days to weeks to months, Washington was not grateful for the respite. Few of the great movers on the world's wide stage have ever loved their native acres with the passion he felt for the home, on its high bluff over the lake-like Potomac, which he had known since childhood and had enlarged to suit his manhood desires. In August 1775, Washington urged his estate manager to "quicken" the installation of a chimney piece at Mount Vernon "as I could wish to have that end of the house completely finished before I return." He still refused to abandon the hope that he would be home, his task accomplished, before the snow flew.[1] Could he not end the stalemate by mounting an attack?

To the major generals and brigadier generals who constituted his Council of War he wrote in early September pointing out that the enlistments of the patriot troops would come to an end either in December or on January 1. All lacked winter clothes. If they were not clothed before the cold struck, they certainly would not re-enlist, and if they were clothed and did not re-enlist, two armies would have to be clothed. Indeed, there would have to be for a time two armies in service, so that there would be no hiatus at the shift-over. Weather-tight barracks would have to be supplied, and also, if the local fences and barns were not to suffer, vast quantities of firewood. What about blankets? What about powder for the long months ahead? "To sum up the whole, in spite of every saving that can be made, the expense of supporting this army will so far exceed any idea that was formed in Congress of it, that I do not know what will be the consequences. . . . These things are not unknown to the enemy: perhaps it is the very ground they are building on."

Washington urged on his generals that a surprise invasion of Boston Neck "by means of boats, cooperated by an attempt upon their lines at Roxbury" would be "hazardous" but "did not appear impractical." However, some of his generals argued that the men could only be counted on to fight if protected by breastworks (with this Lee disagreed); and Washington could not deny that the British position was "surrounded with ships of war, floating batteries, etc., and the narrow necks of land leading to them fortified in such a manner as not to be forced without a very considerable slaughter, if practicable at all." Furthermore, it was pointed out that, since the London government had petitioned the King against the "despotism" of the ministry, a ship might arrive any day with news that the friends of America had come into power. Washington gave in, as he was to do again in October when, at another council of war, he failed to persuade his generals to attack.[2]

Not only were councils of war a standard eighteenth-century military practice, but Congress, so copiously assured by Washington of his lack of military skill, had, in giving him his commission, ordered him to consult his officers. He still felt himself not "a military genius and the officer of experience," and he believed that should he act "under the sole guidance of my own judgment and self-will," failure would make him "a fit object for public resentment." However, he was to write that had he been able to foresee the future, "all the generals upon earth should not have convinced me of the propriety of delaying an attack upon Boston."[3]

If British spies told Howe of the meetings and their outcome, the enemy general would, like Washington, have been disappointed, as he believed that his own only hope of escaping from a very difficult situation was "to tempt them to attack us."[4]

Finding it humiliating to have nineteen thousand* soldiers idle, Washington turned his eyes toward Canada. Congress had been trying to induce the Canadians to join the revolt, but the French inhabitants, so recently conquered from their own mother country, felt little concern with English constitutional disputes, and, as Catholics, they had considerable fear of New England Protestantism. They seemed torpid. This was dangerous to the revolting colonies since, if the conflict continued, a supine Canada would be in effect a huge British base.

---

* In any accounts of military actions, it is necessary to indicate the sizes of armies, but the reader should keep in mind that no figure can hope to be accurate. Both the American and British commands rigged their statistics to fool enemy spies, or to make their own successes seem sensational, their own defeats trivial. Lower officers also had their motives for falsification. They might have accepted bounties for more men than they had actually recruited, and, when companies drew rations according to the number of mouths reported, temptation was to strike neither the absconded nor the dead from the rolls. And there were built-in errors of bookkeeping: in the American army, incompetence and lack of system; in the British, the traditional addition of dummy soldiers the value of whose rations were perquisites of various high officers and officials of the war office. Add the question as to how many men actually present were well enough to fight and how many belonged to the fighting branches of the service.

While Washington was still only a delegate to the Second Continental Congress, an unofficial force, spirited up secretly in Connecticut and Massachusetts, had surprised and taken the royal fort at Ticonderoga that presided over the Lake Champlain route—the best one—between Canada and the northeastern colonies. Congress had at first been horrified because this attack on a royal post from which no hostilities had emanated carried the "loyal protest" a step closer to war. However, after Washington was off to Cambridge, constitutionalists decided that to send an army north could be construed as a defensive move that need not outrage the Crown if the Canadians could be said to have invited it in. This sounded well, but when it came to ordering an actual invasion, the Congress preferred to pass the buck. They expanded the responsibilities Washington had given Schuyler as commander in New York. He was ordered to determine Canadian sentiment and, if he found it favorable to the patriot cause, advance along the inland routes that ran north from his colony.[5]

Schuyler had been selected as a conservative. Being a conservative, he hesitated, all the more because this New York patrician, whose orders had always been scrupulously obeyed, had not been prepared by experience for the lack of discipline and subordination of the troops—many from New England—who were gathering in the Albany-Ticonderoga region. To Schuyler's complaints, Washington replied that he was experiencing in "miniature" what Washington faced as "a portrait at full length." The Commander in Chief urged "patience and perseverance," to which Schuyler replied, "If Job had been a general in my situation, his memory had not been so famous for patience."[6]

The total result was that the march into Canada showed few signs of getting underway. As Washington fretted, New Englanders told him of a back route—it involved mounting and descending wilderness rivers, with marches across rugged heights—along which an army could perhaps struggle from the mouth of the Kennebec River (in northern Massachusetts, now Maine) directly to the St. Lawrence opposite Quebec.

That this route had always been considered passable only to lightly laden canoes increased its interest to Washington, since he reasoned that an army disgorging from a wilderness where it was assumed no army could travel might capture by surprise the fortress city of Quebec which, on its high cliff, was almost impregnable to siege. And there had appeared in camp a squat, powerfully built Connecticut officer whose light blue eyes stared passionately from a dark, hook-nosed face. Benedict Arnold had signalized himself at Ticonderoga. He was resourceful if overaggressive; he was efficient as well as flamboyant; he seemed the ideal man to lead frontiersmen up brawling rivers, along desperate trails.

Washington's letter suggesting to Schuyler that the Kennebec River route be used as a second prong in conjunction with an attack mounted from New

York along the conventional Lake Champlain passage, was, in effect, a pitchfork in the reluctant conservative's back. When Schuyler finally agreed, the season was late—winter would soon block the mountain passes—but Washington ordered Arnold to proceed with over a thousand picked woodsmen. The wild colonel was to remember the transcendent importance of conciliation. Propitiate the Indians! Washington wrote. Eschew all disrespect for the Catholicism of the Canadians: "While we are contending for our own liberty, we should be very cautious of violating the rights of conscience in others, ever considering that God alone is the judge of the hearts of men." Brutality of any sort "will disgrace the American arms and irritate our fellow subjects against us."[7]

Arnold disappeared into the wilderness. But the invasion up Lake Champlain, which was supposed to draw British forces away from Arnold's objective, did not move. Washington wrote Schuyler of his anxiety for "poor Arnold, whose fate depends upon the issue of your campaign." However, when Schuyler's expeditionary force, having finally got going, halted again to besiege the British fortress at St. Johns, Washington would not extend his authority beyond a mere suggestion that the American army detour around the strongpoint and, by taking Montreal, leave St. Johns to wither on the vine. He knew, he wrote, the absurdity of judging a military operation without detailed information: "I only mean it as a matter of curiosity and to suggest to you my imperfect idea on the subject."[8]

Although the wildly unorthodox strategy might have succeeded, it did not impress Schuyler's combat general, Richard Montgomery, who had served as a British regular and knew that you should not endanger your supply line by leaving a strongpoint in your rear.

In the first week of November, Washington received a cheerful dispatch from Arnold written at the head of the Kennebec. "I think he must be in Quebec," Washington wrote on the 8th. "If I hear nothing more of him in five days, I shall be sure of it." In the meanwhile, St. Johns fell and Montgomery advanced on Montreal: all seemed well. Washington scolded his troops for intending to observe on Guy Fawkes Day "that ridiculous and childish custom of burning the effigy of the Pope": Catholic Canada might be coming into alliance! Then he heard that a quarter of Arnold's army had reappeared at the wrong end of the wilderness, having turned back in discouragement. He was now afraid that Arnold was "in a bad way."[9]

Montgomery took Montreal, and on December 5 Washington learned that Arnold had emerged and was on the other side of the St. Lawrence from Quebec, "with his men in great spirits after . . . almost insuperable difficulties. . . . The merit of this gentleman is certainly great, and I heartily wish that Fortune may distinguish him as one of her favorites."[10]

Washington's daring strategy would almost certainly have succeeded in taking Quebec by surprise had not Arnold been struck in the wilderness by a hurricane. Among those of his troops that did not turn back, many died of starvation and exposure in a maze of fallen trees and risen water. And the survivors were so delayed that Quebec had been reinforced on the very eve of their arrival. Yet there was still hope. Montgomery was advancing from Montreal to join Arnold under Quebec's high walls. Their combined efforts might well, by capturing the fortress city, break what was left of British resistance in Canada.[11]

Washington not only expanded the war into Canada: he was sniffing the ocean breezes. In harbors up and down the New England coast, merchant vessels were, because of the hostilities, rocking in idleness. The owners expressed eagerness to assign them for nominal sums to any governmental bodies that would give them official status as armed privateers, the owners to get a share in the value of all captures. This was a standard naval arm in those days and could contribute greatly to the blockade of Boston.

Having, with the help of John Adams, secured the jittery approval of Congress to a briny escalation of hostilities, Washington put army guns and an army crew on the seventy-eight-ton coasting schooner *Hannah* out of Marblehead. On September 2, 1775, Washington inaugurated the American navy with his orders to Captain Nicholson Broughton. The sailor was to seek out and capture vulnerable vessels in the service of the ministry, to treat prisoners "with kindness and humanity as far as is consistent with your own safety," and not to confiscate personal belongings. One-third of the value of the rest of the prize, military and naval stores excepted, was to be divided among the captors.[12]

There were soon six ships in what has been called "George Washington's Navy." He sent the captains word when his spies reported that a British vessel was expected in Boston, or his lookouts saw one clearing the harbor. The patriot raiders were fast enough to overhaul the ponderous supply ships which the ministry had failed adequately to arm, and small enough to flee danger into shallow water where warships could not follow. Washington estimated in December that their prizes so far were worth nearly £20,000 sterling.[13]

The wife of the new director general of hospitals, Dr. John Morgan, was having tea at headquarters, when a messenger rushed in with a dispatch box. The anxious look with which Washington opened it changed into a broad smile. He announced that the schooner *Lee*, commanded by Captain John Manley, had taken the British ordnance brig *Nancy*.

"What delighted me excessively," Mrs. Morgan wrote, "was seeing the pleasure which shone in every countenance, particularly General Gates's: he was in an ecstasy. And as General Washington was reading the invoice [2000 muskets, 100,000 flints, more than 30 tons of musket bullets, a brass mortar, etc.] there was scarce an article he did not comment upon, and that with so much warmth as diverted everyone present."[14]

Washington made Manley commodore of his little fleet, hoping thus to get some of the difficulty off his own back. "The plague, trouble, and vexation I have had with the crews of all the armed vessels is," he wrote, "inexpressible. I do believe there is not on earth a more disorderly set." Every time they came to port "our rascally privateersmen" tended to mutiny "if they cannot do as they please." Washington rose to a fury when "a blundering lieutenant of the blundering Captain Coit, who had just blundered upon two vessels from Nova Scotia, came in with the account of it, and before I could rescue" a letter he was writing, "without knowing what he did, picked up a candle and sprinkled it with grease."[15]

On being driven from the seacoast in 1776, Washington (to his vast relief) turned the ships over to the naval committee of Congress, and after that he had, as he wrote, "nothing to do with the naval department." However, he had shown great natural gifts as an admiral.[16]

Howe complained that the privateers—not only Washington's but also those commissioned by colonial legislatures—"which in great numbers infest the bay of Boston" increased his "very alarming apprehensions" concerning "provisions and stores." They could not be stopped on the high seas. Nor could his own navy block the ports from which the privateers came unless given the assistance of land forces which Howe ruled "could not possibly be spared." Retaliatory raids on the offending seaports were the obvious move.[17]

However, the British, who blamed the rebellion on a small group of rabble-rousers, did not wish to supply these subversive characters with atrocity stories. Before British vessels set fire with incendiary shells to the three hundred houses that constituted the town of Falmouth, Massachusetts (now Portland, Maine), the inhabitants were warned. All escaped unhurt.

In an emotional recruiting appeal, Washington linked the destruction of Falmouth with reports then coming in that the British were negotiating to hire from Russia or Germany mercenaries for service in America: "When life, liberty, and property are at stake; when our country is in danger of being a melancholy scene of bloodshed and desolation; when our towns are laid in ashes and innocent women and children driven from their peaceful habitations . . . and a brutal and savage enemy (more so than was ever yet found in a civilized nation) are threatening us and everything we hold dear with destruction from foreign troops, it little becomes the character of a soldier to shrink from danger and condition for new terms [of enlistment]."[18]

The enlistment of the Connecticut line—thirty-seven hundred rank and file—would run out on December 1, and that of almost all the other troops on the 31st. All would have to be replaced by an army secured entirely anew.

Congress* had decided that this force should be recruited for only one year —till the end of 1776—when presumably, if the war was still going on, a third army would have to be created. What would happen in 1777 was, however, too distant a problem for Washington to bother with now. His immediate concern was that, unless he could get many of the soldiers in his camp to re-enlist, on New Year's Day he would have almost no army. Inquiry revealed that the men, most of whom had come from small villages and were used only to neighbors, were afraid that they might have to serve under officers who were strangers. The first task thus was to determine the new officer corps.

That the army was regarded as "an entire new creation" did not make this easier, but compounded the problem. The number of regiments was being reduced to get a full complement of men in each. Thus some of the best and most influential officers were in danger of being set adrift: to moor them again was extremely difficult, since officers could not be shifted from the regiments of one colony to another, or even between sections of the same colony. As for getting in officers from outside New England, that remained impossible. Add to this that, although all were as green as saplings and actual order of seniority was often extremely difficult to determine, no officer would serve under another whom he suspected of being his junior, if only by twenty-four hours.[19]

At one despairing moment, the Commander in Chief decided wearily that there was no way of getting the arrangements completed. However, memory brought back to him how he had been just as much of a problem to his commanders in the French and Indian War, and with memory came understanding that tempered irritation. He realized that he had "to give in to the humor and whimsies of the people, or get no army." And also he developed a procedure: he gathered officers together into battalions and then set up a board to determine who within the group should command whom. The New Englanders were great disputers but used to compromise. After everyone had "an opportunity of advancing all his reasons for precedence," a decision could be reached "to the satisfaction of them all."[20]

When it became time to enlist the men, every Yankee became a shrewd bargainer for his service. "Such a dearth of public spirit and want of virtue," wrote Washington, "such stock-jobbing and fertility in all the low arts to obtain advantages . . . such a dirty, mercenary spirit pervades the whole that I should not be at all surprised at any disaster that may happen." He promised—to the weakening of his supplies and numbers—that those who re-enlisted should have new clothes and could go home on furloughs.

---

* Early in October, Congress had sent a committee—Benjamin Franklin, Benjamin Harrison, and Thomas Lynch—to confer with Washington and his generals on setting up the army for the following year. Such committees, which reported back to their parent body, became an annual feature of Washington's Revolutionary career.

But in the meanwhile, he had no money to meet the back payroll, which gave rise to rumors that the southern command were holding back money to line their own pockets. When at last sheets of crisp new bills arrived, they were useless for lack of the "signers" whose scrawls were needed to make them legal.[21]

The troops in his encampments, Washington complained, showed one common "desire of retiring to a chimney corner." And Congress had been deaf to his urgings that they, in cooperation with the governments of the various colonies, replenish the army with some kind of a draft. All he could do was to send a lieutenant from each company to its home country to try to lure in new men. That would take a long time before it produced results. To make matters more depressing for the Virginian commander, heavier snows than he had ever seen were falling, turning the ground into an unpleasant white waste.[22]

Washington confided in a letter to Reed that "the reflection on my situation, and that of this army," gave him "many an uneasy hour when all around me are wrapped in sleep. Few people know the predicament we are in, on a thousand accounts; fewer still will believe, if any disaster happens to these lines, from what cause it flows. I have often thought how much happier I should have been if, instead of accepting of a command under such circumstances, I had taken my musket on my shoulder and entered the ranks, or, if I could have justified the measure to posterity and my conscience, had retired to the back country and lived in a wigwam."

Should he be able to get through January without a catastrophe, "I shall most religiously believe that the finger of Providence is in it," for surely, if the enemy did not take advantage of his weakness, "it must be for want of their knowing the disadvantages we labor under."[23]

Washington realized that this letter would cause much trouble if it fell into enemy hands—"I shall be somewhat uneasy" until he heard that Reed had received it—but he could not resist confiding in his absent aide whom he regarded as his intimate friend. "I know no persons," he wrote Reed on another occasion, "able to supply your places (in this part of the world) with whom I would choose to live in unbounded confidence." If only Reed would come back to him: "You cannot but be sensible of your importance to me." His continuing to stay away gave Washington pain.[24]

He would have been even more hurt had he realized that Reed was regarding the Commander in Chief's indiscretions and his appeals as a sign that Washington was not worthy of the post entrusted to him. Reed sent back his resignation from the army: he had accepted election to the Pennsylvania Assembly.

Others could make choices but, however handicapped and lonely, Washington had to stay. Around his headquarters in Cambridge, New Year's Eve was like a carnival, for thousands of men were in the best of spirits as they set out for home. But Washington felt only foreboding. He had made what plans he could to replace the departing men on the widely extended lines in as silent and orderly a manner as possible, but he knew that not enough troops would remain. Some of the defenses were being left unmanned. Now, if ever, was the time for the British to attack!

The Commander in Chief was all alertness, his military senses on the stretch. On the hills, men stood by fresh, fast horses, staring through telescopes. Before twilight deepened into impervious darkness, Washington may himself have ridden to an eminence to look: the enemy camp seemed somnolent; too quiet, perhaps? In any case, it was his duty to return to headquarters, where all dispatches came. How late did he pace the floor; how restlessly did his long body turn in bed? Certainly his ears strained and strained. Was that a shout of warning or the drunken call of a released soldier? Horses' hoofs: far, nearer, passing by. A door slam or a shot? And then it was dawn. Telescopes again, and Boston still quiet.

Although the new army was as narrowly New England as the old (most of the troops from elsewhere on active service were in the Canadian campaign), Washington announced bravely that his force "in every point of view is entirely continental." From a cupboard at headquarters there was extracted a large oblong of colored cloth. Halyards were tied to it, and, as Washington wrote, "We hoisted the union flag in compliment to the United Colonies." The Union Jack of Great Britain was marked on the flag, but only as an oblong in the upper left-hand corner. The rest of the flapping bunting showed thirteen stripes, red and white. The British in Boston rejoiced at first as they thought it was a flag of surrender.[25]

CHAPTER

7

Foreign War or Social Revolution

WASHINGTON had hoped for so long that the crisis would ease before winter, enabling him to return at once to Mount Vernon, that he had allowed the season to become too far advanced, raising the danger of snow-clogged roads, before he wrote his wife to come from Virginia and join him.

Martha Washington had never been far from home. Even in a familiar countryside she awoke with terror when the dogs barked. Now the timid housewife procrastinated about obeying her husband's summons until the estate manager, Lund, wrote his employer censuring her "ill-judged" behavior. "I suppose in one way or another she will make it the 20th [of November] before she will get off."[1]

When Martha did finally get off, she surrounded herself with friends. Near her head in the rocking coach bobbed familiar heads: she saw her son, John Parke Custis, and his wife; General Gates's wife; and her nephew, George Lewis, who wished to serve his uncle as aide. The attention they were accorded on the road surprised Martha. She was met on the outskirts of Philadelphia with "as great pomp as if I had been a great somebody." A military escort of horsemen led her into town.[2]

After the untraveled lady had settled in her lodgings, she was subjected to a severe test of her ability to get on in a strange environment with people whose ideas differed radically from her own. She had been invited to a ball to be given in her honor by leading citizens. She was enjoying anticipations of the dance and had her mind (so we may assume) half on what she would wear, when callers were announced. In came a delegation, four soberly dressed citizens who were obviously torn between embarrassment and a sense of their own importance. The plump, diminutive Virginian chatted with them good-humoredly till they found their tongues. Then they expressed "great regard and affection to her." She thanked them prettily.

They requested her "to accept their grateful acknowledgment and respect due to her on account of her near connection with our worthy and brave general, now exposed in the field of battle in defense of our rights and liberties." She thanked them again. Then came a tightening of their faces. They had come to "request and desire her not to grace that company to which, we are informed, she has an invitation this evening."

It developed that the more radical patriots had threatened to wreck the tavern where the ball was to be held rather than permit the more conservative patriots to involve the Commander in Chief's wife in an excess they considered unsuited to "these troubled times." Robert Hanson Harrison of Maryland, the aide Washington had sent to Philadelphia to meet Martha, was to engage in an angry argument with Samuel Adams of Massachusetts about such bluenosed proceedings. But Martha responded to the request of her gimlet-eyed callers with, as one of them remembered, "great politeness." She sent her "best compliments" to those objecting to the ball, with assurance "that their sentiments on this occasion were perfectly agreeable unto her own." The ball was canceled.[3]

Martha and her party reached Cambridge in mid-December heralded by a letter from Reed stating that Mesdames Washington, Custis and Gates were "very agreeable ladies. . . . No bad supply, I think, in a cold country where wood is scarce. . . . The face of your camp will be changed."[4]

Washington had by now moved into the house of a rich Tory, John Vassall, who had fled to Boston leaving fine furniture behind. As was always the case at his headquarters, his aides lived in, sleeping several to a room. Through the front hall there was a perpetual bustle: the drawing room was the Commander in Chief's office. When a vast quantity of papers had to be prepared, Martha lent a hand, but for the most part she brought what her husband called "the softer domestic virtues" to a household which had previously been altogether masculine. In particular, ladies could now be better entertained. They were "treated with oranges and a glass of wine" in midmorning, or asked to dinner which was held fashionably at two.[5]

When Mercy Warren, who was not only a housewife like Martha but also a bluestocking, authoress, and politician, came to call, the Virginia matron received her terrifying visitor, so Mrs. Warren wrote, "with that politeness and respect shown in a first interview among the well-bred, and with the ease and cordiality" of older friendship. "The complacency of her manners speaks at once the benevolence of her heart, and her affability, candor, and gentleness qualify her to soften the hours of private life, or to sweeten the cares of the hero, and smooth the rugged pains of war."[6]

Martha wrote one of her lady friends at home: "Every person seems to be cheerful and happy here. . . . I confess I shudder every time I hear the sound of a gun. . . . To me that never see anything of war, the preparations are very terrible indeed, but I endeavor to keep my fears to myself as well as I can." She added cattily that "there are but two ladies in Cambridge" who got much attention from men, "but neither of them is pretty, I think."[7]

Washington's headquarters was, even before it had to take to the road with an army on the move, a most complicated domestic operation. However, it was organized to run independently of Martha. The purse was always held by one of Washington's aides, who paid bills and kept accounts for presentation to Congress. Unless one left before another could be found, there was a steward: in Cambridge, Ebenezer Austin, who got on (as some others did not) without the assistance of a housekeeper.

At the moment, Washington employed two cooks. Adam Foutz had the *panache* of being French, but he soon shifted to guarding headquarters with a musket on his shoulder, we know not whether because he yearned for gunpowder or his sauces did not please. The other cook was called Edward Hunt. Mrs. Morrison served as kitchen maid. The washerwoman, Mary Kettel, probably only did rough work, as large bills were paid for outside washing. Washington was soon to acquire a tailor, Giles Alexander, who seems to have traveled with headquarters throughout the war.

The duties of Eliza Chapman, Timothy Austin, James Munroe, and the Negroes Dinah and Peter were not specified. This staff was soon augmented by more Negroes: Servant Jack and Sailor Jack; Hannah, who belonged to a minister and was working to buy her freedom; and a seamstress who appeared in February 1776 and became more entwined with Washington's life than he found agreeable.[8]

She was Margaret Thomas, a free mulatto. Her charms smote the heart of Washington's mulatto body servant, Billy Lee, a slave whom he had bought in 1768 for £61, and who had become inseparable from his owner. Billy claimed that he and Margaret had married. This Washington doubted, but as long as the servant who had "followed my fortunes" for so long with such "fidelity" remained attached to the lady, he could not ban her from his family, although he came to long for the happy day when he would "see her no more."[9]

Since he rose with the dawn, Washington was usually through with routine business by dinnertime. Each day his table was more crowded than it had been at Mount Vernon, and, food being plentiful in Cambridge, a large variety of meats and vegetables tempted the guests. In the presence of the ladies, Washington was always courtly, lighthearted, if sometimes a little formal. When the dessert was finished, the ladies withdrew. Then Washington, his aides, the other officers, and what male citizens were present sat over their wine.

Madeira flowed plentifully. The largest single item in the headquarters accounts for September 1775 was £35.6.11 for this liquid necessity. More

Top: Washington's camp knife and fork; handles with horn insets and made to fit into each other. *Bottom left:* Camp towel; homespun linen embroidered in cross-stitch. *Bottom right:* Leather pack bag. Courtesy of the Mount Vernon Ladies' Association of the Union.

was bought on October 6 for £28. Early in December there is another entry, £37.18.10 for 108 bottles delivered on October 11, and 109 on October 22. Washington believed that wine brought "cheerfulness" to his table.[10]

Nineteenth-century writers would have us believe that, if the conversation got a little rough, the Father of Our Country would rise, his cheeks becomingly mantled with blushes, and say in the manner of Queen Victoria, "We are not amused!" Here is a letter he wrote a year after the war concerning the marriage of an elderly veteran to a younger bride:

"I am glad to hear that my old acquaintance Colonel Ward is yet under the influence of vigorous passions. I will not ascribe the intrepidity of his late enterprise to a mere *flash* of desires, because, in his military career, he would have learned how to distinguish between false alarms and a serious movement. Charity, therefore, induces me to suppose that, like a prudent general, he had reviewed his *strength*, his arms, and ammunition before he got involved in an action. But if these have been neglected, and he has been precipitated into the measure, let me advise him to make the *first* onset upon his fair del Toboso* with vigor that the impression may be deep if it cannot be lasting or frequently renewed."[11]

The pratfalls of ordinary living, rather than fantasy or exaggeration, most amused Washington. We may thus credit an anecdote that comes to us via gossip rather than document. He was sitting, so the story runs, with his generals over wine when they heard, echoing from the distant lines, gunshots and alarm bells. As they sprang to their feet and started for the door, General Greene cried out that he could not find his wig. He was much agitated. By contrast a monument of martial coolness, General Lee urged, "Look for it behind the mirror, sir!" Greene hurried to the mirror and saw in the glass the missing wig firmly on his own head, and behind him General Washington doubled up with mirth.[12]

However, Washington did not countenance excesses that undermined discipline. Another believable anecdote is that when he heard some drunken soldiers squabbling in the yard outside his headquarters, he rushed out and flattened a few of the brawlers with his own fists. One of his general orders read, "The vile practice of swallowing the whole ration of liquor at a single draught is also to be prevented by causing the sergeants to see it . . . mixed with water. . . . In which case, instead of being pernicious, it will become very refreshing and salutary."[13]

Washington was now regularly offering hospitality to the New England politicians, particularly John Adams, who was temporarily back from the Continental Congress. The Massachusetts men were charmed by the gra-

---

* Don Quixote took a simple country girl, whom he called Dulcinea del Toboso, as his fair lady.

cious southern commander and his equally gracious wife, charmed by the high-spirited young outlanders on his staff who could propose a toast so elegantly and hold their liquor like gentlemen; but yet the attitude that had opposed Martha's ball in Philadelphia made this society seem, in its very seductiveness, disturbing.

John Adams had actually heard that there was a whispering in coffee-houses that the people wanted an American king. He wrote half playfully to Mercy Warren: "Monarchy is the genteelest and most fashionable government, and I don't know why the ladies ought not to consult elegance and the fashion." For his part, he preferred a republican "virtue and simplicity of manners." Monarchy entailed "so much elegance in dress, furniture, equipage; so much music and dancing, so much fencing and skating, so much cards and backgammon, so much horse racing and cockfighting, so many balls and assemblies, so many plays and concerts that the very imagination of them makes me feel vain, light, frivolous, and insignificant."

Untraveled John Adams had no conception of what life was really like at a royal court: his vision much more closely resembled a gay week at Mount Vernon broken with a visit to the Annapolis races. He felt that this was the life with which George Washington was familiar, and the very thought of that life made him feel what he most hated to be: insignificant.[14]

Washington would have liked to give to the press, "as a compliment" to the poetess, an ode to him by the colored versifier Phillis Wheatley, but he decided it was wiser to suppress the effusion which ended:

A crown, a mansion, and a throne that shine
With gold unfailing, Washington be thine!"[15]

However, arguments concerning a native royalty were mere anticipations of distant possibilities. The immediate issue was what to do about enthusiastic supporters of the existing royal government. They were legally justified, since independence had not been declared, but they presented active dangers to the cause.

The Massachusetts loyalists were for the most part in Boston with the British, and whatever problems of subversion remained were being efficiently handled by the local government. It was not until the British threatened to spread out the war that the handling of Tories rejoined the crowd of quandries that were ranked around Washington.

After the burning of Falmouth, the ministerial command announced that similar destruction awaited New England's other seaports. No one could foresee that this would prove to be an empty threat. Calls poured in on Washington for soldiers. Although he could not send the various towns Continental garrisons without tearing up his army and violating an order of Congress that local defense should be undertaken by local militia, he dispatched to the communities most menaced a few of his magic-makers, the riflemen, and also high officers to superintend the defenses. These officers found, resident in the towns they were supposed to protect, royal officials surrounded with Tory supporters. The matter should have been handled by the provincial authorities. However, almost all the civilian governments were still skating on the thin ice of a loosely defined cause. They lacked the unanimity to act with effect.[16]

As Washington realized, the fundamental danger, more menacing even than the ministerial soldiers and ships, was the fact that the cause was not monolithic but double. Two quite different issues were clasped together like a pair of hands which, if pulled apart, would become fists striking at each other. Ostensibly, the cause was no more than a protest against injustice coming in from England. However, the seas on which everyone had been launched were unexplored, and no one knew what port would in the end be found. Social revolution might take over from foreign war.

Rebellions appeal naturally to pushing spirits whom the status quo least favors, but tend to frighten those who have the most to lose. Thus, despite innumerable exceptions like Washington himself, the more determined patriots usually came from the middle or lower strata, while, among the native-born, violent loyalists tended to be the socially correct and the well-to-do. The majority of the population were still undecided; they needed time to make up their minds. If too greatly hurried, they might scurry in panic toward the haven most obviously indicated by their social and economic ranks. Thus, there was ever present the danger that the cause would break in half, the prosperous fleeing for protection into the arms of the ministry as the revolt became the cause of the lower classes and was directed against American as well as British men of property.

"There are the shelves," Washington wrote in nautical metaphor, "we have to avoid, or our bark will split and tumble to pieces. Here lies our great danger, and I almost tremble when I think of this rock. Nothing but disunion can hurt our cause. This will ruin it, if great prudence, temper, and moderation is not mixed in our councils, and made the governing principles of the contending parties."[17]

Washington's problem was to deal with the present without upsetting the future. Since the civil governments could not take the lead, it devolved on him to find the best middle ground between leniency that would permit damaging aid to the enemy and stringency that would disgust and frighten the moderates. His ratiocinations were further troubled by a moral issue: he did not believe that men should be persecuted for beliefs which had not led to inimical actions.

This he explained some years later in writing to a former neighbor and present Tory sympathizer, Bryan Fairfax: "The friendship I ever professed and felt for you met with no diminution from the difference in our political sentiments. I know the rectitude of my own intentions, and, believing in the sincerity of yours, lamented, though I did not condemn, your renunciation of the creed I had adopted. Nor do I think any person or power ought to" interfere "whilst your conduct is not opposed to the general interest of the people, and the measures they are pursuing. . . . Our actions, depending upon ourselves, may be controlled, while the powers of thinking, originating in higher causes, cannot always be molded to our wishes."[18]

The mildest possible step in relation to the Tories seemed to Washington the most advisable. As he sent off the New Hampshire brigadier John Sullivan to lead the defense of Portsmouth, he urged the legislature of that state and, indeed, "every other government on the continent" to arrest officials of the Crown who had given "pregnant proofs of their unfriendly disposition." They were to be banished to the interior and their paroles taken that they would stay where they would do no harm. Other suspected Tories were only to be warned.[19]

This seemed milk-and-waterish to the Massachusetts leaders and their intimate, the English radical General Lee. When Lee was sent to arrange the defense of Newport, he on his own authority demanded that all suspected Tories sign an oath stating that they would not assist the enemy. Three who refused were arrested. Washington recognized, probably with reluctance, the expediency of Lee's action, writing Congress that to imitate it in every province would have "a good effect."[20]

At the very end of 1775, shocking news came in across the ocean. The colonists had pinned their hopes on George III intervening for them with his ministry. But the King had now publicly declared that, having received, as he put it, "the most friendly offers of foreign assistance," he was determined to smash by force "a rebellious war" manifestly being carried on for the purpose of establishing "an independent empire." This speech was a turning point in American history, for it forced into innumerable reluctant minds the unwelcome conclusion that "an independent empire" might, indeed, become necessary. Washington was to remember that the speech made a great change in his own thinking.[21]

Early in January 1776, spies reported that the British in Boston were preparing an expeditionary force. General Lee thereupon wrote Washington that "the consequences of the enemy's possessing themselves of New York have appeared to me so terrible that I have scarcely been able to sleep." The city, Lee continued, was controlled by Tories who would welcome any invader and Tory bands were actually operating on Long Island. Congress, with its powerful delegation of New York conservatives, could take no steps, but Lee (who was in daily contact with the Massachusetts leaders) believed that the "best members" of Congress expected Washington to step into the breach by ordering that the city be secured and its Tories suppressed or

[65]

expelled. Lee now proposed that he collect Connecticut volunteers, secure aid perhaps from New Jersey, and march into New York.[22]

Having consulted John Adams, who vehemently backed the suggestion, Washington ordered Lee to proceed. By authorizing a Connecticut force to enter New York and disarm any persons "whose conduct and declarations have rendered them justly suspected of designs unfriendly to the views of Congress," Washington, on the advice of members of the radical wing, took the responsibility for what could be considered the invasion of a middle colony by New England. He was every day thinking more in continental than regional terms.[23]

The Connecticut revolutionaries, who had already made one unofficial (and deeply resented) foray into New York City, flocked to Lee's banners. But the Continental Congress acted quickly to protect New York's independence. They ruled that any troops who went into that colony to arrest Tories became subject, the instant they crossed the border, to the commands of the local authorities.[24]

In ordering Lee to disband his force, Washington expressed his continuing belief that "the period is arrived when nothing less than the most decisive and vigorous measures should be pursued." To Congress, he wrote that he was not fond of stretching his powers and wished they would say, "Thus far and no further you shall go."[25]

Lee, about whom farce always hovered, came down with gout and had to be carried into New York City, where he met with the local authorities and a committee Congress had sent there. He instantly changed his mind about the Yorkers: "I really believe that the generality are as well affected as any on the continent." John Adams thereupon wrote Lee. "A luckier, happier expedition than yours to New York never was projected. The whole Whig* world is blessing you for it." As for Washington, he expunged New York from his immediate, compulsive worries. He had plenty of others.[26]

Trying not to enlarge but to shrink his responsibilities, he urged Congress to appoint anyone they pleased as an additional brigadier; and he did not object when that body set up two military commands semi-independent of his own. The "middle department," under Schuyler, was to include, in addition to New York and Canada, all the states from New Jersey through Maryland. A "southern department" was to extend from Virginia through Georgia.[27]

As usual, Washington was responding to needs rather than precedents. When he heard in mid-January that the Canadian army had been shattered in an unsuccessful assault on Quebec—Montgomery killed and Arnold wounded—he felt the crisis was too great to wait on action from Congress

---

* The use of the words "Whig" to represent the patriots and "Tory" for the loyalists grew out of Whig support in England for the Revolution and the contention in America that the armed protest was only against the Tory ministry.

[66]

or the commander of the middle department. He urged the three major New England states each to raise a regiment and rush it northward.[28]

Montgomery and Arnold had been forced to attack when they did because the enlistments of their men were due to expire in a few days with the New Year. Washington himself had lived through a desperate New Year's Eve, and had no desire to try to live through another. He had hoped before the end of 1776, when his whole existing army would be free to go home. But now he had abandoned that hope.

How everything had changed since George III's truculent speech! During the previous October, Washington had, in his optimism, lightly dismissed a congressional suggestion that two companies of marines be enlisted not just for a year but for "the continuance of the war." Now he wrote Congress that all troops should be enlisted for that continuance.

Even if high bounties had to be paid to secure such soldiers, the cost, Washington argued, would in the end be less than paying smaller sums perpetually for replacements; and surely the army would be more effective. It took time to establish "such a subordinate way of thinking as is necessary for a soldier." Furthermore, "men who are familiarized to danger, meet it without shrinking, whereas those who have never seen service, often apprehend danger where no danger is."[29]

The Adamses were strong in disapproval. John stated that he did not know what the transported convicts and indentured servants who inhabited other colonies might accept, but it was inconceivable that freeborn New Englanders would give up for so indefinite a term as the duration of the war "better living, more comfortable lodgings, more than double the wages." Samuel Adams added that standing armies were "always dangerous to the liberties of the people."[30]

However, now that Washington was converted to long terms of service, he believed in them passionately. He was, in subsequent years, to blame what then seemed to be an interminable prolongation of the war on Congress's refusal to authorize enlistment for the duration at this time when, "the passions [being] inflamed," men flew "hastily and cheerfully to arms." Those early months of 1776 were, indeed, for the more convinced patriots months of great excitement. A new sun seemed to be bursting into the sky.[31]

Like his lesser contemporaries, Washington read Thomas Paine's just-published *Common Sense* with the feeling that the arguments for establishing an independent nation were being spoken by an eloquent voice in his own mind. And, as if to confirm this rising surge of feeling, Governor Dunmore of Virginia, who had once been Washington's friend, initiated war in Washington's home province: he superintended the bombing and burning of Norfolk. And he announced that this was just a beginning. It was hard to doubt that Mount Vernon, so easily available to British warships operating up the Potomac, would suffer from British spite. Well, if the past must go up in flames, it must: there remained the future.[32]

On January 31, 1776, Washington first acknowledged in writing the possibility of independence: "A few more such flaming arguments as were exhibited at Falmouth and Norfolk, added to the sound doctrine and unanswerable reasoning contained in the pamphlet *Common Sense* will not leave numbers at a loss to decide upon the propriety of a separation." He added ten days later that Congress should tell the ministers of Great Britain that "the spirit of freedom beat too high in us to submit to slavery, and that, if nothing else could satisfy a tyrant and his diabolical ministry, we are determined to shake off all connections with a state so unjust and unnatural."[33]

8

Providence Rides a Storm

T HE snow might fall in Cambridge as almost never at Mount Vernon, imposing silence, dimming out the world; yet as he lay sleepless in the dark, Washington felt "the eyes of the whole continent fixed with anxious expectation" upon him. He knew that he was being criticized for allowing a large and expensive army to sit motionless month after month. Although he did not put the whole blame on Congress for chronic shortages of money, arms, tents, gunpowder, engineers—"I dare say the demands upon them are greater than they can supply"—he nonetheless found it hard that Congress seemed "to look upon this as the season for action, but will not furnish the means."[1]

When morning came, he would go out to the bay and jump up and down on the ice in the harbor. It was strong enough to carry his army all the way to the British. Shortages or no, surely this was an opportunity to be improved!

In mid-February, Washington notified a council of his general officers that their army had, or expected soon to have, 16,077 men. His spies reported that the enemy had only 5000 fit for duty. These would be kept so busy by a "bold and resolute push" across the ice that the Americans would have to leave only a skeleton garrison to protect their camp: they could bring their whole force to bear, overwhelming the British. The battle might well "put a final end to the war and restore peace and tranquillity so much to be wished for."

As he argued for such a battle, Washington scanned the faces of his generals without seeing any satisfactory kindling in their eyes. The reply came that with Tory irregulars the British numbered many more than 5000 (this was correct); that 2000 of the patriots lacked arms; that, in fact, a strong force would have to be left to hold the American lines. And, in any case, an assault should be preceded by several days of bombardment.

Washington then asked whether the bombardment could be begun "with the present stock of powder." His officers voted to wait for an adequate supply.[2]

The decision to postpone everything, Washington commented to Congress, "being almost unanimous, I suppose must be right," yet he was still in favor of an immediate assault. Of course, "the irksomeness of my situation . . . might have inclined me to put more to the hazard than was consistent with prudence." Yet he had considered the matter very carefully. How the planter and wilderness fighter, long used to improvisation, emphasizes will over means is revealed by his "firm hope" that if the men would stand by him, an assault would triumph "notwithstanding the enemy's advantage of ground, artillery, etc."[3]

Washington had developed an artillery corps of his own. Since he perpetually urged his officers to make up for their lack of experience by reading, he had been impressed to see "a very fat but very active young man" with an artillery manual almost always in his hand. On better acquaintance, Henry Knox proved very strong despite his obesity, clever, and possessed of "a jubilant personality." Furthermore, if the former Boston bookseller was given the least to work with, he would improvise something that would function at least pretty well. The Massachusetts leaders also admired Knox: Washington put him in charge of the artillery.[4]

When snow had smoothed rutty roads so that heavy objects could be pulled over them on sledges, Knox was sent off to Ticonderoga to fetch the cannon that had been captured with that royal fort. By early February, he had succeeded in dragging to Cambridge, across several hundred miles, fifty-nine fieldpieces. Although many were rusty, cumbersome and antiquated, the patriots felt they now had "a noble train of artillery."[5]

With his officers, Washington now worked out a plan for using this artillery. Penetrating into the bay to the southeast of Boston Neck was still another peninsula, Dorchester. Inland on this broad neck, but still within two miles of Boston, were heights from which, so Washington wrote, cannon could "command a great part of the town and almost the whole harbor." Furthermore, jutting out from the Dorchester Peninsula on the Boston side was another eminence, known as Nook's Hill, which was separated from the city only by a half-mile-wide channel. The Council of War decided to prepare so that, when the necessary powder arrived, they could plant the cannon first on Dorchester Heights and then, if possible, on Nook's Hill.[6]

The strategic importance of the hills had long been recognized by both commands. However, the Americans had been incapable of making effective use of them until Knox appeared with the cannon. And for the British to have occupied them would have overextended their lines, which were already large in relation to the size of their army. Furthermore, any force

General Henry Knox, by Charles Willson Peale. Courtesy of the Independence National Historical Park Collection.

they placed on Dorchester would have been vulnerable to a surprise assault, since the peninsula abutted on the patriot-held mainland but was separated from Boston by water barely passable in bad weather.

Even after his spies had told him that Washington intended to fortify Dorchester Heights, Howe reasoned that he should let the rebels try, and then by blasting or driving them out before they could get a foothold, return the hills to their role as no-man's-land. He knew that the rebels were good at burying themselves like moles, but the ground was frozen too solid for such digging.[7]

Washington had for two months now been preparing means for fortifying on frozen earth. Men not guarding the lines or building barracks had been kept busy tying together "fascines"—bundles of sticks three feet thick and four long—or nailing up "chandeliers"—frames in which these would be placed. Others had been collecting hay and screwing it into great bundles. Carts were now mobilized to carry all to Dorchester Heights, and spades sharpened so that at least a little earth could be moved to hold the equipment down.

As these American preparations went on, enemy preparations seemed to be for evacuating Boston. Four or five hundred men actually sailed away under the British second in command, Sir Henry Clinton. The rest of the shipping in the harbor was being mobilized, and some mortars were taken down from Bunker Hill.[8]

Although Washington feared a "feint" to put him off his guard, there was the possibility that the British actually intended to move away. A few months before, this prospect would have delighted Washington; he would have assumed that they were returning to England. But since then, public statements by George III had made it clear that the British would not end the war until they were defeated in battle. Should they really evacute Boston, they would surely sail over the ocean they controlled to some more strategically promising American harbor, probably New York. The patriots would then be in a less advantageous position than they were now; more would be lost than gained by simply dislodging the British from Boston. Washington concluded that he should crush the British before they could get away.

British regulars, Washington reasoned, would not cravenly embark under the threat of guns placed on Dorchester. If the patriot positions could withstand the cannonading which would certainly be the enemy's first reaction—and Washington intended to see that they should—surely Howe would feel that the honor of his army required an assault with musket and bayonet. This would create another Bunker Hill. Washington had agreed with the criticisms of Ward for not taking advantage of the confusion the slaughter at Bunker Hill had created in the British camp. He had no intention of imitating his predecessor.

The ice having melted, he collected a flotilla of small boats in the Charles River which flowed past Cambridge into the harbor. If the British attacked Dorchester Heights in sufficient numbers to weaken the Boston garrison, four thousand patriots were to climb into the little boats and cast off in two divisions.

After three "floating batteries" (each consisting of one twelve-pounder) had been rowed into position and had softened up the beachhead, the first wave was to land on Boston Common and seize the two hills there: "Beacon Hill and Mount Horam." The second wave would then land a little farther south; the two forces would meet, advance against the unfortified rear of the British lines on Boston Neck, smash those lines, and let into town another patriot force that would be waiting at Roxbury. Then it would be just a matter of mopping up the British army.

Considering the plan "well digested," reassured by "the cheerfulness and alacrity" of the subordinates to whom he had entrusted the preparations, Washington saw "reason to hope for a favorable and happy issue."[9] Yet he had dark forebodings. To his brother-in-law, Burwell Bassett, he expressed concern about his title to some wilderness lands at the confluence of the savage Kanawha and the wild Ohio: "In the worst event" they would serve him "for an asylum."[10]

On February 27, Washington's general orders sent quakes of excitement and fear through the thousands of human bodies around him: "As the season is fast approaching when every man must expect to be drawn into the field of action, it is highly necessary that he should prepare his mind." The troops should remember that they were engaged in "the cause of virtue and mankind," and also that every man who skulked, hid, or retreated without orders "will be *instantly shot down* as an example of cowardice."[11]

Washington managed to procure a moderate stock of powder. He called in the local militia whom he planned to have occupy his fortifications while the troops were out fighting. He recruited nurses, had two thousand bandages prepared. His Council of General Officers having ruled that several days of preparatory bombardment would weaken the enemy and divert their attention from Dorchester, the guns opened up from the opposite side of the line from the true American objective at about midnight on March 2. After many months of almost unbroken quiet, the sounds were shocking. Abigail Adams rushed to her door in nearby Braintree and ascertained that the firing was from "our army. . . . No sleep for me tonight!"

"From my window," jotted Colonel Webb of Massachusetts, "[I] have a most pleasing and yet dismal view of the fiery ministers of death flying through the air. Poor inhabitants, our friends, we pity most sincerely, but particularly the women and children."[12]

[73]

Washington counted the shots—only about twenty-five had been authorized because of the need to conserve powder—and was pleased to see that they carried well and seemed to be well aimed. However, there were several too-bright flashes and too-loud bangs which revealed that his inexperienced artillerymen had overloaded and burst their guns. Eventually, the British artillery answered. Their guns did not carry far enough to reach the American barracks. There was little call on the two thousand bandages.[13]

The next night the patriots staged a similar bombardment, but the British were more active, making the roaring incessant.

On the third night—it was March 4—the American batteries really let go. Webb thought he heard from Boston "the cries of poor women and children."[14] Washington was too busy for such hallucinations. As soon as darkness laid its sooty hands across British telescopes, movement throbbed through the American camp.

Regiments were paraded and only then told their mission. (Spies had to be frustrated.) Safety, the officers pointed out, would depend on the enemy seeing no light, hearing no shout or accidental musket shot before the fortifications were completed.

Off the men went under a fine moon. The riflemen, who led the advance across the neck, spread out along Dorchester's shore in the direction from which glowed the lights of Boston. They stared below those lights, scanning the sibilate lapping of little gray and silver waves for a possible black intervention of enemy prows.

Now file after file of soldiers carried tools and muskets across the neck and up the heights. Intermingled with them came hundreds of wagons, wagons loaded with fascines, with chandeliers, with tight bales of hay, with barrels filled with stones that could be rolled down the slopes on invaders. After eager hands had unloaded, the wagons turned; later they appeared again. More than a thousand men carried the portable ramparts into position; others scratched up with spades a little earth to hold the ramparts down.

All was shadowy, although the moon "shining [as Washington wrote] in its full luster" cast enough glimmer to enable the men to see what they were doing and to ascertain that a tall figure on a dark horse was General Washington, riding it seemed everywhere.[15]

His nerves were tensed for the blow of noise that would warn the enemy, but Washington heard only the creak of wheels, the plod of horses, the rustle of men, the thud of axes as fruit trees came down to make an abatis. The real noise came from the far side of the harbor where cannon were fixing attention with their continuous roar. At one moment, Washington could have seen seven shells all together in the air.

At three A.M., there began an eerie movement of silent bodies along the exposed causeway to and from the mainland. Three thousand tired, work-stained men marched toward their barracks through the half-mile-wide neck, while about twenty-four hundred fresh men came in to man the fortifications that had already taken shape on the two highest hills and on the tableland between.

The moon sank. The dark tightened. Then light became a wan infusion into mist. The firing at the far end of the lines ceased. Finally, the fog dispelled to reveal the half-circle of bay. On Dorchester Heights, there was a springing of birds. Away and below, Boston seemed quiet, since patriot starers could not discern the newly awakened enemy officers staring back up toward them out of windows.

The British commanders had still been drinking toasts the night before when they had received a report that the enemy were active on Dorchester. However, the officers had gone to sleep contentedly, sure that whatever the yokels were up to could be handled easily the next day. But, lo! when the mist rose they saw revealed such a fortification as they could not believe possible. The engineering officer, Archibald Robertson, stated that this "most astonishing night's work must have employed from 15,000 and 20,000 men," while a more poetic soldier, identified only as "an officer of distinction," was inclined to blame "the geni belonging to Aladdin's wonderful lamp."[16]

The first step in Washington's plan had been sensationally successful. Now for the second and what he considered the more important step! Four thousand fresh men waited on the banks of the Charles River to invade Boston, waited only for a major part of the British garrison there to get into boats, sail away, and assault Dorchester Heights.

Surely, Washington stared through his military telescope from a convenient hill. What Boston streets he could descry were filled by soldiers and civilians gaping with raised heads. He knew that if an attacking British force wished to avoid a long wade through mudflats, they would have to take advantage of the high tide at noon. However, there was little bustle on the wharves. Instead, cannon were being wheeled out, pointed at Dorchester, elevated, fired. The balls struck the hills below the forts. Troops then labored to get more height by burying the rear wheels. More reports, but the balls still did not reach. After some hours the effort was abandoned, but not until it was too late to achieve anything on the noon tide. In the meanwhile, the patriots had been strengthening their position by planting in the Dorchester works six twelve-pounders and bringing up fieldpieces.[17]

Finally, augmenting activity on the waterfront made Washington's heart leap with eager anticipation: troops—they seemed to be several thousands—were getting into small boats and were being rowed out with fieldpieces to transports. The transports fell down to Castle William, a fortified island well situated to be the jumping-off place for an attack on Dorchester.

[75]

All was going according to Washington's plan. The next high tide, which would be about midnight, would surely float the British to the peninsula. General Thomas would keep his twenty-four hundred Americans in their fortifications awaiting the advance up the hillsides which could be expected at dawn. By then, Putnam, Sullivan, and Greene would have their men on the boats in the Charles River, ready to move on Boston as soon as the battle raged on Dorchester. The future of the continent seemed up for grabs.

But before the fateful night was due, the sky created its own unnatural night and there swooped down from overhead a majestic storm. "A wind more violent than anything I ever heard," was the verdict of a Briton. "I never before felt such cold and distress," wrote the rifleman Daniel McCurtin. On Dorchester Heights, Lieutenant Isaac Bangs lay under an apple tree: "What I suffered this night, I shall ever bear in mind." But no one suffered at dawn. The British had not even tried to land on Dorchester.[18]

The storm blew itself out at about eight the next morning, leaving behind a cerulean, translucent, windswept sky, but also huge waves that made any amphibious landing still impossible. And, indeed, when troops left Fort William, it was to return to the inner harbor. From bobbing small boats, the expeditionary force disembarked into town. Boston was again too well defended to be successfully attacked.

Homer would have been sure that some god had ridden in that storm. Washington considered the storm "a remarkable interposition of Providence." His philosophy did not permit him to doubt that Providence had intervened "for some wise purpose. . . . But," so he continued, "as the principal design of the maneuver was to draw the enemy to an engagement under disadvantages, as a premeditated plan was laid for this purpose and seemed to be succeeding to my utmost wish, and as no men seemed better disposed to make the appeal than ours did upon that occasion, I can scarce forbear lamenting the disappointment."[19]

Howe might have felt differently had he known what Washington had planned, but, as he understood matters, he was grateful for the storm. He had ordered an assault on Dorchester not because he believed it militarily wise, but because he "thought the honor of the troops [was] concerned." Now he could blame everything on the weather, a force obviously beyond the regular army's control, which had given the enemy time to make their position impregnable.[20]

That Washington put cannon on Dorchester Heights is taught to every American schoolboy, but even military historians gloss over the fact that this famous maneuver was only the first (and to him the less important) step in his plan. Thus the great storm of March 5 to 6, 1776, is assigned no role in the American historical saga. Yet it was one of the most crucial events in the entire American Revolution.

Had the storm not intervened, there would have been such a battle as the Continental Army actually engaged in only once, at Fort Washington, when the entire American force that was engaged fell to the enemy. In all other battles, the patriots had access to escape routes through which, if they found they could not stand up to the trained European regulars, they could scuttle for safety. But the troops Washington had intended to land in Boston could never have regained their boats. They would have been trapped. They would either have had to annihilate the British or be themselves entirely defeated.

In planning this assault, Washington assumed (it was long to be his strategic fault) a precision in the synchronization of differently advancing groups which it was almost impossible to realize in an actual combat. However, the British, any one of whose officers would have been sent to a lunatic asylum for such a plan, had not the slightest inkling of what Washington intended. The surprise would have been as complete as the time it took to row a mile permitted. This would have been Washington's greatest hope: the regular army mind was not at its best in improvising reactions to what their training told them could never happen.

Yet the odds would have been greatly against the American assault. The patriots would have had to cross a mile of open water into the mouths of British cannon. Had all succeeded in getting ashore, they would have been four thousand against the thirty-six hundred Howe had left to garrison Boston. Only if the columns aimed at different points did not stray but succeeded in joining up according to plan and then successfully broke down the British barrier at Roxbury, would the patriots have had any real numerical superiority. And, as was to be proved again and again in the next few years until it became the basic rock on which Washington built his strategy, the raw Americans were no match in close combat for professional foes trained in maneuvering under fire and in the use of bayonet.

At Dorchester Heights, the situation would have been very different. The patriots had demonstrated at Bunker Hill how deadly they could be when they had protecting walls from which to fire on an exposed enemy. Since then they had become a better disciplined and officered force. At Bunker Hill, they had been outnumbered, but at Dorchester the two sides would have been equal at about twenty-four hundred men each. The chances were thus excellent that, even if the enemy had finally taken the heights, the British would have suffered many more casualties than their army could afford.

It thus seems reasonable to contend that Washington should have been satisfied with this almost certain gain, instead of trying to win the war immediately in a second engagement where the odds would all be on the British side. Had he at this early stage of the contest, well before the Declaration of Independence when so many Americans were still undecided, lost half of his army and with it his own prestige, the cause could either have collapsed or shriveled away.

Perhaps it was the Genius of America who rode that storm, delaying action until her amateur general had time to become more proficient in the art of war.

CHAPTER

9

The Taste of Victory

A LTHOUGH he had correctly guessed that the insult would gall Howe into planning an attack, Washington had not realized how grievously guns on Dorchester Heights would terrify officers well trained in artillery warfare. Kept by Washington's security precautions from discovering that the Americans lacked the powder to improve their advantage with a heavy bombardment, the British admiral Molyneux Shuldham notified Howe that he could not keep his ships in the harbor under the threat. He was so eager to get away that he offered the general a month's supply of naval stores to support the retreat.

Seen from whatever hillside, the Boston streets were, as Washington wrote, full of "great movements and confusion amongst the troops the night and day . . . in hurrying down their cannon, artillery, and other stores to the wharfs with the utmost precipitation." If you looked at the right moment you could see big guns being shoved off into deep water. Even the fine coach, in which spyglasses had seen Howe trotting down the street, disappeared with a derisive splash. Refugees stated that the rich Tories were desperately trying to reserve space on boats, so that they would not be left behind when the British withdrew.[1]

Since the privateers which constituted the American navy had to scuttle if they saw a British warship, the enemy could move unopposed wherever the ocean led. To the reports of his spies that the British objective was their naval base at Halifax, far north in Nova Scotia, Washington reacted with indignation that the enemy should feed him so obvious a canard in the belief that he would accept it. Those aspects of military organization that made the rumor completely accurate had, although called to his attention when he had served with regulars during the French and Indian War, never entered his own active experience as a commander. Such soldiers as he had always led were ready to fight if they only had a musket and its ammunition. If cold, they would light a fire; if hungry, they would eat what came to hand. But the British regular army depended on the complicated inter-relationships of neatly fitting parts. Howe had been in too much of a hurry to load so that he could unload logically, and Halifax was the only place on the continent where an army could reorganize in complete safety.[2]

New York seemed to Washington Howe's obvious objective. The city could house a large army; was painfully vulnerable to a power that could control the surrounding waters; would, if once captured, be a fortress for such a power; and from it the Hudson flowed north. Since that great river was navigable to oceangoing vessels and extended to the very edge of the wilderness, it could (particularly in conjunction with an invasion from Canada) be used to cut the rebellion in half.

Once the British got moving, they could advance by water much more rapidly than Washington could by land. He wished he could start most of his army toward New York, but feared to do so lest Howe's conspicuous preparations for embarkation prove no more than a ruse to make him weaken his defenses outside Boston.

As he waited to see how events would turn, Washington wrote to Phila-delphia for a light wagon with a secure, hinged cover that could be locked. It should contain space to store dishes, plates, eighteen campstools, and two folding tables. Congress, he assumed, would pay for this and "a pair of clever horses of the same color," as they must realize that "after I have once got into a tent, I shall not soon quit it."[3]

During the night of March 9, Washington tried to pull the knot tighter by sending men to Nook's Hill on the edge of the half-mile channel that sepa-rated Dorchester from Boston. The British heard the sounds and their cannon had already established the range. The patriots were forced to flee. But six days later, after many more enemy cannon had been dismantled, Washington tried again. This time the cannon fire was too feeble to stop the operation.

The result was electric. The next morning, the ships at the Boston docks were seen raising their sails, while armed men swarmed into small boats. Washington gave orders to prepare Nook's Hill and Dorchester Heights for attack. However, horsemen appeared to say that the vessels had proceeded into the outer harbor where the men were clambering onto transports.[4]

Washington must have longed to see for himself, but the documents imply that he stayed, so as to be ready for anything, at the desk that was the center of his command web. A dispatch: Boston was quieter but otherwise as usual. A dispatch that brought him to his feet: the sentinels who were visibly manning Bunker Hill had proved, after a gingerly approach and close inspection through glasses, to be dummies holding ruined muskets. Americans had swarmed unopposed onto the height and not a redcoat had appeared, even to stare, in the Boston streets below.[5]

The wave of Washington's elation divided around the word "smallpox." Since the disease had been rife in the city, he hurried horsemen to all the regiments with orders that civilians might, if they wished, go into town, but no soldiers. Then a sorting began to collect a thousand pockmarked men who were immune. Washington, too, was immune; but when the advance guard entered recaptured Boston "to the great joy of the inhabitants," the Commander in Chief was not with them. He went to church in camp and heard the chaplain of Knox's artillery regiment preach from Exodus XIV: 25: "The Egyptians said, Let us flee from the face of Israel; for the Lord fighteth for them against the Egyptians."[6]

Most annoyingly, the British remained anchored in the outer harbor: it could still all be a ruse. However, Washington ordered most of his riflemen to dash for New York.[7]

No Roman triumph was ever staged in the Boston streets, the conqueror acknowledging cheers. Washington slipped into town so quietly on the 18th that only those who recognized him as he rode by with his aides knew that he was there.[8]

Military inspection was Washington's objective. He saw that "the hurry in which they have embarked is inconceivable." Strewn in confusion were "provisions and stores, vessels, rugs, blankets, etc.; near thirty pieces of fine, heavy cannon are left spiked . . . shells, etc., in abundance; all their artillery carts, powder wagons, etc., etc., which they have been twelve months about, are left with such abuse as their hurry would permit them to bestow; whilst others, after a little cutting and hacking, were thrown in the harbor, and now are visiting every shore." He remembered back to the darkest days he had seen in the French and Indian War, writing General Lee, "The destruction of the stores at Dunbar's camp after Braddock's defeat was but a faint image of what was seen at Boston."

Washington examined with admiration the professionally laid out works on Bunker Hill: "Twenty thousand men could not have carried it against one thousand. . . . The town of Boston," he added, "was almost impregnable, every avenue fortified." However, he was still not grateful for the storm that had kept him from throwing troops against those impregnable avenues. He still wrote: "I can scarce forbear lamenting the disappointment, unless the dispute is drawing to an accommodation, and the sword going to be sheathed."[9]

The question of what the British had done to the houses of the patriot leaders had a particular poignancy for Washington since his beloved Mount Vernon was threatened by naval raiders. He had written Lund, "I have no doubt of your using every endeavor to prevent the destruction of my house, if any attempts should be made thereon by the men of war or their cutters, but I would have you run no hazards about it, unless an opportunity presents of doing some damage to the enemy. The height of the hill and the distance from the channel gives it many advantages." However, Lund had thought it wiser not to try to protect the house, but rather to pack all the glass and china in preparation for instantaneous removal, and to reserve a neighbor's cellar as a hiding place for the wine. At any moment, Washington might receive word that Mount Vernon had been overrun. It was with trepidation that he passed through the door of the man next to himself most conspicuous in the cause, John Hancock, the President of Congress. What a relief to find everything, even the family portraits, intact![10]

The houses of those rich Tories who had not left their women behind to protect their property stood empty, shutters hastily closed, sometimes a front door swaying in the breeze. More than a thousand civilians, with hardly any of their possessions, were crowded on the ships that rocked in a nine-mile-long line from the outer harbor to Nantasket Roads. These refugees included most of Boston's richest and most cultured citizens, the New England equivalents of Washington and his Virginia peers. Concerning their disappearance, Washington wrote, "One or two have done, what a great many ought to have done long ago, committed suicide. By all accounts, there never existed a more miserable set of beings than these wretched creatures now are." Believing that the power of Great Britain was superior to all opposition and that, in any case, foreign mercenaries were at hand, "they were even higher and more insulting in their opposition than the regulars. When the order issued, therefore, for embarking the troops in Boston, no electric shock, no sudden clap of thunder—in a word, the last trump—could not have struck them with greater consternation. They were at their wits' end and conscious of their black ingratitude. . . . Unhappy wretches! Deluded mortals! Would it not be good policy to grant a generous amnesty, and conquer these people by a generous forgiveness?"[11]

Men who had stayed behind but were suspected of anti-Congress leanings flocked to Washington for countenance; he was courteous but not friendly. He ordered that they and all Tory property be protected by the army until the Massachusetts Legislature decided what should be done. Reluctantly, he returned a beautiful horse Dr. John Morgan had given him when he discovered it had belonged to a vanished Tory.

But not vanished far enough. Day after day, the British remained at their anchorage, which, Washington wrote, "surpasses my comprehension* and awakens all my suspicions." They must be planning a stroke—perhaps they would land below Roxbury and try to march around his rear—that would "retrieve the honor they have lost by their shameless and scandalous retreat."[12]

---

* The enemy had embarked with such precipitation when the patriots appeared on Nook's Hill, that it was necessary to make the boats shipshape by shifting cargo, to take on water, and so forth.

After Washington had fretted for ten days, on March 27, 1776, he was informed that the ocean was becoming white with lifted sails.[13] When it became certain that the fleet was truly standing out to sea, surely he rode to a headland and stared until the last trace was lost over the horizon. His spirits had never been higher.

"No man perhaps since the first institution of armies," he wrote his favorite brother Jack (John Augustine Washington), "ever commanded one under more difficult circumstances than I have done. . . . I have been here months together with what will scarcely be believed: not thirty rounds of musket cartridges a man. . . . We have maintained our ground against the enemy, under the above want of powder, and we have disbanded one army and recruited another within musket shot of two and twenty regiments, the flower of the British army, when our strength have been little if any superior to theirs; and at last have beat them, in a shameful and precipitate manner, out of a place the strongest by nature on this continent, and strengthened and fortified in the best manner and at an enormous expense."

Washington then harked back to his worry on accepting the command that his reputation would be ruined, and to his subsequent anguish when he could not, without giving valuable information to the enemy, defend his character and conduct by describing the shortages that hobbled him: "I am happy, however, to find, and to hear from different quarters, that my reputation stands fair, that my conduct has hitherto given universal satisfaction. The addresses which I have received, and which I suppose will be published, from the General Court of this Colony (the same as our General Assembly) and from the Selectmen of Boston" exhibited "a pleasing testimony of their approbation of my conduct, and of their personal regard, which I have found in various other instances, and which, in retirement, will afford many comfortable reflections."[14]

That the road to that retirement would probably be long and bloody, Washington now realized, but he was turning his face to the future with the self-confidence of a commander who had undertaken an almost impossible task and won. He had won, but the army under his command had not yet faced the test of battle.

II

Fires of Despair

CHAPTER

10

Awaiting the Blow

A FTER the British had disappeared out into the ocean, Washington and most of his army advanced overland to New York, half expecting to hear that the enemy was there before them.

The General's traveling wagon had not arrived, yet he advanced in some pomp, being escorted by the headquarters guard he had just established with orders asking for forty volunteers. They were to be between five feet eight and five feet ten inches tall, "handsome and well made . . . neat and spruce."[1]

Now that he was leaving Massachusetts, Washington brought into his intimate circle, as captain of the guard, an officer from that state. Caleb Gibbs was to capitalize on being the only New Englander in Washington's military family by playing goodnaturedly the comic Yankee—pinched humor, pinched voice, pinched pocketbook, and all—to the eternal mirth of the Commander in Chief.[2]

When Washington arrived in New York City on April 13, 1776, nothing had been seen of the British fleet. Martha being with him, he bought a featherbed, a bolster, some pillows, and bed curtains. He also acquired a large dining marquee, a living tent with an arched chamber, eighteen walnut campstools, three walnut camp tables, some crockery and glassware, and "a green baize bookcase."[3]

Washington's explorations confirmed what he already knew. The city he wished to hold was at the tip of a long, thin island (Manhattan) that was surrounded, except for a narrow channel at the extreme north (Harlem River), with waterways easily navigable by British warships. To the south was the Bay; to the east, the East River, which was really an estuary leading into Long Island Sound; to the west, the great waterway inland that was alternately known as the Hudson or the North River. Across the East River was the southern end of that considerable land mass Long Island. Across the Hudson was New Jersey, a part of the mainland.

[87]

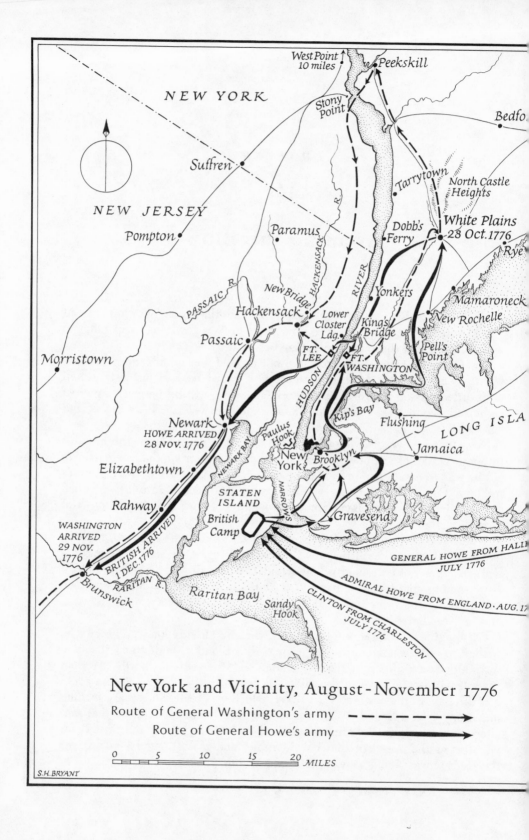

West Point
10 miles
Peekskill

NEW YORK

Stony
Point

Bedfo[rd]

Suffren

NEW JERSEY

Pompton

Paramus

Tarrytown

North Castle
Heights

Dobb's
Ferry

White Plains
28 Oct. 1776

Rye

New Bridge

Yonkers

Mamaroneck

Hackensack

Lower
Closter
Ldg.

King's
Bridge

New Rochelle

Passaic

FT.
LEE

FT.
WASHINGTON

Pell's
Point

Morristown

Kip's Bay

Flushing

LONG ISLA[ND]

Newark
HOWE ARRIVED
28 NOV. 1776

Paulus
Hook

New
York

Brooklyn

Jamaica

Elizabethtown

STATEN
ISLAND

British
Camp

Gravesend

Rahway

WASHINGTON
ARRIVED
29 NOV.
1776

GENERAL HOWE FROM HALI[FAX]
JULY 1776

Brunswick

Raritan Bay

Sandy
Hook

ADMIRAL HOWE FROM ENGLAND · AUG. 17[76]

CLINTON FROM CHARLESTON
JULY 1776

S.H.BRYANT

New York and Vicinity, August - November 1776

Route of General Washington's army - - - →

Route of General Howe's army ——→

0   5   10   15   20 MILES

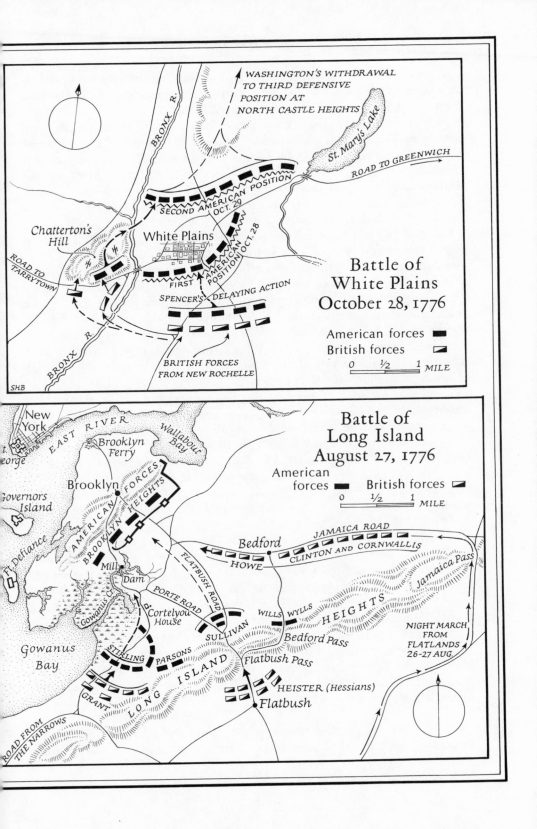

**Battle of
White Plains
October 28, 1776**

WASHINGTON'S WITHDRAWAL
TO THIRD DEFENSIVE
POSITION AT
NORTH CASTLE HEIGHTS

BRONX R.

St. Mary's Lake

ROAD TO GREENWICH

SECOND AMERICAN POSITION OCT. 29

Chatterton's
Hill

White Plains

FIRST AMERICAN POSITION OCT. 28

ROAD TO
TARRYTOWN

SPENCER'S DELAYING ACTION

BRONX R.

BRITISH FORCES
FROM NEW ROCHELLE

American forces ■
British forces ◩

0   ½   1   MILE

SHB

**Battle of
Long Island
August 27, 1776**

New York

EAST RIVER

Wallabout Bay

Brooklyn Ferry

Brooklyn

AMERICAN FORCES

BROOKLYN HEIGHTS

Governors Island

Ft. Defiance

Mill
Dam

Gowanus Cr.

American forces ■   British forces ◩

0   ½   1   MILE

JAMAICA ROAD

Bedford

HOWE   CLINTON AND CORNWALLIS

FLATBUSH ROAD

PORTE ROAD

Cortelyou House

WILLS WYLLS   HEIGHTS

Jamaica Pass

SULLIVAN

Bedford Pass

NIGHT MARCH
FROM
FLATLANDS
26-27 AUG.

STIRLING   PARSONS

LONG ISLAND

Flatbush Pass

Gowanus
Bay

GRANT

HEISTER (Hessians)

Flatbush

ROAD FROM
THE NARROWS

General Lee had started to build the fortifications it was now Washington's labor to complete and defend. Obstructions had been sunk in the East River at a point near its mouth where any ship that tried to clear the channel would be under fire from cooperating batteries on Brooklyn Heights, Governor's Island, and the southern tip of Manhattan. This defensive complex was doubly important because Manhattan Island turned its soft underbelly—a level, sylvan shoreline—to the East River. Most of the Hudson shore was protected by high bluffs, which was fortunate. Because of its width, depth, and current, the Hudson could be neither effectively controlled by cannon nor blocked with sunken objects.

Lee had labored to make the city itself "a most advantageous field of battle" that would cost an invader thousands of men. Washington found in every street which led to the river a barricade, and saw obstructions in the shallows wherever it was considered that enemy troops might try to land. The strongest chain of redoubts crossed Manhattan above the city but far below the island's northern tip, leaving above it woods and fields virtually unprotected. This wall, which could easily become the top of a trap, was considered, when later inspected by a British conqueror, "tolerably well finished. . . . All the rest of their works, which are innumerable, appear calculated more to amuse than for use."[4]

There was no hope of keeping the British fleet out of the Bay, which meant that Staten Island, in the harbor some six miles below New York City, awaited them as a large and fertile jumping-off place. Since neither of the rivers could be blocked unless both shores were held, Washington had to cut up his army by keeping considerable forces not only in the city but on Long Island and in New Jersey. The upper part of Manhattan had also to be occupied, as it offered the only reasonable escape route from the city should the British succeed (as would probably eventually take place) in operating on either of the rivers.

If military expediency were alone considered, the obvious course for a small army devoid of naval protection would have been to abandon Manhattan Island and block the Hudson River farther up, where the rugged hills known as the Highlands rose in cliffs on both shores. Two small forts were being built there (some four miles below the future post of West Point). However, as a civilian soldier, Washington was often, like the legislators that gave him commands, more attuned to civilian reactions than military necessity. Giving up without a fight a major city that presented an ideal base for the enemy's operations would have had so disastrous an effect on patriot morale that neither Washington nor Congress seems, at this time, seriously to have considered it.

After tragic events had taken place, Washington wrote his brother Samuel: "It may be asked how we come to take possession of and continue so long in a place thus circumstanced. To the first I answer that the post was taken and the works advanced before I left Boston, and to the second, that if our strength had been equal" to what Congress had authorized, "we should have had men enough to defend the city, and secured the communication" with the mainland.[5]

Washington's thinking was colored by military inexperience which kept him from realizing how indefensible New York truly was. He actually breathed optimism. The enemy were far off: he knew by April 24 that the fleet that had sailed from Boston had gone to Halifax. They were said to be awaiting fresh British regiments coming from Ireland and the German mercenaries George III had hired. Eventually, they would all descend on New York—but Washington had got there first. If he had only seven thousand men when his Council of General Officers felt he needed ten thousand, had he not called for the militia of New York and New Jersey? There would surely be time for them to assemble. As for the fortifications, he believed at the end of April that "a fortnight more will put us in a very respectable posture of defense."[6]

Washington was most worried by the "too many inimical persons" who were still in the city. A gilded lead statue of George III on a very fat horse grinned down at him whenever he rode through Bowling Green, and he saw "within pistol shot of the wharves" several British warships that were being supplied by the inhabitants.[7]

Carefully, he phrased a letter to the New York Committee of Safety: "There is nothing that could add more to my happiness than to go hand in hand with the civil authority." It was his duty to put "an immediate stop" to intercourse with the British vessels, and he would be happier if he had the committee's concurrence. The committee agreed. The warships, unable to secure supplies, withdrew, one to the outer harbor, the others way out to Sandy Hook where the restlessness of their small boats, "always going out and returning," implied they were expecting a fleet.[8]

Tryon, still officially governor of the colony, held his state on one of the warships, and kept in touch with the disaffected "no one can well tell how." Washington's efforts to persuade the Provincial Congress to empower the arrest of "the suspected and dangerous persons" opened, as he complained to the Continental Congress, a subject so "delicate" that "nothing is done in it. We may therefore have internal as well as external enemies to contend with." As long as the leaden king surveyed Bowling Green from his leaden horse, the New York leaders hesitated to bother any loyal subject, and, as for independence, "the people," so wrote one of Washington's officers, "seem to quiver at the word."[9]

Of course, there were mobs in the city who enjoyed roughing up the "hair caps," as they called those they suspected of being Tories. Washington regarded this activity as being so dangerous that, when he was told of a far-reaching Tory plot against his own life and the very existence of the army, his principal concern, after taking necessary precautions, was to hush up a matter so suited to rabble-rousing.[10]

It had all started when two members of Washington's guard, having been jailed for counterfeiting, tried to enlist a fellow prisoner in a Tory corps which, they stated, was growing within the army. Seven hundred men, they said, were receiving royal pay from Tryon and the yet undeposed mayor of New York City, David Matthews. The prisoner notified the Provincial Congress, starting an investigation which soon brought pale officials rushing through Washington's door afraid they would find him vanished or dead.

Rumor in New York stated, at the time that the plot was discovered, that a dish of peas Washington had fortunately refused to eat had killed some chickens to which it was fed. Also, that when an invading British army arrived, a drummer in Washington's guard would stab His Excellency, while Tories in the artillery turned the cannon on their fellow soldiers. However, investigation revealed that although some of the headquarters guard had actually been reached, the plot had not matured far beyond such an incoherent seething as was inevitable when in certain taverns men openly drank the King's health.

The most active conspirators, including Mayor Matthews, were quietly rounded up and confined. Washington publicly ordered a court-martial for Sergeant Thomas Hickey of his guard "and others." The others were never tried. And when Hickey was hanged in the presence of a large crowd, Washington, in his orders on the occasion, tried to turn attention away from all political issues. "The most certain method," he stated, to keep from being tempted into the crimes of "mutiny, sedition, and treachery," was "to avoid lewd women who, by the dying confession of this poor criminal, first led him into practices which ended in an untimely and ignominious death."[11]

Since Boston was in no immediate danger, the news from there gave Washington wry amusement. That great warrior Ward, who had so huffed at having a mere Virginian put over his head, had resigned rather than follow (as Washington wrote) the war away from "the smoke of his own chimney." And the Massachusetts politician Josiah Quincy, who had in Cambridge regularly favored Washington with interfering advice, now wrote complaining that fortification of Boston Harbor was languishing under Colonel Richard Gridley, whom Massachusetts had once forced down Washington's throat as chief of the engineers. Washington replied that he had been taught to view Gridley "as one of the greatest engineers of the age. If things have gone wrong, I can only express my concern." However, to Gridley himself he wrote sternly: "Who am I to blame for this shameful neglect but you, sir?"[12]

The news from Canada was appalling. Under orders from Congress,

Washington had sent ten regiments to reinforce the little army that was wintering under the still-unbreached walls of Quebec. The new mouths had merely increased the threat of starvation; the new bodies had added fuel to the smallpox which raged in the American camp. Since Congress had failed to send not only supplies but also money, necessities had to be taken from the inhabitants at bayonet point. This impelled waves of pro-British sentiment. And then, on May 6, several thousand British regulars, newly arrived from England, came sailing up the St. Lawrence. Those of the skeleton-like besiegers who were well enough took to their heels. It was a question whether they could make a stand before they disgorged from Lake Champlain into northern New York. It was a question whether they could get to Lake Champlain.[13]

Now that the war had moved away from New England, Washington was achieving his ambition of having an army that represented more than one area of the rebellion. Although he had conquered his own aversion to the New Englanders—at least to the extent of never referring to them insultingly again—he could not have been, considering the emotions he had himself felt, surprised that the mixing of regions did not go smoothly. On August 1, he read the army a lecture in his general orders on the unity of the cause, and threatened with punishment "any officers or soldiers so lost to virtue and a love of their country" as to engage in regional dissension.[14]

More serious than any friction caused by different mores were the illnesses caused by swapping of diseases. In those days of difficult communication, when men rarely got far from home, groups built up immunities to diseases endemic in their own areas, but had no specific resistance to other ills. Typhus, typhoid, and dysentery stalked through the camp under the leadership of the ubiquitous smallpox. Washington told Martha she would have either to go home or be inoculated. She agreed to "taking the smallpox," but her husband doubted "her resolution."* [15]

Finally facing firmly the fact that there lay ahead a long war, the Congress summoned Washington to Philadelphia. For the first time, he left his army. Martha went with him, and set the grim tone of the visit by submitting to inoculation. Before a week had passed, Washington was complaining that Congress's inattention to army affairs was keeping him too long from his command.[16]

Congress, indeed, was deep in the most absorbing of questions: should they declare the United States independent of Great Britain? On this issue, the General made no public statements, but he regretted in private that "the representation of whole provinces are still feeding themselves upon the dainty food of reconciliation."[17]

His own role as a creator of one of the world's major governments lay in

---

* In those days, inoculation was dangerous, since the patient was given an actual (it was hoped, light) case of the disease.

the unforeseeable future. Yet he was concerned as a Virginian with that colony's emerging constitution. He wrote his brother Jack: "To form a new government requires infinite care and unbounded attention; for, if the foundation is badly laid, the superstructure must be bad. Too much time, therefore, cannot be bestowed in weighing and digesting matters well. . . . My fear is that you will all get tired and homesick, the consequence of which is that you will patch up some kind of constitution as defective as the present. . . . Every man should consider that he is lending his aid to frame a constitution which is to render millions happy or miserable."[18]

When Washington could actually get the attention of the committee of Congress appointed to meet with him, they agreed to recommend that 10,000 militia be sent to the rescue in Canada. This was cut by Congress to 6000, with the doubly fatuous proviso that Washington be empowered to recruit "not exceeding" 2000 Indians. The most that could be expected with the Indians, who were being protected by the Crown from the encroachments of land-hungry Colonials, was that they could somehow be bamboozled into remaining neutral.

Turning to the problems of Washington's own army, the Congress resolved that he should receive 13,800 militia recruited from Connecticut, New York, and New Jersey until December 1. For the same short period, a separate "Flying Camp" of 10,000 was to be raised from Pennsylvania, Maryland, and Delaware, to protect the middle states or, if necessary, come to Washington's assistance. The south was to handle its own problems, which had been complicated by the British expeditionary force that had sailed from Boston under General Clinton. It was attacking Charleston, South Carolina. General Lee had been sent to command the defense.[19]

Washington came out of his conferences with Congress not reassured: "We expect a very bloody summer of it at New York and Canada . . . and I am sorry to say that we are not, either in men or arms, prepared for it." However, he was encouraged by an enlarged sense of the importance of victory.

When Washington had first assumed the command, he had thought of the cause primarily in terms of enlightened self-interest and American patriotism. But by February 1776, he had concluded that the American example would point the way to the triumph of freedom everywhere. The Americans were fighting "the cause of virtue and mankind," which made it all the more probable that divine Providence would not permit them to fail.[20]

Washington stayed away from his army only fifteen days. However, the men had become so used to seeing him always with them that even this brief absence gave rise to a rumor that he had resigned. The consternation was so great that General Heath marched his brigade into the city to take their alarm posts. His column was still in motion when there was a sound of cheers and who should come riding along but the Commander in Chief, back once more with his army.[21]

By letter, Washington continued to press for reforms, two of which Congress finally enacted. It set up as one of its innumerable committees a Board of War entrusted with keeping records, helping with recruiting and supply. Even if the president of the new board was the congressman already most overburdened with responsibilities, John Adams, there was now a group in Philadelphia specifically concerned with the army. More importantly, Congress finally gave Washington a chance to develop an accomplished army. They relaxed their opposition to a long term of military service. They offered a bounty of ten dollars to men who would enlist for three years.[22]

However, the army was to face its test of fire before these laws would have the least effect. On June 29, a rifleman wrote: "This morning, as I was upstairs in an outhouse, I spied, as I peeped out the bay, something resembling a wood of pine trees trimmed. I declare at my noticing this, I could not believe my eyes, but keeping my eyes fixed at the very spot, judge you of my surprise, when in about ten minutes the whole bay was as full of shipping as ever it could be. I do declare, that I thought all London was in afloat. Just about five minutes before I see this sight, I got my discharge."[23]

The terms of three companies of riflemen had just expired. Despite the arrival from Halifax of General Howe's army, the riflemen went home.

More than fifty sail were counted in the harbor. Washington had fewer than eight thousand men fit for duty (almost a thousand were too sick to fight). He bustled Martha back to Virginia. He supervised the placing of sandbags and ordered the collecting of cart horses to pull the artillery. He ordered the men to load muskets with one ball and four to eight buckshot according to the strength of their pieces: in case of an attack, they were not to fire until the enemy entered circles of small brush laid out within the best musket range around stationary posts. He sent out renewed calls for militia. If only Howe would not attack until he was more ready![24]

On July 4, 1776, Washington breathed easier—but not because of any news brought on birds' wings (it would have been the only way quick enough) of the action taken in Philadelphia that was to make that date famous. Washington was relieved because Howe, far from undertaking an immediate assault, was settling down on Staten Island. The British general, so spies reported, awaited a fleet and convoy of reinforcements coming directly from England under the command of his brother, Admiral Lord Howe.[25]

For the moment, Washington's major problem was what he called "the treachery" of the Tories. The farmers on Staten Island were jubilantly exchanging their produce for British hard money, and were even, so it was said, offering to take up arms for the King. All along the coasts around New York—New Jersey, southern New York, Long Island—the "disaffected" were reported to be making ready to welcome the British. Now Washington felt forced to move without waiting for the civil authorities, although he continued to petition them to act for themselves. He ordered that officers of the royal government and others "notoriously disaffected" be forcibly moved from the coast "to less dangerous places."²⁶

"My tenderness has been often abused," he explained angrily, "and I have had reason to repent the indulgence shown them. . . . Matters are now too far advanced to sacrifice anything to punctilios!" Yet, when he sent some Long Island leaders for internment in Connecticut, he wrote Governor Trumbull that "as they are apprehended merely on suspicion," he had promised them "every indulgence which your good judgment will permit you to allow. . . . Your humanity and politeness will most effectively prevent their being liable to any unnecessary hardships."²⁷

Military historians have criticized Washington for using up, as a crucial battle impended, his time on scruples like this, and also in correspondence with such querulous British prisoners as Major Christopher French, who had been captured in Canada and was free on parole but never satisfied with his privileges. On one occasion, Washington thus meticulously phrased his refusal of one of French's unreasonable requests: He found it a "painful" duty "to disappoint you in an expectation which you seem to have formed in full persuasion of being right, and in which, on mature deliberation, I am so unhappy as totally to differ from you." When French again complained, Washington wrote in some distress: "You may assure yourself, sir, that both duty and inclination lead me to relieve the unfortunate."²⁸

A waste of time? Or was this ever-alive attention to the feelings of others one of the qualities that enabled Washington to lose many battles but win the war?

On July 9, Washington received from Philadelphia a resolution of the Congress stating, after an eloquent preamble, that "the UNITED STATES OF AMERICA" were "free and independent . . . absolved from all allegiance to the British crown."

The Declaration of Independence sliced through innumerable tangles that had previously been Gordian knots. Royal officials, no longer men in office, were now but foreign representatives subject to legal arrest; Tories were no longer "loyalists"; the laws and the money and the armies of the Colonists sprang into legitimacy—that is, if the war were not lost. If the war were lost, treason would clamp down with double certainty on American shoulders. However, Washington saw this increased danger could be an advantage: greater *sacrifices* could be expected from the man "who believes he must conquer or submit to . . . confiscation, hanging, etc., etc."

[96]

Yet, as Washington held in his hands the document he had once dreaded but had recently desired, his emotion was not elation but rather the sadness with which, "impelled by necessity and a repetition of injuries unsufferable," one breaks at long last and forever with an old love. In acknowledging to the President of Congress the Declaration of Independence, Washington launched into no panegyric, but repeated back almost exactly the phrases Hancock had used in sending the Declaration to him. Washington agreed that the measure was "of the most interesting nature." Hancock was right in stating "that it is not with us to determine in many instances what consequences will flow from our councils, but yet it behoves us to adopt such as, under the smiles of a most gracious and all-kind Providence, will be most likely to promote our happiness." Then Washington added that he hoped Congress's action "is calculated for that end, and will secure us that freedom and those privileges which have been, and are, refused us contrary to the voice of Nature and the British Constitution."[29]

One thing was sure: Washington was irrevocably embarked on the ship of Independence. It was much less certain how his army would react.

"The several brigades," Washington stated in his general orders, "are to be drawn up this evening on their respective parades at six o'clock, when the Declaration of Congress, showing the grounds and reasons of this measure, is to be read with an audible voice.

"The General hopes that this important event will serve as a fresh incentive to every officer and soldier to act with fidelity and courage, as knowing that now the peace and safety of his country depends (under God) solely on the success of our arms; and that he is now in the service of a State possessed of sufficient power to reward his merit and advance him to the highest honors of a free country."

The Commander in Chief stayed in his headquarters. For him, six o'clock was undoubtedly a time of anxiety. Was it a bad omen that this was the twenty-first anniversary of the most frightful experience he had ever suffered through: Braddock's defeat? Finally, he heard cheering—but was the sound heartfelt, was it loud enough?

Eventually, officers began to return to headquarters from the various parades. Washington was pleased to be told of "expressions and behavior of both officers and men testifying their warmest approbation." However, he was not pleased when soldiers joined a mob that pulled down and smashed the statue of George III: "It has so much the appearance of riot and want of order in the army." Such things should be left to the civil authorities.[30]

11

The Carrot and the Big Stick

O N the morning of July 12, 1776, the sound of cannon rolled down the bay from the British anchorage. Lookouts reported to Washington that the fleet had been firing salutes on the arrival of a ship with St. George's flag at her foretopmast. The long-awaited naval commander, Admiral Lord Howe, had finally appeared.

Washington had hardly concluded that operations would soon start when five vessels—the *Phoenix*, forty guns, the *Rose*, twenty guns, and three tenders—shook loose their furled sails and aimed for the city. They neared the end of the island, swung left and up the Hudson, moving rapidly before a brisk breeze on a favorable tide.

To stop just such a passage, cannon had been laboriously placed. However, when drums beat to summon the artillerymen, many failed to respond. They ran instead to the riverbank and stood there, "gazing," so Washington wrote, "at the ships. . . . A weak curiosity," he added angrily, "at such a time makes a man look mean and contemptible."

Now the boats fired at New York. Cannonballs bounded down streets among the disheveled women who had come popping out of their houses. Washington found that "The shrieks and cries of these poor creatures running every way with their children was truly distressing." The scene had "an unhappy effect on the ears and minds of our young and inexperienced soldiery."

Only a few of the patriot guns were manned and fired. These, as far as Washington could determine through his glass, had no effect on the British ships, which continued upriver until they vanished. So much for Washington's hope that he had succeeded in blocking the Hudson waterway.[1]

Having captured or sunk what shipping they met, the British flotilla finally dropped anchors in that broadest part of the Hudson, slightly below the Highlands, called the Tappan Zee. If they had intended to encourage local Tories by sending parties ashore, this hope proved vain, as militia gathering on the banks kept any tars or redcoats from landing. The enemy did prevent the patriots from using the river to supply their army—but only for a short while. One dark night, floating fires appeared from beneath overhanging branches and moved across the water. Paddling passionately from the sterns of rafts as the bows flamed, the patriots bore down on the little enemy fleet. One fire raft was grappled to the *Phoenix* for "ten minutes in a light blaze." The *Phoenix* cut loose, but a tender was burned and the scare sent the British boats dashing downriver. Using a favorable wind and tide, they again passed Washington's batteries without visible damage.[2]

While British might continued to gather on Staten Island, the news from the other theaters of war was good and very bad. Good from South Carolina, where the patriots led by General Lee had repulsed Clinton's amphibious expedition. Very bad from Canada, where the American army was in full flight as much from disease as from the enemy. Under the impact of this disaster, which threatened to open the frontiers of New England as well as New York to invasion, latent fissures widened in the patriot cause.

Schuyler, the general responsible for the northern army, had long outraged with his aristocratic ways the New England regiments that had been assigned to him. Now Connecticut and Massachusetts frontiersmen passed resolutions breathing suspicion that he was a Tory and a traitor: they wished him removed from command. The New England delegation in Congress wanted to see Schuyler replaced by Gates.[3]

Massachusetts had already sponsored Gates's promotion to major general. The former British regular had, during the siege of Boston, impressed observers in Cambridge with his skill, and also his democratic principles. Having suffered so from snobbery when he had served in the army he was now fighting against, the housekeeper's son disliked American aristocrats as vehemently as did any Yankee leveler. In his own behavior, he was not, like Schuyler, elegant, distant, and courtly. He had the figure of a strong, clumsy bear and bent forward to peer, with nearsighted eyes, through thick glasses. He was accessible and superficially aggressive, eager to argue with people's representatives, happy to swear at them, and then often willing (being not really sure of himself) to give in. New England saw in him a savior, but aristocratic New York had no intention of letting their own general be sacrificed.

Congress hedged by dividing the command. Schuyler should keep his authority in New York, while Gates took over in Canada. However, Gates had hardly joined his army when it came pouring back over the border into New York. Each general now claimed that he ranked the other; and in Congress, as the radicals backed Gates and the conservatives Schuyler, a controversy developed which most participants recognized as tending dangerously to divide the cause.

Washington tried to short-circuit the political currents by attributing the charges that Schuyler was a traitorous Tory not to the radicals who were actually sponsoring them, but to Tory traitors trying to sow disunion. He scolded both generals for squabbling and wrote Congress that he would welcome whichever of the two was not needed in Canada as a valuable addition to his own army.[4]

Washington's private feelings were certainly mixed. On one hand, he could not doubt that Gates was the more experienced soldier; on the other, Schuyler was personally the more agreeable to him. Schuyler had been loyal to Washington, while Gates seemed to be setting up as a rival: "I discovered very early in the war," Washington wrote, "symptoms of coldness and constraint in General Gates's behavior to me. These increased as he rose into greater consequence." Washington had expressed hurt feelings when Congress, in first sending Gates to Canada, had allowed him greater autonomy in making appointments than they had ever accorded the Commander in Chief. "His recommendations will always be readily complied with," Congressman Richard Henry Lee had written Washington of Gates. "You will find that great powers are given to the commander of that distant department."[5]

Congress sought refuge from the deeper implications of the Schuyler-Gates squabble by recourse to local option. The combined army being in New York, the command was confirmed to Schuyler. However, New England was mollified by having Gates kept as second in command and combat general.[6]

The northern army continued to fall back toward Fort Ticonderoga. When they passed a more northerly fort on Lake Champlain, Crown Point, without waiting for any enemy to appear, Washington, who dreaded to see Ticonderoga become the only strongpoint between the advancing British and the headwaters of the Hudson, felt "chagrin and consternation." His general officers advised him to exert his Commander in Chief's authority by ordering a return to Crown Point. However, in his letters to the northern commanders, Washington began by admitting that distance made it difficult to understand the situation. He then stated that the move seemed to him and his officers unwise: he hoped it could be undone. When even these mild sentiments brought Schuyler and Gates together in protests against such interference, Washington backtracked, stating that he had intended to do no more than to express his concern and that of his officers.[7]

Since the surrounding forests were impenetrable to cannon, the British would have to come by water down Lake Champlain: they were preparing boats. The Americans were building from green wood a defensive flotilla. If

General Horatio Gates, by Gilbert Stuart. Courtesy of Mrs. Charles A. Pfeffer, Jr.

that command were given to General Arnold, Washington urged, "none will doubt of his exertions."[8]

Gates's promotion had left open the adjutant generalship with its rank of brigadier. By offering Reed this plum, Washington had succeeded at long last in luring his confidant back into his military family. He had need for the lawyer-politician in a complicated exercise of protocol when, two days after Admiral Lord Howe had arrived off Staten Island, a British boat rowed down the bay with a letter for Washington. Having hastily consulted what general officers he could round up, Washington sent Reed to the waterfront with orders not to accept the letter unless it was properly addressed.

After an hour or so, Reed returned to state that the letter had been addressed to "George Washington, Esq." He had refused it. "You are sensible, sir," he had explained, "of the rank of General Washington in our army."

The envoy had replied: "Yes, sir, we are. I am sure Lord Howe will lament exceedingly this affair, as the letter is quite of a civil nature and not a military one. He laments exceedingly that he was not here a little sooner."

This seeming reference to the Declaration of Independence made Washington assume that Lord Howe brought some suggestion for an accommodation. And, indeed, word soon came in that the Howe brothers had been appointed as peace commissioners.[9]

The Howes, in the meanwhile, were trying to think of some way to get a letter delivered without admitting, by giving Washington a title, that the rebel represented a constituted authority. They decided that "the most unexceptional mode of address" was "George Washington, Esq., etc., etc., etc." However, a letter so addressed was refused.

"For the attainment of an end so desirable," the Howes finally resolved to make an exception—but only verbally. They sent another emissary who asked whether "His Excellency, General Washington" would receive the Adjutant General of the British army. Why, of course![10]

Washington selected for the meeting General Knox's headquarters, which was so close to the waterfront that the English envoy could, without gaining any useful intelligence, be allowed to walk there unblindfolded. An American ensign noticed that Lieutenant Colonel James Patterson strode along cheerfully until he saw, flanking the door he was approaching, smartly uniformed members of the headquarters guard. Then "he looked very wild, with his boots pleated, no lace only round his hat."

Washington was gratified to be addressed as "Excellency." But the letter Patterson pulled from his pocket was addressed to "Esq." with the et ceteras. The English officer laid it on the table between them and argued that the et ceteras implied everything that should follow. Washington answered that they "also implied anything." He refused to touch the letter.

The envoy then said: "General Howe would not urge his delicacy further"; Patterson would try to remember the import of the letter. He launched into some complaints about the treatment of some prisoners taken in Canada. Charges induced countercharges and assurances from each side that humanity was the intention.

This sparring over, Patterson said "that the goodness and benevolence of the King had induced him to appoint Lord Howe and General Howe his commissioners to accommodate this unhappy dispute; that they had great powers, and would derive the greatest pleasure from effecting an accommodation, and that he [Colonel Patterson] wished to have this visit considered as making the first advances to this desirable object."

Washington replied that he was not vested with any authority on this subject. However, he understood that the Howes' powers "were only to grant pardons; that those who had committed no fault wanted no pardon; that we were only defending what we deemed our indisputable right."

"That would open a very wide field of argument," Colonel Patterson said, and he shifted the discussion back to prisoners and their exchange.

After a little more talk, Washington "strongly invited" Patterson "to partake of a small collation provided for him." But the Englishman "politely declined, alleging his late breakfast." Patterson departed and the war went on.[11]

The ministerial plan was to alternate negotiation with terror until negotiation was accepted on British terms. Wishing the terror to be unanswerable, they were supplying Howe with what is said to have been the largest expeditionary force sent out by any nation in the eighteenth century. When all the ships were in, there would be more than thirty thousand men, about a third of them those mercenaries known to history as Hessians, although they came from four other German principalities in addition to Hesse-Cassel and Hesse-Hanau. Lord Howe's fleet was to include ten ships of the line and twenty frigates.[12]

About nine thousand men had come from Halifax with General Howe. After successive arrivals—of which the most frightening to patriot watchers were the tall, mustachioed Germans who moved under their high helmets like murderous puppets—had brought Howe's forces (so spies reported) to between twenty thousand and twenty-seven thousand, Washington could not understand why the enemy bothered to wait for any more. Despite all his passionate appeals—"since the settlement of these Colonies there has never been such just occasion for alarm"—he had been able to collect by August 19, only twenty-three thousand men fit, and these had to be strung out along all the waterways. A further complication (which he hoped was not familiar to Howe) was that the troops from the middle states who were occupying the Flying Camp on the Jersey shore insisted that they would not under any circumstance cross the Hudson. They would not leave the area they had been mobilized to protect. To add to everything, so many of Washington's soldiers were so green that the only way to keep his sentries awake was to remove everything on which they could sit down.[13]

Washington suspected that, as his spies reported, the enemy's first attack would include Long Island. A landing could be made too far from patriot positions to be opposed. The American post at Brooklyn Heights would then be attacked. If it were captured, the enemy would have opened the East River and would also hold a position from which New York City could be bombarded.

Even on the colonial scale of competence, Washington's general officers were less impressive than they had been outside Boston. Congress had siphoned off to other commands his ablest generals: Thomas (who had died in Canada), Lee, and Gates. Of the major generals he had left, only Putnam, who was at fifty-eight somewhat superannuated, had ever been present at an important battle. Reed, who admitted his own lack of qualifications to be adjutant general, mourned that "we have neither such an army nor such a council as last year, and yet we want it more."[14]

Washington had entrusted the defense of Long Island to Major General Nathanael Greene. He was slightly crippled, limping with a stiff knee. Writers like to cite this infirmity to explain Greene's sensitivity to criticism, which, however, was no greater than Washington's own.

As a civilian, Greene had helped manage his father's prosperous iron foundry. Although he was devoid of any military experience when the war started, his gift for leadership was so obvious that, despite his infirmity, the Rhode Island authorities raised him in one stroke from militia private to commander of the state forces. Like most of Washington's generals, Greene was large and heavy. He had a broad, high forehead, fleshy cheeks and chin, a surprisingly large, rich, sensuous mouth. However, his thin handsome nose and narrow eyes seemed more suited to a spare Yankee face. Although his brown eyes were small, they dominated his other features as he stared from between his slit-like lids with passion and intensity, and also with cold, calculating intelligence. Washington was greatly impressed with that intelligence, writing that Greene was studying military books and had the makings of a first-class soldier.

However, Greene was taken ill. It could not have been without forebodings that Washington entrusted the Long Island command to Major General John Sullivan. Sullivan had all of Greene's fiery temper but little of his judgment. The son of Irish indentured servants who had bettered themselves on the New Hampshire frontier, he had become a contentious backwoods lawyer eager to sue rather than compromise. Washington wrote that he "does not want abilities"; that he was "active, spirited, and zealously attached to the cause," but too much swayed by vanity and the desire to be

[104]

General Nathanael Greene, detail of portrait by Charles Willson Peale. Courtesy of the Independence National Historical Park Collection.

General John Sullivan, detail of portrait by Richard M. Staigg after unknown artist. Courtesy of the Independence National Historical Park Collection.

popular. He lacked "the sound judgment and some knowledge of men and books" that would help him overcome "the want of experience to move upon a large scale . . . common to us all." And Sullivan was totally unacquainted with the geography of Long Island. However, Washington had no other choice.[15]

Whenever he could, the Commander in Chief sought solace in thoughts of Mount Vernon, the beloved home he might never see again. "There is no doubt," he wrote his manager with the incoherence of haste, "but the honey locust, if you could procure seed enough, would come up, will make (if sufficiently thick) a very good hedge. So will the haw or thorn, and, if you cannot do better, I wish you to try these, but cedar or any kind of evergreen would look better."[16]

On August 21, purposeful movement was at last descried in the British anchorage. Ships took on troops and, having fallen down toward the ocean through the Narrows, swung east to the tip of Long Island that extended far beyond Manhattan and was so far from Washington's position that he could not oppose a landing there. Providence struck again with a great thunderstorm—"when God speaks," wrote a New Englander, "who can but fear"— but this time the British advance was not to be thwarted. The enemy dropped anchor in Gravesend Bay (behind Coney Island) and on the 22nd began to land.[17]

A few patriot skirmishers watched and then fell back through the smoke of wheat fields they had set on fire. As the wind dissipated the smoke, brightly arrayed regiments could be seen advancing, stately and to music.

Washington sent all his records to Philadelphia for safekeeping. However, he wrote concerning the enemy, "I trust, through divine favor and our own exertions they will be disappointed in their views, and, at all events, any advantages they may gain will cost them very dear. If our troops will behave well, which I hope will be the case, having everything to contend for that freemen hold dear, they will have to wade through much blood and slaughter before they can carry any part of our works, if they carry them at all, and at best be possessed of a melancholy and mournful victory. May the sacredness of our cause inspire our soldiery with sentiments of heroism."[18]

CHAPTER

12

The Enemy Strikes

T HE British objective was the American position which covered
Brooklyn Heights. Almost two square miles of rocky bluff that protruded into New York Harbor opposite the lower tip of Manhattan,
the Heights guarded, like a little Gibraltar, the access to the East River.
Where the bluff adhered to Long Island, marshes, rivulets, and coves cut in
from the sides to reduce the passable ground to less than a mile. The
American ramparts crowned the different levels of the bluff and protected
the entranceway.

About a mile and a half beyond Brooklyn Heights in the direction of the
British advance, a rough spine of heavily forested hills extended from close
to the harbor shore some nine miles northeastward. The nearer part of this
natural barrier had been strengthened with ditches and parapets. Washington stated sometimes that this would be the scene of his principal stand,
sometimes that he would only use the hills to "harass and annoy," making
his principal defense from the more strongly fortified base.[1]

The whole position would, of course, be cut off from the main army if the
British navy established control of the East River. However, obstructions
had been sunk in the channel, while batteries on both shores and on
Governor's Island between waited to sink ships that would be forced to
come to an almost complete halt if they tried to batter their way through.

Himself obsessed with the strategy of striking at several widely separated
points, Washington believed that Howe would attack Manhattan simultaneously with Brooklyn Heights. Even when, after successive landings at
Gravesend Bay, it became clear that Howe had moved most of his army to
Long Island, Washington, fearing a feint, kept most of his on Manhattan.[2]

Leadership on Long Island continued to present problems. When Sullivan
demonstrated inadequacy, Washington could only put over his head the one
more senior major general available, Israel Putnam. However, he feared that

such a semi-independent command was not really suited to "the old gentleman's temper." Putnam was "a fine executive officer . . . active, disinterested, and open to conviction," but needed someone of more judgment and more imagination to tell him what to do.[3]

As the two armies eased toward each other, what skirmishing took place was minor. In five days, the total American casualties were one colonel mortally wounded in the breast, one private who had his leg removed by a cannonball, and another shot in the groin. "We have always," Washington boasted, "obtained an advantage."[4]

The British, whose officers were being picked off from ambush by riflemen, protested against this new form of warfare which they characterized as "assassination." The word had for Washington a familiar sound, for after his first military engagement, when he had ambushed a French party in the Ohio Valley wilderness, he had been accused of having assassinated an ambassador. Now he ordered Putnam to see that the riflemen skirmished under proper command in a manner that "will be agreeable to the rules of propriety."[5]

Various diaries report that Washington spent on Long Island the fifth day after the British first landed there. Toward that evening of August 26, he cantered to the edge of the line of hills and looked down on the plain below. It was white with tents which extended out in front of him almost all the five miles to Gravesend Bay, and also ran parallel with the hills almost the complete width of Long Island, from the harbor shore on his right through the village of Flatbush below him and on past another village, Flatlands, five miles to his left. Unfortunately, he did not distinguish from the general clank of arms and pound of drums that came faintly to him through the evening air an ominous stir at Flatlands, a post he considered too far off and in the wrong position to be of any importance. As darkness fell, he rode back to the East River, entered a boat, and returned to Manhattan.[6]

That night the less experienced troops, some four thousand strong, encamped behind the fortifications on Brooklyn Heights under Putnam's immediate command. The thirty-five hundred men on the hills were accountable to Sullivan, who gave himself specific charge of the center overlooking Flatbush. Brigadier General Alexander Stirling* commanded the

---

* Born plain William Alexander in New York City, Stirling claimed a presumably extinct Scots earldom. Although the House of Lords refused to accept this pretension, a Scottish jury backed it, and he was known in America as Lord Stirling. A social leader by birth, marriage, and inclination, Stirling had been before the war a successful merchant, with a great house in New Jersey where Washington had stayed. He was considered by an admiring lieutenant to have "the most martial appearance of any general in the service." However, the French general Chastellux was to write him down as "brave without capacity," a man not ill-informed but "old and dull." Despite an addiction to the bottle, Stirling served Washington adequately throughout the war as a wheelhorse general.[7]

right flank which abutted on the bay: it was here that an attack was expected, since the British could advance under the guns of their ships. The left flank, entrusted to Colonel Samuel Miles of Pennsylvania, had to remain in the air because the hilly spine extended too far to permit complete occupation.

Jamaica Road ran along the top of the ridge. After it had emerged from the American position, it divided, one prong sinking through a pass to Flatlands. Exactly what forebodings this configuration raised at the time in American minds is obscured by hindsight: after the tragic event, many officers claimed that they had vainly tried to impress other officers with the importance of Jamaica Road. Yet no fortification had been built to block the open end of the road. Washington seems to have assumed that the area would be patrolled, and Sullivan certainly sent out a party of five mounted officers.

At three the following morning, as they were scanning the byway for some impertinent enemy patrol, to their utter amazement, these mounted scouts happened on the main British army. Instantly captured, they could not warn their compatriots of the great danger that was moving on the American camp: General Howe and General Clinton were leading ten thousand men and fourteen fieldpieces on a circuitous march. If their secret approach were not discovered, this major enemy force would enter by surprise, along the lightly guarded Jamaica Road, into the unprepared left of the American camp. Although this the scouts could not know, the British had planned, as further cover for their stealthy approach, to distract attention from it by making noisy displays in front of other parts of the American lines.[8]

Washington was asleep in his Manhattan headquarters. At about one in the morning, he was awakened by firing from the direction of Long Island. He soon learned that an action had started along the shore on the opposite side of the American position from Jamaica Road. This was what he had foreseen, and his conviction that the battle would be fought there was strengthened (as Howe intended it should be) when, as dawn widened a clear, cool sky, he saw headed for that sector British warships under full sail. One managed to exchange a few shots with the battery on Brooklyn Heights before the wind shifted and the ships, after fluttering into a series of tacks, gave up the effort and sailed away.[9]

As no sign had developed of a second action against Manhattan, Washington ordered more regiments to Long Island and himself sprang into a small boat. On his arrival, he was told that the American left on Jamaica Road was undisturbed. In the center, Sullivan had advanced with his men across the continuation of Jamaica Road to the edge of the hilly spine. They were looking down on Hessian regiments who were standing motionless in

[109]

formation on the plain staring up. The main action was still on the right, beside the harbor. Sullivan had sent part of his detachment there to reinforce Stirling.

Riding to the right, Washington exhorted the troops. To some white-faced rookies: "If I see any man turn his back today, I will shoot him through. I have two pistols loaded. But I will not ask any man to go further than I do. I will fight as long as I have a leg or an arm." To a colonel: "Let them approach within twenty yards before you fire." To a regiment: "Quit yourselves like men, like soldiers, for all that is worth living for is at stake!"[10]

Nine in the morning, and all was well! Then Washington's hands jerked on the reins when a cannon shot sounded to the left and deep in the American position where he knew there could be no cannon. A second shot sounded from the same place, followed by a burst of martial music. As if these had been a signal, a great roar broke out at Sullivan's center position, indicating that the Hessians were suddenly charging up the slope.

In a few minutes, Washington received a frightened messenger who blurted out that a strong British force had miraculously appeared on the American left and was continuing to advance on Jamaica Road along Sullivan's rear. They were sandwiching Sullivan's force between their own might and the Hessians who were coming up the slope. In a few minutes, it became clear that the enemy column had cut Flatbush Road, which was Sullivan's main line of retreat to the fortified position on Brooklyn Heights. If the British advance were not stopped, it would close a complete trap on Sullivan's men and then come in behind Stirling, who was still fighting along the shore.[11]

Although the surprise was as complete as the surprise that had defeated Braddock, Washington was by no means despairing. He had blamed that earlier rout in the wilderness not on the strategic situation, but on the cowardice of the men. Now he believed that steadfastness could still save the day. The appearance of the British where they had not been expected was admittedly a check, but needed to make no real difference if the men did not "flee precipitously." An enemy soldier was, after all, no more than an enemy soldier whether he was on your front or your rear.[12]

The men did not seem to agree with Washington. Beyond Flatbush Road, there was a lesser road from the hills to Brooklyn Heights which the enemy had not yet cut. It filled from edge to edge with running men. On the hills the sound of firing sank to a whisper and shredded away.

No evidence indicates that Washington tried personally to rally the men. His place, he realized, was within Brooklyn Heights. The greater the rout outside, the more important the fortification would become as a refuge. And in the fortification, panic threatened. The four thousand men garrisoning the works were among the greenest rookies in the amateur army. Washington found them terrified by the sounds and sights outside, and also by the influx of fugitives, all horrorstruck, many of them bearing gruesome wounds, twitching with pain, gushing blood, falling down dead. Washington had his hands full keeping the ramparts manned, trying to hold the spirit of resistance afloat. He could not doubt that the enemy would, as soon as they could reach there, assault walls so quaveringly defended.

Looking out over the walls, Washington saw a sight that filled his heart with exaltation and pity. To keep open an escape route for Stirling's command, Colonel Smallwood's Maryland regiment, grouped tiny and determined on a hillside, were buying time with their blood. Standing off the total British might, they even charged the enemy. "Good God," Washington is quoted as having exclaimed, "what must my brave boys suffer today!"[13]

One of Smallwood's officers appeared suddenly at Washington's side. His colonel had sent him to request reinforcements. Washington must have found it very bitter to refuse, but he could not send living men to certain death in an effort to save heroes as good as dead.[14]

In the meanwhile, Stirling's men were trying to struggle in on the extreme right across a waste of rivulets and marshes. The British fired at the fugitives as they swam, waded, floundered. Washington ordered riflemen and fieldpieces to set up a protective fire. Many fugitives got through, but many, as Howe noted with satisfaction, "were suffocated or drowned."[15]

The firing outside the walls slackened into almost complete silence. Then like the spokes of a multicolored wheel the enemy regiments—the British in red, the Hessian grenadiers in blue coats and their Yagers in green—converged on the open space in front of Washington's ramparts. They halted with their advance detachments just beyond musket shot. They ignored what cannon Washington could bring to bear. After a tremendous force had gathered, more men than Washington had ever seen together in one place, officers passed among them on horseback and there were visible preparations for motion. In whatever confusion, Washington's army would surely have now to meet an assault!

From among the seemingly boundless enemy ranks, shouted orders rang. Thousands of red or blue or green figures straightened, a gleaming bristle of bayonets rose as they shouldered arms, their right knees lifted in unison, they advanced a few feet, they wheeled, and withdrew out of cannon range. It was unbelievable, but it was true! Howe had allowed the most favorable moment for an assault to pass, was giving Washington time to straighten out his army. Washington could only conclude that Howe did not intend under any circumstances to attack that day—unless, of course, the foe was behaving peculiarly to fool the unwary.

Had Howe been told that the historians of the future would scorn him for not having overwhelmed, as they are sure he would have done, Washington's army by an immediate assault, the British commander would have been flabbergasted. To his government, he boasted of "the repeated orders" he had given his officers to curb "the rash impetuosity" of the common soldiery who were eager to attack.

As he scanned Brooklyn Heights through his glasses, Howe's impressions were probably similar to those of the Hessian major Baurmeister, who noted that the rebel works rose "one work behind another as far as the sea . . . strong enough to withstand an assault of fifty thousand men." Howe had not forgotten the lesson of Bunker Hill or that casualties were for him almost irreplaceable. Had the troops "been permitted to go on," he wrote, "it is my opinion they would have carried the redoubt, but, as it was apparent that the lines must have been ours at a very cheap rate by regular approaches, I would not risk the loss that might have been sustained in the assault." He assumed that some of Washington's army would escape across the river whatever he did, and whatever he did, he would catch many before they could embark.[16]

Taking advantage of the lull, Washington sent riflemen into the woods to harass the British flanks, and then joined his soldiers in the mournful examination of faces, the discouraging counting of numbers. Sullivan, Stirling, Miles—all the commanders of the advance forces—did not report at headquarters. It seemed possible that more than a thousand men had disappeared.[17]

That was the past: the present need was to establish order. All afternoon, all evening, all night Washington labored. Not only were there the dazed survivors—some wounded, all bereft of comrades; not only were there the inexperienced troops who had watched the carnage over the ramparts and dreaded the morrow. There were farmers who had sought sanctuary and were standing with their families around wagons loaded with goods. More than a thousand horned cattle had been brought into the fortified isthmus to keep them from the British. Missing their pastures, nervous from gunshot, they lowed passionately through the night and stampeded around the campfires. There was human weeping, and sometimes shouts of joy when men considered dead appeared black with the mud in which they had lain hidden.

All afternoon, all evening, all night Washington moved through the encampment, pale but sleepless, keeping the sentries on their rounds, trying to see that everyone had something to eat, gathering stray officers and men into military formations which he hoped would function with need. As his exhausted troops lay in irregular huddles under the sky, he had seen over the walls British tents being raised. A white city bloomed miraculously about the skirts of the woods.

In the blackness of night, Washington surely rode often to the ramparts; he listened for the sounds of a sneak attack. And when dawn broke, he was there peering as the dusk dissolved. He saw no unusual movement in the British camp. Convinced that the confrontation was firmly established, he ordered more troops over from Manhattan.

This order has down the years filled historians with outrage. Washington, they insist, was boneheadedly throwing more men into a trap, which could be snapped shut if the wind changed. Then the British navy would, so it has been argued, sail up the East River, cutting off from the augmented regiments in the vulnerable fortifications on Brooklyn Heights all hope of escape.

Since the wind did not change, the matter was never put to the test. However, the British high command agreed not with the future historians but with Washington, who believed that the East River had been effectively blocked. Baurmeister tells us that the channel was so clogged with sunken ships, their masts protruding from the water, that only rowboats could pass. As long as the Americans held the batteries on Brooklyn Heights, these obstacles could be removed only at the greatest hazard; and any British warship that was damaged would have to weather, in its broken condition, the long ocean voyage either to Halifax or England before she could be mended. The Howe brothers, as their dispatches and later explanations demonstrate, did not take seriously any possibility of cutting Washington's line of retreat across the East River.[18]

The day after the battle passed to skirmishes: cackles of fire that led to no more than individual tragedies. In the afternoon, a cold rain began to fall. In some places sentries stood up to their middles in water, while their mouths complained loudly that they had no rum to keep the cold out. Lack of baggage meant no one had dry clothes. Some tents were brought over from Manhattan, but not enough. Under the feet of the men and the hoofs of the cattle, the ground turned to mud—but there all the men had to sleep. Sickness stalked through the camp, dropping bodies that had not been touched by the enemy.[19]

Not till 4:30 on the second morning after the battle did Washington find time to write Congress. (He had ordered an aide to notify them of the battle.) The letter was somewhat incoherent: he did not know how many men he had lost. He believed the enemy's loss had been considerable. He had heard the sounds of heavy skirmishing the previous evening, but the "event I have not yet learned." He hoped to get more tents, as the defeat and the weather caused "the men to be almost broke down." This much he dictated. He scrawled his signature and (we hope) allowed himself a moment of rest.[20]

When dawn seeped into a foggy drizzle, it was possible to see something outside the ramparts that had not been there before: the British had dug a trench parallel to the American works, so angled that it could not be fired into. It was sixty rods long and had been placed arrogantly within a hundred and fifty rods of the principal American redoubt, Fort Putnam.[21]

This was the first in a foreseeable series of scientific approaches. Soon there would be cannon in that trench. Then another trench would be dug even closer. Then the Americans, if they wished to hold Brooklyn Heights, would have to sally out over the walls and drive the British from the trenches.

As Washington rode among his men, he inspected ammunition boxes: the powder had been spoiled by the wet. He found the troops "dispirited by their incessant duty and watching." Complaints were so violent that he wondered whether the drenched, starved, sick, depressed men could be kept much longer on the lines. And now some Cassandras were warning him, how justifiably he could not tell, that the defenses which kept the British ships from the East River might possibly not suffice.[22]

Probably before he called (on the afternoon of the 29th) the Council of General Officers that agreed with him, Washington resolved that the army must be moved across the river to Manhattan. But how was this to be done when the British were within earshot and eyesight, when Tory spies abounded, and when, if the British caught the army half on water and half still on Brooklyn Heights, the ramparts would fall and the result be pure disaster?[23]

George Washington handled the security problem with a series of brilliant lies grounded on the fiction that fresh troops from the Flying Camp in New Jersey were coming over to relieve the tired troops on Long Island. In preparation for the shift, he explained, all the small boats on the rivers had to be gathered and manned by Massachusetts fishermen from the Salem and Marblehead regiments. And as evening approached, the troops on Brooklyn Heights were ordered to prepare to be relieved at midnight by the mythical fresh troops.

The night came in dark with continuing rain. As they waited on the East River by the Manhattan shore for the Jersey troops to appear, sailors were amazed by orders to take their boats empty to Long Island. When on Brooklyn Heights regiments were withdrawn from the lines, the men still in position were ordered to spread out and fill the empty space until—it would be any minute now—the fresh troops appeared. Even high officers were for as long as possible kept in ignorance of what was actually taking place, although everyone was warned from the start that safety in so complicated a shiftover required silence that would not alert the enemy.

As the final regiments slipped away from the ramparts, mysterious figures came in to give the cries of sentries and feed the campfires. The orders of this skeleton force were to seek, should the maneuver be discovered, to delay enemy attackers until the retreating troops could be turned around.

Behind the retreating men their deserted fires cast a halo into the rain-soggy sky, but ahead there was not a ray of light. Guides whispered how to proceed. Then there would come through the silence the squishy sound of hoofs in mud, and the troops would see, on a tall gray horse, the tall glimmering figure of General Washington.

When ten thousand to twelve thousand men and much equipment must be moved to landings and placed on boats, all does not go smoothly. Fickle winds turned the sailboats off their courses, but for once collisions produced no profanity. The cattle, used to shouts, refused to be driven in silence: They had to be abandoned. The heaviest guns sank so deep in the mud that even oxen could not extract them. There were moments of panic when men tried to climb on the backs of those before them. And for Washington there came two moments of sheer terror.[24]

At about two A.M., a cannon spoke horribly in an American redoubt. Washington galloped there to find that the gun had unaccountably exploded. Then he listened through the throb of rain to discover whether the British had been alarmed. Silence. Thank God, silence![25]

Even more frightening was the sight of a friendly face. At the head of a regiment that was moving through the press toward the ferry landing, Washington recognized Colonel Hand. Hand's regiment was part of the picked corps that was supposed to remain on the ramparts till the last. Investigation revealed a mixup in orders.

"It is a dreadful mistake," Washington mourned. He watched Hand's regiment pushing back through the crush, and calculated the time it would take them to mount again behind the ramparts. The time passed without catastrophe.[26]

Back and forth over almost a mile of water the motley fleet—rowboats, flatboats, sloops, schooners—moved. Men were still crowding toward the shore when Washington calculated that dawn was near. To add to his anxiety, although the rain continued to fall, the fog was rising.

There were still troops waiting on the shore when light began to seep overhead, but, before day really broke, the fog, as if summoned by an enchanter, came back so thickly that the boats vanished after they had traveled six feet.

Finally, the forlorn hope was called in from the ramparts; finally, George Washington himself stepped on a boat. He heard shots behind him. The British had discovered what had happened in time to chase the last of the rear guard onto the last of the boats.

At his headquarters in New York with the retreat triumphantly completed, with not a living man left behind, Washington collapsed. More than twenty-four hours passed before he notified Congress of the escape. He had been, he explained, "quite unfit to write or dictate till this morning." For the six days that began with the battle, "I had hardly been off my horse and had never closed my eyes."[27]

13

If Only the Troops Will Stand By Me

W ITH the deepest concern," Washington wrote Congress after he had fled from Brooklyn to New York City, "I am obliged to confess my want of confidence in the generality of the troops. . . . Till of late, I had no doubt in my own mind of defending this place, nor should I have yet, if the men would do their duty. But this I despair of." He hoped that, "whatsoever the event," it would be remembered that he had done the best he could with troops enlisted for such short terms that they could not be trained.[1]

For Washington, the Battle of Long Island had been deeply disillusioning (if in the long run educational). His military thinking had been grounded on the hope that his virtuous citizen-soldiers would prove in combat superior, or at least equal, to the hireling invaders. He believed that Howe's strategic coup would have come to little if the majority of the men had stood up to the attackers the way Smallwood's one brigade did. That instead they quickly surrendered or took to their heels was to Washington a shock which his successful final escape from Long Island did nothing to alleviate.

Washington had not yet discovered that one of the greatest advantages of his army was its superior mobility, nor was he ever to admit (at least publicly) that one favorable aspect of this mobility could be their address in running away. So few men had survived years before at Braddock's defeat because the men had been trained against disorderly flight and the officers had been unwilling to countenance a withdrawal until it was too late. Indeed, those who attempted to run were, if the officers could get at them, beaten back with swords. Washington's troops were very different. When they felt (wrongly, as well as rightly) that their position was untenable, they did not even look around for an officer. They took off with all the alacrity of men used to moving rapidly over rough ground.

During the orderly withdrawal across the river, the ability of each

American soldier to think for himself had proved beyond controversion invaluable. Each understood, when notified, what he was doing and its importance: they flowed around difficulties that would have blocked columns able to operate only at the end of chains of command.

Indeed, the escape from Brooklyn Heights seemed to trained military minds miraculous. As *Dodsley's Annual Register* (London, 1776) put it: "Those who are best acquainted with the difficulty, embarrassment, noise, and tumult which attend, even by day and no enemy at hand, a movement of this nature with several thousand men, will be the first to acknowledge that this retreat should hold a high place among military transactions."[2]

In telling of events on Long Island, Washington wished to give the Tories as little as possible to smile about. However, rather than boast of a miraculous retreat, he played everything down. In accounts that never exceeded five hundred words, he referred to the battle as a "skirmish," and contrasted the bravery of some of the troops with the cowardice of others. And he made remarkable use of the fact that, after chasing him into his fortifications, the British had stepped slightly back: "During the engagement, a deep column of the enemy descended from the woods and attempted an impression upon our lines, but retreated immediately on the discharge of a cannon and part of the musketry nearest them." After some vacillation, during which he got the figure as high as a thousand, Washington fixed for publication the American loss, including prisoners, at about eight hundred: the enemy's loss "I could never ascertain, but believe it . . . exceeded ours a good deal."* [3]

However effective such glossing over of the defeat may have been in distant parts, gloom reigned in New York City. Wet clothes, accouterments, and tents were laid out on every street, "dampening the spirits of the army. . . . The merry notes of the drum and fife," a diarist noted, "had ceased." Instead, the soldiers (who had before the battle shared Washington's optimism, considering themselves almost invincible) were whispering to each other that they had been "sold out": if only Congress would recall General Lee from the south to replace General Washington![4]

Washington wrote Congress that the militia, "dismayed, intractable," were deserting in large numbers, "in some instances almost by whole regiments" (eight thousand Connecticut militia shrank within a week to two thousand), and "their example has infected other parts of the army." His orders reflected the state of discipline when he wrote that the General "not only commands but most earnestly exhorts" the troops to stop "rambling about."

---

* British statistics enumerated the prisoners they captured as 1097, and estimated the total American loss at 3297, a ridiculous figure considering that only some 3500 were engaged outside the walls. A fair guess puts the American casualties in killed, wounded, and captured at 1500. Howe gave his loss as 367.[5]

Imposing control was nearly impossible because the troops were owed two months' pay. And the officers were too confused to send Washington returns that would let him know what force he had to rely on.[6]

Trying to find an escape from the solid horror of his dilemma, Washington turned to his texts and his fellow officers, coming to the conclusion that history, experience, "and the advice of our ablest friends in Europe" dictated "that on our side the war should be defensive: it has even been called a war of posts." The Americans should never risk "a general action: . . . it would be presumptuous to draw out our young troops into open ground against their superiors both in number and discipline." The answer was to curb the enemy by fortifying suitable positions in the face of their advances. Although Washington agreed that such a war of posts offered the greatest hope of success, he was not truly sanguine: "I have never spared the spade and pickax. I confess I have not found that readiness to defend even strong posts at all hazards which is necessary to derive the greatest benefit from them. . . . but I doubt not this will be gradually attained."[7]

Concerning making New York City a defensible post, Washington's pessimism now outran his optimism. Possession of Brooklyn Heights had enabled the British to open the East River and given them control of Long Island, whence they could ferry their troops to any of the coves and fields that faced them on the extensive, all too inviting Manhattan shore. If they came in above the city and marched quickly across the island, they might well trap any troops that had been stationed below.

Manhattan stretched about thirteen miles from north to south. At the southern end, which was occupied for about a mile and a half by the city, and for the next seven miles of variegated farmland, the island was some two miles wide. Then the Harlem River began to cut northwesterly from the East River to the Hudson, shaping the top of the island into a rough wedge. As the land narrowed, the rocky heights that extended along the Hudson shore occupied more and more of the wedge until at last the whole north end of the island was rough, easily defensible ground. The region was known as Harlem Heights. From the northern tip, Kingsbridge, the exit from Manhattan, stretched across the Harlem River to Fordham Heights on the mainland.

Militarily, the obvious move was for Washington to abandon the city and retire to Harlem Heights. However, many circumstances, including the failure of the British to bombard from captured Brooklyn Heights, persuaded Washington that the enemy hoped to capture the city intact as a permanent military base. New York could comfortably house their whole army, and could be supplied indefinitely by ships. Furthermore, because of the surrounding rivers, a naval power could hold the city with only a small land garrison, leaving most of the British army free to adventure elsewhere.

Washington asked Congress for permission to forestall the enemy by burning New York City. Congress refused. "This in my judgment," Washington wrote Lund, "may be set down among one of the capital errors of Congress."[8]

Many of Washington's officers, including his intimate Reed and also Greene, for whom he was developing an increasing admiration, urged him to abandon the city anyway. This he could not bring himself to do. Handing over as a free gift to the enemy a city considered by some defensible, and on the fortifying of which so much labor had been bestowed, would, he feared, "dispirit the troops and enfeeble our cause." Dispatches he received from Congress made him conclude that that body wished the city held "at all hazards." Furthermore, despite his recent experiences, he could not get it out of his head that if his men acted rapidly and bravely, they could bounce any British spearhead back off the island before the enemy had a chance really to bring their power to bear.

The confusion into which contrary conclusions spun Washington's exhausted brain is revealed by a sentence he wrote to Congress: "We are now in a strong post, but not an impregnable one—nay, acknowledged by every man of judgment to be untenable."[9]

By a majority vote and with Washington's concurrence, a Council of War decided to "pursue a middle course." Nine thousand troops were to withdraw to the comparative safety of Harlem Heights, where they were to build barracks. Work was to be speeded on three forts: Fort Independence, guarding the Kingsbridge crossing to the mainland, and two strongpoints facing each other across the Hudson, in the hope of closing that river. These were Fort Washington on Harlem Heights and Fort Constitution (soon to be called Fort Lee) on the Jersey shore. Five thousand troops were to remain in the city. What was left of Washington's army—perhaps another five thousand—were to occupy the lowlands between the city and the Heights. They were to man a defensive line along the East River shore, and hold off any invaders until larger forces could converge from the Heights and the city.

Leaving thus in the city a large force which could be cut off by a successful invasion of weakly held territory above might well be considered foolhardy. However, Washington felt called on to defend himself to Congress not against rashness but against overcaution in retiring so much of his army to Harlem Heights. He realized, he wrote, how greatly a "brilliant stroke" would cheer the cause after the defeat on Long Island. Yet, "when the fate of America may be at stake on the issue," he did not "think it safe or wise" to refuse to follow "the wisdom of cooler moments and experienced men."[10]

Washington stationed lookouts on all commanding heights; he urged skirmishers to capture prisoners who could be interrogated. "Leave no stone unturned nor do not stick at any expense" to procure spies, he ordered. He had "never been more uneasy" for lack of information: all would be lost if an enemy incursion were not turned back before it could mature.[11]

The British remained poised, as it were, for the kill, while the Howes made another effort to see if the rebels were yet scared into submission. General Sullivan was released on parole to tell Congress that the negotiators had wide powers. Congress thereupon sent a commission, headed by Benjamin Franklin, to meet the brothers and assay their olive branch. It developed (as Washington put it) that "Lord Howe had nothing more to propose than that, if we would submit, his Majesty would consider whether we should be hung or not." The congressional commissioners returned to Philadelphia; and bullets were once more in order.[12]

A group of Washington's generals, led by Greene, requested a new Council of War to reconsider the decision to keep a force in the city, and Congress notified Washington that it had never been their intention to urge him to try to hold the place against his judgment. Washington now joined with the majority who decided that the present situation was "extremely perilous": the city should be completely evacuated as soon as the stores, cannon, and sick could be removed.[13]

Now that the issue had at last been faced up to, Washington felt a passionate anxiety to get out before the British took the advantage. Wagons were the desperate need. In procuring them and, indeed, doing anything, Stephen Moylan, the quartermaster general, proved utterly incompetent: he was soon to be removed from office. Washington, an aide wrote, "is obliged to see into and in a manner fill every department, which is too much for one man." Washington wrote: "You cannot conceive how we are put to it for conveniences to transport the sick, the stores, the baggage, etc." He allowed one of his riding horses to be put to a baggage wagon, but to no purpose— the animal died.[14]

When there was a choice between moving artillery and sick soldiers, Washington did not hesitate. He could not bear to have "my eyes and ears too shocked with the complaints and looks of poor creatures perishing for want of care." To justify his decision on practical grounds, he argued that leaving their sick comrades behind would discourage the entire army, and thus expediency seconded humanity.

The medical department was caught in the universal shortage: no medicine, no milk, no facilities for setting up hospitals. Washington was forced to order that the sick who could walk be taken by their surgeons to the best place they could find. This removed invalids from the jurisdiction of the army and spread disease through the countryside.[15]

At moments when he felt one new problem would destroy him, Washington was assailed with the cries of women. Surrounded with squads of children, the wives of Long Island and New York City soldiers insisted that should they be left behind, "we must all starve together or commit acts which may involve us in ruin." Washington reasoned that if his men ever received their pay they could pay the women for doing their washing. Awaiting that time, he put on rations and accepted as an army responsibility a domestic contingent that was to clog operations until the end of the war.[16]

From across the East River, the enemy were fascinated spectators of the rebel scramble to get out of the city. The Hessian major Baurmeister writes that Washington was often seen riding along the shore. "This provoked Captain Krug of the artillery to fire two shots at him and his suite, and he would have fired a third if their horses had not kept moving."[17]

Sixteen days after the evacuation of Long Island, on September 14, Washington moved his headquarters to Harlem Heights. Many of the stores and cannon had been gathered there, but enough remained below to force a continuation of the old pattern: Putnam commanded the five thousand men in the city, and the other five thousand were still strung along the East River shore, the strongest detachments being toward the north, guarding the Plains of Harlem, where Washington expected the enemy's attack.

September 15 dawned clear and hot. The day had hardly begun when Washington heard cannon speak from the Hudson River. The sound moved rapidly northward and then halted at about the middle of the island. A messenger reported that three British warships were now anchored in the river out of the range of any American guns. No preparation was being made for a landing, but the boats were in a position to block any further withdrawal of goods from the city by water.[18]

Washington's prophetic soul may have told him that when the Howes started on one side they usually ended on the other. In any case, he rode down from the Heights and southeast to the old Dutch village of Harlem (First Avenue and 125th Street). Looking out over the East River, he was relieved to see that the redcoats on Buchanan's (now Ward's) Island and Montresor's (now Randall's) Island were sunning themselves in sylvan calm. Less shipping was present than usual. There were no signs of the expected assault.

It was about eleven in the morning when Washington's ears were assailed by "a most severe and heavy cannonade." He turned toward the sound, staring south down the East River, and soon saw a cloud of black-powder smoke billowing high into the sunlight. It augmented but remained stationary, while the roar continued: clearly the British were trying to batter out a beachhead. Washington estimated that they were attacking a spot guarded only by rudimentary entrenchments that were thinly occupied by his greenest militia (some had served only a week). However, stronger and more experienced regiments were close enough to get there quickly. Washington set off for the battle at a gallop.[19]

Although no one had bothered to notify the Commander in Chief, the British maneuver had been visible since the light of dawn had revealed five warships anchored broadside. They were within musket shot of Kip's Bay, a cove which scooped into Manhattan between the present Thirty-second Street and Thirty-eighth Street almost to Second Avenue. Eventually, there appeared from a Long Island creek eighty-four sixteen-oared barges, each filled with red- and blue-clad British and Hessian troops. Spreading out, they made the surface of the river look, a militiaman wrote, like "a large clover field in full bloom." Facing this phenomenon were some four hundred fifty farmboys who had never fired at a human being. To protect them they had only shallow trenches with the earth that had been dug out thrown up ahead as a parapet. They watched in trepidation.

After the "clover field" had come to a stop, flashes brightened the batteries on the boats. "I thought my head would go with the sound," wrote the militiaman. "I made a frog's leap from the ditch and lay as still as I possibly could, and began to consider which part of my carcass was to go first." Finally the cannonading eased. The militiaman and his companions raised their heads to see hundreds of soldiers, steel blades extended in front of them, marching in rows through the shallows stolidly for the shore. Outnumbered by horrible-looking fighters with bayonets and unmatchable firepower—cannon grapeshot was now coming from the boats and men were shooting down from the rigging—the militiamen, some of whom were armed only with scythe blades hammered into poles, took "merrily" (so the irrepressible militiaman wrote) to their heels.[20]

Washington was galloping down the Post Road (it wandered to one or the other side of the present Lexington Avenue). Some distance from the firing, "to my great surprise and mortification," he met militiamen coming toward him at a run. He reined in his horse sideways across the road; his staff and General Mifflin did likewise. Topping what was now a wall of horses, the officers waved their swords and ordered the men to turn around. They shouted that the men were running from nothing. If the men would look over their shoulders, they would see that they were not being pursued. The men veered off the road to avoid the blockade and proceeded through the fields, "retreating," Washington wrote, "with the utmost precipitation."[21]

The choking dust, thrown up by so many desperate feet, yellowed the hot, windless air. Through the strained sunlight stragglers loomed, but the crowd had passed. Washington spurred ahead, coming quickly to a crossroad which ran (at about Third Avenue and Fortieth Street) west from the Post Road to the other main north-and-south road on the island, Bloomingdale Road (Broadway). The crossroad stopped when it joined Washington's road but pointed eastward across fields and down a slope toward the Kip's Bay shore on which the British were consolidating their beachhead.

Washington rode up a hill (where the Public Library now stands) to survey the situation. He was pleased to see coming up the Bloomingdale Road in good order Fellows's brigade of Massachusetts militia and Parsons's Connecticut Continentals. Washington dispatched orders that these troops turn into the crossroad. When they came level with him, he shouted, "Take the walls! Take the cornfield!"[22]

Abandoning all formations, the men scrambled for the positions. Some having tried one, shifted desperately to the other. Riding among them, Washington "used every means in my power to rally and get them into some order, but my attempts were fruitless and ineffectual."

All was still "disordered" when a party of the enemy came in sight, approaching up the slope from the river. They were not, Washington estimated, "more than sixty or seventy in number." They were the first foes Fellows's and Parsons's men had seen that day—and they were to be the last. Washington heard noises behind him and turned to see soldiers running away "in the greatest confusion." Turning back, he found that the men who had a moment before seemed steadfast under his gaze were now taking off after their companions. Down on the ground came a shower of guns, muskets, powderhorns, coats, and knapsacks, thrown away in an agony of fear. The men had fled "without firing a single shot."[23]

Washington galloped after the men, struck at them with his riding whip, shouted for them to turn. They ducked and continued their run. He threw his hat on the ground and cried out, "Are these the men with whom I am to defend America?" And again, "Good God! Have I got such troops as those?"[24]

Finally, Washington was alone in the crossroad. He saw some fifty of the enemy about eighty yards away and advancing at a run. He stared at them blankly. He did not move. From behind, aides came galloping up. They seized the bridle of the commander's horse, turned him around, and hurried him out of mortal danger.

George Washington, General Greene wrote, was "so vexed at the infamous conduct of his troops that he sought death rather than life."[25]

When Washington regained some composure, he realized that organized resistance was necessarily at an end. He joined his fleeing troops, trying, while rumors that the British horse were approaching created hysteria around him, to make the retreat as orderly as possible. He was in an agony of apprehension for the thousands of soldiers who would be cut off in the city if the British took advantage of the collapse of all resistance at Kip's Bay to draw an impassable line across the island to the Hudson shore.

As the troops he had been accompanying scrambled passionately for the comparative safety of Harlem Heights, Washington stopped some distance below (Ninety-first Street and Broadway) at an important crossroad. From the white farmhouse of Charles Apthorpe, he directed rearguard actions aimed at protecting the escape routes of the various detachments still out

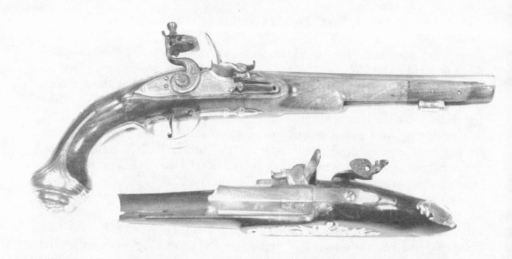

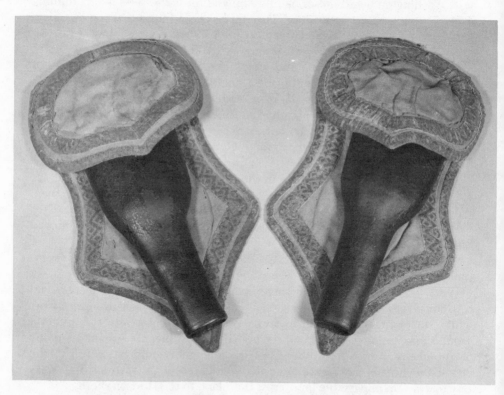

Washington's pistols and holsters. Length of undamaged pistol, 15½ inches.
The holsters are of black leather, ornamented with scarlet braid. Courtesy
of the Mount Vernon Ladies' Association of the Union.

below. He surely stood at the door of the house, staring anxiously at the fugitives who came in.

At first, the bodies of men were all from the East River posts which had been above the landing. Then there appeared exciting faces: officers Washington recognized as belonging to the New York garrison. They came in about nightfall, leading little groups of soldiers, all exhausted from their flight of more than ten miles.

They had, so they told Washington, scurried from the city along the Hudson shore through fields and copses and little farmers' lanes. When they had come level with the Kip's Bay landing place, they had heard band music and sporadic firing off to their right, but had seen not a single enemy. Eventually (about Columbus Circle), they had met Bloomingdale Road as it inclined westward toward the river. It proved empty. The going was then easier, and here they were! More members of the New York garrison came in, and then more and more and even more until Washington became convinced that practically none had been captured.* Not until the very last of the garrison was hurrying by did a small British column loom from the dusk. They fired a few shots, killing a lieutenant colonel.

However, the garrison had not been able to bring with them anything heavier than their muskets. Washington mourned bitterly that, as he put it, "the dastardly behavior of our troops" had caused the loss of irreplaceable artillery—numerically more than half of the patriot cannon—tents, baggage, wagons, and camp equipage, "which would have been easily secured had they [the troops] made the least opposition" to the British landing.[26]

Writers have commonly assumed that if the British had only had the gumption to march across the island directly after their landing had resulted in the collapse of American opposition, the roughly three thousand men still below Kip's Bay would certainly have been captured. That this seemingly obvious maneuver was not undertaken has made historians accuse the British high command of softheadedness, and has given birth to many legends, the nicest of which is a glowing compliment to the charms of American womanhood. Mrs. Robert Murray had an elegant house on the British line of advance. She appeared, so the story goes, at the door with a Circe-like smile and an invitation to tea. Having lured the British high command inside, she bemused them with her beauty and wiles until they forgot they were supposed to be fighting a battle. Finally, a wink from her butler communicated that the garrison from the city had passed into safety. Then, her loveliness heightened by a now manifest glow of American patriotism, she coldly put the lobsterbacks out. Another legend is that General Howe, as a Whig who had been opposed to the war, purposely let the Americans escape.[27]

---

* The British captured in total only some twenty officers and three hundred men.[28]

Actually, Howe's tactics had been, if not venturesome, correct and hardheaded. He had agreed with Washington, who had hoped to dislodge the enemy before they could establish themselves, that the crucial time of the invasion was when the first wave had landed and the second was still on the way. As any professional strategist would have done, he had ordered Clinton, who was in command of the first wave, to use his full strength in creating and holding a beachhead. Whether Howe should have provided in his orders for further action should the American opposition collapse is open to argument, since collapse can be simulated as a ruse.

Clinton later claimed that he had been prevented, when he saw Washington's army in full flight, from "stretching . . . immediately across the island" by the orders of Howe (whom he loved to put in the wrong). Perhaps Clinton was also deterred by personal forebodings. His landing party totaled four thousand men.[29] He could not conceivably have stripped the beachhead of more than half of these. Beyond Bloomingdale Road, which was here at the center of the island, there was no further thoroughfare. His detachment of no more than two thousand would have had to penetrate and hold against some three thousand Americans a three-quarter-mile-deep strip of rough ground: that mixture of fields, woods, farmhouses, stone walls, rocks, watercourses, and gullies most suited to American fighters, least to British and Hessians.

That the second wave of the invasion, which comprised nine thousand men, moved more slowly than had been intended is the one aspect of the British behavior on that day which is open to firm criticism. The total force had not gathered on the beachhead until about 5 P.M.[30] Howe, who was now present and in personal command, probably assumed (as was the fact) that the garrison from the city had already got by. He might have bagged some stragglers, but would this have been worth exposing his irreplaceable troops to sharpshooters lurking behind walls? He resolved to send no detachment directly west across the island. One part of his force would go south and occupy the city while another would move gradually in the direction of Washington, going northward on the Post Road which inclined gently towards Harlem Heights.

The historical fact that, when the matter was put to actual test, almost all of Washington's army succeeded in getting away could be taken to indicate that his leaving much of his army in the city was not so completely foolhardy as the history books would have us believe.

As for Howe, he did not recognize, then or later, any need to make excuses for the escape of the rebel garrison.[31] He had, indeed, carried out the operation brilliantly according to the rules of that war of posts which Washington wished to learn and in which the Englishman had been trained. He had by maneuver occupied the major rebel metropolis which he desired as a base for future action. Since he had driven the enemy back, he was correct to have avoided serious fighting that would, however successfully it was carried through, have weakened his army with some casualties, and which might have resulted in the destruction of all or part of the city which he had skillfully captured completely undamaged.

For the rest of the war, Washington was to rue the day that Howe got into New York.

CHAPTER

14

Blood on the Bushes

A FTER his discouraged army had drawn itself in, like a wounded spider, on Harlem Heights, Washington, who always expected the enemy to act as rapidly as he would have done in their situation, prepared as best he could for an immediate attack. Sure that the enemy would take advantage of the confusion around him, he set some men manning the earthworks and others digging to strengthen them. Then he certainly rode to the Point of Rocks (127th Street and Saint Nicholas Avenue), a natural lookout extending from the southeastern edge of the Heights. The plains of Harlem swung below him in a wide semicircle. There were no unusual sounds or lights, and horsemen he had sent out to scour the flat terrain reported no enemy advance.*

However, there was one close approach to the encampment where neither eyesight nor horsemen could penetrate. Along the Hudson shore, Harlem Heights came to an abrupt end, falling into the Hollow Way, a flat break in the cliffs (around 125th Street) that was a quarter of a mile wide. Then the uneven tableland rose again abruptly to form Bloomingdale Heights (Grant's Tomb, Columbia University, etc.). A major British advance could be building under the thick foliage on Bloomingdale Heights.

Before daylight on the 16th, Washington sent out a hundred and twenty New Englanders who had volunteered as "rangers" to discover what was happening on Bloomingdale Heights. Then he wrote to Congress a report on the battle of the day before. Having explained his present position, he added, "I should hope the enemy would meet with a defeat in case of an attack, if the generality of our troops would behave with tolerable resolution. But experience, to my extreme affliction, has convinced me that this is rather to be wished for than expected."[1]

---

* True to the strategy he had been taught, Howe was taking no risks as he completed his occupation of the city and consolidated his other gains.

[128]

Washington had just finished writing when a messenger rushed in to say that the British were advancing across the Harlem Plains in three powerful columns. Shouting to an aide to copy the letter and sign it, Washington leapt on horseback and galloped to the Point of Rocks. Bright daylight showed the plains empty. The report had clearly been a phantasmagoria thrown up by terror. However, firing sounded from under the obscuring trees on Bloomingdale Heights. Washington sent Reed over to reconnoiter.

The firing continued, becoming louder as if the fighting were moving towards Washington. Then Reed and the rangers popped out of the forest on the far cliff, scrambled down into the Hollow Way, hurried across through fields, and clambered up to the American-held Heights. Some British light infantry appeared on the lip of the other cliff. A bugler raised his instrument, and through the early morning air there came to Washington's ears the call used in the chase to indicate that the fox had skulked into his hole. The insult was only too plain to the foxhunting Virginia squire. Even the Philadelphia lawyer Reed "never felt such a sensation before. It seemed to crown our disgrace."[2]

His face hot from the insult, Washington questioned Reed and the rangers. They told him that the enemy numbered only three hundred and were dangerously far in advance of the rest of their army. According to Reed, Washington was so discouraged that he had to be "prevailed upon" to take advantage of the situation. Washington's own version was that, feeling even a tiny victory might help recover his army's "military ardor," he "immediately" ordered some troops down into the Hollow Way to decoy the bugler and his companions there, while another force started on a circuitous march that would get them up on the opposite cliff behind the mockers.

The maneuver started out excellently. "On the appearance of our party in front," Washington wrote, the enemy "immediately ran down the hills, took possession of some fences and bushes, and a smart firing began, but at too great distance to do much execution either side."

As Washington strained his eyes to see his secret posse appear dramatically above the enemy, his ears were unpleasantly assailed by firing "rather on their flank than in their rear. . . . By some unhappy mistake" the posse had let itself be seen.[3]

Up the far cliff the British scrambled. (Washington may have longed for a bugler to give some fox calls of his own.) The Americans in the Hollow Way scrambled up after them and all disappeared under the trees. The firing rapidly became more distant as the British continued to flee.

Messengers soon appeared from the woods to clamber up to Washington and ask for reinforcements. In order to send more men, Washington had to use some of the troops who had fled so cravenly the day before. In anguish lest they again misbehave, he collected high officers to go with them; a galaxy of generals, including Putnam and Greene, with most of Washington's own staff, led the reinforcements across the Hollow Way. And the news that came back was so good it was almost unbelievable. Yesterday's skulkers "charged the enemy with great intrepidity." Washington had soon committed eighteen hundred men.[4]

As the Americans (in the words of a Maryland colonel) "engaged in the true bush-fighting way," the British continued, despite some reinforcement, to fall back. Then there came to Washington's ears the deep voices of British cannon. He reasoned (correctly) that the enemy must be "sending in a large body to support their party." He longed to respond with further reinforcements who might "improve" this encounter into a major victory. However, he was held back by "a want of confidence in the generality of the troops."

Washington had given his men free rein for an hour and a half when he finally dispatched orders that they should disengage and come back. Then the firing frayed away. The American troops disgorged into the Hollow Way below Washington, dragging along some wounded but in high spirits and good order. Thus ended what has gone down in history as the Battle of Harlem Heights.* [5]

"This little advantage," Washington wrote, "has inspirited our troops prodigiously. They find that it only requires resolution and good officers to make an enemy (that they stood in too much dread of) give way." However, he himself was not much "inspirited."[6]

In its first three weeks of actual fighting, his army had revealed what seemed to him mortal weaknesses. That the troops had shown in retreat immense nobility, that they had fought bravely when in the woods and not convinced they were outmatched, seemed to Washington hardly any compensation for their unwillingness to stand when they felt themselves in real danger, for the fact that his army had twice been shoved aside by the enemy as easily as a giant would push away a child. If only he could resign!

---

* Washington estimated the American loss at 60 killed and wounded. Howe put his casualties at 168. To his government, the Briton claimed a victory—3000 Americans repulsed with more than 300 killed—but one of his subordinates noted that the British had got in trouble through overconfidence and had been "rather severely handled. . . . This was an unfortunate business and gave the General [Howe] a good deal of concern, and nothing was intended or gained by it."[7]

A Heavy Heart

WASHINGTON was, upon occasion, sick—"much indisposed"— his mind, as he put it, too much "on the stretch," and his feelings wounded "by a thousand things." He wrote his confidant Lund Washington from Harlem Heights, "I am resolved not to be forced from this ground while I have life," but he felt it necessary to add, "if the men will stand by me, which, bye and bye, I despair of."[1]

For the moment, Howe showed no signs of putting Washington's worst fears to the test. Although the British lurched from Staten Island across the intervening narrow channel to New Jersey, capturing the port of Amboy and five hundred of its garrison, the English general clearly considered Harlem Heights too formidable to storm. And one midnight Washington saw a red glow to the south that brightened until there was no doubt that New York City was on fire. "Providence or some good honest fellow," Washington commented, "has done more for us than we were disposed to do for ourselves." Although it was disappointing to learn that only a quarter of the occupied city had burned, the confusion caused by this loss could be counted on to delay any major British march.[2]

The menace of an attack was, however, always there, like a gnawing toothache that colors every perception; yet for almost a month after the Battle of Harlem Heights no major enemy maneuver pulled Washington's mind from the internal problems of his army.

Washington secretly begged his aides to assure him that the cause would go better, would go at all, if he resigned. To Lund, he wrote, "If I were to wish the bitterest curse to an enemy on this side of the grave, I should put him in my stead with my feelings; and yet I do not know what plan of conduct to pursue. I see the impossibility of serving with reputation, or doing any essential service to the cause by continuing in command, and yet I am told that if I quit the command, inevitable ruin will follow from the distraction that will ensue. In confidence, I tell you that I never was in such an unhappy, divided state since I was born. To lose all comfort and happiness on the one hand, whilst I am fully persuaded that under such a system as has been adopted, I cannot have the least chance for reputation, nor those allowances made which the nature of the case requires; and to be told, on the other, that if I leave the service all will be lost, is, at the same time that I am bereft of every peaceful moment, distressing to a degree. But I will be done with the subject, with the precaution to you that it is not a fit one to be publicly known or discussed." However, if he fell in battle, it might not be amiss that how he was being hamstrung might be made known in justice to his character.[3]

The people, Washington complained, were being led to believe that the enemy was "scarce a mouthful for us." And a committee Congress sent to Harlem Heights alarmed Washington by refusing to be alarmed. Seeing a bustling camp and plenty of vegetables, they expressed relief that things were not worse.[4]

Outside his own immediate circle of intimates, Washington said nothing about his daily and nightly dreams of resigning and returning to Mount Vernon. However, he was determined to alarm Congress. Once he wrote the President of that body in his own hand: "From the hours allotted to sleep, I will borrow a few minutes to convey my thoughts. . . . Unless some speedy and effectual measures are adopted by Congress, our cause will be lost!"[5]

Discipline had completely broken down. "Every hour" his headquarters filled with civilians, including women in tears. They enunciated "the most distressing complaints of the ravages of our own troops who are becoming infinitely more formidable to the poor farmers and inhabitants than the common enemy." Despite Washington's commands and exhortations, the soldiers ruled anything worth stealing fair game as Tory property. When a brigade major tried to stop a party that was making off with four large mirrors and a bundle of women's clothes, the looters drew up in battle formation and offered to kill the major.[6]

Washington complained to Congress that he needed a greater variety of punishments, since for most offenses the military code prescribed thirty-nine lashes which "many hardened fellows" said they would gladly suffer again for a bottle of rum. Congress responded, authorizing a hundred lashes, as well as death for an enlarged group of offenses; but in his heart Washington doubted the efficacy of punishment as an influencer of men.[7]

He continually threatened that troops who skulked during battle would be shot, and he had written that fear of punishment distinguished long- from short-term soldiers and kept men brave. However, he could not bear to carry out his threats. What more perfect example could be found than Ebenezer Liffenwell who, when Reed tried to keep him from fleeing during the Battle of Harlem Heights, had tried to shoot Reed? Washington ordered Liffenwell to be shot in the presence of the army on the Grand Parade, but pardoned him on the day of the execution, threatening that the next such miscreant "shall suffer death without mercy."[8]

Troops were improved, Washington was convinced, not by punishment but by training. Being prevented from keeping men long enough to train them inspired his loudest protests to Congress. He again faced the dissolution of the entire army with the end of the year, and it was now mid-September. He insisted that the measures Congress had taken to bring in the three-year men they had already authorized were woefully inadequate. To begin with, the service would have to be made financially attractive.

"When men are irritated and their passions inflamed," Washington wrote, remembering the halcyon days in Cambridge, "they fly hastily and cheerfully to arms: but, after the first emotions are over . . . a soldier reasoned with upon the goodness of the cause he is engaged in and the inestimable rights he is contending for, hears you with patience and acknowledges the truth of your observations, but adds that it is of no more importance to him than others. The officer makes you the same reply, with this further remark, that his pay will not support him, and he cannot ruin himself and his family to serve his country, when every member of the community is equally interested and benefited by his labors."[9]

Let not Congress feel that, if enlistments lagged, they could with safety continue to fill in with recurring temporary levies of militia. The result would be "certain and inevitable ruin."

"Just dragged from the tender scenes of domestic life," militiamen were "ready to fly from their own shadows." The sudden change in their manner of living made them receptacles and spreaders of sickness. "Accustomed to unbounded freedom and no control," they resisted all discipline, in the process corrupting whatever more regular troops Washington had been able to gather. The unforeseeable "fluctuation" in their numbers "deranges every plan as fast as adopted." And in battle, so they had tragically demonstrated, they started stampedes that unnerved the regulars. "If I was called upon to declare upon oath," Washington stated with the exaggeration he often applied to passionate argument, "whether the militia have been most serviceable or hurtful upon the whole, I should subscribe to the latter."

"Certain I am that it would be cheaper to keep 50, or 100,000 men in constant pay than to depend upon half the number and supply the other half occasionally by militia." Not only did each set of militiamen have to be equipped anew, not only did they have to be paid for time lost in coming and going, but high bounties had to be given them for each enlistment. And, alas, such bounties, which could repeatedly be collected for short service, hindered enlistment in the regular army, since it was more profitable to come and go.[10]

Washington then argued for further distinction between officers and men, and for an anti-equalitarian and anti–states' rights reorganization of the medical service.

[133]

The epidemics in Washington's New York encampments, coming on top of the debacle in Canada, were proving only too conclusively that disease was a monstrous eater of armies. (The Americans were, indeed, to lose many times more men to germs than they lost to bullets.) Edinburgh-trained Dr. John Morgan, who served as director general of hospitals, was America's most distinguished physician, and he had worked hard to surround himself with doctors of competence. However, the regiments, each of which had been recruited in a specific locality, had their own surgeons, usually country practitioners who had been known at home to the officers and men. When Morgan tried to establish authority over these surgeons, they insisted, often with the loyal backing of their regimental commanders, that they were autonomous, if not actually superior to the perfumed dandies of the central hospital department. And Morgan, having more the character of Schuyler than of Washington, added social rancor to medical disagreement by making clear his disdain for the lowborn, apprentice-trained empirics.

The regimental surgeons insisted that the hospital department supply them with drugs and instruments (which were almost irreplaceable, since the Colonies had imported such things from England), yet they would give no accounting of how the supplies were used. Morgan was alarmed, but could not refuse as long as the sick were treated in the surgeons' own improvised hospitals. Efforts to move the sick to general hospitals were unavailing until some action of the enemy sent the regimental surgeons scurrying to dump all their sick suddenly on Morgan's staff.

Having described this situation to Congress, Washington added that many of the regimental surgeons "are very great rascals, countenancing the men in sham complaints to exempt them from duty, and often receiving bribes to certify indispositions." He urged that the country practitioners "should undergo a regular examination," and, if not actually appointed by the hospital department, be under its orders.[11]

Although many of Washington's recommendations were bitter pills for them to swallow, Congress did their best to back him up. They voted pay raises and liberal bounties for enlistment in the regular army, going in this beyond their own judgment (and their ability to achieve). They voted that the men be given, as an additional inducement, free uniforms. They agreed that the regimental surgeons should be accountable to the hospital department. And they wrestled with Washington's double insistence that the militia should not be relied on and that the term of enlistment for the Continental Army be expanded from three years to the duration of the conflict.[12]

The conception of a people's army, virtuous yeomen dropping their ploughs to repel a tyrant's Myrmidons, was dear to the hearts of philosophical democrats. They refused to believe that their faith in so noble an idea was altogether visionary, but they had to admit that it was not working under the command of Washington. Since Washington was still indispensable to the cause, they agreed (although some nurtured the hope of seeing better times under a more satisfactory general) that it was necessary to give him, as far as safety permitted, the weapons he could best use. But how far did safety permit?

If Washington commanded an army which had through the years been welded into a unit under his command, would he not, with peace, do what so many Roman generals had done: make himself king or dictator and oppress civilians? The conservatives were less haunted than the radicals by this fear; but all the members of Congress were appointed by their states, and most cherished the autonomy of the states which gave them their power. They recognized that the Continental Army, if allowed to become through long service a unit apart from state control, might open the way to a continental government.

Although necessity forced them to empower the enlistment of eighty-eight regiments for the duration of the war, Congress added a provision which may well have made Washington wish that the bill had never been passed: the states were to keep control of the regiments they raised, not only supplying them but by appointing the officers.[13]

Washington's officers, like his men, had been enlisted only till the end of 1776, and now, if they were to be reappointed, they would have to call themselves to the attention of the politicians in their state capitals. Some, wishing to leave nothing to chance, took off for home without consulting Washington, and it was clear that those who stayed and attended to their duty were placing their military careers in jeopardy. As for Washington, he wrote Congress: "I see such a distrust and jealousy of military power that the Commander in Chief has not an opportunity, even by recommendation, to give [his officers] the least assurances of reward for the most essential services."[14]

Congress rushed off letters suggesting that the states send commissioners to consult with Washington on what appointments should be made. Washington—"I entreat you . . . I beseech you!"—passionately begged the upper officers from each state to send lists of recommendations to their legislatures. However, it would all take time, and Washington knew from the experience of the previous year that the men would not enlist until the officers they would serve under had been determined. He foresaw a gap between his old and his new army, which would have to be filled by those militia "with whom no man who had any regard for his own reputation can undertake to be answerable for the consequences."[15]

To cap Washington's misery, reports were coming in that the British were offering higher bounties for enlistment than Congress could afford, and

[135]

were being highly successful in drawing to their banner Americans whom Washington called "parricides." He could not be sure "whether any rubs in our way of our enlistments or an unfavorable turn in our affairs, may not prove the means of the enemy recruiting men faster than we do. . . . The certain and absolute loss of our liberties will be the inevitable consequence."[16]

The one favorable circumstance Washington could see was a refilling of his depleted reservoir of generals. An exchange of prisoners having been negotiated—"officer for officer of equal rank, soldier for soldier, and citizen for citizen"[17]—he got back Sullivan and Stirling. And there came riding up, accompanied as always by his dogs, the old wizard himself, General Charles Lee.

Fresh from his triumph at Charleston, Lee had collected thirty thousand dollars from Congress to make certain he would not lose by his army service, and had privately expressed his opinion that congressmen were all useless "cattle" and that Washington was remiss in obeying their orders. He also believed that Congress, having lost faith in Washington, had ordered him to hurry to New York because they wanted a new savior.[18]

For his part, Washington was enchanted to have again the assistance of his experienced military friend. He gratefully gave Fort Constitution, the twin on the Jersey side of the Hudson of Fort Washington, a new name: Fort Lee.

16

British Might Displayed

O N the night of October 12, 1776, after the Continental Army had remained undisturbed on Harlem Heights for almost exactly a month, a fog obscured the southern end of New York State. As Washington lay asleep in his headquarters, no unusual sounds or lights penetrated to him through the mist. But farmers residing on the banks of the upper East River were conscious of ghostly stirrings out on the water: voices, the creak of rigging. The next morning a British fleet and army showed plain.

The enemy had sailed up the East River through the rapids of Hell Gate, followed the river easterly away from Manhattan (they would now have gone under the Triborough Bridge), and advanced with the part of Long Island that is now the Borough of Queens on their right, and on their left the part of the mainland that is now the Bronx. Where the river disgorged into Long Island Sound there projected from the mainland, like a soft palate hanging in the watery mouth, a point of land known as Throg's (or Frog's) Neck. On this the British made their landing. They would have only to march nine miles westward to cut, at the mainland end of Kingsbridge, Washington's escape route from Manhattan Island.[1]

Washington's first reaction when notified was that he "wished to God" that he was more familiar with the geography of that part of New York. Out on horseback, and off with his aides behind him! He was glad to discover the ground between Kingsbridge and Throg's Neck was "strong and de-fensible, being full of stone fences." It was a good omen that the men sent out to guard the passes "seemed to be in good spirits."[2]

On Harlem Heights, the orders were for the butchers to keep killing and one man in every mess to keep cooking until four days' provisions for all had been dressed. However, the British did not advance. Probably because of faulty maps, Howe had landed eleven thousand men not on a solid point, but on an end of land isolated from the shore by marshes. Americans had quickly dismantled the causeway and now fired with rifles at engineers who tried to replace it. And the second wave of the advance—Hessians with the necessary stores and provisions—was being kept by contrary winds from getting through the rapids at Hell Gate, "a very horrid place to pass."[3]

The fact remained that Howe's move made Harlem Heights a potential trap. A Council of War held at Lee's headquarters concluded that the army should withdraw—but not entirely. Since Congress had ordered them to hold the Hudson River, the generals decided to leave a garrison at Fort Washington, which, in cooperation with Fort Lee and with hulks sunk in the channel between, was the best block to navigation of the lower Hudson the patriots had. The theory was that, in case of an irresistible attack, the garrison, which was put under the command of General Greene, could escape across the river to New Jersey.[4]

Washington was convinced that the British objective was "to form a line in our rear," separating his main army from its supplies, and either pinning it against Long Island Sound or forcing it to flee westward across the Hudson, which would leave Connecticut and the rest of New England unprotected. The enemy, he wrote, "must never be allowed, if it is possible to avoid it, to get above us."[5]

The theater of war was now a long, narrow (ten-mile-wide) slab of land between the Hudson River and the Sound. It was cut lengthwise by four rough parallels. After the Hudson shore came the Upper Connecticut Road. Next was the Bronx River. Then came Hutchinson River, the Lower Connecticut Road, and finally the shore of the Sound. Fifteen miles north of the British landing at Throg's Neck and twenty north of Harlem Heights, the broken, hilly area around White Plains gathered in like a fist the interior strands. White Plains appealed to Washington "as the first and most convenient stage" of his retreat. He ordered that his supplies be taken there.[6]

After the British had been quiescent for five days, the reinforcing ships got through Hell Gate and helped Howe's expeditionary force break from Throg's Neck. The British then advanced north along the Lower Connecticut Road, with their left protected by the Hutchinson River. Washington came down from Harlem Heights and off Manhattan Island. He moved parallel with the enemy on the Upper Road, his right on the Bronx River. By leaving parties behind him on every advantageous piece of ground, he kept open as long as possible his communications with the garrison at Fort Washington. Then, as his own force mounted near White Plains, he systematically drew his detachments in. Lee, who commanded the exposed American rear, undoubtedly advised Washington. No maneuver could have been better managed. Despite its complication, it cost almost nothing in men and supplies.

On the British side of the no-man's-land between the Hutchinson and

Bronx rivers, there was more action. "The Rebels," so an officer complained, "appeared drawn up in our front behind all the fences and high stone walls."[7] Falling back expertly, they inflicted casualties. However, when the British, having marched some ten miles from their landing place, approached the town of New Rochelle, the garrison there fled without attempting resistance. Such contrasts Washington blamed on good or bad leadership by the officers.

At White Plains, Washington set his men to digging entrenchments on a tongue-shaped bluff that jutted out in front of the village in the direction of the British advance from New Rochelle. The left side of the bluff was protected by a stream issuing from a local pond; the right side, by a gully through which the Bronx River washed.

Until Lee had brought the last of the troops in, Washington found little time to reconnoiter. The next morning—it was October 27—he led a group of general officers across the Bronx River to examine Chatterton's Hill which rose directly west of the gully. Some militiamen who had been lounging behind stone walls came raggedly to a salute, but the eyes of the generals were on something else. They were looking down from a superior height on the American encampment: suppose the British put cannon on Chatterton's Hill?

Then the eyes of the officers turned, as if by common consent, northward to where higher hills rose behind White Plains. "Yonder," said Lee, pointing toward New Castle, "is the ground we ought to occupy."

Washington replied, "Let us then go and view it."

They had hardly started when, so General Heath* remembered, a horseman appeared, his steed panting. "The British are on the camp, sir!"

"Gentlemen," said Washington, "we have now other business than reconnoitering." He led a gallop for the camp. On his arrival, he was told that the American advance guard had been beaten in. "Gentlemen, you will repair to your respective posts and do the best you can."

However, the British did not appear. They encamped at a distance of four miles. The sound of firing came from farther away and in the direction of Fort Washington. Before nightfall, the news came in that a contemptuous British gesture with a small naval and land force against Fort Washington had been repulsed. So far, so good![8]

At dawn on the 28th, Washington sent two regular regiments to join the militia on Chatterton's Hill, making the total force there about sixteen

---

* General William Heath had been a successful Massachusetts farmer who had raised large herds of cattle to be sold as ships' provisions. Although he had climbed up the political side of the militia ladder, he read military books. He described himself as being of "middling stature, light complexion, very corpulent and baldheaded." Chastellux characterized him as "frank and amiable," more suited to the countinghouse than the field. Washington found him useful in garrison posts.[9]

hundred. He also dispatched skirmishers to harass the British if they should march. As the hours passed, he heard firing in the distant woods, and then his skirmishers emerged into the mile-long plain which fronted on the American position. They ran back through open fields. Soon several enemy columns emerged from under the distant trees. Field artillery was brought up and began to fire. Washington's guns answered, but the range was long.

As the enemy infantry marched stolidly down the long clearing, a troop of about twenty horse exploded suddenly into action, galloping and brandishing their sabers. They seemed bent on charging the American position, but when almost at the fortified bluff, they veered. Gracefully the horses leapt over a fence. The cavalcade flashed as they proceeded through a wheat field. Then an American cannonball tumbled a trooper off his mount. At this, the rest of the horsemen galloped out of the field and disappeared behind a hill.[10]

The infantry column kept coming on. The solid blocks of red and blue, bayonets rising above, advanced with an undulating motion. One after another they turned left by platoons, passed through "a bar or gateway," to come directly in front of the American position. "The sun shone bright," Heath remembered, "their arms glittered, and perhaps troops never were shown to more advantage." The head of the line had traversed the fields and disappeared under flanking trees while the rear was still emerging from the distant wood. Finally, all those who were visible halted. In solid blocks, the units lowered as the men sat down. There was no straggling, as when the Americans were at ease. Each man sat as motionless as a pebble.

More and more British cannon were being brought into closer range. "The scene," a Pennsylvania soldier wrote, "was grand and solemn. . . . The air groaned with streams of cannon and musket shot; the hills smoked and echoed terribly with the bursting of shells; the fences and walls were knocked down and torn to pieces, and men's legs, arms and bodies mangled with cannon and grape shot all around us."[11]

After a considerable pause, the blocks of Britons and Hessians on the American right rose from their sitting posture. They forded the Bronx River and filed into the gully which separated the Patriots' main camp from Chatterton's Hill that commanded it. Washington could not see what was happening, but, as the British cannon fire in that sector ceased, he concluded that the enemy troops were advancing into a position where they could be hit. This reasoning was confirmed when from the far side of Chatterton's Hill the fire of small arms burst out so heavily that it was a continuous noise "without distinction of sounds." Although the enemy attackers were still not visible, Washington knew that they were charging up the slope.

This was now a little Bunker Hill, the kind of engagement in which Americans had always given the best account of themselves. True, they had

had no time to prepare redoubts, but, since the war was no longer static, such would surely be the continuing situation. The men had stone walls and trees to crouch behind. Washington was straining his every sense to follow what was more important than an immediate skirmish: the result would indicate whether the war of posts to which he wished to commit himself—the effective defense of successive strong positions—could be made part of the war of movement that the enemy was now forcing upon him. How he longed to have the auguries be good!

But they were not. After about a quarter of an hour, Washington saw his troops come welling over the crest of the hill. They hurried down the near side toward the main encampment. They were not in full flight, it is true, but although no enemy was visible at their heels, they were not in the best order. A considerable time was to elapse before helmeted heads rose over the crest to be followed by the blue-clad bodies of Hessians. The German mercenaries lined up in drill formation and stood there, triumphant against the afternoon sky.[12]

Washington expected British field artillery to appear on Chatterton's Hill. Cannon fire would then infiltrate his camp, while fresh enemy troops assaulted his center. But, as the anxious minutes dragged slowly into hours, this did not happen. The enemy infantrymen, wherever visible, sat down again beside their muskets, and the wheeled vehicles that emerged from the far forest were not more cannon but wagons bearing tents.[13]

As usual, Washington was greatly puzzled by the British strategy. General Howe, in defending his actions before Parliament, was to explain that forcing the very strong ground on which Washington was posted would have gained nothing beyond "some baggage and provisions," since the rebels had heights behind them to which they could flee.* Howe stated that his objective in his march into Westchester County had been double: to force the rebels to quit their stronghold on Harlem Heights "and, if possible, to bring them into action." The first objective had, except for the continued presence of the garrison of Fort Washington (which seemed ripe for capture) been achieved. In Howe's lexicon, the second should not involve a bloodbath where heavy American casualties would be accompanied by heavy British.

Howe was beginning to realize that the conquest of territory was not as important in America as in smaller and more centralized Europe. To win this unusual war it might well be necessary to destroy Washington's army. But Howe did not intend to risk destroying his own army. Professional skill in maneuver would sooner or later open an opportunity to eliminate, in an inexpensive manner, the ridiculus amateur by whom Howe was opposed.

---

* Howe also told Parliament that "political reasons" had entered into his decision not to attack further. Despite various guesses, this statement has never been elucidated.

In the meanwhile, the British general seems to have been confused on how to proceed: He was not used to relying on improvisation growing out of unforeseeable movements of the enemy.

The night after the conquest of Chatterton's Hill, Howe kept his troops sleeping on their arms. Washington kept his up all night digging entrenchments. The next morning, Howe, "observing their lines . . . much strengthened by additional works," deferred what he now called "the designed attack upon them."[14]

Thus ended what history has portentously called the Battle of White Plains. However depressing to Washington, it was really a skirmish in preparation for a battle that never took place.*

Washington's immediate yearning was to get his army back and up into the higher hills at New Castle. He kept everyone who could be spared from the lines employed in carrying stores from White Plains to that haven. Then an enemy deserter reported that Howe intended to attack during the night of the 31st.[15]

The night of the 31st was black and horrid with rain. Howe did not move in such weather, but Washington did. Despite "infinite difficulties and delays"—the main problem had been the usual lack of wagons—he had already succeeded in getting out most of the stores. Now he withdrew his army. When they were safe on the New Castle heights, he signaled his successful retreat by setting fire to some barns and one house that contained forage and other bulky things he had had to leave behind.

Howe responded by advancing in the early morning with a bristle of arms and a roar of cannon. However, he quickly came on a strong rear guard embedded in the rocky banks. A "cunningly hid" fieldpiece removed a Hessian's head. Again Howe encamped.

The British general was to explain, "All these motions plainly indicating the enemy's design to avoid coming to action, I did not think the driving their rear guard further back an object of the least consequence."[16] It was the Boston-Cambridge situation over again. Even if Howe advanced a hundred miles, he would come on nothing to capture, which Washington could not whisk away, the loss of which would cripple or even seriously damage the rebels.

From his new position, Washington saw the British camp a long cannon shot away. The weather growing cold, they lit at night (so Heath wrote) "a vast number of fires . . . some on the level ground, some at the foot of the hills and at all little distances to their brows, some of which were lofty." All "seemed to mix with the stars and to be of different magnitudes."[17]

---

* Howe stated his loss as very slight and set the American at 250. Washington estimated publicly the British loss at 300 and his own at less than 150.[18]

[142]

This strangely Arcadian scene, this interlude in terror, soon faded. As November 5 dawned, there came into view a great stirring in the British camp. Washington gave orders; bugles blew; drums beat; men rushed to their battle posts; and now thousands of eyes were staring below. During the night, the British had dismantled and packed their tents. Did this mean that Howe intended to dislodge the Americans from their hills?[19]

Now the British might was on the move toward the American lines. Now the columns were turning inexplicably to their left and again to the left. They were marching off in the direction of New York City.

Some of Washington's generals almost leapt with pleasure. The campaign was done, they exclaimed; the British, they told Washington, "are going into winter quarters, and will set down in New York, without doing more than investing Fort Washington."

"That they will invest Fort Washington," Washington replied, "is a matter of which there can be no doubt." However, he suspected that Howe also would make some other, more aggressive move, perhaps dash across New Jersey to take Philadelphia. "He must attempt something on account of his reputation, for what has he done as yet, with his great army?"[20]

One thing was certain. Wherever Howe went, there a patriot force must also be. But how, in the present uncertainty and confusion and weakness, could that be managed?

17

The Blackest Defeat

W ASHINGTON suspected that the enemy would now invade New Jersey with the intention of crossing the state and capturing Philadelphia. However, their disappearance from in front of New Castle might be a trick to make him leave that strong post, opening their way for a countermarch into New England. The worst aspect of the situation was that these alternative theaters of war were separated by the Hudson River, an obstacle which, under the best of circumstances, could not be quickly crossed. He concluded that he would have to station a force on each bank of the Hudson, so that whichever way the British pushed, they would not get away unopposed. If the river were kept free of British ships, the part of the army that was away from the action could, when the enemy showed their hand, dash across to join the part that was delaying the enemy.[1]

With the approval of a Council of War, Washington worked out a four-way division of the army. The garrisons under Greene already at Fort Washington and Fort Lee would try to continue to hold shut the lower Hudson. As a second line of defense for the essential waterway, three or four thousand men under Heath were to be stationed at the Highlands forts, thirty miles upriver. Some seven thousand troops from the New England and New York regiments would guard New England by staying at North Castle. Their commander was to be General Lee. Washington himself would lead across the Hudson the regiments that had originated west of that river. These proved to number only two thousand fit for duty, but he hoped to find in the Flying Camp on the Jersey shore across from Manhattan Island five thousand soldiers whom Greene did not need for the defense of his forts.[2]

For almost two centuries Washington has been damned right and left because he thus divided his army. However, the contemporary military historians R. Ernest Dupuy and Trevor N. Dupuy point out that much of what Washington did was dictated by his situation. Certainly, to place delaying forces on the opposite sides of the river was the only way to keep the British army from running free in one direction or the other. The slowness of British movements in comparison with the American could with some justice be relied on, when the need developed, to enable the Continental Army to come together again. Washington could not have foreseen what was in fact to prevent such a rapid junction: the insubordination of General Lee.[3]

Since a Hudson crossing would have to be kept open, the garrison at the Highlands forts was dictated. But even the Dupuys do not support the decision to try to hold Fort Washington. No one in Washington's council could have failed to realize that this involved great risks; Washington himself expressed misgivings. However, Congress had indicated its desire that the fort be not abandoned. The Council could not face up to ordering a withdrawal that would bring to an end all efforts to hold the more than twenty strategic miles of the Hudson above Manhattan and below the Highlands. Lee was later to claim that he had argued that Fort Washington should be evacuated and that his "proposal" had been "slighted." Perhaps he did not expostulate too loudly, lest he force reconsideration of a plan which gave him semi-autonomous control of the lion's share of the army. He found the possibilities thus opened exhilarating. Quit at last of his amateur superior, Lee would be able to demonstrate how an experienced military genius could save the mismanaged cause.[4]

Washington himself was so exhausted, so puzzled and depressed, that he did not find it in his heart to give peremptory orders. In entrusting most of his men to Lee, he "requested"; he "suggested"; he stated that he had "the most entire confidence in your judgment and military exertions." Even concerning the probable strategic rejoining of the armies, Washington cracked no Commander in Chief's whip: "If the enemy should remove the whole or the greatest part of their force to the west side of Hudson's River, I have no doubt of your following with all possible dispatch, leaving the militia and invalids to cover the frontiers of Connecticut, etc., in case of need."[5]

Washington's decision to divide the army four ways was pursued in the face of a continued and foreseeable diminution in the total force. After every alarm, so complained his aide Harrison, the roads were crowded with men "returning to their homes in the most scandalous and infamous manner." And, desertions aside, the enlistments of the Massachusetts militia would expire on November 17 (in eleven days), while almost all the Continental regiments were to disband either on November 30 or December 31. Because of the congressional proviso that the officers be appointed by state governments, hardly any were yet qualified to re-enlist their troops.[6]

Despite his distrust for militia, Washington was forced to urge a general

Major General Charles Lee, engraved by A. H. Ritchie after a drawing by B. Rushbrooke. Courtesy of the Prints Division, New York Public Library.

call. How many would respond and whether these would stay was problematical, for the temporary soldiers resented the new war of movement. New York's militia commander, General George Clinton,* complained that it was "most horrid" to "lay in cold trenches, uncovered as we are. Daily on fatigue, making redoubts, fleches, abatis and lines, and retreating from them and the little temporary huts before they are well finished, I fear will ultimately destroy our little army without fighting." The existing militiamen, Clinton continued, would not re-enter the service, and would, by their complaints, prevent others from joining up. This was confirmed by General Greene, who sent Washington a report stating that when they were asked to serve, the New York militia replied that General Howe "had promised them peace, liberty, and safety, and that is all they want."[7]

On abandoning his pursuit of Washington, Howe had marched down the east shore of the Hudson to Manhattan, driving in the outposts which the garrison at Fort Washington had maintained on the mainland. The American position was now completely surrounded except to the west where high cliffs fell to the river. It was an extensive post, since the fort itself was merely the strongest point in a series of defenses that covered all Harlem Heights. Patriot possession of this ridge, which was almost four miles long and three-quarters of a mile wide, had not yet been seriously challenged. However, since Fort Washington was now embedded like a cancer in the middle of the British flank, an assault could be only a matter of time.

A further ominous note was added to the situation when three British ships braved the Hudson River defenses over which Fort Washington presided, and moved past without visible damage. Washington then wrote Greene, asking: "What valuable purpose can it answer to attempt to hold a post from which the expected benefit cannot be had? I am therefore inclined to think it will not be prudent to hazard the men and stores at Mount Washington, but, as you are on the spot, leave it to you to give such orders as to evacuating Mount Washington as you judge best." To this strong nudge, Washington added the equivalent of an order concerning Fort Washington's twin across the river, Fort Lee, which was being used as a general supply depot and was in the way of the expected British advance into New Jersey. "You will therefore immediately," Washington wrote, "have all the stores, etc., removed which you do not deem necessary for your defense."[8]

Greene replied that the garrison at Fort Washington pinned down twice its number of British troops and kept the enemy from free communication between Manhattan and the New York mainland. "I cannot conceive the garrison to be in any great danger. The men can be brought off at any time."

---

* There was a General Clinton in both armies: Sir Henry (British) and George (American). There were also opposing generals named Howe: Sir William (British) and Robert (American).

Concerning Washington's order that he remove the stores from Fort Lee, Greene replied only that he would keep an eye out for enemy threats to that sector. In sum, he would "pursue such measures for the future as circumstances render necessary."[9]

Washington, who expected soon to be on the scene himself, let matters rest there.

News was arriving from the north, where a major British army under Sir Guy Carleton had been coming down from Canada. Before the Battle of White Plains, Washington had heard that the improvised fleet on Lake Champlain which Benedict Arnold had built and was commanding had been swept aside by an infinitely superior British naval force: only Fort Ticonderoga remained between Carleton and the headwaters of the Hudson on Washington's distant rear. But now more complete dispatches revealed that Arnold had inspired his floating soldiers to fight hour after hour against hopeless odds with such heroic ferocity that the British had become discouraged. They had returned to Canada. Tortured by the unwillingness of his own men to stand up to the enemy, Washington filed away in his mind that he had an endlessly valuable officer in Brigadier General Benedict Arnold.[10]

On November 12, Washington led his part of the army across the Hudson to the Highlands. They marched down the west shore, passing the northern end of the British position across the river and eventually coming to Greene's headquarters at Fort Lee. Washington was met there by three frightening pieces of intelligence.[11]

He found that the Flying Camp, which he had counted on to add five thousand to his own two thousand men, contained less than one-half that number and that these showed "no disposition to afford the least aid." Greene, he further discovered, had completely ignored his orders to remove all extra stores from Fort Lee. And—most worrisome of all—far from accepting his advice about withdrawing from Fort Washington, Greene had actually sent in more men and supplies.[12]

Led by Reed, Washington's staff officers urged him to override Greene with summary orders that the troops be brought back across the river. However, Washington, so Reed wrote, "hesitated more than I ever knew him on any other occasion, and more than I thought the public service permitted."[13] And, indeed, in recalling two years later what his thinking had been, Washington still expressed himself confusedly. "When I considered that our policy led us to waste the campaign without coming to a general action on the one hand, or to suffer the enemy to overrun the country on the other, I conceived that every impediment that stood in their way was a mean to those purposes." He had, so Washington's recollection continued, a high opinion of Greene, who was more familiar with the immediate situation than he was. Furthermore, Congress had recently re-

[148]

solved that he should "use every art and whatever expense" to hold the post "if it be practicable." And so, Washington, after what he remembered as "warfare in my mind and hesitation," finally acquiesced in Greene's policy, although it was "repugnant to my own judgment."[14]

Washington, who felt he could not spare the time to cross the river and examine for himself, intended his acquiescence, so he wrote his brother Jack, to stand only "till I could get round and see the situation of things." For the moment, the point of major crisis seemed to him not so much Fort Washington as the route through New Jersey, which lay completely open to a British march. Surely Howe lusted for the American capital; surely he would mount his main attack that way. Washington assumed that the Briton would leave behind a detachment that would in a leisurely manner besiege Fort Washington. Against such an attack, the fort could hold out at least long enough to permit an orderly withdrawal.[15]

After spending a day with Greene, Washington rode on to prepare for the defense of the Jersey crossing to Philadelphia. However, he had hardly reached Hackensack when a messenger galloped in with news that action had started at Fort Washington. The British had delivered an ultimatum to Colonel Robert Magaw, the commander there: they threatened that if the Americans did not surrender in two hours, they would put the entire garrison to the sword. Magaw had defied the enemy.[16]

Washington sprang again on horseback. As he neared the Hudson, he listened vainly for sounds of battle. The silence could mean that the fighting had not started, or just possibly the garrison had escaped across the river. Or it could mean that the garrison was already lost.

Dusk had fallen when Washington pounded up to Fort Lee. Junior officers met him to say that so far there had been no serious combat. General Greene and General Putnam were across the river. They were not trying to bring the men off. They had sent over even more men.

Washington called for a boat and, in great agony of spirit, embarked over ripples that glistened faintly in the darkness. From across the flood, a black shape approached. It proved to be another rowboat, and the other generals were aboard. Oarsmen leaned over gunwales to hold the boats together. As they all heaved gently in the tide, Washington conferred by lamplight with his subordinates. They said that the troops were "in high spirits and would make a good defense." Washington, who counted so heavily on morale, was reassured. "It being late at night," he returned with his generals to Fort Lee.[17]

Early the next morning, Washington and three generals—Greene, Putnam, and Brigadier Hugh Mercer—launched out again on the Hudson. "Just at the instant we stepped on board the boat," so wrote Greene, the sound of cannon fire echoed from the cliff across the river. Oars bent frantically; the keel scraped at last on pebbles; and up the steep path the generals ran. As they emerged on the bluff, birds twittered unconcernedly around them. The firing was still distant: two miles to the south, where a British and Hessian attack had been mounted over the Hollow Way which had been involved in the Battle of Harlem Heights. Washington was notified that the first line of redoubts there at the very bottom of the American position had been quickly overwhelmed, but the second was holding.

The Commander in Chief had not been on this ground since he had marched off for White Plains. He saw that the earthworks had been augmented and strengthened. They seemed well manned. On its familiar crag, two hundred and thirty feet above the Hudson, stood Fort Washington, a high pentagon of earth walls. Enemy engineers were to consider it crude, as it had no palisades without, no barracks within. Washington's thoughts, as he examined it, are unrecorded. Did he realize that most of its cannon were useless in the present emergency since they were fixed to fire out over the river? Did he worry that the fort was much too small to serve as a final refuge for the men assembled on the bluff?

Messengers came riding in from many directions to report enemy movements. Washington, so it quickly became clear, had guessed wrong in assuming that Howe would attack the fort with only a detachment. The assault to the south across the Hollow Way was merely a beginning: the whole British army seemed to be in motion around the beleaguered post. To the extreme north, near Kingsbridge, a major Hessian force was preparing to cross the narrow Harlem River. Further down the Harlem on Long Island, beside the center of the American position, British were marching, perhaps, as Greene surmised, "to reconnoiter the fortifications and the lines"; perhaps to make more crossings of the stream.

"There we all stood," Greene wrote of Washington and the other generals, "in a very awkward situation. As the disposition was made, and the enemy advancing, we durst not attempt to make any new disposition. Indeed, we saw nothing amiss. We all urged His Excellency to come off."[18]

Washington had concluded, so he later wrote, that it was "too late" to get the men out as the post was "invested."[19] However, he hoped that, if the troops would resolutely man the lines, the position could be defended. All three of his generals offered to stay behind and help. But Washington, in agreeing to withdraw, ordered the generals to come with him. Magaw, who had made the preparations, was to keep the command.

The generals filed down the cliff and were rowed back to the Jersey shore. Washington posted himself on "the high bank at Fort Lee." He stared across the river; he listened. The troops, he gathered, were returning the British fire both to the north and the south "in such a manner as gave me great hopes [that] the enemy was entirely repulsed." But these hopes faded in a very few minutes. Puffs of smoke rising from the middle of the cliff revealed that the enemy had successfully crossed the Harlem River into the American center. (Washington later discovered that "they landed inside of the second lines, our troops being then engaged in the first.") The powder smoke began drawing in from the south and east toward the high fort on the cliff. To the north, as Washington noted, the troops continued to stand for "a considerable time." However, "at length they were also obliged to submit to a superiority of numbers and retire under the cannon of the fort," where the rest of the Americans were, Washington realized, now huddled.[20]

The firing came to a sudden halt. Washington assumed that the British must have raised a flag of truce so that they could reiterate their demand for the surrender of the fortress. "At this time," he reported to Congress, "I sent a billet to Colonel Magaw directing him to hold out, and I would endeavor this evening to bring off the garrison, if the fortress could not be maintained as I did not expect it could, the enemy being possessed of the adjacent ground." The messenger ran down to the river, pushed off in a small boat, landed on the far bank, ran up to the fort, reappeared, clambered down, was rowed back, and told Washington that Colonel Magaw had "entered too far into a treaty to retract."

Washington hurried over another messenger urging Magaw to insist on liberal terms. Back came the word that they had been "able to obtain no other terms than to surrender as prisoners of war."[21]

"This is a most unfortunate affair," Washington wrote, "and has given me great mortification, as we have lost not only two thousand men that were there, but a good deal of artillery and some of the best arms we had." Perhaps it was just as well that he did not discover, until the first shock was past, that his loss of men was closer to three thousand than two thousand.* [22]

The catastrophe was due in part to Washington's belief that Howe would invest the fort with a detachment rather than bring his entire force to bear in an assault. It was also due to the overconfidence which he had not yet overcome in what patriot soldiers could do if adequately inspired. He was still committed, having thought of no more effective strategy, to "a war of posts," and Fort Washington was the most powerful post the Americans had.

Perhaps most to blame was the ignorance of military engineering Washington shared with his army. Always good at digging, the Americans had spread over a wide plateau works too extended to be held even by the large numbers of men Greene had sent over. Coming in from several directions and making a feint in another, British columns had penetrated to the backs of some of the fortifications, causing confusion followed by a general retreat.

---

* Official American figures put the number captured at 2634; official British, at 2818. Neither total, of course, included those killed. The British gave their loss as in the neighborhood of 500 killed and wounded.[23]

Then a second fault of the American planning had become manifest: the size of the main fort had no relation to the number of men who now needed to use it as a refuge.

Although it was doubtful that Washington would have understood much of what was wrong—this defeat was the lesson that made him sophisticated on the subject of forts—he had made no inspection until it was too late to make changes. The situation of Fort Washington when it was besieged cannot thus be altogether blamed on him. Yet his was the top responsibility: he was the Commander in Chief and he had been in the area for three days. That he had not ordered the fort to be evacuated before it was attacked was the worst blow his prestige had suffered since, as a twenty-two-year-old greenhorn, he had surrendered to the French that ridiculous wilderness stockade Fort Necessity.

General Lee was quick to take advantage of the issue. To Washington himself, he wrote, "Oh, General! why would you be overpersuaded by men of inferior judgment to your own?" And, with such consciousness that he was scheming that he urged, "let these few lines be thrown into the fire," Lee wrote the radical congressman Benjamin Rush that his last words on parting with Washington at New Castle had been advice to "draw off" the garrison from Fort Washington "or all will be lost." Lee added to Rush, "A total want of sense pervades all your councils. . . . Had I the powers, I could do you much good."[24]

As the chorus of criticism swelled, Washington could not defend himself by insisting that no blunder had been made. Always oversensitive to situations which might take away from that public esteem which he desired as his sole reward, less sure than ever that he possessed the military skills requisite to his station, Washington did not generously shoulder the blame. He pushed the blame off on Greene.[25] For this there was, of course, some justification. Greene had been on the ground and had augmented the crisis; he had ignored Washington's urging that he withdraw from the fort; and he had persuaded Washington, when the Commander in Chief appeared in person, to fall in with his policy. Yet the Commander in Chief had allowed himself to be persuaded.

Almost ten years later, Washington responded to a query sent him by the Rev. William Gordon, who was writing a history of the Revolution, by sending Gordon as a justification of his own role at Fort Washington, a copy of his letter to Greene urging withdrawal. However, Washington suppressed the fact that he had subsequently been on the scene for several days during which he could have overruled Greene. Uneasily, he added to Gordon that he had supplied the document "because you desire it, not that I want to exculpate myself from any censure which might have fallen on me by charging another."[26]

If Washington did shift more of the burden onto Greene than was altogether just, he did not try further to decontaminate himself by driving the scapegoat into the hills. On the contrary; he kept Greene in his inner councils, making the disgraced general ever more his close friend and intimate counselor. Thus he allowed the criticisms he had shunted off on his subordinate to rebound on him personally in the form of charges that he incompetently relied on advisers proved unworthy.

Actually, it is questionable whether any act of Washington's after his arrival at Fort Lee could have saved the situation at Fort Washington. Although historians tend to assume that all that was necessary to get the troops out was to give an order, the fact was that the British were watching, and if they had got wind of any embarkation, they would have been present in a most unpleasant manner. Yet it is also a fact that Washington made no preparations—and they would have had to be extensive—for a possible withdrawal in advance of the battle or even as the battle raged. The most he could write Magaw, in urging that officer not to surrender, was that he would "endeavor" that evening to bring off the garrison. He would have needed, at that last minute, to improvise something.

Why did Washington depart with his three generals after the battle had started? That he was motivated by cowardice his behavior on many other occasions makes inconceivable. Although he underestimated the number of men engaged, he knew they were more than were usually entrusted to a colonel. Furthermore, he believed that a patriot detachment fought more valiantly if overweighted (as had been done at Harlem Heights) with high officers. Of course, it would have been silly, as Greene stated, for the generals to try to rearrange things in the face of the enemy; yet, as the situation developed, able and experienced commanders could have been useful. If Washington (who had so hated as a young man to have authority snatched from his hands) had felt that Magaw had a right to keep command of the battle he had prepared for, the Commander in Chief was certainly putting a lesser consideration over a major. If he had assessed the situation as so desperate that to leave members of the high command there would have been to doom them, surely he should, after he got back to Fort Lee, have hurried preparations to mitigate the defeat rather than just watch in agony from his hillside.

We can only conclude that Washington, who had not given himself a full day's rest since he had accepted the command a year and a half before, whose mind had been for so long without intermission "on the stretch," was not thinking clearly. He confided to his brother Jack that he was "wearied almost to death with the retrograde motions of things." He needed a breathing spell—but would it be allowed him?[27]

Washington rode again to Hackensack to see what could be done for the defense of New Jersey. He soon wrote Congress that, since Fort Lee could not by itself block the river, he was removing all stores in preparation for withdrawal. By the time this was achieved, the enlistment of most of his men would be on the point of expiring. He was planning to post what small forces remained to him—they would be about two thousand—at Brunswick, on the direct road to Philadelphia, and such intermediate posts as seemed most likely to prevent the enemy from making "an irruption."

Before he could dispatch this letter, Washington scrawled on it a P.S.: "The unhappy affair of the 16th has been succeeded by further misfortunes."[28]

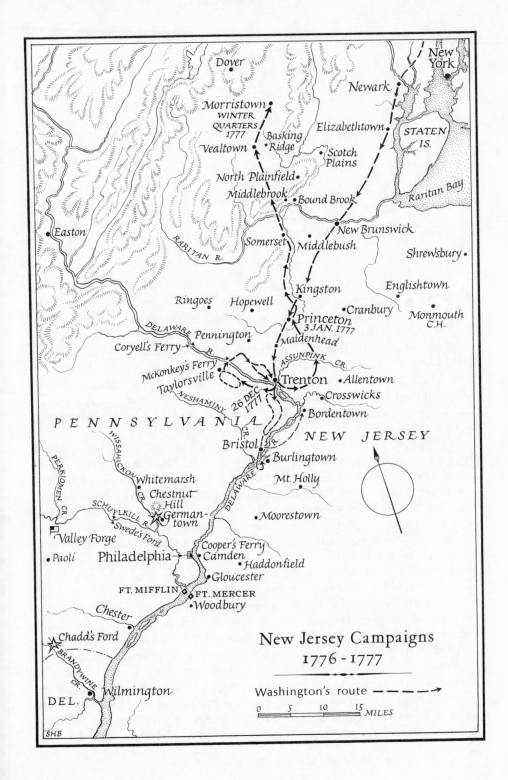

Dover

New York

Newark

Morristown
WINTER
QUARTERS
1777
Basking
Ridge

Elizabethtown

STATEN
IS.

Vealtown

Scotch
Plains

North Plainfield

Middlebrook

Bound Brook

Raritan Bay

RARITAN R.

Easton

Somerset

Middlebush

New Brunswick

Shrewsbury

Englishtown

Ringoes

Hopewell

Kingston

Cranbury

Monmouth
C.H.

DELAWARE

Pennington

Princeton
3 JAN. 1777

Coryell's Ferry

R.

Maidenhead

ASSUNPINK CR.

McKonkey's Ferry

Taylorsville

NESHAMINY CR.

26 DEC.
1777

Trenton

Allentown

Crosswicks

Bordentown

NEW JERSEY

P E N N S Y L V A N I A

Bristol

DELAWARE R.

Burlingtown

PERKIOMEN CR.

WISSAHICKON CR.

Whitemarsh

Chestnut
Hill

Mt. Holly

SCHUYLKILL R.

German-
town

Swede's Ford

Moorestown

Valley Forge

Paoli

Philadelphia

Cooper's Ferry

Camden

Haddonfield

Gloucester

FT. MIFFLIN

FT. MERCER

Chester

Woodbury

Chadd's Ford

New Jersey Campaigns
1776 - 1777

BRANDYWINE CR.

DEL.

Wilmington

Washington's route - - - - →

0   5   10   15
                    MILES

SHB

18

The Mutiny of General Lee

THE third morning after the fall of Fort Washington—November 19, 1776—had dawned with the pungent freshness of sunlight after a night of drenching rain. From the moist, gleaming landscape, a rider emerged bearing bad news. The British had taken advantage of the dripping blackness of the previous night. They had secretly crossed the Hudson, landing on the west bank six miles above Fort Lee, and were now advancing on the fort. The strength of the enemy column was not yet clear. Greene was preparing the fort for defense, and had sent out delaying skirmishers.[1]

Washington knew that the fort, being fortified primarily against an attack from the water, lay almost open to the British. The enemy were coming down through the long, narrow sliver of land that lay between the Hudson and Hackensack rivers. Even if the garrison fled successfully from the fort, they would still, if they were not to be cornered, have to cross the Hackensack into the main part of New Jersey. Their only reasonable escape route was across a bridge six miles from Fort Lee but (alas!) considerably closer to the advancing British. It was hard to believe that the enemy would not send a quick column to cut the bridge. Yet the Americans would, if (as seemed probable) they were greatly outnumbered, have to get there first.[2]

Washington's powerful horse traversed the six miles to the fort in three-quarters of an hour. He was greeted with the information that the hostile column numbered from six to eight thousand.* Fort Lee had only two to three thousand defenders. Washington shouted orders for immediate flight. The men who were cooking lunch over their campfires should not wait to eat it or for the kettles to become cool enough to carry. Of the cannon, there was only time to hitch up two twelve-pounders. Two or three hundred tents, about a thousand barrels of flour, much baggage (thank God, the stores of ammunition had already been removed!) had to be abandoned. So did more

---

* A more correct figure would have been four thousand.

than a hundred men whose response to the crisis had been to break into the sutler's liquor. As these weaved away from their officers stating thickly that they would not risk their lives by obeying any orders, Washington saw to the lining up of the rest.[3]

To a quick drumbeat, off the line went at double-quick for the bridge. The fear that they would not get there in time filled every informed mind. Reed was in despair. This catastrophe, coming on top of the Fort Washington fiasco, had made him lose the little confidence in Washington he still possessed. He sought out a horseman who would agree to carry a message to General Lee. The man had a scrap of paper. Reed had a pencil. "Dear General," he wrote, "we are flying before the British. I pray—" He could write no more, for his anguished pressure had broken the pencil. He finished his message verbally to the horseman: Lee must come at once and rescue an army otherwise surely lost. The horseman rode off to spread consternation wherever he stopped at a tavern and told what he had been told.[4]

Washington, in the meanwhile, was leading his troops as rapidly as possible toward the bridge. He fully expected that before he got there, he would run into an English column. However, the woods and fields, where his scouts moved and which he anxiously scanned, remained innocent of anything but autumn. At last, he saw the bridge, standing silent over sibilant water. At a trot, their breaths aching in parched throats, the garrison of Fort Lee dashed over the Hackensack into what was, for the moment, safety.*

Back in the village of Hackensack with his troops collapsed around him, Washington sat down to write Lee: "This country is almost a dead flat, and we have not an entrenching tool, and not above three thousand men, and they very much broken and dispirited, not only with our ill-success, but the loss of their tents and baggage. I have resolved to avoid any attack though, by so doing, I must leave a very fine country open to their ravages."

Washington then stated that he could not be an accurate judge of Lee's situation. However, "I am of opinion, and the gentlemen about me concur in it, that the public interest requires your coming over to this side" of the Hudson. He thought his reasons "must have weight with you." The enemy was evidently changing the seat of war to New Jersey. Expecting what protection the Continental Army could give, the state would "cease to depend upon or support a force" which made no effort to save them. Since dissatisfaction in New Jersey would spread to Pennsylvania, it was politically "of the utmost importance that at least an appearance of force should be made to keep this province in the connection with the others." Even if Lee could not bring many troops, rumor could be encouraged to exaggerate their numbers.[5]

When Washington's back was turned, the man in his military family on

---

* The enemy had not altogether grasped the importance of the bridge, and had, in any case, mistaken a tributary, Overpeck Creek, for the Hackensack.[6]

whose friendship he most relied slipped into the cover of this letter a secret one: "I do not mean to flatter or praise you at the expense of any other," so read Reed's words to Lee, "but I confess I think it is entirely owing to you that this army, and the liberties of America, so far as they are dependent on it, are not totally cut off. You have decision, a quality often wanted [lacking] in minds otherwise valuable, and I ascribe to this our escape from York Island, from Kingsbridge and the [White] Plains, and have no doubt had you been here the garrison of Mount Washington would now have composed part of this army. . . . Oh! General, an indecisive mind is one of the greatest misfortunes that can befall an army; how often have I lamented it in this campaign! . . . Every gentleman of the family, the officers and soldiers generally, have a confidence in you. . . . I must conclude with my clear and explicit opinion that your presence is of the last importance."[7]

Lee had other ideas. There were British detachments near his post at White Plains. He was determined to overwhelm them in a way that would make clear to all his military superiority to Washington. For this, he would need all the men he had. The fleeing force in New Jersey would have to find help elsewhere. Why not the Highlands? Lee ordered Heath to send Washington two thousand men from the garrisons there. When Heath replied that he was not under Lee's orders and had received no such command from Washington, Lee flew into a fury. Nor did Lee recede from his demand that Heath should obey him, even after Washington had backed Heath's contention that there should be no weakening of the Highlands, on the control of which the ability of the Continental Army to reunite depended.

Washington benignly attributed Lee's usurpation of command over Heath to an excess of patriotic zeal. He knew nothing of a letter in which Lee stated to the Massachusetts Committee of Safety that "indecision bids fair for tumbling down the goodly fabric of American freedom and, with it, the rights of mankind. . . . There are times when we must commit treason against the laws of the state for the salvation of the state. The present crisis demands this brave, virtuous kind of treason." Lee wished Massachusetts to send troops she was raising not to Washington, but directly to his own encampment.[8]

"I have received your orders and shall endeavor to put 'em in execution," Lee wrote Washington. However, he doubted that he could lead many men across the river as his troops lacked shoes, stockings, blankets, and zeal. He would have marched already had he not seen an opportunity to cut off an exposed force of British and Tories.

"My former letters," Washington replied, "were so full and explicit as to the necessity of your marching as early as possible that it is unnecessary to add more on that head. . . . Having formed an enterprise . . . I wish you may have succeeded."[9]

Reports of large Tory forces mobilizing in Monmouth County on the

Jersey shore to the south of him made Washington fear that the time had come, which he had so long dreaded, when the enemy would recruit faster than he did: only some four or five hundred New Jersey militia had joined his army. He dispatched Reed to Burlington to plead with the New Jersey authorities for troops, and Mifflin to Philadelphia to plead with Congress. These emissaries did not dare, lest they extinguish the will to fight, reveal the whole truth of Washington's situation. As Mifflin put it, he confided to Congress as much "as their sensibility and *my own delicacy* would justify."[10]

Washington was trying—by personal exploration on horseback, by studying what few maps were available, and by interviews—to master the geography of the situation in which British initiative had placed him. Manhattan Island lay like a huge pickerel between the Jersey shore and Long Island, while below, shaped more like a flounder and out in the bay, Staten Island was separated from New Jersey by only a narrow channel. The main British position covered both islands. In Jersey, they possessed Fort Lee (opposite the northern tip of Manhattan) and Amboy (opposite the southern tip of Staten Island). A large British force under General Lord Cornwallis was advancing southward from Fort Lee parallel with the Hudson and in the direction of Amboy.

Washington fell back before Cornwallis and then, having met the road that stretched for some fifty-five miles from Amboy to Philadelphia, turned inland. He was passing through, as he complained, "a level champaign country": no crags for militiamen to hide behind, no stone walls (only open fences), hardly any trees. The one natural impediment between Amboy and the Delaware was the Raritan River. The town of Brunswick surmounted the Raritan's west bank.[11]

On November 29, Washington arrived in Brunswick with his little force. The next day, there was a great stirring in camp, but it was no preparation to battle. Several thousand men—including many Pennsylvanians who should by rights have stayed for another month—were preparing to go home. As Washington tried to keep his spirits up, a messenger rode in from General Lee. Washington's heart jumped—perhaps Lee was at long last on his way with those desperately needed troops. The dispatch was addressed to Reed, but that aide was away trying to inspirit the Jersey authorities. Assuming the letter was official business, Washington broke the seal and innocently ran his eye down the page.

Lee began by thanking Reed for "your most obliging, flattering letter." He agreed with Reed in lamenting "that fatal indecision of mind which in war is a much greater disqualification than stupidity, or even want of personal courage; accident may put a decisive blunder in the right, but eternal defeat and miscarriage must attend the man of the best parts if cursed with indecision." Lee then rehearsed the opportunities he saw which kept him from marching, and stated that as soon as he had made his effective stroke against the British, he would "fly to you, for to confess a truth, I really think our chief will do better with me than without me."[12]

That the phrase "fatal indecision of mind" referred to himself, Washington could not doubt, and it was clear that, as Washington later put it, the letter he held in his hand was "an echo" of one Reed had written Lee. Washington had relied on Reed for that intimacy which he so needed as he stood up to such terrible difficulties so far from home. Washington had humored and loved and leaned on Reed as an indulgent and admiring father might have done. So this was what Reed thought of him! Was the charge against him true? Washington was far from sure that it was not true.

Several years later, Washington explained to Reed, "I was hurt not because I thought my judgment wronged by the expressions contained in it, but because the same sentiments were not communicated immediately to myself." Washington's "unreserved manner" to Reed, "entitled me, I thought, to your advice upon any point in which I appeared to be wanting." Reed's "withholding that advice from me and censuring my conduct to another was such an argument of disingenuity that I was not a little mortified at it."[13]

On the day that he made the discovery, Washington forwarded Lee's letter to Reed with the unadorned statement, "The enclosed was put into my hands by an express from the White Plains. Having no idea of its being a private letter, much less suspecting the tendency of the correspondence, I opened it." Washington then thanked Reed "for the trouble and fatigue you have undergone in your journey to Burlington. . . . My best regards to Mrs. Reed. I am, dear sir, etc." When he lay down to what surely was a sleepless night, he must have realized that Reed's reaction to this cold epistle would be to resign.[14]

The next morning was December 1, the day when so many of his troops would be legally free. It proved also to be the day when Cornwallis's army caught up with Washington's. A report came in that the van of an enemy force of six thousand to seven thousand men was only ten miles away. Washington hoped that the crisis might persuade the New Jersey militia to stay. They all departed, leaving Washington with scarcely thirty-four hundred effectives.

Washington's rear guard came in across the Raritan into Brunswick closely pursued by Cornwallis's advance guard. Hessian Yagers, the enemy answer to the American riflemen, were able by their rifle fire to prevent the patriot engineers from completely destroying the bridge. However, American riflemen were able to keep the enemy from crossing the bridge. It was a stalemate—but not one that could last. The enemy field artillery galloped up and began, as Washington wrote, "a smart cannonade. . . . It being impossible," he continued to Congress, "to oppose them with our present force with the least prospect of success, we shall retreat to the west side of [the] Delaware."[15]

As he drew up his army for further flight, Washington wrote Reed describing his desperate situation, begging his old friend not to resign but to come, despite everything, back to him.[16]

In the expectation that the British would aggressively chase him, Washington retreated rapidly across an open landscape too suited to European armies. He sent ahead calls that all the boats on the Delaware be gathered so that after he had crossed in what vessels there were, none would be left that would enable the British to follow. He was in Princeton on December 2, and beside the Delaware at Trenton on the 3rd. Then, like a fox at the door of its lair, he looked (so to speak) over his shoulder and saw that the British were not following.[*] He sent his baggage over the river and returned with a considerable part of his army to Princeton in the hope that something would turn up.[17]

Perhaps the officers he had sent out in the hope they could find Lee would discover that the general, of whom Washington had heard nothing for a week, had actually crossed the Hudson and come near enough to cooperate on some bold stroke. Perhaps from the bare landscape dripping in winter rain would suddenly appear the five regiments which, with Congress's approval, Washington had ordered Gates to bring down from the now quiescent Canadian border. Perhaps he would be gladdened by the sight of considerable New Jersey militia. But the only news that came to him was that the British were advancing, if with deliberation, in great strength.[18]

Utterly unreinforced, Washington hurried back to the Delaware and ferried his troops into Pennsylvania. The British van appeared as his rear guard disappeared across the water. No supplies were left behind except for a few boards.[19]

For the moment, the army was safe, but it was in a desperate condition. Watching the sick, exhausted, starved, and naked men stagger up the bank after they had crossed the river, the painter Charles Willson Peale decided it was "the most hellish scene I ever beheld." As he stood there horror-struck,

---

[*] Cornwallis had not further pursued Washington on the day when he had caught up with him at Brunswick because the main British force had already covered twenty miles in a forced march and were considered too exhausted to go any further. Although writers have criticized Cornwallis's slowness in this entire campaign, according to British army standards he moved fast. Howe wrote that he deserved special praise for "the ability and conduct he displayed in the pursuit of the enemy from Fort Lee to Trenton, a distance exceeding eighty miles, in which he was well supported by the ardor of his corps, who cheerfully quitted their tents and heavy baggage as impediments to their march."

The British were not really in a hurry. Only after American resistance in New Jersey had entirely collapsed did they seriously consider the possibility that this late autumn campaign could carry them all the way to Philadelphia.[20]

Peale was accosted by a soldier who "had lost all his clothes. He was in an old, dirty blanket jacket, his beard long, and his face so full of sores he could not clean it." Only when the man spoke did Peale realize, from the sound of the voice, that this was his beloved brother James.[21]

Reed was again present. On receiving Washington's curt letter he had dispatched his resignation to Congress. However, he had withdrawn the resignation at Washington's request. When he reappeared at headquarters, he had foreseen an emotional explanation and reconciliation. But Washington preferred to pretend that nothing had happened. This angered Reed. He never forgave Washington. Yet the two worked together, however strainedly, from day to day.[22]

The British had extended their lines on the Jersey side of the Delaware some fifteen miles both north and south from Trenton, and they could, of course, march even farther in either direction. Their lack of boats might not stop them for long: they could bring boats on wagons from New York, or they might be supplied with some that Tories had hidden. They would not need very many, since the Delaware, although swift, was narrow, a pygmy compared to Washington's Potomac.

Since, in principle, the enemy could strike wherever they willed, the American force should have been, for effective defense, twice the British. It was at first only a quarter, and then when reinforced by all the Philadelphians who could be recruited for a last-ditch defense, it was only a half. Washington ordered his outlying generals to keep a watch on every likely crossing, do the best they could against a British advance, and, if routed, meet him at Germantown on the far side of Philadelphia.[23]

Again and again Washington had written that the greatest danger to the cause was that it might fall apart from the inside. He had tried to make the army a pin that would hold all together. Now, despite his every effort, the pin had slipped. The New Jersey legislature disbanded so each member could save himself, and the Continental Congress fled Philadelphia to Baltimore. Important patriot leaders—Richard Stockton of New Jersey, Joseph Galloway of Pennsylvania—recanted and urged their compatriots to follow their lead. All across New Jersey, the inhabitants queued up, swore renewed allegiance to George III, and pocketed royal pardons. Washington was notified that units of the Pennsylvania militia "exult at the approach of the enemy": he was wondering how these traitorous soldiers could be disarmed. And when his commissaries tried to buy necessary supplies with the only currency they had, Continental paper, they were pushed away by farmers convinced that the government which issued the paper would soon be no more.[24]

As they moved too far from the fighting to respond to emergencies, Congress voted Washington "full power to order and direct all things rela-

tive to the department and to the operations of war." Even those congressmen who distrusted the prestige Washington already possessed had voted
for the measure as, alas, "necessary." In forwarding the resolution to
Washington, a committee stated, "Happy it is for this country that the
general of their forces can safely be entrusted with the most unlimited
power, and neither personal security, liberty, or property be in the least
degree endangered thereby."[25]

That a dictator be empowered to cut the Gordian knots of congressional
confusion and indecision had been advocated to radical congressmen by
General Lee, who had eagerly volunteered to take the responsibility. "But,"
so Lee added sadly, "I am sure you will never give any man the necessary
power." Washington had now been given the necessary power. Like Lee, he
was dissatisfied with much that had been done and not done. Would he
grasp the opportunity to decapitate error with a reaper's scythe?[26]

Washington had been a legislator before he was a general, and an
independent planter more than either. He felt that he had been given
"powers that are too dangerous to be entrusted. I can only add that
desperate diseases require desperate remedies; and with truth declare that
I have no lust after power, but wish with as much fervency as any man
upon this wide, extended continent for an opportunity of turning the sword
into a ploughshare."[27]

Congress's resolution, of course, altered not a particle the fact that any
step taken without virtually unanimous approval of the leaders of different
areas and views would further the disharmony that was more actively than
ever the new nation's greatest danger. Pressure was put on Washington by
individuals and groups to promulgate various controversial matters, but he
knew these same people would scream in protest if his fiats should serve not
their own ends but those of their doctrinal or regional opponents. Better to
face renewed charges of indecision than to incite discord and risk the blame
he felt he would deserve if he should engage in headstrong measures that
failed. He would proceed as usual, except where necessity absolutely
required.

What necessity seemed absolutely to require was in its implications highly
revolutionary: it presaged, indeed, a much later America. Because of his
desperate lack of soldiers, he added twenty-two regiments to the eighty-
eight that had been authorized. Even if the regiments were not completely
filled, he explained to Congress, having so many more officers on the recruit
would bring in more men. Almost as an aside, he added, "If any good
officers offer to raise men upon Continental pay and establishment in this
quarter, I shall encourage them to do so, and regiment them when they have
done it."

Although he did not emphasize this purpose to Congress, his action
enabled him to get around waiting for commissions to come in from the state

capitals. He also failed to stress that the new regiments would have no specific state ties. On his own authority, he had laid down the organizational beginnings of a truly united army suited to a United States that was not a regional alliance but a single unified nation. This seemed natural to Washington. Learning from his daily experience in camp, he had become one of the first Americans truly to take the continental view.

"It may be thought," he continued to Congress, "that I am going a good deal out of the line of my duty. . . . A character to lose, an estate to forfeit, the inestimable blessing of liberty at stake, a life devoted, must be my excuse. . . . If Congress disapprove of this proceeding, they will please to signify it, as I mean it for the best."* [28]

Washington also created apart from the state lines a special corps of artillery: three regiments with (as was universal army practice) a twenty-five-cent premium in pay. Rather than himself appoint a commander, he pressed Congress to appoint (as they did) Knox.[29]

Concerning further needs, Washington did no more than to urge, in the old manner, that Congress act. He wanted a corps of engineers. He asked for more major generals and brigadier generals, a clothier general, a commissary to supply prisoners of war, and other officials who would keep him from being "obliged to attend to the business of so many different departments." He asked for more military supplies and better provisions.[30]

Washington could have used his new powers to take at bayonet point from the inhabitants what his army needed. He preferred to make as much capital as the obedience of his troops would permit out of a contrast between good behavior in the patriot army and the "licentiousness" of the enemy. Jerseyites were discovering that Howe's pardon in the pocket did not keep the Hessian from the door. The Hessians and the British, too, looted and smashed. How many young ladies were actually raped history will never discover, but the possibility was in every mind as heavy footsteps crunched through the snow accumulating in dooryards. Patriot propagandists—with Washington's assistance—were making every use of every atrocity, true or imagined.[31] But there was no hope of really getting the cause rolling again unless there was a victory, even a small one, to restore, with the prestige of the army, hope.

If all his forces could only be made to converge, Washington wrote Governor Trumbull, he could "attempt a stroke," as the enemy "lay a good deal scattered and to all appearance in a state of security. A lucky blow in this quarter would be fatal to them, and would most certainly raise the spirits of the people." However, Washington could do nothing with the forces he had. In his desperation, he finally weakened the post in the

---

* In their terror and desire to be protected, Congress approved the "additional regiments" (as they came to be called). However, roadblocks were soon to be inserted in the way of so great a portent of federal union.[32]

Highlands by ordering Heath to join him with a regiment. He dreamed of the regiments coming down from Canada. And, above all, he needed the large force of regulars under Lee.[33]

Finally he received a letter from that laggard general stating that, since the British outposts near White Plains which he had hoped to attack had "contracted themselves into a compact body very suddenly," he was coming across the Hudson to help Washington. However, instead of joining, as ordered, his Commander in Chief, he intended to march to the heights at Morristown. He had sent messengers to intercept the regiments coming down from Canada and order them to join him there. He would then have five thousand men, a force strong enough to induce the New Jersey militia to rise and join him. The British, Lee continued to Washington, would not dare continue across New Jersey and on to Philadelphia "with so formidable a body hanging on their flanks or rear." Washington should tell this to "the troops immediately under your command; it may encourage them." Lee ended by beseeching Washington to "take out of the way of danger my favorite mare" stabled at Princeton.[34]

Washington was in later campaigns to follow Lee's strategic conception, using the heights at Morristown to protect Philadelphia. However, at the moment he was unfamiliar with the strategy and the geography involved. He wrote Lee that he would have highly approved of "your hanging on the rear of the enemy" were it not for the feebleness of his own force that was actually blocking their path. Under existing circumstances, "I cannot but request and entreat you, and this too by the advice of all the general officers with me, to march and join me with all your whole force with all possible expedition." Otherwise, there would be "little, if any, prospect" of saving Philadelphia, "whose loss must prove of the most fatal consequences to the cause of America."[35]

After a final flirt at trying to find an opportunity to land on the enemy an independent blow, Lee at long last gave in to Washington's orders and began a slow march toward the Delaware through upper New Jersey, north of where Howe's army was stationed. However, as Lee relinquished the effort to prove himself superior to Washington, Washington freely handed to Lee everything that insubordinate subordinate had schemed for.

Not only Lee's army, Washington now learned, but the two other forces he was expecting—Gates's from Ticonderoga and Heath's from the Hudson Valley—were approaching, on separate routes, through the hills of northern New Jersey. Surely, since they all were on the British right flank, it would waste time and opportunity to have them continue across the Delaware to Washington's camp.

He sent out riders to find the various forces in Jersey and order them to rendezvous at Pittstown, in the hills some twenty-five miles north of Trenton. General Stirling was to go directly to Lee, who as senior officer

[165]

would be in command. The generals were to work out "what probable mode of attack can be attempted. . . . Weigh every circumstance of attack and retreat properly [so] that nothing that can be guarded against may be unprovided for. . . . I do not mean to tie you down to any rule," Washington's orders continued, "but leave you free to exercise your own judgments of which, as I before said, I only want timely advice."[36]

For what he conceived to be the good of the cause, Washington had placed the power to overreach him in his rival's hands. Although he did not know the extent to which Lee was intriguing against him—Lee had just written Gates, *"Entre nous,* a certain great man is most damnably deficient"—he must have known, if only after the incident of the letter to Reed, that powerful men, with Lee's own agreement, were casting the Englishman as the new savior of the cause. Furthermore, he realized that Lee was "rather fickle, and violent, I fear, in his temper."[37]

Washington's surrender of power was dictated by no necessity: it would surely have been reasonable for the Commander in Chief to move across the river to join the larger part of his army. His decision may well have grown from diffidence. He had undoubtedly taken to heart the defeats he had been suffering, the criticisms of him that were broadcast even by his dear companion Reed. Lee was considered by Washington's entourage what Greene called him, "a most consummate general"[38]—and no one could doubt that he was more experienced than Washington. Perhaps Washington concluded that, whatever the effect on his own reputation and, indeed, his continuance in the command, it would be better for the United States if this desperate effort were entrusted to Lee.

Although its importance has been overlooked, this magnanimous decision was surely one of the most signal acts of Washington's entire career.

It was not the last time that Washington put too much confidence in an officer of whom a less noble nature would have been more suspicious—there would be, for instance, the matter of Benedict Arnold and West Point—but perhaps this was the most dangerous time. Not because Lee might have been defeated, but because he might have won. Supposing he, not Washington, had received the credit for the turning of the tide which was actually to be turned by Washington at the battles of Trenton and Princeton? When many influential patriots doubted Washington's military skill, Lee might well have been elevated into Washington's command.

The American Revolution would then have been pulled in directions made only too familiar by the almost universal course of other revolutions. Lee was a European radical, less close in temper and ideas to Washington than to Robespierre and Napoleon. Scornful of civil authority, critical of Washington for obeying Congress, he would quite willingly have sent a recalcitrant legislature scuttling with "a whiff of grape." He believed not in the conciliation but in the punishment of his political enemies. He saw no reason why the army should not live by looting Tories (which meant, in effect, anyone who was disliked by someone in power). If such a man had become the commander of the American army, the foreign conflict with England would rapidly have become an aspect of civil war. Unless he were quickly unhorsed, the eventual result would have been a British victory, or a dictatorship of the right or a dictatorship of the left.

Providence or fate or luck had intervened even as Washington was taking his selfless and dangerous step. Lee had a propensity for sleeping in strange places (and with strange women). He had spent the night of December 12 some distance from his army in an inn kept by a widow. The next morning, he was lounging in his shirtsleeves when British light horse came galloping up. Seeing them through the window, Lee cried, "For God's sake, what shall I do?"

The widow hurried him upstairs and tried to hide him between the chimney and the breastwork over a fireplace. Lank as he was and push as he could, Lee could not make himself fit into the tiny space. As he pulled in his breath again and again in efforts to shrink, bullets shattered the glass in the windows. Then Lee heard a British voice order that the house be set on fire. At this, Lee sent down word that he would "resign himself."

The British were delighted with their coup, convinced that they had struck a major blow by carrying off the only competent general in the rebel service. During the resulting celebration, Lee's captured horse was made to drink so many toasts to George III that (to the real or assumed horror of American propagandists) the animal became staggering drunk.[39]

Concerning his captivity, Lee wrote that he did not so much mourn for himself as for "a great continent . . . frustrated in the honest ambition of being free." When Washington heard "the melancholy intelligence," he expressed "the utmost regret. . . . This is an additional misfortune, and the more vexatious as it was by his own folly and imprudence (and without a view to answer any good) he was taken," having gone "three miles out of his own camp for the sake of a little better lodging. . . . I know his feelings upon the occasion and I know the loss our country must sustain in his captivity. The event," Washington continued bitterly, "has happened."[40]

Having no other officer in New Jersey to whom he was willing to entrust a major move, Washington ordered the various forces to meet him in Pennsylvania. He would have to find some promising way himself to lead an attack by recrossing the Delaware.

III

The Rising Phoenix

19

An Icy River

THOMAS PAINE had come to have a look at the army and had found it in flight across New Jersey. Observing Washington, he concluded that he had never seen the General appear to such advantage. "There is a natural firmness in some minds which cannot be unlocked by trifles, but which, when unlocked, discovers a cabinet of fortitude, and I reckon it among those kind of public blessings which we do not immediately see that God hath blessed him with uninterrupted health and given him a mind that can even flourish upon care."[1]

From the far side of the Delaware, Washington wrote his estate manager, Lund Washington: "Matters to my view, but this I say in confidence to you as a friend, wear so unfavorable an aspect (not that I apprehend half so much danger from Howe's army, as from the disaffection of the three states of New York, New Jersey, and Pennsylvania) that I would look forward to unfavorable events." Lund was to "prepare accordingly in such a manner, however, as to give no alarm or suspicion to anyone."

Washington, however, was not deterred from urging plans for the long-range future of Mount Vernon. He was sending a stallion, who was "very vicious," having been badly cut," but "as much, so I think, after mares as any stallion I ever met with." Washington hoped that Lund would prepare for the horse's arrival by exchanging "the old grays for young mares."

Washington then ordered Lund "to plant locusts across from the new garden to the spinning house. . . . Let them be tall and straight-bodied and about eight or ten feet to the first limbs. Plant them thick enough for the limbs to interlock when the trees are grown—for instance, fifteen or sixteen feet apart." And so forth, over several pages.[2]

The troops from Lee's and Gates's armies, whose slow approach Washington had so long observed in an anguish of impatience, finally came in.

Washington had assumed that they had already been re-enlisted: "to my great distress and mortification," he found that this was not the case. If they could not somehow be persuaded to stay, the long-expected reinforcements would vanish again in two weeks. Washington tried to comfort himself with the thought that "inquiry and investigation" usually served to "point out a remedy." However, he only uncovered "more and greater difficulties. . . . You may as well attempt to stop the winds from blowing or the sun in its diurnal as the regiments from going when their term is expired."[3]

Instead of offering reinforcements, New England was begging for some. The British had opened a new phase in the war by embarking some six thousand troops from New York and establishing them on the island a few miles offshore in Narragansett Bay where stood the flourishing city of Newport, which they easily captured.* To prevent their moving to the mainland, what levies New England could raise were gathering around Rhode Island's other city, Providence, under the command of "Granny" Spencer. Washington contributed to the defense all he could spare: one man who seemed a legion, Benedict Arnold.[4]

In the meanwhile, the enemy Washington faced across the Delaware seemed to be relaxing into winter quarters. The main British army had returned to New York, while the force left behind in New Jersey was cozying down in stationary posts. However, Washington was only slightly reassured. Realizing that on January 1 he would be left with a mere twelve hundred regulars, having himself little confidence in the militia who were being passionately recruited to fill in, notified that in extremely cold weather the Delaware froze so hard that the enemy could cross it on foot, Washington could hardly doubt that Howe would return to the offensive.† But in the meanwhile, the British Jersey posts were—presumably to protect residents who had accepted Howe's pardons—widely separated from each other. Furthermore, since naval supremacy consists in having the boats, however small, that will navigate the body of water involved, Washington possessed it for the first time in the war.[5]

The commander of the advance enemy positions was Major General

---

* This island now called Aquidneck, was then commonly referred to by the name of the state in which it was comprised: Rhode Island. As a naval and military base, it menaced all of New England, and its strategic value was greatly enhanced by a harbor considered the best in America because, unlike New York, it could only with the greatest difficulty be blockaded. The nearest anchorage for enemy ships, Gardiner's Bay at the top of Long Island, was miles away and supplied only partial shelter from storm. Newport Harbor was also less likely than New York to freeze up in winter.

† Actually, Howe had abandoned, when he had been prevented by a lack of boats from immediately crossing the Delaware, what had never been more than an opportunist effort to take Philadelphia that year. Professional armies do not pull themselves apart with winter campaigns, and British intelligence had faltered or been fooled on American strength. In mid-December, Howe believed that the shift-over in Washington's army had already taken place, leaving behind eight thousand men.[6]

James Grant. This Washington found most reassuring, since he remembered an idiotic maneuver Grant had executed with considerable loss eighteen years before when they had served together during Forbes's march on Fort Duquesne. Grant was a fatty, whose beetling brows, protruding lips, and double chin were dwarfed by puffing cheeks and swelling neck. He could be counted on to take the minimum precautions, since his disdain for the rebels was notorious.[7]

The posts immediately opposite the Delaware were garrisoned by Hessians, whose ignorance of English made them the more liable to surprise. There were said to be two or three thousand at Trenton, a village directly opposite the center of the American position but slightly inland from the Delaware on a tributary stream, the Assunpink.[8]

Trenton had only two main streets and these, as they sank down to the Assunpink, could be almost completely dominated from a hill at the top of the town. The road from upper Jersey to Princeton ran sideways across this hill, bringing the main streets, which met it at right angles and a few hundred yards apart, to their ends. A second road from the north, called River Road—it was closer to the Delaware which it roughly paralleled— came into Trenton near the middle of the town. At the bottom, about half a mile below the Princeton Road, the two main streets joined to cross the Assunpink over a bridge. Thence a road turned southeast to run along the Jersey bank of the Delaware to the next British post at Burlington, some fifteen miles away.

Washington's plan of attack envisioned several columns that would cross the Delaware at different places and make Trenton into a trap by simultaneously blocking all the roads. Starting some distance south of the town, eighteen hundred men under Brigadier General John Cadwalader, and (if it should come up in time) a force expected from Philadelphia under Putnam, would cut the road to Burlington, preventing an arrival of reinforcements from that post. Embarking directly across from Trenton, six hundred to eight hundred militia under Brigadier General James Ewing were to seize the bridge across the Assunpink. In the meanwhile, the main army of twenty-four hundred would have crossed the Delaware at McKonkey's Ferry, some nine miles upriver. They would march in two columns, that commanded by Sullivan coming into the center of town on the River Road, and that led by Washington and Greene appearing on the Princeton Road across the top of the two main streets.

After the Hessians had been disposed of, the whole army would come together, examine the situation, and decide what enemy force to take on next. (Unlike Howe, Washington did not aim only at limited objectives that could be foreseen; but, on the other hand, Howe would have known at a glance that Washington's plan of attack was much too complicated to work out as intended.) The whole maneuver was to start on Christmas Day, when the Hessians would probably not be paying much attention, and before the patriot enlistments had run out.[9]

On Christmas Day, Washington led his main detachment upriver far enough inland so that they would be invisible to enemy lookouts. They halted behind low hills, and then, as dark blotted out the enemy shore, advanced to McKonkey's Ferry, where they were met by large cargo boats which had just emerged from hiding up creeks and under overhanging foliage. These "durham" boats, named after their maker, had been especially designed for ferrying goods across the Delaware. Shaped like huge canoes—forty to sixty feet long, but only eight feet wide—they were double-ended and they drew not more than two feet even when carrying loads of fifteen tons. Along the gunwales ran narrow promenades, since the method of propulsion was for men to stand at the bows, firmly establish poles in the bed of the shallow river, and then walk toward the stern, pushing the vessel forward.[10] Because a pole against the river bottom gives more purchase than oars, this was, before steam power, a common expedient for fighting strong currents.

The air was chilly, discouragingly damp with a foretaste of storm, but the wind was still moderate. The ice chunks that moved wanly in the dark flowing river were few and did not seem menacing. Trained seamen from Glover's Marblehead Regiment manned the boats (as they had at the escape from Long Island); they felt it safe to crowd men aboard until the gunwales were almost awash. The first contingent of Washington's army got across in jig time.

Then the wind stiffened, bringing a terrible cold that formed ice in the shallows: a man would turn to scratch himself, and when he looked back sheet ice was a full foot further out in the river. The soldiers had to break through the crust to get to the boats, and, as soon as their clothing became wet, it froze as solid as armor. When the wind made the boats lurch, unshod horses slithered and beat with their hoofs to regain their footing. The men, pushing on the poles they had pressed against the river bottom, had difficulty balancing on their narrow decks, all the more so because as they walked they had to avoid the sticks with which other men were trying to ward off the floating cakes of ice that augmented dangerously with the freeze. The going became slower and slower.

According to the timetable on which cooperation between the various attacks depended, Washington's army should be across by midnight; but at midnight the laborious ferrying was still in full swing. Then it was three in the morning and the artillery was not yet over. Not till four was the whole detachment huddled on the Jersey shore. "This," Washington remembered, "made me despair of surprising the town, as I well knew we could not reach it before day was fairly broke. But, as I was certain there was no making a retreat without being discovered and harassed on repassing the river, I determined to push on at all events." He could only hope that the other expeditions had been similarly delayed, particularly Ewing's column, which was supposed to take the bridge and which was too weak to stand by itself.[11]

That this desperate effort to save the cause might turn into a defeat that would finally erase American independence became more probable when, toward the end of the ferrying, a great storm struck: rain, snow, and hail mixed together. In an anguish of anxiety, Washington watched from the Jersey shore for the last boats to come in. At last, the troops were all landed. Riding among them, he saw in vexed lantern light familiar rag-covered bodies, familiar weather-scarred faces under anything that could be folded into a hat. The officers reported that the storm "did not in the least abate their ardor." Then Washington was surely glad of the murderous weather that might well counteract the dreaded effects of daylight. Not only would the saturated air veil his army, but surely the Hessians would, after their Christmas celebration of the day before, doze in fancied security. Mercenaries would never suspect that any soldiers would budge from their quarters in such a storm.[12]

After Washington had given the order to march, the men and horses slithered every whichway on ice flowing with yet unfrozen rain. It was difficult to move, but deadly in the horrible cold to stand still: two men who went to sleep during a halt could not be wakened.

After two hours, the army had traversed the four miles to Birmingham, where the River Road down which Sullivan was to march turned off to the right from Washington's Princeton Road. A final hurried conference between the generals, a synchronizing of watches, and the columns separated. Each had about five miles to go.

As Washington moved with his detachment, he sent out whispered orders that from now on no one was to show a light. On through dark! Sleepers in roadside farmhouses, wakened by multitudinous muted sounds of moving men, remembered old superstitious fears, for they could see nothing outside their windows but storm. On and on! Then a glimmer appeared in the eastern sky. As Washington rode, a horseman materialized by his side. He was from Sullivan. Sullivan had met no opposition, but most of his men would be unable to fire: their powder was drenched. Washington replied that they would have to fight with their bayonets. There could be no turning back.[13]

On and on! As day lightened the almost solid mass of snow and rain, Washington could see silhouettes of men advancing with bowed heads. A shout in front! Washington spurred his slithering horse forward. A group of human figures were approaching across a field. To Washington's utter amazement, they proved to be a company of Virginians. The captain explained that they had been sent across the river the day before to reconnoiter. They had just been at Trenton and had shot a sentry. Shot a sentry! "You, sir," Washington rumbled in an anguished whisper, "may have ruined all my plans by having put them on their guard!" When the army arrived at Trenton, they would surely find the Hessians all lined up in battle array. But it was too late to turn back now.[14]

More light. The leafless trees on both sides of the road stood in ice like giant skeleton princesses encrusted with diamonds. Their branches rattled in the wind. Guides told Washington that his column was now within a mile of Trenton. He started a chain of whispered orders. As it reached each group, the men took off in a slipping, ungainly lope.

The skeleton princesses fell back behind Washington and daylight came in strongly over white cleared ground. Ahead was a one-story shack that angled out behind into a lean-to. Washington had expected the shack to be there. It was the cooper's shop which the advance pickets were said to inhabit. Sure enough, Washington heard a cry in gutturals. He heard and saw American muskets reply. More shouting in German, and then Hessians came running out of the house.[15]

The Americans loped ahead in such numbers that the Hessians fell back— but not in disorder. Other houses now stood beside the road; Washington could not help being impressed by the way the enemy pickets withdrew from behind one structure to another, keeping up all the while "a constant retreating fire." But most of his mind was listening for sounds elsewhere to the south. At last they came, dull and torpid through the heavy air. That was it! Sullivan's division had arrived and was attacking along the River Road.[16]

Washington's detachment quickly reached the area where the Upper Road cut across and topped the two main streets of the town. Moving among his men, he could sight first down one street and then down the other, and also see to some extent the yards behind and between the rows of houses. Everywhere Hessians boiled like bees emerging from a disturbed hive. Staring in Washington's direction, they had to cover their eyes, since the wind which came from behind the Americans' backs blew the snow and sleet full in their faces. "From their motions," Washington concluded, "they seemed undetermined how to act."* [17]

---

* The Hessians had been caught completely by surprise. When he had been urged several days before to take precautions, the commanding officer, Colonel Johann Gottlieb Rall, had (according to a Victorian translation of testimony at the official Hessian investigation) stated "Fudge! These country clowns cannot whip us." The skirmish involving sentries which Washington had feared would alarm the enemy had seemed to them, when guerrilla attacks were so common, too trivial to notice. Convinced that no strong force would move in such weather, the officer of the day had, on the morning of the battle, failed to send out the usual patrol. And after Washington had appeared so unexpectedly, the Hessians found themselves unable to achieve the formations from which they had been trained to fight.[18]

The air was so thick that Washington's straining eyes could not hope to penetrate the half-mile to the bridge across the Assunpink which Ewing's independent party had been supposed to take and hold. It was difficult to distinguish sounds, but, as far as he could tell, there was no firing there.

Washington ordered two regiments to continue on the Princeton Road far enough to block any Hessians who tried to flee in that direction through fields on his left beyond the village. He halted the rest of the men on the high ground that dominated the two streets and formed them so that the artillery could be brought forward. First two guns and then others—so many that they were crammed wheel to wheel—were aimed down the streets. When they boomed, the great increase in the level of sound made Washington realize the fire of small arms was petering out. Clearly what powder his men had had that was not too wet to fire had been expended. But he knew that Sullivan was active somewhere below and that some of his men, bayonets in place, had gone into the fields to the right of town and were breaking into the backs of the houses the Hessians occupied.

Two Hessian guns appeared on King Street with dim shapes behind them that seemed to be companies forming. American artillery fire dispelled the wavering shapes, and then a charge down the street took the cannon before they could be fired.[19]

The Hessians now came out of the town into the fields to the left just as Washington had expected they would. When they saw the regiments that were blocking that escape route to Princeton, they moiled around in confusion. Some of the patriot units in the town came out after them and harassed their left flank. The Hessian officers were now desperately trying to draw up the bewildered men. Washington ordered the cannon beside him on the hill to fire at the emerging formations. There was no shelter on the snowy slope, and the cannon range was point-blank.

The snow capered, opening and dimming sight. Washington heard some artillery explosions and a little crackling fire. Then a young officer appeared at his side. "Sir," he shouted, "they have struck."

"Struck?"

"Yes. Their colors are down!"

Washington wiped his field glasses and stared. Then he said with the laconism of great emotion, "So they are."

This concluded the battle at Washington's end of the town, but he assumed that Sullivan was still engaged: he spurred his horse down King Street. He had not gone very far before he met a horseman who bore the news that the Hessians down below had also surrendered. "This," cried Washington, "is a glorious day for our country."[20]

Surely, he continued his ride to the bridge. Sullivan's men were in possession. They told him that before they had been able to fight their way there, a platoon of British light horse and an undetermined number of Hessians had crossed and disappeared down the road to Burlington. There was no word of Ewing's force. Had they arrived, Washington stated, "not a Hessian would have escaped."[21]

Perhaps none had entirely escaped. If Cadwalader had crossed the icy river according to plan and cut the Burlington Road, the fugitives would be bagged after all. But, strain as he would, Washington could hear no firing in that direction. It seemed increasingly clear that the other two detachments had failed to get over through wind and cold and storm and floating ice. Only Washington's twenty-four hundred men were on this side of the Delaware.

In the Trenton streets, so recently rocked with gunfire, sound had shrunk to voices and the rustling of snow. Trying to count his dead, Washington discovered to his amazement that he had none: the red-spotted snow hummocks covered enemy casualties. He saw Hessians standing disarmed in such crowds that frowning officers were in despair how to count them. (They finally decided there were about 920.) This was the first victorious battle Washington had commanded since the Jumonville Affair of more than twenty years before.[22]

Howe would have thought it absurd even to consider marching instantly on for another attack, but Washington called a Council of War to discuss the possibility of chasing after the Hessians along the Jersey bank of the Delaware. If they could reach the next post of Burlington while it was still in the confusion caused by bad news and the pelting in of the fugitives, they might achieve a second victory. However, there were too many arguments against. Although Washington had ordered—certainly with regret, for he knew how tired and cold his men were—that the hogsheads of rum in the Hessian storehouses be smashed in the gutter, some of the men had anticipated him and were tipsy. All were exhausted, and the storm which showed no signs of abating might make the Delaware completely uncrossable. Then this part of the army would be permanently separated from the rest. His numbers, so he explained to Congress in justifying his reluctant decision, were inferior to the forces the enemy could pull together in the neighborhood if given a little time.[23]

And so the army marched back to McKonkey's Ferry (where their boats were) with the prisoners, with six captured pieces of brass artillery, with a thousand stands of arms and many other supplies loaded into captured wagons, and with four of those regimental flags that meant so much to European armies. Recrossing the river was slow and had its hardships—even more floating ice than before had to be fended from the boats—but everyone was in too high spirits to mind difficulties. After a day and two nights of continuous marching and fighting, during which there had been no pause for sleep, the men finally collapsed cheerfully into their quarters.[24]

Washington had achieved such a coup as he had long realized was

[178]

needed to bring new life to the ailing cause. But perhaps even more cheering to the Commander in Chief—it gave him, he wrote, "inexpressible pleasure"—was the fact that he had not seen "a single instance of bad behavior either in officers or privates. . . . Each seemed to vie with the other in pressing forward. . . . If any fault can be found, it proceeded from too great eagerness."[25]

20

Where No Sensible General Would Go

THE victory at Trenton was to reverberate down the corridors of history, but in that frozen December of 1776, Washington felt only that he had made a good start which should be improved by further action. As for Howe, he expressed disbelief: it seemed inconceivable that "three old, established regiments of a people who make war a profession should lay down their arms to a ragged and undisciplined militia."[1]

To worsen matters for the British, other Hessian units, on learning the fate of their compatriots, had retired with great alacrity toward the British base at Amboy, leaving the Jersey bank of the Delaware and, indeed, all the western part of the province unguarded. With what oaths we know not, Howe dispatched Cornwallis and a powerful force of British regulars to re-establish the situation and avenge the honor of his army.[2]

Although Washington's own force had got safely back across the river, other prey awaited Cornwallis on the flat fields of Jersey. After the great storm had broken on Christmas night, Ewing's party that aimed for the Assunpink bridge had made no effort to cross the Delaware, and Cadwalader's expedition to cut the Burlington Road had, when already partly across the river, turned back, sure Washington would do the same. On learning that Washington had persevered and beaten up Trenton, and that the Hessians in the neighborhood were in confusion, the two generals finally crossed the river. Finding neither Washington or any enemy, they had encamped with their fifteen hundred to eighteen hundred men at Bordentown, five miles below Trenton.[3]

Historians have criticized Cadwalader, who was the senior officer, for putting Washington on the horns of a dilemma, but Washington himself praised the Pennsylvania brigadier as "a military genius of a decisive and independent spirit." The Commander in Chief ordered more Pennsylvania militia over into Jersey, and on December 29, when his men were somewhat rested and he had been able to collect two days' provisions, he led his own force on their third crossing of the Delaware in four days. He encamped at Trenton.[4]

The enlistments of most of Washington's men would expire in forty-eight hours. One of his motives in bringing the army dangerously back to the scene of their victory was to establish an emotional base for a recruiting drive. Using the dictatorial powers granted him by Congress, he promised every man who would stay for six weeks a bounty of ten dollars, and also a share in whatever goods might be captured. In his orders, he praised their achievements at Trenton and mourned that such men should abandon the cause "for the sake of a little temporary ease." Then he had the regiments paraded one after another and made to each a personal appeal.

A sergeant remembered that His Excellency came up to a Pennsylvania regiment on a fine charger. From the saddle, he "in the most affectionate manner entreated us to stay." Then Washington rode off to one side and ordered the drummer to beat for volunteers. Rat-a-tat-tat!—but no man stepped forward.

"The General," so continued the sergeant's reminiscence, "wheeled his horse about, rode in front of the regiment, and, addressing us again, said, 'My brave fellows, you have done all I asked you to do, and more than could be reasonably expected, but your country is at stake: your wives, your houses, and all that you hold dear. You have worn yourselves out with fatigues and hardships, but we know not how to spare you. If you will consent to stay . . . you will render that service to the cause of liberty and to your country which you probably never can do under any other circumstances. The present is emphatically the crisis which is to decide our destiny.'"

The drums beat a second time. One soldier said to another, "I will remain if you will." The other, "We cannot go home under such circumstances." A few stepped forward and then more and more until some two hundred, nearly all the regiment that were fit for duty, had volunteered. (Our informant adds that because of wounds or smallpox, within a few weeks nearly half the volunteers were dead.)[5]

In urging recruiting drives at other posts, Washington stated that the regiments with him had re-enlisted "to a man." To Congress, he wrote of "half or a greater proportion." His estimates in numbers of those who had agreed to stay ranged from one thousand to fourteen hundred.[6]

While Congress was in flight, the capitalist Robert Morris represented the legislature in Philadelphia. To Morris, Washington sent a request for paper money to meet the bounties he had promised, and also some "hard money to pay a certain set of people." (Spies would not risk their lives for paper.) If necessary, so Washington continued, money should be borrowed. "We are doing it upon our private credit. Every man of interest and every lover of his country must strain his credit upon such an occasion. No time, my dear sir, is to be lost."

With a speed which inclined Washington to be forever Morris's admirer, a messenger appeared carrying fifty thousand paper dollars and two knobby canvas bags. Emptied on a table, the bags disgorged four hundred and ten Spanish silver dollars, a French half crown, two English crowns, and ten and a half English shillings. "The time and circumstance," Washington wrote, were "too remarkable ever to be forgotten by me."[7]

Hard coins placed in mysterious palms brought a report that the enemy was concentrating about five thousand men at Princeton, only ten miles away. Washington considered his situation "most critical" and his force "small"—yet to retire again behind the Delaware would ground the rising hopes of the Jersey militia. He would have to make a stand, but where? There were no extensive rocky regions, no redoubts.[8]

Calling to him the other troops in Jersey, Washington resolved to post the five thousand men who came together—mostly raw recruits—on a hill directly across the Assunpink Creek from Trenton. The bridge was in front of his center. To his left, the creek angled toward the Delaware which it met at a distance of about a mile. To his right, the creek pointed gradually inland. Shaped like an irregular slice of pie, the land which the Americans occupied presented opportunities for defense, since the Delaware River, which flowed by about half a mile to the rear, was impassable to the boat-less British, and the Assunpink could only be forded at a series of specific places. However, the area could also be a trap. Should the British succeed in crossing the creek, they could pin Washington, whose boats were elsewhere, against the river. Washington considered the position was too exposed; critics then and still have branded it foolhardy. However, Washington undoubtedly relied on his troops' extreme mobility to evade any blow from the enemy's ponderous paw.[9]

The British commander was still Cornwallis, although Washington thought it was Howe. Cornwallis left his baggage and three regiments behind in Princeton when he advanced just before dawn on January 2, 1777, down the Post Road from Princeton to Trenton. His numbers—a good estimate is fifty-five hundred—were only slightly greater than Washington's, but they were expert fighters well supplied. This professional army responded with such careful might to harrying from the flanking woods and ravines that it took them the whole day to cover ten miles. Dusk was in the air when Washington espied, from the hill on which his army was encamped, his skirmishers come spilling down Trenton's two parallel streets. They disappeared into the houses to harass the British advance guard that also came in view. By the time the British had flushed the Americans out, the dusk had proceeded so far that the sounds of firing were preceded by visible flashes of light.

The American pickets now ran for the bridge, while Knox's cannon sent shot and shell over their heads to delay the pursuers. The crossing was a narrow way between stone parapets: it became solid with men. A soldier remembered that as he pushed his way along, he saw that "the noble horse of General Washington stood with his breast pressed close against the end of the west rail of the bridge, and the firm, composed and majestic countenance of the General inspired confidence and assurance." The soldier eventually found himself pushed against the horse's shoulder and Washington's boot: both remained motionless as iron.

The British made a gesture at following across the bridge and dipped their feet in various of the nearby fords, but withdrew when greeted with vigilant shots. They fired some of their own cannon, but camped out of range. As darkness took over, the flash of guns gave way to the more even burning of campfires. Temporary peace, a pause in carnage, descended.[10]

The British engineer Robertson, who noted that the Hessians should have retired at the Battle of Trenton to the position Washington now held, stated that the British "durst not" attempt a frontal assault. When Howe eventually reported home that the Americans had occupied "a strong position beyond a creek," he felt it unnecessary further to explain why Cornwallis did not attack that night. Cornwallis himself was in no hurry. He is reputed to have stated, "We've got the old fox safe now. We'll go over and bag him in the morning."[11]

"Having," Washington wrote, "by this time discovered that the enemy were greatly superior in numbers and that their drift was to surround us, I ordered all our baggage to be removed silently to Burlington soon after dark."[12] Washington—how Howe would have sneered!—had prepared no preconceived plan: he had all along intended to see what the British would do, and then to react accordingly. It did not now escape him that the size of the force he faced implied that only a weak garrison had been left at Princeton.

A tour of Washington's own campfires revealed that the men were a little uneasy, but still confident—if only that the Lord would somehow protect them—and eager to act. Some grumbled as the night became increasingly cold, but Washington saw with joy that the roads, which had been muddy, were freezing solid. His own headquarters at a Trenton tavern having been overrun by the British, he called a Council of War in the combined parlor, dining room, and kitchen of the two-story shanty that was the headquarters of St. Clair.* It was agreed that fires should be kept up and loud noises made with entrenching tools, while the army slipped silently around the

---

* This encouraged St. Clair to claim credit for the strategy decided on.

British left flank and attacked Princeton. Should they succeed at Princeton, they could advance deeper into enemy territory, perhaps to Brunswick, the main British depot for stores.[13]

If Washington realized how impossible what he was planning would be for a conventional army, that made him the more eager, since it would increase the likelihood that Princeton would be surprised. However, no one could doubt that the scheme was very dangerous. Even if the patriots could count on moving faster than the enemy, even if they had no supply line which it was essential (as it would be for European regulars) to keep open, the fact remained that they were planning willfully to sandwich themselves between the large enemy forces in New Jersey and New York. They were placing Cornwallis across their line of retreat. "To run the hazard of the whole army's being cut off," he reported to Congress, "was unavoidable, whilst we might, by a fortunate stroke, withdraw General Howe from Trenton, [and] give some reputation to our arms. . . . One thing I was sure of, that it would avoid the appearance of a retreat."[14]

At about midnight, in response to whispered orders, the men left their fires and moved out into the cold, going they knew not where, or whether to retreat or bloody action. Above the stars were dim; below ice was changing slow rills into pale, eerie lines. Men with a good sense of direction realized that they went east of south and then veered to north-northeast. Having made a wide sweep, they joined a secondary road that some miles to the east ran parallel to the Post Road from Trenton to Princeton. When there was a halt, whole files of men fell asleep on their feet, to be bowled over when more wakeful men behind them stepped forward.

Washington's aides rode back and forth, keeping him in touch. After about six or seven hours of marching, bright day revealed a motionless landscape aglitter with hoarfrost. Now Stony Brook hurried on Washington's left, rushing water rippling around ice-clad rocks. The road was angling in toward Princeton. Soon the front of the column came to a crossroad that was only a mile from the town. Straight ahead, Quaker Road ran to the Post Road, joining it just where it crossed Stony Brook on a bridge. Washington ordered General Mercer to lead his brigade down Quaker Road and, by destroying the bridge, cut contact between the main British army at Trenton and the regiments assumed to be in Princeton. The rest of the American army was, under Washington's immediate command, to turn right and advance toward the village on Old Road, which paralleled the section of the Post Road that extended from the bridge to Princeton.[15]

Discreet silence reigned, and then from the direction of the bridge, whence Washington had expected to hear at the most a scattered exchange of fire with sentries, there exploded a roar of small arms. Riding toward the sound, Washington saw Mercer's few hundred men withdrawing across an

[184]

orchard and up a hill in the direction of Old Road. They were being driven by a powerful force of redcoats—it seemed several regiments—who held before them naked bayonets.

Washington ordered the unit nearest him, Cadwalader's Pennsylvania militia, into the battle. As they advanced a little hesitantly, the troops already engaging the enemy suddenly broke. Mercer's men ran pell-mell in among the Pennsylvanians, creating confusion. While the British line advanced in perfect formation with steady might, brandishing sharp steel, the Americans were milling in an agonized bewilderment that could only too quickly eventuate in a rout.

However, the appearance on a hill of two American fieldpieces brought the British to a halt, and then a big man on a white horse appeared at a gallop with generals and aides around him. Washington had come, like Achilles, to rally his hosts. "Parade with us, my brave fellows!" he shouted. "There is but a handful of the enemy, and we will have them directly."[16]

The Pennsylvanians lined up again to face the enemy, who were now established behind a fence on the crest of a little ridge. Washington gave orders that extended the patriot line to the right with riflemen and New England Continentals. His aides spread the word that no one was to fire until given the command. Then Washington came in front of his troops and galloped along the line to the very center. He waved his men forward and, as they advanced, continued to move before them, a towering target on horseback. The enemy were ever closer. Now Washington and his followers began to mount the rise and were within musket range: although most of the enemy held their fire, a few bullets zinged around them. Washington continued to lead the quick, silent patriot advance. Within thirty yards of the British line, he shouted, "Halt," and gave the order to fire. Both sides fired simultaneously, with Washington between them.

Washington's aide, Colonel Edward Fitzgerald, covered his face with his hat, for he could not bear to see the Commander in Chief killed. When, all the guns having been emptied, the firing ceased, Fitzgerald lowered his hat. Around him, many men were writhing in their last agonies. But Washington sat solidly on his horse, untouched. The aide rode up to him, and, tears streaming from his eyes, gasped, "Thank God, your Excellency is safe!"

Washington took Fitzgerald's hand. "Away my dear Colonel, and bring up the troops. The day is our own."* [17]

The enemy had broken and were in full flight. Washington did not know how many more British detachments were in the neighborhood; however, he could not resist leaving that problem to his subordinates. Now, at long last,

---

* This anecdote, which Washington's stepgrandson, G. W. P. Custis, said Fitzgerald often told him many years later, has been generally accepted despite Custis's unreliability. That Washington should have behaved thus is within his character—he had ridden between firing troops in 1757.[18]

The Battle of Princeton. *Above:* Detail from Charles Willson Peale's *Washington at the Battle of Princeton.* Courtesy of The Art Museum, Princeton University. *Below:* Sketch by John Trumbull. Courtesy of Princeton University Library.

he had a chance to chase regulars across open fields. Perhaps he heard again, somewhere in his subconscious, the bugle call, signaling that the fox had gone to earth, with which the enemy had insulted him at the Battle of Harlem Heights. Having paused only to give a few quick orders, he was off after the enemy. He was heard to shout, "It's a fine fox chase, my boys!"[19]

On the day before, Cornwallis had left three regiments at Princeton. However, as he prepared to attack Washington beyond Trenton, he had called two of the regiments to him. They had just set out when they had stumbled into Mercer's men by the Stony Brook bridge. Washington was now chasing some of the survivors; others joined the remaining British regiment which had been approaching the battle from the town of Princeton.

This force soon discovered that the rebel army coming toward them along Old Road was so large that it had to be Washington's. But the British knew that this was impossible: Cornwallis was holding Washington's army pinned against the Delaware many miles away. The situation made no sense: the British were too flabbergasted to put up more than a token resistance. Some fled. The rest surrendered themselves and the town.

So happily victorious, the Americans looked around for his Excellency. Where was he? Anxiety mounted. Had Washington been captured or killed?

The Commander in Chief had continued his whooping fox chase until the prickings of his conscience became too strong. Then he reined in and rode back across the field where his men had just fought. He saw more than a hundred corpses. Those of Americans had been brutally mangled, stabbed and stabbed again. He found General Mercer being attended to, still breathing despite seven deep wounds. An eighteen-year-old lieutenant bled in every part of his body: from his head where his skull was fractured, from his breast where there was a bullet hole, and elsewhere from innumerable bayonet gashes. Resolving angrily that he would protest such brutality to the British command, Washington chased away a marauder who was trying to rob a prone, feebly gesturing British officer.

Looking up, he saw on a rise what one of his captains described as "a very pretty little town. . . . The houses are built of brick and are very elegant, especially the college, which has fifty-two rooms in it." Many men were milling around but there was no firing. Cheers erupted as Washington galloped in clearly unharmed.[20]

As he rode from regiment to triumphant regiment shouting congratulations, he was notified that a large British army was coming from the direction of Trenton "in a most infernal sweat, running, puffing, and blowing and swearing at being so outwitted." They were forced to stop where the bridge across Stony Brook had been destroyed, but even under the protection of patriot artillery fire, the watery gap could not be expected to hold the infuriated English army for long.[21]

Washington yearned to gather in the lovely enemy supplies in Princeton warehouses. However, there was only time for the men to swap their old blankets for new British ones. In good order and (except for those mourning dead companions) in the best of spirits, driving between two and three hundred prisoners, the patriot army marched off proudly to the fifes and drums. They were going deeper into New Jersey.[22]

Washington's own enthusiasm was so great that he felt he had perhaps within his grasp a chance to end the war that very day. If he could get to Brunswick that day and take the wealth of stores and supplies and specie (he later heard there had been £70,000) which the British had hoarded there, surely the enemy would give up. He sent out horsemen with tinder and flint and steel to burn the bridges on all roads to Brunswick except the one he intended to take.

But, as he and his top officers rode in a gaggle together, they remembered "the harassed state of our own troops, many of them having had no rest for two nights and a day," and meditated on "the danger of losing the advantage we had gained by aiming at too much." If only they had six or eight hundred fresh troops! As it was, when they came to a crucial crossroad, they turned away from Brunswick, left toward Somerset Court House. They hoped to find a consolation prize there: a garrison of thirteen hundred. But the town proved empty of soldiers, the garrison having ridden off to Trenton.[23]

Washington proceeded by slow stages to the heights around Morristown, two-thirds of the way back across New Jersey. The British made no serious effort to molest his march.

Enemy behavior, indeed, increasingly revealed how correct had been Washington's judgment that it was worth a great risk to follow up the victory at Trenton with another stroke. The British historian George Trevelyan was to write concerning Trenton: "It may be doubted whether so small a number of men ever employed so short a space of time with greater and more lasting effects upon the history of the world." But such would not have been the result if Washington had not gone on to overwhelm Princeton.[24]

Had the British succeeded in re-establishing their lines on the Delaware, Trenton would have just been another of those stinging raids in which the history of inconclusive warfare abounds. But after Princeton, the British reasoned that it was unsafe to keep forces spread out in western Jersey. They made Brunswick, less than ten miles from their fastness on Staten Island, their most advanced post. The upshot placed in serious doubt the effectiveness of a combined military and political strategy with which the British had hoped progressively to damp out the rebellion.

Tory exiles, of course, had encountered little difficulty in persuading the King and his ministers that the Revolution had been forced on a predominantly loyal population by armed brigands: drive away the brigands and love for the Crown would bubble to the surface. It followed that it would be effective to conquer an area, grant pardons to those who reaffirmed their allegiance to the Crown, and then, leaving a small force to assist the now loyal province in protecting itself from the rebels, go on to the similar liberation of an adjacent area.

This surely was the best British hope in a country too scattered to be dominated from a few captured centers. And the crowds who had sought pardons after the British had established control in New Jersey had seemed to prove the feasibility of this conception. Washington had been worried to the point of despair. Then Trenton and Princeton had demonstrated a fact as profoundly discouraging to the British as it was inspiring to the patriots: what had seemed an upflooding of Tory sentiment had commonly been no more than self-preservation. His Majesty's newly declared loyal subjects did not come to the assistance of the King's forces or retreat with them. As soon as royal pardons were no longer needed, the papers went into the fire. Guns which had remained motionless under British control were taken down from hundreds of walls in preparation for shooting at redcoats and Hessians who had been proved not invincible. It seemed that the British must hold an area primarily through their own unassisted military might—and that this might would have to be considerably greater than those who despised Washington's army had supposed.

News of Trenton and Princeton traveled across America like a rainstorm across a parched land, lifting bowed heads everywhere. The *Pennsylvania Journal* wrote of Washington, "Had he lived in the days of idolatry, he had been worshiped as a god." And John Hancock named a son George Washington Hancock.* [25]

However, the memory of the preceding months could not be altogether erased. The American losses have been estimated by Freeman at between four thousand and forty-five hundred killed or captured, with several thousand more dead of disease, casualties equaling perhaps half the number of men engaged. Although Washington, who spread exaggerated accounts of enemy losses—two thousand to three thousand, for instance, at Trenton and Princeton—played down his own, there were empty firesides in every village and returned veterans had tales to tell. [26]

After the victories, Washington dinned into the ears of his generals that the new prestige of the army was as precarious as it was precious. Thus he wrote angrily to Sullivan, who had taken a position where he could be

---

* Accounts of the engagements created an even greater military reputation for Washington and his men abroad than had been created at home. Europeans found it doubly amazing that orthodox professionals could be outgeneraled and overcome by undersupplied amateurs. Frederick the Great was quoted as stating that the marches "were the most brilliant of any recorded in the annals of military achievement." This réclame proved useful to American negotiators seeking European support—and word of it eventually came back across the water further to impress Washington's compatriots. [27]

[189]

surprised by the British: "Our affairs at present are in a prosperous way; the country seems to entertain an idea of our superiority, . . . and a belief prevails that the enemy are afraid of us. If . . . you should be drove, which nothing but the enemy's want of spirit can prevent, the tables will be turned, the country dispirited, and we shall again relapse into our former discredit."[28]

21

A Hopeful Pessimist

WASHINGTON had hardly holed in at Morristown after the Battle of Princeton before his army was threatened by celestial action. On January 8, 1777, he wrote the Pennsylvania Council of Safety, thanking them for "your notice of the eclipse of the sun which is to happen tomorrow. This event, without a previous knowledge, might affect the minds of the soldiery."[1]

Although he knew that General Lee had considered the heights around Morristown strategically very important, Washington, who had never before been there, had planned only a temporary stop to "accommodate and refresh" his march-weary troops before moving on to a better position. However, riding and interviewing soon persuaded him that he could not hope for a better position. Twenty-five miles due west of New York City, Morristown was roughly the same distance from the three main British posts in Jersey: Brunswick, Newark, and Amboy. The heights near the village had as an outer rampart a chain of sharp hills which overhung the flat through which the New York–to–Philadelphia roads ran. And in the rear were not only further defiles to cover a possible retreat, but also farm country abounding in provisions. Washington decided to make Morristown his headquarters for the rest of the winter.[2]

The most immediate problem was what to do about the inhabitants of New Jersey who had during the British occupation sworn allegiance to the Crown. There was no lack of fire-eaters who wanted to punish them in various ways. But Washington considered that "'tis bad policy" to make "martyrs."[3]

Although he could still sometimes view with alarm the possibility that "parricides" would copiously refill Howe's depleting legions, the events of the last month made Washington regard this as a secondary danger. He issued a proclamation: all who had taken the British oath should come to the nearest military headquarters and swear "allegiance to the United States." Those who refused, and who had not been caught in inimical acts for which they deserved punishment, were to be politely escorted to the British lines.

Protests in Congress were led by the Jersey delegates. Despite the powers accorded him, Washington should not, they insisted, grasp executive or legislative powers. His proclamation would enable Tories to escape just prosecution by merely mouthing an oath. And surely "an oath of allegiance to the United States . . . is absurd before our confederation takes place." Congress referred the matter to a committee. The committee reported that Washington's action had been required by military necessity, on which the house tabled the whole matter in order to avoid an angry debate.[4]

For his part, Washington regretted that he needed to act as rigorously as he did. "In the adoption of any measure for general operation," he mourned, "individuals may and will suffer." To minimize the suffering, he ruled the wives and children of exiles could stay in their homes "if their behavior warrants," and that the refugees could take with them personal possessions that would be of no assistance to the enemy.[5]

The wisdom of a serpent could not have devised a more effective weapon than was forged by the kindness of Washington's heart. Tories imprisoned, Tories exiled to the frontier, would have been strengthened in their hatred of the patriot cause. But the Tories Washington sent to New York City were subjected to British military rule. The generals felt vastly superior to Colonials. Influential Tories who had given up wealth and power for their King were permitted hardly any role in the government of the city and accorded only tiny stipends on which to subsist themselves. It was considered natural that the daughters of lesser Tories should contribute to the family support by catering to the lusts of British soldiers. When shortages developed that endangered the bill of fare at officers' messes, ordinary refugees were hardly allowed to eat at all. Since everything that the most extreme patriot orators said about British tyranny was more than exemplified there, New York City became the most effective reformer of Tories on the continent.

To the shortages that plagued New York, Washington was gleefully contributing. His spies reported that Howe, confident that a pacified New Jersey would serve during the winter as his granary, had not amassed any quantity of supplies within his base. No way existed to block him from whatever Long Island offered—but Washington intended that this was all he should have without fighting for it.

Orders went out that in New York's Westchester County above Manhattan Island and in eastern New Jersey all supplies close to the British lines should be removed or destroyed: the deeper the British foraging parties would have to penetrate into patriot territory, the more enemy soldiers would have to make the march. And wherever parties penetrated, militiamen were to surround them like clouds of bees, stopping them if possible, otherwise falling back before them. Such continuing activity would, Washington noted, "in a manner harass their troops to death."

Washington had discovered the ideal way to use the militia, about whom he was henceforth to complain much less strongly. Often inhabitants of the terrain they guarded and thus letter-perfect on its geography; engaged in a service where discipline and subordination were of secondary importance; having (as Washington put it) "superior skill in firearms" which enabled them to make the enemy "always sustain the greatest loss"; the militia were perfectly suited for what came to be called, when the Spanish reinvented it during the Napoleonic Wars, guerrilla warfare.[6] And also the militia, being spread across the countryside, were kept away from the Continental troops, whom they therefore could not, with their lawless example, corrupt.

However, such utilization of the militia did not one whit reduce Washington's concern with the Continental Army as the heavy fist of the patriot war effort. The militia could only be counted on to make going uncomfortable for enemy detachments. Unless a strong Continental Army were enlisted for long enough to be disciplined and trained, the British could move anywhere in force, capture whatever they seriously desired.

After the troops who had accepted at Trenton a brief extension of service had gone home, Washington had very few regulars. And more difficulties than the most fertile brain could possibly imagine stood in the way of his replenishing the ranks. He often was not supplied the money with which to pay bounties, and when he did have money, he had to compete with larger bounties paid by states for home defense.* (Washington wrote the governor of Rhode Island that unless he stopped interfering thus, the Continental Army would not "bestow any extraordinary attention to the defense" of Rhode Island.) When states tried to help by adding their own bounties to

---

* Another formidable rival for recruiting in the Continental Army was service in privateers, which was more financially rewarding since the crews got a share of the value of prizes. Washington (who himself owned a share in at least one privateer[7]) did not complain of this competition. Much more effective than America's embryo navy, the private enterprise fleet was of tremendous value to the patriot war effort. Since America had almost no manufactures, most military supplies had to be imported either from the Indies or from Europe; and to pay for those supplies, goods had to be shipped from the United States. It would have been a disaster had the British been able to establish an effective blockade of American ports. The privateers, it is true, could not fight major British warships, but they could keep those warships busy convoying the freighters that brought supplies for the British army, and, for that matter, British merchant vessels anywhere, since the privateers sailed even into the mouth of the English Channel. The seamen captured British munitions Washington's army could use, and furthermore disrupted enemy communications by taking the boats that carried dispatches back and forth between the ministry in London and the British command in America.

those offered by Congress for Continental enlistments, Washington's troops went home to collect the money. He had to threaten the death penalty for enlisting several times to collect several bounties. Then he became convinced that officers were collecting bounties for enlistments that had never been secured, as their returns for desertion were so high. Having growled for several months that he would accept no men who would not stay for the duration or at least three years, he was forced to appeal for one-year men.[8]

He wrote Congress bitterly that he saw none of the military ardor which he had hoped would inspire the officers when their pay was "genteelly augmented and the army put up on a respectable footing." It seemed "as if all public spirit was sunk into the means of making money by the service or quarreling upon the most trivial points of rank."[9]

Whenever any department of the army wavered, the responsibility devolved on Washington. He was carrying out the duties of adjutant general, since Reed had insisted on returning to Pennsylvania politics and it seemed impossible to find anyone else. Finally, the job was given to Timothy Pickering, a fierce, handsome New Englander Washington had not previously met, but who was said to have made a deep study of war in books (and who was to make Washington trouble for the rest of his life).[10]

Joseph Trumbull, the commissary general, sat in his native Connecticut balancing his books, and when he finally gave in to Washington's importuning and came to camp, he was instantly summoned by Congress. The legislators thereupon reorganized the commissary department in such a way that most of its officers resigned or threatened to—a situation which Washington protested to Congress as more dangerous than the enemy.[11]

Washington had no love for the French who had inspired the Indians to devastate the Virginia frontier during his previous war. However, the very rivalry with England which had created the older conflict now made France the natural ally in the revolt of the United States. Washington could not believe that France would actually declare war on the English in the American cause or go beyond their present "underhand assistance" of selling supplies for American money. These munitions—sixty-eight hundred stands of small arms, for instance, which arrived in March—were so invaluable that Washington was to write in April 1778, "France by her supplies has saved us from the yoke so far."[12]

A more equivocal French import from France were individual volunteers: officers who claimed to have served in the French army and were now arriving at Morristown from Europe and the Indies in "swarms." As Washington complained to Congress, for days together it filled "half my time to hear their pretentions and explain to them the reasons why it is impossible for me to gratify them in their wishes."[13]

They would march into his presence stiff-legged and aggressively uniformed. They were very ceremonious and superlatively martial in bearing.

Through interpreters—Washington spoke no more French than they did English—each insisted that he was entitled, because of his glorious record on European battlefields, to one of the very highest commands in the American army. Washington suspected that most of them were "hungry adventurers." But in no individual case could he be sure, and his feelings as a gentleman were always lacerated by having to deny the claims of men who had come so far and often had exhausted their funds in the journey. He found it embarrassing to be forced to pay for the mending of proud foreigners' torn breeches.[14]

Many of the intruders vociferated that they had claims which were binding on Washington. Romand de Lisle insisted that he had been assured by Congress the command of the artillery, which was one of the incidents that made Washington—to the rage of some of the members—accuse Congress of getting rid of the Frenchmen's importunities by dumping them on him. Most embarrassing of all were those arrivals who had been given commissions in Paris by the officious but undeniably official American representative, Silas Deane. Philippe du Coudray, who had brought with him a retinue of eighteen officers and ten sergeants, had in writing that Deane had put him in control of the artillery. Congress felt obliged not only to make du Coudray a major general, but to back-date his commission in a manner which gave him seniority over many American generals. Greene, Knox, and Sullivan thereupon petitioned Congress for redress and threatened to resign if the newcomer were inserted over their heads. Congress reacted with rage at this interference with their prerogatives which they considered synonymous with the liberties of the people, and it looked for a while as if Washington would lose three of his very few valuable generals. John Adams wrote angrily, "I wish they would all resign. For my part, I will vote upon the genuine principles of a republic for a new election of general officers annually."[15]

Tempers were, however, soothed; and then du Coudray, with his Gallic dash, galloped his horse onto the Schuylkill Ferry so lustily that he landed in the water on the other side. Having neglected the plebeian exercise of swimming, he drowned.

The French influx was the more straining because Washington kept taxing the interpreters in an effort to find individuals who could be really useful in the technical departments where the American lack of conventional training crippled most. The fiasco at Fort Washington made him realize that his greatest gap was in that specialty that involved the designing of fortifications: military engineering. Here Silas Deane (or was it Providence?) came beautifully to his rescue, sending him three competent experts led by Colonel Louis le Bèque Duportail, who was to prove one of the most useful officers in Washington's entire army.[16]

Another of his acquisitions Washington was greatly to regret, although for the moment he was pleased. What a relief it was to have one of the French officers who confronted him speak to him in good English: Colonel Thomas Conway was, indeed, an Irishman who had been driven into international military service by English oppression. "From what I can discover," Washington wrote, "he appears to be a man of candor, and, if he has been in service as long as he says he has, I should suppose him infinitely better qualified to serve us than many who have been promoted." Congress made Conway a brigadier.[17]

Although himself a devoted and brilliant horseman, Washington had been, during the early phases of his command, glad to have little cavalry. In the first place, he considered that the "broken country full of stone walls" where the Massachusetts and New York campaigns were fought made "no enemy more to be despised" than a man on horseback. Since cavalry could not "leave the road," they could be fired at with impunity from any thicket. And, in the second place, keeping any considerable numbers of horsemen greatly complicated problems of supply. Even if grass were plentiful—only during summer and rarely even then in wooded America—the mounts of a company of horse would soon eat themselves out of protected grazing at a stationary post. And, when unable to live off the land, each horse should be given daily fourteen pounds of hay, ten of oats, and four of straw. Maintaining cavalry thus involved transport and storage facilities and only too often foraging expeditions which placed troops in jeopardy. It was, indeed, even more to fill the bellies of horses than of men that the British kept popping out of New York that winter of 1777.[18]

When he had himself been in the city before the Battle of Long Island, Washington had dismounted four hundred militia cavalrymen from Connecticut. He explained that since he only had enough forage for absolutely necessary work and artillery horses, cavalry mounts would be "a moth and a check on the service." However, he urged the various states to maintain, at a distance from his army, "troops of light horse* . . . in constant readiness" to "throw succors to a place in case of emergency." He visualized such troops not as true cavalry (who fight on horseback) but as mounted infantry (who ride to the battle but dismount before they fight).[19]

On first concluding that the enemy intended to operate in New Jersey, Washington tried to take advantage of the fact that they had cavalry horses to feed while he had not: he ordered the destruction of all forage in the area over which the armies would maneuver. But as soon as he himself was on the Jersey plains where horsemen could gallop freely, he quickly discovered a need for cavalrymen of his own.[20]

One type of mounted activity came naturally to American riders. They

---

* All the cavalry used during the Revolution were known as "light horse" in contradistinction to the heavy dragoons who, as they trundled along under ponderous equipment reminiscent of ancient chivalry, were the tanks of the epoch.

were good at speeding over the countryside to find some enemy detachment or supply train which they could attack, usually dismounting if the enemy gave battle. These raids not only harassed the enemy, but often resulted in the capture of supplies that the ever-impoverished Continental Army badly needed. And the army quickly developed—in a young Virginia neighbor of Washington's, Henry (Light Horse Harry) Lee—a leader of such skirmishing whose skill as a mounted raider seemed to Washington to reveal "great resources of genius."[21]

However, Light Horse Harry (unlike his son, Robert E. Lee) had no "economy," no ability to organize on a large scale, and such groups of mounted planters and farmers as he commanded could not check in mounted combat the trained British cavalry. The enemy horse could scour at will the flat reaches of Jersey, where there were no woods or rocks or stone walls for the patriots to skulk behind. "From the experience I have had this campaign of the utility of horse," Washington wrote Congress, "I am convinced there is no carrying on the war without them." In particular, his own skirmishers, the riflemen, were very vulnerable to cavalry, because once they had fired, it took them some time to drive new bullets down the long, tight, rifled barrels of their guns. Supplying them with spears did not, alas, enable them effectively to protect themselves when they were unable to fire. And the psychological impact of the enemy cavalry on the American troops was even greater than their actual destructiveness.

Washington now dreamed of establishing true cavalry of his own that would be capable of fighting from the saddle—this involved special equipment and much training of both men and horses—and that could serve as a shock force able to ride down infantry in battle. He induced Congress to establish on paper several regiments of horse. Then he offered the command with the rank of brigadier to Reed. Reed refused. "My arrangements," Washington wrote his old companion, "have been a good deal disconcerted." Surely, Reed realized that despite what had happened in relation to General Lee, he still held "the same place in my affections that you ever did."[22]

Washington was lonely. Since the 1776 campaign had continued until winter had closed the roads from Virginia, Martha had been unable to join her husband as she had done the year before. No person in the army, Washington wrote, "suffers more by an absence from home than myself." He was oppressed by the erratic post from Virginia. He explained that although he was too busy to write often, his family wrote him regularly. Receiving the letters irregularly was "rather mortifying, as it deprives me of the consolation of hearing from home on domestic matters."

Sometimes, however, the news was far from consoling: "The smallpox . . . has got into my family." There were three hundred persons to be inoculated. That June, Washington anticipated modern medical practice by urging on Virginia "a law to compel the masters of families to inoculate every child born."[23]

Washington's claims to vast lands on the far Kanawha River, to those dream acres his exploring feet had actually walked and which he envisioned as a refuge should the Revolution fail, had been left in a legal tangle when he rode off to war. Now his old friend and former surveyor, Colonel William Crawford, offered his services. Washington could only reply that his time was so "engrossed by public matters that I scarce bestow a thought on my private affairs, beyond my family at Mount Vernon."[24]

Among the many public matters that continually vexed Washington was an outrageous squabble in the medical department that grew out of an ancient personal hatred between the two most distinguished doctors from Philadelphia. Dr. John Morgan had founded America's first medical school in a way that deeply offended Dr. William Shippen. Washington, who was an old friend of Shippen's, had hoped that he would become the Continental Army's director general of hospitals. However, Shippen had shown no interest until the job went to Morgan. Then he began intriguing. He secured an appointment as director general in New Jersey, and when, in the fall of 1776, the army moved across the Hudson, he insisted that he was now in charge: Morgan should stay behind in New York. As the two physicians tussled over which medicines belonged to whom and commanded each other to depart, the ill-tended hospitals were undoubtedly the most dangerous places on the whole American continent. One attending physician complained that he had known "from four to five patients to die on the same straw before it was changed, and that many of them had been admitted only for slight disorders." Here was a picnic for the typhus lice, who, when a dead body became cold and unpleasant, had only to crawl a few inches to find a new living man.[25]

Morgan, although Washington believed he had done his best, was finally discharged and Shippen put in his place. That would have been an advantage if it produced unity—but now the politician-physician Rush got into a herculean fight with Shippen that angrily involved groups of congressmen.

The fundamental problem was, of course, that medicine was not ready to deal effectively with most infectious diseases: inevitable failure produced slothfulness and personal accusations which increased the deadly impact of the underlying ignorance. Poor Washington, seeing his hard-earned men dying pitifully around him, called for unity in the medical department and did what he himself could. With brilliant pragmatism, he stressed those measures that could really help: hygiene in camp and order in the hospitals, and, above all, inoculation, the one answer to epidemics which the eighteenth century knew that actually worked.

However great the temporary risk, so Washington decided, future smallpox epidemics must be prevented by having all new levies halted on their way to camp to be inoculated. This added to all other recruiting delays an additional four weeks. It encouraged and perpetuated that drought of men which was forcing Washington to violate his new strategy by mixing in militia with what regulars he had at Morristown. Even after that had been done, his force usually fluctuated at around a mere three or four thousand effectives.[26]

An eyewitness tells us that he distributed his troops so thinly through the various hamlets around Morristown that the inhabitants believed three thousand men were forty thousand. When an officer rushed into head-quarters demanding authority to arrest a spy, the Commander in Chief urged him to make friends with the spy, invite him in to dinner, and then give the miscreant, as if by inadvertence, a chance to steal a return Washington enthusiastically prepared that gave the patriot number as twelve thousand.[27]

But surely Howe could not be fooled forever. He would eventually realize Washington's weakness. Then he would attack. Washington's army might well be so completely routed as to prevent it "from making a junction of any consequence" during the whole year of 1777. Philadelphia would, of course, fall to the enemy. These thoughts filled Washington with such anguish that he repined, "I think we are now in one of the most critical periods which America ever saw!"[28]

The protests and warnings with which Washington bombarded Congress kept that body skulking at Baltimore, away from the capital their general insisted he was too weak to defend. Then in mid-February Howe actually entered New Jersey with a force which, so Washington reported, outnumbered his army two to one. The news threw Congress into an excess of resolutions, calling for nonexistent troops from everywhere. A vote which admonished Washington that he should not only confine the enemy "but with the blessing of God entirely to subdue them" persuaded Thomas Burke of North Carolina of "a great desire in the delegates of the eastern [New England] states and in one of New Jersey to insult the General."[29]

After the British action proved to be no more than a forage in force, Robert Morris advised Washington that if he would be optimistic sometimes "it would draw forth the exertions of some good men. . . . Heaven (no doubt for the noblest purposes) has blessed you with a firmness of mind, steadiness of countenance, and patience in sufferings that give you infinite advantages over other men. This being the case, you are not to depend on other people's exertions being equal to your own. One mind feeds and thrives on misfortunes by finding resources to get the better of them; another sinks under their weight." He begged Washington to present Congress with "the best side of the picture frequently."[30]

Washington replied that to deceive Congress "with false appearances and assurances would in my judgment be criminal and make me responsible for consequences." It was his duty to give Congress the exact picture.[31]

Yet it is true that from the very start of his command, Washington had, in his letters to Congress, pictured the cause as perpetually dangling, like that heroine of silent screen serials, Poor Pauline, over one precipice after another—and that the cause had never been dashed to pieces, and had often stepped back completely unscathed.

Washington knew that Congress, afflicted with infinitely more business than it was organized to handle, tended to postpone any problem not in crisis: he perpetually cried crisis. The possibility that he might put himself in the position of the boy who called "Wolf! Wolf!" until his shouts were ignored, does not seem to have bothered him. He was a passionate man and was in fact perpetually on one brink or another, even if because of his sensational skills (and Howe's conservatism) he rarely took a fall. Perhaps he should shout even louder! Despite everything he could say, Congress never seemed to realize that he could hardly "by every means in my power, keep the life and soul of this army together. In a word, when they are at a distance, they think it is but to say, 'Presto! Begone!' and everything is done."[32]

That it was truly hard to persuade Congress is shown in a letter that John Adams wrote General Sullivan that very February when Washington was in an agony for lack of men: "Are we to go on forever this way, maintaining vast armies in idleness and losing completely the fairest opportunity that ever was offered of destroying an enemy completely in our power?"[33]

However, persuading Congress was not the only motivation for the dark pictures Washington drew. His letters to his relations in Virginia exhibit even more pessimism. That he found relief in thus unburdening himself unofficially we cannot doubt, but this was not the explanation he himself gave. He stated that in order to fool the British and bolster American morale, he was forced publicly to minimize all his difficulties and exaggerate his army's strength. Thus, if he failed, the fault would seem altogether his own. He wished for the protection of his ultimate reputation to have in the hands of his relations a record of the difficulties that had been forced upon him.

A lesser man would undoubtedly have seen fewer difficulties. Washington was like a fine watchdog perpetually protecting his sheep, recognizing every avenue through which a wolf might come, agonizing over every opening he could not close.* His senses were all the sharper because he was the wolf

---

* He urged one of his officers not to "conceal any circumstance from an unwillingness to give pain, especially as the knowledge of them to a man determined not to sink under the weight of perplexities may be of the utmost importance."[34]

too, probing for chinks that might give him access to the enemy's fold. Washington would have exulted at one-tenth the possibilities he was forced to leave to Howe. He could not understand why the professionals did not make use of the opportunities he could not help spreading before them. Surely General Howe could not be so "unfit for the trust reposed in him" as not to take advantage of weakness, if not today, then tomorrow, or surely the day after. "It is our business," Washington wrote, "to prepare for the worst."[35]

There were also, as Morris suspected, personal explanations for Washington's catalogues of "misfortunes." The letters he had written to his English agents from Mount Vernon in peaceful years bear startling resemblances in mood to his screeds written from military camps: nothing is well done, nothing is going right. After each indignant letter it would seem that its successor ought either to discharge the factor or to announce Mount Vernon had become bankrupt. Washington did finally slip away from the factor, but only after years of complaints—and Mount Vernon prospered.

Although Washington's anxieties were heightened by the actual dangers and crises of wartime, anxiety had always been his companion, even when he moved in peacetime through a gentle world on the banks of the slow-flowing Potomac. It was natural for Washington to be haunted from day to day by dark forebodings. But, for this very reason, he took his worries less to heart than would a man whose temperament was normally flooded with sunshine. Experience had taught him that he need not be too upset by the prophecies of doom his nerves uttered. Despite them all, he had risen at home to affluence and in the wide world to a position of greatness. His body was strong, his mind and will also. He would not fail.

Washington, who combined in his character so many opposites, exhibited to the world pessimism in detail and optimism in the large. "Our affairs," he wrote typically, "are brought to an awful crisis that the hand of Providence, I trust, may be more conspicuous in our deliverance." The man who had so often cried havoc could, in another mood, state, "I have seen without despondency (even for a moment) the hours which America have styled her gloomy ones."[36]

22

Recapture of a State

ARLY in March 1777 (although the fact was hidden from all but his close associates), Washington came down with an illness so severe that he could only attend to the most necessary business.[1] This was his first real sickness since he had taken the command, an amazing record, considering how much contagion there had been around him and how often he had been seriously ill during civilian life. After ten days, he was back at his desk again, a recovery which may well have been speeded by good news from Virginia: a one-woman reinforcement was on the way.

Martha had set out before the roads had really emerged from winter. She reached Morristown in the middle of March. She was all the more welcome because Washington's housekeeping arrangements had gone awry.

His Excellency had taken it upon himself to fire Mrs. Thompson—"the old woman" as he called her—whom Martha had on a previous stay hired as housekeeper. And he had hired Patrick Maguire, newly arrived from Ireland, as steward. However, Patrick proved "given to liquor," and, when properly elevated, dared "take the liberty" of being "very insolent" to the Commander in Chief. Washington now wrote to the captain of his guard, Gibbs, who was visiting in Philadelphia, to locate Mrs. Thompson if he could, and also to try to find him a steward who had experience "as a butler in a gentleman's family." A man without such experience, Washington explained, "would be diffident and suffer himself to be imposed upon by our servants, who stand so much in need of being checked for their extravagance and roguery in making away with liquor and other articles." Washington added that his family needed wine and sugar.[2]

Martha's arrival made headquarters blossom with ladies. One of them, the wife of a Virginian colonel, Mrs. Theodorick Bland, gives us a picture of the encampment as it softened into springtime. Morristown was "a very clever little village situated in a most beautiful valley at the foot of five mountains.

It has three houses with steeples, which give it a consequential look." However, except for two families of refugees from New York, it was "inhabited by the earnestest rustics you ever beheld."

You could not travel three miles without passing another village with steepled meetinghouses and courthouses, "which gives them a pretty, airy look, and the farms between the mountains are the most rural sweet spots in nature. . . . They present us with just such scenes as the poets paint Arcadia: purling rills, mossy beds, etc., but not crying swains and lovely nymphs, though there are some exceeding pretty girls, but they appear to have souls formed for the distaff rather than the tender passions." The farmers, "the most inhospitable mortals breathing," served visitors only "dreadful good water."

Mrs. Bland and her husband visited headquarters two or three times a week by invitation and almost every day by inclination. "Now let me speak of *our* noble and agreeable commander," she continued, "for he commands both sexes, one by his excellent skill in military matters, the other by his ability, politeness, and attention." Washington was generally busy in the forenoon, but "from dinner till night he is free for all company. His worthy lady seems to be in perfect felicity when she is by the side of her *Old Man* as she calls him. We often make parties on horseback." Then "General Washington throws off the hero and takes on the chatty, agreeable companion. He can be downright impudent sometimes—such impudence, Fanny, as you and I like."[3]

Mrs. Bland considered the general's aides "all polite, sociable gentlemen." There was a new face. On March 1, Washington had announced, "Alexander Hamilton, Esq., is appointed aide-de-camp to the Commander in Chief, and is to be respected and obeyed as such."[4] Although no one could yet realize the importance of this statement to the future of the United States, Washington quickly realized that in this quick, proud, bony-faced young man, with cold blue eyes and a smiling mouth, he had acquired a towering assistant. Hamilton had come from the West Indies to New York as a boy; had at seventeen blossomed as an able propagandist for the patriot cause; and, although now only twenty, had behind him considerable experience in the Continental artillery. He was a super-Reed, of much the same temperament, but a genius where Reed had only been very able.

When spring warmed hearts and the earth, the new Continental Army began coming in. Washington made his general orders a serial textbook on the duties of everyone from the general officers to the fifers and drummers, whom he admonished to practice regularly: "Nothing is more agreeable and ornamental than good music." For the first time he included in his orders such personal appeals as "the General wishes it on these accounts and for his own ease and satisfaction."[5]

[203]

The trees were leafed out and the flowers bright when, at the end of May, Washington moved his force from their winter quarters at Morristown to Middlebrook, which was at the very edge of the hills that overhung the Jersey plain. He was endlessly busy directing spies, analyzing the information they brought in. On the enemy's movements, Washington's movements would depend. They had the initiative.[6]

Only one thing was absolutely certain: they would keep a garrison in New York. From there on, the possibilities were endless, but Washington's reasoning and his spies made him believe that the British would probably either try to cut the United States in half at the Hudson River or try to take Philadelphia. Although in the middle of the previous campaign a British force had come down from Canada as Howe moved through New Jersey, Washington saw this as too illogical to be repeated as a deliberate plan. If there were another invasion from Canada, Howe would certainly advance up the Hudson to meet it. If, on the other hand, Philadelphia were to be the object, the Canadian army could be expected to sail down the coast and join Howe. The logical routes to Philadelphia were two: either overland through New Jersey or around by the ocean and up the Delaware River.

Washington's reasoning defined four areas of danger that should be defended: the Jersey plains; the Hudson Highlands; Lake Champlain, down which a Canadian army would sail; the Delaware between Philadelphia and the sea. Although his plight of the previous autumn had given him a bellyful of divided armies, he felt that he could station major forces at two of the key positions without so far extending his interior lines that he would be, should the British unite for a single thrust, prevented from quickly bringing his own army together. He stationed the troops from the eastern states at Peekskill in the Highlands and kept those from New Jersey and the states farther south at Middlebrook under his own command. At the other spots, the reliance should be on forts.

If the northern British army invaded from Canada, Fort Ticonderoga, which dominated Lake Champlain, should delay them until Washington could counter the British move with the necessary reinforcements. Since Philadelphia was some seventy miles up the Delaware from the ocean, forts on that river could presumably keep out any British amphibious force until highly mobile Continental troops completed a dash across New Jersey.[7]

In ordering the Delaware forts, Washington revealed that he had well pondered the lessons presented him at Fort Washington and Fort Lee. Strongpoints should be compact rather than extensive. No more men should be assigned to an installation than could get within its walls—he urged only three hundred men for Billingsport—and forts should not be made depots for any "large quantity of stores." The general who had a short time before relied so much on his troops' ability to dig and pile now wrote, "I begin to consider lines as a kind of trap" which were useless except to block "passes that cannot be avoided by an enemy."[8]

On the night of June 17, the British, reinforcements having swelled their number to twenty-seven thousand men, made their first major move of the campaign: a large force crossed the narrow channel from Staten Island into New Jersey and started along the road to Philadelphia.[9]

In the previous campaign, Washington would probably have left the heights at Middlebrook and dashed through northern New Jersey in an effort to get across the Delaware before the British could get over, so that he could make a stand at that defensible line. But now he realized that the British, with their need for sophisticated supply lines, would not advance while a powerful force menaced their rear. Nor would they sandwich themselves between two American forces as Washington had done at Princeton. He ordered Benedict Arnold, who happened to be in Philadelphia, to lead the Pennsylvania militia in guarding the Delaware crossing. This inept force could not, even under such brilliant command, stop the British, but it could delay them if they ignored the supply-line problem and tried to cross. Washington's highly mobile army would then have time to catch the enemy half on one side of the river and half on the other.[10]

Washington's best guess was that Howe did not really intend for Philadelphia, but wished "to maneuver us out of our present encampment into action upon disadvantageous terms." Far from intending to give battle on the flatlands, where British techniques would prove so great an advantage, Washington planned to retire, if Howe should attack Middlebrook, into the higher hills to his rear. Such refusal of action would, he knew, invite criticism from those—politicians and some of his own generals—"who wish to make themselves popular at the expense of others, or who think the cause is not to be advanced otherwise than by fighting." But that would have to be borne.[11]

As it turned out, Howe made no effort to cross the Delaware or to assault Washington. When the van of the British army had gone about nine miles beyond Brunswick, the whole enemy line became stationary. The Pennsylvania militia had risen in force to man the far side of the Delaware. The New Jersey militia was bubbling up all around the enemy. John André, the British staff officer who was later to become so famous, noted that all the avenues to the camp "were infested by ambuscades." Washington now yearned to have the British stay in Jersey as long as possible, drawing out ever more militia, "which will be a great discouragement to the enemy by showing that the popular spirit is at such a height, and, at the same time, will inspire the people themselves with a confidence in their own strength, by discovering to every individual the zeal and spirit of his neighbors."[12]

When the British retired to Brunswick on the 18th, burning "many valuable houses in their route," Washington assumed that they had been frightened by the popular uprising in a state where they had seemed to be welcome the year before. He believed this would be "a greater shock to the enemy than any event which has happened in the course of this dispute, because it was altogether unexpected." Howe had, however, no such sense as Washington's of the importance on war of public attitudes. Having ruled Washington's camp too strong for a frontal attack, he had hoped by making a feint at Philadelphia to lure the Americans into a battle on the plain. When Washington would not be decoyed, Howe had seen no reason to continue that maneuver.[13]

However, he tried another. Embarking all of his army except the garrison at Amboy, he carried the troops across the Arthur Kill to Staten Island. This withdrawal lured Washington to a relatively exposed position near the Kill, the main American army on a minor height at Quibbletown, while a large detachment under Stirling encamped in the plain below. On the night of June 25–26, Howe crossed secretly back from Staten Island and marched to get behind the American position. He succeeded in beating up the advance guard of Stirling's detachment, but all the rest of the quick-marching Americans got away.[14]

Having again failed to trap the old fox, Howe retired again to Staten Island. Now he abandoned even Amboy. Not a single British soldier was left in New Jersey. This complete recapture of a state the British had almost completely overrun seemed to John Hancock "the most explicit declaration to the whole world that the conquest of America is not only a very distant but an unattainable object." However, other New England leaders were outraged because Washington had not assaulted Howe: "I long," Joseph Warren wrote John Adams, "to hear of enterprises, of battles fought and victories gained on our side." It was incontrovertible that the snake had not even been scotched. Being an amphibious reptile, it might descend on any part of America to which water led. "They have it much in their power," mourned Washington, "to lead us a very disagreeable dance."[15]

IV

A Very Disagreeable Dance

23

The Enemy Vanishes

WASHINGTON'S spies reported that British transports were being "fitted up with stalls over their main decks for the reception of horses." Weighed with other data, this indicated strongly that Howe intended for Philadelphia. However, dispatches from the north stated that the British second in command, General John Burgoyne, was starting down from Canada with a large army. The best way to resolve this seeming contradiction was to conclude that the Canadian movement was a feint to pull the Continental Army northward so Howe could march unimpeded across New Jersey while his baggage train went around by water. Washington responded no further to the Burgoyne threat than to advance a few regiments from Morristown toward the Highlands. He counted on Fort Ticonderoga to block Burgoyne's route should that officer actually come down Lake Champlain.[1]

Indications increased that Burgoyne's threat was a serious invasion—and then Washington received dreadful news. Because it was "not apprehended nor within the compass of my reasoning," it flooded him with "chagrin and surprise." The garrison at Ticonderoga had, without firing a shot, abandoned the fort at Burgoyne's approach and disappeared into the forest. Lake Champlain was now a British highway! Except insofar as they were impeded by forests and would be harassed by what militia would spontaneously arise, the enemy had free access to the northeastern section of the United States: both the headwaters of the Hudson and western New England.[2]

Although his own army was minimal for the defense of Philadelphia, Washington rushed four regiments up the Hudson to reinforce Schuyler, who still held the northern command. It would also be necessary, Washington decided, to send a combat general who could do what Schuyler, who was best at organizing supply, could not do: integrate the militia with regulars, and make the whole force fight against odds. Washington believed that the ideal officer for this desperate assignment would be Benedict Arnold—but Arnold had reasons for not serving that seemed even to Washington valid.[3]

Since Arnold had been the senior brigadier and also the one with by far the most impressive record, Washington had been amazed, some four months before Ticonderoga fell, to learn that Congress had passed over Arnold and promoted to major general five less outstanding officers. Washington urged Arnold not to resign until the matter could be straightened out: "My endeavors to this end shall not be wanting."

Arnold replied, "Although I sensibly feel the ingratitude of my countrymen, every personal interest shall be buried in my zeal for the safety and happiness of my country."[4]

Washington's protests to Congress were met with the information that Arnold had been ignored because of states' rights sentiment: his native Connecticut already had her share of major generals. Remembering, perhaps, how he himself had been slighted during the French and Indian War as a Virginian, Washington felt that he could no longer importune the injured officer not to resign. "The point," he wrote, ". . . is of so delicate a nature that I will not even undertake to advise; your own feelings must be your guide." However, when Arnold's feelings only carried him to unhappy inactivity in his home town of New Haven, Washington was thankful that the army had not lost so valuable an officer. And Arnold quickly proved again his value.[5]

On April 25, 1777, some two thousand enemy landed from the Sound near the Connecticut town of Norwalk and marched twenty-five miles inland to Danbury, where they burned an American supply depot. Arnold galloped from New Haven and so successfully spirited up the inhabitants that the British had to fight their way back to their boats with heavy losses. The enemy, Washington exulted, "will engage in such enterprises in future with much caution and circumspection."[6]

Congress could not ignore Arnold's new exploit, but they had too great a sense of their own dignity to make complete restitution. In promoting him to major general, they allowed him to continue to rank below the five officers they had raised over his head. Arnold was not satisfied, nor did Washington think he should be. The Commander in Chief warned Congress, "He will not act, most probably, under those he commanded but a few weeks ago."[7]

General Arthur St. Clair, who had deserted Ticonderoga but was still up north, was one of those. Nonetheless, hoping that the injured officer would magnanimously agree, Washington urged Congress to send Arnold to the rescue: "I am persuaded his presence and activity will animate the militia greatly." Arnold soon appeared in Washington's camp to state that (in Washington's paraphrase) "he generously, upon this occasion, lays aside his claim, and will create no dispute should the good of the service require" him to serve under St. Clair.[8]

Although intelligence reports still pointed Howe at Philadelphia, Washington could hardly believe that the Briton would fail to go up the Hudson toward Burgoyne. To be as prepared as possible for either move, he led his army from the Morristown region to the Clove, a "very difficult and rugged gorge" which bit through the Highlands on the west bank of the Hudson, giving access to upper crossings of the river. This pass had been "scarcely known before the war": a traveler typically considered it "the wildest and most deserted country" he had ever seen. There was "a lake so solitary and concealed that it is only visible through the trees by which it is surrounded." It had banks so steep that a deer who took one false step would inevitably fall into the water.* [9]

For some ten days, Washington inclined his army one way or the other in the eleven-mile pass as indications pointed to Howe going north towards Canada or southwest to Philadelphia. Although the Clove was lower than the country around it, Washington's men had to mount and descend what seemed to aching legs "very high mountains." His Excellency could find no better headquarters than a dilapidated log cabin. He slept in the one bed with his staff on the floor around him. "We had plenty of sepawn [boiled cornmeal] and milk, and all were contented," so wrote the New Englander Pickering. But Washington poked up the commissary general concerning four casks of cane spirits, one of Madeira, and a large cheese, all long promised. [10]

To Washington, the reports of his lookouts and spies were "puzzling and embarrassing beyond measure. . . . At one time, the ships are standing up towards the North [Hudson] River. In a little while, they are going up the Sound [toward New England], and in an hour after they are going out of the Hook" into the Atlantic. Howe tried to help along confusion by arranging for a letter to fall into Washington's hands in which he presumably told Burgoyne that he was aiming for Boston. Recognizing the stratagem, Washington regarded it as the surest proof that Boston was not menaced, but he was still so torn as to write, "Our situation here is distressing." [11]

On July 24, "one hundred and seventy topsail vessels and about fifty or sixty smaller ones" actually sailed from New York Harbor into the ocean. Leaving only a strong garrison at the Highlands, Washington started the rest of his army on a rapid march across New Jersey to protect Philadelphia. However, he kept "casting my eyes continually behind me" since "General Howe's in a manner abandoning General Burgoyne is so unaccountable." Perhaps Howe, having tricked the Continental Army into moving away, would dash back and sail up the Hudson after all. [12]

When, during the preceding late autumn, it had taken Cornwallis three

---

* This is Tuxedo Lake. Travelers now move through part of the Clove at a mile a minute on the New York Thruway—some fifteen miles after they cross the Tappan Zee Bridge to the west bank of the Hudson.

weeks to move from Fort Lee to Trenton, Howe had loudly praised his men for traversing some eighty miles so rapidly. Now, in the varying heat of July, the advance section of Washington's army covered during two days a greater distance—from the Clove to Flemington, a village within eleven miles of the Delaware. At Flemington, Washington heard that some seventy sail had been seen off Egg Harbor on the sea lane to Philadelphia. However, they had vanished as suddenly as they appeared—and Washington's supermen were very tired. Cautiously, he halted his army on the New Jersey side of the Delaware.[13]

On July 31, Washington had just finished his breakfast when a rider from Congress brought word that the fleet had been sighted off the capes at the mouth of the Delaware. Washington assumed that, much of the river being blocked, the enemy would sail up as far as they could. Their army would then disembark and march for Philadelphia. He ordered his own army "to cross the Delaware with all possible dispatch and proceed for Philadelphia."[14]

With a sense of relief that he was at long last coping with a solidified situation, Washington galloped ahead to find between the ocean and the city a good place for his army to make a stand. But he awoke the next morning to receive the "surprising" news that the enemy had disappeared again into the ocean. This was frightening. He reasoned that Howe had sailed back to New York to support Burgoyne. But his army was too tired to follow—and his guess might be wrong. He allowed his men to collapse in the "extreme heat" at the Falls of the Schuylkill, five miles above Philadelphia. Believing in the eighteenth-century manner that much bathing was bad for the health, he warned them to wash only "moderately."[15]

Washington himself rode into Philadelphia, where Congress was wrangling over the northern command. The New England delegates and their allies blamed Schuyler, as St. Clair's superior, for the fall of Ticonderoga, and returned to the old agitation to have him replaced by Gates. New York, as before, refused to abandon her general. Congress as before tried to dump the matter into Washington's lap, and Washington, as before, refused to compromise his nonpartisan political position by getting into the squabble. From a purely military point of view, he was probably glad when Congress plumped for Gates, who could command combat as well as supply, but he foresaw personal problems. Gates had become increasingly insubordinate. He had accused Washington, in a very rude letter, of trying to engross "every tent upon the continent," and had, in what Washington considered "a most extraordinary manner," intercepted some uniforms intended for one of Washington's regiments. Washington's premonitions made him ask Congress to make it completely clear who would command should British movements force a junction of his own command and Gates's northern army. Although (as later events indicate) there may have been some secret hesitation in the minds of some delegates, Congress endorsed Washington's authority.[16]

A cautious commander menaced by an aggressive rival does not weaken his own army to strengthen the potential usurper. However, since Burgoyne was making much use of Indian fighters, Washington sent to Gates his own best skirmishers, Morgan's riflemen.

At a dinner given him at Philadelphia's City Tavern, Washington, still much plagued by French volunteers, met yet another, but this one was most certainly no hungry adventurer. The Marquis de Lafayette was so well connected in Louis XVI's Court that his coming to America had provoked an international incident, England protesting to France. Congress had tried to help the international quarrel along by making the twenty-year-old aristocrat, who had no military experience whatsoever, a major general. Washington was told that the title was supposed to be altogether honorary, but he had "found by experience that however modest they [the French arrivals] may seem at first . . . they soon extend their views, and become importunate for offices they have no right to look for."[17]

Lafayette's reddish hair had retired prematurely up his receding forehead; he had a narrow, oval face, bright hazel eyes, a long, pointed nose, and a protruding cleft chin; he was remarkably blond for a Frenchman. Although he was far from handsome, he was engaging: his slight body trembled with temperament as Washington had seen the bodies of highbred chargers do. He was struggling to become proficient in English, a compliment that the less aristocratic volunteers rarely paid Americans. Although he made no secret of his conviction that the greatness of his family, and the fact that the eyes of all Europe (as he believed) were upon him, required of him the accomplishment of great deeds, he was becomingly modest in admitting his lack of military knowledge.

Washington invited Lafayette to join his military family as honorary aide. The Marquis was all enthusiasm.

A week or so later, Lafayette came to the army. Writing in the third person, he was thus to describe his impressions: "About 11,000 men, ill armed and still worse clothed, presented a strange spectacle to the eye of the young Frenchman: their clothes were parti-colored and many of them were almost naked. The best-clad wore *hunting shirts:* large gray linen coats." The tyro ruled the American method of drill too complicated, and his eye was offended that "no other distinction of height was ever observed" than that the smaller men were put in the front rank. (This was for a utilitarian purpose: to make it easier for the rear rank to fire over the heads of the front.) The officers (although they had powdered their hair to impress the Marquis) drew from him only the adjective "zealous." Lafayette concluded that in the American army "virtue stood in place of science," and he wondered why, being himself virtuous, he should not at once assume the

The Marquis of Lafayette, by Charles Willson Peale. Courtesy, Henry Francis du Pont Winterthur Museum.

command his rank as major general implied. But for the moment he held on to his modesty.

"We must feel embarrassed," so he quoted Washington as saying to him, "to exhibit ourselves before an officer who has just quitted French troops."

"It is," Lafayette replied, "not to teach but to learn that I come hither."[18]

However, after only eleven days with the army, Lafayette asked Washington to commission two of his aides as the first step toward his actually taking command of a division. Both embarrassed and annoyed by this request from a young man he was beginning to revere, Washington burst out to a friend in Congress that if the legislature had intended Lafayette's commission to be entirely honorary, "I wish it had been sufficiently explained to him." If, on the other hand, the commission was meant to be operative, "Why have I been led into a contrary belief?" Washington had no more idea how to proceed "than the child unborn."[19]

As Washington and Lafayette came nearer each other in increasing intimacy, this problem, like all that subsequently developed between them, resolved itself according to a procedure that perpetually deepened their mutual admiration and love. Instinct with ambition and ebullient self-esteem, the younger man remained as fertile with schemes for contribution to the cause and his own personal glory as an imaginative child, but he submitted his inspirations to Washington for a final judgment, expecting that his elder would strike many of them down.

The two men were better able to understand each other because they both possessed the same transcendent ability to learn from experience. Lafayette quickly recognized what most of the other French volunteers never saw: that however unorthodox the military methods of the American army and its Commander in Chief, they were highly effective in the kind of warfare in which everyone was now engaged. Having great intelligence and no conventional military knowledge to unlearn, Lafayette became, with sensational rapidity, one of Washington's most successful military pupils.

Lafayette was to explain to his wife that Washington, "surrounded by flatterers or secret enemies . . . finds in me a sincere friend, in whose bosom he may always confide his most secret thoughts, and who will always speak the truth." Unlike other young men Washington had encouraged, unlike Hamilton and Reed, Lafayette never turned on his patron. His affection became to Washington a poultice for loneliness. The childless general and the French aristocrat who had been orphaned at the age of three came, as they both boasted, to fill the roles of father and son. Washington spoke of Lafayette as "the man I love."[20]

But all this Washington could not, during that August of 1777, foresee. At that moment, Lafayette was one of the many secondary problems that made more vexing his main quandary: where was Howe?

As the British fleet remained invisible, Washington's fears ranged along the entire coast from Boston (where mysterious shadows seen by fishermen incited a desperate panic) to Charleston. However, the conclusion that Howe was on his way to support Burgoyne was so much the most logical that on the 10th Washington started his army on a slow march eastward.[21]

That afternoon Washington stopped at a tavern called the Billet. He and eight companions consumed with their dinner a bottle of wine and a punch made from two pounds of sugar and "two quarts spirit and brandy." (His servants and the protecting light horse drank two bowls of toddy and three quarts of rum.) The whole party was on the road again when word came that the enemy had been sighted "off Sinepuxent Inlet, about sixteen leagues to the southward of the Capes of [the] Delaware." Charleston now seemed the objective, but Washington decided that he would ruin the army if he tried to march there in the heat.

Everyone encamped. Washington splashed his horse across a little stream to occupy a low fieldstone farmhouse near what is now Hartsville, Pennsylvania. Here he fretted for eleven days before there was another report on British movements. They were off Chesapeake Bay and seemed to be standing in. Washington ordered that the whole army should prepare to march the next day, and then, since he could see no reason why the British should advance up the Chesapeake, revoked the order.[22]

On August 22, the news came that finally established the British destination past doubting: the fleet was now far up Chesapeake Bay. Howe, Washington wrote, "must mean to reach Philadelphia by that route, though to be sure it is a very strange one."[23]

Howe had, as a matter of fact, intended to advance on Philadelphia via the Delaware, but, when the fleet had paused off the Capes, reconnaissance had revealed patriot defenses on that river so formidable that the British decided to proceed to the Chesapeake. Under the best of circumstances, Howe pointed out, the boats could not have hoped to get up the Delaware above Wilmington, and to Philadelphia from Wilmington was only a negligible twenty miles shorter than from the head of Chesapeake Bay. He could not, of course, foresee that contrary winds would make the trip to the Chesapeake take three weeks. However, he felt that this might have been for the best, since he had a European's idea of the unhealthiness of the American climate: the troops were less likely to be ill on the ocean than on the continent during the sickly hot months of July and August.[24]

Howe added that the major reason for his strategy was that, to preserve the capital, Washington would "have to risk a battle." This time the regulars would, once and for all, smash the Continental Army under its amateur general, whom the British professional command considered no more than "a blockhead."[25]

CHAPTER

24

A Failure of Intelligence

THE Continental Army was not a parading force. It had never before
marched through the streets of a city, and Washington, having seen
British regulars dress and wheel, authorized this parade with misgivings.

To ward off the enemy the army had to move to the other side of Philadelphia. Washington reasoned that it could hearten the patriots and awe the
Tories if the crossing were made a display of might. However, there was a
risk; the army's free style of marching and lack of uniforms might seem not
powerful but pitiful. Washington used his general orders to stage-manage as
best he could.

After the highest officers, who would lead the parade, there should be a
clattering of light horse. Then, in contrast, a wilderness touch: pioneers
carrying axes. Then, regiment after regiment, each preceded by its field
artillery. In the very middle of the procession, the heavy artillery was to
advance, surrounded by the artificers belonging to it. Then more regiments
and a final burst of light horse. Drums and fifes should be massed in the
center of each regiment, and "a tune for the quickstep played, but with such
moderation that the men may step to it with ease, and without *dancing*
along or totally disregarding the music as too often has been the case. . . .
Great attention [should be] given by the officers to see that the men carry
their arms well, and are made to appear as decent as circumstances will
permit. . . . Not a woman belonging to the army is to be seen with the
troops." Every man should wear in his hat, or (if he had no hat) in his hair,
a leafy green sprig to indicate hope.[1]

As Washington led on horseback, with beside him that symbol of French
assistance Lafayette, the crowds cheered but no one felt truly festive. The
citizens were all anguishedly judging how capable the army would be of
protecting the city. That the line, although sometimes twelve abreast, took

[217]

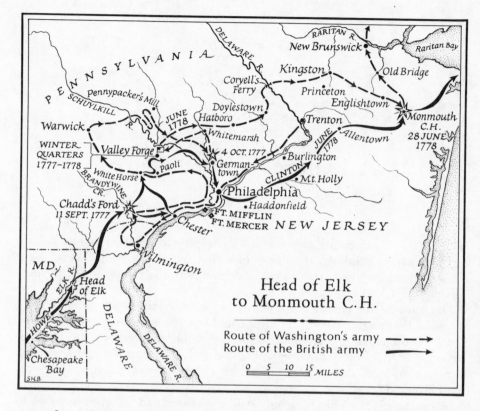

Head of Elk
to Monmouth C.H.

Route of Washington's army — — — →
Route of the British army ——————→

0   5   10   15 MILES

more than two hours to pass was considered by patriots a good omen. That
there was much nakedness and that what hats existed were all cocked at
different angles were bad omens. A lady was pleased when she concluded
that the men carried their firelocks in a way which seemed to show training,
but John Adams noted that the troops did not "turn out their toes so exactly
as they ought."[2]

The parade over, Washington aimed the army for Wilmington and then
galloped ahead with Lafayette and an escort of light horse to reconnoiter a
countryside in which he had never expected to maneuver and try to make a
stand. An express met him with the news that the enemy had begun to
disembark at the head of the Elk River (Elkton, Maryland), which was the
extreme northeast corner of Chesapeake Bay. Washington rode in that
direction, learned from the natives of two overlooking hills, stationed the
local militia on them as advantageously as possible, and secured in the
process a distant view of some tents being raised.[3]

Darkness had fallen when, still accompanied by Lafayette and the troop
of horse, Washington started back toward his army. Soon a storm changed

the air to ink and drenched them to the skin. They all rode toward a glimmer of light; they knocked on a farmhouse door. The face of the man who answered did not break into such a glow at learning that here was Washington as Lafayette would have liked. However, the party entered.

Inconspicuously attentive, Lafayette heard the unexplained closing of a door that could mean a messenger sent to the British. He led Washington to one side and whispered that it was necessary to move on. (Remember what had happened to General Lee!) When Washington smiled at Lafayette's fears, the Marquis blamed a stubborn unwillingness to admit to having made a mistake. There was little sleep for the Frenchman that night. All rose before daybreak. After they were safely away, Washington (so Lafayette was to insist) "acknowledged that any one traitor might have caused his ruin."[4]

However, as the story was repeated in camp, Washington denied that he had been rash: "I was, as I afterwards found, in a disaffected house," but "I had a strong party of horse with me." To this statement, Washington added a sentence which seemed to reflect irritation with those spreading the story: "I was equally guarded against friend and foe."[5]

Having much reduced his numbers with reinforcements sent to the northern army, Washington needed to depend heavily on militia that gathered slowly; he was glad that the British were held up because—so it was reported—their horses had suffered much on the voyage. Now, for the first time, he had a considerable body of cavalry of his own. They skirmished perpetually and brought in prisoners. Washington himself was daily in the saddle, scouring the smoothly rolling countryside for some geographic configuration that would help him to achieve the almost impossible: save the capital; fend off, with his inadequate means in this terrain unsuited to his irregulars, a mighty regular army. But even the crops would not cooperate: Indian corn, growing ten to fifteen feet high, changed roads into narrow channels from which the exploring eye could see nothing. Only infuriating noises came through. "The country," General Greene reported, "all resounds with the cries of the people—the enemy plunders most amazingly."[6]

Reports came in that the British fleet had sailed off with the army's baggage. This seemed so crazy that Washington would not at first believe. Then he concluded that the fleet intended, after the army had marched overland to Philadelphia, to break its own way to the city through the Delaware River defenses. "A strange maneuver indeed," Washington commented. Should the vessels be scattered by a storm, the army might be ruined.[7]

On the night of September 7 the skies throbbed with a vast, eerie display of northern lights, as the enemy, some fourteen hundred strong, began their advance from the Head of Elk. Washington wrote of his army, "The troops are in good spirits." And spurred on by British plundering, "the people of the country show an universal good will to oppose the common enemy."[8]

Now the two armies maneuvered toward each other in a cautious dance. On September 9, Washington gave his men comfort. "Such of the troops as have not been served with rum today are as soon as possible to be served with a gill a man."* For once in an admiring mood, John Adams wrote, "General Washington sets a fine example. He has banished wine from his table, and entertains his friends with rum [a New England product] and water. This is much to the honor of his wisdom, his policy, and his patriotism."[9]

By September 10, Washington had decided to make his stand behind the Brandywine River, which Howe would have to pass over to reach Philadelphia and which could only be crossed at a series of fords. Wherever the Americans placed their main army, Howe would, so Washington's spies reported, try to get across the river elsewhere and surprise a flank in a maneuver similar to that which had worked so well on Brooklyn Heights. This time Washington intended to turn the tables. The enemy strategy would include sending a detachment to make a rumpus in front of the American center, holding attention there while the flanking march achieved its circle. As soon as he was certain that the main British army was off maneuvering, Washington intended to dash across the river and beat up the detachment demonstrating in front of him.[10]

This plan dictated keeping his army as close together as possible so that it could unite for the thrust. Washington decided to place his main force behind Chad's Ford, which faced the main road along which the British would normally advance: he had his own headquarters there, although the detachment was specifically under Greene. A little back, Stephen's† and

---

* Washington had just written Congress, "I would beg leave to suggest the propriety of erecting public distilleries in different states. The benefits arising from the moderate use of strong liquor have been experienced in all armies and are not to be disputed."

† Adam Stephen had been Washington's second in command of the Virginia Regiment during the French and Indian War. The two had been close friends, but had subsequently fallen out, becoming violent political enemies. Stephen had come into the Continental Army in February 1776 as a Virginia colonel and had been promoted by Congress through brigadier to major general. Washington habitually upbraided him for disobeying orders, making false reports, etc. To take one example, "Your account of the attempt upon the enemy at Piscataway is favorable, but, I am sorry to add, widely different from those I have had from others (officers of distinction) who were of the party. I cannot by them learn that there is the least certainty of the enemy's leaving half the slain upon the field [as] you speak of in your letter of this date; that instead of an orderly retreat, it was (with the greatest part of the detachment) a disorderly rout; and that the disadvantage was on our side not the enemy's, who had notice of your coming and was prepared for it, as I expected."[11]

Stirling's divisions served as a mobile reserve. Downriver to the southeast, the fords were surrounded with declivities: they could be entrusted to the Pennsylvania militia. Upriver, Sullivan commanded the American right. He kept his strongest force between the two fords above Chad's. Weaker brigades and then mobile cavalrymen were stationed farther upstream. It was concluded that they did not have to extend very far, since local inhabitants had assured Washington (he did not know that this intelligence was wrong) that after the Brandywine had divided six miles upstream, there was no ford across the two branches for twelve miles and that anyway the going there was extremely rough. Washington assumed that if the British did march for these distant crossings, he would be notified by scouts he had ordered to ride through the area and by two commands whom he sent prowling the enemy side of the river: Colonel Bland's 1st Dragoons and some local militiamen, who were supposed to be familiar with the terrain, under Major Spear. Also across the river were Maxwell's light infantrymen, whose assignment was to harass the British as they advanced.[12]

The dawn of September 11, 1775, was heralded by a crackle of small arms sounding from the road to Chad's Ford. Washington undoubtedly rode to where he could stare across the river. Maxwell's skirmishers fell back; the British front came in view; the skirmishers crossed the ford protected by Knox's cannon; more enemy appeared; horses dragged up enemy artillery; the cannon were expertly placed in position and an artillery duel began. The British fanned out so that their flanks were hidden by what Lafayette called "the skirts of the wood"; it was impossible to tell what part of the army was actually facing the American center. Washington, with Lafayette beside him, rode through his troops to "acclamations." Such British as were visible stayed where they were. The hours passed to a somewhat desultory firing of large guns.[13]

Pacing at his headquarters or riding nearby, Washington was all eagerness for word that a British flanking movement was setting the stage for his stratagem. At about eleven in the morning, a hint came: the defenders of one of the upper fords reported considerable enemy movement on the far side of the Brandywine. Washington dispatched a messenger to cross the river, find Colonel Bland, and order him to "send up an intelligent, sensible officer immediately with a party to find out the truth." In the meanwhile, he ordered Stephen's and Stirling's divisions to fall back three and a half miles to the low hills, near Birmingham Meeting House, which contained the road along which the British flanking party would appear after they had crossed the river high up.[14]

In came a confirming dispatch: five thousand men with sixteen or eighteen fieldpieces had been seen on the far side of the river proceeding to the upper Brandywine. The news now seemed certain enough to act on. Washington ordered Greene's and Sullivan's divisions to prepare for a

[221]

charge across their respective fords against the presumably weakened British center.[15]

As Washington watched, Greene's men were about to enter the water when in came a rider with a dispatch from Sullivan. It read: "I saw some of the militia who came in this morning from a tavern called Martin's on the forks of the Brandywine. The one who told me, said he had come from thence to Welches Tavern and heard nothing of the enemy above the forks of the Brandywine, and is confident that [they] are not in that quarters." Sullivan concluded that Washington's previous "information must be wrong."[16]

Washington seems not to have been sure where the taverns mentioned were located in relation to the Valley Road on which the British had been reported, but he knew the militiamen Sullivan referred to were Spear's corps of local inhabitants who were familiar with the countryside. In any case, he could not take a chance of leaping into the maw of the main British army. He stopped the troops that were about to cross the river, and ordered Stephen's and Stirling's divisions to halt where they were. He sent only Maxwell's skirmishers to the far bank. They were to feel out the British center.[17]

Washington was awaiting further word in his office when he heard voices outside. His aides were trying to interview a man who insisted in urgent shouts that he must see General Washington. He had just been ignored by General Sullivan, he vociferated; he would have nothing further to do with subordinates. Then there appeared through Washington's door a tremendous stranger who was so dark that he looked like an Indian (the neighborhood joke was that he had been suckled by a squaw). He bellowed in great excitement that the army must retire at once or be surrounded. He had ridden up a hill on this side of the river, on the American right, and found himself face to face with a horde of redcoats. They had fired at him, but his horse was swift—and here he was to give the warning!

Washington needed to make an immediate judgment as to whether the stranger was telling the truth or had been sent by the enemy for the worst purposes. The information the man had brought was, he replied in an angry voice, impossible: he had opposite and certain information. Who was it who dared thus lie to him? The man replied that his name was Thomas Cheyney. Did not, Washington then asked, Thomas Cheyney know that spies were hanged?

The threat elicited not cringing but a torrent of indignation. According to one account, Cheyney exclaimed, "If you doubt my word, put me under guard until you can ask Anthony Wayne or Persie Frazer if I am a man to be believed. I would have you know that I have this day's work as much at heart as e'er a blood of you!"[18]

Washington concluded that the report was worth investigating. He had hardly mounted his horse before the dispatches began coming in pell-mell. There could no longer be any doubt that a major British force, led by an advance guard of about two brigades, was on the American side of the river, moving rapidly toward the patriot rear. Was this to be the Battle of Long Island over again?[19]

Washington cursed the "uncertain and contradictory" intelligence which, "notwithstanding all my pains to get the best," had prevented him from carrying out his plan of attacking across the Brandywine. It was now too late: the British could come down from the hills behind him and fall on his rear as he crossed. The best hope was to drive back the army that was advancing into his right flank. He ordered Stephen and Stirling to complete at a trot their arrested move to Birmingham Meeting House. Sullivan was to hurry his regiments there also and take command. Until the total British maneuver became clearer, Washington felt his own duty was to stay at the main position by Chad's Ford.

At five in the afternoon, he dictated a report to Congress: Sullivan had made contact with the enemy a half-hour before "and the action has been very violent ever since. It still continues. A very severe cannonade has begun here too, and I suppose we shall have a very hot evening. I hope it will be a happy one."[20]

Balancing what he saw and heard nearby with the sound behind him and the dispatches he received, Washington finally decided that the party advancing in his rear must contain the lion's share of the British army. Leaving General Lincoln to hold Chad's Ford, he ordered Greene's regiments back to the rescue and decided to go himself.

Washington galloped on his powerful charger toward the sound of battle, reaching at last a ploughed hillside on which Americans were trying in confusion and difficulty to make a stand, while ahead the whole landscape seemed alive with red- and blue-coated men whose bayonets gleamed silver over their smoking muskets. The British advance was being slowed by American cannon fire, but as the artillerymen and horses went down under British bullets, fewer and fewer cannon spoke. The side of the American line closest to Washington—the left—seemed on the point of breaking when he heard from over his shoulder the sound of many men. Weedon's brigade of Greene's division came pounding in through the copses Washington had just traversed.* [21]

As Sullivan, who was in immediate command, ordered Weedon to strengthen the crumbling American line, Washington turned his horse back

---

* Washington's statement that he saw "no part" of the action "until the retreat commenced" does not make clear the exact moment of his arrival. I here follow Freeman's informed guess.

in the direction from which more of Greene's men should be appearing: he had decided he could contribute most by "hurrying on reinforcements." Lafayette rode up to him, pale and wavering in the saddle, his leg spurting blood. Seeing a surgeon, Washington called out (or so Lafayette wrote years later), "Take care of him as if he were my son, for I love him the same."[22]

It quickly became manifest that, reinforced or not, Sullivan's men could not stand against the stronger and better-organized British force. Washington galloped to the road on the crest of the rolling hills which offered the best line of retreat. He sought in the partially wooded countryside fresh positions on which to form the troops for temporary stands. The British engineer Captain John Montresor writes of the Americans' "covering their retreat with their light troops from one patch of woodland to another, firing upon us, as we advanced into the cleared intervals, until our cannon surmounted the summits from one to another, which drove them beyond" immediate range. In the meanwhile, the five thousand British who had been facing Chad's Ford streamed across the Brandywine, forcing the troops left there under Lincoln to retire, abandoning their artillery.[23]

The Americans were in full retreat, but the British did not follow far. Their cavalry were mostly dismounted since so many horses had died during the long ocean passage to the Chesapeake. The flanking party—some eight thousand men under Cornwallis—had marched, in order to cross the Brandywine above the forks, seventeen miles on a hot day, and Howe did not send his fresher troops after the murderously retiring Americans. As we have seen, the tactics of destructive pursuit had not in the 1770's been effectively developed. Howe was to explain that "a due regard for the wounded, the importance of possessing the post at Wilmington for their accommodation and for the security of the prisoners" precluded his "following up the victory more closely."[24]

After the British thrust had faded out, Washington's concern was to reassemble his scattered army. We have a glimpse of him riding up to some officers on the Wilmington Road and asking whether they knew the way to Chester. When they answered that they did know, he ordered them to round up as many troops as possible and conduct them there.[25]

Washington himself rode into Chester about midnight. He was too fatigued to write Congress; Harrison was too "distressed." Pickering put pen on paper: "I am sorry to inform you that in this day's engagement we have been obliged to leave the enemy masters of the field." The battle was then briefly described and the opinion expressed that the enemy's casualties had been the more considerable. The draft was handed to Washington, who added to Pickering's statement, "Notwithstanding the misfortune of the day,

I am happy to find the troops in good spirits and I hope another time we shall compensate for the losses now sustained."[26]

Although efforts were continued to make those losses seem smaller than the enemy's, it remained clear that the Continental Army had failed dismally in its main objective: effectively to interpose between the British and Philadelphia. Blame was widely distributed: on a French brigadier in Sullivan's division, Preudhomme de Borre, who was suspended; on Sullivan, who would have been suspended if Washington had not intervened; on General Maxwell, who was said to have been drunk; on the Maryland colonel William Smallwood, who was said to have been drunk or mad—but, although for the moment few said it out loud, the responsibility had been clearly Washington's.[27]

"Washington," wrote Freeman in 1951, "conducted the Brandywine operation as if he had been in a daze." He had not, Freeman continued, seen to it that the ground was adequately reconnoitered so that intelligence reports could be evaluated. And he had allowed his plans to be disjointed by the report from Spear's militiamen, which Sullivan had forwarded to him, without ascertaining their specific route and the exact times at which they had traversed it. Information on these scores would have revealed that their evidence did not actually contradict the other reports that a flanking expedition was under way.[28]

Perhaps the real blame should go to Washington's lack of a staff adequate in numbers and differentiation. Although, as a former surveyor, he was especially conscious of the importance of maps, hardly any existed of the wide American countryside, and he could not command enough cartographers to draw even a small fraction of what was called for by a war of movement. His map of the Brandywine area, which he had annotated with his own hand, failed to include the information he was most crucially to need. As for reconnoitering, he and his staff rode and rode, but they had other tasks as well; and, in any case, visual exploration is no adequate substitute for good maps. That interviews with local inhabitants could turn up unreliable information, the Brandywine debacle emphasized. Furthermore, Washington had always been, whether or not he should have delegated the task, his own chief of intelligence. Lacking, in the middle of a battle, time for an evaluation of conflicting reports that would have involved securing additional information, Washington had based his judgment on the reliability of witnesses, preferring the report from Major Spear's militiamen because "the Major's rank, reputation, and knowledge of the country gave him a full claim to credit and attention."[29]

Despite charges often found in history books, Brandywine was not the Battle of Long Island all over again. The differences were, indeed, much more significant than the similarities. The new failure had been due to a slip-up, rather than a crude lack of foresight. The surprise had been only a half-surprise and Washington had been half prepared to meet it. When the unfortunate thrust had actually developed, the Continental Army had not, as before, given way to panic. They had fought like regulars, although of an American rather than a European stamp.

That there had been a change in the patriot army had not been altogether lost on the more perspicacious British officers. Some denounced Howe for having allowed Washington the time to develop his more effective force. But among many of Washington's own compatriots the fact of defeat seemed all that really mattered. Few generals in history have held on to so much prestige through as many disappointments and checks as Washington had done? Was there to be no end of failure? many an influential American now asked. And those political leaders who had long been dubious of Washington were not altogether sorry to feel that they were seeing their worst fears realized.[30]

Benjamin Rush, the Philadelphia physician-politician, was sent by Washington to treat in the British camp the prisoners captured at Brandywine. Rush returned with his eyes starry from a view of the British regulars, walked briskly into Washington's headquarters, gestured toward the ragged and dispirited patriot armies, and made comparisons that, he noted happily, "gave offense." In his notebook, Rush jotted his summary of "The state and disorders of the American army:

"1. The Commander in Chief, at this time the idol of America, governed by General Greene, General Knox, and Colonel Hamilton, one of his aides, a young man of twenty-one years of age. 2. Four major generals, Greene, Sullivan, Stirling, and Stevens [sic]. The first a sycophant to the General, speculative, without enterprise. The second weak, vain, without dignity, fond of scribbling, in the field a madman. The third a proud, vain, lazy, ignorant drunkard. The fourth a sordid, boasting, cowardly sot. The troops undisciplined and ragged, guns fired a hundred a day, pickets left five days and sentries twenty-four hours without relief; bad bread, no order, universal disgust."[31]

CHAPTER

25

The Prize: Philadelphia

PHILADELPHIA occupied the point of land at the confluence of the Delaware and Schuylkill Rivers. The Delaware was on the far side from the British advance. However, the Schuylkill, as it flowed southeastwardly from distant mountains became, once the British had overrun the Brandywine, the last major obstacle between the enemy and the American capital. An impressive stream, it could, nonetheless, be crossed at any one of a long series of fords.

Washington's first use of the Schuylkill was to dodge behind it. Although not shattered by the recent defeat, the Continental Army was staggered. Congress tried to raise morale by voting the army thirty hogsheads of rum in consideration of their "gallant behavior" at Brandywine. For two days, Washington "refreshed" his men at Schuylkill Falls.[1]

Most of the men had jettisoned their blankets and camp equipage during the battle. In the long marches of the previous six weeks, they had worn out their shoes. Philadelphia was full of goods—four speculators were said, for instance, to have three to four thousand shoes—but little was for sale. The merchants realized that if they only waited a few weeks, the city would probably be captured, and they would be paid in British gold rather than almost worthless Continental paper. In this predicament, Washington turned to his brilliant aide, Alexander Hamilton. Although (as Washington wrote) "I feel and I lament the absolute necessity," he sent Hamilton to the city with orders to requisition what the army needed, by force if necessary, and give in return certificates promising future payment. However, the merchants hid their goods so craftily that Hamilton got little. The defenders remained unshod and half-naked.[2]

Ammunition was also hard to come by, but Washington managed somehow to collect forty rounds per man. Then he took his force back across the Schuylkill at a ford a dozen miles or so above the city. The water was so high that the men had to lock arms to keep from being swept away.[3]

As the public saw it, Washington's task was to save Philadelphia, but he knew that the British had a second objective—to trap his army—and he realized that the army was more important than the city. If he interposed in front of the enemy, they would surely march around his right flank, driving him east or southeast, across the Schuylkill or down along it, in either case pinning him against the unfordable Delaware. The most he could then hope for was to flee from below Philadelphia into the southern states, away from the theater of war. To avoid catastrophe, he needed, whatever else happened, always to keep above the enemy. If they pursued, he must retreat north or west. However, he must be ready to turn at an instant if the enemy turned their march for the city: then he would attack their rear as they crossed the Schuylkill. And he must always be on the lookout in the hope that he could catch a hostile detachment at a disadvantage. Speed in maneuver would be so essential to this strategy that Washington ordered all his soldiers who still had personal possessions to leave them behind. Wishing "to share every hardship to which his army is exposed," he would, he announced, abandon all his own baggage except blankets.[4]

As Washington had foreseen, the British made for him, not the city. He retreated west, with the enemy following. After two days and twenty miles, he saw "a convenient opportunity" to strike a moving enemy column. However, he had hardly given the order and heard the first shots, when a huge rain pelted down. The enemy had canisters that kept their powder dry; his own men had not; there was nothing to do but flee. If Washington cursed the downpour, so did Howe, who mourned to see the Americans disappear "by a forced march into a very rough, mountainous country."[5]

Washington hurried his men to Warwick Furnace in the foothills of the Alleghenies, more than forty miles west and a little north of Philadelphia. He was too far from the city to defend it, but the troops were "so much fatigued" that they could not move, and there was no food with which to revive them. Washington could only halt and hope that the enemy would make another snatch at him, rather than take at once the completely exposed capital.[6]

He felt almost as helpless as a hawk that had been blinded. Required by his circumstances not to initiate strategy but to counteract enemy moves, he always relied heavily on gathering intelligence that would enable him to anticipate the enemy. Hitherto, he had found little difficulty in securing from patriot informants floods of information which, if correctly interpreted, kept him forewarned. But now the British were maneuvering in the greatest Quaker settlement in the world. Whether or not they had (as many suspected) Tory leanings, the Quakers were doctrinally opposed to war: they would have been untrue to their beliefs had they encouraged bloodshed by sending Washington information. The British were now in an area as dead to the patriot listening devices as if they had been in the middle of the ocean.[7]

From where he was, Washington could not hope to receive the news of a British effort to cross the Schuylkill in time to fall in their rear. He decided that he would have to march all the way back to the river, cross it himself, place detachments and mounted messengers at every ford, keep his main army in a central position, and try to dash to any point of enemy advance in time to catch them in the water.

Having scrambled up enough food to get the army mobile again and powder to replace in part the rain-drenched ammunition, Washington brought an end to the two-day halt. On their unshod, blistered feet again, "wet to the breast" in dripping weather, hungry and thirsty, returning east when they had so recently dashed west, the men marched with curses on their lips. The officers were confused and unhappy. Pickering remembered that "on one of these dreary nights" he found himself beside Greene as their horses were drinking from a creek. "Before I came to the army," Pickering remarked, "I entertained an exalted opinion of General Washington's military talents, but I have since seen nothing to enhance it." According to Pickering, Greene replied, "Why, the General does want decision. For my part, I decide in a moment."[8]

Still keeping north of the British, Washington took his army across the Schuylkill high up, some thirty miles as the crow flies from the city. He left behind on the enemy shore a brigade of light infantry commanded by the Pennsylvania brigadier Anthony Wayne.

Wayne, who came to be called "Mad Anthony" by his troops, was mocked by the British as "the tanner," because of his occupation before the war. A born military killer like Arnold and Light Horse Harry Lee, Wayne would shout, "I believe that sanguine God is rather thirsty for human gore!" This aggressive officer with his burning brown eyes had manifested gifts as a combat general in Canada and, since he had recently joined Washington's army, at Germantown. Now Washington wrote him, "The cutting the enemy's baggage would be a great matter, but take care of ambuscades." Wayne did not take care. He woke one morning near Paoli to find the British in his camp, operating silently with nothing but bayonets. On hearing (an exaggeration) that two hundred and forty of their compatriots had been skewered like pigs when they cried for mercy, many farm boys vanished from Washington's army.[9]

Congress was still in Philadelphia, though poised for flight, when Hamilton went on a mission across the lower Schuylkill. He happened on a large group of British and rushed a dispatch to Philadelphia: "The enemy have the means of throwing a party this night into the city." Waked from their beds at two or three in the morning, the congressmen went hightailing away. In effect, over his shoulder, John Adams cried, "Oh! Heaven grant us

[229]

one great soul! . . . One active, masterly capacity would bring order out of this confusion and save this country."[10]

As Washington prepared to reinforce the fords nearer Philadelphia to the south, an echo from the dead intelligence zone reported that the British were marching north on the other side of the river. Washington could only guess that the enemy objective was Reading, which was from a military point of view more important than Philadelphia, as it was the main army supply depot. He set his men shambling northward, and was thirty miles from the city when he learned that the enemy had countermarched, crossed the Schuylkill at a lower ford, and were advancing unopposed on the capital. Washington wearily ordered his men to halt. They had been too "harassed" by their weaving march since Brandywine, were too devoid of shoes to reach the capital and fire even one defensive shot.[11]

Howe's acceptance of Philadelphia marked his abandonment of the hope that he could taunt, lure, or trap Washington into a decisive battle; yet the final bagging of the capital was done with a strategic snap that made Washington, after his long series of inconclusive marches and vain counter-marches, seem outwitted, even foolish. And then, as if to underline Washington's humiliation, news came in of a great triumph won by the northern army under Gates.

Burgoyne's troops, as they had traversed the long wilderness route from Canada, had got farther and farther off base. Guerrillas cut their supply line; detachments (including major ones) were beaten up by bands of backwoodsmen; and the more the British floundered, the more numerous were the frontiersmen who came out to oppose them. Since Burgoyne could not winter in the forest, he had either to fight his way back to Canada, or successfully carry his slowing thrust to Albany. And now the thrust had been brought to a bloody halt when the advanced part of his army was fought to a standstill at the Battle of Freeman's Farm.

To celebrate the victory, which made him foresee "success in that quarter equal to our most sanguine wishes," Washington ordered that the men in his encampment be paraded and each served a gill of rum while thirteen cannon rumbled. However, he was as conscious as was everyone else of the contrast between Gates's successes and his own impotence. His troops, so he exhorted them, would suffer "disgrace" if they continued to allow themselves to be "outdone by their northern brethren."[12]

26

To Bring the Men to This

HOWE had sent a detachment under Cornwallis into Philadelphia, and other detachments on various strategic missions, while he himself encamped with the main British army at Germantown, a suburb that lay between the Continental Army and the city. Washington, whose intelligence had revived, was delighted to learn that Howe was publicly demonstrating his scorn of the rebels by leaving his camp unfortified. Why not stage another and larger Trenton? Washington told his associates that he would always rather give than receive an attack.[1]

It was a matter of resting his troops, inspiring them—"Covet! my countrymen and fellow soldiers! covet! a share of the glory due to heroic deeds!"— and of getting into his camp every militiaman or regular (and also shoes) that could be scratched up anywhere. By October 2, he had roughly eight thousand Continentals and three thousand militia. He estimated the British at three thousand in Philadelphia and eight thousand at Germantown.[2]

Washington had previously explored Germantown. He knew that the houses were strung on both sides of Main Street. A continuation of roads coming down parallel with the Schuylkill, this street ran through the center of the village for about a mile before it came to an important crossroad, and then continued some five miles to Philadelphia. Spies reported that the British outposts and light infantry were stationed along Main Street on the near side of the crossroad, while the bulk of Howe's army was encamped just beyond the crossing.[3]

In addition to Main Street, there were two other entrances from the north into Germantown. A series of lanes ran close to the Schuylkill and passed the crossroad at its western end. Seven miles inland, Shippack Road joined the eastern end of the crossroad.

As he had planned (and failed) to do at Trenton, Washington intended to use all the available roads. The Pennsylvania militia under General

Armstrong were to come down the riverbank lanes; one prong of the Continentals—Sullivan's division, which Washington would accompany—was to advance in the center down Main Street, and the other prong, under Greene, down Shippack Road. A further division of militia, under Small-wood and Forman, was also to start on Shippack Road, but was to take from it a wider arc into town.

The plan was that the division Washington and Sullivan led would drive the British back, while Greene, coming in from the left, would pin the fleeing enemy against the Schuylkill. The militia on the two flanks would confuse the enemy without (since they were kept separate) confusing the Continentals, and conceivably they could close a trap by coming together in a pincer movement behind the British.

Since, as at Trenton, success depended on surprise, Washington could not alarm the enemy by coming too close to them before his army took off on their purposeful march. From the starting point in Worcester Township, his own division would have to plod fifteen miles, Greene's nineteen. The whole army was to get in motion at seven P.M. on October 3; they were to be at their separate objectives, within two miles of the enemy, at two A.M. They would then halt till four A.M.; at five A.M. they were simultaneously to overrun the outposts, using only bayonets so that shots would not awake anyone who was snoozing.

Writers who dare laugh at Washington have found cause in the road directions he expected the leaders of the various groups to follow in the dark. For instance: "Smallwood and Forman to pass down the road by a mill formerly Danl. Morris and Jacob Edge's mill into the White Marsh road at the Sandy Run; thence to White Marsh church, where take the left hand road which leads to Jenkin's Tavern on the Old York Road below Armitages, beyond the seven mile stone half a mile from which turns off short to the right hand, fenced on both sides, which leads through the enemy's encampment to Germantown market house." Horsemen riding back and forth to keep all in touch were supposed, since no lights could be shown, to find the shuffling columns by bits of white paper glimmering in every hat.[4]

More or less when planned, the army sets out for its various objectives. At about one A.M., a detachment is plodding in the dark down a seemingly interminable road when, unseen by any patriot eyes, the branches in a thicket part and hostile eyes stare. After the American detachment is out of hearing, a British patrol leaps on its horses and gallops off to warn General Howe.[5] This, of course, Washington does not know.

Although Washington does everything he can to hurry the men, the column he and Sullivan lead falls irrevocably behind schedule. At two A.M., when they are supposed to begin their two hours' pause at the jumping-off place, they are still, so the guides inform Washington, far away. Before they even reach the jumping-off place, it is five-thirty, and dawn has begun to stain the sky. At about six A.M., the column is advancing along the Main Road down a hillside toward another rise called Mount Airy. It is on Mount Airy that the first British picket is supposed to be posted. However, although day should be streaming in, Washington can see only a short distance ahead. The rising sun has sucked up a heavy fog. Washington surely welcomes the fog as it increases the hope of achieving surprise, but he is soon to wonder whether the vapor was sent not by a benign "Providence" but by "some unaccountable something."[6]

Now is the time for the advance party, under the command of the Irish-French volunteer Brigadier General Thomas Conway, to remove the British pickets with bayonets. Off they go! Bayonets are silent. Washington hears from ahead shouts and then an alarming explosion: mass firing, as if an important British force had been waiting on the alert.

With, as he later admitted, "great anxiety," Washington strains his ears to hear the other columns coming up: the militia coming in on his right, or, more importantly, Greene dashing in on his left.[7] However, the sounds of firing are all concentrated ahead. The fog remains impenetrable. Washington agrees that his second in command, Sullivan, should find the battle and join it with most of the troops present, while other brigades deploy into the flanks where the militia and Greene should be. A small further force should be held motionless in reserve. Washington makes himself stay with these, accessible to all dispatches in the very center of the rear.

Sullivan's advance adds fuel to the firing. Dispatch riders and sound reveal that a major engagement, against what must be at least several regiments, is going on around Mount Airy. Cannon speak. For twenty minutes the noise swells along the corridors of mist. Then, without becoming less constant, the noise diminishes and softens.

As soon as he is sure that the enemy is retreating, Washington wishes that the sound would abate even more. He knows the men have only forty rounds apiece. He says to Pickering, "I am afraid General Sullivan is throwing away his ammunition. Ride forward, and tell him to preserve it." Pickering gallops ahead.[8]

After what seems to him a long time, Washington decides that he is justified in himself leading the regiments he has been holding in reserve slowly forward. On both sides of Main Street he sees an eerie glow: the retreating British have set on fire fields of buckwheat. Powder smoke and the smoke from this burning make the fog, as he was later to remember, "so infinitely dark." However, his heart sings within him when, having left the burning fields behind, he dimly descries on the right side of the road untended cannon, deserted tents, all the silent accouterments of a military camp. His troops have dislodged a sizable section of the British army! And the firing still recedes before him.

Then, startlingly close, directly in front, there comes a burst of musket fire. He spurs his horse, and sees a looming something. But the fog closes in, leaving his mind bewildered and his eyes aching in an effort to recover what he has seen. A rift in the fog, and he is facing a large brick mansion. Flames flickering in the cracks of shuttered windows precede the patter of bullets and sometimes the fall of a screaming man. Washington and his staff rein in. This, he is told, is the mansion of the Chew family; clearly some of the enemy fugitives have taken refuge there.

When Pickering returns from his embassy to Sullivan, he sees the rear part of the army standing still just out of range of the fire from the house. A knot of high officers on horseback are gathered around Washington and arguing: some want to bypass the house, but others agree with Knox that it would be "unmilitary to leave a castle in our rear." No one knows how many of the enemy are lurking there.

A lieutenant volunteers to carry up to the house a white flag and to demand surrender. As he approaches, a sharp report sounds; the emissary is struck and sinks in blood to the ground. Knox now has cannon in position. He lets them loose, but the balls bound obliquely from the Chew house. A command sends a platoon of infantry running for the windows. The windows flick murderously with gunfire; some men scream and fall; the others dash back out of range. More men are lined up; another command; anguishedly rushing feet, the cry of muskets, human screams; bodies drop or flee. The attempt is made again and again until the environs of the house are, as the Briton John André wrote, "strewn with a prodigious number of rebel dead."[9]

Ahead the firing has become increasingly dim with distance. Washington decides at last that he must seal off the Chew house by surrounding it with a small detachment. He orders the rest of the reserve to the support of Sullivan. Unable to any longer control his own eagerness, he gallops on faster than his troops toward the main battle.

His horse's hoofs are loud in the fog. Although the wounded stir and the dead lie still around him, there is no enemy fire. The main battle remains far ahead. To have gone so far, the British must have fled in panic.

Finally, some bullets do begin to sing out of the houses on the two sides of the twenty-yard-wide street. Washington reins in his horse, veers to one side, and comes out in a succession of backyards. Ahead of him some of Sullivan's men are pulling up a fence by the roots. A whole rank has lined up along the barrier; they press the fence backward and forward several times, and then lift the posts out of their holes. Other Continentals are firing from behind orchard trees, over flower beds and hedges. "With a degree of gallantry that did them the highest honor," Washington was to write, they were "driving the enemy from field to field."[10]

The attack has now carried almost the entire two miles to the crossroad behind which is the major camp of the British army. Looking up, Sullivan sees that his commander has not only arrived at the head of the advance, but is exposed "to the hottest fire of the enemy." Sullivan canters over and remonstrates; others join in with their voices; and Washington, to "gratify" the protesters, withdraws a short distance. But he is soon back at the very front, and there he remains.

For some time now Washington has been hearing sounds from his left—crackling like thorns under a pot, rumblings like thunder—which indicate that Greene's powerful force has come and is also pushing its way toward the British camp. Now the sound moves into the area ahead of Washington: some of Greene's men must actually be among Howe's tents! The British, Washington reasons, are "in the utmost confusion and flying before us in most places. . . . Victory," Washington decides, is "declaring herself in our favor." He is on the point of ordering the men around him to charge and drive the British back toward Philadelphia, when through the phantasmagoria of fog he descries a shocking sight.[11]

Out of the British camp, over the narrow crossroad, patriot soldiers appear at a panicky run. In the few seconds it takes Washington to comprehend this altogether unexpected happening, the panic is communicated to the troops around him. The highest hopes change without insulating pause into nightmare.

Now the fog through which he spurs his horse with all the suddenness of despair is filled with the fleeing forms of his own men: faces blackened with powder, breaths shrieking from nostrils, shoulders beating against the sides of his horse like so many huge bats. Washington shouts but they do not hear; he threatens with his sword but they do not duck; they flee like a landslide after rain has eroded a sandy cliff. And firing has broken out behind on the left flank where Washington knows there is no enemy. He can only conclude that elements of Greene's and Sullivan's divisions, confused by the foul, impenetrable vapor, have come together and are shooting at each other. Washington spurs his horse toward the new ominous sound, reflecting bitterly that "the most flattering hopes of victory" have for reasons "which as yet cannot be well accounted for" turned into a rout.[12]

The fratricidal battle quickly ceases, and the men stop running as soon as they escape from the immediate proximity of the enemy. But Washington's army is now in such confusion that his one thought is to get the men, as quickly as possible, out of danger. He orders a rapid retreat, the objective being Pennypacker's Mill at a distance of twenty miles. (Should it successfully get there, the army will, in addition to fighting for two and a half hours, have marched, since the previous afternoon, more than thirty-five miles.)

At first, fear of immediate pursuit spurs the men, but it eventually becomes clear that the enemy is not following in strength.* Then the monotony of exhausted movement is only broken by occasional false rumors

---

* Howe did not wish to risk his troops in a country "so strongly enclosed and covered with woods."[13]

of an incursion of British cavalry. Some officers, suffering from "almost an unspeakable fatigue," fall asleep in their saddles. Others have such recourse to their flasks that General Stephen and two lieutenants are to be subsequently cashiered for drunkenness. The ditches are full of sleeping men.[14]

His own head nodding over his horse's, Washington tries wearily to work out in his mind what has happened. Even when, his columns safe at Pennypacker's Mill, he can himself lie down in his camp bed, he cannot sleep. His long body stirs feverishly as his mind toils to discover why "in the midst of the most promising appearances . . . the troops began suddenly to retreat."

He is inclined to blame the fog, which, "by concealing from us the true situation of the enemy, obliged us to act with more caution and less expedition than we could have wished, and gave the enemy time to recover from the effects of our first impression; and what was still more unfortunate, it served to keep our different parties in ignorance of each other's movements, and hindering their acting in concert. It also occasioned them to mistake one another for the enemy, which I believe, more than anything else contributed to the misfortune which ensued." Another difficulty was that Sullivan's division ran out of ammunition.[15]

That the complication of the original plan (neither of the militia wings ever reached the battlefield and Green's column was late because it had lost its way) did as much as the fog to keep his parties from acting in concert, Washington never stated. Nor, strangely enough, did he regard as more than an "annoyance" the British occupation of the Chew house, of which historians have made so much. The resulting sound of firing behind the lines had been shocking to the advance troops. It had made Wayne, who commanded on the left of Sullivan's thrust, hold back, and had lured Stephen, in command on Green's right, to come blundering cross-country and get into a skirmish with Wayne and the patriot besiegers of the Chew house.[16]

Three days after the battle, Washington wrote Congress that "every account confirms the opinion I first entertained" that his army had been on the very point of victory when they fled. "The tumult, disorder, and even despair which it seems had taken place in the British army was scarcely to be paralleled; and it is said, so strongly did the ideas of a retreat prevail, that Chester was fixed on as their rendezvous" after they had been driven from Philadelphia.[17]

Washington was to learn better. Three years later, he told some French officers, "This famous day could have had the most unfortunate consequences if the English (and Cornwallis especially) had profited by their advantages."[18]

When, during the night before the battle, Howe had been notified that

Americans were on the march, he had assumed that his scouts had seen "a mere flying party. . . . I did not expect," he remembered, "the enemy would have dared to approach after so recent a defeat as that at Brandywine." Thus, he alerted only those light troops who, in making the first stand, had startled Washington by emitting so well-organized a sound. After finding themselves overpowered by a much superior American force, the light troops had retreated very rapidly, and they did create some confusion when they came pelting into Howe's camp. However, and it was to this Washington referred when speaking to the French officers, Howe was able to rally to the counterattack regiments that had not yet been engaged, while Cornwallis came pelting in from Philadelphia with several thousand additional men. The Americans, particularly as many were without ammunition, may well have saved their skins by fleeing when they did.[19]

Washington attributed to the British fantastic losses—"the lowest say it was 1500 killed and wounded, other 2000 and some as high as 2500"*—and eventually fixed his own at 1000, including deserters. He wrote that his troops had not been "the least dispirited" and had "gained what all young troops gain by being in actions." They had, in addition, been convinced "that when they made an attack, they can confuse and rout even the flower of the British army with the greatest ease." Yet Washington could not deny that the whole affair had been "unfortunate"—the Americans had fled and the British had not been dislodged from the capital.[20]

In Europe, it seemed almost inconceivable that an untrained rabble would attack a mighty regular army so effectively and so soon after they had been defeated. (Germantown had followed Brandywine by only twenty-three days.) The French foreign minister, Vergennes, when discussing a possible alliance with American commissioners, stated that "nothing struck him so much" as the Battle of Germantown: "To bring an army, raised within a year, to this, promised anything." However, Congressman Burke of North Carolina blamed the "miscarriage" on "the usual source: want of abilities in our superior officers and want of order and discipline in our army."[21]

And, in that autumn of 1777, Germantown had an unfortunate backlash. When planning the attack, Washington had strengthened his army by calling in, over Putnam's widely broadcast protests, several regiments from that general's defensive command on the Hudson Highlands. Almost instantly, some British reinforcements sailed into New York, and the commander there, Sir Henry Clinton, decided to take pressure off Burgoyne by attacking the Highlands. He completely outmaneuvered Putnam, capturing the forts that blocked the Hudson. As far as American defenses were concerned, the river was opened to a British advance from New York City

---

* The official British figure was 534.

that would threaten the rear of Gates's army while the front was still engaging Burgoyne.[22]

Washington admitted that "this stroke would have perhaps proved fatal to our northern affairs" had not Gates, with a major assist from Benedict Arnold, defeated Burgoyne on Bemis Heights in a second battle. It now seemed too late for Clinton to prevent the complete capture of the British northern army.*[23]

Despite his elation at another major victory in the north, Washington continued to feel humiliated by the contrast between Gates's achievements and his own. He again admonished his troops to remember that they were "the Grand American Army. . . . What shame then and dishonor will attend us if we suffer ourselves in every instance to be outdone."[24]

Did Washington already feel the girths weakening that held him in the saddle of the top command? Those who feared or disliked or distrusted His Excellency were pleased to see rising in the military firmament a second star that promised to rival or even outshine the man who had singly dominated the skies for so long. John Adams wrote that he was glad Burgoyne's predicament was "not immediately due to the Commander in Chief nor to the southern troops. . . . If it had been, idolatry and adulation would have been unbounded, so excessive as to endanger our liberties."[25]

Rush wrote Adams that Gates's army was like "a well-regulated family," while Washington's "imitation of an army" was like "an unformed mob." He asked Adams to compare the "characters" of the two generals: Gates "on the pinnacle of military glory, exulting in the success of schemes planned with wisdom and executed with vigor and bravery." Washington "outgeneralled and twice beaten, obliged to witness the march of a body of men only half their number through 140 miles of a thick-settled country, forced to give up a city the capital of a state. . . . If our Congress can witness these things with composure and suffer them to pass without an inquiry, I shall think we have not shook off monarchical principles, and that, like the Israelites of old, we worship the work of our own hands."[26]

---

* Actually, Clinton, who felt that the force Howe had left him was too weak both to hold New York City and advance up the Hudson, had never intended to do anything more than create a diversion by attacking Highland forts.

V

Plots Against Washington

27

George Washington Eclipsed

O UT of the bloody battlefield at Germantown a phoenix had risen who was not at all to Washington's liking. Earlier in 1777, when he was being overrun with French volunteers, Washington had selected among them, for cautious recommendation to Congress, Thomas Conway, largely because the Irish-born French colonel spoke English. After Congress had made Conway a brigadier, he never stopped talking. To Benjamin Rush, Conway described his own role at Germantown all the more volubly because, although one of the most junior brigadiers, he wanted to be made a major general, and wished Congress to be properly frightened by his threat to resign if immediate promotion were denied him.

Deeply impressed, Rush wrote his friend John Adams: "General Conway wept for joy when he saw the ardor with which our troops pushed the enemy from hill to hill." But when he saw Washington "passive" at having his orders countermanded by "an officer low in command . . . his distress and resentment exceeded all bounds. For God's sake, do not suffer him to resign! He seems to possess [General] Lee's knowledge and experience without any of his oddities and vices. He is, moreover, the idol of the whole army."[1]

Conway had led the first charge at Germantown. His division commander, Sullivan, who considered that Conway's "knowledge of military matters in general far exceeds any officer we have," had been much impressed, but not so Washington. Washington had, indeed, considered court-martialing Conway for attacking in the front instead of the flank and being "a considerable time separated from his brigade."[2]

When seen in profile, Conway's features were shaped like a half-moon: receding forehead, jutting aquiline nose, and receding chin. There was, however, a firm bump on that chin. He pulled his mouth in like a prissy governess, had popeyes, and wore on his face a look of irritable elegance. Washington hated him as he hated few men his whole life long.

General Thomas Conway, engraving reproduced in James Bennett Nolan's
George Washington and the Town of Reading in Pennsylvania.

Exiled from Ireland with his Catholic family at the age of six and enrolled in the French army at fourteen, Conway professed no allegiance except to the military life and his own star. Washington, who believed that the strength of the American cause lay in its justice, was disgusted to hear the Irish-Frenchmen talk as a Hessian might. Conway stated frankly that he had come to America "for to increase my fortune and that of my family." He wished to be made a brigadier on his return to France, which meant he would have to be a major general in the inferior American service.[3]

What many another foreign officer thought but kept more or less to himself, Conway openly expressed. Convinced that Washington was too ignorant in military matters to have any real competence, he believed that only the American's stupidity and anti-French prejudice kept him from following exactly the advice of the real professionals. Among these he cast himself as the most experienced, "the elder officer you have in your army." At Councils of War he expostulated so endlessly about what his former chief, Frederick the Great, would have done, that he irritated the Rhode Island brigadier James M. Varnum into shouting, "There are some men in this continent who know more about maneuvers than the King of Prussia." Conway commented, "This made me dumb." It was the only time he ever was dumb.[4]

Conway was cringingly submissive to Lafayette, whose influence at the French Court he feared, but he broadcast his opinion that Washington's "talents for command" were "very miserable indeed." Washington's reaction was to believe that Conway's "ambition and great desire to be puffed off as one of the first officers of the age could only be equaled by the means which he used to obtain them." When Washington would not indulge him to the detriment of the service, he became "my inveterate enemy," practicing every damaging intrigue because of the "absurd resentment of disappointed vanity." In particular, Washington resented his "reprobating a measure which did not succeed that he himself advised me to."[5]

Early in November 1777, Washington heard rumors that Congress, afraid that so valuable an officer would carry out his threat of resigning, intended to promote Conway over the heads of the many brigadiers who were his seniors.[6]

As Washington angrily meditated on this threat, Putnam relayed from the Hudson Highlands an unofficial report that Burgoyne had actually surrendered to Gates.* Washington forwarded the good news to President Thomas

---

* Much has been made in the history books of the fact that the British ministry neglected to notify Howe that Burgoyne was going to march down from Canada to the northern Hudson Valley. It is usually assumed that had he known in time, Howe would have moved north to converge with the other British column. Although this seemed to Washington the reasonable strategy, Howe might well not have gone. Since Burgoyne's army was designed to be strong enough to take care of itself, Howe would have been

Wharton of Pennsylvania, adding, "It remains for us to play a counterpart, and to enable me to do it effectually, I hope the whole force of your state will pour forth."[7]

Washington turned from commenting on Gates's victory to venting his indignation against Conway's proposed promotion in a letter to Richard Henry Lee which was one of the most violent he had ever written a congressman. To raise a man without "conspicuous merit" over the heads of the other brigadiers would, he warned, "give a fatal blow to the existence of the army." Though his officer corps did not dispute the authority of Congress to make appointments, "they will judge the propriety of acting under them. In a word, the service is so difficult, and every necessary so expensive, that almost all our officers are tired out. Do not, therefore, afford them good pretexts for retiring." Every day he had to dissuade several who came to him for that purpose from going home. He conjured Congress that they should not, by a "real act of injustice, compel some good officers to leave the service, and thereby incur a train of evils unforeseen and irremediable.

"To sum up the whole, I have been a slave to the service; I have undergone more than most men are aware of to harmonize so many discordant parts; but it will be impossible for me to be of any further service if such insuperable difficulties are thrown in my way."[8]

Did this passage contain a threat that Washington might resign if Conway were promoted? It certainly could be read that way. During the French and Indian War, Washington had often growled that he would go home, and twice had actually done so. But during the Revolution he had never before, whatever had been his privately expressed dreams of retirement, even implied to a congressman that he was considering such a move. He could not now have given the hint to a more unfortunate correspondent, since Lee

---

open to the charge of interfering in a rival commander's campaign. Furthermore, his appearance would not have radically altered the balance of power, since if he had gone Washington would have gone too, reinforcing Gates as he reinforced Burgoyne.

Hindsight tells us that the Burgoyne expedition was doomed before it started, since he was sent hundreds of miles from his base through wild country suited to American fighters where he could not rationally hope either to keep his supply line open or live off the land. Even if he had reached Albany, it is doubtful that he could have been supplied. Had Howe's army been there too, the problem would have been the more grievous unless the British could have made the Hudson into an open highway.

Washington feared British access to all parts of the Hudson because this would have enabled them to disrupt his own supply lines, if only by the destruction of all patriot boats that could not be kept hidden from British raiders. However, the British would have had a hard time themselves making free use of the river. This was most dramatically demonstrated when, in 1776, the *Phoenix* and the *Rose* had been driven from the Tappan Zee, the very widest section of the Hudson, by fire rafts. To keep the river safe for wind-powered ships that could at any moment be becalmed, the British would have had to establish posts on both banks that could control the whole 150 miles from New York City to Albany. What an opportunity for cutting them up piecemeal this would have given the Washington of Trenton and Princeton!

belonged with Rush and others to a political group who sincerely believed that the cause would do better under a new commander in chief. Lee must have noticed the clear implication that Conway could be used as a lever to pry George Washington loose.

In replying to Washington, Lee stated that he doubted Congress would take any action "whilst it is likely to produce the evil consequences you suggest." However, the "advocates for the measure" stated that Conway's promotion would "be very agreeable to the army, whose favorite Mr. Conway was asserted to be."[9]

The day after Washington wrote his angry letter to Lee, corroboration, though still unofficial, came in for Burgoyne's surrender. "Let every face brighten," Washington's general orders read, "and every heart expand with grateful joy and praise to the supreme disposer of all events, who has granted us this signal success." After the chaplains had had time to deliver "short discourses," the cannon in the artillery park would fire (did Washington smile to think how this would drown out long-winded sermonizers?) thirteen salutes.[10]

Feeling a need to justify himself to his own state, Washington wrote Governor Henry of Virginia that, because of the reinforcements he had sent north and the apathy of the Quakers and the Tories in Pennsylvania, his numbers (propaganda announcements to the contrary notwithstanding) had in this campaign always been inferior to Howe's. On the other hand, Gates had possessed many times Burgoyne's force. Had Washington not sent part of his own army to help rescue the north, and had the same spirit prevailed in Pennsylvania as in New England and northern New York, "we might before this have had General Howe nearly in the situation of General Burgoyne, with this difference, that the former would never have been out of reach of his ships, while the latter increased his danger every step he took."[11]

Washington's emotions were in a turmoil. He did his best to be fair to Gates, discountenancing (as Wayne noted) those of his officers who were inspired by envy to belittle Gates's achievements. Washington did welcome reports that greatly exaggerated the strength of his rival's victorious army; but he took on his own shoulders the blame of the aspect of the surrender for which Gates was most criticized.[12]

At the Saratoga Convention, Gates had agreed that the surrendered troops could return to England on condition that they never serve again in America. Not only would this enable them to replace other troops who could be sent across the ocean, but it was known that during the Seven Years' War, George II had, as soon as he got his troops back, repudiated a similar proviso ratified at the Convention of Klosterzeven. Washington was among the patriots who feared that if Burgoyne's troops were once put on transports, they would sail to New York. (This was, in fact, the British plan.) "Do they not declare, many of them," Washington asked, "that no faith is to be held with rebels?" Washington publicly regretted the provision in the convention: he urged that every subterfuge be used to keep from abiding by it; but he admitted that Gates had been forced to the unfortunate agreement by the British capture of the Highlands forts he had himself weakened. That Gates's rear was open to attack placed Gates "in a critical situation" that "would not allow him to insist on a more perfect surrender."[13]

Although Howe had reacted to the Battle of Germantown by withdrawing his entire army behind the fortifications he was erecting around Philadelphia, the situation had not yet solidified to a point where Washington could no longer hope to achieve something before winter closed the campaign. The fleet that had sailed around from the Chesapeake with the British baggage had been able to penetrate up the Delaware only as far as Chester. The navy could not join the army; the army was cut off from the rest of the British Empire until the enemy could overcome fortifications planned by French engineers under Colonel Duportail. Fort Mifflin in Pennsylvania had opposite it on the New Jersey shore Fort Mercer. Chevaux-de-frise were sunk in the channel between them, and gunboats hovered above the obstruction waiting to shoot across the barrier with heavy cannon. Effective as these defenses were, they could not be expected to hold indefinitely. However, they might not be taken without land as well as naval action, and in this Washington's last opportunity of the year lay.

He realized that to attack any strong force sent out from Philadelphia against the forts would involve serious risks, since the countryside was flat and the patriots could, if defeated, be pinned against either the Delaware or the ocean. Washington would need more soldiers than he had, and, for once, it seemed clear how he would get them. Gates should return the troops Washington had lent the northern campaign, and also send the many other regiments that would not be needed up north since Burgoyne had surrendered. He wrote urging that the troops be dispatched at once, but hoped to be notified that Gates had already started them efficiently on their way. If the reinforcements did not arrive soon, Washington's opportunity would vanish with the fall of the Delaware forts.

However, as Washington waited eagerly from day to day, from one week to the next, no word of any sort came in from Gates: not even a confirmation of the surrender. It seemed very strange. Convinced that it had been his subordinate's duty to send him, at the very least, "the earliest authentic advice of the victory," Washington had moments when he wondered whether the reports he had received were not a mirage, whether after all no surrender had actually taken place. He burst out to Richard Henry Lee that he could not "help complaining most bitterly of General Gates's neglect," especially as troops from the north might "give an important turn to operations in this quarter."[14]

Sixteen days after the presumed surrender, Washington decided to send Hamilton up north to find out what was going on. He entrusted to his aide a reproachful letter to Gates and a list of the twenty regiments he desired. Suspecting the worst, he empowered Hamilton to require, in the name of the Commander in Chief, that the regiments "be immediately put in march to join this army."[15]

Hamilton met, coming down the Hudson Valley on their way to join Washington, Morgan's riflemen, a Continental brigade, and some militia—a much smaller force than the Commander in Chief desired. In the Highlands, he found regiments Gates had sent to reinforce Putnam. As the aging Connecticut general pouted, Hamilton ordered these on to Pennsylvania. Then the aide proceeded to Albany, where he found that Gates had sent most of his militia home but was holding on to three Continental regiments, two more than Washington intended to leave in that quiet sector.

From Hamilton in Albany, Washington received letters that were both discouraging and frightening. Discouraging, because he reported Gates's insistence that since the British still held the Highlands forts and could dash upriver from New York, he needed a strong army to protect New England and guard the stores in Albany. Frightening, because Hamilton had decided that it would be "dangerous" to insist on anything "diametrically opposite [to] the opinion of a gentleman whose successes have raised him into the highest importance," and who "has won the entire confidence of the eastern [New England] states" plus "influence and interest elsewhere." Hamilton had agreed to Gates's relinquishing one brigade instead of two. He was convinced that Gates would not, if he thought he could get away with it, send a single man.[16]

Gates, who was a more noisy than resolute controversialist, in the end gave Hamilton more troops than he had at first agreed to. However, Washington's aide had correctly judged Gates's mood of insubordination. The housekeeper's son who had been driven from the British army by his equivocal social position had been flooded with self-satisfaction by his victory over that army. If "old England is not by this taught a lesson of humility," he wrote his wife, "then she is an obstinate old slut." As for Washington's idea that the force outside Philadelphia was the "Grand American Army" led by the Commander in Chief, Gates no longer subscribed to it. He saw two armies under equal commanders, the northern and the southern, and foresaw that he might, for the good of the cause, have to take over both. Did he not receive letters like that from Philadelphia (it was unsigned but probably from Congressman John Lovell) which stated that Washington's army "will be totally lost unless you come down and collect the virtuous band who wish to fight under your banner and with their aid save the southern hemisphere"?[17]

Discussing the matter with his ingratiating young aide, Colonel James Wilkinson, Gates had decided to underline the situation by sending no official notification of the surrender to Washington.[18] As became an independent commander, Gates would report only to Congress. However, even Congress now loomed so small in the vision of the conqueror of Burgoyne that when he entrusted the dispatch to Wilkinson, he did not urge the twenty-one-year-old to hurry.

Wilkinson, whose handsome if suety face slanted forward from a high, receding forehead to a mightily protruding chin, had a soft outside and a hard inside; he was to play a long, equivocal role in American history. Now he made a leisurely trip, playing the role of conquering hero in many a taproom.

At Reading, the last major stop before York, Pennsylvania, where Congress was sitting, Wilkinson found that the large and select society of refugees from Philadelphia was alive with criticisms of Washington. General Mifflin was there, "considerably malcontent," according to a contemporary memoir, "and apparently not high in favor at [Washington's] headquarters." Mifflin said that it was common gossip that Washington was a mere puppet in the hands of Greene, who was in turn unpatriotic and incompetent.[19]

As it was raining, Wilkinson decided that Congress could wait another day. He took "pot-luck" dinner with General Stirling. In this household, he was among Washington partisans, but, as the rain kept coming down, he stayed late and "in the warmth of social intercourse" (as he later put it) he took a great fancy to Stirling's aide, Major William McWilliams. He told McWilliams of a letter from Conway to Gates, which Gates had read aloud to some of his officers and which listed thirteen reasons, many to Washington's discredit, for the defeat at Brandywine. After Wilkinson had weaved off, Stirling wrote a letter to Washington.[20]

In the meanwhile, Washington, although still unreinforced, had moved his army closer to the enemy. His new camp at Whitemarsh, which covered "two commanding hills," was only twelve miles from Philadelphia. Headquarters was a farmhouse so simple that the Commander in Chief's staff spent the nights, as Washington had done when a frontier surveyor, lying on the floor in a tight circle around the fire. Having not recovered their baggage since Brandywine, they had one tin plate apiece.[21]

The packet arrived from Stirling. Opening it, Washington came on two sheets of paper. One read: "The enclosed was communicated by Colonel Wilkinson to Major McWilliams. Such wicked duplicity of conduct I shall always think it my duty to detect." The other read: "In a letter from General Conway to General Gates, he says, 'Heaven has been determined to save your country, or a weak general and bad councillors would have ruined it.' "[22]

Up until the moment that he read these words, Washington (as he later remembered) had assumed that Conway and Gates were strangers to each other. The discovery that the two officers—one hateful and the other insubordinate—were not only correspondents, but that he himself was the subject of their "confidential letters" came to him as a revelation. What he had previously assumed were unrelated menaces were, he reasoned, aspects of a single plot to destroy his reputation. His enemies intended to demonstrate him as incompetent by reducing his army to impotence. Gates would keep every soldier he could, while Conway was demanding promotion as a means to force the resignations of what officers Washington actually had.[23]

After a night during which rage and frustration surged through his powerful frame, Washington sat down and wrote Conway:

"Sir: A letter I received last night contained the following paragraph: 'In a letter from General Conway to General Gates, he says, "Heaven has been determined to save your country, or a weak general and bad councillors would have ruined it."'

"I am, sir, your humble servant, George Washington."[24]

If Washington expected this icy epistle to cow the Irish Frenchman, he was disappointed. To headquarters came a reply that glowed with pleasure in the controversy. Conway doubted that the expression "weak general" had "slipped" from his pen, but if it had, he had only been referring to Washington's "excess of modesty." Although such an "inquisition" as Washington was trying to establish concerning letters between his officers was a proceeding "of which there are few instances in despotic and tyrannical governments," Conway would be willing to let Washington see his letter to Gates. But Washington should beware of how he would figure in an account of the war which Conway intended to publish in France.[25]

Into headquarters at long last came a brace of letters from Gates. He stated that he would in the future report directly to Congress: he was sure that Congress would keep Washington informed. He expressed resentment at having a young whippersnapper like Hamilton sent to him with the power to give Washington's orders, and referred to the troops now on the march—he gave the number as five thousand—as being "succor" generously sent from the northern to the southern army.[26]

Washington was now all expectations. If the reinforcements* arrived immediately, the year's last opportunity might yet be grasped.

Due largely to a cocky disdain for American soldiers which the Hessians seemed unable to get over, an attempt on October 22 to take Fort Mercer in a combined land and sea raid had ended in disaster for the enemy: two

---

* To add insult to intrigue, Putnam was holding, despite the orders relayed by Hamilton, all the troops he could in the Highlands. The superannuated general had the idea that, in a vaguely planned attack on New York, he could make better use of them, than could Washington.

British ships were lost and Washington estimated the Hessian casualties as four hundred out of twelve hundred engaged. Finding some comfort in this little victory, Washington had referred to it in his letters over and over again.[27]

The British then mounted a careful siege of Fort Mifflin. Soon the commander there wrote Washington that the fort had become so battered that it should be abandoned. However, in his revived hope that he would be reinforced from the northern army, Washington sent back a plea for the men to hold on "to the last extremity." Blood fountained from many a mortal wound in patriot flesh, but it was too late. On the night of November 15–16, Fort Mifflin finally fell. This enabled the British to breach the chevaux-de-frise and drive away the American row galleys.[28]

Fort Mercer was now ready to be shaken from the vine. For this purpose, two thousand men under Cornwallis came out of Philadelphia, crossed the Delaware, and marched through lower New Jersey to join with some further British troops that had been landed from New York at the mouth of the river. Before this overpowering force, Fort Mercer, that last block in the river, would be helpless unless rescued.

Washington leaped at the report that several thousand of the reinforcements expected from the north were at last approaching through New Jersey. He hurried Greene's division over the river in the hope that they could cooperate with the newcomers in an attack on Cornwallis. But Greene could not find the new arrivals in time, and Fort Mercer had to be evacuated. On November 22, British sails appeared at long last in the Philadelphia harbor.

Washington's army had kept the British army and navy apart for almost two months after Philadelphia had fallen, yet what he had done seemed to the public little more than the delaying of a total defeat. He was informed that, while Gates's praises were on every tongue, "it is a matter of amazement" that, with the troops propaganda had attributed to him, he had done so little.[29]

Washington harbored a brief dream of attacking Philadelphia while Cornwallis's detachment was still below. The main army would dash overland from Germantown, while Greene would cross the Delaware from New Jersey in small boats. With Duportail, Washington rode around the outskirts of the city. They stared through field glasses in the crisp, clear winter sunlight. The French engineer finally ruled that five thousand men could hold the British fortifications against any imaginable force. Washington could only resolve that however "distressing" it was to be unable to answer "the expectations of the world without running hazards which no military principles can justify . . . patience and a steady perseverance in such measures as appear warranted by sound reason and policy must support us against . . . censure."[30]

Criticism of Washington was coming in from another quarter as the result of a controversy with the civil authorities in which each took the position that would normally be expected of the other. Supply had completely broken down. When Washington complained to Congress that his army was starving and freezing as the winter snowstorms began, Congress urged him to take what he needed at bayonet point. The justification was that the inhabitants near his camp were Tories and Quakers, and, in any case, the British would get their hands on whatever Washington failed to requisition. But the British could buy, while Washington would have to grab. Taking, as he had previously tried to do, from urban speculators was, he believed, one thing—from farmers was another. However convenient it might seem at the moment, it would confirm Tories and undermine the faith of Whigs. Furthermore, ordering the troops to requisition encouraged them to undertake on their own authority "plundering and licentiousness."

Washington continued to call on Congress for supplies, and Congress retaliated with "a resolve which," so the Massachusetts delegate James Lowell crowed to Samuel Adams, "was meant to rap a demi-G—[God] over the knuckles." Washington was formally accused of "too great delicacy in exerting military authority."[31]

There being no other way out, he was in the end forced to obey Congress and take from the farmers, but with continuing protests and foreboding. Why did not the state governments undertake the task? he queried. He dreaded the results of encouraging "the prevalent jealousy of military power" which might undermine the support of the army altogether.[32]

Howe, who had a taste for final flourishes (and may have been informed of the pressure being put on Washington to save his reputation and perhaps his command by a fight), began maneuvering in front of the American lines on December 5. Washington rode around as if half demented in an effort to find some opening in the British positions, but he could find none and was not demented enough to attack at his own disadvantage. On December 9, Howe took his army back into Philadelphia and began putting it to bed for the winter.[33]

Where was the Continental Army to go to bed? "The General," Washington announced in his general orders, "ardently wishes it were now in his power to conduct the troops into the best winter quarters." However, as he explained to his weary men, if the army sought comfort in the villages of interior Pennsylvania, they would leave quantities of fertile country as a granary to be ravaged by the enemy. Furthermore, the villages were already crowded with "virtuous citizens" who had sacrificed all their possessions by fleeing from Philadelphia: "To their distresses, humanity forbids us to add."

The troops must build, at the approaches to Philadelphia, their own villages, construct for themselves out of raw wood "the best shelter in our power. With activity and diligence," Washington assured them, "huts may be erected that will be warm and dry." Washington ("our truly Republican general," as Laurens called him) announced that he would set the example by living himself in one of the improvised huts.[34]

Scouts examined the countryside to find the least unlikely spot, inhabitants were interviewed, and then, in mid-December, the army was on the march through snow. Washington had offered ten dollars to the "artist" who could "produce the best substitute for shoes made of raw hides." However, all the ingenuity the army could muster did not blot out that trail of bloody footsteps which the shivering men left behind in reality and also in ever-continuing American legend. Led by a general whose right to command was about to be vigorously assaulted, the rabble in arms approached bleak hillsides whose name was ever to be synonymous in the United States with hardship. Washington began heading his letters "Valley Forge."[35]

28

Make Washington Resign

THE man who was now to emerge as George Washington's most dangerous enemy had long seemed his friend. When Washington had first left Philadelphia to assume his command of the Continental Army, a crowd had gathered outside his lodging to watch him depart. He was about to mount his horse when an elegantly uniformed figure ran lithely toward him, knelt with an elegant swoop, and held his stirrup. As the crowd cheered this histrionic gesture, the startled Washington looked down to see smiling up at him the handsome, mobile face of Major Thomas Mifflin, the Philadelphia politician and member of Congress whom he had just appointed his aide-de-camp.[1]

As Washington had joined his army at Cambridge, Mifflin had been at his side; the orator could not forget that, with Reed, he had inaugurated Washington's staff. And he had proved very useful in the twin capacities of businessman and inspirational speaker. Washington had soon appointed him quartermaster general, and when he had resigned that post out of a desire to smell more gunpowder, everything had gone so badly in the quartermaster department that he had to be called back. "There is not another man in the army," Washington explained, "who could carry on the business upon the present large plan."[2]

His ability to inflame *"their* passions," as he put it, made Mifflin a brilliant recruiting officer, particularly in Pennsylvania where his personal popularity was great. He had made a great contribution to the Trenton-Princeton campaign by scooping out with his silver tongue much of the militia that marched and fought. At the start of the 1777 campaign, he had been largely responsible for the crowd of Pennsylvanians who had appeared on the far side of the Delaware when Howe had made his feint in New Jersey.[3]

Before Washington was chosen Commander in Chief, when Pennsylvanians were first persuaded to support New England, John Adams had

Thomas Mifflin, detail of portrait by John Singleton Copley. Courtesy of the Historical Society of Pennsylvania.

said of Mifflin that he "ought to have been a general, for he has been the animating soul of the whole." Mifflin had kept his close connection with the Adams–Richard Henry Lee–Benjamin Rush wing in Congress; other politicians admired him as a brilliant manipulator of men; Congress elected him first brigadier and then major general. Incommensurate with his role as quartermaster general, these ranks implied important commands, but the very temperament that enabled him to address crowds "most pathetically" made Mifflin slightly ridiculous as a soldier. Abigail Adams describes how, when he had heard some shots, he "flew about as though he would have raised the whole army."[4]

Mifflin could not at first understand why Washington did not give him combat assignments and lean on him for military advice—and then it became manifest to him that the Commander in Chief had been hypnotized by a snake in the grass, that latecomer to his councils, Nathanael Greene. When Greene's bad advice brought on the catastrophe at Fort Washington, Mifflin, who was convinced that he had known better, expected Washington to turn with relief to him, but, so he wrote, "the ear of the Commander in Chief" continued to be "exclusively possessed by Greene," who was "neither the most wise, the most brave, nor the most patriotic of counselors."[5]

As Mifflin was becoming increasingly dissatisfied, Washington's passion for horses induced the commander to write Mifflin, as quartermaster general, one of the few self-seeking letters he penned in the entire war: Should some cavalry horses become so worn down that they would have to be sold, he would like to buy fifty or a hundred mares to put on his farms. He did not wish, Washington continued, any step taken that was not for the good of the service, yet he would prefer not having his name mentioned, "well knowing that the most innocent and upright actions are often misconstrued." Although Mifflin (as Washington had at one time suspected and he had denied) made purchases in a way that helped feather his own nest, yet this letter, which seemed to show the Commander in Chief coming down to his own level, could hardly have raised Washington in his eyes.[6]

Things had come to a head when, during the July before Philadelphia fell, Washington's army was in that wild pass through the Jersey Highlands, the Clove, oscillating back and forth as intelligence reported that Howe was going up the Hudson to join Burgoyne, or through the ocean to Philadelphia. When Greene argued that protecting Philadelphia was "an object of far less importance than the North [Hudson] River" and the communications across it with New England, Mifflin replied that Greene was "indifferent to the fate of Philadelphia" because he was a provincial New Englander. Greene's comment was sarcastic: "Philadelphia," he sneered, "is the American Diana" to be "preserved at all events." Washington's ruling was between the extremes—he would wait till Howe showed his hand and then try to counter whatever move the enemy made; but Mifflin, whose property and heart were in Pennsylvania, was now too high in the ropes to accept this compromise. He insisted that Washington march at once to the defense of Philadelphia, and when Washington refused, he announced that he was sick, too "indisposed" to stay with the army.* He rode off to Philadelphia where, according to Greene, he "raised a prodigious clamor," excoriating Washington's behavior and Greene's role in it.[7]

During the rest of the campaign, during the long, tiring marches that carried the army from New York to the Chesapeake, at the Battle of Brandywine, during the loss of Philadelphia and the Battle of Germantown, and subsequently at Valley Forge, Washington, as he put it, "experienced the greatest difficulties and inconveniences for want of a person of activity and authority at the head of the [quartermaster] department." Furthermore, his lack of success in rallying the Pennsylvanians was to some extent caused by the way the famous local recruiter had skulked and expressed his disapproval of the army. Paine believed that Philadelphia could have been saved had Mifflin exerted himself. Mifflin, however, remained full of outrage. He fled with other refugees from the city to Reading, and sent in to Congress his resignation both as major general and quartermaster. Congress not only begged him to stay on as major general, but substituted for his role as quartermaster a more influential post.[8]

In response to Washington's requests that some "new expedient" be found to relieve the army's distresses, Congress had decided to reorganize the Board of War, changing it from one of their innumerable committees to an executive organization made up with men of special qualifications in the realm of military supply. Richard Henry Lee, having secured Washington's delighted approval for the change, saw to it that his friend Mifflin was appointed to the board. As for the post Mifflin had deserted, Congress made no effort to fill it, leaving Washington to struggle on the snowy hillsides of Valley Forge without a quartermaster.[9]

His appointment to the Board of War cured Mifflin's "indisposition" in a jiffy. As the other positions on the board were slowly filled, Mifflin used his political address and his influence in Congress to establish control over the new agency. He labored successfully to have its powers extended from merely assisting with supply to reorganizing, independently of the Commander in Chief, whom he considered incompetent, all aspects of the military. And, working in close collaboration with Lee, he succeeded in having Congress elect, as president of the board, none other than the hero of Saratoga, Horatio Gates, who was to keep his rank as a senior major general in the army he was to supervise. Mifflin and Lee had agreed in considering "the military knowledge and the authority of Gates necessary to procure the indispensable changes in our army."[10]

---

* The sentiments here attributed to Mifflin and Greene are summaries of their arguments taken from later writings.

Congressman Eliphalet Dyer of Connecticut wrote Gates that Washington's "army in every department wants a total reform and regulation, both internal and external. We are determined by the blessing of Heaven to have it effected." Appointing Gates "meets with universal applause; great expectations are from it."[11]

However, despite its recent actions and such letters, Congress was not on the whole anti-Washington, or indeed committed to any consistent policy. The founding legislators, who had first steered the Revolution and selected the Commander in Chief, were for the most part no longer present. Many had returned to their states to deal with governmental reorganization in those theoretically independent sovereignties: John Hancock, for several years the President of Congress, was one of these. Others, like John Adams, who was about to sail on a diplomatic mission to France, were serving the confederation in various ways. And the congressmen newly elected by the state legislatures were, as Washington complained, often men of "contracted abilities" who took their federal responsibilities so lightly that they attended at Congress or not as personal whim indicated. Whole states were commonly completely unrepresented. A newcomer of less than four months' experience in Congress had succeeded Hancock as President: this was Henry Laurens of North Carolina, who was typically drawn both ways on issues affecting Washington. Although his normal political alliance was with the Adams-Lee-Rush faction, his brilliant son John had recently joined Washington's staff and adored the Commander in Chief. The same Congress could one day vote to force an exterior reform of the army on Washington, and the next day to increase his personal control over the appointment of officers.[12]

Such a political landscape offered good ground for the manipulative talents of Mifflin and Lee, even if they had to proceed warily. Since loyalty to Washington persisted in the minds of even those leaders who wished that he were more gifted as a soldier, the conspirators would have to undermine, slowly and without raising suspicions, that "idol worship" which seemed to them so dangerous and irrational. For the surest result, the situation should be so manipulated that Washington would, in fury or discouragement, resign of his own volition. And Washington had indiscreetly revealed to Lee that the intriguers had in hand a weapon toward making him depart: the promotion of Conway.

Everything seemed to be going with suitable subterranean smoothness until Mifflin saw a piece of paper that filled him with alarm. Conway had taken Washington's letter of rebuke so lightly that three weeks passed before he showed it to his friend Mifflin. He must have been amazed when he saw Mifflin's face.

The letter indicated only too strongly that Washington had somehow penetrated the secret councils of the intrigue. In an effort to determine the source and size of the leak, Mifflin read the document over and over. Except for a conventional opening and closing, he saw only: "A letter I received last night contained the following paragraph: 'In a letter from General Conway to General Gates, he says, "Heaven has been determined to save your country, or a weak general and bad councillors would have ruined it." ' "[13]

Had Washington been the most accomplished intriguer in the world, he could not have forged a more destructive weapon than this laconic little epistle. Whether by chance, or out of literary instinct (explanations weaken words intended to coalesce into a bullet), or with calculation to throw his enemies off balance, Washington had given no hint as to the source of his information, had not mentioned Wilkinson or Stirling or the convivial evening at Reading. His object had been (as he put it) to notify Conway "that I was not unapprised of his intriguing disposition." In so doing, he had allowed his opponents every opportunity to draw false conclusions and become suspicious one of another.[14]

To Gates, who was still up north at Albany, Mifflin rushed off a warning: "An extract from General Conway's letter to you has been procured and sent to headquarters." The extract contained "just sentiments," but might make trouble. Gates should take better care of his papers.[15]

Gates replied that Mifflin's news "inexpressibly distressed" him. No man took better care of his papers than he did. He kept them locked and the key in his pocket. It was hard to imagine who could be "the villain that has played me this treacherous trick."

Gates's best guess was that Hamilton had somehow got into his files when in Albany as Washington's emissary. This conclusion encouraged Gates to believe that he could further discredit Washington by making an issue of the theft of private letters. He wrote Washington, "Those letters have been stealingly copied. . . . I conjure your Excellency to give me all the assistance you can in tracing out the author of the infidelity which put extracts from General Conway's letters to me into your hands." Having expressed his horrified sense of what "crimes of that magnitude" could do to "the safety of the states," he added that in order to speed up detection he was sending Congress a copy of his letter to Washington. He privately forwarded another copy to Mifflin. It would, so he wrote his ally, "enable you to act with all possible propriety."[16]

Gates's letters were moving down from Albany when Conway, annoyed by the promotion to major general of another foreign officer whom he insisted had been his junior in France, penned an outraged resignation. Distressed at the prospect of losing an officer considered so valuable, Congress referred the problem to the Board of War.[17]

The moment had come to do what Lee, and surely also his friend Mifflin, knew might (if Washington really meant what he had implied) induce

Washington to resign. Conway must be promoted to major general! Flying directly in the face of the Commander in Chief's official stand would, of course, be crude and might backfire—but there was a way to get around Washington's stated objection to the promotion and at the same time enrage him the more. Washington had put his opposition to Conway on the grounds that the other brigadiers would refuse to serve under an officer who had been their junior. But the brigadiers could have no complaint if Conway's promotion were in the staff, not in the line. And Washington himself had pointed a way. He had recommended that an experienced foreign officer be designated inspector general and empowered to establish in the army a uniform and sophisticated system of drill and maneuvers.[18]

Under Mifflin's leadership (Gates was still in Albany) and with the subsequent approval of Congress, the Board of War established the office of inspector general on a much wider base than Washington had recommended. The inspector would exercise overall supervision of Washington's army. However, he would not be under Washington's orders. Acting independently, he would report directly to the Board of War, which could then by its own authority force on Washington the reforms he suggested. The office would carry the rank of major general. Meet Major General Conway![19]

Either through carelessness or to make the shock as unpleasant as possible, the board did not notify Washington of what they had done. When the new inspector general got to headquarters, he would do that himself. And so, very pleased with himself and blithe as a cricket, the man Washington most hated set out for Valley Forge eager to twist the Commander in Chief's tail.[20]

29

The Batteries of Intrigue

THE Valley Forge encampment, eighteen miles northwest of Philadelphia, was on a succession of hills between Valley Creek and the
Schuylkill River. Both watercourses were escarped by bluffs. Only a
few scattered farmhouses rose on a camping ground so extensive that, when
Washington established markets to encourage the neighborhood to bring
in supplies, he set different days for different areas. Plenty of woodland
supplied timber for the meager redoubts needed to protect a terrain so
naturally strong, and for the huts which the men had been ordered to build
for themselves.[1]

Washington's orders had specified that each hut should measure fourteen
by sixteen feet, the roof six and a half feet high. The inflammable laths from
which fireplace and chimney were constructed were to be coated with clay a
foot and a half thick. Unless boards could be procured, doors were to be
made of oak slabs split with an axe. The ordinary soldiers' cabins, each
housing twelve men, were to be laid out by regiments along improvised
streets. Behind would be the huts of the officers, which were to differ from
the men's by being floored not with earth but with boards. Some of the
cabins were partially sunk in the ground. There were hospitals and storehouses, and the "necessary houses" were carefully placed at a distance from
the wells.

What would the British army have done if forced to create out of raw
wood a sudden city capable of withstanding a more severe winter than Old
England knew? Only the engineers could have lifted an effective finger, and
they would have been baffled by the lack of nails. But American farmers
were familiar with erecting their own buildings, and the classic log cabin, as
used at Valley Forge, dispensed with nails by laying the logs in reciprocal
notches. Because of a lack of sawmills to supply boards for roofing,
Washington offered a hundred dollars to any officer or soldier who could

invent cheaper covering, quicker in construction than small logs made tight with laths. Some soldiers roofed their huts with earth or turf, which proved unhealthy.[2]

Thomas Paine described the troops as resembling "a family of beavers, everyone busy: some carrying logs, others mud, and the rest fastening them together."[3] Yet it took time to create a city from standing trees. In the interim, the men lived in tents which their fires filled with smoke until their eyes "started out of their orbits like rabbits' eyes." So wrote Dr. Albigence Waldo of the Connecticut Line, who continued, "Poor food—hard lodging—cold weather—fatigue—nasty clothes—nasty cookery—vomit half my time —smoked out of my senses—the devil's in it—I can't endure it. . . . A pox on my bad luck. There comes a bowl of beef soup—full of burnt leaves and dirt, sickish enough to make a Hector spew—away with it boys—I'll live like the chameleon upon air! . . .

"There comes a soldier, his bare feet are seen through his worn-out shoes, his legs nearly naked from the tattered remains of an only pair of stockings; his breeches not sufficient to cover his nakedness; his shirt hanging in strings; his hair disheveled; his face meager; his whole appearance pictures a person forsaken and discouraged. He comes, and cries with an air of wretchedness and despair, 'I am sick, my feet lame, my legs are sore, my body covered with this tormenting itch . . . and all the reward I shall get, will be—"Poor Will is dead." ' "[4]

Washington drew up plans for an attack on the British in Philadelphia—it might be staged on the first anniversary of the Battle of Princeton—but even as he wrote down the terse paragraphs, he knew that his army could not move. The clothier general had given him so little assistance that 2898 of his men were "barefoot or otherwise naked," a figure that was soon to rise to 4000. He found himself designing clothes: the tailors among his troops should use "the pattern of the sailor's pea jacket," as cheap and quick to make, warm and saving of cloth.[5]

To top Washington's frustration, the Pennsylvania legislature publicly protested the army's having gone into winter quarters. "I can assure those gentlemen," he wrote in anger, "that it is a much easier and less distressing thing to draw remonstrances in a comfortable room by a good fireside than to occupy a cold bleak hill and sleep under frost and snow without clothes or blankets. However, although they seem to have little feeling for the naked, distressed soldiers, I feel superabundantly for them, and from my soul pity those miseries which it is neither in my power to relieve or prevent."

Again and again he expressed admiration for his army that was under such civilian attack because it had not made Howe's beautifully appointed force bite the dust. "Without arrogance or the smallest deviation from truth it may be said that no history, now extant, can furnish an instance of an army's suffering such uncommon hardships as ours have done, and bearing them with the same patience and fortitude. To see men without clothes to cover their nakedness, without blankets to lay on, without shoes—by which their marches might be traced by the blood from their feet*—and almost as often without provisions as with, marching through frost and snow, and at Christmas taking up their winter quarters within a day's march of the enemy, without a house or hut to cover them till they could be built . . . in my opinion can scarce be paralleled."[6]

As Washington walked the camp at night, he heard the hills echo with melancholy shouts, "No meat! No meat!" combined humorously with imitations of crows and owls. What little food there was trickled in from day to day as foraging parties returned from oppressing, to Washington's deep regret, farms that had to be ever more distant as the nearer ones were stripped clean. A heavy snow which blocked the roads might bring pure disaster. "I am now convinced beyond a doubt," Washington shouted at Congress, "that unless some great and capital change suddenly takes place . . . this army must inevitably be reduced to one or other of these three things: starve, dissolve, or disperse in order to obtain subsistence."[7]

The capital change Congress had in mind walked into Washington's tent at the very end of November with a triumphant smile on its chinless, popeyed, supercilious face. Thomas Conway announced that he was now a major general.

Washington stated that the promotion was "extraordinary" and would outrage all the brigadiers in the army.

Not so, said Conway. The promotion was not extraordinary. It was suitable to the post which he now occupied, the post of inspector general. He handed Washington the resolution of Congress.

Having read the paper, Washington pointed out that the Board of War was to furnish a set of instructions according to which the troops were to be maneuvered. Did Conway have the instructions?

Conway cared little for instructions from other people. With a shrug, he admitted that he had not brought them with him.

Then he would have to wait, said Washington. He could not serve as inspector general until the instructions arrived. An aide would show him the door.† [8]

Conway belonged to that class of men who, although they permitted themselves to be as rude as they pleased, were convinced of their popularity

---

* The army was unshod at Valley Forge partly because thousands of imported French army shoes proved too small for American feet. And when the French shoes did fit, the Continentals wore them out in a few weeks.[9]

† This interview has been reconstructed from letters that subsequently passed between Washington and Conway.

and were hurt if they found themselves not liked. He departed hurt at the way Washington had spurned him, but confident that Washington's officers would rally eagerly to his comfort and support. Some of the French volunteers did, it is true, produce some clucks of outrage, but the native brigadiers got grimly to work drawing up a petition of protest against his promotion. Conway could think of no other rational explanation but that Washington was basely intriguing against him.[10]

Hearing of the scene between Washington and Conway, Lafayette hurried to headquarters but was told that Washington was too busy to see him. Worried, he explained in writing to his chief that he had until recently been a supporter of Conway (whom he had known in France) because he considered him "a very brave and good officer." However, he now realized that achieving military skill "is not so very difficult for any man of common sense who applies himself to it"; and Conway was proving himself a dangerous man. Parties in Congress, Lafayette went on to warn Washington, "are infatuated with Gates . . . and believe that attacking is the only thing necessary to conquer. These ideas are entertained in their minds by some jealous men, and perhaps secret friends to the British government, who want to push you, in a moment of ill-humor, to some rash enterprise."

Lafayette went on to insist patriotically that Conway was not French but Irish. The controversy had, it is true, "made a great noise" among the French officers, but Duportail and several others had assured Lafayette that they supported Washington. "I wish your Excellency could let them [the French officers] know how necessary you are to them." However, whatever happened, "I am now fixed to your fate, and I shall follow it and sustain it, as well by my sword as by all means in my power. . . . I feel the greatest concern at all what happens since some time."[11]

Washington replied with assurances of his "sentiments of the purest affection" for Lafayette, a violent diatribe against Conway, hurt feelings relative to "the tongue of slander," and agreement that "the fatal tendency of disunion is so obvious." Then his pen turned lyrical: "It is much to be lamented that things are not now as they formerly were, but we must not, in so great a contest, expect to meet with nothing but sunshine. I have no doubt but that everything happens so for the best, that we shall triumph over all our misfortunes, and shall, in the end, be ultimately happy; when, my dear Marquis, if you will give me your company in Virginia, we will laugh at our past difficulties and the folly of others."[12]

Conway's spirits were now as low as a short time before they had towered. "Greatly disappointed and chagrined," he took lodgings some distance from camp. Thence he wrote a letter which indicates that, although the movement that was developing to replace Washington with Gates was to go down in history as the "Conway Cabal," the foreigner did not know of the use which more subtle minds were trying to make of him. The letter was to Gates himself. In it Conway complained that he was being accused of "intriguing at Congress with General Mifflin and you in order to remove General Washington, and that I gave myself the merit of the Germantown affair. Such low calumnies I do not think worth answering. . . . I am stopped in functions, cannot be useful, and do not choose to struggle with cabals. I wish I could be sent somewhere else."[13]

With no suave Mifflin at his shoulder to restrain him, Conway fired off at Washington an insulting, sarcastic letter: "The general and universal merit which you wish every promoted officer might be endowed with is a rare gift. We see but a few men of merit so generally acknowledged. We know but the great Frederick in Europe and the great Washington in this continent. I certainly never was so rash as to pretend to such a prodigious height. . . . But you, sir, and the great Frederick, know perfectly well that this trade is not learned in a few months. I have served steadily thirty years."[14]

Receiving no immediate answer from Washington, Conway wrote him again. "I understand that your aversion to me is owing to the letter I wrote General Gates." Expressing opinions of superior officers was common in Europe, and no notice was taken.* Must Washington, who commanded "this army raised for the defense of liberty," introduce "such an odious and tyrannical inquisition?" Conway then implied, not too subtly, that Washington might yearn to be king, and ended on his former note of military disdain: "I do not pretend, sir, to be a consummate general, but . . . an old sailor knows more of a ship than admirals who have never been at sea."[15]

Washington sent the first of Conway's letters to Congress, and undoubtedly allowed the second to be circulated in camp and talked about. Officially, he made no comment except to defend himself as a gentleman from having been rude to Conway. He had received his enemy he insisted, if not "in the language of a warm and cordial friend . . . with proper respect to his official character." It was Washington's aide, John Laurens, who underlined how upset his chief was. Laurens wrote his father, the President of Congress, that Congress would have to determine "whether General W. is to be sacrificed to General C., for the former can never consent to be concerned in any transaction with the latter, from whom he has received such unpardonable insults."[16]

Washington, as he wrote, had "borne much for the sake of peace and public good," allowing "but few differences" to develop between him and

---

* Conway's statement was factually correct. In the aristocratic world, a soldier's social rank was more important than his military, his civilian patrons more valuable for his advancement than his military superiors. As a result, subordination was almost impossible to establish: every important officer was intriguing against his superiors with people in power back home. During the Revolution, the process resulted in a great weakening of the British high command: Clinton intrigued against Howe, Cornwallis against Clinton, and so on. Washington was, as in so many other situations, groping toward the methods of organization that were to grow up with people's armies.

his officers—but now he gave way to all the anger he had for so long suppressed. Although he knew he had personal enemies, few people had ever dared be insolent to his face, and Conway's scorn of him as an amateur soldier opened old wounds that had been left by the behavior of British regulars during the French and Indian War. He seems to have wished he could challenge Conway to a duel. "It is such an affront," so young Laurens explained to his father, "as Conway would never have dared to offer if the general's situation had not assured him of the impossibility of its being revenged in a private way."[17]

As his anger surged, Washington received Gates's letter implying that he had suborned a "traitor" to steal documents from private files. Gates had, of course, opened himself to a brief, factual reply that would have crushed him as a hysterical fool, but Washington was too wrought up fully to appreciate the opportunity. He did expose the ridiculousness of Gates's accusations by revealing that his source of information was the indiscretion of Gates's own aide, Wilkinson—but then, in a manner far from his usual behavior, he tried to score specious debater's points. Although he himself had just sent Conway's letter to Congress, he criticized Gates for spreading dissension by bringing the same body into their controversy. And he wrote most disingenuously that, until Gates had complained of a confidential leak, he had assumed that Wilkinson had acted under Gates's orders "with a friendly view" to warn Washington against Conway. "But in this, as in other matters of late, I have found myself mistaken."[18]

As Washington snapped at Conway and Gates, warnings came into his headquarters of a major plot to displace him. Many were verbal, but enough written ones remained to reveal that Washington was given good reason during the first month of 1778 to feel the ground sifting away below his feet.

President Laurens wrote his son, "I hinted some time ago my discovery of party in our councils; the events which I dreaded and in many instances predicted, are now coming to maturity. . . . Our whole frame is shattered; we are tottering; and without the immediate exertion of wisdom and fortitude, we must fall flat down. Among the causes of this melancholy state are to be found some men in whom your friend [Washington] reposed an implicit confidence. I do not mean in the army."[19]

Washington's oldest friend in the army and a true one, his Virginia neighbor Dr. James Craik, set out for home early in January, and by the time he reached Port Tobacco in Maryland felt it necessary to pause and write Washington. He had been asked before he left camp "by a gentleman whom I believe to be a true friend of yours," to warn Washington "that a strong faction was forming against you in the new Board of War and in the Congress." Craik had decided to wait to say anything "until I reached home, as perhaps I might make some further discoveries on my way. At my arrival in Bethlehem, I was told of it there. . . . At Lancaster, I was still assured of it. All the way down, I heard of it, and I believe it is pretty general over the country. No one would pretend to affix it on particulars, yet all seemed to believe it."

The names most often mentioned as Washington's enemies were, Craik continued, R. H. Lee and Mifflin. The method was to hold Gates up to admiration and make out that Washington's army had been three or four times greater than the British, and that he had, despite "many opportunities of defeating the enemy," lost Philadelphia through incompetence. "It is said they dare not appear openly as your enemies, but that the new Board of War is composed of such leading men as will throw such obstacles and difficulties in your way as to force you to resign."[20]

President Laurens sent Washington an unsigned paper entitled "Thoughts of a Freeman," which had been found on the steps of Congress: it was voluminous and lambasted Washington from every direction. In his acknowledgment to Laurens, Washington wrote, "My enemies taken an ungenerous advantage of me. . . . They know I cannot combat their insinuations, however injurious, without disclosing secrets it is of the utmost moment to conceal. But why should I expect to be exempt from censure, the unfailing lot of an elevated station? Merits and talents, with which I can have no pretensions of rivalship, have ever been subject to it. My heart tells me it has been my unremitted aim to do the best circumstances will permit; yet I may have been very often mistaken in my judgment of the means, and may, in many instances, deserve the imputation of error." But, in any case, "I would not desire in the least degree to suppress a free spirit of inquiry into any part of my conduct that even faction itself may deem reprehensible." The paper "exhibits many serious charges, and it is my wish that it should be submitted to Congress."[21] (This was not done.)

To the Reverend William Gordon, whose warning had been that the faction intended to put General Lee (if he could be got back from the British) at the head of the army, Washington wrote, "I did not solicit the command, but accepted it after much entreaty," and with realization that he lacked "ability and experience equal to the discharge of so important a trust." He had "pursued the great line of my duty and the object in view (as far as my judgment could direct) as pointedly as the needle to the pole. So soon then as the public gets dissatisfied with my services, or a person is found better qualified to answer her expectation, I shall quit the helm with as much satisfaction and retire to a private station with as much content, as ever the wearied pilgrim felt upon his safe arrival in the Holy Land, or haven of hope; and shall wish most devoutly that those who come after may meet with more prosperous gales than I have done, and less difficulty." * [22]

* Let those who subscribe to the canard that Washington could not write well read this paragraph a second time.

When Patrick Henry forwarded to Washington an anonymous letter he had received—Washington's army was "a mob" but "a Gates, a [Charles] Lee, or a Conway would in a few weeks render them an irresistible body of men"—Washington recognized the handwriting of Dr. Rush and was hurt, "having always received from him the strongest professions of attachment and regard." Although the criticism of error was "the prerogative of free-men," Washington added, he could not help crying out against such "secret, insidious attempts . . . to wound my reputation!" From another letter, he scratched out as too revealing a reference to "the most painful sensations" he felt at being "the object of persecution to men who are embarked in the same general interest, and whose friendship my heart does not reproach me with ever having done anything to forfeit." Washington's aide Tench Tilghman stated that Washington had had no higher opinion of any man than Mifflin. "I have never seen any stroke of ill fortune affect the General in the manner that this dirty underhand dealing has done."[23]

Washington was, as his biographer Rupert Hughes states eloquently, "a lonely farmer caught in an endless war." And now his enemies beckoned to his most beloved friend.[24]

With hesitation, as if he feared he was being overswayed by affection, Washington had finally given Lafayette, who was learning so fast, an active major general's command under his immediate eye. Then came a missive from the Board of War: Lafayette had been assigned the command of a winter expedition against Canada that had been determined on without Washington's knowledge. "The Board," so the dispatch added grandly, "will be happy on this, as well as every other occasion, to receive your opinion and advice."[25]

Washington summoned Lafayette, placed the letter in his hand, and said (so the Frenchman later quoted him), "I prefer its being for you rather than for any other person."

The Board of War's first conspicuous independent act, making Conway inspector general, had misfired. When Washington had bluntly refused to honor the appointment, Conway's presumed popularity with the army had foundered; and then the Irish-Frenchman had written Washington insulting letters. The board, even with Gates down from Albany and in the chair, did not dare make further efforts to force Conway on Washington. If they were not to lose face, they would have to find some other prominent role for their protégé, who was noisily exhibiting his bruised feelings around the little improvised capital of York. Furthermore, a second coup to follow up Burgoyne's surrender would be a patriotic contribution and also solidify Gates's eminence.

Burgoyne's surrender had left few British regulars in Canada. The province could not be reinforced before spring opened the icebound St. Lawrence. If a quick invasion were welcomed by the inhabitants, Canada would fall. The inhabitants were mostly French. Surely they would welcome an army led by Frenchmen: the exalted Lafayette could be cast as figurehead with the veteran Conway, as second in command, supplying the military brains. In the process, Lafayette, who was influential overseas and at home with the corps of foreign officers, could be won over to Gates. The vision was so incandescent that the projectors failed to consider whether adequate supplies could be quickly gathered at Albany, the frozen jumping-off place in northern New York. As for Washington, he believed that the expedition was "the child of folly, and must be productive of capital ills." However, "as it is the first fruit of our new Board of War, I did not incline to say anything against it."[26]

Lafayette assured Washington that he wished no post independent of his friend: the title of aide-de-camp suited him better than any other. But the conspicuous young nobleman, who felt with some justice that Europe expected much of him, yearned to distinguish himself. Washington persuaded his spiritual son to accept the honor. Lafayette then spurned the idea that Conway could be his second in command. When the Board of War tried to argue, the Marquis threatened to lead most of the foreign officers back to France. Washington and his disciple must have had a good laugh when the board was forced to put over Conway's head the French general he was most determined to outrank: the self-styled baron Johann Kalb.[27]

Pampered and groomed by Washington like a high-mettled charger before a tournament, Lafayette set out in late January for Albany. So few of the necessities for a winter march proved to be available that the expedition had to be abandoned. Loudly Lafayette blamed the Board of War for "recommending a measure of such consequence without certain assurance of the means."[28]

The Board of War's chickens were coming home to roost. Conway's letters, in which the foreigner had insulted not only Washington but through him all America's self-taught officers, were becoming daily more and more celebrated. It was an aspect of Washington's leadership that his emotions tended automatically to parallel those of the mass of the people: the very qualities that had made Conway hateful to him proved when publicly displayed to make the bullying braggart hateful to almost everyone. Realizing that they had tied an albatross around their own necks, the conspirators tried to cut loose. When on April 22 Conway wrote one of his habitual complaints to Congress, in which he threatened to resign unless indulged, to his amazement and horror his resignation was accepted. He could not believe it! He ran to his former friends and was received with stony faces. He complained to Gates that Richard Henry Lee and Samuel Adams had turned their backs on him, considering it "vain to oppose the torrent."[29]

But Gates was also turning his back. His false charge that Washington had been tampering with his papers had put him in an unfortunate light, and a subsequent pettifogging correspondence between the two men, although to the credit of neither, did Gates the more harm since the tone was obviously less typical of Washington than of his enemies. It seemed as if His Excellency were being forced to stoop to protect himself from pygmies. Thus, Washington responded to a defense of Conway by Gates in a sarcastic style that resembled Conway's own: "The United States have lost much from the unseasonable diffidence which prevented his embracing the numerous opportunities he had in council of displaying those rich treasures of knowledge and experience he has since so freely laid open to you. I will not do him the injustice to impute the penurious reserve which ever appeared in him upon such occasions to any other cause than an excess of modesty . . ." and so forth through a long, heated passage.[30]

Gates finally assured Washington that he had had no correspondence with Conway before the offending letter (which was a lie). Washington's enemy was no particular friend of his; he hated controversy; he hoped Washington would drop and forget the matter. Washington replied that he would bury what had happened in "oblivion . . . as far as future events will permit."[31]

As for Mifflin, he wrote Gates that due to "wicked suspicions," he no longed dared confide his thoughts to paper. Publicly he stated, to the guffaws of Washington's supporters, that Washington was "the best friend he ever had in his life."[32]

His enemies were in full flight, but Washington, who had, after resisting so many provocations down so many years of command, given way to rage, continued to behave in a manner of which he would normally have disapproved. He showed Wilkinson some letters he had received from Gates which contained passages to the young officer's discredit. Wilkinson thereupon wrote Gates that he would "hasten on the wings of resentment to assert my *wounded* honor at the point of my sword and ratify my integrity in blood. . . . May the God of justice help you!" A duel between the general and his protégé was only averted when, on the field of blood, instead of firing they fell into each other's arms in tears.[33]

Unchecked by Washington, his officers prowled the capital threatening to challenge loose talkers. Richard Peters, the civilian member of the Board of War, found himself being trailed to his intense terror by the gigantic rifleman Daniel Morgan. Major John Clark, Greene's aide, warned Greene's critics: "I believe a few ounces of gunpowder diffused through proper channels will answer a good purpose." To Washington's expressed amusement, Mifflin had to engage in some fancy footwork to keep from being called out by General Cadwalader. The only duel that seems actually to have been fought was between Cadwalader and Conway. A ball passed through Conway's mouth and neck.[34]

Bandaged, sitting up wanly in bed, Conway asked for paper and wrote

Washington: "My career will soon be over. . . . I find myself just able to hold the pen during a few minutes. . . . Therefore justice and truth prompt me to declare my last sentiments: You are in my eyes the great and good man."[35]

Washington was not moved by these piteous words. He was sure the Irish-Frenchman was merely engaging in more histrionics. And Washington was right. Conway did not die. He lived to return to a distinguished career in the French service.*

---

* Conway was sent to India, where he served as maréchal de camp and then as governor of the French possessions. Having espoused during the French Revolution the royalist cause, he spent his last years in exile.

30

What Was the Conway Cabal?

THE movement in opposition to Washington that raised its head in December 1777 and tried to duck out of sight again during February 1778 came to be referred to as the Conway Cabal, partly because of the swing of the phrase. ("Mifflin Cabal" sounds scruffy.) Down the years, there has been a continuing confusion as to exactly what took place. Some historians have envisioned a formal conspiracy of traitors that almost succeeded in toppling Washington, while the modern iconoclast Bernhard Knollenberg would have us believe that Washington was being hysterical in the manner of an old maid who sees imaginary burglars under her bed.[1]

At the time, even the best informed were confused. President Laurens could state one day, "Our whole frame is shattered; we are tottering"; and four days later, "The whole amounts to little more than tittle-tattle."[2]

As the pressure receded, in March 1778, Washington wrote Patrick Henry, "I cannot precisely mark the extent of their views, but it appeared in general that General Gates was to be exalted on the ruin of my reputation and influence." Mifflin, it was commonly supposed, "bore the second part," while Conway was "a very active and malignant partisan." In May, Washington stated, perhaps at least in part to quiet rumors, "Whether any members of Congress were privy to this scheme, and inclined to aid and abet it, I shall not take upon me to say; but am well informed that no whisper of the kind was ever heard in Congress." However, as an old man, he recalled that "the attempt was made by a party in Congress to supplant me in that command."[3]

Hamilton was convinced that a plot against Washington existed "in the most extensive sense." (He believed that it failed because "it unmasked its batteries too soon.")[4] There were surely doubts and discontent for the conspirators to work on. One can hardly dig into any extensive archive of letters exchanged by either the politicians or the soldiers of the period without coming on expressions of dissatisfaction with Washington's management of the army. Such criticism, even a desire to remove him from the command, was not, of course, in itself either treasonous or disgraceful. Washington was in public office. Any man who became convinced that the cause could be better served by supplanting him possessed not only a right but a duty to labor for that end.

Much of the dissatisfaction had been building up for a long time. Although Washington had in this particular long since reformed his thinking, New Englanders could not forget that the Virginian had insulted their civilization (which they did not doubt was the greatest in America) and their troops in letters from Cambridge. These indiscretions, by encouraging New Englanders to doubt the soundness of Washington's judgment and the goodness of his heart, added fuel to the fear that he might, in the manner of overpowerful Roman generals, in the end destroy free government. He would, of course, be assisted in this if he led a coherent army of long-enrolled veterans.

Although events had forced Congress to agree to enlistment for three years and even for the duration of the war, the continuing uneasiness of the civilian leaders was revealed by the way they threw roadblocks between Washington and the achievement of the results he insisted were necessary for victory. Congress failed to vote adequate bounties, and the states dragged their feet on securing long-term enlistments, craftily filling in the gaps with short-term men and militia. In providing necessary ordnance and supply, the fear of too powerful a military was a deterrent. From Valley Forge, Washington found it necessary to point out to Congress that the Continental Army was a new phenomenon not subject to historical parallel. Then he added a threat which the politicians could not have found reassuring.

Standing armies, so Washington wrote, were dangerous to the state only if the soldiers were "mercenaries, hirelings," who lacked "any of the ties, the concerns, or interests of citizens," and had "no other dependence than what flowed from their military employ." The Continental soldiers were "citizens, having all the ties and interests of citizens, and in most cases property totally unconnected with the military line." No other group in the thirteen states had paid "more sanctimonious regard" to civilian authority. However, they should not be pushed too far. Making legislative distrust of the army manifest was "impolitic in the extreme. Among individuals, the most certain way to make a man your enemy is to tell him you esteem him such: so with public bodies."[5]

But the legislators, particularly those most concerned with state sovereignty, could not help being worried. Despite every precaution Congress took to segregate the various state lines and keep the officers dependent on their local legislatures, long Continental service did tend to drown local loyalty in continental thinking. Washington had personally established the Additional Regiments that mixed men from all the states. After the war, he was to comment with approval that "a century in the ordinary intercourse" would not have done for continental unity "what seven years' association in arms did."[6]

How far Washington's thinking had sped beyond the political consensus is revealed by the vicissitudes of the efforts to get the states to agree to even a minimum of common government. Before Independence was declared, the Congress had started working on Articles of Confederation. Not till November 1777 could they agree on a draft to refer to the states. Although the document established little more than "a league of common friendship," it had not yet received the unanimous ratification necessary to put it in effect. There might be a Continental Congress, a single Commander in Chief and a Continental Army, but the states still had no legal connection with each other.

The solution to the dangers seen in a standing army and too much Continental unity was so obvious and so deeply rooted in American tradition that the civilian leaders found it maddening that Washington could not or would not fight successfully with a force largely made up of one-year men reinforced by waves of short-term militia. A most encouraging aspect of Gates's victory over Burgoyne seemed to be that it had been largely accomplished by militia. Overlooking the facts that Burgoyne's most lethal enemy had been geography, and that the militia had only flocked when the British were already in trouble, Gates's supporters argued that what Gates had done with militia up north, he could, if put in control of Washington's army, do against Howe.*

Washington's insistence that he could not triumph with short-term soldiers was blamed by his critics in part on his background as a Virginia planter, which was supposed to have prejudiced him against a people's army, and in part on a lack of that true military skill which, it was assumed, could quickly make invincible a random gathering of virtuous, patriotic American citizens.

Anyone who had worked with Washington since the start of the war, as Mifflin and Lee and Gates and the Adamses had done, had heard him state over and over that he lacked both ability and training. Even while his right to command was under attack, he continued to point out that he had never claimed to be a military genius. And certainly he had, since the British had evacuated Boston, been defeated at every meeting with the main British army. The victories at Trenton and Princeton had been against outposts.

Although the strategic conceptions Washington had been developing were

---

* "Collecting militia," Washington noted, "depends entirely upon the prospects of the day. If favorable, they throng in to you. If not, they will not be moved."[7]

to be greatly admired in the future by military historians, they ate away at British power rather than smashing it; they showed no signs of ending the war; and he had lost Philadelphia. Not only those whom his propaganda fooled as to his strength thought that he ought to have done better. Man is a buck-passing animal. The civilian leaders who watched his army dwindle and who failed to keep it supplied were naturally inclined to believe that his force, if not ideal, was plenty strong enough. In any case, they saw no practical way of achieving more strength: a great general overcomes difficulties.

Whoever dominates anything as Washington dominated the Continental Army is sure to make enemies, not only those who truly resent his power, but also those who are frustrated in their attempts to share it. Washington's concern with intelligence, his fear of gossip that would result in informing the enemy, kept him from even hinting at his plans to any but his most intimate collaborators: a French officer was surprised at how much less "talk about operations of war" circulated in the American than in the French armies.[8] Even major generals were kept uninformed. This increased the sense that the army was being run by a little group of favorites gathered around the Commander in Chief. Mifflin was far from alone in resenting Washington's reliance on Greene and Lafayette, Laurens and Hamilton. Actual jealousy encouraged a line of criticism which was politically effective since it attacked Washington in terms of admiration: it was charged that, because of his often acknowledged diffidence, he was controlled by men less able than he.

Malcontents exist at all times but most copiously in times of violence and rapid change. All the more because Congress was so amorphous a body, spawning few conspicuous leaders, Washington was the natural target for all those displeased with any aspect of the ever-shifting political scene. He was blamed by farmers whose cows had been stolen or died of natural causes, by businessmen who had lost money, by underfed soldiers and officers not promoted, by childless women and men with stomach ulcers.

The labor of channeling this chaotic dissatisfaction into an effective current had just begun when Wilkinson's indiscretion and Washington's cryptic note to Conway not only unmasked but confused the batteries of his opponents. They were still an informal pressure group of scattered men with similar views. Gates had not yet come down the river from Albany, and Richard Henry Lee was soon drawn by his personal affairs to Virginia. Mifflin's brain seems to have been the central office of the enterprise.

Mifflin's closest collaborator seems to have been Lee. Gates, temperamentally less a subtle schemer than a noisy controversialist, was playing an opportunist role: he felt he deserved the top command and was glad to help pull it his way. Conway was no more than a willing tool. Rush was a strong (and indiscreet) partisan. Lovell, always Washington's most outspoken enemy in Congress, and Pickering, who had resigned as adjutant general to join the Board of War, came along eagerly. John Adams had done much to foster a political climate unfavorable to Washington, but was now on his way to France. Samuel Adams would have enjoyed the unhorsing of New England's former critic.

Washington was to claim that the officers of the northern army remained loyal to him, but certainly Gates's staff was a hotbed of intrigue. Among the other army officers who were violently critical of Washington was General Wayne, whose one military conception was attack. President Laurens stated that there were men involved who respected Washington but "want the honor to defend. . . . In all such juntas," Laurens continued, "there are prompters and actors, accommodators, candle snuffers, shifters of scenes, and mutes."[9]

By the time the cabal collapsed, no strings still visible had been pulled to have Washington discharged from the command; that would not have been at the moment practical politics. Some of Washington's opponents wished merely to reduce his authority by dividing the army between regional commanders of whom he would remain one. However, it seems clear that the active leaders intended to create a situation where Washington would be forced either to knuckle under or, what seemed more probable for his proud spirit, remove himself through resignation.

Before anyone else paid much attention, the conspirators achieved on paper brilliant results: they established what seemed on the face of it all the necessary machinery to force Washington out. The Board of War was placed over his head and kept in the control of his enemies, with Gates as president and Mifflin as star manipulator. Both these men held, furthermore, major general's commissions in Washington's line. And the crowning touch was supplied by appointing Conway, the man Washington so hated, to supervise his army as a representative of the Board of War.

After it had been reported to him that the prime object of the plot was to make him resign, Washington denied that he had ever threatened to do so.[10] However, he had implied as much, and the bald threat had emerged from his headquarters. The conspirators seemed to have leapt on the hints and broadcast them.*

This proved very unwise, since it made a public not prepared for the idea try to envision the cause without Washington.

At the center of the cause since it had assumed true continental scope, Washington's role had grown with the surrounding growth of events and institutions as a strong tree rises within a new forest. Such a tree both shapes and is shaped by the vegetation around it: a branch which extrudes

---

* On February 5, Greene wrote McDougall, "Great pains have been taken to give the public an idea the General was about to resign, and that I governed him in all cases."[11]

crookedly does so to fit into an existing gap. The tree becomes locked into the woods like a piece in a three-dimensional puzzle. To cut it down would involve a great tearing in the objects around it, and, however carefully the tree was replaced, the hole could only partially be filled in.

Washington's presumptive successor Gates would not have been a replacement but a new departure. He was an altogether different kind of man: a controversialist, an extremist. He was bitter against the upper classes who had thwarted his career in England, and he had sharp elbows. Backed by the New England radicals and their allies elsewhere, he had allowed his battle for the northern command against the conservative Schuyler to be fought not only on military but on ideological grounds.

The opposition to Washington tended to come from the very ideological groups—those who most wished a social as well as a national revolution— who most admired Gates. However, when faced with the actual possibility that their hero might replace Washington, they usually had second thoughts. In all political controversies (even in the Gates-Schuyler fracas that involved army command), Washington had done his best to be neutral. If he had been slow in coming round to Independence, no one was now its more staunch supporter. If he seemed unsound on the militia and states' rights, he had kept an army in the field and had shown himself much more eager to refuse than to grasp civil power. His aristocratic air and tendency to protect the conservatives might be annoying to restless spirits, but gave him great value as an anchor that helped hold the more propertied patriots to the cause.

Should Gates replace Washington, extremism on the left would be encouraged. The right would feel a necessity to defend itself, and the whole cause would be sent spinning toward that internecine controversy and perhaps warfare which all responsible leaders, left as well as right, knew must above all things be avoided.

But there was still more to it than that. When Washington was insulted by Conway and slandered by Gates, innumerable people who had been vocal in criticism found their hearts surprisingly suffused with love.

Even as the cabal was still fulminating in the temporary capital at York, Washington was given at Valley Forge a touching demonstration of loyalty of his men. The foraging on which he was forced to subsist the army was bringing in less and less food as farms were stripped as bare as humanity allowed.* Washington had at last sent Greene out with a force large enough to protect itself far from the main army—two thousand men—on an extensive search for eatables. They had found little. New Jersey, Pennsyl-

---

* Washington ordered: "Leave as much forage to each farm as will serve the remaining stock 'till next grass, as much grain as will support them 'till harvest, some milch cattle and a reasonable number of horses."[12]

7 — DELEGATION

vania, and Maryland were indeed completely exhausted of beef and pork. There were not enough wagons to bring salt provisions from the south. Perhaps New England would send some wagons, but that would take time. To top all, the troops were owed four to five months' pay. When Washington complained again to the Board of War, Pickering asked why, if the troops had no meat or vegetables, they could not substitute bread?[13]

Soon the troops had no bread. As Washington paced melancholy through the camp, soldiers called from their huts in voices sad but not loud, "No bread, no soldier!" Unable to deny to himself that such violence would be justified, Washington tried to prepare his mind for a mass desertion, or even the mutiny of unpaid, unfed, naked troops suffering to protect fat civilians who either criticized or ignored them.[14]

When an aide reported that a delegation of enlisted men was at the door of his office—something heretofore unheard of—Washington tightened his nerves for what was to follow. But soon his eyes were swimming with tears. The men stated that they realized the difficulties under which he labored, and had only come to make sure that their own difficulties were completely understood. "Naked and starving as they are," Washington wrote, "we can not enough admire the incomparable patience and fidelity of the soldiery." And in his general orders he congratulated the army for proving themselves "worthy [of] the enviable privilege of contending for the rights of human nature."[15]

The ragged varlets on their bleak hillside relished such sentiments from their general because they knew that he truly believed in them himself and that he every day did his best to live up to his ideals.

VI

Toward a More
Effective Army

31

The Other Valley Forge

ALTHOUGH American legend dwells only on that aspect of army life at Valley Forge which is symbolized by bloody footsteps in the snow, a later and opposite aspect existed. It featured rough comfort, jolly companionship, and the forging of a more effective army. The change happened at about the time the Conway Cabal deflated: in mid-February 1778, when, due to "the exertions of our friends in different quarters," the army became, as Washington wrote, "pretty well supplied."[1]

Since there was always plenty of wood to burn, the troops could, when food was added, enjoy the snugness of the cabins with neatly drawing chimneys they had built with their own hands. Nakedness could then be taken as a joke. A group of young officers gave a dinner to which no one was admitted who possessed a whole pair of breeches. Clubbing their rations, they feasted on tough steak plus potatoes, having hickory nuts for dessert. With what could only be described as "some kind of spirits," they made a salamander, "set the liquor on fire and drank it up, flame and all. Such a ragged and at the same time merry set of fellows," reminisced a French volunteer, "were never before brought together."[2]

On first reaching their empty hillsides, the troops had complained of being (in Dr. Waldo's phrase) locked away from the world like "Jonah in the belly of a great fish." Now they enjoyed "a spacious city" inhabited exclusively by men very like themselves. In the previous winter encampment at Morristown, militiamen had clamorously come and quickly gone, but there were now enough long-term soldiers for Valley Forge to contain no others. The entire community belonged, as Washington observed, to "that class of men whose tempers, attachments, and circumstances disposed them" to long military service. Even the ministers mixed gunpowder with their sermons. The soldiers might drink lachrymose toasts to "sweethearts and wives," but, on the other hand, no one made them change diapers or keep their chins shaved.[3]

The bakehouse housed at night amateur theatricals. How strangely Washington's heart must have beat to watch, in this situation which his wildest youthful imaginings could not have foreseen, other youngsters performing Addison's *Cato,* the play concerning which he had written from another military camp to his unattainable love, Sally Fairfax, that he would find "myself doubly happy in being the Juba to such a Marcia as you must make."[4]

After the men had completed their huts, Washington moved from his own tent into the farmhouse of one Deborah Hewes. He wrote around in an effort to find the baggage which he had abandoned before the fall of Philadelphia in his desire to share the hardships of his troops. "I do not know in whose care and possession it is, but am satisfied I ought to have a good deal there, among other things a bed, end irons, plates, dishes, and kitchen utensils. . . . Hire or impress proper wagons for bringing these things." Washington was expecting Martha and feared that she would find his headquarters "a dreary kind of place, and uncomfortably provided." He knew she would arrive in deep depression because of the death of her beloved sister, Fanny Bassett.[5]

Martha had already lost her father, her first husband, and three of her four children. She wrote Burwell Bassett from Mount Vernon that Fanny had been "the greatest favorite I had in the world. . . . If to meet our departed friends and know them was certain, we could have very little reason to desire to stay in this world. . . . Nothing in the world so I wish for more sincerely than to be with you, but, alas," she could not. Washington had stated that he would send for her. "If he does, I must go."[6]

Arriving in early February, Martha found that "the General's apartment is very small." The entire farmhouse was, indeed, so tiny that the bedchambers in which many aides slept crowdedly at night had to be used during the day as sitting rooms for visitors. Her husband, Martha was to write, "has had a log cabin built to dine in, which has made our quarter much more tolerable than they were at first." The clothing shortage precluded elegance. "I cannot get as much cloth as will make clothes for my servants," Washington complained, "notwithstanding one of them that attends my person and table is indecently and most shamefully naked."[7]

Martha's presence was, as always to her husband, a joy and strength: not only for the comfort her very presence brought a man who so longed for domesticity and his own hearth, but because wherever she was, human difficulties were smoothed over. George Washington, as had just been demonstrated, had his enemies; no evidence exists that Martha ever made a single one. She possessed dignity but was utterly unassuming. She was not brilliant. Men could not remember anything she had said but remembered her affability and charm. Women found her domestic and chatty: full of conversation about household details and grandchildren. Her discretion was unfailing—and everyone felt more pleased with themselves after having talked to her.

The French general Chastellux was to write of the diminutive lady—she was about five feet tall—"I find that she looks like a German princess." A Hessian prisoner, indeed, considered her "pretty," while another Frenchman stated, "She is small and fat; her appearance is respectable; she was dressed very plainly and her manners were simple in all respects."[8]

What strangers did not recognize was her courage. Her temperament was apprehensive. She was certain when a letter did not arrive that the delay indicated disaster; she was terrified of travel and strange places and guns. Yet she came when summoned; complained only a little; spoke with "raptures" about the discipline of the army; and stated bravely that she preferred "the sound of fifes and drums . . . to any music that was ever heard."[9]

The perpetual strain of having her husband away at battles—why did he not keep her better informed of what he was doing?—and of her annual marches, to wherever headquarters had roosted and then back again to Virginia, had told on her appearance. Her mouth, which was always tiny, was now drawn so tight with nervous strain that her lips were pulled under, almost completely hidden. Her expression was rather sad than happy, a little lost-looking, yet quiet, contained, and without self-pity. She drew her dark hair back firmly from a high forehead and combed it down behind to cover the tips of each ear. Her chin, although narrow, was double. She had a mole on her right cheek, and a hooked nose, strong with high nostrils.

Her presence attracted to the Valley Forge headquarters other ladies who, as female society always did, lightened His Excellency's cares. The French volunteer Pierre Étienne Du Ponceau thus described the inner circle: Martha "reminded me of the Roman matrons of whom I had read so much, and I thought that she well deserved to be the companion and friend of the greatest man of the age." He found Mrs. Greene, who could speak to him in French, "a handsome, elegant, and accomplished woman." He admired Mrs. Stirling and her daughter Lady Kitty Alexander, but reserved for Lady Kitty's friend Miss Nancy Brown the phrase "a distinguished belle."

The female set, with Washington often in attendance, met at each other's quarters, or gathered at headquarters where "the evening was spent in conversation over a dish of tea or coffee. There were no levees or formal soirees; no dancing, card playing, or amusements of any kind except singing. Every gentleman or lady who could sing was called upon in turn for a song."[10]

Pickering's departure to make Washington trouble at the Board of War lightened his evenings, since the replacement as adjutant general, Colonel Alexander Scammell, was "full of ludicrous anecdotes." At the general's table after the ladies had left and when the wine circulated, Scammell "was allowed to take the command and to excite beyond any other man, the general himself."[11]

The office of quartermaster, from which Mifflin had resigned, still lay vacant. Wishing to have in that crucial post a friend he trusted (and certainly with realization of how much the appointment would anger his enemy), Washington secured the selection for the man Mifflin most resented: Greene. The position was lucrative, but Greene insisted that he had accepted it largely out of "compassion" for the harried Washington. He rode out to find army property dispersed all over the countryside. Wagons lay abandoned by every road, and he pulled back the creaky door of a dilapidated barn to disclose a towering white pile of tents and tent cloth.[12]

Washington sent Congress fusillades of suggestions for reorganizing various army services; and he conferred for days with a committee Congress sent to camp. When the legislature had done nothing much by mid-April about recruiting or almost anything else, he shouted, "At no period since the commencement of the war have I felt more painful sensations. . . . I shall make no apology for the freedom of this letter. . . . My agreement with the committee entitled me to expect upwards of forty thousand Continental troops, exclusive of artillery and horse."[13]

Washington still dreamed that he might pull his scattered cavalry raiders together into a striking force that could determine the outcome of battles, and his ambitions in this direction were encouraged by the appearance as a volunteer of the highborn Polish patriot and exile Casimir Pulaski. His imagination fired with Pulaski's tales of cavalry exploits on the plains of Poland, Washington induced Congress to make the Pole brigadier general in command of the horse.[14]

However, equipping real cavalry proved beyond the means of the impoverished cause. Sabers, carbines, and also saddles suitable for fighting from horseback were almost unprocurable, and what necessities the country could provide were made by inflation impossibly expensive. Suitable horses cost so much that the government could not buy them in adequate quantity, and, should a regiment by hook and crook become adequately mounted, how could the animals be kept fed in seasons or places that did not supply green forage? Add that Washington, since fighting from horseback was a skill unknown to American riders, appointed as Pulaski's subordinates other foreign officers.

Not only did the foreigners—all hungry for rank and personal glory—feud among themselves and with the American generals who tried to command them, but, as they rode around the countryside, they demonstrated aristocratic disdain for American mores. Peasants who annoyed them were summarily punished; if they suspected a citizen of being a Tory, they would string him up without a trial. Poor Washington could only protest after the event. "The temper of the Americans and the principles on which the present contest turns," he would write, "will not countenance proceedings of this nature."[15]

Having got into innumerable personal squabbles, Pulaski resigned in March 1778 as commander of the cavalry.* [16] And Washington, despite occasional flareups of renewed interest, largely abandoned his dream of horsemen who were more than mounted infantry, who would fight from the saddle and shock the enemy in battle with massed charges.

For not moving heaven and earth to establish mounted power, Washington has been criticized by various writers. However, he was probably right in concluding that in the rough and wooded terrain over which he operated, formal cavalry would not be worth the expense. The British, and also the French who were soon to arrive, had trained and equipped cavalry legions, but neither made really effective use of them in the campaigns Washington fought. Riders were, it is true, to play a major role in the south, where the terrain was much better suited to unmolested galloping, but even there the horses were used more for rapid transport than as powerful adjuncts to battle.

While Washington was at Valley Forge, military activity was largely confined to attacks on British foraging parties and efforts to turn back American farmers who wished to sell produce in Philadelphia for the enemy's hard money. This second labor was, despite the activity of Washington's mounted guerrilla patrols, so imperfectly performed that Howe suspected Washington was blinking at the trade, which brought needed specie to the rebel economy, served as a cover for spies, and would, in any case, be extremely difficult to stop. Washington stated that it could not be stopped without doing what "the horror of depopulating a whole district" prevented—creating a barren strip around the city—and he did use the farmers' wagons to keep contact with the spy network he had set up before the city fell.[17]

A continuing problem was created by the Quakers, whose religious disapproval of all fighting prevented them from cooperating in any blockade and who thus in effect assisted the British. Probably to embarrass Washington, Howe allowed four wives to leave Philadelphia on a mission to beg Washington for the release of their rich and influential husbands who had been imprisoned after the defeat at Brandywine. The Hessian Major Baurmeister reported that Washington "received these courageous Quaker women in the most cordial manner, kept them to dinner, and for the rest of the day they were entertained by the General's wife." Through her intercession, all the Quakers were released. "The joy among the members of this powerful sect . . . was extremely great."[18]

---

* Assigned a small independent corps, Pulaski was killed in 1779 during an attack on Savannah.

Washington's winning gentleness toward defectors combined with British ineptitude to frustrate Howe's efforts to recruit in Pennsylvania a powerful Tory militia. The British general complained that, despite the great promises of members of great American families, eight months' effort yielded only 974 men.[19]

However, Washington was caused much "anxiety" by word that the British ministry had introduced into Parliament two "reconciliation bills" which, in effect, offered the Americans all they had petitioned for in 1775. How he would have welcomed such news then! Now, not knowing that the move had been forced on the British by the imminence of a French entry into the war, Washington interpreted it as a propaganda ruse: "the most wicked, diabolical baseness, meant to poison the minds of the people and detach the wavering, at least, from our cause." His hatred for the enemy boiled over: "Great Britain understood herself perfectly well in this dispute but did not comprehend America. . . . They meant to drive us into what they termed rebellion that they might be furnished with a pretext to disarm and then strip us of the rights and privileges of Englishmen and citizens. . . . What name does such conduct as this deserve? and what punishment is there in store for the men who have distressed millions, involved thousands in ruin, and plunged numberless families in inextricable woe?"[20]

Washington's favorite plan for that winter had been, now that the core of his army was on long-term enlistment, to drill them under an experienced European inspector general into a really efficient force. The interposition of Conway, who had not yet resigned and still ranked as inspector general, was serving as a block, but Washington, who never allowed the shadow to keep him from the substance, hoped to get around that somehow. He thus read with special interest a letter, signed by Benjamin Franklin and Silas Deane, which stated that a certain Baron von Steuben, who was arriving in America as a volunteer, had been an aide-de-camp and quartermaster general to Frederick the Great. An accompanying letter from Steuben linked Washington's name with that of the great European general without any of Conway's sarcasm. "Your Excellency is the only person under whom, after having served the King of Prussia, I could wish to pursue an art to which I have wholly given up myself."[21]

Even Conway had agreed that the Prussian system was superior to the French: why not have it taught by a man who had actually associated with the great Frederick? That is, unless the nobleman who styled himself Lieutenant General Frederick William Augustus Henry Ferdinand Baron von Steuben should prove one of those toplofty foreign officers who scornfully refused to make even the least concession to American ways.

Washington rode out to meet Steuben some miles from headquarters. He could not have been reassured to see the lieutenant general appear, followed by crisp aides and a high-stepping greyhound, as a figure of striking martial aspect. On his broad chest gleamed a highly polished medal the size of a saucer and a gargantuan jeweled star. However, when the Baron dismounted, he shrank, for his legs were very short. On close view, he proved to be an elderly German with a jowled, guileless, humorous face. And his high-stepping greyhound, Azor, was soon contributing to the mirth of the camp by his skill as a music critic. If, as a convivial evening advanced, an officer sang well, the dog would wag his tail, but he responded to a false note with howls.[22]

Washington was soon warned that Steuben was a fraud. The self-made son of poor parents, he had dubbed himself Baron so that he would have a chance of promotion in European armies.* The report that he had been quartermaster under Frederick was a mistranslation; he had never risen above major in that service. His rank as lieutenant general had been an honorary title in the court of a minor German princeling.[23] But Washington discovered that the German was, in truth, an extremely able drillmaster, and the fact that he had raised himself by his own bootstraps made him appreciative rather than scornful of American soldiery.† No European army, the bogus baron pointed out, would have stayed together under such hardships. To a European comrade in arms, he wrote, "The genius of this nation is not in the least to be compared with the Prussians, the Austrians, or French. You say to your soldier, 'Do this,' and he doeth it, but I am obliged to say, 'This is the reason why you ought to do that,' and then he does it." Steuben proved himself a true disciple of liberty rather than another foreign adventurer by agreeing "with the greatest cheerfulness" to function as inspector general while deprived of the title which Conway still pre-empted. However, as Washington put it, "he ingenuously confesses" that he could not afford to serve without pay.[24]

Steuben considered the English method of army organization very inferior, but soon decided that the Americans were too used to it to change. The need was to establish any kind of uniformity. He discovered, so he said, that a regiment might be formed of three, four, eight, or nine platoons, while the Canadian Regiment had twenty-one. A regiment could be larger than an average brigade or contain only some thirty men. Accurate figures were, indeed, almost impossible to procure, since once a man's name was on the roll of a company, the captain continued to swear to it whatever happened, unless the man had died under his very eyes.

---

* Being attractive to warriors who could not climb the ordinary aristocratic ladder, Washington's army was full of bogus noblemen: not only the home-grown Lord Stirling, but "Baron de" Conway, "Baron de" Kalb, and others.

† Du Ponceau, who had arrived as Steuben's aide, claimed that his general invented, as an affectionate appellation for the American soldiery, the term *"sans culotte,"* which took on an almost religious significance in connection with the next people's army: that of the French Revolution.[25]

Untrained in hand-to-hand fighting, the men had no faith in bayonets, which they used to roast beef but did not take to battle. Arms were often in very bad condition, and drill, which did not go beyond manual exercise, varied from regiment to regiment according to the whims of the colonel. Maneuvering was uniform primarily in an unfortunate tendency to march, as on Indian trails, single file, which was one explanation of Washington's complicated battle strategy. To get power in his attacks, he coordinated several columns.

Desiring to find the plan most suited "to the spirit of the nation," Steuben consulted Greene, Laurens, and Hamilton, all of whom could communicate with him (he spoke no English) in French. Washington assisted in the final perfecting.[26]

When Washington announced the result in general orders on March 28, he did not hesitate to use for effect the bogus baron's exaggerated credentials. He referred to Steuben resoundingly as "a lieutenant general in the foreign service." And Scammell argued unashamedly that seeing a gentleman who had been dignified with so high a rank under Frederick the Great "condescend" to act "in the capacity of a drill sergeant" could not help impressing all with the importance of what he was teaching and making all learn fast.[27]

Washington added to his guard a team of one hundred men whom Steuben was personally to drill so that they could serve as an object lesson for the entire army. The German memorized, parrot-like, the commands in English. When the team did not perform to his mind, or he forgot the English words and thus helplessly saw the soldiers running into a stone wall, he would swear in German, then in French, then in both together. Finally, he would call to his aides, "My dear Walker, and my dear Du Ponceau, come and swear for me in English. These fellows won't do what I bid them!"[28]

Steuben confined himself to the essentials, eliminating more than half of the Prussian manual of arms. He taught the soldiers how to carry a musket on the march, load and fire, fix bayonet and charge. He also showed them how to "form in a column, deploy, and execute little maneuvers with excellent precision." One of Washington's general orders read: "In order to correct the vicious step which our soldiers have contracted and induce a natural march easy to the soldiers and calculated to gain ground," the fife and drum corps were to be silenced until they could learn the new rhythm.[29]

When the team was expert and Steuben's assistants had by watching him been trained, drill began for the whole army, each regiment on its own parade. Steuben galloped around, flying often into "whirlwinds of passion" which the army came lovingly to expect. One evening, a captain said to him, "You halloed and swore and looked so dreadfully at me once, when my platoon was out of its place, that I almost melted into water." Steuben blushed crimson and replied, "Oh fie, *donc*, fie, *Capitaine!*"[30]

Drilling with Steuben became the crowning amusement at Valley Forge. It enabled the troops to do easily what they had formerly done badly, and opened chances for rivalry and display. Ensign George Ewing remembered that "we had a great deal of diversion in trying the delinquent officers": those found guilty were each fined a quart of peach brandy. And Du Ponceau tells us that after a sham maneuver between two divisions "a huge bowl of punch" was handed around at Washington's headquarters.[31]

When the army was ready to stage a sensational review, history politely supplied a sensational occasion.

"France," Washington had written, "by her supplies has saved us from the yoke." He had long known that efforts were being made to bring France, and perhaps Spain also, into the war on the American side, but Congress failed to keep him informed on foreign affairs and he suspected that the royal courts of Europe were too full of intrigue and sloth to take any action beyond "underhand assistance." Mid-April was bringing warm days to Valley Forge before he gathered enough gossip from gentlemen who wandered into headquarters to expect that France would take the crucial step of enraging England by recognizing American independence.[32]

On April 30, Washington received two letters, neither of them official, stating (as he summarized it) "that the court of France has recognized us free and independent states; that Britain is in a greater ferment than she ever was since the Revolution, and that all Europe is getting into a flame. . . . I believe no event was ever received with a more heartfelt joy"—all the more because the treaty recognizing the United States contained extensive provisions for a military alliance should France's political act embroil her in a war with England.

Washington wrote Congress laconically that he would like official notification so that he could officially notify the troops. On the fifth morning thereafter, there was still no word from Congress: the general orders Washington issued were routine. But then someone brought to headquarters a copy of the *Pennsylvania Gazette* of three days before. It included a whole supplement devoted to the treaty. He issued a postscript to his orders: "It having pleased the Almighty ruler of the Universe propitiously to defend the cause of the United American States and finally, by raising us up a powerful friend among the princes of the earth, to establish our liberty and Independence up[on] lasting foundations, it becomes us to set apart a day for gratefully acknowledging the divine goodness and celebrating the important event which we owe to his benign interposition."[33]

The celebration was set for the next day. At nine o'clock a cannon shot summoned the soldiers to line up unarmed at the various parades for ceremonies presided over by the clergy. Washington, attended by his staff, rode to the parade of the second line to hear a minister read a précis of the treaty and then wax (so Kalb wrote) "most eloquent, very touching" in praise of the King of France. After an hour and a half had been thus spent, a cannon boomed and the men went to their huts to get their arms in preparation for the martial pageant to be staged by impresario Steuben.[34]

As Washington cantered to the central position from which he was to review all, he heard rising from every hill and dale around him professionally barked commands. Everywhere, the men were being lined up by the brigade inspectors, put through their preliminary motions. Finally, the brigade inspectors stalked stiff-legged to the commanding officer of the brigades, and, one after another, snapped efficiently, "The battalions are formed." The brigadiers then appointed field officers to command the battalions. The field officers, having strutted to the various parades, ordered the men to load and ground their arms.

A portentous silence. Another signal gun! Shouted commands! Young Laurens, who was beside Washington, reports that "the several brigades marched by their right to their posts in order of battle." This brought them all together under Washington's eye. A murderous-looking line was formed "with admirable rapidity and precision. . . . The martial appearance of the troops gave sensible pleasure to everyone present."

Another pause, while the men glared horribly at an imaginary enemy, but stood as motionless—how they had once fidgeted!—as a landscape of rocks. Then from the artillery park, one after another, thirteen shots. As the last reverberation died, the men launched into that progressive fire with muskets, each man shooting singly and in turn, which was known as a feu de joie. Down the long first line and back along the second the running noise and smoke went, thousands of men each waiting with mounting tension for the moment when he would shoulder his musket and pull the trigger, firing all by himself in the presence of His Excellency and the whole army. Steuben began to relax as the maneuver was "executed to perfection."

The last shot fired, the officers led a succession of prearranged huzzas: "Long Live the King of France! And Long Live the Friendly European Powers." Finally: "To the American States." Then the cannon spoke again— thirteen rounds—and everyone cheered at will, and to everyone's delight there was an encore of the feu de joie. The hills, so a poetical soldier wrote, struck to ecstasy by all the sounds, mingled them, reverberated them, kept them lovingly in the spring air until everyone was enchanted by the "beautiful effect."[35]

At last the troops marched back to their encampments where rum awaited them. Washington rode to a many-domed ampitheater which had been raised in front of the artillery park. The covering had been picturesquely improvised out of dozens of officers' marquees. Tables flanked by benches numbered in the hundreds. In the center was an open space where His Excellency and "Lady Washington" received.

Having seen to their men, the officers approached in columns, thirteen abreast, the arms of each rank linked together to signify "most perfect confederation." They were joined by distinguished exiles from Philadelphia, mostly male, and that little galaxy of ladies—Mrs. Greene, the Alexanders, etc.—that circled around "Lady Washington." A band of the army's most accomplished musicians roared out excellent music, but the greatest pleasure, a guest wrote, was the warmth and affability with which Washington greeted his officers.

Then came the "cold collation." Kalb, who had better things to do than adulate Washington, noted that there was "a profusion of fat meat, strong wine and other liquors." For Ewing, the excitement was that Washington "did us the honor to eat and drink with us, where many patriotic toasts were drunk." According to Laurens, "the general received such proofs of the love and attachment of his officers as must have given him the most exquisite feelings."

"I was never present," wrote another of Washington's officers, "where there was such unfeigned and perfect joy as was discovered in every countenance. The entertainment was concluded with a number of patriotic toasts attended with huzzas. When the general took his leave, there was a universal clap, with loud huzzas, which continued till he had proceeded a quarter of a mile, during which time there were a thousand hats tossed in the air. His Excellency turned round with his retinue and huzzaed several times."[36]

It had been a wonderful day. But back in his own headquarters, the happy smiles and the huzzas of his officers a memory now, Washington gave way to a softer, more alluring dream. He believed that since England would probably soon be embroiled in a European war with France there might not be another campaign in America. "Calmness and serenity," he wrote, "seems likely to succeed in some measure those dark and tempestuous clouds which at times appeared ready to overwhelm us. The game, whether well or ill played hitherto, seems now to be verging fast to a favorable issue."[37]

He rushed off a letter urging his stepson under no circumstances to sell any acres: "Lands are permanent, rising fast in value, and will be very dear when our independency is established and the importance of America better known."[38]

Land; his land; Mount Vernon where his heart was; peace with Martha by a shining river!

32

General Lee Rides Again

THE machinery which Mifflin and Lee had set up to dominate Washington had not been abolished: it had merely stalled, as machines will when overloaded. Conway, although he made no effort to serve in that capacity, kept the title of Inspector General until he was finally completely separated from the army. Although they now dared do little more than growl to each other against "the Image" in private letters, Gates and Mifflin continued to lead a Board of War which, as far as its paper powers went, could still dominate Washington.

When the return of fighting weather became imminent, Congress ordered Washington to invite Gates and Mifflin to represent the Board of War at a council on the strategy to be followed in the coming 1778 campaign. Washington was furious. Only after consulting with his intimates did he acknowledge that his duty required him, out of respect for Congress, to treat the interlopers "with civility." He did not intend to let them get away with anything. Assuming that at the council his enemies would keep silent so that they could subsequently criticize any decision that might prove unfortunate, he resolved that he would require them to put down their opinions on every matter in writing.[1]

After the council had convened at Valley Forge on May 8, Washington reported that the British had 4000 troops at New York; about 2000, mostly Germans, in Rhode Island; and 10,000, "the flower of their army," behind strong fortifications in Philadelphia. He had not been adequately informed on "European intelligence" to know whether the enemy expected fresh troops, but he assumed that, as England would now be interested in protecting her homeland from France, reinforcements "will probably not be very large or very early."

The American forces at Valley Forge (11,800), below Philadelphia at Wilmington (1400), and at the Hudson forts which Clinton had abandoned when he went into winter quarters (probably about 1800), were slightly less numerous than the enemy, totaling some 15,000 exclusive of artillery and horse. "Destitute of any information from the different states on which dependence may be placed," he could not report on what reinforcements to expect, but past experience indicated that the army would not go above 20,000. What temporary assistance might be secured from militia was unforeseeable. There would not be enough cannon to batter down any fortifications, and perhaps not enough for "the contingencies of the field." The outlook for provisions was "tolerably good."

Washington then asked whether the army should attack the British in Philadelphia, attack the British in New York, or await contingencies. The council agreed with the conclusion Washington had already reached in one of his elaborate pro-and-con memoranda: The army should "remain on the defensive" awaiting "a fairer opportunity."[2]

Congress had ordered Gates to proceed to the Hudson, where he was "to command very largely" but nonetheless receive instructions from Washington. Gates was soon insisting, in reply to an icy letter from the Commander in Chief, that it was not on his orders that some arms on their way to Valley Forge had been pre-empted by one of his subordinates.[3]

As for Mifflin, Congress ordered Washington to give him a major general's command in the line. Washington pointed out in reply that Mifflin had wanted to resign "when a cloud of darkness hung heavy over us. . . . But if *he* can reconcile such conduct to his own feeling as an *officer* and man of *honor,* and Congress hath no objection to his leaving his seat in another department [the Board of War], I have nothing *personally* to oppose it, yet I must think that gentleman's stepping in and out, as the sun happens to beam forth or obscure, is not *quite* the thing, nor *quite* just with respect to those officers who take the bitter with the sweet." Soon Congress—Mifflin claimed it was persecution due to Washington's influence—ordered an investigation of his acts as quartermaster general. Washington blandly gave him permission to leave camp so that he could collect evidence.[4]

Although Washington balked at accepting men he did not trust, he was suffering from a severe shortage of generals. He was thus delighted when negotiations got underway to secure by exchange the return from British captivity of General Charles Lee. That experienced soldier, he stated, was never more needed than at this moment.[5]

Whatever doubts had been raised in Washington's mind by Lee's disobedience of orders during the 1776 campaign had undoubtedly been assuaged by the realization that Lee had been right in insisting that the way to hold New Jersey was to lurk in the strategic hills around Morristown. And Washington could not know that during Lee's captivity, when he had been in presumptive danger of being executed as a traitor to the army in which he had previously served, Lee had presented the British with a plan for winning the war which was treasonous to the American cause.[6]

Notified that the British were releasing Lee, Washington met him on the road. As His Excellency embraced his old friend, the massed bands of the army, which had been waiting, burst into a march. The two generals rode side by side the four miles to Valley Forge between troops who, as Steuben had taught them to do, wheeled and presented arms. If Washington expected Lee to be in raptures about these new skills, he was disappointed.

Washington had during Lee's year and a half of captivity worked out his own strategy, gained military self-confidence, and raised about him advisers who shared his newly acquired conceptions. He now preferred to Lee's ideas those of Greene, whom Lee could remember as a civilian just commissioned. The returned prodigal could only be horrified. Mifflin, having not yet left Valley Forge, wrote Gates that Lee was "almost sick of his station" because he found the Commander in Chief surrounded by sycophants. And Lee was soon in personal correspondence with the leaders of the dying Conway Cabal. He did not hide his opinion that Washington was "not fit to command a sergeant's guard." He had found the army "in a worse situation than he had expected" and was convinced that it was his duty to straighten everything out. Washington could not "do without me . . . considering how he is surrounded."[7]

Moving on from camp to the temporary capital at York, Lee presented to Congress a plan he had himself drawn up for reorganizing the army. He explained lightly to Washington, "I am mounted on a hobby horse of my own training, and it runs away with me. Indeed, I am so infatuated with it that I cannot forbear boasting its excellencies on all occasions to friends or enemies." Equally playfully, Washington replied that he hoped soon to have "the pleasure of seeing you in circumstances to mount your hobby horse, which I hope will not, on trial, be found quite so limping a jade as the one you set out to York on."[8]

Lee's plan warned Congress of a possible·British advance up the Susquehanna, which he had himself recommended in his treasonous paper to the enemy command. For the rest, he brushed aside everything that Washington had induced Steuben to do. At drill and formation, he wrote, the American could only "make an awkward figure, be laughed at as a bad army by their enemy, and defeated in every encounter which depends on maneuvers." Some of his suggestions implied pure guerrilla warfare undertaken by semi-autonomous battalions.[9]

That this conception had not occurred to Washington is impossible to believe, nor is it necessary to look far to work out why he had never considered embracing it as official policy. Whatever would have been its effect militarily, politically it would have spelled disaster. With each region fighting by itself its own battles, continental unity would have fallen apart.

Sir Henry Clinton, by Thomas Day. Courtesy of Vincent Freed-
ley. Photograph from the Frick Art Reference Library.

Sir William Howe, published by John Morris, London, 1777. Courtesy of
the New-York Historical Society.

And on the local level animosities were at their sharpest. Self-contained bands of radical militia would menace the neighborhood conservatives, who would in turn join together for self-defense. The left and the right would fight not only the invaders but also each other.*

Lee was soon back at Valley Forge, where Washington gave him the command of the first division. His tongue and his pen were never quiet. Washington finally wrote him, "I shall always be happy in a free communication of your sentiments upon any important subject relative to the service," but would Lee please bring his criticisms "directly to myself." Having officers openly reprobate matters that could not be remedied did no good and damaged morale.[10]

Word came from across the lines that Washington had outlasted yet another enemy commander in chief. After an elegant farewell ball had been given him by his officers, Sir William Howe left for home. Sir Henry Clinton, formerly his top subordinate, moved from New York to Philadelphia to assume the command.

By mid-May, Washington's intelligence sources—"deserters, townsmen, women of different qualities, spies"—were unanimous in reporting that the British were planning to depart from the American capital which they had captured with such fanfare. Washington's spirits leapt with the hope that they might "withdraw altogether from the continent," going to the West Indian islands which so needed protection from the French.† However, intelligence sources in New York reported that preparations were being made there to receive the Philadelphia regiments, and that boats suitable for ferrying were being gathered in the channel between New Jersey and Staten Island. Washington concluded that Clinton intended to march to New York, sending his baggage around by water. This seemed confirmed when most of the British shipping in Philadelphia harbor, "upwards of one hundred sail," fell down the Delaware, leaving most of the army behind.[11]

If the British were going to march across New Jersey, did this not present an opportunity to strike them with Washington's newly trained army, to bring the war in an explosion to a close? How Washington yearned to think that the moment was at last at hand. However, the plains of Jersey were just the kind of terrain, suited to the maneuvering of massed forces and

---

* Guerrilla warfare had, because of the weakness there of the Continental Army, its greatest tryout in the south during 1780 and 1781; the result was much infighting between Whigs and Tories, indescribably bloody.

† Since their products and needs fitted so well into the European economy, the various colonies in the Indies were more valuable financially to the Old World than any part of the North American continent. That extensive chain of islands, where the usual European belligerents had contiguous possessions, had, down the years, been the main seat of warfare in the Western Hemisphere. It was, indeed, common for English statesmen to believe that the loss of the North American colonies would be a less serious blow than the loss of the sugar islands.

amenable to shock attacks by the enemy horse, which he had learned to avoid as a scene of battle. He asked himself whether his army was now really so strong as to be thus risked, and the answer he reluctantly reached was no.

Washington remembered that the states had not filled their requisitions for new men, that some two thousand of his troops were down with various diseases, and that he lacked every kind of supply. However regretfully, he resolved to adhere to his established strategy. He sent the New Jersey regiments across the Delaware in preparation for molesting the enemy flanks, and planned himself to cross with the main army as soon as the British crossed. However, he would stay north of them, trying to move as rapidly through the hills as they marched through the lowlands, so that he could, at about the time they entered New York City, join Gates for a defensive stand on the Hudson.[12]

Washington's active temperament was always lacerated by British slowness. With the fleet gone, why did the army stay? At last, what seemed the answer disembarked from a boat that had come up the river: off stepped commissioners who had been empowered by the ministry in London to offer the rebels everything but independence. Because of the French alliance and the British weakness exemplified by the planned evacuation of Philadelphia, they had clearly come too late, but they would probably be given a decent interval in which to attempt their mediation. However, on June 16, "a faithful fellow" whose mother was a washerwoman in Philadelphia reported that the commissioners had ordered their linen delivered at once, "finished or unfinished." And sure enough, at 11:30 on the morning of June 18, the British moved out of Philadelphia and into New Jersey.[13]

Washington did not lead a conqueror's parade through the regained capital. He sent in a small detachment (commanded by the wounded Benedict Arnold) to keep order "till some kind of civil government can be established." He himself led his army into New Jersey north of the British.[14]

His detailed orders to Lee as the commander of a division must have galled that veteran. Lee was to march exactly in accordance with the instructions given him by the quartermaster general, so that Washington would "know precisely your situation on every day. . . . Be strict in your discipline. . . . Begin your marches at four o'clock in the morning at the latest that they may be over before the heat of the day, and that the soldiers may have time to cook, refresh, and prepare for the ensuing day."[15]

Washington expected that he would have to dash for the Hudson to make his movements counter the enemy's, but the enemy, once they were in New Jersey, hardly advanced at all. He began to "suspect that General Clinton, desirous of a general action, was endeavoring to draw us down into the lower country, in order by a rapid movement to gain our right, and take possession of the strong grounds above us." This consideration, plus the fact that the weather was both murderously hot and unusually rainy, induced Washington to halt his troops at Hopewell, some twenty miles north of the dilatory British. He restlessly asked that marksmen in all the regiments volunteer, and sent them off to help the Jersey troops harass the enemy flanks.[16]

Washington's Parthian tactics were always the result of self-control. Since he yearned with all his heart for action that would bring the war to a rapid end, the British as they dawdled there on the Jersey plains were a constant temptation.On June 24, he called a Council of War.

The enemy, he announced, numbered 9000 to 10,000. The Americans had 10,648, not counting 1200 regulars and 1200 militia hovering on the British flanks and rear. "It is now the seventh day since the enemy evacuated Philadelphia, during which time they have marched less than forty miles. . . . The obstructions thrown in their way by breaking down bridges, felling trees, etc., were insufficient to produce so great a delay.* . . . Under these circumstances, and considering the present situation of our national affairs and the probable prospects of the enemy," Washington wished answers to the following question:

Would it be advisable "to hazard a general action?" If so, should it be done by "making a general attack upon the enemy, by attempting a partial one, or by taking such a position—if it can be done—as may oblige them to attack us?" If no general action was indicated, what measures should be taken to annoy the enemy?[17]

General Lee pre-empted the floor, arguing with the eloquence always at his command that the British had never been in such excellent condition or so well disciplined. Would it not be idiotic, when the French alliance could be counted on to assure in the long run American independence, to put all to the hazard and to do so at a disadvantage? Washington looked disappointed; Lafayette and Greene objected; Steuben and Duportail, struggling with their inadequate English, urged an attack; and Hamilton shook an angry head at seeing approach a result "which would have done honor to the most honorable society of midwives." However, Lee carried a close vote against attempting a full-scale battle. It was decided as a compromise— although Lee objected to this too—that an additional fifteen hundred men be sent under Brigadier Charles Scott "to act as occasion may serve on the enemy's left flank and rear . . . the main body to preserve a relative position, so as to be able to act as circumstances may require." All officers present except Wayne signed the report.[18]

That evening, Wayne, Lafayette, and Greene each sent Washington letters urging that he override the decision and order stronger action than

---

* Again Washington failed to realize how easily a well-organized army is disconcerted: Clinton blamed his slowness on the destruction of bridges.[19]

mere skirmishing around the edges of the British column. "I would a Council of War would never have been called," wrote Lafayette; and he added that he would risk all he owned on the outcome of a fight. Greene argued for a specific plan (which had undoubtedly already been discussed).

Since the enemy line of march necessarily stretched for miles—the baggage train by itself was twelve miles long—it should be possible, Greene wrote, to make "a serious impression" on their flank and rear with the light troops "without suffering them to bring us into a general action." However, the main army should be in supporting distance ready to move up to help the light troops escape if that became necessary, or to take advantage of any confusion which setting fire to its tail might cause in the main British army. Although the primary object would be "a partial attack . . . if it should amount to a general action," Greene stated, "I think the chance is greatly in our favor."[20]

Despite his dislike for taking on himself the responsibility of overriding a Council of War, Washington hesitated no longer. He eagerly adopted the plan. And, as was always the case when he finally came to a firm conclusion, he erased from his mind all his former doubts. He had decided what was to be done. It only remained to do it.

Word came that the enemy were on the march toward Monmouth Court House. Washington advanced his own army to Kingston, within twelve miles of the road along which the enemy would have to pass. He sent another thousand men to join the detachments hovering around the British. He intended that the augmented force should, if a "fair opportunity" offered, attack the enemy's left flank or rear.[21]

The operation had now grown beyond the point where a brigadier should be left in charge. Washington would have, of course, to stay with the main army. To what major general should be entrusted in the planned attack? Lee, his ranking subordinate, had denounced what was intended, as foolhardy. Greene was now a staff officer and thus ineligible; and Stirling, who ranked after Lee in the line, was more proficient as a drinker than a fighter. Then came Lafayette, a brilliant youngster, but utterly without experience.

As military protocol required, Washington offered the command to Lee. Lee refused. Washington then passed over Stirling to choose Lafayette. Stirling fumed but seems to have been ignored. Lee hurried into headquarters to say that his friends were blaming him; he had changed his mind; he would take the command. Under questioning from Washington, his doubts reappeared, and he again agreed to Lafayette. But not for long. He reappeared at headquarters, so Hamilton wrote, "recanted again and became very importunate." Washington "grew tired of such fickle behavior, and ordered the Marquis to proceed."[22]

Lafayette was soon fully occupied sending out horsemen to find the various skirmishing groups and bring them together. Morgan's riflemen, who were on the other British flank, proved too far off to be gathered in, but the rest assembled. In the meantime, Washington ordered the men he had held in the main army to leave their possessions behind so that they could quickly reach a position from where they could support the intended attack. However, his troops wilted as they marched through the intense heat, and then rumblings growled in the sky. "Unluckily," as Washington wrote, a heavy storm forced him to halt. Lafayette, who was not impeded by the storm, got within five miles of the enemy's rear. When Washington received word that the Marquis planned to attack the next morning, he hurried back the information that the main army was too far away. Lafayette should withdraw and wait.

Clinton had his spies out, and the result of the intelligence they brought in became visible to Lafayette's horsemen who were staring from hills. There was a great shuffling around in the long British line. The best troops —all the grenadiers, light infantry, and chasseurs of the line—were moved to the rear where they could ward off Lafayette. When this was reported to him, Washington responded by reinforcing his advance corps with another thousand men. It now consisted of about half the army.[23]

One of Lee's aides delivered to Washington a letter. Lee had written that when he agreed to Lafayette leading the detachment, "I considered it as a more proper business of a young, volunteering general than of the second in command in the army; but I find that it is considered in a different manner. They say that a corps consisting of six thousand men, the greater part chosen, is undoubtedly the most honorable command next to the Commander in Chief, that my ceding it would, of course, have an odd appearance. I must entreat therefore (after making a thousand apologies for the trouble my rash assent has occasioned to you) that if this detachment does march that I may have the command of it. So far personally; but to speak as an officer, I do not think that this detachment ought to march at all." He added that, if he were not given the command, "both myself and Lord Stirling will be disgraced."[24]

Washington was truly fond of Lee, with whom he had shown a patience he had never shown with Gates. He had no reason to doubt Lee's loyalty to the patriot cause or, despite the criticisms Lee had broadcast, to himself. (Lee had always been a prodigious talker and carper.) The English veteran was a much more experienced soldier than Lafayette and, in any case, his seniority gave him a clear preference. If an officer were to be disqualified from a command to which he had a right because he had opposed the strategy in council, Councils of War would be an impossibility. Such an officer might, indeed, carry through with more care what seemed to him dangerous.

There remained to consider the "distress of mind" from which Washington recognized that Lee was suffering. Lee's confusion inspired in Washington not fear for the cause but rather pity for an individual he admired. (Washington was to make the same mistake over again when he entrusted West Point to an obviously disturbed Benedict Arnold.) Glad to be able to "ease" the unhappiness of his old companion, he gave Lee the command of the corps that was to open the attack in what became famous (or infamous) in history as the Battle of Monmouth.[25]

CHAPTER

33

The Battle of Monmouth

I N sleeping in the open fields, under trees exposed to the night air and all changes of weather," so wrote Washington's aide, James McHenry, "I only followed the example of our general. . . . When I joined His Excellency's suite, I gave up soft beds, undisturbed repose, and the habits of ease and indulgence which reign in some departments, for a single blanket, the hard floor or the softer sod of the fields, early rising, and almost perpetual duty."[1]

On the night of June 27, 1778, no one of Washington's staff slept soundly, for Washington had sent Lee the order that he should, as soon as the British began to move the next morning, "attack their rear if possible."

It was, indeed, now or never.* When the British set out with daybreak from their strong encampment around Monmouth Court House (now Freehold, New Jersey), they would have to string out their line in a terrain where they were highly vulnerable. But if they were permitted to proceed unimpeded, they could, in ten or twelve miles, reach the heights of Middletown where they would be safe from assault.[2]

The head of Washington's army was within three miles of Englishtown, which was in turn within six miles of the British. Lee's select command of five or six thousand encamped around Englishtown. Washington assumed that Lee was engaged in perfecting, at his headquarters on a hill above a little brook, his orders for the battle. Instead, Lee was riding or pacing or sitting or trying vainly to sleep, his mind in a turmoil of nervous agony. He did not even appear at the council he had himself called of his top subordinates.[3]

Rising early on the 28th, Washington awaited dispatches with all the eagerness of an impetuous nature that had been shackled to inaction month

---

* Washington had been criticized not without reason, for hesitating so long that he allowed himself no chance at a second try, should this day's adventure miscarry.

[302]

after month. On being finally notified that at dawn "the front of the enemy had begun their march," he instantly, as he later wrote, "put the army in motion and sent orders by one of my aides to General Lee to move on and attack them unless there should be very powerful reasons to the contrary; acquainting him at the same time that I was marching to support him."[4]

Washington's men had left behind their blanket rolls and they stripped off their shirts, but the muggy heat was so intense that as the columns advanced, men dropped as if hit by invisible bullets. Those that could not be roused were rolled like cordwood into the bushes; some, Washington noted, "died in a little time after."[5]

At 11:30, Washington was at Englishtown. He dictated a hurried report to Congress expressing fear that the British would get away before Lee could catch them. But then in came a favorable dispatch: although the enemy were moving off at a quick pace, their rear guard was in reach and much less numerous—only fifteen hundred to two thousand—than Lee's detachment. Further news was that Lee, having discovered a shortcut, had "a great certainty of cutting off" this rear guard. In high spirits, Washington sent Lee another assurance that he was coming up. He led his own seventy-eight hundred men ahead as fast as steaming weather and sandy roads would allow.[6]

Now he was listening for sound that would indicate that Lee had caught up with the enemy and was engaged. At last he heard cannon shots and the distant crackle of small arms. Confident of a triumph, he felt his heart leap at this overture to the symphony of battle. But where was the symphony? Instead of augmenting, the noise petered out until only the clanking of his own troops disturbed the hot oppressive air.

Washington sent one aide ahead to discover what was going on, and another to find Lee with the message that he should "annoy the enemy as much as in his power, but at the same time proceed with caution and take care the enemy don't draw him into a scrape."[7]

Washington was advancing at the head of his column, puzzled but still confident, when a farmer appeared beside him with a strange message: "He had heard our people were retreating." Washington's reaction was anger, because the statement was clearly untrue. Lee's strong force could not have been driven back, as there had been only the most restricted sounds of battle, and Lee had sent him no notification of any change of plan. Sternly, Washington asked the farmer where he had got his information. The man pointed to a soldier whose insignia indicated he was a fifer.

When brought before Washington, the fifer "appeared to be a good deal frighted." Washington asked him "whether he was a soldier belonging to the army, and the cause of his returning that way."

The fifer admitted that he was a soldier and added "that the Continental troops that had been advanced were retreating."

Washington, so his aide Colonel Harrison remembered, "seemed to be exceedingly surprised and rather more exasperated." Lest the discouraging rumor spread through the army, he "threatened the man, if he mentioned a thing of the sort, he would have him whipped." He ordered a light horseman to keep the fifer in custody. Then he galloped ahead to find out for himself what was happening.[8]

He had gone some fifty yards when he saw coming toward him two or three persons, one of whom seemed to be "in the habit of a soldier." Washington asked "whence they came and whether they belonged to the army." The reply was that "all of the troops that had been advanced—the whole of them—were retreating."[9]

But there was still no sound of fighting. Through a rolling landscape, somnolent in the misty heat, past steaming, infertile fields from which the thin voices of insects sounded clear, Washington rode ahead, finally crossing a morass on a bridge. Then he heard, first dim but rapidly closer, a multitudinous rustle of feet and voices. The heads of two Continental regiments came in sight. They were "in some disorder. The men were exceedingly heated and so distressed with fatigue they could hardly stand." Lieutenant Colonel Tench Tilghman, who was riding beside Washington in his role as aide, thought he recognized one of the officers as a Captain Moore.[10]

Under questioning, the captain proved confused. He first said that the regiment had been ordered to withdraw because they were exhausted, but then talked of a mission to retrieve two cannon. Having told him to lead his men into the shade and give them some rum, Washington asked the officer one more question: Was Lee's entire force retreating?

The captain replied that he thought it was.[11]

As if to confirm this statement, there came in view several more columns, so many that they thronged not only the road but the flanking sandy fields. Washington exclaimed to his aides that he was "exceedingly alarmed" to find "the advanced corps falling back upon the main body, without the least notice given to him." Recognizing among the newcomers Colonel Israel Shreve and Lieutenant Colonel David Rhea, he galloped over to Shreve and asked "the meaning of the retreat."

Shreve answered "in a very significant manner, smiling, that he did not know, but that he had retreated by order." Tilghman noticed that "he did not say by whose order."

Washington told Shreve to march his men on across the morass, halt them on a hill overlooking it, "and refresh them."

In the meanwhile, Rhea had taken Tilghman aside to say that he "knew the ground exceedingly well, and that it was good ground, and that, should General Washington want him, he should be glad to serve him."[12]

Now there appeared, at the head of more retreating regiments, a familiar scarecrow figure followed by the usual dogs. General Lee was riding slowly towards them, vociferating to his aides. Washington dug spurs into his horse's sides. In a moment, he was next to Lee and shouting, "What is the meaning of this?"

Lee looked up in amazement. He said, "Sir? Sir?"

"What is all this confusion for, and retreat?"

Lee was to remember that he had been "flattering myself" that he would receive "congratulations and applause" for extricating the army from a situation of great danger. "I confess I was disconcerted, astonished, and confounded by the words and the manner in which His Excellency accosted me." That manner, Lee continued, "so novel and unexpected from a man whose discretion, humanity, and decorum" he had always admired, was "much stronger and more severe than the expressions themselves. . . . I was for some time incapable of making any coherent answers to questions so abrupt and in a great measure to me unintelligible."

When Lee finally found his tongue, as always it ran on. He began by saying that he knew of no confusion "but what naturally arose from disobedience of orders, contradictory intelligence, and the impertinence and presumption of individuals." He gave some particulars of how various officers had disrupted his strategy by disobeying him. He added that, to his surprise, he had found himself "in the most extensive plain in America,"* where his troops would have been helpless before the enemy horse.

Washington broke in: He "had certain information that it was but a strong covering party of the enemy."

That might be so, Lee replied, but the enemy was rather stronger than he was, and he did not consider it proper to risk so much. Besides, the whole action had been undertaken "against his own opinion."

Washington shouted, "All this may be very true, sir, but you ought not to have undertaken it unless you intended to go through with it!"

Lee returned to expostulating that his whole plan of attack had been vitiated because his orders had been disobeyed, but Washington had heard enough.† [13] He started to ride back to establish order among the troops who had retreated past him. However, he did not get very far.

---

* Clinton tells us that the plain was one mile wide and three long.

† All the more because it was made at a court-martial where Lee was trying (among other things) to justify his eventual use of insulting language to Washington, his statement that Washington's manner was stronger "than the expressions themselves" gives the quietus to anecdotes of Washington battering Lee at their confrontation with sensational profanity. The several other earwitness accounts presented before the same court also make no mention of swearing. The legend, indeed, has no greater basis than supposed statements said to have been made verbally, after many years had passed, by two officers, Scott and Lafayette, who had not even been present.

In any case, it is highly improbable that Washington could, even if he had let himself go, have sworn with the stunning eloquence legend has attributed to him. To be a good profane swearer (like a good anything else) requires practice, and, although Washington is known to have been irked on other occasions into an isolated oath, the cultivation of profanity did not appeal to his rational and pragmatic intellect. Four months after Monmouth, he attacked in his general orders "the wanton practice of swearing" as a disgusting and indecent vice "productive of neither advantage or pleasure."[14]

Colonel Harrison came galloping up to say that the enemy would be there in fifteen minutes. Washington received the information with dismay. Till that moment, he had assumed that the British, having brushed Lee aside, were continuing their interrupted march toward the safe ground at Middletown. Now he realized that unless he could rally for an almost instantaneous stand the confused soldiers who were streaming by him, blood would fountain out of chaos. It could be a replay of Brooklyn Heights or Kip's Bay. It could be even worse, prove "fatal to the whole army."[15]

Washington's nerves flexed passionately for action, but, so Tilghman remembered, he "seemed at a loss, as he was on a piece of ground entirely strange to him. I told him what Lieutenant Colonel Rhea had told me of knowing the ground. He desired me to go and bring him as quick as possible to him."[16]

As Tilghman rode off, Washington looked around. He drew in his breath with wonder. He saw that "that bountiful Providence which has never failed us in the hour of distress" had placed him at a position which could be held, if not forever, at least until he could achieve something better. The ground sloped in the direction of the enemy. A hedgerow bordered the road like a green rampart, and on the left a wooded hill overlooked the road. At its most extensive, the entire passage was narrow, and it sank to an even narrower crossing over a swamp.[17]

Rhea was now by his side. The local officer reported that the slope continued upward to their rear, entering a protective wood, and that there were even stronger wooded heights farther to the left.[18]

Washington was suddenly all sparkling action. Hamilton, who was by no means always enthusiastic about his commander, wrote, "I never saw the general to so much advantage. His coolness and firmness was admirable." According to the more poetic Lafayette, who came riding up at this moment at the head of his own detachment, "General Washington seemed to arrest fortune with one glance. . . . His presence stopped the retreat. . . . His graceful bearing on horseback, his calm and deportment which still retained a trace of displeasure . . . were all calculated to inspire the highest degree of enthusiasm. . . . I thought then as now that I had never beheld so superb a man."[19]

Colonel Henry Beekman Livingston's regiment was lined up behind the hedgerow. Forming two of the retreating regiments into one, Washington stationed them in the skirts of the wood. As he opened his mouth to call for artillery, there was Lieutenant Colonel Eleazer Oswald with several cannon. Washington ordered that they be placed to command the road.

The next regiments that appeared were in considerable disorder. Washington told them to continue to the rear and pull themselves together. Then a force became visible far to the left of the passage Washington was preparing to defend. Fearing it was an enemy column bent on turning his flank, he

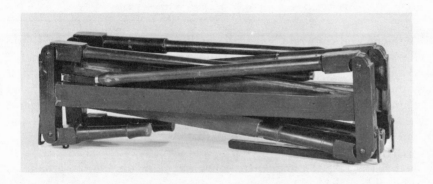

Washington's camp bed, folded and extended, with fixtures for attachment of canopy.

sent Tilghman and General Cadwalader galloping to investigate. As Washington watched anxiously, they cheerfully waved their hats. Washington relaxed a little.[20]

Now there came the unmistakable sound of expertly marching feet hitting the ground in unison. British regulars? No; it was Wayne's Pennsylvania division approaching in excellent order. Washington rode up to Wayne and told him (as that officer remembered) that he was preparing to make a stand with three regiments and two pieces of artillery. He wished Wayne to add his division, take the immediate command, and "dispute the ground as long as possible till he had time to form the army."[21]

Wayne had just posted his men when the sultry air was split with loud sound: British cannon had opened up from across the marsh. Washington waited to see redcoated infantry come in view and line up with cavalry on their flanks. Then the Commander in Chief accepted his greater duty by spurring his horse toward the rear to find the stronger ground of which Rhea had told him, and range defensive forces there.[22]

Washington had not gone very far before he came on General Lee. The officer was in such a state of bewilderment that he had just asked Hamilton, "Do I appear to be out of my senses?" Washington asked him curtly whether he wished to exercise his rightful authority by commanding the rear guard that was holding off the enemy. Various witnesses ascribe to Lee various answers. One reports that he stated that the army was in a desperate situation because of the enemy's "great superiority in cavalry." Another account makes him emote, "Your Excellency may rely upon it that I myself will be one of the last men off the field." Washington rode on to the rear, and Lee wandered off to the right.[23]

Washington soon saw Greene and Stirling at the head of that main part of the army with which he had himself set out that morning. A glance and a quick consultation made clear that, despite the heat under which they had been sagging, the men were in good spirits and eager for the fray. Washington decided to make his major stand with these fresh troops, allowing Lee's disordered regiments to continue their withdrawal to Englishtown, where they were to be re-formed. Happening again on Lee, Washington ordered him to superintend this operation.

Greene, Washington wrote, took "a very advantageous position on the right"; Stirling found almost as strong a post on the left which he further protected with some cannon. According to Hamilton, while both these generals rendered "very essential service," Washington was the "master workman. . . . A general rout, dismay, and disgrace would have attended the whole army in any other hands but his."[24]

The front of the new position was a fence. Two regiments had hardly lined up behind it when the sound of firing in front grew louder. Wayne's men, having finally been forced to abandon a brilliant rearguard defense, came retreating up the slope, moving rapidly but in good order, some turning to fire in the direction of the enemy, others dragging along the pale, limp bodies of companions. When the fugitives came to the fence, they leapt over or struggled bloodily under. Without flinching, the defending regiments allowed the battered, heat-exhausted men to pass by them.

With a wild tattoo of hoofs, the British horse came pelting up the road. The regiments behind the fence only moved to raise their muskets. They held their fire until the cavalry were within forty paces. Then, on command, they all simultaneously pulled their triggers.

Men and horses fell to mingled screams of anguish. Red-fountaining lumps lay contorting or motionless as riderless horses galloped off in all directions. If man and steed were still together, the brightly topped centaurs turned and fled. After them scurried on foot the yet mobile men who had lost their horses. Some sagged to the ground before they got very far; others were brought down bloodily by renewed fire.

The British infantry now appeared in deliberate and ponderous might. "Finding themselves warmly opposed in front," so Washington reported to Congress, they "made an attempt to turn our left flank; but they were bravely repulsed and driven back by detached parties of infantry. They also made a movement to our right, with as little success, General Greene having advanced a body of troops with artillery to a commanding piece of ground, which not only disappointed their design of turning our right, but severely enfiladed those in front of the left wing. In addition to this, General Wayne advanced with a body of troops and kept up so severe and well directed a fire that the enemy were soon compelled to retire behind the defile where the first stand in the beginning of the action had been made."

Under Washington's delighted eyes, "The officers of the army . . . seemed to vie with each other in manifesting their zeal and bravery." The artillery "distinguished themselves in a remarkable manner." Indeed, "the behavior of the troops in general, after they recovered from the first surprise occasioned by the retreat of the advanced corps, was such as could not be surpassed."[25]

This was what Washington had longed for and worked for; this was the fruit of the longer enlistments he had beaten out of Congress, of Steuben's efforts and of Valley Forge. He could not resist a renewed effort to achieve, with his finely forged new weapon, the victory of which he felt Lee's retreat had robbed him. It was only five o'clock in the afternoon. Although his men were gasping and some even dying from the heat, hours of light still remained to fight by.

"The enemy," so Washington continued his report to Congress, "had both their flanks secured by thick woods and morasses, while their front could only be approached through a narrow pass. I resolved nevertheless to attack them, and for that purpose ordered General Poor with his own and the

[309]

Carolina brigade to move round upon their right, and General Woodford upon their left, and the artillery to gall them in front. The troops advanced with great spirit to execute their orders, but the impediments in their way prevented their getting within reach before dark."

Still Washington would not give up. He directed the advance column to remain where they were "with the intention to begin the attack early the next morning." The main army "continued lying upon their arms in the field of action, to be in readiness to support them."[26]

That night, Lafayette and Washington slept on the ground under the same mantle, "talking over the conduct of General Lee." Dawn found Washington staring through his telescope towards the area where he hoped to see his prey. However, the thinning of the dark revealed only scattered dead bodies and, laid out in orderly ranks, prone figures that sometimes moved. Clinton had done what Washington had so often been forced to do: he had disappeared silently in the night. He had carried with him all his wounded except the fifty-four he had left behind because too badly hurt to be transported.[27]

How Washington longed to follow! However, "the extreme heat of the weather, the fatigue of the men from their march through a deep sandy country almost entirely destitute of water, and the distance the enemy had gained by marching in the night, made pursuit impracticable and fruitless."[28]

Washington sent out burial squads who reported that they found the bodies of some 300 English soldiers and four officers, while newly made graves testified to the demise of more officers. Arguing that the usual proportion was four or five wounded to one killed, Washington estimated that Clinton had carried off with him between 1000 and 1200 injured men. (Clinton admitted to 294 killed, wounded, or dead from the heat; 64 missing.) For the American army, Washington's figures were 62 killed, 161 wounded, and 132 missing.[29]

That the army had been saved from a disastrous rout by miraculous intervention stuck in Washington's mind: surely, it was more than blind chance that the very spot where he had met the retreating forces had been designed by nature for defense. Two mornings after the battle, as his troops rested in Englishtown, he published these general orders: "The men are to wash themselves this afternoon and appear as clean and decent as possible. Seven o'clock this evening is appointed that we may publicly unite in thanksgiving to the supreme disposer of human events for the victory which was obtained on Sunday over the flower of the British troops."[30] Yet Washington knew that the victory had been only partial—the British could claim a successful if expensive rearguard action—and for this Washington, in the privacy of his headquarters, bitterly blamed General Lee.

34

Monmouth's Aftermath

W ASHINGTON was holding in his anger, making no public statement concerning Lee's behavior at Monmouth, although he was
convinced that the miscreant had come between the Continental
Army and a major victory. Lee was pacing up and down in his headquarters.
He stated over and over to his aides that he had extricated his part of the army
from certain destruction at the sabers of the British cavalry on a level plain,
"the very element of the enemy," where, "by the temerity, folly, and contempt of orders of General Wayne . . . a large part of the force had rashly
exposed themselves." Had he not, in a brilliantly executed retreat, "maneuvered my antagonists from their advantageous ground into as disadvantageous a one?" He contended that he had meant to make a stand at the
very spot where Washington had rallied the troops after unjustly brushing
him aside. "By all that's sacred," Lee would burst out, "General Washington
had scarcely any more to do in it than to strip the dead!" And, to top
everything, Washington had—could anyone believe it!—ordered him behind
the lines to rally the troops who had retreated there: "sent me out of the
field when the victory was assured! Such is my recompense for having
sacrificed my friends, my connections, and perhaps my fortune; for having
twice extricated this man and his whole army out of perdition; and now
having given him the only victory he ever tasted!"[1]

Sometimes, as his mind swirled, Lee entertained "sanguine hopes" that
Washington would send him an apology. For two days, he waited with what
seemed to him superhuman patience. Then he called for paper and wrote
Washington.

He had, he pointed out, saved the whole army at a moment of terrible
risk. To him "the success of the day was entirely owing." And yet, when they
had met on the field of battle, Washington had used "very singular expressions." He wanted to know exactly what Washington accused him of so that

he could justify his conduct "to the army, to the Congress, to America, and to the world in general. . . . Sir, I have a right to demand some reparation." Surely, what had happened "was not a motion of your own breast but instigated by some of those dirty earwigs who will forever insinuate themselves near persons in high office."[2]

Washington called in Wayne and Scott, who had commanded the spearhead of Lee's advance force, and asked them for a written statement of what, we may assume, they had already told him. The two brigadiers claimed that they had caught the enemy "in full march, moving with great haste and confusion." They themselves had taken a position which, though near to the enemy, was protected by a deep morass. Far from being exposed, "the ground we now occupied was the best formed by nature for defense of any, perhaps, in this country." Having repulsed a charge of the enemy's horse and foot, they saw before them "the most pleasing prospect, from our numbers and position, of obtaining the most glorious and decisive victory." However, to their amazement, the troops to their right, who were under the immediate command of Lee, started to fade away. Wayne sent twice to Lee "requesting that the troops might return to support him," but Lee did not deign to dispatch any reply, and the withdrawal continued. Since their right was being exposed, the brigadiers had to join the retreat. "We also beg leave to mention that no plan of attack was ever communicated to us, or notice of a retreat until it had taken place in our rear."[3]

With this information, which was backed by other witnesses, in hand, Washington finally unleashed his anger.

"Sir," he wrote Lee, "I received your letter (dated through mistake the 1st of July), expressed, as I conceive, in terms highly improper. I am not conscious of having made use of any very singular expressions at the time of my meeting you, as you intimate. What I recollect to have said, was dictated by duty and warranted by the occasion. As soon as circumstances will permit, you shall have an opportunity either of justifying yourself to the army, to Congress, to America, and to the world in general; or of convincing them that you were guilty of a breach of orders, and of misbehavior before the enemy, on the 28th instant, in not attacking them as you had been directed, and in making an unnecessary, disorderly, and shameful retreat."[4]

Lee remembered that he had hoped that his letter would elicit an apology from Washington. When, instead, "these thundering charges were brought against me, comprehending the blackest military crimes of the whole black catalogue, I was more than confounded. I was thrown into a stupor. My whole faculties were, for a time, benumbed. I read and read it over a dozen times, and thought it still a delusion, but when I waked, and was convinced of the reality, I sat down and wrote the second letter."[5]

Again Lee got the date wrong, writing this time the 28th rather than the 30th. He would welcome, he stated, an "opportunity of showing to America the sufficiency of her respective servants. I trust that the temporary power of office, and the tinsel dignity attending it, will not be able, by all the mists they can raise, to offiscate [obfuscate] the bright rays of truth. In the meantime, your Excellency can have no objection to my retiring from the army. I am, sir, your most obedient, humble servant."[6]

No sooner had the messenger departed with this letter than Lee sent Washington another. It stated that he desired a court-martial, and warned that there should be no delay lest a controversy between his adherents and Washington's disrupt the cause.

Washington replied, "I have sent Colonel Scammell, the adjutant general, to put you in arrest, who will deliver you a copy of the charges on which you will be tried. I am, etc."[7]

The strength of Washington's anger did not permit him to draw up the charges carefully. The first—"disobedience of orders in not attacking the enemy on the 28th of June agreeable to repeated instructions"—would have been truly applicable only if Washington had been so idiotic as to order Lee to attack under all circumstances, no matter what the situation proved to be when he actually confronted the enemy. As a matter of fact, Washington's orders, while making his intention plain, left room for Lee to exercise judgment. Thus, the true question was not obedience or disobedience of orders, but of good or bad judgment exercised in good or bad faith.

Washington's second charge was "misbehavior before the enemy on the same day by making an *unnecessary, disorderly,* and *shameful retreat.*" Whether the retreat had been "unnecessary" or "shameful" went back to the matter of judgment. Only whether it had been "disorderly" was capable of factual trial.

Of the third charge—"disrespect to the Commander in Chief in two letters"—was Lee clearly guilty.[8]

The court Washington appointed under the presidency of Stirling was made up not of lawyers but of soldiers. They were willing to ignore the specific wording of the indictment and make their rulings according to their assessment of Lee's tactics. After about a month of hearings, they found Lee guilty of all three charges, with the provision concerning the second that the retreat had been disorderly only in "some few instances." Having thus supported the Commander in Chief, the possibility of victory and the fighting spirit of the army, the court laid down a sentence strangely mild: Lee was to be suspended from any command for twelve months.[9]

This verdict was referred to Congress for what Washington assumed would be instantaneous and enthusiastic approval. Two months later, he wrote his brother Jack that there was a "mystery" he could not explain in the fact that Congress had not acted. "There are," he commented, "moles among men as well as beasts, and their ways are as impervious to the view."[10]

Lee himself less resembled a mole than a rooster perpetually on the crow.

He stated publicly that he had been tried not in a fair court but by an "inquisition" as tyrannical as any ever sponsored by Mazarin or Cardinal Richelieu; and he published a detailed defense of his behavior at Monmouth abrim with jibes at Washington. Reviving the issue of Conway, insisting that the Irish-Frenchman had also been a sacrificial victim, Lee concluded thunderously that Washington, as a military incompetent, was jealous of and determined to wreck any officers with real skill.

Lee's public behavior forced Congress to face the issue at last in terms not of the actual charges but of Lee's loudly insisted-on rivalry with Washington. The Englishman was demonstrating all over again his eccentricity and lack of judgment; Congress could not accept the consequences of allowing him to be exalted over Washington. However, the decision to endorse the verdict of Lee's court-martial was far from unanimous: of the eight states present and voting, two voted for Lee.[11]

As the matter had hung in the balance to the endless blaring of Lee's voice and pen, Washington had fretted mightily that his principles would not let him say anything in his own defense that could prejudice an undecided judicial proceeding. Yet he feared for the effect on his reputation: would not his silence be taken as a "tacit acknowledgment" that he was incapable of answering Lee's charges? In his bitterness, Washington forced from his memory how fond he had once been of Lee, how he had relied on the advice of that veteran. He had never felt more than "common civility," he wrote, for a man whose "temper and plans were too versatile and violent to attract my admiration."[12]

After Congress had voted, Washington's aides swung into action. Accusing Lee of having insulted His Excellency, Laurens challenged Lee to a duel. Hamilton served as Laurens's second. Lee was slightly wounded in the side. However, the wound to his reputation and feelings was more deep. Continuing to fulminate from his enforced temporary retirement, he wrote Congress during July 1780 a letter they considered so insulting that they dismissed him completely from the service.[13]

In the top echelons of the army, the opposition to Washington was now reduced to a single survivor: Horatio Gates. However, Washington's old enemies of the Conway Cabal had not been won over; they had merely been driven underground. They agreed among themselves that Lee, who had been right at Monmouth, was sacrificed to Washington's incompetence and pride.

Historians have almost unanimously excoriated Lee's retreat. His hysterical attacks on Washington prejudiced them against his contentions from the very first, and the later discovery of his treason (or near treason) when a British captive seemed to clinch his guilt at Monmouth.

Had Lee been engaged in treason he would not have tried to extricate the army but to deliver it at a disadvantage. Actually, his behavior at the battle which elicited Washington's angry reaction stemmed from a basic strategical disagreement. Although the matter had not been tested in battle, and Washington (as his hesitations before he ordered the attack revealed) could still doubt, the Commander in Chief believed that the Continental Army had been so improved that it could now stand up to the British and German regulars in open battle. Lee was unimpressed by anything Washington had achieved since he himself had been captured in 1776, when the army had been at its lowest ebb. His unvarying opposition to the attack was based on his conviction that the Americans would surely be routed.

Under the circumstances, Lee should never have accepted the command of the advance force, all the more because his nervous organization was at the best not stable. That he was confused both before and during the action the evidence makes abundantly clear. Although not spilling over into treason, his divided loyalties surely created tensions, if only because he was extremely anxious to make a good impression in his role as commander* on the British regular officers he admired and with whom he had fraternized during his captivity. His realization that his opponents would be shocked made him doubly unhappy about the unconventional maneuvers engaged in by the American-trained generals—Wayne and Scott—who led the front of his advance. Convinced that the Americans could stand up to the enemy, even the British horse (one charge of which they did, indeed, dissipate), they considered the terrain they occupied "the best formed by nature for defense of any perhaps in the country." Lacking their confidence, Lee believed that his subordinates were getting him into a desperate scrape by placing his army in what seemed to his anxieties "the most extensive plain in America," a disastrous terrain where the incompetents would be chewed up by the regulars, particularly the light horse. Wayne and Scott felt victory was in their hands, and Washington, resolute as always once he had finally made up his mind, agreed that only Lee's pusillanimousness had prevented a major American triumph. He scorned Lee's claim to have saved the army from disaster. Who was right?

As Washington himself said on another occasion, no one can foretell the outcome of a battle. However, the way the Continental Army, when Washington had finally rallied them, stood up to the enemy implies that Lee's mental confusion and lack of confidence in the American soldiery had served the enemy well.

The actual strength of the British force before which Lee fell back remains a subject of unresolved controversy. Washington believed that it had been no more than a weak rear guard that could easily have been overwhelmed; Lee visualized it as large and made up of the flower of the British army. Clinton insisted, of course, that he had prepared for the rebels

---

* As Freeman has pointed out, for all his extensive military experience, Lee had never before commanded a battle in the field.

[315]

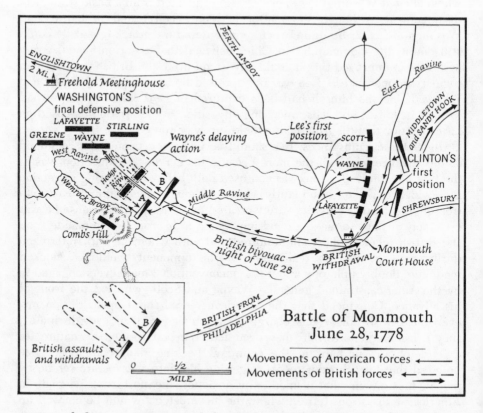

an overwhelming reception and that had it not been for the judgment and skill of Lee, the patriot rabble would have been smashed.

However, Clinton revealed by his subsequent actions that Monmouth had taught him a depressing lesson. He had learned that he was facing something which his predecessor Howe had never faced: an army which could fight European regulars on their own terms. This realization by the British commander in chief was to have a major effect on the future of the war.[14]

The Wheel Turns Full Circle

I N the steaming weather, Washington made no further effort to attack
the British as they moved from the Monmouth battlefield to the shipping that awaited them at Sandy Hook and were then ferried to their
long-established positions on Staten Island, Manhattan, and Long Island.
The obvious post for the Continental Army was now at the Hudson River
to block off that inland waterway and be prepared to march, if need be,
to New England. However, the British were not arriving at New York in
any condition to undertake an immediate offensive: for once, there was no
pressure to move fast.

Washington gave his men two days in which "to breath themselves" at
Englishtown. He was able to allow two days more for the advance to
Brunswick. Even at this slow pace, as he reported, the march was "incon-
ceivably distressing . . . about twenty miles through a deep sand
without a drop of water except at South River, which is half way." When the
army collapsed at Brunswick, Washington feared, in the eighteenth-century
manner, that the men might damage their health by immoderate splashing
in the nearby Raritan River. The sergeants were ordered to see that their
charges did not bathe in the heat of the day or remain long in the water.[1]

At Brunswick, the army celebrated the second anniversary of the Declaration of Independence. The men enjoyed a double serving of rum, and, as a
member of Washington's guard noted in emphatic spelling, "At night, his
Exelency and the gentlemen and Ladys has bawl at Head Quarters with
grate pompe."[2] How could it help being a cheerful occasion? There was so
much to be thankful for. France had declared on the American side. The
British were drawing in their horns: they had been forced to abandon the
capital of the American cause, and their retreat had proved very expensive.
In addition to the casualties at various skirmishes and Monmouth, the
enemy had lost through desertion about a thousand men, mostly Germans.
At long last, what the patriots had foreseen was taking place. Having got a

[317]

true whiff of freedom (and having made friends and sweethearts in Philadelphia), Hessians were abandoning in droves the mercenary service to which they had been sold by their princes.

As his own army resumed its leisurely move toward the Hudson, Washington found time for sightseeing. With his aides around him, he crossed the Passaic on a dilapidated bridge and rode on to where he could see rising high in the air what he would have thought was smoke had he not known it was spray. He was soon staring down into a fissure to see white water dropping some thirty feet through a very narrow cleft and then, where the cleft widened, taking a second fall of about seventy feet. Far below, the semi-gloom was colored by "a beautiful rainbow in miniature."

His traveled aide McHenry gave it as his opinion that these Falls of the Passaic were well enough, but not comparable to Niagara or even the Falls of the Mohawk. Washington, nonetheless, stared happily, for they were the most impressive falls he had ever seen.*

The party made themselves comfortable where a cool spring bubbled up under the shade of a huge oak. From their traveling canteens they unpacked a modest repast of cold ham, tongue, and some biscuit. "With the assistance of a little spirit, we composed some excellent grog. Then we chatted away a very cheerful half hour."[3]

On they rode, through charmingly fertile country to the village of Paramus. The plan was for them to sleep at the house of a Mrs. Watkins, but they had hardly entered this modest dwelling when up rode a servant with an invitation for them to stay with Mrs. Theodosia Prevost (the future wife of Aaron Burr) in her elegant mansion, Hermitage. Not wishing to offend Mrs. Watkins, Washington remained with her for dinner, and was rewarded, so McHenry tells us, by having "her two charming daughters" sing "several pretty songs in a very agreeable manner."

The party moved on to Hermitage, which they found inhabited by belles of a more prismatic brilliance. Mrs. Prevost, the rich widow of a British army officer, had staying with her "some fair refugees from New York. . . . With them," McHenry continues, "we talked—and walked—and laughed— and danced and gallanted away the leisure hours of four days and nights."[4]

They all danced with the more abandon, Washington leading many a measure, because good news kept coming in. The Continental commander, who suffered so much from jealousies between the states, could not help being delighted to hear that nine states had signed the Articles of Confederation, which established a legal basis for continental union. Four more states would have to sign before the Articles became operative, yet it had been a great step forward.[5]

And then, on the morning of July 11, there penetrated to Hermitage a

* The Falls of the Passaic, so celebrated in the eighteenth century, are now buried in the industrial bowels of Paterson, New Jersey.

stunning rumor: a French fleet, come to fight the British at the patriots' side, was actually off the coast. This was almost too thrilling to believe, but before the day was out a horseman appeared from Philadelphia with official word that "on the 15th of April a French fleet sailed from Toulon consisting of twelve sail of the line, seven frigates, and four xebecs [lateen-rigged three-masters indigenous to the Mediterranean], which we hourly expect to arrive in Chesapeake Bay."[6]

This fleet, which outweighed the British ships stationed in North American waters, would give the patriots what their cause had never had, control of local ocean. However, a sobering postscript to the news made clear that the naval superiority might be only temporary: eleven British ships of the line were said to be speeding across the ocean behind the French.

On the 13th, Washington heard that the expected French fleet, commanded by an admiral called Count d'Estaing, had actually arrived in the Chesapeake. He dispatched Laurens, who spoke French, to concert plans with the admiral.

Most of the army had already marched ahead when on the 15th Washington rose early and said good-by to the amenities of Hermitage. With his staff, he rode through narrow and stony roads to Colonel Hay's at Haverstraw. The house was a mile back from the Hudson but on an eminence that looked down on the river where it broadened into the Tappan Zee. Washington could see the opposite shore and heights beyond it. Although more extensive and more rugged, the prospect was not unlike the view that in all the world spoke most deeply to his heart. If he half closed his eyes, he could imagine himself at Mount Vernon, looking down on the dear tidal expanses of the Potomac. And when he opened his eyes, he felt joyfully that he was closer to Mount Vernon than at any time since he had accepted his command. Even before the French fleet had arrived, he had speculated that the British would have to abandon their campaign in America to protect themselves in other parts of the world. Surely he would soon be able at long last to lay aside the soldier.[7]

Already his situation, with the British fortifying in New York and his army free outside, was one that would quite recently have seemed beyond his wildest hopes. "It is not a little pleasing nor less wonderful to contemplate," he wrote, "that after two years maneuvering and undergoing the strangest vicissitudes that perhaps ever attended any one contest since the Creation, both armies are brought back to the very point they set out from, and that that which was the offending [offensive] party in the beginning is now reduced to the use of the spade and pickax for defense. The hand of Providence has been so conspicuous in all this that he must be worse than an infidel that lacks faith, and more than wicked that has not gratitude enough to acknowledge his obligations—but it will be time enough for me to turn preacher when my present appointment ceases, and therefore I shall add no more on the Doctrine of Providence."[8]

[319]

VII

The French Alliance

36

New Cards in an Old Game

T HE word from Europe was that France's acceptance of American independence had set her fighting with Great Britain. And the arrival in America of the French fleet was tangible proof that George Washington's war had entered a new and radically different phase.

Up till now, all the soldiers on Washington's side had been more or less under his orders. The ocean had been controlled by the enemy. And decisions reached in Europe had affected his strategy only by their effect on enemy plans and forces. But now Washington would fight beside warriors who would never be truly under his command. The possibility that his allies might (as at this moment) dominate the ocean lanes opened up a whole new range of strategic thinking. And decisions made abroad would have effect on his own manpower as well as that of the enemy.

Washington had a passion for intelligence that would enable him to foresee, and, as far as his possibilities went, he was an excellent spymaster. But his possibilities ended at the seaboard. Americans were at best ill-informed concerning the ancient diplomatic ganglia that had been set into frenzied activity by the outbreak of war in Europe. As old alliances and enmities interwove in the memories and emotions of princes and ministers with present considerations of balance of power, Congress was too often confused as to what was going on. And the little the Congress did find out, it was careless about communicating to Washington. "I am," he complained, "destitute of information with respect to the present state of European politics."[1]

No spies reported to Washington British decisions which had already established the strategic pattern that was to dominate the rest of his war. When European guns had begun to fire, the French Atlantic Fleet had been at Brest and their Mediterranean Fleet under d'Estaing at Toulon. Although England's existing naval superiority to France offered the possibility of corking d'Estaing up in the Mediterranean, the British feared that Spain would join the French, tipping the naval balance against them. The safety of the British Isles, it was decided, required England to keep her fleet united and near home unless an enemy squadron actually removed itself from European waters by sailing for America. Then the English could send a pursuing detachment. Thus d'Estaing had been allowed to leave the Mediterranean unopposed, and only after it was certain that he was headed for North America did the British send a squadron to counter him: thirteen ships of the line under Vice Admiral John ("Foul Weather Jack") Byron (the poet's grandfather). Naturally, d'Estaing arrived first. Until Byron reinforced the weaker British squadron already in North American waters, the ocean would be a pro-patriot highway. This situation was to repeat itself at various times in various campaigns as French squadrons appeared in advance of their British equivalents.[2]

A second major British decision was that the North American aspects of the war had become, with the entrance of France, secondary to the control of the West Indies where both European powers had extremely valuable possessions. Clinton had abandoned Philadelphia because he had been ordered to send eight thousand men—about a third of his command—to the Indies and also Florida.

Clinton was still waiting to get these off. He had been forced to use all his shipping to transport the army baggage from Philadelphia to New York, and then d'Estaing had appeared outside New York Harbor. Washington urged the Frenchman to sail in at once and attack the British at their anchorage. However, a French "sixty-four" drew twenty-seven feet to the British twenty-two. D'Estaing encountered sandbars which he believed he could not cross.[3]

Franco-American attention turned to Newport, where almost six thousand enemy soldiers, mostly Hessians, were pinned down on an island a mile off the mainland because d'Estaing's presence bottled up all British shipping. Washington considered the odds one hundred to one that these soldiers could be captured. The French fleet had brought four thousand marines. Washington quickly swelled Sullivan's Continentals, who had been watching the enemy from the mainland of Rhode Island, with so many regulars and militia that the patriot force numbered nine thousand.[4]

Sullivan loomed as a problem. He could not reasonably be removed from a command he had held for some time, but Washington knew that the New Hampshire frontiersman was impetuous, vain, cantankerous, and voluble. How would he get on with the newly arrived allies? Even for the courteous Washington this was proving a problem. In the letters he received from d'Estaing, the admiral tortured every sentence until it contained, in addition to the idea it was supposed to convey, a complimentary reference to Washington, however irrelevant, strained, ritualistic, or even fatuous. In his own efforts to reply in something like the same manner, Washington produced paragraphs of such overpolite and manifestly embarrassed clumsiness as he had not indited since he had tried to please his highborn (and eternally displeased) English superiors during the French and Indian War.[5]

Then there was d'Estaing's representative, Major André Michel Victor, Marquis de Choin, a near relative, as Washington was copiously informed, of the French minister of marine. The highborn major made it so clear that everything about the American camp and His Excellency's table was so below his usual standard that Washington praised Choin to d'Estaing for the "sacrifice" he had made "in accommodating himself to a manner of life" which he did not find "the most agreeable."[6]

It seemed to Washington his obvious move to send as a buffer between d'Estaing and Sullivan his own highborn French general, Lafayette. And to smooth any difficulties that might arise with the local authorities, he also dispatched the Rhode Islander Greene, who agreed to waive for the occasion his seniority to Sullivan.

Hearing that d'Estaing had safely anchored off Rhode Island, Washington entertained "the fairest hopes that ever were conceived." Surely, the capture of so large an enemy force would give "the finishing blow to British pretensions of sovereignty over this country." The rest of the enemy would disappear from America "as fast as their canvas wings could convey them."[7]

Then came news as puzzling as it was disturbing. Lord Howe, who still held command of England's American squadrons, had sailed his fleet out of New York harbor. Washington could not believe that they would attack d'Estaing at numerical disadvantage; but supposing—direful possibility!—they were on their way to join somewhere offshore Byron's expected fleet? Then it would be the French who were in danger! Washington begged Sullivan to report every day: "Just to hear that all is well will be a relief to me."[8]

For a while, all went well. Sullivan and d'Estaing successfully landed their troops and marines on Newport Island. Everything was prepared for an attack on the main British installations, when d'Estaing's lookouts reported a British fleet in the offing. The French admiral reacted violently. He pulled his marines back onto his ships, lifted sails, and set out after the enemy, leaving the Americans sitting on the island by themselves, face to face with the British.

Washington still hoped for the best. Since the British fleet had fled at the approach of the French, he assumed that they were still the weaker: Admiral Howe, it seemed, had not joined up with Byron. Therefore, d'Estaing would probably defeat or drive away the enemy flotilla. He would return to Newport and the siege would continue.

The next news was written in the sky over Washington's head: an easterly gale piled dark clouds and a great storm broke. Both fleets would certainly be scattered, and it might well take some time before the French could get their sailing vessels back to Rhode Island. Washington suffered from "a disagreeable state of suspense and anxiety."[9]

Finally, Washington heard that d'Estaing had returned. The French admiral stated that there had been no naval battle. However, his storm-battered ships needed to be refitted. Furthermore, some of Byron's fleet had joined Howe and the rest were daily expected. His orders under such circumstances were to take refuge in Boston Harbor. Despite anguished patriot screaming, the French sailed off, leaving Sullivan's men without naval support, facing a strong British garrison and a mile offshore. So much for the first effort at Franco-American cooperation! So much for "the fairest hopes that ever were conceived"![10]

Washington was very angry. He had no reason to love the French. They had been his enemies in his previous war and had incited the Indians to great brutality against Virginians. He could not doubt that France had entered the war for no high-minded motives but because it was to her "interest" to weaken Great Britain. As for the volunteers who filled his Councils of War with foreign jabbering, he had just been incited to a new rage against them: the good-natured Steuben had finally succumbed to the infection of transatlantic arrogance. Although a staff officer, Steuben wished a command in the line, and he was off junketing to Congress in an effort to have most of the supervision of the army taken away from Washington and put in his own hands. In a fury, Washington wrote, "I do most devoutly wish that we had not a single foreign officer among us except the Marquis de Lafayette."* [11]

And now, to top everything, an altogether foreign force had lured his men into exposing themselves, and then vanished, leaving them in the greatest danger!

The address of Americans in moving around enabled Sullivan to get his men back to the mainland before the British could take advantage of their plight. However, the situation had stirred up a catfight of major proportions that endangered all future Franco-American cooperation. From the first, d'Estaing and Sullivan had got on badly. The French courtier-admiral had complained that the shortset, ruddy, rough Irish-American frontiersman "has shown towards me the manner of a commander to his servant; he styles himself my general. . . . I was forced to show an austere firmness to make the allies understand that while their troops were good for a defensive, they had no qualities necessary for attack." The Americans, indeed, were "a curious lot" who accused the French of being "thin, polite, and always dancing."[12]

After the French had sailed away, Sullivan insulted them in his general orders. This, so Greene wrote Washington, opened "the mouths of the army

---

* Fortunately this most indiscreet letter was not intercepted by the enemy.

in very clamorous strains" against France. Lafayette took offense and insulted the American officers back, becoming, as he angrily reported to Washington, "more upon a warlike footing in the American lines than when I come near the British lines at Newport."[13]

To various patriot leaders, Washington wrote that "whatever private opinions may be entertained," it would be politic to state that the French fleet had been forced to go to Boston because of "the damage suffered in the late storm." He chided Sullivan: "First impressions, you know, are generally longest remembered, and will serve to fix in a great degree our national character among the French." Americans should take into consideration that the French "are a people old in war, very strict in military etiquette, and apt to take fire where others scarcely seem warmed." Having complimented Lafayette by reminding him that his influence was great, Washington went on: "I, your friend, have no doubt but that you will use your utmost endeavors to restore harmony." Strictures uttered "in the first transport of disappointed hope" should be ignored.[14]

Fears Washington expressed as to how the French fleet would be received in Boston proved only too well founded: disorders mounted until rioters who were pillaging a French bakery mortally wounded a French officer who tried to protect his *bon pain*. Then all responsible individuals leapt back from the yawning abyss. D'Estaing offered to land troops from his fleet and lead them on foot to Rhode Island, where he would put himself under Sullivan's command, an offer which was, of course, politely refused. Washington wrote d'Estaing that the French officer could only have been murdered by some stray Englishman; he praised the admiral's forebearance as flowing "from a great mind."[15]

In the next international crisis, Washington and d'Estaing were on the same side. The British peace commissioners, who were still hanging around New York, included in a declaration to Congress slurs on France. Lafayette, still too far up in the high ropes to climb down quietly, challenged to a duel the head of the commission, the Earl of Carlisle. The Marquis failed to notify Washington, but d'Estaing got wind of what was happening. Terrified lest he be blamed if the darling of the French court were killed, the admiral rushed off an appeal to Washington to intervene.

In writing Lafayette, who was still in New England, Washington, as he reported to d'Estaing, "omitted neither serious reasoning nor pleasantry." He stated to his young friend that "the generous spirit of chivalry, exploded by the rest of the world, finds a refuge, my dear friend, in the sensibility of your nation *only*. But it is in vain to cherish it, unless you can find antagonists to support it. . . . It is to be feared that your opponent, sheltering himself behind modern opinion and under his present public character of commissioner, would turn a virtue of such ancient date into ridicule." Furthermore, "experience has proved that chance is as often as much con-

[327]

cerned in deciding these matters as bravery, and always more than the justice of the cause."[16]

Surely remembering that Washington's aides had, without incurring their commander's displeasure, recently fought several duels for Washington's honor, Lafayette did not allow himself to be cajoled into withdrawing his challenge. However, the Earl of Carlisle refused to cooperate.

Washington had never met d'Estaing. He wrote the admiral that since enough of Byron's fleet had arrived to give the British unquestioned naval superiority, any discussion of possible offensive cooperation "would be premature." Otherwise Washington would "count it a singular felicity" if "personal intercourse should afford me the means of cultivating a closer intimacy with you."[17]

D'Estaing clamored to have troops sent to Boston to protect his base from land attack. Washington replied that since it was essential that supplies should be able to cross the Hudson, he had to protect the river with a force almost equal to the British in New York. He pointed out that to attack Boston in adequate strength, the enemy would have to withdraw from New York, a move which could not be concealed and would give Washington time to establish effective countermeasures.[18]

The British were, on the whole, quiescent. To what extent Clinton had been weakened by the detachments he had finally succeeded in sending to the Indies, how deeply he had been impressed by the American stand at Monmouth, became clear from the change which had taken place in the strategic situation around New York. Washington, who had had to skulk for so long, could now write (although perhaps with a touch of rhetorical exaggeration) that his army "had been the whole summer inviting them out of their stronghold"—but in vain.[19]

British action was limited to skirmishing. The navy raided New Bedford and Martha's Vineyard, losing more in the hate they engendered than they reaped in rebel fright or in supplies. The enemy professionals surprised and cut up with bayonets several patriot outposts to Washington's loudly expressed "chagrin and amazement" that any of his officers could, as they indulged themselves "in good quarters," have been so careless. Tory irregulars descended on an occasional sleeping farmhouse to bayonet or capture some nightshirted rebel leader they particularly disliked. During mid-September, the enemy foraged in New Jersey, covering their flanks so expertly with geographic barriers that Washington had to put up as "cheerfully" as he could with the "inconvenience."[20]

Wholesale carnage was limited to the northern frontier. The torch which had been dropped by Burgoyne's surrender had been taken up, during that summer of 1778, by Indians, primarily from the powerful Iroquois League, operating with Tory exiles from the Mohawk Valley. July 4 had seen

Pennsylvania's Wyoming Valley flowing with the blood of several hundred scalped inhabitants. In September, the settlements around German Flats on the Mohawk River were laid waste, and in November the Cherry Valley massacre depopulated the northern end of that Susquehanna Valley where, farther south, Washington had suffered through much of his French and Indian War service.

As the commander responsible for protecting the Virginia frontier from Indian raids, but without enough troops to effect anything, Washington had, at the age of twenty-four, burst out, "The supplicating tears of the women and moving petitions of the men melt me into such deadly sorrow that I solemnly declare, if I know my own mind, I could offer myself a willing sacrifice to the butchering enemy. . . . If bleeding, dying! would glut their insatiate revenge, I would be a willing offering to savage fury, and die by inches to save a people!" But now Washington had a larger canvas to scan, and although he could "lament," he could express "distress," he could only send north and west what riflemen and few regiments he could spare from operations of more importance to the cause. He did not fool himself into believing that this could protect the long frontier. Since Indians always struck where guarding soldiers were not, "the only certain way of preventing Indian ravages is to carry the war vigorously into their own country." However, he was too weak to attempt this unless more major British detachments departed from the continent. Slipping into a repetition that revealed inner urgency, he wrote, "I fear we must content ourselves for the present with defensive precautions, for the present."[21]

The complete solution would be to pull the Indians' bases out from under them by adding Canada to the thirteen states. Lafayette, Washington knew, was hoping for a more successful replay of the previous year's plan to send a winter expedition under the leadership of Lafayette himself and other French officers whose presence would presumably win over the French inhabitants. To his disciple, Washington wrote in late September, "If you have entertained thoughts, my dear Marquis, of paying a visit to your court, to your lady, and to your friends this winter, but waver on account of an expedition to Canada, friendship induces me to tell you" that there was no point in waiting. He hinted that Lafayette could most contribute by using his influence in Europe to help get Spain into the war beside France.[22]

Lafayette had already taken steps to force Washington's hand. Without notifying his friend and commander, the Marquis had departed from New England to Philadelphia carrying a scheme for presentation to Congress. The idea was that twelve thousand Americans should in various expeditions capture "Detroit, Niagara, St. John's, Montreal, etc.," while a French fleet sailed up the St. Lawrence and (reversing the triumph of General Wolfe that had ended French control of Canada) took the fortress city of Quebec.

Lafayette wished to be empowered to make the necessary arrangements in France.

Congress was enthralled with the prospect. They ordered Lafayette to ride to Washington's headquarters on his way to the shipping, and ordered Washington to add his suggestions to the sheaf of papers the Marquis would carry to Versailles.[23]

Referring to himself in the third person, Lafayette thus describes what happened next: "Heated by fatiguing journeys and overexertion, and still more by the grief he had experienced in Rhode Island; and having afterwards labored hard, drank freely, and passed several sleepless nights at Philadelphia, M. de Lafayette proceeded on horseback in a high state of fever and during a pelting autumnal rain. Fetes were given in compliment to him throughout his journey, and he endeavored to strengthen himself with wine, tea, and rum; but at Fishkill, eight miles from headquarters [which was now at Fredericksburg, New York], he was obliged to yield to the violence of an inflammatory fever. He was soon reduced to the last extremity."

If another cause of Lafayette's illness was his knowledge that his secret trip to Congress had been disloyal to his adopted father, that the Marquis never admitted. He wrote rather in an explosion of sentiment, "General Washington came every day to inquire after his friend, but, fearing to agitate him, he only conversed with the physician, and returned home with tearful eyes and a heart oppressed with grief."[24]

Even if he did not ride thus "every day" sixteen miles from his duties, Washington was, of course, worried. And the alarm from which he was suffering was by no means only for his friend's health. After he had read the dispatches Lafayette had been bringing, he suspected a dangerous French plot against the future of the United States. He was soon to write privately to President Laurens:

"As the Marquis clothed his proposition when he spoke of it to me, it would seem to originate wholly with himself; but it is far from impossible that it had its birth in the Cabinet of France, and was put into this artful dress to give it the readier currency. I fancy that I read in the countenances of some people on this occasion more than the disinterested zeal of allies. I hope I am mistaken."[25]

Officially to Congress, in a many-thousand-word letter, Washington demolished the scheme as a practical enterprise. More money, men, and supplies would be needed than the country had ever succeeded in raising. To make commitments to France that could not be lived up to could only endanger the alliance. Better to plan "something less extensive" within the possibilities of self-reliant, purely American action. Washington added that he could not obey Congress's orders to send his comments to Versailles, since that would reveal weaknesses in the American cause that "ought only to be known to ourselves."[26]

In his private letter to Laurens, Washington expounded an "insurmountable" objection which could not be openly stated to Congress, but which "alarms all my feelings for the true and permanent interests of my country." His thinking was now not only military but political; it harked back to the desperate years during which he had tried to drive the French and their allies from Fort Duquesne. Surely it would be madness, he wrote, to allow the French to take possession of Quebec, the capital of a huge province "attached to them by all the ties of blood, habits, manners, religion, and former connections of government. I fear this would be too great a temptation to be resisted by any power actuated by the common maxims of national policy." He wrote in his draft but scratched out a reference to "that spirit of ambition and love of domination which the enemies of France have pretended to be particularly characteristic of that enterprising nation."

"Let us realize for a moment," Washington continued, "the striking advantages France would derive from the possession of Canada." Not only would she be able to monopolize the valuable fur trade with the Indians, but she would find in Canada a base that would help her hold and supply her West Indian possessions. She would then have "ports of her own on this continent, independent on the precarious good will of an ally." Furthermore, "possessed of New Orleans on our right, Canada on our left, and seconded by the numerous tribes of Indians . . . whom she knows so well how to conciliate," France would "have it in her power to give law to these states." She would be anxious to do so since the United States would become with independence "the most natural and the most formidable rival of every maritime power in Europe."

Should they once become implanted in Canada, the French, so Washington apprehended, would, after the war was won, stay on "as a pledge and surety" for the debts owed them by the United States, "or under other specious pretense . . . till they can find a bone of contention." Let Congress not assume that France would be afraid of driving America back into the arms of the English, for by then France and her ally Spain would probably have established control of the seas. "Resentment, reproaches, and submission seem to be all that would be left us."*

Then Washington wrote—he did not know how prophetically of problems he would have to face some twenty years later when he was officially President—that "men are very apt to run into extremes. Hatred to England may carry some into an excess of confidence in France, especially when motives of gratitude are thrown into the scale. Men of this description would be unwilling to suppose France capable of acting so ungenerous a part. . . . But it is a maxim founded on the universal experience of mankind that no nation is to be trusted further than it is bound by its interest; and no

---

* However prudent he may have been to urge precaution, Washington's suspicions were incorrect: the French government had not instigated Lafayette's plan. They had no immediate designs on Canada.

prudent statesman or politician will venture to depart from it." America should be "particularly cautious, for we have not yet attained sufficient vigor and maturity to recover from the shock of any false step into which we may unwarily fall."[27]

The situation, Washington realized, was ticklish, since policy would not permit Laurens to show his private letter widely, and the official letter, for all its length and strength, might not convince. In the meantime, his spies reported that New York City was "in a general fermentation." He longed for believable reports that the enemy were planning a complete evacuation, but the mercantile houses which had been established under the British aegis showed no signs of packing up. To his brother Jack he wrote that the enemy would probably stay if only because he was convinced they should not: they "almost invariably run counter to all expectation. . . . I begin to despair of seeing my own home this winter."[28]

A report that the heavy linings were being taken out of the coats of ten enemy regiments and made into waistcoats or breeches suggested that the troops were destined for a warmer climate, Washington guessed the West Indies.[29] In discounting a rumor that their destination was Charleston, South Carolina, Washington reasoned in a manner which, had the British agreed with him, would have saved them their eventual defeat at Yorktown:

"I am well convinced myself that the enemy, long ere this, are perfectly well satisfied that the possession of our towns, while we have an army in the field, will avail them little. It involves *us* in difficulty, but does not, by any means, insure *them* conquest. They will know that it is our arms, not defenseless towns, they have to subdue before they can arrive at the haven of their wishes, and that, till this end is accomplished, the superstructure they have been endeavoring to raise, 'like the baseless fabric of a vision,' falls to nothing.

"But this, though a reason operates powerfully with me in deciding upon the point, is by no means the most weighty consideration in my mind." An invasion of the south had seemed "probable" before the appearance of the French fleet, "as their whole conduct was full of unaccountables, but to attempt now to detach 10,000 men (which is, I suppose, half their army) and to divide their naval strength for the protection of it, would, in my judgment, be an act of insanity, and expose one part or the other of both land and sea force to inevitable ruin. I therefore conclude they will go there wholly or not at all. Nevertheless, I may be mistaken."[30]

During early November, Byron's fleet, which had been prowling outside Boston harbor, was scattered by another storm, and d'Estaing took the opportunity to slip past the blockade into the ocean. He did not notify his ally, Washington, where he was going, but Washington assumed the Indies. Logic indicated the same destination for the British fleet, which, after it had reassembled, disappeared from New York convoying some five thousand soldiers. Although other detachments sailed later,* strong garrisons remained at Rhode Island and New York. They were refurbishing their winter quarters.[31]

Getting the Continental Army also into winter quarters was delayed by a congressional decision to move Burgoyne's surrendered troops from New England to Virginia: Clinton might recapture the lost regiments if Washington did not protect their Hudson crossing. The German officers among the captives were all eagerness to see the American hero. One noted that His Excellency watched their march "from in front of a plain house . . . with a serious look and without any pose." Another, who had been told that "an important general of His Majesty Frederick of Prussia" would be with Washington, failed to recognize that bogus baron Steuben. Washington served the German staff "a drink made of whiskey, water, and sugar" which they understood was called "toddy." They refused his invitation to dinner. Being used to the frosty aristocrats of Europe, they ruled Washington "very nice," but could see in him "nothing extraordinary or great."[32]

When Washington received a letter from Congress placing further pressure on him to support Lafayette's scheme for a joint Franco-American conquest of Canada, he decided that he would have to go to the capital "for a few days." He set out on December 21, 1778. A week later, he wrote Lafayette that there was no further reason why the Frenchman should delay his return home: "A certain expedition, after a full consideration of all circumstances, has been laid aside." Washington enclosed a letter of introduction to Franklin in which he praised Lafayette's services to America: "I have a very particular friendship for him."[33]

It is highly significant that Washington did not hold against his psychological son his suspicions that the Frenchman was placing above the interests of the United States the interests of his own nation. This attitude reveals that Washington's belief in patriotism was not chauvinism but rather a general principle which he considered equally applicable everywhere. It also helps explain his reluctance to entrust power in his army to volunteers from abroad. He did not believe that a non-American worthy of trust could be untrue to his own country by giving his first allegiance to the United States.†

To Lafayette, Washington now wrote that only if the war continued could

---

* Both fleets and the largest of the departing British land forces did go to the Indies, where the enemy captured St. Lucia before d'Estaing arrived. Other detachments from New York carried out orders from overseas by reinforcing Halifax and West Florida.

† Washington applied a similar attitude to recent immigrants. Although he often made exceptions (among whom Hamilton was one of the most marked), Washington tended to place less reliance on the fidelity to the cause, on the willingness to make sacrifices for America, of men not truly acclimated here. An ameliorating factor seemed to him the possession of property: if an immigrant had valuable possessions to lose in an American defeat, he was the more to be trusted.

he expect to share "fresh toils and dangers with you in the plains of America." Should peace return, "I can entertain little hopes that the rural amusements of an infant world or the contracted stage of an American theater can withdraw your attention and services from the gaieties of a court; and the active part which you will more than probably be called upon to share in the administration of your government. The soldier will then be transformed into the statesman, and your employment in this new walk of life will afford you no time to revisit this continent, or think of friends who lament your absence. . . .

"Adieu, my dear Marquis. My best wishes will ever attend you. May you have a safe and agreeable passage, and a happy meeting with your lady and friends."[34]

37

The Measure of Iniquity

T HE desperate situation of his supply services determined Washington's selection of quarters for the winter of 1778–1779. If his army were not all in one area but spread widely there would not be so much pressure on the almost non-existent wagons. And, as there would probably be less food available to the east of the Hudson, the larger part of his army should be posted to the west. So Washington bedded his army down in a zigzag line some seventy-five miles long from Danbury in Connecticut southwesterly to Middlebrook and Elizabeth in New Jersey. Since the largest cantonment would be at Middlebrook, he intended to establish his headquarters there. As at Valley Forge, the troops would build their own huts.

"Were I to give in to private conveniency and amusement," Washington wrote, "I should not be able to resist the invitation of my friends to make Philadelphia (instead of a squeezed up room or two) my quarters for the winter, but the affairs of the army require my constant attention and presence . . . to keep it from crumbling. As peace and retirement are my ultimate aim, and the most pleasing and flattering hope of my soul, everything advancive of this end contributes to my satisfaction, however difficult and inconvenient in the attainment, and will reconcile any place and all circumstances to my feelings whilst I continue in service."[1]

However, once Washington had journeyed to Philadelphia to deal with Lafayette's Canadian scheme, Congress asked him to stay so that he could discuss with them the innumerable problems of the army. What he saw as he walked the streets and sat in the drawing rooms made him write that he would never "be again surprised at anything."

Washington saw great coaches rolling by, surrounded with powdered lackeys; he saw great tables displaying five times as many dainties as the sated guests could eat. He thought of the brave men he had seen march in rags and die, on empty stomachs, of bullets and disease and cold, and he thundered, "Speculation, peculation, and an insatiable thirst for riches seem to have got the better of every other consideration and almost of every order of men."[2]

Inflation was the master of the revels, and the revelers were those who had so manipulated inflation as to profit by it. The value of money was sinking five per cent a day. A few months might put a total stop to its circulation. "And yet, an assembly [dance], a concert, a dinner, or a supper that will cost three or four hundred pounds will not only take men off from acting in but even thinking of this [the national] business, while a great part of the officers of your army from absolute necessity are quitting the service, and the more virtuous few, rather than do this, are sinking by sure degrees into beggary and want. . . . A rat in the shape of a horse is not to be bought at this time for less than £200, a saddle under thirty or forty." In such a situation, "what funds can stand the present expenses of the army?"[3]

Hostesses vied with each other to entertain "our great Fabius Maximus" and his consort, "Lady Washington," who had reluctantly joined him for the winter. During the previous November, she had written to her brother from Mount Vernon, "I am very uneasy at this time: I have some reason to expect that I shall take another trip northward. The poor General is not likely to see us [in Virginia] from what I can hear. I expect to hear certainly by the next post. If I do, I shall write to you to inform you and my friends, if I am so happy to stay at home."[4]

However strained and uneasy they felt, it would have been contrary to Martha's and particularly her husband's nature not to have enjoyed some of the grand Philadelphia parties. At one, given by the beautiful Mrs. Samuel Powel, who was eventually to become his close friend, George and Martha confessed happily to Benjamin Franklin's granddaughter, Mrs. Bache, that this was the twentieth anniversary of their marriage. Martha no longer danced, but she smiled—it is hoped benignly—to see her husband romp through the measures with younger ladies.* There were surely agreeable evenings, but General Greene, who was usually present, wrote that the "luxury and profusion" with which he was surrounded gave Washington "infinitely more pain than pleasure."[5]

He was worried not only for the nation but for his own personal fortunes. When some land he had long coveted on "my own neck" (beside Mount Vernon) came up for sale, he found he possessed no fluid assets.[6]

He had refused any salary as Commander in Chief. The six thousand to seven thousand pounds which he had invested in bonds had been reduced by inflation to the equivalent of as many hundreds. His creditors were grasping the opportunity to pay off their debts at a tenth of value and,

---

* Shortly after his return to camp, Washington "danced upwards of three hours without once sitting down" with Mrs. Greene.[7]

because of his "fear of injuring by any example of mine the credit of our paper currency if I attempted to discriminate between the real and nominal value of paper money," he did not know how to protect himself. He first instructed Lund, his estate manager, vaguely, "You will do the best you can to have justice done me; their impositions afterwards I must submit to as a tax to dishonorable men." But after his virtue had "sunk me a large sum," and Lund had again pointed out how desperately he was being cheated, he decided that those who took such advantage of him must lack "common honesty." And surely no law "could be intended to make a man take a shilling or sixpence on the pound for a just debt." He instructed Lund still to accept paper for debts contracted after the inflation began, but no longer for "old debts."[8]

However, he added with a touch of irritation that his manager should not have appealed to him, since he had no way of ascertaining what was in Virginia legal or "common usage." Lund should consult neighbors, "men of honor, honesty, and firm attachment to the cause." If they took almost worthless paper for old debts, and "if it is thought to be advancive of the great cause . . . for individuals to do so, thereby ruining themselves while others are reaping the benefit for such distress; if the law imposes this and it is thought right to submit," he would agree, as "no man has, nor no man will go further to serve the public than myself."[9]

Washington's mother was a continuing financial drain. That December, she wrote Lund, "I should be much obliged to you to send me forty pound cash to buy corn for they have not made more at Little Falls Quarter than will serve the plantation. There is terrible doings there. Charles [another son] never goes over. I shall be ruined. Corn at five pound a barrel. As for flour, I don't know the taste of it. I never lived so poor in my life, but if I can get corn, I am contented. . . . I hear poor Mrs. Washington had gone off [to join George]. God bless you. Spare your health or poor George will be ruined."[10]

Washington became convinced that inflation had made his manager's salary inadequate. He wrote Lund, "I wish you to say what you think is just and right. This it is my full wish to give, and more I do not think you would ask. Therefore we cannot disagree."[11]

Lund beseeched Washington to come to Mount Vernon while the troops were in winter quarters: for all his employer's faith in him, the manager was able to produce hardly any of those crops which brought those "fortunate enough" (as Washington wrote wistfully) to have any to sell four times their peacetime value.[12]

An agrarian who even now had spent almost no time in cities, Washington liked to blame the inflation on the traditional enemies of farmers: those moneymen, those "monopolizers, forestallers, and engrossers" who bought

goods at a low price and held them for a rise. Such individuals, he wrote his
brother Jack, were enough to make men "curse their own species for possessing so little virtue and patriotism." He fulminated that "those murderers of
our cause" should be brought "to condign punishment. . . . I would to God
that one of the most atrocious of each state was hung in gibbets upon a
gallows five times as high as the one prepared by Haman. No punishment in
my opinion is too great for the man who can build his greatness upon his
country's ruin."[13]

Outbursts like these, which blamed the inflation on the business community, seemed to put Washington on the extreme left of the political
controversy rocking Philadelphia, but his verbal explosions reflected nervous
anger and despair rather than true partisanship. The most conscipuous conflict was a slugging match between Silas Deane and Arthur Lee, two Americans who had contracted for goods in France. Lee accused Deane of peculation. As the battle widened to include the blame for inflation, and that
most conspicuous manifestation of financial dislocation, poverty contrasted
with luxury, the radicals and the agrarians gathered behind Lee, the conservatives and the moneymen behind Deane, Washington's reaction was to
glimpse the old, horrifying specter of a division in the cause.

This controversy is said by some historians to have marked the start of
political parties in the United States. Washington, who as President was to
oppose political parties, now wrote, "It is also most devoutly to be wished
that faction was at an end, and that those to whom everything dear and
valuable is entrusted would lay aside party views and return to first principles. Happy, happy thrice happy country if such was the government of
it!" But, alas, "party disputes and personal quarrels are the great business of
the day, whilst the momentous concerns of an empire, a great and accumu-
lated debt, ruined finances, depreciated money, and want of credit (which
in their consequences is the want of everything) are but secondary considerations and postponed from day to day, from week to week, as if our
affairs wore the most promising aspect."

Washington urged an effort to get the "ablest and best men" back from
their state governments, where many were now serving, to Congress, where
"the great and important concerns of the nation are horribly conducted for
want either of abilities or application in the members. . . . If the great
whole is mismanaged," he pointed out, all "must sink in the general wreck."
Then let America's leading minds appear, investigate public abuses, and
work "an entire reformation."[14]

Here Washington's cool intelligence rather than his anger and prejudice
were speaking. Himself regretting that he did not have farm produce to sell
at the type of price that he had to pay for what he bought, he was capable
of realizing that men whose assets were primarily in what fluctuated—
money and credit—were even more grievously trapped than he, as a

landowner, was. They had to rise with the tide or be drowned. The idea that prices could be regulated by law had once seemed to him a panacea and still appealed to his emotions. However, he gradually became convinced that such legislation was "inconsistent with the very nature of things." He came to believe that it would be like trying to stop the smallpox by making it a crime to show the symptoms. The agrarian who had always shuddered away from such considerations was being forced to put his already overburdened mind on problems of finance. And to learn, he had to consult the people who knew: members of the financial community. The most important were two men, both of whom were named Morris, although they were not related.[15]

It was generally agreed, even by those who regarded him as therefore the more pernicious, that the ablest financier on the continent was Robert Morris. Brought to America from England at the age of thirteen, Morris had voted in Congress against Independence. However, he had continued to throw his shoulder to the wheel; he became invaluable to the cause because of his practical energy and his financial skills. Concerning him, the sophisticated French soldier-philosopher Chastellux was to write, "It may safely be asserted that Europe affords few examples of perspicacity and facility of understanding equal to his, which adapts itself with the same success to business, to letters, and to sciences." Chastellux described Morris as "a large man, very simple in his manners, but his mind is subtle and acute. . . . His house is handsome, closely resembling the houses in London. He lives there without ostentation but not without expense, for he spares nothing which can contribute to his happiness or that of Mrs. Morris, to whom he is much attached. A zealous republican and an epicurean philosopher, he has always played a distinguished part at table and in business."[16]

Robert Morris's close collaborator Gouverneur Morris came from a leading family in aristocratic New York. He had been a fiery patriot from the first. He was able, witty, talkative, extreme, much of a dandy, and so celebrated as a ladies' man that when he lost a leg in a carriage accident, rumor reported that he had injured it jumping, on the husband's return, out of a charmer's bedroom window. His high spirits kept Washington amused, and he had a sound business head over the elegant lace that beautified his chest. As the years passed, he became one of Washington's most intimate friends.

Under the tutelage of such men, Washington came to realize that the inflation was caused by a fundamental flaw in the financial policies of the government. When Congress had resolved to take over the direction of the war, they controlled no assets with which to pay for anything. Recourse was thus taken to an expedient which had been a favorite in the colonies (although often opposed by the Crown): the printing of money. The theory was that a legislature should vote, at the same time as the money was issued, specific taxes which would bring the currency, after a planned period of circulation, back to the government for cancellation. The total result was supposed to be the establishment of a temporary medium of exchange, which would at the same time enable the government to anticipate taxes.[17]

For the Continental Congress the problem was—and it was here that Washington was instructed to find the nub of the situation—that, although the legislature could set presses rolling, it had no power to tax, nor did the states have the least intention of granting that power. All that Congress could do was to call on the states to send to Philadelphia tax revenues that would enable Congress to redeem, in due course, the Continental paper. This the states rarely succeeded in doing.

Washington thus summarized what he had learned: The paper could be counted on to continue to depreciate unless it was sunk "with heavy taxes."[18]

Since during the Colonial period governmental expenses had normally been very small—the government offered few services and officials were paid not out of taxes but by collecting fees—the Americans were used only to very light taxation. Even Washington, although experience was bringing home to him daily the necessity of revenue, believed, when taxation fell heavily on him, that somehow he was being discriminated against. He would, he insisted, pay taxes "with cheerfulness" if they were "equally laid and judiciously applied, but flagrant partiality is enough to sour the minds of any people, and bring curses on the authors of it." He then launched into an attack on the official most responsible for Virginia's tax policy, Governor Patrick Henry: "A man may err once and he may err twice, but when those who possess more than a common share of abilities persevere in a regular course of destructive policy, one is more apt to suspect their hearts than their heads." Such sentiments did not encourage politicians to vote taxes.[19]

Washington's financial mentors also pointed out (and this he could well understand from his own experience) that an agrarian society produced little capital, which was one of the reasons why taxes were so hard to collect. A sound national economy, which could support a triumphant war, needed trading on a large scale, manufactures, and so forth. Washington was impressed to the point of writing his brother Jack an admission that his continuing desire "to have my property as much as possible in lands . . . is not consistent with national policy."[20]

Mixed up in Washington's reactions to the choice between an agrarian and a business economy was the disturbing issue of Virginia's labor pattern. A moral man perpetually stating that he was fighting to preserve himself and his descendants from slavery could not help being uneasy about the slaves on his own estate. When the war started, Washington's attitude had been paternalistic: the Negroes had a right to their food, clothes, and lodging as long as they earned them, and he would not shirk his part of the compact by selling a Negro without first procuring the slave's consent.

However, his slaves had always refused to agree to being sold to other owners. This increased Washington's financial plight, since the midwives kept calling at his slave quarters, supplying him with a population that ate up all the food Mount Vernon could produce. (This was a major reason why he had no produce to sell.) To free unproductive slaves without assets or education would be cruelty, not kindness. He was in a bind that became so serious that as his tax bill increased, he had at last to abandon his paternalism: he ordered Lund to sell slaves, which were indeed his only fluid asset, to raise the necessary cash to pay the taxes.[21]

This decision made, Washington felt in part of his mind a desire to go further. Since he had left the south to lead the army, he had come on many men who regarded the whole institution of slavery as evil: not only individuals he found personally inimical like John Adams, but such of his beloved associates as Lafayette and young Laurens.* The whole matter was so disturbing that he broke out to Lund, "I every day long more and more to get clear of" all his Negroes.[22]

Glimpsing the advantages both to the individual investor and the nation of fluid capital, Washington began asking himself whether he would be better off if he sold the crops his slaves produced or sold the slaves and invested the returns in government loan certificates, "collecting the interest." To Lund, he stated, "If a negro man will sell at or near one thousand pounds and woman and children in proportion, I have not the smallest doubt on which side the balance, placed in the scale of interest, will preponderate. My scruples arise from a reluctance in offering these people at public vendue, and on account of the uncertainty of timing the sale well. In the first case, if these poor wretches are to be held in a state of slavery, I do not see that a change of masters will render it more irksome, provided

---

* Laurens, who came from South Carolina but was no longer part of that environment, having been educated in Geneva as a lawyer, wished his father, President Laurens, to give him his patrimony now in male slaves of fighting age. He would organize them into a military corps and free the survivors after the war. The father objected, partly on the grounds that the colored people had been too debased by servitude to fight. Young Laurens replied that Washington "is convinced that the numerous tribes of blacks in the southern part of the continent offer a resource to us that should not be neglected. With respect to my particular plan, he only objects to it with the arguments of pity for a man who would be less rich than he might be."[23]

By refusing to cooperate, the father torpedoed this plan, but young Laurens kept urging as a matter of public policy the arming of southern plantation slaves. (Negroes had long been used, particularly in Rhode Island, to swell out the northern regiments.) In March 1799, Washington wrote Laurens objecting that if the patriots did what he suggested, the British would do it too, and, being possessed of more arms, might be the more successful. Furthermore, the escape from slavery of some would make the condition "more irksome to those who remain in it" since "most of the good and evil things of this life are judged of by comparison." Having gone this far, Washington was overcome by a desire to escape from the issue. "As this is a subject that has never employed much of my thoughts," he wrote, "these are no more than the first crude ideas that have struck me upon the occasion."

However, in 1782 Washington finally backed Laurens's effort to have South Carolina establish a "black corps."[24]

that husband and wife, and parents and children, are not separated from each other, which is not my intentions to do."

However, the problem was not an immediate one, as it would obviously be madness to turn any real goods into capital until the moment when "the tide of depreciation is at an end . . . and everything runs in a contrary direction." And Washington probably knew in his heart that he would never thus flee his responsibility to his slaves, at the same time utterly changing the way of life he had inherited from his ancestors and in which he had himself been raised. Since there was no free labor for hire in Virginia, he would have to give up his plantation, all the delights of farming, all those soothing occupations of which he dreamed every day as he suffered through the heavy routines of war. Despite the experience he was having in military camps and in the cities, Washington remained to the bone an agrarian whose emotions continued to tell him that the moneymen—at least the worst of them—preyed upon the farmers who were "the least designing and perhaps most valuable part of the community."[25]

The education Washington was beginning in economic matters was, since general financial policy was not now his responsibility, to bear little fruit in action until years later when he had, as President, to adjudicate disputes between the agrarian Jefferson and the moneyman Hamilton. For the moment, Washington's problem was somehow to keep the inflation from destroying his army.

His officers were in a desperate state. When their salaries would hardly pay for patches on their torn uniforms, they could send nothing home to their families, who were thus forced to seek support by dissipating whatever assets they had in civilian life. Eventual starvation for their families, penury on their return home faced Washington's officer corps.

At conferences in Philadelphia, Washington pointed out that had it not been for the hope of a speedy end to the war raised by the announcement of the French alliance he would now have only "the shadow of an army." But the hope had vanished, and the unhappiness of the officers was being daily exacerbated by the contrast between their poverty and the luxuries enjoyed by profiteers. Unless steps were taken to make "the officers *take pleasure* in their situation," the army would quickly become "an insipid mass incapable of acting with vigor, and ready to tumble to pieces at every reverse of fortune."

To insure the officers from a disastrous future, Washington had from Valley Forge urged that Congress establish for those who would serve till the end of the war a system of pensions similar to the half pay which was a usual perquisite of retired European officers. The idea had proved shocking to those politicians who feared a strong military establishment, but Congress had hesitantly endorsed pensions for seven years after the peace. They now voted to recommend to the states that half pay be offered for the lifetime of the officer. They also agreed, although no one knew how this would be financed, that the officers should be at once clothed at public expense, and that large bounties should be paid to secure long-term enlistments of common soldiers.[26]

The strategy Washington fixed on for the coming campaign shows him thinking not as a military man clamoring for strength and opportunity, but as a statesman balancing every aspect of the situation. Although he wished to have replaced the 4380 regulars whose enlistments were expiring, he did not ask Congress for an army strong enough to undertake on its own initiative any major action. Unless d'Estaing should reappear with his marines, the only offensive should be a march by a few thousand men through the "Long House" of the Iroquois in the northern frontier. The Continental Army would sit tight in defensive positions that would keep the weakened British from breaking out of their posts. Inaction during 1779 would save expense, give Congress a breathing spell during which they could revive the national finances in a way that would make possible vigorous measures in 1780.

The possibility that Spain might join France as a belligerent and England react by removing all her troops from the United States bothered Washington's planning, for if that happened it might be possible to invade and capture Canada. Washington would find it "extremely disagreeable to be unprepared for improving the opportunity, but when I consider the necessity of economy in our present circumstances . . . it will be the safest and most prudent way to suppose the worst and prepare for it."

The positive part of Washington's program he thus stated, "The army, though small, should be of a firm and permanent texture."[27]

A major cause of dissatisfaction among the officers was that the army, recruited erratically and organized by states, had each year a different number and usually smaller number of regiments into which a theoretically permanent officer corps had to be fitted without violating seniority or overleaping state lines.* To make matters worse, the arrangements were being allowed to dangle and the resentments to fester: a Committee of Congress, which had started at Valley Forge to reorganize the 1778 army, had never completed the task. On August 3, Washington had written "almost the whole of my time is now employed in finding temporary and inadequate expedients to quiet the minds of the officers. . . . We can scarcely form a court-martial or parade a detachment in any instance without a warm discussion on the subject of precedence."[28]

Washington begged that the reorganization be completed. And he asked —it was usually far from his first request—that immediate attention be

* Between 1777 and August 1781, the regiments on the Continental establishment shrank from one hundred and sixty to fifty.[29]

given to the stores that would be needed in the summer; that the clothier general's department be replanned and the clothes bought from foreign powers by government contract rather than by private individuals; that more brigadiers be appointed; that something be done about the cavalry; that the artillery be improved according to a plan presented by Knox; that the hospital organization be renovated; etc.; etc. Congress voted that Washington should have the power to decide most of these matters on his own initiative. During the French and Indian War, Washington had welcomed, when he could get them, such blanket grants from his civilian masters. Now he was more politically astute, and also he recognized buckpassing when he saw it. He asked Congress to give him a committee to consult.[30]

On January 13, Washington had begun stating that he wanted to return to his army. On February 11, he was at last released. Although Martha was beside him, he rode off through New Jersey with a heavy heart. He was carrying back to camp no plan for effective action, no scheme for ending the war. He seemed doomed to what was for his temperament the most difficult of all tasks: inaction, helpless waiting. And the prospect was made more frightening by his suspicion that "it is now consistent with the views of speculators, various tribes of moneymakers, and stockjobbers of all denominations to continue the war for their own private emolument. . . . The measure of iniquity," Washington concluded sadly, "is not yet filled."[31]

CHAPTER

38

The Fleet That Never Came

IN previous years, there had been a sharp break between winter quarters
and campaign; rough weather had abated and then, however deliberately, the British lion had awakened: Great movements had been afoot.
But in 1779, the seasons imperceptibly merged. There had been hardly any
snow or frost since mid-January. By April 1, the fruit trees had budded, and
they were in full bloom on the 10th. In Newport and New York, the British
continued the routines of garrison life, and even the fine flarings of Washington's strategical imagination could find little in the reports of his spies to
alarm.

The quiet in the American camps was rarely disturbed by the arrival of
new recruits, since the mounting inflation kept the offered bounties, however sensational in sound, from being effective lures. Washington had "little
more than the skeleton of an army," but it was a robust skeleton, well
housed in homemade huts made by experience superior to those at Valley
Forge: sickness had been reduced by not sinking the cabins in the ground or
roofing them with turf. Although the men's blankets tended to be too small,
there were enough shoes—out with bloody footsteps!—and 20,011 new
uniforms had arrived from France. These were blue and red and brown
and red; the colors were assigned to the various regiments by lot; but
whichever they secured, the men had been kept warm.

Supplies, if sparse, had proved adequate for men long inured to a
pauper's diet, while individuals who had not become immune to the
endemic camp diseases had long since gone home or been buried. The
troops, Washington summarized, were "better clad and more healthy than
they had ever been since the formation of the army." Although his soldiers
signed occasional petitions and sometimes sassed their officers, there were
none of the mutinies Washington foresaw sometimes in dark moments. The
war had become somnolent.[1]

[345]

Washington tried to keep himself active by laboring on the rearrangement of the army which Congress had entrusted to him, and by making the most thorough possible examination of military possibilities on the frontiers. He collected old diaries of wilderness explorations. Commanders at frontier posts received his orders to allow mysterious individuals "to pass and repass without interruption and without search of their canoes or baggage." Scouts on routes Washington thought useless alarmed the Indians by their presence, but his scouts examining trails the army might use moved less visibly than the flitting deer.

In studying all the campaigns of the French and Indian War, Washington could not help realizing how restricted had been his view when, as Virginia commander, he had emoted on his local frontier, resenting all military activity elsewhere. Now he realized that the enemy fort at Niagara was, because it controlled navigation westward on the Great Lakes, the key to the whole Ohio frontier. How he wished he had the men and supplies to grasp that key! But no: he could only hope to overrun the towns in upper New York of the six Iroquois nations.[2]

The Delawares had been, with the Shawnees, the authors of the atrocities on the Virginia frontier—the murdered mothers with bloody children at their breasts—that had wrung Washington's bowels. However, they could now be useful since they were traditionally resentful of the Iroquois. He invited six Delaware chiefs to his camp and staged for them a military review. Martha, who with Mrs. Knox and Mrs. Greene watched from a carriage, wrote to her daughter-in-law, "Some of the Indians were fine looking, but most of them appeared worse than Falstaff's gang. And such horses and trappings! The General says it was done to keep the Indians friendly towards us. They appeared like cutthroats all."[3]

Despite his preparations, Washington did not intend actually to dispatch an expedition into the Indian country until he was sure that d'Estaing's fleet would not sail up from the Indies, presenting the possibility of achieving more important objectives. There were rumors, and then late in April the French ambassador, Conrad Alexandre Gérard, announced that he would come to camp bringing important news and accompanied by Spain's unofficial observer, Juan de Miralles. Washington was all anticipation, but the functionaries had nothing specific to communicate. The most positive result of the conference was that Miralles, horrified at the plainness of Washington's fare, decided to symbolize the bounty of his royal master by sending presents: crystal flasks and wine with which to fill them, chocolate, sugar, guava jelly, candies, a box of lemons to make punch with, and a hundred-pound sea turtle.[4]

The first purposeful stirring among the British in New York City took place in early May. A flock of loaded transports—they proved to hold about

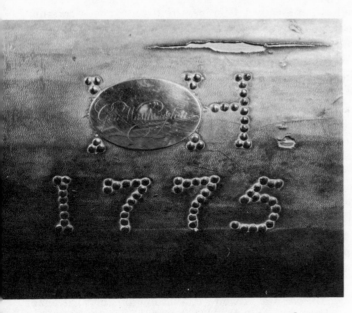

Top: Washington's trunk, covered with deerskin, hair side out, iron bound, studded with brass tacks; 15 inches high, 36 inches long. *Bottom left:* Detail of trunk. *Bottom right:* Washington's telescopes, both made in England of brass and wood, with large diameter 2¼ inches. Opened length: top, 33 inches; bottom, 31 inches. Courtesy of the Mount Vernon Ladies' Association of the Union.

two thousand men—set out into the ocean under naval escort. When Washington heard that they were raiding the Virginia shore of Chesapeake Bay, he must have worried for Mount Vernon, so near the scene of destruction. However, he ruled that the Continental Army could do nothing to protect his homeland from such "precarious and desultory attacks." The British returned quickly from Virginia and word arrived a little later that they had not touched Mount Vernon.[5]

The next enemy move was in force up the Hudson. Washington was dismayed, since Duportail had just warned him that the defenses at West Point were feebly incomplete. Packing Martha off to Virginia, he led the army in New Jersey toward the river through the upper Highlands along that wild pass the Clove. However, the British stopped short of West Point. They pounced on King's Ferry, the crossing of the Hudson at the bottom of the Highlands, where two patriot forts faced each other across the river from Stony Point and Verplanck's Point. Designed only to scare away small British raiders, the forts were tiny, each garrisoned with less than a hundred men. Clinton's major force captured the crossing easily, and then, with what Washington considered "astonishing industry," they set about strengthening the works.

For once, Washington approved of Clinton's strategy: "It was certainly one of the wisest measures they had yet pursued," since it not only cut the easiest American communication across the Hudson, but assisted the British in bringing in supplies and sending out Tory conspirators.[6]

To be closer to the enemy activity, Washington set up headquarters at New Windsor on the east side of the Hudson some miles above West Point. As he mourned that the British advance was a source of "great perplexity to us," he became conscious that they were boasting mightily over their capture of Stony Point, trying to make it seem as if overrunning that anthill had been a major coup. Surely, one propaganda coup deserved another! Clinton's main army had returned to New York, leaving no more than a strong garrison in the forts. And some action on the part of the Continental Army was surely needed "to satisfy the expectations of the people and reconcile them to the defensive plan we are obliged to pursue."

Washington rode downriver and stared at Stony Point through his spyglass; spies moved in the night. A deserter reported that the sandy beach running along the south side of the new British works was obstructed only by a slight abatis. A surprise seemed possible![7]

In selecting an officer to lead the adventure, Washington revealed again his willingness to use an imperfect instrument if the strengths it possessed fitted the task in hand. General Wayne had made an ass of himself at Paoli and had subsequently plagued Washington with ridiculous suggestions to attack, *attack,* ATTACK! Washington's final judgment on him was that he was "more active and enterprising than judicious and cautious; no economist it is feared; open to flattery; vain; easily imposed upon; and liable to be drawn into scrapes; too indulgent (the effect perhaps of the causes just mentioned) to his officers and men." But send Wayne, with "good advice," into a fight, and he showed his "many good points as an officer."[8]

Washington closeted himself in secret with Wayne. And then, on July 10, he sent Wayne written orders concerning what he referred to only as "the enterprise in contemplation." "Under the cover of night" a picked corps of light infantry should advance down the shore, capturing and taking with them, to enforce secrecy, every human being they met. Finally, they would come to a dark wood where boats would be waiting under overhanging branches. Into these boats "a vanguard of prudent and determined men" would climb with fixed bayonets but no ammunition in their muskets, so that no one could tip off the enemy by mistaken fire. Off with muffled oars and with the tide. A pale line in the glistening dark would be the vulnerable beach. For as long as possible sentries should be secured or silently skewered. Of course, in the end the enemy would fire, and, at the sound, the larger American force which had been listening in the wood should start pelting toward Stony Point down the causeway.

Two years before, Washington would have planned a simultaneous attack on the facing fort at Verplanck's Point. But experience had taught him "the uncertainty of cooperating in point of time"—and he feared that a complicated plan might vitiate the surprise on which the capture of Stony Point depended.[9]

On the night selected, July 15, Washington stayed where his duty was, at headquarters. Dawn came up to the greeting voices of birds. The uncommunicative river flowed ever more brightly between its long ramparts of hills. Not till 9:30 did a messenger dash up on a foam-flecked horse. The letter he brought was terse: "Dear General, The fort and garrison with Colonel Johnston are ours. Our officers and men behaved like men who are determined to be free. Yours most sincerely, Anty Wayne."[10]

Washington leapt on his freshest horse and pounded toward the scene of action. He hoped that he could now attack Verplanck's Point—surely the enemy there would be in confusion; he hoped somehow to hold both posts against counterattack. But the confusion he came on as his horse strode the dusty roads was in his own army: dispatches had been missent; there had been "accidental delays in bringing on the heavy cannon and entrenching tools." Verplanck's Point clearly could not be taken, and when Washington galloped into Stony Point, a quick look revealed that the British had, in strengthening the defenses, done nothing to protect the fort from the side where they were supreme, the water. And in rode a messenger to say that downriver British vessels, moving passionately to the flash of oars and the pull of sail, were "heaving in sight." The American move was to load everything in the fort that could be pried loose into one of the small boats that were bobbing beside Stony Point.

In the end, all but one of the cannon were successfully removed; all the patriot boats but one got off under an enemy cannonade; all the soldiers scuttled successfully away by land. Washington was back in New Windsor by the 19th, "very fatigued" but on the whole jubilant.[11]

The blow had been a little one, but in quiet times small noises resound. The beating up of Stony Point raised American morale and dented the British. So did Light Horse Harry Lee's exploit of surprising a British garrison at Paulus Hook, a peninsula on the Jersey shore opposite the very heart of the enemy's New York base.

On May 31, Washington, having heard nothing of d'Estaing, ordered Sullivan to lead the long-planned expedition against the Iroquois into the Finger Lakes region of New York: "The immediate objects are the total destruction and devastation of their settlements, and the capture of as many prisoners of every age and sex as possible." Washington realized that the Indians, being less agriculturists than nomadic hunters, could rebuild their villages in a few weeks and would only be stung by the destruction of their crops and orchards. And to kill or capture warriors would be difficult, since war parties kept out of the way of superior numbers: only "in a sudden way" could "an enemy so vigilant and desultory" be surprised into battle. The most that Washington really hoped for was that rapid movement would permit the capture of some old men, women, or children whom the Indians had carelessly left behind. The possession of these would supply a bargaining point with the Iroquois.[12]

To Washington's "inexpressible concern," Sullivan's men carried more supplies than Washington approved of, and moved more slowly. Having fought off the one ambush the Indians attempted, they entered at will villages that were always empty: not even a sick grandmother to capture. Eventually announcing that forty Indian towns—one a metropolis of 128 houses—had been burned, innumerable fruit trees girdled, and crops estimated at 160,000 bushels destroyed, Washington publicly hailed (whatever he thought privately) Sullivan's expedition as a "full success."[13]

The news coming in from faraway places was good. In the Indies, d'Estaing had forced on a British fleet greater losses than his own had suffered; and he had captured the two Windward Islands of Grenada and Saint Vincent. Furthermore, the international development for which Washington had most hoped had taken place. Although not acknowledging American independence (she had colonies of her own in the New World which she did not wish to lose), Spain joined her traditional ally, France, in the war against their old enemy, England.*

All summer long Washington's spies had brought him rumors of reinforcements expected in New York from England. On August 25, they sailed in, as did a new commanding admiral for the American station, Marriot

---

* Spain wished to wrest from embattled England Gibraltar and Minorca.

Arbuthnot. Washington could not know that this coarse, senile sea dog would prove a great contribution to American independence. However, spies did state that the reinforcements—some five thousand men—were so sickly that they set an epidemic raging in the enemy-held city. Although now considerably outnumbered, Washington's troops were "remarkably healthy." He did not foresee any important enemy eruption. To his stepson, he wrote, "Our affairs at present put on a very pleasing aspect, especially in Europe and the West Indies."[14]

Washington found himself more relaxed than he had been since he had assumed the command: there now rose to the surface of his mind a gaiety, a playfulness that had been suppressed by the endless iteration of labor and crisis. To Dr. John Cochran, he wrote:

"I have asked Mrs. Cochran and Mrs. Livingston to dine with me tomorrow, but ought I not to apprise them of their fare? As I hate deception, even where the imagination only is concerned, I will.

"It is needless to premise that my table is large enough to hold the ladies: of this they had ocular proof yesterday. To say how it is usually covered, is rather more essential, and this shall be the purport of my letter. Since our arrival at this happy spot, we have had a ham (sometimes a shoulder of bacon) to grace the head of the table; a piece of roast beef adorns the foot; and a small dish of greens or beans (almost imperceptible) decorates the center.

"When the cook has a mind to cut a figure (and this I presume he will attempt to do tomorrow) we have two beefsteak pies or dishes of crabs, in addition, one on each side the center dish, dividing the space, and reducing the distance between dish and dish to about six feet, which without them would be near twelve apart. Of late, he has had the surprising luck to discover that apples will make pies; and it's a question if, amidst the violence of his efforts, we do not get one of apples instead of having both of beef.

"If the ladies can put up with such entertainment, and will submit to partake of it on plates once tin but now iron (not become so by the labor of scouring) I shall be happy to see them."[15]

Another of Washington's effusions of high spirits was sent to Lafayette in France. The Marquis had written, "I have a wife, my dear general, who is in love with you. . . . She begs you would receive her compliments, and make them acceptable to Mrs. Washington."[16]

Washington replied, "Tell her (if you have not made a mistake and offered your *own love* instead of *hers* to me) that I have a heart susceptible of the tenderest passion, and that it is already so strongly impressed with the most favorable ideas of her, that she must be cautious of putting love's torch to it, as you must be in fanning the flame. But here again, methinks, I

[351]

hear you say, 'I am not apprehensive of danger. My wife is young, you are growing old, and the Atlantic is between you.'

"All this is true, but know my good friend, that no distance can keep *anxious* lovers long asunder, and that the wonders of former ages may be revived in this. But, alas! will you not remark that amidst all the wonders recorded in holy writ no instance can be produced where a young woman from *real inclination* has preferred an old man. This is so much against me that I shall not be able, *I fear,* to contest the prize with you, yet, under the encouragement you have given me, I shall enter the list for so estimable a jewel."

However, Washington turned a deaf ear to Lafayette's suggestion that he visit France (where he could actually meet the Marquise) once the war was over. He was too old to learn the language, he wrote, and "to converse through the medium of an interpreter upon common occasions, especially with the *ladies*, must appear so extremely awkward, insipid, and uncouth, that I can scarce bear it in idea." Lafayette and his consort should cross the ocean to "my rural cottage, where homely fare and a cordial reception shall be substituted for delicacies and costly living."[17]

In early September, there came into Washington's ears, that were ever eager to catch the slightest rumor that might have significance, reports, vague but yet repeated, that a mysterious fleet, which could be d'Estaing's, had been sighted off the coast. Supposing it were d'Estaing, and supposing the British had not heard the news and were thus liable to surprise! Not confiding his hopes even to his division commanders, Washington dispatched Light Horse Harry Lee, on what was announced as a routine mission, to a post overlooking the entrance to New York harbor. Lee was to keep a fast whaleboat hidden in a cove, and deliver, should the heaven-sent opportunity arrive, a letter in which Washington urged the admiral to attack New York instantly. He was at at the same time to announce his presence by "firing a number of guns in quick succession," at which Washington would move to cut off any British retreat by land.[18]

Rumors of sightings kept coming in, but no firm intelligence. No cannon shots sounded from the harbor. After twelve days, Washington began to suspect that the reports had been floated "to answer the villainous purposes of speculating and stockjobbing."[19]

By September 29, Washington had received definite news. D'Estaing was indeed on the coast, but far away: he was off Georgia, preparing to attack Savannah in conjunction with American forces under General Lincoln. Washington now had grave doubts of d'Estaing's "coming this way." However, Congress leapt into a fever of anticipation, ordering Washington to call out thirteen thousand militia and prepare for instantaneous cooperation with the French fleet. Obediently, the Commander in Chief beat the militia tocsin. In urging Sullivan to hurry back with his force from the Indian campaign, he wrote dramatically, "the occasion may be the most important that America has seen during this war." However, several days later, he quietly advised Sullivan not to harass his troops with forced marches.[20]

The British in New York suddenly sprang into action. They drew in their lines, although that meant abandoning the forts at Stony Point and Verplanck's Point; they strengthened their fortifications at the harbor approaches and sank large ships in part of the channel; they dispatched transports that returned with the troops that had for several years occupied Newport. All this could either mean, Washington reasoned, that they were afraid of d'Estaing, or that they were preparing to dispatch a large part of their army to some other theater.[21]

On November 10, Washington wrote his stepson that having heard nothing of the French fleet since its arrival off Georgia, "We begin to fear that some great convulsion in the earth has caused a chasm between this and that state that cannot be passed."[22]

On November 15, Washington learned that more than a month before, d'Estaing had attempted an assault on Savannah, had been bloodily repulsed, and had set sail back to the Indies. Soon a large British detachment floated out of New York, its destination only to be guessed at. That seemed to be that. In Washington's theater, another fighting season had come to an end, with almost nothing accomplished.[23]

39

Rattlesnake Road

T HE winter of 1779–1780 replayed the darkest days at Valley Forge, but this time there seemed much less excuse. Then Philadelphia had just fallen. Despite the defeat of Burgoyne up north, the British lion had been rampant in the middle states. Now, in that central region the British occupied only their New York base, and the force that remained there seemed too weak to do more than cower behind its defenses. As for the large expeditionary force which had sailed from New York the day after Christmas, it eventually came to roost off Charleston, South Carolina, more than seven hundred sea miles from Washington's army.

But in New York and New Jersey winter came in like a British agent. On January 3, there was a blizzard—"no man," Thacher wrote, "could endure its violence many minutes without danger of his life"—that left behind snow four to six feet deep. And the snow was kept on the ground by cold weather which, so the Virginian Commander in Chief insisted that he was told by the oldest inhabitants, "exceeded anything of the kind that had ever been experienced in this climate before."[1]

Relying on West Point to hold the Hudson River line, Washington encamped most of his army—it did not cover a large area as it was not large—in rolling country around Morristown. Fortunately, the men, who had become skillful in such construction since their "monstrous" difficulties at Valley Forge, had completed their huts before the blizzard broke. However, the army remained unfed, naked.[2]

As early as November 24, Washington had warned of serious famine. By mid-December, he was crying in anguish to the Congress and the governors of the middle states that the shortages did not result from "accidental obstructions" as in former cases, but from a total want of means for securing supplies. He wrote the local New Jersey magistrates that he could no longer punish men for plundering the inhabitants, that was now "only to be lamented as the effect of an unfortunate necessity." To prevent complete chaos, the magistrates would have to force the acceptance of written promises to pay, and in the meanwhile, Washington would order that what was needed would be officially requisitioned "with as much tenderness as possible." An aide tells us that he found giving these orders "very disagreeable," but he was certainly angry, too.[3]

As Greene put it, "a country overflowing with plenty are now suffering an army employed for the defense of everything that is dear and valuable to perish for lack of food." Colonel Webb wrote, "I damn my country as void of gratitude!" And Colonel Ebenezer Huntington expressed a wish to bathe his hands in the blood of the villains who were starving the army.[4]

Stern measures, in which the magistrates cooperated, improved matters for a while, but by mid-March, hunger was again stalking the camp. Day after day for several months, Washington spent much of his time scrounging for food. On May 5, he wrote Congress, "I was much alarmed yesterday on account of our stock of meat," when, lo! there appeared a blessed messenger to report that "a few cattle" had come in from Connecticut. But nine days later, he was again "melancholy"—no meat. And four months' pay was due the army.[5]

Behind the shortage lay a recent major revolution in the official relationship between the army and the civilian governments. As long as the money the federal presses printed retained at least some purchasing power, Congress had been enabled to assume the main burden of the war. But the states had continued their failure to pay into the treasury the funds necessary to support the Continental currency. At last, the end had been reached: The Continental bills became so valueless that there was no point in printing any more. Congress was forced to urge a new system in which all expenses would fall directly on the political entities which had the power to tax: on the states.[6]

Each state was to pay its own line, and also supply the army, according to a pre-established quota, with those necessities which it could most easily produce or procure. Federal officers, it was resolved, would no longer purchase: they would merely receive goods and transport them to the army.

Having now relinquished to the states virtually all powers except those related to foreign transactions, Congress had become, as far as the army was concerned, no more than a medium through which requirements were called to the attention of the states. In protesting, Washington stated succinctly, years before that document was created, the basic principles of the Constitution of the United States:

"Unless the states will content themselves with a full and well-chosen representation in Congress, and vest that body with absolute powers in all matters relative to the great purposes of war and of general concern by which the states unitedly are affected, reserving to themselves all matters of local and internal polity for the regulation of order and good government, we are attempting an impossibility and very soon shall become (if it is not already the case) a many-headed monster, a heterogeneous mass, that never will or can steer to the same point."[7]

The new system was, as Washington foresaw, from the start a failure. Since enough goods did not arrive from the states, he had to requisition at bayonet point. Having nothing else to offer, he was forced to give, in return for the produce he took, "certificates" which, although not technically money, added to the weight of obligations under which all federal credit was foundering. Furthermore, if a state did act, it was usually only in favor of its own line, which added to the hardships of the men from other states, the humiliation of inequality and the bite of injustice.

And then there was the situation—"the most disagreeable," as Washington put it, "that can be imagined"—of the Additional Regiments which Washington had established by his own authority on a truly continental basis. A few were adopted, as an act of generosity, by specific states. The sixteen others had to be disbanded for lack of support, setting adrift officers who were among the very best in the service.[8]

"There has never been a stage of the war," Washington cried out to Congress, "in which the dissatisfaction has been so general or alarming." The army had been kept together by "patriotic virtue" seconded by "the unremitting pains that have been taken to compose and reconcile them to their situation. But these will not be able to hold out much longer against the influence of causes constantly operating and every day with some new aggravation. . . . The officers resign. . . . The men have not this resource: they murmur, brood over their discontents, and have lately shown a disposition to enter into seditious combinations."[9]

On May 26, Washington received unpleasant news which he had long expected: the enlisted men from two unfed Connecticut regiments had emerged from their huts in the night carrying their arms. They were, they announced, determined to "return home or, at best, to gain subsistence at the point of the bayonet." However, when their officers appeared, a debate developed which might have been at a New England town meeting. "The troops," so Washington reported to Congress, "very pointedly mentioned besides their distresses for provisions, their not being paid for five months; and, what is of a still more serious and delicate nature in our present circumstances, they mentioned the great depreciation of the money." The officers used "every argument" they "could devise, either to interest their pride or their passions; they were reminded of their past good conduct; of the late assurances of Congress; of the objects for which they were contending." In the end, although one angry soldier struck an officer, most of the men returned to their huts.

Only a few months before, Washington had argued that spreading fear by punishing the ringleaders was the only way to put down a mutiny. Now he wrote, "The men have borne their distress with a firmness and patience never exceeded . . . but there are certain bounds beyond which it is impossible for human nature to go." If the Connecticut regiments had actually marched off, he warned Congress, the rest of the army might have followed.[10]

Greene wrote Reed, "The great man is confounded at his situation, but appears to be reserved and silent." Washington himself wrote Steuben, "The prospect, my dear Baron, is gloomy and the storm thickens." However, "I have been so inured to difficulties in the course of this contest that I have learned to look on them with more tranquillity than formerly. Those which now present themselves no doubt require vigorous exertions to overcome them, and I am far from despairing of doing it."[11]

In a similar vein of resignation, Washington wrote Robert Morris that only on convivial occasions did he "wish for and feel the want" of wine, "having, so far as my own gratifications are interested, resolved to be equally contented with grog should it even be made of New England rum and drank out of a wooden bowl." But then, as he went on to Morris, his optimism frayed away into true blackness at last. When his "public duty" came to an end, "I may be incapable of . . . social enjoyments."[12]

How well Washington's economic education was proceeding is revealed by an argument he wrote Joseph Reed, then president of the Supreme Executive Council of Pennsylvania, to demonstrate that the state could not relax on the assumption that, now Spain had joined France, the war was as good as won.

"In modern wars," Washington wrote, "the longest purse must chiefly determine the event." The French financiers had by wise administration and loans so far avoided additional taxes, but he was "well informed" that if the war continued into another campaign, they would have to impose taxes "which the people of France are not in a condition to endure for any duration." As for Spain: "Commerce and industry are the best mines of a nation; both are wanting to her." Her treasury was not as well filled as Americans believed, and was going rapidly down. Furthermore, "the temper of the nation is too sluggish to admit of great exertions."

Although the British government was in debt, England was rich and her system of public credit was capable of greater extension than any other nation's. It would probably last out the conflict. And once the war was won, the Crown might welcome a general bankruptcy which could be used as "the ladder to climb to absolute authority." Their desire to "pave the way to triumph more effectually over the constitution" might well be an added reason why the ministry would push the war to its last extremity.

At the moment the combined French and Spanish fleets were stronger than the British, but this situation could not be expected to last into another campaign. Not only was England financially more sound, but "it is an axiom that the nation which has the most extensive commerce will always have the most powerful marine." Thus every exertion, Washington concluded, must be made by the American patriots to end the war that summer.[13]

Martha had arrived in Morristown a few days before Christmas. She joined her husband and his military family in the house of Mrs. Theodosia Ford, which was not commodious and was made less so by the fact that the landlady continued to occupy two of the four downstairs rooms, while some of the upper rooms were not finished. Washington promised Martha carpentry work and a separate log kitchen, but on January 22, after all the servants seemed to have been turned into mutes, he wrote angrily to his old friend Quartermaster Greene:

"I have been at my present quarters since the first day of December, and have not a kitchen to cook a dinner in." Eighteen of his servants "and all Mrs. Ford's are crowded together in her kitchen, and scarce one of them able to speak for the colds they have caught." His guard had cut the necessary logs: the trouble was over boards, which he had been told were unprocurable. "To share a common lot and participate the inconveniences" of the army "has with me been a fundamental principle"—but he saw other officers' quarters being made snug with boards. "Far, very far is it from me to censure any measure you have adopted for your own accommodation, for the immediate convenience of Mrs. Greene," who was pregnant. He would "with great willingness have made my conveniences yield to hers, if the point had lain there."[14]

Tempers were getting frayed. Washington had recently upbraided Major Gibbs, the commander of his guard, on some matter concerning a tent. Gibbs passed the scolding on to a lieutenant, William Colfax, in a manner which seemed unjust and redoubled Washington's anger. He wrote Colfax that he intended "to act coolly and deliberately myself, and will therefore give him [Gibbs] an opportunity of recollecting himself. He has been guilty of a piece of disrespect, to give it no worse term, such an one as I much question if there is another officer in the line of the army would have practiced; and because I would not suffer my orders to be trampled upon, a supercilious and self-important conduct on his part is the consequence. . . . I am led from a regard to my own character and by principles of justice to yours to inform you that I consider you as the instrument not the cause of disobedience to my orders." Colfax should not stay away from Washington's dinner table any longer.[15]

Washington's good humor was not being increased by his business relations with his stepson. The soft young man, whom Martha had so spoiled, had shown little concern with imitating his stepfather as a champion of liberty, and he was blandly taking advantage of his absent parent. Having agreed to purchase a herd of Washington's cattle, he culled out the forty-eight best, had the dregs appraised, and applied the resulting low price to the valuable beasts. Furthermore, he delayed paying Washington anything at all while the value of money dropped four to one.

Holding onto the idea that Jackie did not understand what he was doing, Washington sent him a lecture—it was by no means the first—on the meaning of inflation. Then the stepfather burst out angrily, "You might as well attempt to pay me in old newspapers and almanacs with which I can purchase nothing."[16]

Movement on horseback was for Washington an essential of his task and a release from nervous tension. However, as winter came on, his favorite charger, Blue Skin, had a fistula, the sorrel had hardly fleshed out since the previous winter, and the mare was with foal. He wrote to his Virginia neighbor Alexander Spotswood for a truly tremendous addition to his stable: no mount he had was "completely master of my weight." Spotswood did his best, but Washington commented unenthusiastically after his first look at the recruit that he would accept the steed "as men take their wives, for better or worse, and if he should prove a jade and go limping on, I must do as they are obliged to do: submit to the bargain."[17]

For the first time in the war, the principal military action was in the south. The expeditionary force that had sailed from New York in December was under the command of the enemy's top officers: Clinton, Cornwallis, Arbuthnot. It had included most of the local British fleet and 5000 to 6000 soldiers. In March, another 2500 men had sailed. They all appeared off South Carolinia and laid siege to Charleston.

Clinton, Washington believed, would never have dared leave only 11,000 rank and file—two-thirds Hessians, the rest Tories—in New York, had the Continental Army not been allowed to become so weak. As April pointed to true fighting weather, the Americans had in New Jersey and on the Highlands only 10,400 men, of whom 2800 would have completed their three-year enlistments with the end of May. However, since the Hessian commander, Knyphausen, could make no major eruption without endangering his post, Washington and his council decided that they could detach 2000 of their soldiers to join the southern regiments who were defending South Carolina under the command of Lincoln.[18]

Washington considered that Congress and the Board of War had taken the southern department completely out of his jurisdiction. However, Lincoln wrote that he desired "the advantage of your advice and direction," while young Laurens, who was serving as Lincoln's aide, urged Washington to journey south and take charge. There could be no objection, Laurens argued, since Washington's British equivalent, Clinton, was already there.

"If it were proposed by Congress," Washington replied, "I confess to you I should not dislike the journey, did our affairs in this quarter permit it." However, he had "scruples which forbid me to let the measure in question originate with me."[19]

Remembering the debacle at Fort Washington, Washington expressed to both Lincoln and Laurens his concern at their keeping their forces in Charleston, where all would be captured if the city fell. However, it would take his letters a long time to arrive.[20]

On the evening of May 6, the dishes had been cleared from the supper table, and the candles had been lighted. Washington may well have been sitting with his staff cracking jokes over rum punch, when a messenger appeared with a letter. It was headed "at the entrance of Boston Harbor" and plunged on without any formal heading: "Here I am, my dear General, in the mist [midst?] of the joy I feel in finding myself again one of your loving soldiers. I take but the time of telling you that I came from France on board of a frigate which the King gave me for my passage. I have affairs of the utmost importance that I should at first communicate to you alone. . . . Adieu, my dear General; you will easily know the hand of your young soldier, Lafayette."

Washington replied:"I . . . shall embrace you with all the warmth of an affectionate friend when you come to headquarters, where a bed is prepared for you."[21]

When the Marquis arrived, his news proved indeed sensational: the French were sending across the ocean not only a navy—six sail of the line under Chevalier Tenay—but an army under the command of an officer named the Count de Rochambeau. Seven thousand to ten thousand French regulars were to fight beside Washington on American soil.[22]

CHAPTER

40

Enter a Gallic Army

AND so it was again a new spring of hope! After Washnigton had, as Lafayette remembered, received him with sentimental tears, the friends vied with each other in excitement and enthusiasm. Lafayette repeated (and may have believed) the official French statement that Rochambeau and his army were to be under Washington's orders. Washington, remembering his resentments during the French and Indian War at the way the lowest British officers had insisted on ordering around the highest provincials, was gratified to be told of a French ruling that if officers of the same rank served together, the American was to have the precedence. He was not told that Rochambeau had also been ordered to keep the armies so distinct that such a situation could not arise.[1]

In working out plans with Lafayette, Washington put forward the conception that was to remain the anchor of his strategic thinking: although other coups could weaken the enemy, the only blow that would by itself end the war would be to capture the British anchor base in New York. Word should be sent by any possible means to Admiral de Ternay and General Rochambeau "urging them in the strongest terms to proceed both fleet and army with all possible expedition to Sandy Hook" outside New York Harbor, "where they will be met with further advices." If Clinton and Arbuthnot were still away besieging Charleston, New York should be ripe for capture. If, on the other hand, the British expedition had returned, the French should sail on to Newport, where they would establish their permanent base on the island the British had until recently held.[2]

Since the enemy would certainly hear from European sources of the impending French arrival, Washington set to work to fool them concerning where to expect the blow. He instructed Heath to ask questions at Boston— spies could be counted on to listen—about the state of the British defenses at Halifax; and he ordered translated into French (under a spurious parade of secrecy) a proclamation urging the Canadians to rise to the support of a Franco-American invasion.[3]

In his arguments with Congress that his troops must be clothed, Washington now had a new talking point: it would be "mortifying . . . distressing to our feelings" to offend the aristocratic sensibilities of French regulars by having their soldiers serve side by side with naked men. He ordered his own officers to "endeavor" to procure such uniforms as he gleefully (he always enjoyed designing regalia) described. A major general should, for instance, be resplendent in "a blue coat with buff facings and lining, yellow buttons, white and buff underclothes, two epaulettes with two stars upon each, and a black and white feather in the hat." All officers should sport a cockade and, as "side arms, either a sword or genteel bayonet."[4]

He urged the states to prepare him for cooperation with the impending French arrivals by supplying him with an even larger army than he had been given at the optimistic opening of the war: twenty-five thousand Continentals and seventeen thousand militia. "We have the means of success . . ." he exhorted. "It only remains to employ them." And he warned that if the states failed to rise to the occasion, "the succor designed for our benefit will . . . in all probability precipitate our ruin. Drained and weakened as we already are, the exertions we shall make, though they may be too imperfect to secure success, will at any rate be such as to leave us in a state of relaxation and debility, from which it will be difficult if not impractical to recover. The country exhausted, the people dispirited, the consequence and reputation of these states in Europe sunk, our friends chagrined and discouraged, our enemies deriving new credit, new confidence, new resources."[5]

On May 31, Washington heard that Clinton had captured Charleston, and with the entire garrison of twenty-five hundred Continentals and two thousand militia, an even heavier loss than that at Fort Washington. This, he commented, would "give spirit to our enemies" and discourage the patriots. However, his gift for prophecy enabled him to reason that the check "may be attended in the end by happy consequences. The enemy, by attempting to hold conquests so remote, must dissipate their force, and, of course, afford opportunities for striking one or the other extremity."[6]

It was instantly brought home to him that, for all his grandiose plans, his own army was as weak as a sucking baby. From the depleted garrison in New York, the commander, Knyphausen, sent into New Jersey a detachment so strong that Washington could do nothing but watch them "ravaging a fine country below the mountain" where he had to keep his troops defensively huddled. "To such indignity we must, as often as they please, submit," he wrote angrily, "till we receive the quotas of men required from the different states." He insisted that he had so far that season not received "a single recruit to the army."

Le Comte de Rochambeau, by Charles Willson Peale. Courtesy of the
Independence National Historical Park Collection.

At first, Knyphausen's move seemed to Washington inexplicable, since the enemy did no effective foraging and continued to maneuver on the Jersey plain long after it was clear that Washington would refuse a battle. Then an excited rider came in from the coast to report that some sixty-five sail had emerged from a fog off Sandy Hook. They had advanced unopposed into New York harbor, which meant that they could not be the expected French expedition.

Washington now reasoned that Knyphausen had been ordered to hold him in Jersey while Clinton, making a surprise return from South Carolina, dashed up the Hudson. However, if Washington hurried for the river, Clinton might switch and land behind him in Jersey from British-held Staten Island. Washington could only move a little closer to the Hudson and then wait and see, hoping that if a major thrust actually developed up the river, West Point would hold until militia could assemble and he could get there.[7]

The arrivals had, indeed, been a large part of the British army back from Charleston, and Clinton did lead them in a gesture up the Hudson. However, he quickly retired to New York City, at the same time calling Knyphausen back.*

To his loudly expressed outrage, Washington had not been notified by the various state governments as to what reinforcements, if any, he could expect. Admittedly, the reappearance of four thousand British soldiers and most of Arbuthnot's fleet made a combined Franco-American attack on New York less feasible. Yet Washington realized that the French, who might appear off the coast any day, would instantly "look to me for a plan of the measures to be pursued. . . . I cannot even give them conjectures." Washington dispatched a brigadier to each state to bring in what soldiers they could find, and wrote Jack that "the accursed policy" of the governments "is to be lamented, bitterly lamented, and in the anguish of soul I do lament."[8]

Rumors reached Washington that a British naval reinforcement was expected in the wake of the French fleet, and then he heard that the French had actually arrived at Newport on the afternoon of July 10. He began arranging for transport to carry to his army "a quantity of clothing, arms, and ammunition" which it had been reported they would bring, and he wrote Governor Trumbull that, despite the continued unpreparedness of his army, he still intended to "hazard" joint operations that would break the

* Knyphausen had gone into Jersey on his own initiative because he had been told by deserters that the state needed only the presence of an army to return to its old allegiance. He had stayed because once the Hessian had got an idea in his head, it was hard to knock it out. Finding him there, Clinton had tried to take advantage of the situation, but had abandoned the attempt when he became convinced that Washington would do nothing rash. The total result, so Clinton's aide André wrote, was that several hundred Hessians took the opportunity of deserting.[9]

long stalemate. "A regard to our national character obliges me to it, and I hope the same motive will stimulate the states."[10]

The day after he had learned of the French arrival, Washington saw a newspaper, brought out of New York City, which stated that Rear Admiral Thomas Graves had sailed into that harbor with six capital ships. This, he commented with wild understatement, was "rather an unlucky circumstance." However, he wrote Congress that it ought not "to have any effect upon our exertions. It ought on the contrary to excite in us a determination to be prepared at all events. We do not yet know the force which Chevalier de Ternay has brought with him." If it remained superior to the British, "we may be able to operate in some other quarter if not against New York." If it were "no more than equal [he did not hint to Congress that it might be inferior, which actually proved to be the case], we should not lose sight of the great superiority of the French and Spanish fleets in the West Indies, which may perhaps enable the commanders in those seas to turn the balance decidedly in our favor."[11]

In came a letter from Rochambeau abrim with those orotund compliments which flow easily from a courtier's pen: "I have arrived here with all the submission, all the zeal, and all the veneration I have for your person and for the distinguished talents which you reveal in sustaining a war forever memorable." Washington could only read such epistles in translation, and found it painful to answer them in the same style. However, he had once more at hand the man he considered the perfect instrument for communicating with the French commanders. In parallel effusive letters to Rochambeau and de Ternay, Washington stated that in the future he would communicate to them through Lafayette, "a friend from whom I conceal nothing. . . . I entreat you to receive whatever he shall tell you as coming from me."[12]

Washington would have been flabbergasted could he have read the thoughts of the French commanders on receiving these missives. Lafayette had intrigued in court to get the command Rochambeau now held; although a general in the American army, he was merely a captain of the reserve in the French; Rochambeau, who was only moderately wellborn, had down the years had his fill of bumptious young aristocrats. The Marquis's fire and passionate ambition to distinguish himself, which Washington found so charming, grated on the elderly professional soldier whose body bore the scars of many wars.[13]

Lafayette set out for the French at Newport carrying with him a memorandum in which Washington continued to urge a combined attack on New York. It would be necessary, he pointed out, for the French to guarantee naval superiority. Then he admitted that the required American troops had not yet gathered and that he could not state precisely when they would. Yet, "to fix some epoch to it," a tentative date for the attack should be set: he suggested August 5.[14]

Washington was soon "greatly disappointed" to hear that most of the supplies he had expected the French to bring had been left behind because of a shortage of transports. Furthermore, there could be no doubt that de Ternay's fleet was clearly inferior to the British now in New York. But there was still hope: the rest of the supplies and a second French land and naval force was expected in a few weeks. Washington in no way relaxed his posture of preparing to attack New York. "The die is cast," he wrote Congress, "and it remains with the states either to fulfill their engagements, preserve their credit, and support their independence, or to involve us in disgrace and defeat."[15]

Six years later, Washington explained that he had determined "at all hazards to give out and cause it to be believed by the highest military as well as civil officers that New York was the destined place of attack, for the important purpose of inducing the eastern and middle states to make greater exertions in furnishing specific supplies than they otherwise would have done, as well as for the interesting purpose of rendering the enemy less well prepared elsewhere."[16]

Thinking thus in his own terms, Washington did not realize that he was greatly embarrassing his French allies. Probing always for a hole in the enemy defenses, for a chance of action, the Fabian leader tossed up trial balloons in the realization that only a very rare one would fly. Rochambeau's thoughts were less volatile. As an official of an autocratic government, he did not understand the mixing with strategy of propaganda to excite the home front, and, being used to operating from power not weakness, he saw no reason to dance around problems like a lightweight boxer. You remained quiet in your might until you saw a chance for a knockout blow, and then you struck. You did not expose yourself to the mirth of your fellow professionals by publicly endorsing crackbrained schemes. To make matters more difficult for Rochambeau, he had been ordered by his king to take no unwarranted risks and yet, at the same time, give the impression that he was obeying Washington's orders.

Rochambeau reported to his government that the country was "in consternation." Washington had only three thousand men (this was roughly accurate) and paper money had fallen to sixty to one. "Send us troops, ships, and money, but do not depend on these people nor upon their means: they have neither money nor credit; their means of resistance are only momentary and called forth when they are attacked in their own homes." Puzzling over Washington's expressed desire, under such unpropitious circumstances, to attack New York, he concluded that the American leader felt a desperate need to strike because he "really believed . . . that, on account of the late great decline in the finances of Congress, this campaign was the last struggle of expiring patriotism." But even taking all that into account, Rochambeau found it hard to believe that Washington could actually wish to be so foolhardy. The basic trouble, the French general reasoned, must be "mischief-making" on the part of Lafayette. Surely,

Rochambeau's rival was exaggerating Washington's desires in order to make it out that Rochambeau was afraid to attack. If only Washington had not "sent Lafayette to me with full powers from him!"[17]

Admiral de Ternay, who was less on the spot, agreed to take the onus: he notified Washington that he would under no circumstances risk his fleet in New York harbor. And Rochambeau begged Washington to meet him and de Ternay halfway between their two camps. "In an hour of conversation, we shall be able to settle things far more definitely than in volumes of writing."

Washington replied, "There is nothing I should more ardently desire than to meet" the Frenchmen. However, "my presence here is essential to keep our preparations in activity, or even going on at all."[18]

Discussion of such matters was brought to a sharp halt when Arbuthnot's fleet and transports bearing Clinton with a large land force sailed for the French position in Rhode Island. Washington assured Rochambeau that he would march to the rescue could he hope to get there in time. As it was, he was taking his army across the Hudson from New Jersey to menace New York in conjunction with the militia who were coming out to meet the emergency. If Clinton had embarked enough men really to endanger the French, Washington reasoned, he would have to return to New York or face the possibility of losing his most important base.

Washington proved right. Although the British fleet remained off Newport to blockade de Ternay, Clinton came popping back.[19]

The crisis enabled Washington to increase his force to 6143 continentals and 3700 militia. The effort this had involved, he wrote Lafayette, would add to the bad impression that continuing inaction "will make on the minds of the people. . . . Let me intreat you to ascertain the probability of a succor coming from France and the West Indies!" Succor from France would be the second squadron that had been slated to follow Rochambeau. From the Indies, a combined French and Spanish fleet might, after it had achieved its immediate objective by capturing Jamaica, sail northward.[20]

The increase around Washington's campfires of fighting right arms was matched by an increase in eating mouths—and even if there was food to put in them, it often could not be cooked because the quartermaster department could not procure kettles. And Congress, instead of coming effectively to the rescue, picked out as a scapegoat the man who was, perhaps, Washington's most valuable subordinate.

Greene had become quartermaster general in response to the Commander in Chief's pleading. Battling inflation as best he could, he had operated to Washington's satisfaction. However, after Congress's decision to turn supplying the army over to the states had compounded confusion, the civilian leaders had blamed the quartermaster. Personal hatred was added to the brew when Washington's enemy Mifflin, whom Greene had superseded, was put on the committee to straighten things out. Greene was charged not only with gross incompetence, but also with having gone beyond the line of duty to line his own nest.[21]

This was a difficult matter really to determine, since no sharp distinction then existed between public and private interest. Lacking any permanent official organization through which to work, a supply officer was considered the more valuable if he could throw his personal credit into a breach, if he had reliable partners and established business connections whom he could call on to help at their own—and by extension his own—profit. The situation was, indeed, very similar to that with which Washington had become familiar when as a young man he had observed William Fairfax's activities as the land agent of Lord Fairfax. It was assumed that the agent would make his labors worthwhile by taking care of his own interests; the question was really one of degree. This had been the situation with Mifflin (who was never actually found guilty of any fraud), as it was now with Greene. Greene himself stated that he was being attacked because it was believed that he had been making money "too fast."

Washington rushed to Greene's support, but his intervention did not altogether help, since the belief that Greene was too much His Excellency's favorite was already a cause of resentment. Schuyler reported to Washington that Greene's supporters had been greatly embarrassed when an imprudent speaker in Congress had attributed to Washington the wish that should anything happen to him, Greene should succeed as commander in chief.* [22] Finally, Greene resigned the quartermastership peremptorily and with the supercilious rage of a high military officer.

Congress, angered in turn, was inclined not only to accept Greene's resignation as quartermaster but to discharge him as major general. When warned of this, Washington fired back one of his angriest letters. If Greene were actually removed, it would exhibit, he wrote, "such a stretch of arbitrary power—" Then he scratched out the phrase and began again: "such a specimen of power, that I question if there is an officer in the whole line" who would not resign. Each would ask, "May it not be my turn tomorrow, and ought I to put it in the power of any man or body of men to sport with my commission and character?" Congress should not forget that no body of men (Congress could take that!) had made such sacrifices to the cause as the officers.[23]

Allowing Greene to continue as major general, Congress satisfied itself by appointing to be his successor as quartermaster a man who had long been openly vocal against Washington, Timothy Pickering. Greene wrote, "The

---

* Washington may well have believed that Greene would make his most promising successor, but, all legend to the contrary, no unimpeachable document indicates that Washington ever said so. He would undoubtedly have regarded any such statement as an encroachment upon the prerogatives of Congress.

army are not pleased with his coming. They begin to consider him a congressional spy."[24]

On sailing back to New York after the capture of Charleston and General Lincoln's army, Clinton had left Cornwallis as British commander in South Carolina. Needing a new general to oppose Cornwallis, Congress elected Gates. This isolated Washington even further from the southern theater. He considered himself in such a "delicate situation . . . with respect to General Gates" that he was unwilling to make, "even in a confidential way," any comments on the management of the southern campaign "lest my sentiments, being known, should have an unfavorable interpretation ascribed to them by illiberal minds."[25]

Having assumed the leadership of some fourteen hundred regulars and two thousand militia, Gates advanced into South Carolina. Cornwallis faced him with a slightly smaller but much better-disciplined force. They met at Camden on August 16. Gates's militia took to their heels; the regulars who tried to stand were overwhelmed; the Americans suffered about two thousand casualties in one of the worst routs of the war, which brought to an end all organized resistance in both Carolinas.

Whatever were Washington's private emotions, he put on paper the criticisms of his rival. To Congress, he wrote that Camden was an object lesson concerning "the fatal consequences of depending on militia." To Gates, he wrote soothingly, "The behavior of the Continental troops does them infinite honor. The accounts which the enemy give of the action show that their victory was dearly bought." And then Washington referred to what was causing the greatest popular outcry: that Gates had separated himself by seventy miles from the battlefield before he paused to report to Congress. "It would answer no good purpose," Washington wrote, "to take a position near the enemy, while you are so far inferior in force."[26]

Accepting no such lenient view, Congress removed Gates from all command and ordered an inquiry into his conduct. In this crisis, their resentment of Washington's power gave way to dependence: they threw the southern command into his lap, empowering him to appoint Gates's successor. Washington happily selected Greene, but, always careful not to grab, preferred merely to "nominate" him to Congress. In writing the legislators, Washington put down and then scratched out the following phrase: "I very sensibly feel this fresh mark of the confidence of Congress in leaving to me the appointment of a general officer to so important a command." Congress approved the appointment of Greene, whom they had so recently struck at.[27]

As Greene's assistants, Washington detailed Light Horse Harry Lee—cavalry was particularly valuable in the flat south—and Steuben—"there is an army to be created." To southern officials and his powerful Virginia

neighbors, he sent praise of Greene—"I think I am giving you a general"—
and arguments against reliance on the militia: "We must have a permanent
force, not a force that is constantly fluctuating and sliding from under us as
a pedestal of ice would do from a statue in a summer's day." If the south
would gird itself, he argued, the enemy's progress could be disastrous to
them, "for they have not a stamina of force sufficient for such extensive
conquests."[28]

Continuing its dependent mood, Congress voted Washington "full power"
to concert military moves with French or Spanish commanders wherever
stationed. Thus the future President was given for the first time authority
that extended beyond the North American continent.

Meditating on his first official plunge into foreign affairs, Washington
decided that the situation was too "critical" for any attempt to hold up the
prestige of the new nation with claims of strength. To the French ambassador, Luzerne, for forwarding to the French commander in the Indies, the
Comte de Guichen, Washington sent an abject appeal. The government of
the United States, he stated, was "without finances, its paper credit sunk
and no expedients it can adopt capable of retrieving it; the resources of the
country much diminished by a five years' war in which it has made efforts
beyond its ability. Clinton with an army of ten thousand regular troops,
aided by a considerable body of militia" was "in possession of one of our
capital towns and a large part of the state [New York] to which it belongs;
the savages desolating the other frontier [of New York]; a fleet superior to
that of our allies, [able] not only to protect him against any attempts of
ours, but to facilitate those he may project against us. Lord Cornwallis with
seven or eight thousand men in complete possession of two states, Georgia
and South Carolina; a third, North Carolina, by recent misfortunes at his
mercy; his force daily increasing by an accession of adherents, whom his
successes naturally procures him in a country inhabited in great part by
emigrants from England and Scotland, who have not been long enough
transplanted to exchange their ancient habits and attachments in favor of
their new residence."

The British, Washington continued, were said to be preparing to send
more troops to the south. "If they push their successes in that quarter, there
is no saying where their career may end. The opposition will be feeble,
unless we can give succor from hence." But distances were so great that
effective succor would have to travel south in ships. Enough troops could not
be dispatched unless Guichen released from the Indies enough ships to give
the Franco-American allies "an unequivocal naval superiority" in North
American waters.[29]

Increasingly annoyed at having to deal through Lafayette, Rochambeau
finally sent Washington a letter, written in English so that no translator

could intervene, repeating his request for an interview. And Gates's defeat at Camden had finally made Washington eager to see the Frenchmen; he now had a scheme to propose. If de Ternay moved his fleet to Boston, where (as was not the case at Newport) it would be safe without special military protection, Rochambeau with his five thousand men could join Washington—who expected soon to be left with only six thousand—outside New York. This additional strength would, Washington reasoned, do one of two things: it would either prevent Clinton from following up his victories in the south by dispatching another detachment there, or, if Clinton did nevertheless reinforce Cornwallis, it would open the possibility of attacking the weakened garrison he left behind. Washington agreed to meet Rochambeau and de Ternay at Hartford, halfway between their respective camps, on September 20.[30]

As Washington prepared to get off, dispatch boxes gave a roller-coaster-like motion to his emotions. Word of unidentified sails moving against not distant horizons filled him with exaltation: "It seems very probable that the Comte de Guichen is really approaching the coast." But then the sails were identified: they were British; twelve ships of the line and four frigates under Admiral Rodney. The ocean was even more completely the enemy's.[31]

However, Washington, surrounded by his retinue and guards, set off on schedule to the hoofbeats of forty horses. Having reached and crossed the Housatonic, he rode through Connecticut hills sometimes as wild as the Shenandoah Valley had been when he had surveyed there: towering forest pockmarked with little stump-filled clearings. Then he would come surprisingly on communities where "the cultivation appears rich and well-managed." One of these—seven or eight houses grouped "in a beautiful situation" around a meetinghouse—proved to be the first geographic namesake he had ever visited: it was called Washington.

On Rocky Hill, Washington surely paused to look out on the wide panorama of the Connecticut River bending, with belts of fields around it, between chains of low mountains. (This was the expansive world for which he fought!) As he approached Hartford, settlements became thicker until a continuous line of farmhouses, "everywhere adorned with trees and meadows," could strike a French traveler as "a *jardin anglais* which art would have difficulty equaling."

Hartford, the same traveler ruled, "is not worth lingering over. . . . It consists of a long, very long street parallel to the river." But now Washington had something more fascinating to become acquainted with than a new countryside. He was to meet, for the first time, his allies.[32]

Rochambeau's aides crowded around Washington in admiration. "His dignified address," wrote the engineer Count Mathieu Dumas, "his simplicity of manners, and mild gravity surpassed our expectation and won every heart." And Count Axel de Fersen, that chivalrous slave of Marie Antoinette, wrote, "His handsome and majestic while at the same time mild and open countenance, perfectly reflects his moral qualities. He looks the hero. He is very cold, speaks little, but is courteous and frank. A shade of sadness overshadows his countenance, which is not unbecoming and gives him an interesting air." Von Closen, who served as interpreter in subsequent conferences with Rochambeau, noted that Washington gave striking evidence of military talents and knowledge: "I could not find strong enough words to describe" what Washington said "as vividly and forcefully as I should."[33]

No such enthusiastic descriptions fell from Rochambeau's pen. To him, Washington was a problem: an officer of great prestige, whom he was supposed to obey but whose judgment he had come to doubt. The difficulty was compounded by the importance to Rochambeau's mission of keeping on the best possible terms with the Americans until the objectives of the French crown had been achieved.

When Washington distinguished among the French officers their commander in chief, Rochambeau, he saw a short, stocky, ruddy man with fleshy features that crowded a long face. Rochambeau had a scar on his temple that grazed the corner of an eye, and he limped a little from another wound. He had spent thirty-seven of his fifty-five years in the army; he had little conversation that did not deal with troop movements; he was brisk; he expressed a concern only with fact. Yet there were moments when his face took on the sensitivity of a world-weary poet: he was suddenly pensive. But the moments would quickly pass. Washington, whose sympathetic imagination usually carried him far into other men's psyches, was baffled by this Frenchman, civilized, efficient, always affable, never cordial.

Rochambeau, convinced that this campaign was as good as over, wished to discuss the following year. It was humiliation for Washington to have to admit that he had been unable "to combine with Congress" on the force he would receive at the commencement of the next campaign, or even on how he was to replace those of his men who would be released on January 1. He went on to express opinions concerning what the French should do: he thought it necessary that they should "complete" their army to fifteen thousand. "He hopes," so the official French minutes reported, "the states, by a new effort, will be able to supply" an equal number.[34]

Rochambeau promised to slip his son through the British blockade so that the young man could ask in France for reinforcements and for hard money, which, after it was paid out for supplies sold to the French army, would bolster the American economy. Since Washington agreed that it would first be necessary to have thirty thousand men and naval superiority, the French commander felt it safe to go along with Washington in stating that the capture of New York should be considered the prime objective. Rochambeau was, indeed, the very model of a cooperative subordinate till Washington proposed his plan, which involved immediate action: that the French ships go to Boston and the French troops join him outside New York.[35]

De Ternay later noted that he had been in favor of this, as he considered Boston the better harbor, but he said nothing. Rochambeau raised various objections. Washington was too wise to venture, in his role of titular commander, on positive orders, but, so he remembered, "I urged, as far as decency and policy would permit," the wisdom of his scheme. Finally, Rochambeau stated that he had instructions of which Washington had not been notified. To avoid a breakdown of discipline and the possible difficulties that might grow from differences of national manners, he had been ordered to keep his army, until an actual battle portended, all together and on an island.[36]

Thus the conference produced "nothing conclusive." Washington was to write Lafayette, "You must be convinced, from what passed at the interview at H—— [Hartford] that my command of the F'—— T——ps [French troops] stands upon a very limited scale."[37]

CHAPTER

41

Tribulations of an Old Friend

AS Washington rode back through autumn foliage from his frustrating
conference with Rochambeau, he remembered how, at the beginning
of the campaign that was now drawing to a close, he had hoped
"that a prospect was displaying which would enable me to fix a period
to my military pursuits, and restore me to domestic life. The favorable
disposition of Spain; the promised succor from France; the combined
[French and Spanish] force in the West Indies; the declaration of Russia
(acceded to by the other powers of Europe, humiliating to the naval pride
and power of Great Britain); the superiority of France and Spain by sea in
Europe; the Irish claims and English disturbances, formed in the aggregate
an opinion in my breast (which is not very susceptible of peaceful dreams)
that the hour of deliverance was not far distant*. . . . But, alas! . . . I see
nothing before us but accumulating distress. We have been half our time
without provision and are like to continue so. We have no magazines [of
munitions] nor money to form them, and in a little time we shall have no
men, if we had money to pay them. We have lived upon expedients till we
can live no longer. In a word, the history of the war is a history of false
hopes and temporary devices instead of system and economy."

Having come to this point in his thinking, Washington tried to find a
bright side: "It is vain, however, to look back, nor is it our business to do so.

---

* Catherine the Great of Russia had in February 1780 called, with considerable
success, on other maritime powers to join in a League of Armed Neutrality that would
protect their claims to trade with belligerents (particularly France) without interference
(particularly by the British navy). In March, Washington had ordered the whole army to
celebrate St. Patrick's Day in grateful recognition of Irish petitions to the English
Parliament which appeared calculated "to restore a brave and generous people to their
ancient rights and freedom, and by their operation to promote the cause of America."
Later Washington had expressed the hope that the "injured and deceived . . . populace
of England as well as Ireland" were preparing to punish the government which had
created the "present mischief."[1]

Our case is not desperate, if virtue exists in the people and there is wisdom among our rulers."

The conclusion was satisfactory, but his mind churned on: "To suppose that this great revolution can be accomplished by a temporary army; that this army will be subsisted by state supplies; and that taxation alone is adequate to our wants, is in my opinion absurd and as unreasonable as to expect an inversion in the order of nature to accommodate itself to our views."* [2]

To escape from the melancholy of his thoughts, Washington could fix his mind on his immediate destination: pleasure seemed directly ahead. He was planning to spend the night with the most brilliant of his combat generals, Benedict Arnold, and with that officer's pretty young wife. He had known the former Peggy Shippen since she was a child. She was spirited and he could enjoy with her such a ceremonious flirtation as it amused him to engage in with pretty young ladies.

But to think for any length of time about the Arnolds was to remember the injustices and difficulties through which the great combat general had suffered. Arnold had again and again demonstrated military brilliance, but what had been his reward? After his impressive achievements at Ticonderoga; in his wilderness march to Quebec; in the siege and attack on that city; as a naval commander on Lake Champlain, he had been denied, because of jockeying between the states, the promotion to which he had every right. Washington had then felt that he would have been justified in resigning. However, Arnold nobly laid aside his injured claims to rank in order to join Schuyler's army that was trying to turn back Burgoyne's menace to northern New York.

Arnold's loyalty to Washington's friend Schuyler made him, after Schuyler had been replaced in the northern command by Gates, feud with the newcomer, whom Washington also did not trust. Gates removed Arnold from all command. However, the fighter could not bear to leave the area of battle. Although Gates gathered in all the credit, Arnold, in disobeyal of orders, commanded from the field the aggressive battle which led directly to Burgoyne's surrender. At the very moment of victory, Arnold was wounded in the leg.

Congress very belatedly restored Arnold's rightful rank, but now the magnificent athlete was a cripple. From his hospital bed in Albany he branded as ridiculous the effort, made at the height of the Conway Cabal by the Board of War, to stage, over Washington's head, a winter invasion of Canada. With the spring of that year, Arnold finally appeared at Valley Forge. How could Washington forget his first sight of his old friend? Arnold could not stand on his leg; he had to be held upright by two soldiers. His

---

* These quotations, which summarize Washington's thinking at the time, are taken from a letter he wrote on October 5 to General Cadwalader.

Benedict Arnold, engraved in Paris, 1781, after a drawing by Pierre Eugène du Simitière. Courtesy of the New-York Historical Society.

Peggy Shippen, by John André. Courtesy of the Yale University Art Gallery.

fine hawk's face had taken on the disgruntled look of a bitter old man; and the light-blue eyes that had once snapped from among his dark features were now dull and fishlike. Seeking a post suitable for the wounded hero, Washington had, on the British evacuation of Philadelphia, made Arnold the military commandant of the capital.[3]

Washington soon heard rumors that Arnold was courting, not without signs of success, the much younger, much better-born belle Peggy Shippen. Peggy had stayed in Philadelphia during the occupation and had danced with British officers. Complaints sounded that Arnold was preferring such suspected Tories to the "virtuous" patriotic maidens who had fled British-held Philadelphia. However, Washington could not find this upsetting: he had ordered Arnold to protect conservatives from persecution and, in any case, believed that women should ever be regarded as immune to the issues of warfare.

Further reports that Arnold was using his official position to make money through illegal partnerships were, of course, bothersome—and when Washington stayed in Philadelphia during the winter of 1778–1779, he saw Arnold living with a grandeur of which he could not approve. But almost everyone was being charged with peculation by somebody else, while the extravagance was too ubiquitous to be charged to the account of any one man. And certainly, no patriot had more right to a little pleasure, more need to put on a good show, than the hero who had suffered such injustices and was courting a young beauty while he remained so crippled that he needed four men to help him in and out of his coach.[4]

Washington had hardly returned to his headquarters at Morristown when Arnold appeared with his leg improved—he could now hop around on a high-heeled boot—but his face working with emotion and in his trembling hand a piece of paper. It proved to be a proclamation in which the Supreme Executive Council of Pennsylvania, with Washington's faithless friend Reed as president, imputed to Arnold eight pieces of malfeasance. These involved illegal business transactions, support of Tories, and defiance of the independent sovereignty of Pennsylvania. No evidence was given, and the document ended with a slap at Washington's powers to appoint his own officers: if Arnold were not removed from the Philadelphia command, Pennsylvania would withhold funds from the army and only call out militia under "the most urgent and pressing necessity."

Arnold assumed (probably correctly) that he had Washington's sympathies. However, Washington's official position made it impossible for him to show any partiality. He found himself forced to administer Arnold a "rebuke before I could convince him of the impropriety of his entering upon a justification of his conduct in my presence, and for bestowing such illiberal abuses as he seemed disposed to do upon those whom he denominated his persecutors." The best Washington could do for his friend was to urge him to lay the matter before Congress. He was greatly "relieved" when he learned that Congress was actually assuming jurisdiction.[5]

However, a most acrimonious row broke out in Philadelphia.

Reed and his Supreme Executive Council led a left wing which blamed the economic collapse on the misdeeds of business speculators and were inclined to punish—even hang—conservatives as Tories. Since Arnold had been conspicuous for luxury and a business collaborator with various merchant-congressmen (particularly from New York), convicting Arnold became for the radicals a holy cause. The conservatives felt that their own safety required that they rally behind him. Further heat was lent the controversy by a local political issue: the Pennsylvania constitution which had put Reed and his friends in power was under attack by revisionists who were friends of Arnold.

It soon came clear that Reed's Supreme Executive Council had little evidence to back their suspicions of Arnold. They could only demonstrate one charge: a misuse of government wagons to carry private property. The other seven impeachments, they stated, were an expression of "their sense of his conduct . . . an opinion operative only as the world shall give it weight." Washington could not fail to conclude that it was unfair for a governmental body to challenge an individual soldier to what was, in effect, a propaganda war.[6]

However, all matters of fairness to an individual, as too often happens in wartime, had to give way to grave matters of public policy. When a congressional committee acquitted Arnold of the six charges they considered civilians competent to try, Reed insisted that the prerogatives of Pennsylvania as an independent nation had been dangerously invaded. Feeling ran so high that it was rumored that Congress would have to leave Philadelphia for another state. Facing a breakdown of cooperation between the states and exacerbation of the latent conflict between the conservatives and the radicals, Congress could only backtrack. They threw out the verdict of their committee, left four charges dangling, and ordered Washington to have the other four, which were considered amenable to such action, tried in a court-martial.

Washington received from Arnold a letter warning that Reed would seek delay—"it is to his interest that the affair should remain in the dark"—and pleading for an early trial. Washington set May 1, 1780, as the date. Instantly a letter from Reed: the early date was an insult to Pennsylvania—witnesses could not be gathered so quickly—and proved that the army intended "a mere formality." Washington wrote Arnold that he had no choice but to postpone the trial.[7]

The reply that came from Arnold did not make happy reading: "If your Excellency thinks me criminal for Heaven's sake let me be immediately tried and if found guilty, executed. I want no favor; I only ask justice. . . . Having made every sacrifice of fortune and blood, and become a cripple in the service of my country, I little expected to meet the ungrateful returns I have received from my countrymen; but, as Congress has stamped ingratitude as a current coin, I must take it. I wish your Excellency, for your long and eminent services, may not be paid in the same coin. I have nothing left but the little reputation I have gained in the army. Delay in the present case is worse than death."[8]

Washington (who was no mean exaggerator himself) was less upset by the hysterical tone of this letter—nothing of which Arnold was accused was a capital crime—than by the fact that his own situation in relation to his friend was, as he wrote Arnold, "truly delicate and embarrassing: on one side your anxiety, very natural in such circumstances, and the convenience of the army strongly urge me to bring the affair to a speedy conclusion; on the other, the pointed representations of the state on the subject of witnesses and the impropriety of precipitating a trial so important in itself, seem to leave me no choice. I beg you to be convinced I do not indulge any sentiments unfavorable to you, while my duty obliges me and I am sure you wish me to avoid even the semblance of partiality."[9]

From Arnold there now came an expression of regret that "my cruel situation should cause your Excellency the least embarrassment or uneasiness." Arnold only desired vindication so that he could take a command in the army: "My wounds are so recovered that I can walk with ease and I expect soon to be able to ride on horseback. . . . The interest I have in the welfare and happiness of my country . . . will, I hope, always overcome my personal resentment."[10]

Washington was surely pleased to conclude that Arnold had got hold of himself. The commander did not particularly notice the strange interjection of the phrase "I hope," and nothing could have been further from his thoughts than that Arnold now wanted a command in the army so that he could betray it.

Although the record that was visible to Washington indicated that Arnold was being hounded in the most unfair manner by the Pennsylvania authorities, the hidden truth was that Arnold had been guilty of the financial peculations Reed suspected but could not prove—and, indeed, many others. However, the wounded hero continued to feel himself persecuted; he had sacrificed so much for the cause, and was, he felt, singled out to be attacked for underground practices in which a large part of the financial community, including many men who had made no sacrifices, were also engaged.

Arnold finally married his Peggy, and on May 1, 1779, the couple sent secret overtures to a young man named John André with whom Peggy had flirted during the British occupation of Philadelphia. This young man was now adjutant general of the British army, and to him Arnold offered to sell, for suitable payment, "his services to the commander in chief of the British forces . . . either by immediately joining the British army, or cooperating on some concerted plan with Sir Henry Clinton." André replied that Arnold should stay in the American service and by "enabling us to attack to advantage," facilitate the "seizing an obnoxious body of men."[11]

Washington felt a load lifted from his conscience when, in December 1779, he was at long last able to order the court-martial for which—as he saw it—a brave and wounded officer, just married to a lovely young lady, was pleading for on the grounds that he desired justice. The court, after more than a month of deliberation, found Arnold guilty of two of the four charges. However, these were little more than misdemeanors: he had given an unsuitable pass to a schooner owned by Tory profiteers, and, in securing wagons to move his own property, he had made "an imprudent and improper" request of the wagonmaster. The court imposed the mildest possible sentence: Arnold should be reprimanded by Washington.[12]

After Congress had approved the verdict, Washington requested that "the whole of the proceedings in the case of Major General Arnold may be transmitted to me." He had not, of course, been present at the trial. He wanted to determine how sternly to word his reprimand. Furthermore, once the reprimand had been delivered, Arnold would be free to take a command. Surely, Washington wished also to see whether anything had been revealed to indicate that his old friend could no longer be trusted. The record proved to be a vast billowing of confusion through which could be discerned some greed on Arnold's part and much bad judgment in dealing with civilians, but no major dishonesty or lack of continued dedication to the cause. Washington phrased his reprimand as gently as possible: "The Commander in Chief," he began, "would have been much happier in an occasion of bestowing commendations on an officer who has rendered such distinguished services to his country as Major General Arnold. . . ."[13]

Washington's wildest imaginings, of course, did not envision the clandestine movements of mysterious couriers that kept communication going across the lines between the Arnolds and Major André. The Arnolds sent intelligence like ordinary spies and demanded large sums of money. However, Washington's universal caution that automatically confined secrets to the smallest possible circle kept Arnold from having any unusually valuable intelligence to send.* And, while Arnold remained under charges, he could not hope to secure a command to betray. The British had refused to promise him any major compensation.

---

* When Washington was first expecting Rochambeau and wanted to fool the British into thinking that an attack was planned on Canada, he had sent Arnold in Philadelphia a proclamation addressed to the Canadian people, with the request that it be translated into French. Far from confiding that this was a trick which would be leaked to the British, Washington gravely warned Arnold that the matter should be conducted with the greatest secrecy. In his role as a spy, Arnold sent the proclamation to André as a genuine indication of Franco-American plans.[14]

Even the outcome of the court-martial, which opened to Arnold active service, hardly warmed up the British spymasters. They reasoned that Arnold would now be given a command in the line, which would not offer good opportunities for treason, since he would be operating under Washington's eye, and since, in the unconventional American army, subordinates could not be counted on to carry out orders that were clearly to their disadvantage.

Seeking something finite to offer, the connubial traitors fixed on the fortress of West Point. If Arnold could secure the command, he could certainly manage to betray to the enemy that all-important bastion of American defense. The suggestion was received by the British with satisfactory enthusiasm.[15]

Fortunately for the plot, the existing commandant was unsatisfactory to the New York State authorities. Arnold talked as veteran to veteran with his former commander, Schuyler, who, having resigned from the army, now led New York's congressional delegation. And Peggy whispered as a flirtatious young woman into the ear of the susceptible young New York congressman Robert R. Livingston.

Schuyler and Livingston urged on Washington that the stationary post was perfectly suited to the half-crippled hero, and added that New York would be pleased to see him there. Schuyler reported back to Arnold that Washington "expressed himself with regard to you in terms such as the friends who love you could wish. . . . He expressed a desire to do whatever was agreeable to you, dwelt on your abilities, your merits, your sufferings, and the well-earned claims you have on your country."[16]

That was in early 1780; Rochambeau was still expected and Washington was all eagerness to concert with the French in an attack on New York. He remembered that Schuyler's suggestion made "little impression on me. . . . I answered that, as we had a prospect of an active and vigorous campaign, I should be glad of General Arnold's aid and assistance. However, the command of West Point would be utterly unworthy of an officer of Arnold's rank and abilities, because Washington intended "to draw my whole force into the field when we were in circumstances to commence our operations against New York, leaving even West Point to the care of invalids and a small garrison of militia." However, if Arnold was really still too crippled for a command in the field, "I should readily indulge him."[17]

As the 1780 campaign remained quiescent, as Rochambeau sat at Newport and Washington called vainly for reinforcements, Arnold's role remained unresolved. Then, as we have seen, Clinton and Arbuthnot moved on Rhode Island, and Washington reacted by menacing New York. The Commander in Chief was standing on a height above Stony Point, watching his troops cross the Hudson, when Arnold came riding up. "He asked me," so Washington was quoted as remembering six years later, "if I had thought of anything for him."

This, Washington felt, was a happy moment. He was at last in a position to welcome back into his martial element the frustrated warrior, who had suffered through years of pain, of physical helplessness, and of civilian controversy. Washington told Arnold that he was to have a post to which his rank and abilities entitled him—"a post of honor" in the main army.

Arnold's reaction amazed Washington: "His countenance changed and he appeared to be quite fallen, and, instead of thanking me or expressing any pleasure at the appointment, never opened his mouth." The soldier, who had always been so eager for service, just stood there in a dreadful silence. Finally, Washington "desired him to go to my quarters and get something to refresh himself, and I would meet him there soon."

As, some time later, Washington approached his quarters, Tilghman intercepted him. The aide reported that Arnold was pacing the floor with a desperate limp, expressing "great uneasiness," growling that his leg would not let him ride horseback long enough for him to succeed at an active command. Only at West Point could he do himself justice.

"His behavior," Washington remembered, "struck me as strange and unaccountable." However, he suspected nothing sinister. He felt pity and concern for a brave man, a great patriot, who seemed to have been so overwhelmed by misfortunes that he had lost his nerve. Going in to Arnold, Washington, with all the courtesy of his nature, all the warmth of friendship, tried to persuade the bold fighter that he was more wounded in spirit than in body. But Arnold continued unhappy and, it seemed, confused. He insisted, beyond all reason, that he must have the post Washington considered unworthy of him. Finally, he limped off disconsolately, conspicuously dragging his short leg.[18]

On August 1, Washington announced "the order of battle for the present." General Arnold was assigned the left wing. (On hearing the news at a Philadelphia dinner party, Peggy Arnold had hysterics, which was interpreted as a young bride's fear that, on active duty, her husband might be killed.)[19]

Then Clinton returned from the Rhode Island expedition, bringing an end to any immediate possibility of an aggressive campaign that would give importance to the command of the left wing. To save transport and forage, Washington decided to take his army back to New Jersey. West Point became again the key to the Hudson Valley that would have to be held, if attacked, until Washington could move his men across many miles. The command no longer seemed piffling—and perhaps Arnold had given Washington an ocular demonstration of his assumed inability to get around on horseback. To his general orders of August 3, Washington added the postscript, "Major General Arnold will take command of the garrison at West Point."[20]

A month and eleven days later, Washington, as he prepared the expedition from which he was now returning, wrote Arnold, "I shall be at Peekskill on Sunday evening, on my way to Hartford to meet the French Admiral and General. You will be pleased to send down a guard of a captain and fifty at that time, and direct the quartermaster to endeavor to have a night's forage for about forty horses. You will keep this to yourself, as I want to make my journey a secret."

Arnold hurried off a message to the enemy: "General Washington will be at King's Ferry Sunday evening next on his way to Hartford, where he is to meet the French admiral and general. And will lodge at Peekskill."

Since Arnold's letter was delayed in passing surreptitiously through the lines, Washington had got safely by.[21]

As Washington talked at Hartford with the French allies, Arnold conducted an interview of his own. It was with Major John André, who had been secretly ferried to the Hudson shore from a British warship. The talk began in the dark under a clump of trees and was continued with daybreak in the house of a local landowner, Joshua Hett Smith. (Smith believed what Arnold told him: that his visitor was John Anderson, a spy in the American service.) Superior in this respect to Washington's conference with his French allies, Arnold's meeting with the British agent resulted in positive plans. The two officers agreed on synchronized stages by which Arnold would deliver up West Point. Then Arnold, not wishing to be away from his headquarters for too long a time, rode up the river, leaving Smith to see "John Anderson" back to the British lines.[22]

September 24, 1780. Washington is riding from Hartford toward the Hudson in the expectation of taking dinner with the Arnolds. Smith appears at Arnold's headquarters to report that he has seen the mysterious Anderson safely into British-controlled territory. Smith rides on to the village of Fishkill and is surprised to find Washington dining there. His Excellency has met Luzerne on the road and has reluctantly decided to postpone his visit to the Arnolds while he confers with the French ambassador. Washington dines at the same table with Smith, but undoubtedly pays little attention to the silly young popinjay.[23]

September 25, 1780. Washington leaves Fishkill at dawn, intending to breakfast with the Arnolds.

42

Treason Most Foul

IT was not a long ride from Fishkill to Benedict Arnold's headquarters, and Washington set out as soon as the autumnal sky began to lighten. However, there were several redoubts along the river which he felt he ought to visit. As he turned off the highroad down lanes rutted by the wheels of cannon, his companions—Lafayette, Knox, and a flock of aides—became impatient. Eventually, Lafayette (so it is reported) reminded Washington that Mrs. Arnold was waiting breakfast for them.

The commander replied genially, "Ah, I know you young men are all in love with Mrs. Arnold. . . . You may go and take your breakfast with her, and tell her not to wait for me." Lafayette and most of the party decided to stay with His Excellency, but two aides, Major Samuel Shaw and Major James McHenry, rode ahead with the message.[1]

Inspection takes time and the morning was far advanced before Washington finally glimpsed through the trees the roof of Arnold's headquarters. On the east bank of the Hudson, Robinson's House (as the building was known) was across the river from West Point and two miles below it. Correct eighteenth-century gentlemen considered that the location—"surrounded on two sides by hideous mountains and dreary forests, [and] not a house in view but one within a mile"—could only appeal to "a taste for romantic singularity and novelty." But Washington looked forward to a warm welcome: the firm handshake of his fellow veteran Benedict Arnold, winning smiles warming the features of sweet, blonde, girlish Peggy.[2]

He spurred his horse slightly and came around the edge of a barn to a lawn overlooking the river that was about a quarter of a mile off to the right. The rambling, capacious two-story mansion house, with its three different roof lines that reflected successive enlargements, was now at his left. Since he had sent four light horsemen to alert the Arnolds of his immediate arrival, he expected that the opening door would reveal that friendly couple in greeting poses. He saw instead a foppish young man standing alone, bowing a meticulously powdered head while embarrassment marked his features. Washington probably recognized Arnold's aide, David Salisbury Franks. In voluble sentences punctuated with nervous giggles, Franks stated that Mrs. Arnold had not yet arisen and that the general had gone by water for West Point. The general had told Franks that he was on his way to prepare a suitable welcome for His Excellency. Had His Excellency breakfasted? When Washington said he had not, Franks bustled off to get food on the table.[3]

This reception was disappointing. However, Washington knew that it was natural for belles to sleep late, and he could not have been displeased that Arnold was preparing a reception for him, since he believed that ceremonies of respect to high officers improved both the appearance and the discipline of the army. He ate a leisurely breakfast. Then, leaving Hamilton behind to receive any dispatches, he rode to the river and walked with a small group down the steep bank to the landing where a barge and its crew of oarsmen were waiting to transport him to West Point.

The oarsmen created ripples and the fortress came ever more clearly into view. It seemed to slant backward as it mounted the precipitous west shore of the river. Not very far above the water, the main redoubt clung to a sheer crag like a monstrous crab. As the surrounding hills billowed higher, they revealed ramparts pierced for cannon, while near the sky three peaks were topped with semi-independent forts. The mazelike interweaving walls were sometimes built of wood, sometimes of turf, and sometimes of stone. Scars on the hillsides spoke of quarrying too recent to be greened over, while piles of rocks and logs indicated construction still only planned. Washington knew that downstream, where the river seemed almost to disappear into the hills, the flow swung into a turn that would slow any sailing vessels which tried to brazen their way by. On this spot the main cannon were trained, and there the river washed, from bank to bank, over the links of a tremendous iron chain.[4]

Washington could not help being moved as the fortress came closer. This was the great engineering feat of his command, the only true strongpoint created by the Continental Army. Volunteer engineers from abroad— Kosciuszko, Duportail—had designed it. During more than three years of hard labor, the soldiers had shaped the towering ramparts. Inflated dollars, anguishedly raised, had been spent by the millions. And there the fortress stood, serene in the pellucid autumn air, while Benedict Arnold—so Washington believed—was preparing the garrison for a military greeting to their Commander in Chief.

When the advance of Washington's barge brought the beach and landing wharf into clear view, these were surprisingly empty. No bustle of officers lining up men: only the usual sentries somnolently pacing. As the intervening strip of water narrowed, Washington saw Colonel John Lamb, the resident commandant of the fortress, coming running down the steep way from the main redoubt. Still out of breath when Washington stepped ashore, Lamb puffed out apologies for having prepared no suitable reception. If only he had been notified!

To Washington's startled query, Lamb replied that he had not seen Arnold that day. This seemed strange—but there were various landing places under the various redoubts. Perhaps Arnold had come another way.

The inspection began. As Washington climbed over the hillsides, ducked through blockhouse doors, visited gun emplacements, he asked everywhere for Arnold. "No one could give me any information where he was. The impropriety of his conduct, when he knew I was to be there, struck me very forcibly." Washington became increasingly anxious. "My mind," as he put it, "misgave me," but he felt only a vague fear. "I had not the least idea of the real cause."[5]

Washington was later to insist that he had found the post in "the most critical condition." However, he probably was not particularly upset until after he had learned what he was about to discover. If some of the redoubts were weak, broken, or unfinished, if work seemed to be progressing slowly, he could hardly have been surprised. Perfection rarely hovered over the Continental Army.[6]

Dinner at the Arnolds' had been set for four. Washington completed his inspection in time to permit his rowers to get him back to Robinson's House by three-thirty. He strode anxiously up the steep bluff from the riverbank, but again the opening door revealed neither Arnold nor Peggy. It was Hamilton who greeted him. No, Hamilton had heard nothing of Arnold. No, Peggy had not emerged from her bedroom; she had sent down word that she was indisposed.

Washington walked along a hallway to the chamber that had been assigned to him, and began to freshen up for the meal. A knock on the door. Hamilton came in carrying a handful of papers. Washington reached out for the packet, separated the papers, and began to read.

As Lafayette primped in another room, Hamilton burst open the door. He begged the Marquis to attend instantly on His Excellency. Lafayette sprinted down the hall to find Washington trembling with extreme emotion. "Arnold," Washington cried out, "has betrayed us!" And then he asked, "Whom can we trust now?"[7]

The first task, as soon as the men had regained enough control to do anything rational, was to determine by a careful examination of the many papers, exactly what the situation was. There must have been (although it is now lost) a covering letter from the outpost commander, Lieutenant John

Jameson, stating that three irregulars had been prowling in the British-dominated territory beyond the Croton River when they had stopped a lone rider in civilian clothes. The rider, who stated that his name was John Anderson, had behaved so strangely that they had stripped him, finding documents in his shoes. Jameson was holding the man and was herewith forwarding the documents.

There was an official pass allowing "John Anderson" to move between the lines and made out by Benedict Arnold. Also in Arnold's handwriting were a transcript of secret information Washington had given a Council of War, pages of material about West Point that would be useful to a besieger, and a rough accounting of the 3086 patriots Arnold had slated for death or capture.

Seemingly a later addition to the packet was a letter, meticulously executed in an elegant script. It proved to be from the prisoner: "What I have as yet said concerning myself," Washington read, "was in the justifiable attempt to be extricated; I am too little accustomed to duplicity to have succeeded." He wished now "to rescue myself from an imputation of having assumed a mean character for treacherous purposes or self-interest, a conduct incompatible with the principles that actuate me, as well as with my condition in life. . . . The person in your possession is Major John André, adjutant general to the British army." The rest of the epistle was given over to an argument in which André attempted, as Washington later put it, "to show that he did not come under the description of a spy."[8]

The documents understood, the next question was what to do. A glance out the window would have shown that the wind, blowing upriver, was ideal for carrying British ships from their anchorages in New York Harbor to West Point. Washington could not know to what extent other officers were in Arnold's plot; he could not be sure that, even though André had been intercepted, alternate advices had not got through to the British. However, overriding emotions kept Washington from deciding that his first duty was to take every possible step to protect the endangered fortress.

The most important consideration, so it seemed to Washington, was to capture and hang the traitor. Although McHenry, who had breakfasted with Arnold, reported that the villain had disappeared immediately after receiving a letter which had thrown him "into some degree of agitation," Washington refused to accept the conclusion that Arnold had been notified of André's capture and had, in the intervening five hours, surely made his escape. Perhaps he was lurking somewhere within the lines, still ignorant of his danger. Under these circumstances, Washington concluded no move should be made that would indicate to anyone—you could not tell who would alert Arnold—that the treason had been discovered. While all else went on as usual, Hamilton and McHenry should gallop, as fast as the swiftest horses could carry them, to King's Ferry, eight miles downriver, where there were forts and forces that could stop Arnold's barge "if she had not passed."[9]

No sooner had Hamilton and McHenry pounded off than Arnold's senior aide, Lieutenant Colonel Richard Varick, who had been in bed with a fever, came into Washington's room, flushed, a little unsteady, and clearly in the grip of strong emotion. He said that Mrs. Arnold seemed to have gone mad. She had run through the halls almost naked and, after he had got her back in bed, she had exclaimed "there was a hot iron on her head, and no one but General Washington could take it off." Would His Excellency please go to the anguished lady?

Washington mounted the stairs to Peggy's room. In her disarranged bed, with her hair flying around her touching face and her nightclothes pulled awry, she exhibited (so Hamilton was told) "all the sweetness of beauty, all the loveliness of innocence, all the tenderness of a wife, and all the fondness of a mother. . . . One moment she raved, another she melted into tears. Sometimes she pressed her infant to her bosom." She dandled her babe wide-eyed and seemed oblivious of her visitors. Finally, Varick said, "There is General Washington."

As Washington leaned over her, his features working with pity, she stared him hard in the face. "No!" she cried, and denied that he was Washington.

He gently assured her that he was.

"No!" she cried again, gesturing with her bare, shapely arms to shield her infant. "No, that is not General Washington! That is the man who was agoing to assist Colonel Varick in killing my child."

Washington labored to disabuse her, but when she finally admitted that he was who he pretended to be, it was only to upbraid him for "being in a plot to murder her child." Her husband, she cried out, could not protect her: "General Arnold will never return. He is gone. He is gone forever, *there, there, there:* the spirits have carried him up there." She pointed at the ceiling. "They have put hot irons in his head."

As the lovely lady raved and gestured, her clothes parted to reveal charms that should have been hidden. Then she would push her baby aside and turn downward on the bed to cling to the mattress in a transport of tears. At last, finding that he could not make her respond to his reassurances, Washington went sadly away, hating Arnold all the more for having caused such anguish to a beauty he never doubted was innocent.

Peggy had been warned by Arnold before he fled that the treason had been discovered. Her performance was majestic, but she had not needed to use such heavy artillery to convince the courtly commander that she was a greatly wronged angel. Washington always shied away from connecting the tender sex with the dark emotions of war. He left Peggy's bedroom determined to protect her from every implication raised by her husband's guilt.* [10]

Washington joined an uneasy group of officers in the living room. "Mrs. Arnold is sick," he said, "and General Arnold is away. We must therefore take our dinner without them."

"I had a high fever," Varick wrote, "but officiated at the head of the table." Both he and Franks, who had taken no part in the plot, had by now inferred that Arnold had gone to the enemy. Unwilling to accuse their superior without real evidence and realizing that if treason had taken place they would be under suspicion, they covertly watched Washington for indications of what he knew and how he felt toward them. Washington and his staff covertly watched them for signs of guilt. "Never," Lafayette is quoted as reminiscing, "was there a more melancholy dinner. The General was silent and reserved, and none of us spoke of what we were thinking about. . . . Gloom and distress seemed to pervade every mind, and I have never seen General Washington so affected by any circumstance." However, Washington's courtesy did not desert him. Varick noted that "His Excellency behaved with his usual affability and politeness to me."

The food, "plentiful" but hardly touched, was finally all served and cleared away. The party separated. After a while, Washington asked Varick to put on his hat. As they walked outside, Washington told him of Arnold's perfidy. Then (so Varick wrote), "with delicacy, tenderness, and civility," Washington stated that, although "he had not the least cause of suspicion of Major Franks or myself," the two aides must consider themselves under arrest. "I then told him the little all I knew."[11]

The inhabitants of Robinson's House were now alerted. It would have been a poor spy network indeed that was not now pulsing out warnings. Any great hope of gain to be achieved through secrecy would seem to be over. The wind was still blowing upriver. If Arnold had placed at key positions officers who were his partners in the plot, they still held their commands. West Point had not been alerted. Yet Washington still took no active steps. The man who had admired and trusted Arnold and within whose own character treason was inconceivable was circling in the murky mazes of what Varick called "the most affecting and pungent anxiety and distress."[12]

Between six and seven in the evening, Washington received a letter from Hamilton at King's Ferry stating that Arnold had escaped to a British warship anchored in the river. "Though I do not believe the project will go on," Hamilton continued, "it is possible Arnold has made such dispositions

* Peggy's active complicity in the plot remained hidden until long after her lifetime. It was not established until Clinton's headquarters papers were acquired by the Clements Library in the 1930's.

with the garrison as may tempt the enemy, in its present weakness, to make the stroke this night. . . . Without making a bustle," Hamilton was notifying the commander of the main army in New Jersey (Greene) "to be in readiness to march and even to detach a brigade this way." He hoped Washington would approve, "as there may be no time to be lost.".

Hamilton enclosed two letters which had been sent from the British warship to King's Ferry. Both were in Arnold's familiar handwriting. The one addressed to Washington contended defiantly that, whatever the misguided might think, it was true patriotism which had carried Arnold to the British. The second letter was addressed to Peggy. Washington sent it upstairs unopened, accompanied by a message that, although it had been his duty to try to capture Arnold, he was happy to relieve her anxiety by telling her that her husband was safe.[13]

Washington could hardly have helped recognizing that he had been derelict in not ordering Hamilton to do what the aide had done on his own: warning the command of the main army to be prepared. This realization, plus the news that Arnold had actually escaped, seem to have shaken him out of his lethargy. In dispatches sometimes headed "seven o'clock," sometimes "seven and a half o'clock," and sometimes just "o'clock" he changed the commands at key outposts where Arnold might have placed collaborators; he alerted West Point, ordering that it be reinforced and put in readiness for an attack. (It was not actually in readiness until 2 A.M.)* [14]

When, during the night, the wind changed, blowing strongly downriver,[15] the possibility was erased that the British could gain direct military advantage from Arnold's treason.† The moment-to-moment tension dropped, but Washington still had to handle his own emotions; and the human flotsam that the wreck had left afloat; and the question whether there were more traitors to be discovered; and the frightening problem of how the treason of so conspicuous an officer could be prevented from psychologically damaging the already dipping cause.

The human flotsam closest to Washington's emotions was twenty-year-old Peggy, "whose face and whose youthfulness [as Lafayette wrote] make her so interesting." In the morning, she admitted to no memory of her hysteria of the day before, and now spoke frankly, if tearfully, of her apprehension that "the resentment of her country will fall upon her who is only unfortu-

---

* Freeman explained Washington's long delay by stating that not until evening did Washington know enough of the situation to take action. However, many of the orders Washington finally gave did not depend on specific information, and, in any case, Lamb, the officer most completely familiar with the situation at West Point, had returned from the fort with Washington and was available for consultation.[16]

† The British had planned no immediate action. They did not know that André and Arnold had concerted a plan until Arnold appeared to their amazement and reported that André's capture had given all away.

nate." Washington was all sympathy and grave reassurance; he offered to send her either to her husband in New York or her father in Philadelphia. She chose to turn her back on the plot that had failed; Franks accompanied her to Philadelphia. "It would be exceedingly painful to General Washington," Lafayette wrote Luzerne, "if she were not treated with the greatest kindness."[17]

On Robinson's House now converged by Washington's order the various individuals known to have been concerned in André's foray behind the American lines. Interviewing them himself, Washington decided that only Joshua Hett Smith was adequately implicated to be tried.* Smith was demonstrated to have been Arnold's dupe, a fool rather than a villain. The conclusion was reached that Arnold had operated altogether as a lone wolf. (This was, except for his wife, mean go-betweens, and spies independently in the British pay, entirely correct.)

After André had been brought to headquarters, Washington found him "a man of the first abilities," and treated him, so the Briton wrote Clinton, "with the greatest attention." André was, indeed, a prisoner to wring Washington's heart. Of French background, although born in London, he had marked temperamental resemblances to Washington's beloved Lafayette. He was also young enough to be Washington's son, quick, mercurial, brilliant, chivalrous, and much concerned with personal honor. In a situation of mortal danger, he was displaying—could Lafayette have done it as well?—almost superhuman control. He behaved in the presence of his captors with charm, grace, almost relaxation.

To Washington, as to all the other officers concerned, André's plight was given particular poignancy because his romantic impetuosity had placed the important officer in a predicament which the eighteenth century considered far below his station. Gentlemen could be spymasters, but they did not themselves wear disguises and rummage behind the enemy lines. André claimed that he had come ashore in his uniform in his high official capacity, meeting Arnold on what was neutral ground, but had been tricked by Arnold into entering an American post: then he had no choice but to try to achieve an escape in those civilian clothes that made him falsely resemble a spy. Hatred for Arnold made this believable, yet the fact remained that he had been caught bearing incriminating papers, functioning as a spy. The established punishment for that was not a gentleman's death—being shot— but the death of a varlet—being dangled from a gallows.[18]

The meanness of his situation spurred André into a high line of "candor." To the Board of General Officers who conducted his trial, he confessed so much that the verdict was inevitable. The board ruled that he "ought to be

---

* Varick and Franks requested a military inquiry to clear their names, which it amply did.

considered a spy from the enemy, and that, agreeable to the law and usage of nations, it is their opinion that he ought to suffer death."[19]

From André, Washington received a letter which the condemned man signed with his proud title, Adjutant General of the British Army: "Buoyed above the terror of death by the consciousness of a life devoted to honorable pursuits and stained with no action that can give me remorse, I trust that the request I make to your Excellency at this serious period, which is to soften my last moments, will not be rejected.

"Sympathy toward a soldier will surely induce your Excellency and a military tribunal to adapt the mode of my death to the feelings of a man of honor.

"Let me hope, sir, that if aught in my character impresses you with esteem toward me, if aught in my misfortunes marks me as the victim of policy and not of resentment, I shall experience the operation of these feelings in your breast by being informed that I am not to die on the gibbet."[20]

The consideration was one that Washington, as a gentleman, could not help finding affecting—and he was always unhappy about executions. To make matters worse, his brilliant young officers were almost aswoon with admiration and pity for André. Hamilton, to whom the prisoner had made a personal appeal, was particularly insistent, even rude, and went off in a rage when Washington would not agree that André be shot. "Some people," Hamilton growled, "are only sensible to motives of policy!" Yet Washington felt he had no choice. The British propaganda machine was already in high scream, and, if André were not executed in the manner of a spy, that would be pointed to as proof that he had not really been a spy but had been wantonly murdered.[21]

André occupied the same position in Clinton's heart that Lafayette did in Washington's. Across the lines came letters in which Clinton insisted that his friend had gone on an official mission to Arnold, and had subsequently merely obeyed orders which Arnold, as commander in the area, had a right to give. This argument was both specious (a spy is not blameless because he obeys the orders of the traitor he is suborning) and also contradicted André's own contention that Arnold had carried him behind the American lines without his knowledge and against his will. However, Washington saw in Clinton's concern a chance of saving the young man whom he considered "more unfortunate than criminal" and who had "much in his character to interest."

Washington might "lament," but he recognized a "necessity of rigor": the army was in effect under trial in the eyes of the American people. To spare the British agent out of hand would be interpreted as softness about treason. But supposing Washington could substitute on the gallows for the unfortunate go-between the real, the heinous criminal?[22]

Captain Aaron Ogden of the light infantry was ordered to appear at

John André, by an unknown artist. Courtesy of James André.

headquarters at the dot of eight o'clock on the morning after André had been sentenced. To his surprise, he found His Excellency waiting for him outside the tent. Washington handed him some letters to take under a flag of truce to the British lines, and then told him to go to Lafayette's tent for further instructions. Lafayette was also eagerly awaiting him. Suggesting what Washington could not because of his high rank suggest, Lafayette urged Ogden to whisper to the commander of the British post "that if Sir Henry Clinton would in any way whatever suffer General Washington to get within his power General Arnold, then Major André should be immediately released."

When Ogden did as he had been told, the British officer who had met his flag leapt on a horse and galloped away. In two hours he was back with a glum face and the verbal answer: "A deserter was never given up." He also brought written information that a high-level British delegation would come to the American lines to intercede for André.[23]

At the resulting meeting, Greene and Hamilton represented the American cause. Hints flew that André would be exchanged for Arnold. The hints were not responded to. The British representatives had nothing more to offer than the specious arguments which had already been submitted to Washington in writing. Grieved and deeply disappointed, Washington set the execution for noon the next day, October 2.[24]

The macabre procession from André's place of confinement to the gallows would pass close to the headquarters Washington now occupied at Tappan, New York: the death march would pound in, even through closed windows. To allow the sufferer hope, Washington had not notified him of how he was to be executed: there would be the dreadful moment when the accomplished young British gentleman saw the gallows. It was not an agreeable moment to contemplate.

If Washington was able to persuade himself that it would not be commented upon, he surely rode out from headquarters. Otherwise, he certainly sat in gloom. And, wherever he was during the actual tragedy, after it was over, he was surrounded by men in tears. Never had witnesses to an execution been more moved by the noble bearing of the victim.

In Washington's headquarters, eyes still wept when a belated dispatch appeared from the British lines. It was a letter from Benedict Arnold threatening that if André were executed, he personally would "think myself bound by every tie of duty and honor to retaliate on such unhappy persons of your army as may fall within my power. . . . I call Heaven and earth to witness that your Excellency will be justly answerable for the torrent of blood that may be spilt in consequence!"

"There are no terms," Washington wrote of Arnold, "that can describe the baseness of his heart." He instigated an elaborate plot (which misfired) to kidnap the traitor from his lodgings in New York City, and bring him out alive for hanging to patriot cheers.[25]

As the British propaganda machine ground out statements attributed to Arnold in which he described his treason as true patriotism and urged his former associates to imitate him, hatred for the traitor swept the nation. Washington, who was not without his enemies, had supported Arnold to the civilian authorities; he had personally put the traitor in command at West Point. And the whole conservative wing of the revolutionary leadership was liable to the charge of guilt by association, since they had backed Arnold against the Pennsylvania radicals. As the leader of those radicals, Reed did make gestures at demonstrating that Washington and the aristocratic Schuyler had shown gross favoritism to the traitor, but even Reed was halfhearted, glad, it seems, quickly to abandon his efforts. In the end, the Pennsylvania radicals contented themselves with banishing Peggy from her father's house in Philadelphia. She was forced against her will to join her partner in treason behind the British lines.[26]

One trembles to think what a modern "super-patriot" rabble-rouser might have done with the issue. However, our forefathers resisted all temptation to shatter, by venting spite or prejudice, the precarious national unity.

Washington's own attitude was expressed in dismissing a rumor that the American general Robert Howe was in the pay of the British. He wrote the Board of War that they ought not to "neglect any clues that may lead to discoveries, but, on the other hand, we ought to be equally circumspect in admitting suspicions or proceeding upon them without sufficient evidence. It will be the policy of the enemy to distract us as much as possible by sowing jealousies, and, if we swallow the bait, no character will be safe. There will be nothing but mutual distrust."[27]

Washington labored to turn the popular emotion to gratitude that the plot had been foiled. "In no instance since the commencement of the war," he stated, "has the interposition of Providence appeared more conspicuous than in the rescue of the post and garrison of West Point from Arnold's villainous perfidy."[28]

CHAPTER

43

More Education for George Washington

THE French were comfortably bedding themselves down for the winter in Newport, whence, indeed, they had not stirred since they had first reached America in July. However, Washington still dreamed of "closing the campaign with some degree of eclat." He embarrassed the French command at Newport (who knew the Spaniards would give no direct help to American independence, of which they disapproved) by suggesting that these supposed allies should, if they succeeded in taking Florida, be persuaded to join with the French and Americans in freeing Georgia and South Carolina.[1] And, when his spies reported that the British intended to send out a large foraging party, his mind kindled with the idea of taking the then weakened city with a surprise invasion from across the Hudson River. "My wishes," he later confessed, "had got so far the better of my judgment" that he had put his troops partially in motion before he allowed himself to recognize that his means were "inadequate to the end."[2]

It was mid-November 1780 when Washington finally allowed his army to relax into winter quarters. Earlier in the war, he had tried to keep as many men as possible in service during the snowy months, but now he ordered his officers to leak away, so gradually that the British would not notice, those men whose enlistments would expire on January 1. The crucial shortages of food had been augmented by the Indians whose farms Sullivan had destroyed the year before. They had returned and set fire to the crops in the Mohawk Valley on which Washington had relied to feed his troops in the contiguous Hudson Valley.[3]

Lack of wagons to bring supplies to a single point again forced Washington to separate his tiny army. He tried to make this necessity serve strategy. The New York brigade he sent to Albany, where it could bolster the frontier; the Pennsylvania line (from which he was soon to hear ominously)

[396]

he stationed at Morristown; the Jersey brigade (from which ominous news was also to come) he put further north at Pompton to protect communications through the Clove; and he hutted the New England brigades around West Point.[4]

Washington established his own headquarters near the fortress at New Windsor. In this "dreary station," he occupied "very confined quarters, little better than those of Valley Forge." For two months he had been unable to get any public money to support his table. He could not keep in close touch with his French allies since he could not afford to feed couriers' horses.[5]

In the fiscal darkness there was one light, still hardly bigger than a candle, yet throwing a gleam into the future which (even if largely ignored by Washington's biographers) does much to explain some of his most important acts as President. A group of merchants, under the leadership of Robert Morris, had organized the Bank of Philadelphia. This private institution was first mentioned in Washington's correspondence (July 4, 1780) when, in trying to inspire the radical Reed to draft recruits, he pointed out that Reed would have to do something effective, since "the bank established for supplying the army" had been created by Reed's conservative political opponents and "will undoubtedly give them great credit with the people." He was soon adding insult to injury by writing Mrs. Reed that "the female patriots" who had taken up a subscription for the army could extend its utility by depositing the money in the bank and receiving for the bank's notes: "I should imagine the ladies will have no objection to an union with the gentlemen."[6]

As Jefferson, that determined opponent of banks, remained in Virginia within the confines of agrarian economic thinking, Washington's financial education was progressing. He had become convinced that the paper which had been printed by the various public bodies, having been based on false economic principles, could never be restored to value. What was therefore called for, if the war effort were not to collapse, was a new and separate paper money system that would not depreciate because it would be guaranteed by actual funds. The funds could be the capital and deposits in a bank. Philadelphia merchants subscribed £1,100,000 in Continental currency to get such a bank started. However, they counted mainly on the convenience which traders would find in buying from them notes permanently exchangeable at face value. Since there would be no reason to cash the notes at once, the receivers would hand them on to their own creditors in the payment of their bills. Thus the notes would circulate as currency, while the money originally used to purchase them remained in the bank and was usable for various purposes that further bolstered the economy and helped supply the army.[7]

In August 1780, Washington wrote the directors of the bank that they were now his principal reliance in securing immediate supplies for the army. He urged on Congress that all the trading towns establish similar "associations"—but in vain. The Bank of Philadelphia remained unique and could not all by itself solve the army's problems. On December 10, Washington complained of his regiments, "never half complete in men, but perfectly so in every species of want. . . . We have neither money nor credit adequate to the purchase of a few boards for doors to our log huts. . . . It would be well for the troops if, like chameleons, they could live upon air, or like the bear suck their paws for sustenance during the rigor of the approaching season."[8]

To General Sullivan, who had resigned from the army and had been elected a member of Congress, Washington wrote that interfering with the organization of the civil government was something he never wished to do, but surely it was now clear that Congress could not help supply the army unless its purely legislative structure was modified by the establishment of executive departments. Individuals or small boards, who could practice "not only close application but a uniform train of thinking and acting," must, if the "great business of the war" were to be adequately executed, replace the old "fluctuating" committees of congressmen who were engaged also in innumerable other affairs. In the meanwhile, to cover the army's nakedness Congress should turn to private enterprise, employing "some eminent merchant of approved integrity and abilities to import (in his own way)" necessary cloth. Tailors in the army would then cut and sew the actual uniforms.

However, the overriding need, Washington continued, was for a foreign loan. To think that the army "can rub through" another campaign like the last "would be as unreasonable as to suppose that because a man had rolled a snowball till it had acquired the size of a horse that he might do so till it was as large as a house."[9]

There now appeared in Washington's correspondence, for the very first time, hints that he would welcome a peace without complete victory. Rumors were afloat that the European belligerents, sick of the expensive war that was sinking into a stalemate everywhere, were considering a compromise in which some of the United States (probably what the enemy at that moment controlled) would be declared still British, the rest free. In a circular to the states, Washington pointed out that "the interpositions of neutral powers may lead to a negotiation this winter," and that nothing would make the English more reasonable than a strong army in America. To Franklin, who was representing the United States in Paris, Washington confided, "Our present situation makes one of two things essential to us: a peace, or the most vigorous aid of our allies, particularly in the article of money." Then, to bolster the American position, he sent Franklin a fallaciously optimistic summary of the military preparations being made by the states.[10]

In late November, before he had moved from New Jersey to his winter quarters at New Windsor, Washington prepared to entertain a terrifying visitor, whom he had met formally during the conference at Hartford. That the Chevalier de Chastellux was a nobleman and a well-known soldier, the third in command of Rochambeau's army, Washington could take in his stride. However, Chastellux was also a famous author, a laureate of the celebrated Académie Française. He was the first European philosopher Washington had ever met. And he was traveling the United States to collect material for a book: Washington could not doubt that whatever impression he himself made on the academician would be immortalized in that toplofty intellectual's pages.

The philosopher appeared with two aides and five servants. He had quantities of dark hair over a high, square forehead, small greenish-brown eyes, and a long, lantern-jawed face. When his face was in repose, he seemed ponderous. However, his gravity soon disintegrated into the eagerness of a universal curiosity. He expressed himself modestly, and was extremely respectful to Washington, who he had decided was "the greatest and the best of men."[11]

The amazement of French officers, marked down in many diaries, when they finally saw Washington leap around and cheer, reveals that, as habitués of a culture where men expressed more emotion than they felt, they had been fooled by Washington's normal reserve into thinking him cold. Chastellux was no exception. Furthermore, the description of Washington he included in his book makes one suspect that in order to bring the Virginian more in line with his sights, he envisioned him to some extent in a traditional classic toga. He compared Washington's to Agamemnon's army. Yet Chastellux's characterization of Washington is one of the most eloquent ever written, and it has been extremely influential in determining the attitudes of posterity toward the hero:

"The strongest characteristic of this respectable man is the perfect harmony which reigns between the physical and moral qualities: . . . a perfect whole that cannot be the product of enthusiasm, which rather would reject it. . . . Brave without temerity, laborious without ambition, generous without prodigality, noble without pride, virtuous without severity, he seems always" to have avoided passing beyond "those limits where the virtues, by clothing themselves in more lively but more changeable and doubtful colors, may be mistaken for faults. This is the seventh year that he has commanded the army and he has obeyed Congress: more need not be said.

"His stature is noble and lofty; he is well built and exactly proportioned; his physiognomy mild and agreeable, but such as to render it impossible to

Chevalier de Chastellux, by Charles Willson Peale. Courtesy of the Independence National Historical Park Collection.

speak particularly of any one of his features, so that, on leaving him, you have only the recollection of a fine face. He has neither a grave nor a familiar air, his brow is sometimes marked with thought but never with worry. . . . He has not the imposing pomp of a *Maréchal de France* who gives *the order*. A hero in a republic, he excites another sort of respect which seems to spring from the sole idea that the safety of each individual is attached to his person. . . . The goodness and benevolence which characterize him are evident in all that surrounds him, but the confidence he calls forth never occasions improper familiarity."

If anything could be more marvelous than Washington's character, it was that so many Americans recognized the value of so unflamboyant a man: "soldier, magistrate, and people all love and admire him." History, so Chastellux continued, would praise Washington not for any specific virtue, but because "at the end of a long civil war, he had nothing with which he could reproach himself."[12]

Chastellux found Washington more romantic as a horseman. Not only were His Excellency's chargers of the highest quality, but he broke them himself. The one Washington lent the Frenchman was perfectly trained, "having a good mouth, easy in hand, and stopping short in gallop without bearing the bit." He noted that Washington always, even when there was no hurry, rode at a gallop: "He is a very excellent and bold horseman, leaping the highest fences and going extremely quick without standing upon his stirrups, bearing on the bridle, or letting his horse run wild."[13]

Having been led to suppose that the Americans were "barbarous in their discipline," Chastellux was agreeably surprised. The officers, "whose functions bring them into public view, unite much politeness to a great deal of ability." Washington's headquarters filled the fields around a small farmhouse, presenting "neither the picture of inexperience nor of want." There were the tents of Washington's guard; nine wagons awaited the headquarters baggage; grooms were attending to horses, sentries were "exactly stationed."[14]

However, the French philosopher viewed with disapproval worthy of a New England minister the length of time Washington and his aides spent at the table. Concerning midafternoon dinner, he noted "the meal was in the English fashion, consisting of eight or ten large dishes of meat and poultry, with vegetables of several sorts, followed by a second course of pastry, comprised under the two denominations of 'pies' and 'puddings.'" After the cloth was taken off, the waiters brought in a quantity of apples and nuts which "Washington usually continues eating for two hours, toasting and conversing all the time." They were hickory nuts, served half open, "and the company are never done picking and eating them. The conversation was calm and agreeable." When Washington suggested a toast, it was given out by an aide who did the honors of the table, being seated at the bottom near the general. This aide was also charged with seeing that the bottles did not cease to circulate.

At seven-thirty, after about three and a half hours, the company rose. However, before Chastellux was out the door, he saw servants shortening the table and turning it into a round one. He was told that they were laying the cloth for supper.

Thinking that Washington might like to do some business, Chastellux mounted to his chamber, but within an hour he was called to supper. "I returned to the dining room, protesting strenuously against this supper." Washington explained that "he was accustomed to take something in the evening." Now only the general's military family were present. There were three or four light dishes, some fruit, "and above all a great abundance of nuts, which were as well received in the evening as at dinner." When the cloth had been removed, a few bottles of good claret and Madeira were laid on the table. The toasts were less solemn than at dinner, "only a sort of refrain punctuating the conversation, as a reminder that each individual is part of the company." Every guest was called on to give "a sentiment, that is to say a lady." Washington and his officers conversed until eleven, "always free and always agreeable."[15]

Washington himself lit the Frenchman upstairs. There being only four bedrooms, Chastellux had to share his with several of Washington's aides. His Excellency apologized, "but always with a noble politeness which was neither embarrassing nor excessive."[16]

Although he found Chastellux "a gentleman of polite and easy manners," Washington (who had great difficulty getting the hang of spelling the Frenchman's name*) had not, when this man "eminent in the literary world" departed after three days, yet overcome a barrier of embarrassment. In congratulating the philosopher on his successful return to Newport, Washington wrote, "I wish I had expression equal to my feelings that I might declare to you the high sense I have of, and the value I set upon, your approbation and friendship. It will be the wish and happiness of my life to merit a continuance of them, and to assure you upon all occasions of my admiration of your character and virtues."[17]

However, the men saw a good deal of each other in the next three years, and came on so easy a basis that in 1787, long after Chastellux had gone back to France, Washington wrote him thus banteringly: "In reading your very friendly and acceptable letter . . . I was, as you may well suppose, not less delighted than surprised to come across that plain American word, 'My wife.'—A wife!—Well, my dear Marquis, I can hardly refrain from smiling to find you are caught at last. I saw, by the eulogium you often made on the happiness of domestic life in America, that you have swallowed

---

* During a few months in 1780, Washington spelled the name Chattelus, Chattelleaux, Chattelaux, Chatelaux, and Chatlies; but never correctly.[18]

the bait and that you would as surely be taken (one day or another) as you was a philosopher and a soldier.* So your day has at length come! I am glad of it, with all my heart and soul. It is quite good enough for you. Now you are well served for coming to fight in favor of the American Rebels, all the way across the Atlantic Ocean, by catching that terrible contagion, domestic felicity, which time like the smallpox or the plague, a man can have only once in his life, because it commonly lasts him (at least with us in America —I don't know how you manage these matters in France) for his whole lifetime. And yet, after all the maledictions you so richly merit on the subject, the worst wish which I can find in my heart against Madame de Chastellux and yourself is that you may neither of you ever get the better of this same domestic felicity during the entire course of your mortal existence."[19]

Chastellux's major work, *De la Félicité Publique, ou Considérations sur le sort des hommes dans les différentes époques de l'histoire* (1772), the book that was so praised by Voltaire and translated into various languages, was a historical disquisition to prove that "there is progress, there is hope for the world." By discovering "sound policy" and "genuine morality," governments were driving away the ignorance and superstitions of the previous centuries. Through the application of man's ability to reason, the art of government was advancing toward the achievement of what Chastellux argued should be its sole aim: "The greatest happiness for the greatest number of individuals."[20]

Chastellux's ideas were also to be found in other books, but Washington was not much of a reader: he did not, for instance, order John Locke's *Essay Concerning Human Understanding* until the Revolution was over. Is it pure imagination to hear echoes of conversations over wine with the French philosopher-soldier in such passages as this one from the farewell circular Washington sent to the states, when he resigned from the army, that came to be known as *Washington's Testament:*

"The citizens of America . . . are from this period to be considered as the actors on a most conspicuous theater, which seems to be particularly designated by Providence for the display of human greatness and felicity. Here they are not only surrounded with everything which can contribute to the completion of private and domestic enjoyment, but Heaven has crowned all its other blessings by giving a fairer opportunity for political happiness than any other nation has ever been favored with. . . . The foundation of our empire was not laid in the gloomy age of ignorance and superstition, but at an epoch when the rights of mankind were better understood and more clearly defined than at any former period. The researches of the human mind after social happiness have been carried to a great extent; the treasures

---

* At fifty-four the philosopher and soldier had, to the rage of his elderly mistress, married a pretty Irish girl of about twenty-eight.

of knowledge, acquired by the labors of philosophers, sages, and legislatures, through a long succession of years, are laid open for our use, and their collected wisdom may be happily applied in the establishment of our forms of government. The free cultivation of letters, the unbounded extension of commerce, the progressive refinement of manners, the growing liberality of sentiment, and above all, the pure and benign light of Revelation have had a meliorating influence on mankind and increased the blessings of society. At this auspicious period, the United States came into existence as a nation, and if their citizens should not be completely free and happy, the fault will be entirely their own."* [21]

---

* When elected in December 1783 to the American Philosophical Society, which was much concerned with scientific studies, Washington wrote, "In the philosophic retreat to which I am retiring [Mount Vernon], I shall often contemplate with pleasure the extensive utility of your institution. The field of investigation is ample, the benefits which will result to human society from discoveries yet to be made are indubitable, and the task of studying the works of the great Creator inexpressibly delightful."[22]

44

The End of Our Tether

A S Christmas approached, Washington's mind harked back to the use he had made four years before of the enemy's relaxation during the holiday season. Crossing the Hudson as he had crossed the Delaware, attacking New York as he had attacked Trenton, were past his powers. But surely something could be done.

Lieutenant Colonel David Humphreys was given secret orders. The party he led was to row with muffled oars downriver in the dark. They would land silently behind the house where General Clinton slept. Up through the garden at a crouching run! Some would go round the two sides of the house and seize the sentries in the street; others would then crash into the back of the house with crowbars. They would capture Clinton and all his papers. At the same time, another party would seize Knyphausen.

The kidnapping parties actually set out on Christmas night, but high winds drove the boats out into the bay beyond the city.[1]

Taking action which, Washington believed, would by now have brought victory had it been taken four years before, Congress "at length" voted officers who served through the end of the conflict half pay for life.[2] This, however, did nothing for the common soldiers, and at nine in the evening of New Year's Day, after rum had flowed free, what Washington had so long dreaded actually took place in the encampment of the Pennsylvania line near Morristown.

He heard about it at about noon on January 3, 1781, when the dispatch from General Wayne reached his headquarters on the Hudson at New Windsor. Tense sentences communicated that most of the Pennsylvania troops, from noncommissioned officers down, had banished their officers and were marching, fully armed and with cannon, on the Congress at Philadelphia. Lest the enemy hear and attack, Wayne had deployed the New

Jersey troops toward the British lines and called out the militia. He heard alarm guns and saw beacons burning, but did not know their meaning. As soon as he had completed this letter, he would gallop after the mutineers, accompanied by two colonels, in an effort to halt their march. "What their temper may be I cannot tell. We had our escapes last night. Perhaps we may be equally fortunate today. Captain Billings is killed; Captain Talbert mortally wounded; some others are also hurt."

A postscript was more encouraging. Not a single officer had joined the mutiny. The mutineers had made no move that implied desertion to the enemy. Since bounties to new soldiers were being given in cash, while no pay was forthcoming to soldiers already in the service, the mutineers, so it was reported, wished to be discharged so that they could secure bounties by re-enlisting, when they would again "fight for America."[3]

As soon as Washington had absorbed the contents of Wayne's letter, he called in those of his officers he most trusted and asked them to find out, without seeming to do so, whether his own troops would be likely, on hearing of the mutiny, to join it. He ordered that a small escort of horse be prepared so that he himself would be mobile. Then he sent Wayne a warning against attempting any forceful opposition to the mutineers. Even the rumor that the Jersey militia were gathering behind them might "drive them to the enemy or dissipate them in such a manner that they will never be recovered." He urged that they be permitted to cross the Delaware unhindered, placing that river between them and possible desertion to the British. Then an effort should be made to stop them, and procure a list of their principal grievances which Wayne would promise to present to Congress. Perhaps, "after the first transports of passion, there may be some favorable intervals which may be improved."

Washington had heard that two Pennsylvania officers had ridden to Congress "to advise them to go out of the way." Congress, Washington insisted, must not flee from Philadelphia. "Waving the indignity . . . the mutineers, finding the body before whom they were determined to lay their grievances, fled, might take a new turn, and wreak their vengeance upon the persons and properties of the citizens, and in a town of the size of Philadelphia, there are numbers who would join them in such a business."[4]

He himself, Washington wrote, intended to gallop to the scene the following morning. However, before morning came, the officers he had sent out came back with frightening reports on the stability of the regiments encamped around New Windsor. Their "want of flour, clothing, and, in short, everything," made it unsafe for Washington to depart. He took every precaution to keep news of the mutiny from spreading in his camp, but he knew that word would soon get there somehow.[5]

Suppose his troops also marched away? He had been grateful for the mildness of the winter, but now he cursed it. There was no ice in the Hudson. The British could sail up easily, and, if the army disbanded, only the New York militia would remain to oppose them. That is, if the levies could be got out in time, which he doubted. He begged New York's Governor Clinton to hurry to headquarters: "your advice . . . would be of infinite service to me."[6]

Always eager to get some profit out of even the worst situation, Washington sent Knox galloping to the New England governments with a circular letter that used the mutiny as the basis of a warning that unless the troops were better supplied and instantly given three months' pay in money that would buy something, the very worst might well happen.[7]

Word that the mutineers had not continued their march across the Delaware, but were lurking at Princeton, may have relieved the anxieties of Congress, but it frightened Washington: Such an "intermediate post between Congress and the enemy" would favor bargaining in which the mutineers played one side against the other. When Major General Arnold had reacted as he did to the injustices with which he had been treated, what was to be expected of unjustly neglected common soldiers, many of whom were foreign-born? The mutineers had, it is true, stated that they "spurned the idea of turning *Arnolds*" and had arrested two agents who had appeared among them with attractive offers from the enemy. However, the British representatives remained, even if in confinement, a menace to be reckoned with, since the mutineers had refused to turn them over to be hanged.[8]

Washington had warned Wayne against the use of force, but he now concluded that it might be necessary to march against the mutineers. This would be "hazarding everything," since his own troops, being equally unpaid, unfed, and naked, might not put down the insurrection but join it. However, a Council of General Officers expressed "the almost universal opinion that their men might be depended upon. I therefore gave directions for a detachment of one thousand to be prepared and held in readiness." These would have to be, at least for a few days, shod and amply fed, a task that could only be anguishing to the commissary department.[9]

The detachment did not have to march, but the price paid for this release from immediate danger was staggering. In return for delivering up the British agents and laying down their arms, the mutineers received, in addition to various financial concessions, the absolute discharge of one-half their number and furloughs for the other half until April. Washington had lost many of the veterans he had so carefully trained, and, for the time being at least, the Pennsylvania line had ceased to exist. What was to keep the other state lines from imitating, with similar results, the disorder that turned out so happily for the mutineers? How was it going to be possible to keep any Continental Army at all in the field?[10]

In great anxiety, Washington awaited another insurrection. But when it came, he surely thanked Providence. The outbreak in the New Jersey line was so minor that it could be put down by force in a manner that would make a lesson for the whole army. Having got their lips around some rum, only a part of the line, only some two hundred men, had defied their officers and set out for the state capital at Trenton with demands similar to those the Pensylvanians had won.[11]

Washington was prepared. He had at West Point a detachment of six hundred men who had been well fed and clothed. He ordered General Robert Howe to lead these on a march against the mutineers. And he fired off warnings to the officers of the insurgents not to treat with them on any basis but unconditional surrender. This time there would be no compromise! He intended to execute some of the ringleaders. Of course, the force he had sent to do so might refuse, when the chips were actually down, to attack their fellow soldiers. However, Washington "thought it indispensable to bring the matter to an issue and risk all extremities."[12]

Washington did not himself accompany Howe's detachment, perhaps because he thought it unwise to involve in so uncertain a gamble his ultimate prestige as Commander in Chief. However, when no approaching figures brought him news across the snowy landscape, he finally found the suspense unbearable. He went to examine his horses. Then he sent a blistering note to Quartermaster Pickering: "My horses, I am told, have not had a mouthful of long or short forage for three days. They have eaten up their mangers and are now (though wanted for immediate use) scarcely able to stand. I should be glad to know if there is any prospect of relief for them." Later that same January 25, he wrote Pickering for a sleigh, a pair of horses, and a driver.[13]

Four days after Howe had marched, Washington started moving swiftly through the white landscape. A courier finally appeared coming the other way. His news was infuriating. The New Jersey officers had disobeyed orders; they had treated with the mutineers and made concessions; they had promised them, if they returned to their duty and their huts at Pompton, immunity from punishment. The mutineers had gone back to their huts. It seemed as if the gift of Providence in supplying so little a mutiny had been refused; as if all hope of violently cutting the string of mutiny had been frustrated.

Washington caught up with Howe at Ringwood, a few miles from Pompton. He found some of the officers there ready to argue that the mutineers could not now be touched, but other informants said the men had only partially returned to subordination. They were obeying some officers and not others, and insisting that only after the promises made them were realized would they lay down their arms. Washington ruled that the men had not kept their side of the bargain and were thus liable to punishment.[14]

While Washington waited nervously at Ringwood, Howe's force advanced, was given a final harangue on the ill effects of mutiny, and ordered to surround the mutineers. The orders were obeyed. The mutineers were terrified into lining up without their arms. Three ringleaders were instantly tried at the drumhead and found guilty. Then one was pardoned. The other two were shot by weeping firing squads made up of their closest companions. "The existence of the army," Washington commented, "called for an example." He also pointed out that "civil liberty" could not survive when armed soldiers undertook "to dictate terms to their country."[15]

The quashing of the New Jersey mutiny brought an end to the protests as effectively as Washington had hoped it would. Rochambeau commented that it was "a most extraordinary trait of patriotism in these times of rebellion" that the mutineers had not treated seriously with the representatives of the enemy.[16] Clearly, Benedict Arnolds were not the natural growth of the United States. Yet the snake of unrest had only been scotched, not killed. It could not die as long as the government remained bankrupt.

In what Washington called "the present infinitely critical posture of our affairs," Congress pushed him along another step toward the role of President. They decided to take advantage of their Commander in Chief's great prestige in France. Explaining that a soldier "could speak knowingly of the state of the army," they appointed Washington's twenty-six-year-old disciple, Colonel John Laurens, envoy extraordinary to the Court of Versailles. In a letter to America's permanent representative there, Benjamin Franklin, Washington introduced Laurens as "one of my aides-de-camp" and made it clear that, although the young warrior was to avail himself "of your advice and assistance upon all occasions," he remained the representative of Washington personally and the army.[17]

In his formal instructions to Laurens, Washington pointed out, as always, the importance of naval superiority. But in rehearsing the agreement he had made with Rochambeau to ask that the French land force be augmented to fifteen thousand, he stated that the money it would cost to raise and send such a force would, if put into American hands, be more useful than the force itself.

With money sent in from Europe, "we should be in a condition to continue the war as long as the obstinacy of the enemy might require." Without financial support, "we may make a feeble and expiring effort the next campaign," which could be "in all probability, the period to our opposition." He added that "if France delays a timely and powerful aid . . . it will avail us nothing should she attempt it hereafter. . . . We are at the end of our tether."[18]

45

Never Go Home Again

AT his "dreary station" among the Highlands of the Hudson, an exile now for almost six years from the southland where his entire previous life had been led, Washington watched from a distance the war increasingly disrupt the world to which, as Greene wrote, he "languished" so often to return.[1]

In December 1780, Clinton had sent to Virginia an expeditionary force of fifteen hundred. What was Washington's rage to hear that it was under the command of a now British brigadier, Benedict Arnold! It would have taken a man of much less imagination not to see in his mind's eye the man he so hated putting the torch to Mount Vernon.

Attending, at whatever distance, to affairs at Mount Vernon, was for Washington a joy. "How many lambs have you had this spring? . . ." he would write his estate manager. "Are you going to repair the pavement of the piazza? . . . Is your covered ways done? What are you going about next? . . . An account of these things would be satisfactory to me, and infinitely amusing in the recital." But surely now he picked up the southern mail with a trembling hand.[2]

In early February 1781, a freak of weather seemed to put Arnold in his power. There was a great storm. The British fleet, which had been watching the French from an anchorage near the tip of Long Island, was damaged and scattered. However, the French had quietly ridden out the storm in Newport Harbor. They had a sudden naval superiority which would last until the British reassembled and refitted.

After a course of plundering and burning, Arnold was fortifying Portsmouth Harbor where the James River joined Chesapeake Bay. Off to Rochambeau, Washington rushed suggestions that the whole French fleet, convoying a thousand soldiers and siege artillery, should descend on the traitor's force. Washington would cooperate by sending a thousand men under Lafayette on a forced march to the head of the Chesapeake, where they could be picked up by French shipping.[3]

On February 14, Washington received from Rochambeau a most disheartening letter, written before the French had received his own urgings of a large-scale attack on Arnold. Washington read Rochambeau's statement that Chesapeake Bay was "generally considered" to have a narrower entrance than was shown on the maps and thus to present dangers to naval attack. However, so Rochambeau continued, "I think that two men-of-war and two frigates" could destroy the shipping accompanying Arnold's expedition, "and that, at this moment of time, we have a fair chance for the accomplishing of that plan."[4]

In anguish of spirit, Washington rushed off another letter urging that a force be sent adequate to attack not only Arnold's shipping but to capture the traitor and rid Virginia of his army.

Two days after Washington had received from Newport discouraging word of minuscule planning, he met, as he climbed the stairs at headquarters, Hamilton coming down. He said that he needed his aide's immediate assistance. Hamilton replied, "I will wait upon you immediately," and continued downstairs.

Washington went to his room, expecting Hamilton any moment. Hamilton did not come. Washington began pacing up and down the hall. When Hamilton finally appeared at the bottom of the stairs, Washington burst out angrily, "Colonel Hamilton, you have kept me waiting at the head of the stairs these ten minutes. I must tell you, sir, you treat me with disrespect."

The young aide's bony, intelligent, intolerant face flared into an answering anger: "I am not conscious of it, sir, but since you thought it necessary to tell me so, we part!" Having thrown his resignation into Washington's face, Hamilton stalked away.

Washington returned to his room fuming, but slowly got control of himself. In less than an hour, he summoned Tilghman. This other aide was to go to Hamilton, state that Washington had the greatest confidence in Hamilton's integrity and usefulness, and that Washington desired "a candid conversation to heal a difference which could not have happened but in a moment of passion."

Tilghman returned, looked unhappy and embarrassed. Hamilton, he reported, had responded to Washington's overture with a tirade: Washington had kept him at menial tasks, always finding excuses to bar him from active military or political service. Since Hamilton's resolution to resign could not be revoked, "a conversation could serve no other purpose than to produce explanations mutually disagreeable." However, the aide would stay with Washington until he could be replaced. During that time, it would depend on Washington "to let our behavior to each other be the same as if nothing had happened."

Washington sent back word that he was willing to forgo a conversation, and that he gratefully accepted the young man's offer to continue, if only temporarily.[5]

Hamilton had just buried deep his illegitimate West Indian birth by marrying into the New York State aristocracy. To his new father-in-law, General Schuyler, he wrote that he had always disliked service as an aide "as having in it a kind of personal dependence." He had accepted Washington's offer because of patriotism, and had quickly discovered that the General "was neither remarkable for delicacy nor good temper." Although he had risen high in Washington's confidence, "for three years past I have felt no friendship for him and professed none." When Washington made cordial advances, he had responded in a manner which showed "that I wished to stand rather on a footing of military confidence than of private attachment." He asked Schuyler to imagine how this "must have operated on a man to whom all the world is offering incense."

Having "resolved, whenever it should happen, not to be in the wrong," Hamilton had been awaiting an opportunity to cause a breach, and now that he had found it, he would not make peace. Any concessions that Washington might offer would obviously be dictated only by his need for Hamilton's services: "His self-love would never forgive me for what it would regard as a humiliation." To that other aide, McHenry, Hamilton gloated, "He shall, for once at least, repent his ill-humor."[6]

Washington had written of Hamilton, "There are few men to be found of his age who has a more general knowledge than he possesses, and none whose soul is more firmly engaged in the cause, or who exceeds him in probity and sterling virtue." Privileged with such a paragon, Washington should, perhaps, have made more effort to secure for him more conspicuous glory. Hamilton functioned as chief of staff but lacked the title. Although Washington did send him on occasional important missions and encourage him to preside at the headquarters table, the young Titan had made no secret of the fact that he considered this not enough. When daring raids were planned, he begged to be allowed to lead them. Washington always replied that it would be bad for morale to insert a staff officer in a line command at the moment when there was special honor to be won. Hamilton had wanted to be made adjutant general; he had wanted to become Congress's superintendent of finance; he had wanted the French mission that was entrusted to John Laurens; but in each case Washington's backing had been too little or too late. And so, month after month, Hamilton had found himself laboring at headquarters.[7]

Washington was not the kind of executive who sits behind an empty desk as details are smoothly handled by subordinates. Only when physically separated from the Commander in Chief could aides—or for that matter, major generals—do much altogether on their own. And, wherever Washington acted, he dominated.

That most of the letters sent out from headquarters were in the handwriting of aides, only the signatures being Washington's, has induced some historians to credit everything but the signatures to the amanuenses. However, papers drawn in other hands—even by as strong a personality as Hamilton—differ from papers altogether in Washington's hand not in kind but in degree. They reveal Washington's characteristic thought construction and prose style, although these are paler, like colors that have, without any exterior admixture, faded.

Routinely Washington drew up "heads" from which an assistant prepared a draft. Washington reviewed the draft and perhaps revised it with interlinear corrections. A new draft was then put on paper. Washington examined it again, and made any further changes he desired. Finally, the fair copy was written out. If suggestions originated by the aides were incorporated, they were by now so digested that they seemed Washington's own—which must have been very irritating to an able, aggressive man like Hamilton.[8]

The force of Washington's personality was so basic a part of his nature that, while he treated those around him with courtesy and often affection, he was unconscious of how he overwhelmed them. And there was the problem created by his temper. He did his very best to keep it in check, but he was by nature irascible and frequently under great strain. Furthermore, as he refused to have infected teeth pulled lest he have nothing left but bare gums to chew with, he often suffered from nerve-racking toothaches. The explosions of so forceful a man must have been terrible to withstand; and then there were occasions when he neither exploded nor immediately forgave: he was "severe in his resentments, often keeping the nearest friend a long time in suspense as to what he thought."[9]

Of another difficulty of his aides, Washington was very conscious. In urging Congress to raise their pay, he explained, "I give in to no kind of amusements myself, consequently those about me can have none, but are confined from morn till eve hearing and answering the applications and letters of one and another. . . . Knowing this, and at the same time how inadequate the pay is, I can scarce find inclination to impose the necessary duties of their office upon them." It was not surprising, he wrote, that his aides sought preferment elsewhere.[10]

Washington, who may well have foreseen that the brilliant Hamilton would not serve him forever, bore no grudge: he approved of ambition when it was, like Hamilton's, "that laudable kind which prompts a man to excel in whatever he takes in hand." And additional shade was thrown over their parting, it is true, by Washington's discovery that the young man had, although "I complied and religiously fulfilled it," violated their agreement that "no mention should be made" of their falling-out. However, Washington continued to employ Hamilton as chief aide for as long as he would stay (several months), happily made Hamilton's bride the hostess of headquarters, and, after the couple had left, gave Hamilton the command of a battalion of light infantry.[11] His continuing belief that his former aide deserved more than this—deserved, indeed, a real opportunity for glory—was to be spectacularly displayed during the siege of Yorktown.

Shortly after his first falling-out with Hamilton, Washington heard that before any of his own communications on the subject had reached them, the French command in Newport had dispatched one ship and two frigates to the Chesapeake. This force was obviously too weak to accomplish anything against Arnold and yet it was so strong that its departure immobilized, as now weaker than the British, the rest of the French fleet. The heaven-sent opportunity created by the storm damage to British ships seems to have been frittered away.[12]

A few days more, and a letter from Rochambeau stated that the little naval expedition to the Chesapeake had, after a successful attack on some minor British naval raiders, returned to Newport. And now—how Washington's heart leapt as he read the words!—the reunited French were prepared to do what Washington had originally asked: set out in force and attack Arnold at his Virginia base of Portsmouth. The whole fleet would sail, carrying 1120 soldiers. There was, however, some objection, which Washington did not understand, to sending transports up the Chesapeake to pick up and ferry down to the fray the force under Lafayette which Washington had sent hurrying overland from the Hudson to Virginia.* [13]

Washington resolved to post as rapidly as he could gallop to the French camp at Newport, where he could personally "level all difficulties." Of course, he might not arrive in time. The French must realize the importance of permitting no delays, since their fleet would have to be in a defensible position off Portsmouth before the British, who were feverishly collecting and repairing their fleet, regained overall naval superiority.

At Bull's Falls near Kent, Connecticut, Washington thundered at the head of his party onto a crude bridge across the Housatonic. His mount, frightened by the springy action of the bridge, jumped sideways and then, in trying to extricate it from between planks, broke his leg. Washington leapt lightly free. He amazed a French officer, who was accompanying him, by calmly looking over the edge to where the horse was now floundering. He remarked quietly, "Well, we must leave him behind." However, he gave

---

* In dispatching Lafayette, Washington had written, "It was with great reluctance I could resolve upon seeing you separated from headquarters." The French regulars wished he had kept the military upstart home. A strong reason why they did not want to pick up Lafayette's forces was that all the French generals but Rochambeau would be outranked by the American major general who was no more than a reserve lieutenant in their own army.[14]

instructions which eventuated in a note in his expense account. "Getting a horse out of Bull's Falls" cost, in inflated money, $215.[15]

Washington rode the two hundred miles from New Windsor to Rhode Island in three and a half days. At the Newport Ferry, he was met by Chevalier Charles René Dominique Sochet Destouches, who had succeeded to the naval command because of the death of de Ternay. "In great state," Washington was escorted onto the admiral's barge and rowed out, as cannon fired salutes and banners waved, to the flagship *Duc de Bourgogne*. He climbed up the side to the sound of martial music and, as his eyes came level with the deck, he saw soldiers and sailors parading. Then he was greeted by Rochambeau, who had behind him a veritable flock of officers. Wrote Commissary Claude Blanchard, "I was presented to him. His face is handsome, noble, and mild. He is tall (at least five feet eight inches)."[16]

Washington was enchanted to see that the fleet seemed ready to sail. He would keep the conference short, so that the ships could get off at once, gaining that much more time on the enemy. In two hours, he had arranged for Destouches to pick up Lafayette and made all the other necessary arrangements.[17]

Now for the grand sailing! But no! Many decorative barges came to the side of the flagship. Not only the officers who were to stay behind but also those who were scheduled to sail climbed down. All were rowed into Newport Harbor, as land batteries thundered and ranks of foot soldiers that were lined up along the waterfront executed magnificent gyrations. Washington was told that he was being received with ceremonies usually reserved for a Marshal of France or a Prince of the Blood. But he could hardly resist turning to stare sadly at the hulls that swung, under sailless spars, at anchor.[18]

Troops were lined up three ranks deep on both sides of the road down which he advanced from the waterfront to Rochambeau's headquarters. So used to emaciated raggedness, Washington stared almost incredulously at the spotless dress uniforms that bore not the slightest tear, at plump faces which revealed that the French had rested well on American soil. That evening, Washington was the hero of a torchlight procession led by thirty boys, each holding up a candle on a staff. All the windows under which he passed were illuminated; all the windows and roofs crowded, so an eye-witness wrote, with "the fair part of creation," who fluttered handkerchiefs and showered favors. That Washington moved along sadly was noted and attributed to the nobility of his temperament—"the voice of adulation never disturbed the equanimity of his deportment"—but in truth, he was torn with anxiety. Gay lanterns hung on rigging that should be glistening with salt spray.[19]

The next day was full of citizens offering complimentary addresses and of French officers "unbonneting" themselves to multicolored undulations of

[415]

plumes—and also of motionless warships. The wind, Washington noted, was now "as favorable to them and as adverse to the enemy as heaven could furnish." However, he felt that protocol would not permit him to ask why the fleet still lay at anchor—and no one volunteered an explanation.[20]

That night, Washington attended a dance at Mrs. Cowley's Assembly Rooms. The chamber was draped with flags; the local hostesses had lent their best silverware. Washington was asked to open the ball. He selected as his partner the "beautiful" Miss Margaret Champlin. The selection of the first number being hers, she called for the tune known as *A Successful Campaign*. When His Excellency stepped out with the belle, the French officers took the instruments from the hired musicians and Rochambeau wielded the baton. Around and around His Excellency stepped with innate courtesy and the powerful grace of an athlete, but in pauses of the music— between *Boston's Delight, Flowers of Edinburgh, Haymaking, Innocent Maid*—he listened to make sure the wind had not died or changed.[21]

The following morning, Washington was enchanted to see sails rising in the harbor to catch a still favorable wind. Anchors splashed out of the bay and the ships were actually in motion. But then the *Fantastique* ran aground. The fleet turned into the wind and waited. Six hours passed. Then, the *Fantastique* having finally been got afloat, the French armada disappeared into a cold winter sunset.[22]

Washington stayed on at Newport to confer with Rochambeau. The French general reported that he had not received final news from France concerning their request, decided on during their previous meeting, for naval superiority, fifteen thousand men, and much money. The Queen Empress, he explained, had died; there had been changes in the makeup of the ministries; and England, by declaring war on Holland,* had created new problems in the European theater. "All these circumstances would not allow of further efficacious attention being paid to the wants of America." France had sent half a million francs to pay the expenses of her army and navy, and Rochambeau's son was still awaiting at Versailles word as to whether anything further would be done. As Washington left the conference, he could only apply to his continuing dream of ending the war by attacking New York the sad adjective "remote."[23]

Washington's plan to inspect some New England bases before he returned to his army was cut away by the news that less than forty-eight hours after the French had finally taken to the ocean, the British fleet had set sail after them. A "meeting," Washington concluded, seemed "unavoidable." Since the fleets were nearly equal in strength, the issue of a naval combat was perhaps "never more interesting." Believing that "much will depend

---

* Rather than permit Holland, which was the most important neutral carrier, to join Catherine the Great's League of Armed Neutrality, Britain had found a pretext for declaring war.

upon which fleet reaches the Chesapeake Bay first," he could not get out of his mind angry thoughts about how the French had delayed.[24]

Posting back to his army, Washington found awaiting him at his head-quarters a letter which could hardly have been, from a personal point of view, more humiliating. It concerned his seventy-seven-year-old mother. She had always been resentful of anything he had done that was not in her service, and she had talked so against George's activities that she was believed by many to be a Tory. Her perpetual complaint was of neglect. The letter Washington held in his hands was from Benjamin Harrison, the speaker of the Virginia House of Delegates. It told Washington that some members, hearing that Mary Washington "was in great want, owing to the heavy taxes she was obliged to pay," had started a movement in the House for the state to come to the financial rescue of the unfortunate mother of the Commander in Chief. "Supposing you would be displeased," Harrison wrote, he had blocked the move, although "I make no doubt but the Assembly would readily grant the request" if Washington wished them to do so.[25]

Washington replied, "I do not delay a moment" to express "surprise" at the idea of "a pension for my mother." He outlined the liberal provisions he had made, "at her request but at my own expense . . . to make her latter days comfortable and free from care. . . . Before I left Virginia, I answered all her calls for money, and, since that period, have directed my steward to do the same. Whence her distresses can arise, therefore, I know not, never having received any complaint. . . . Confident I am that she has not a child that would not divide the last sixpence to relieve her from *real* distress. This she has been repeatedly assured of by me; and all of us, I am certain, would feel much hurt at having our mother a pensioner . . . but, in fact, she has an ample income of her own."[26]

To add to Washington's Virginia humiliations, his stepson, who had been elected to the Senate undoubtedly because of his connections with the Commander in Chief, had instantly put on the mantle of a great statesman and when action was taken which he had opposed, he had conspicuously and grandly boycotted the legislature. His stepfather wrote him a gentle reproof, adding, "I do not suppose that so young a senator as you are, little versed in political disquisitions, can yet have much influence," but it was in Custis's "power to be punctual in your attendance . . . to hear dispassionately and determine coolly."[27]

Washington, who had little to do but worry, was increasingly haunted by the fear that, even if "the divine government" came at long last to America's rescue, "the period for its accomplishment may be too far distant for a person of my years." Older already than his father and his beloved brother Lawrence had been when they died, he feared that he would never experience again "those domestic and rural enjoyments which in my estimation far surpasses the highest pageantry of this world."[28]

Washington's anxiety for the expedition against Arnold increased daily as no firm news came in and rumors grew louder that the English fleet was clearly stronger than the French. In his rage that the French had delayed until they had lost a perfect opportunity and had placed all in jeopardy, Washington sent off a series of the most indiscreet letters he had penned since he had stopped criticizing the New England troops four years before.

He excoriated the French command for having, by refusing his advice, allowed the expedition against Arnold to become "bold and precarious." Of his two specific charges, the first was fallacious and unfair. Forgetting that the original small naval expedition, which had delayed the sailing of the larger one, had departed before the French command had received his urging of the alternate plan, he wrote, "It is to be lamented, greatly lamented" that the French had ignored, "when I first proposed it to them," his suggestion which would have made the defeat of Arnold "inevitable." Washington's second charge was that, after the French fleet had been reunited by the return of the smaller expedition, there had been an "unfortunate and to me unaccountable" delay in the sailing from Newport of the larger force. All this said, he added piously, "But it is our true policy to make the most of their assistance without censuring their mistakes. Therefore it is I communicate this in confidence."[29]

Washington dispatched letters of this import to his estate manager Lund and to four congressmen or ex-congressmen: Schuyler, Joseph Jones, William Fitzhugh, and John Armstrong. He seems to have forgotten, as he marked the passages "private" and wrote them in his own hand so that his aides need not know, that his lack of funds for special couriers would make him use the ordinary mails. These mails were often rifled by the British, who would love to make trouble between the Americans and the French.

On March 30, Washington learned that there had been a skirmish between the two fleets. Satisfied that the English were the stronger, the French had disengaged and returned to Newport, having done some damage to enemy ships but without having thrown even a puffball at Arnold. In reporting this to Washington, the French command expressed anxiety lest they be accused of "want of execution." What an unfounded idea! replied Washington. The French enterprise would, rather, meet with "universal admiration."[30] And then his letter to Lund, so critical of the French, was published in the New York Tory press.

To Washington's headquarters came a mild letter from Rochambeau, expressing surprise, particularly at the passage that misrepresented what had really happened, and also telling Washington for the first time that the delay of sailing he had witnessed in Newport had been due to a lack of supplies.

Politely, Rochambeau gave Washington a way out—perhaps the letter was a forgery—and he repeated his assurances that the King had placed him under Washington's orders.[31]

Washington probably found the restatement of the pious falsehood on the extent of his command, which made him seem responsible for what he could not control, doubly irritating since, had Rochambeau waited for orders, the hampering first small fleet would never have sailed.

In his reply to Rochambeau, Washington expressed "extreme pain" that an "accident" had made public a letter "which may contain an implication the least disagreeable to you or to the Chevalier Destouches. . . . The enemy," he continued, "have fabricated whole letters for me, and even a series of letters." However, although he thought that text might have been edited, "it would be disingenuous in me not to acknowledge that I believe the general import to be true." Rochambeau should consider that the letter was written to a friend "totally unconnected with public affairs." Not mentioning that similar letters had gone to leaders of public affairs, Washington stated, "No idea of the same kind has ever gone to any public body." The letter was "written in haste, and might have been inaccurately expressed. . . . As to the apparent insinuation that the first expedition had been preferred to the one proposed by me, I could not have intended to convey it, because it would have been unjust. . . . With this explanation, I leave the matter to his [Destouches's] candor and to yours, and flatter myself it will make no impressions inconsistent with an entire persuasion of my sincere esteem and attachment."[32]

As Washington's admirers state, this was a "manly" letter, but it was hardly an ingratiating one. It could not have gone very far in propitiating the French general and admiral. Even if his pride kept him from an abject apology, why did Washington, who so often stretched the truth for propaganda ends, not take advantage of the out Rochambeau had suggested by stating that the stinging section of the letter was a forgery? The truth seems to have been that Washington, whose whole life was now so irksome, was still angry. He wrote young Laurens in France (although this time in cipher), "The failure of this expedition (which was most flattering in the commencement of it) is much to be regretted, because a successful blow in that quarter would, in all probability, have given a decisive turn to our affairs in all the southern states; because it has been attended with considerable expense on our part and much inconvenience to the state of Virginia, by assembling its militia; and because the world are disappointed in not seeing Arnold in gibbets; above all, because we stood in need of something to keep us afloat till the result of your mission is known."[33]

The troubles of Virginia had only begun. At the opening of the year, Greene and Cornwallis had faced each other in the Carolinas, where the weather was warm enough for winter fighting. On January 17, Greene's light infantry, commanded by Morgan, so decisively defeated a British detachment at Cowpens that the mobility of Greene's army was impeded by captured cannon, some eight hundred prisoners, and an enemy baggage train. Cornwallis responded angrily: he increased the speed of his own army by burning many of his remaining wagons and all his supplies that were not absolutely necessary—the army would live off the country—and took off after Greene. Unwilling to abandon their booty, the Americans were for once not faster than the enemy—and they were weaker. Greene had some two thousand men of whom only fourteen hundred were Continentals, while Cornwallis had twenty-five hundred to three thousand regulars. Washington lamented to Greene that he would find it difficult to avoid a general action since it would probably result in "the dispersion of your little army."[34]

Greene's precipitous flight was assisted by a suggestion Washington had made the previous November that, since Virginia was so cut by rivers, he should build and drag around with him wheeled flatboats. Greene got across the Dan from North Carolina into Virginia before Cornwallis could catch up with him.[35]

Collecting militia until he had swelled his force to some four thousand— only about one thousand Continentals were still with him—Greene returned to North Carolina and fought Cornwallis at Guilford Court House. Although the British army was now the smaller, it was entirely made up of regulars. In the end, the Americans were forced to flee. However, Cornwallis lost nearly a quarter of his force in killed, wounded, and missing.

The American and the British armies now shifted relative positions. Cornwallis decided to operate in Virginia. He crossed the Dan from North Carolina and called to him from Portsmouth the force under Arnold which had recently been reinforced. Greene thereupon saw an opportunity to repossess the Carolinas, where the British now had only the garrisons of a few seaport bases. Greene marched south. Then Cornwallis was faced in Washington's home state only by the little force under Lafayette which had been dispatched to cooperate with the French fleet's abortive gesture against Portsmouth. Having only three thousand men, more than half of them militia, Lafayette could do nothing but keep out of the way of Cornwallis's seven thousand. Virginia lay helpless.[36]

In April, the British sloop *Savage* anchored off Mount Vernon and trained her guns on the house. Washington's first reaction on hearing what happened must have been relief that his principal losses had only been seventeen slaves, who had fled to the British on a promise of freedom, and a small sailboat. The mansion house stood! However, on second thought he sent Lund a reproof, stern if a little incoherent.

Lund should not have gone on board the *Savage* and bargained with the captain to save the house. He should not have supplied the enemy with refreshments. This "will be a precedent for others and may become a subject of animadversion." Washington had rather "they had burnt my house and laid the plantation in ruins."

Since there was no way of stopping the British from making further raids, Washington urged Lund to hide whatever valuables he could. His remaining slaves and his buildings could not, he believed, be saved. "But I am prepared for the event."[37]

From Thomas Jefferson, the governor of Virginia, Washington received an anguished appeal. Jefferson wrote that the British were in a position "to waste an unarmed country and to lead the minds of the people to acquiescence under those events which they see no human power prepared to ward off." The only hope seemed to be that Washington would "lend us your personal aid. It is evident from the universal voice that the presence of their beloved countryman . . . to whose person they have still flattered themselves they retained some right, and have ever looked up as their dernier resort in distress, that your appearance among them, I say, would restore full confidence of salvation. . . . The difficulty would then be how to keep men out of the field."[38]

"No body, I persuade myself," so Washington wrote, "can doubt my inclination to be immediately employed in the defense of that country where all my property and connections are." Not only Governor Jefferson but "many of my friends" had urged him to come to the rescue of Virginia. However, he saw "powerful objections to my leaving this army," and even more powerful objections to trying to march that army southward hundreds of miles.[39]

While the mails carried overland Washington's reluctant refusals to come to the rescue, the government of Virginia completely collapsed. Richmond being so exposed to the enemy, the capital was moved to Charlottesville. However, it took a long time for a quorum of legislators to find enough courage to appear even at Charlottesville—and then British light horse came galloping in. Although Governor Jefferson fled successfully across the mountains, seven members of the House were captured. Jefferson's term then expired. The legislators were too scattered to elect a successor.

While Washington, "acting [as he put it] on the great scale," resolutely faced a possible complete British capture of his homeland, the first known serious effort was made to persuade him down the path to political dictatorship. There was much talk in Virginia of handing the government to him personally.* [40] Interestingly enough, the proposition was actually con-

---

* Although the larger suggestion may not have been seriously made to Washington, the conception that his personal political direction could save the entire United States kept

veyed to the general by the man whose previous fears that Washington would want to be a dictator had helped make him the leading Virginian in the Conway Cabal. And Richard Henry Lee cast as a collaborator in this effort to give Washington great civil power, the congressman who had always been most vocally suspicious of Washington's ambitions: John Lovell. This proves again that, even as it is the wife with the greatest yen for philandering who most distrusts her husband, it is the individual most personally susceptible to tyranny who most smells tyranny in the breeze. The witch-hunter and the witch are always sisters under the skin.

Lee started his letter to Washington by stating a hope that they were still friends despite "the arts of wicked men." He went on to emote, "It would be a thing for angels to weep over if the goodly fabric of human freedom, which you have so well labored to rear, should in one unlucky moment be leveled with the dust." The scheme for which Lee wished Washington's approval was that Congress order Washington to Virginia with two or three thousand good troops and the power to assume, until the legislature could convene and a governor be appointed, dictatorial powers. Congress would furthermore recommend that the Assembly, after it had convened, continue Washington's powers for an additional six to ten months.[41]

Washington showed no hurry in answering Lee. When he got around to it, he stated that "unconscious of having given you just cause to change the favorable sentiments you have expressed for me, I could not suppose you had altered them. . . . The distresses of Virginia I am but too well acquainted with; but the plan you have suggested for the relief of it, in my judgment, is a greater proof of your unbounded confidence in me than it is that the means proposed would be found adequate to the ends in view, were it practicable to make the experiment."[42]

At this dark time, when so much else also preyed on his nerves, Washington had been unable to escape the conclusion that he had been left no possibility of taking a strong step to rescue Virginia without abandoning his republican principles and his great duty to the United States as a whole. No decision could have been more bitter. It meant turning his back, perhaps forever, on almost everything which had meant most to him in the halcyon days of peace.

How far his thinking had traveled! For almost forty years, Washington had considered Virginia his "country." It was for Virginia that he had fought in the French and Indian War. During that war, his outrage at a military policy that offered advantages in opening the west to the rival country of Pennsylvania had brought him into his worst hassle with the

cropping up in Philadelphia. Thus, the Rhode Island congressman Ezekiel Cornell had written Greene in August 1780, "The necessity of appointing George Washington a sole dictator of America is again talked of as the only means under God by which we can be saved from destruction."[43]

British high command. But quite recently, he had urged on Virginia the relinquishment of her claims to the western empire for which he had once fought.

The issue had been that Maryland—another rival country against whose pretensions Washington had skirmished as a young man—would not ratify the Articles of Confederation as long as the agreement countenanced Virginia in hogging so much wilderness. Only after Virginia abandoned her claims to all lands west of the Ohio did Maryland, by ratifying the Articles, enable them to become, on March 1, 1781, operative. In expressing pleasure over these steps toward unity, Washington wrote, as one would of a lost bride, a eulogy to the relinquished region "which for fertility of soil, pleasantness of clime, and other natural advantages is equal to any known tract of country in the universe of the same extent."[44]

As for the share he had tried before the war to carve out for himself in the wild Elysium, he had found, "since I came into the service," no time to attend to it. How the shifting of claims and boundaries had affected the legality of his patents, he did not know. He feared that his western concerns would sink into "absolute ruin before I am at liberty to look after them."[45]

However, a deeper ruin than the loss of his western lands and the burning of Mount Vernon stared Washington in the face. Even if the Revolutionary War were in general won, his old country of Virginia might be permanently lost. The mediation then being undertaken by the neutral European powers promised to let each side in the American war keep the territory it controlled at the time of the peace. If England continued to control Virginia, Washington would not only be bankrupted (his estates would surely be confiscated) but he would be exiled for the rest of his days from the hills and river and fields he loved.[46]

VIII

Another Man's Gamble

46

Forcing Washington's Hand

A S Washington wandered in mazes of frustration, his nerves grew tenser. "To guard against assassination," he wrote, "which I neither expect nor dread, is impossible," but he admitted that he did lie awake at night worrying for fear that the enemy might try to kidnap him as he had tried to kidnap their generals. Local Tories—there were many in the Hudson Highlands—might sneak up through secret ways they knew only too well, surprise his guard, and carry him off in a boat. Washington did not confide to paper what visions rose in his mind of being pulled through the streets of New York City as a butt of mockery, of being tried in London, of the gallows—or worse—at last. To General Heath, he wrote, "If the water at night is well guarded, I shall be under no apprehension of attempts of this kind." However, he ordered a reinforcement to his guard.[1]

For Washington, the best medicine was activity. As additions to the shrinking tasks of his shrinking army, he resumed the diary jottings he had abandoned on becoming Commander in Chief, and he supervised classification of his military records. He ordered that the sheets, unsightly "in the rough manner in which they were first drawn," should be copied into uniform blank books. Utility should be served with clear indexes, "beauty" by having "clerks who write a fair hand" and preserve identical margins "upon black lines equidistant."[2]

Lafayette being down south, Washington needed to find another English-speaking go-between with Rochambeau. When he fixed on his new admiration, Chastellux, who had in Paris the same "private circle of friends" as Lafayette, Rochambeau and the other Lafayette-dislikers in the French army were not pleased. They were all the more irritated because Chastellux liked to criticize his commander (who did not speak the language) for "incredible ignorance of everything American." Rochambeau's partisans responded by ruling the philosopher *"trop américain."* But Washington, not informed on the parties that divided the French army, was pleased with his correspondent, who sometimes sent him important information which Rochambeau either delayed or withheld.[3]

When Rochambeau's son finally returned from France with dispatches and a new naval commander, Jacques Melchoir, Comte de Barras St. Laurent, a personal interview between the French and American leaders was called for. It was held at Wethersfield, Connecticut, on May 22, 1781. Because of threatening British naval action, Barras did not get there. Rochambeau spoke for the French command, with Chastellux present as interpreter.[4]

French sources, and particularly Rochambeau's own memoirs, have (with amazing acceptance by historians) depicted Washington as myopic at this conference to the possibility, urged by Rochambeau, that Cornwallis's army could be trapped (as it eventually was) on the perimeter of Chesapeake Bay. Actually, there was no way for anyone to know that Cornwallis, who was triumphantly operating in inland Virginia, would come to the coast and roost at Yorktown or any other spot where he could be pinned down and besieged. (Washington suspected that he would return to the Carolinas.) Furthermore, Rochambeau kept from Washington a fact on which the eventual successful plan basically depended. Although Washington was informed that a "numerous" French fleet under Admiral de Grasse would operate that summer in the Indies, he was given no reason to believe that this fleet was more likely to cooperate with his own army than the same admiral's fleet of the previous year, which had never arrived.[5]

Rochambeau, on the other hand, knew that de Grasse had been given orders to come north in July or August. This had been communicated to him by his government in what he called "a confidential message to me alone." He was surely glad to keep the information from Washington, since, as a lecture on secrecy he soon gave the American commander reveals, he had come to doubt (after the interception by the British of Washington's letter so unfairly critical of the French) the American's discretion. He was, indeed, so evasive that Washington wrote Luzerne, "It is not for me to know in what manner the fleet of His Most Christian Majesty is to be employed in the West Indies this summer, or to inquire at what epocha it may be expected on this coast."* [6]

What Rochambeau communicated to Washington was hardly encouraging. A reinforcement of only six hundred men was expected for the army, and the French government was dispatching only a little money. Furthermore, he carried an answer to a question Washington had sent to Barras:

---

* Not till May 14, nine days before the meeting opened at Wethersfield, had a letter started on the long trip from France authorizing Luzerne to tell Washington that de Grasse had orders to come to North America.[7]

the Newport squadron could not be made strong enough to ferry any troops down south. That this question had to be answered refutes what Rochambeau wrote in his *Memoirs:* "General Washington, during this conference, had scarcely another object in view but an expedition against the island of New York." However, Rochambeau was correct in stating that Washington considered a blow at New York "the most capable of striking a deathblow to British dominion in America."[8]

While the conference was in session, Washington received some dispatches that had been intercepted by a privateer and which demonstrated that the enemy's primary intention was to subdue the southern states. This encouraged Rochambeau's argument that a large portion of the combined armies should march south. Washington replied that a major move in that direction would have to await the water transport that was dependent on naval supremacy: the march would ruin his army. He gave reasons which he considered "too numerous" to recapitulate in his diary, but pointed particularly to the expense, and the danger that the New England troops, who were disinclined to go so far from home into a climate they considered unhealthy (and which might be for them), would dwindle through desertion and sickness.[9]

Rochambeau now asked Washington to speculate on what should be done if, by some chance, "a French naval reinforcement" should appear and establish naval supremacy. He wanted Washington to agree that the attack should then be made in the south. However, Washington insisted that the south should remain the second choice, to be embraced only if the combined force proved too weak to overrun New York. In the abstract, a French fleet should steer for Block Island outside New York Harbor, although it might then, should it ever actually appear, "be directed against the enemy in some other quarter as circumstances shall dictate." Rochambeau, however, wanted nothing of the New York plan. He pointed out that in 1779 d'Estaing had found that his boats drew too much to get into New York Harbor. Washington replied that he had investigated further and found that d'Estaing had been misinformed. In the heat of his argument, Washington so overestimated that American force which could be brought to bear on New York that, on cooler thoughts after the conference was over, he was to warn Rochambeau not to regard his estimates "as official or definitive."[10]

During the debate, Chastellux (who had not been told de Grasse was really expected and who agreed that New York was the optimum objective) was horrified to see Rochambeau display to Washington "all the ungraciousness and all the unpleasantness possible."

The French general's nerves were on edge. Not only had Washington insulted the French in his inaccurate letter that became public, not only was Washington unwilling to prefer the south to New York, but Rochambeau's son had brought back news from France the general found personally upsetting. Various of his officers had written to ladies of the Court letters that were critical of him and had been circulated. Nevertheless, there had been a movement to make him secretary of war which would have succeeded had he not been away in America. He could not help, he admitted, comparing this lost opportunity with the "scanty resources and distressing predicament" of his present command. His own officers were finding him hard to get on with. Count Fersen complained that he had become distrustful of his top subordinates "in a way that is disagreeable and indeed insulting." Commissary Blanchard added that he treated those who worked with him as if they were either "rascals or idiots." And now he treated Washington in a way that Chastellux feared gave the American hero "a sad and disagreeable feeling in his heart."[11]

The legend that Rochambeau and Washington enjoyed a friendship of perfection is based on the fact that both labored hard and successfully to present to the public an image of Franco-American unity. Now Rochambeau signed a paper agreeing with Washington that, should de Grasse's fleet arrive, "an operation against New York" seemed preferable "under present circumstances to attempt sending a force to the southward." However, he rushed off to Santo Domingo a surreptitious frigate bearing a dispatch to de Grasse in which he reported the results of the conference, but added that he considered the official conclusion unwise. De Grasse should, he urged, sail not for New York but for Chesapeake Bay. He urged the admiral to secure from the governor of Santo Domingo an infantry brigade that had been intended for other purposes and to raise a loan of 1,200,000 francs in the French colonies. De Grasse was to send back immediate word so that "I might take the earliest opportunity to combine our march with that of General Washington, so as to proceed by land as expeditiously as possible, and join him at any stipulated part of the Chesapeake."[12]

During the Wethersfield conference, Washington's recommendation for immediate action had been that Rochambeau's army join his own on the outskirts of New York: this would remove pressure from the south, since Clinton, thus menaced, could not further weaken the garrison at his most important base, and might, indeed, feel it necessary to call some of Cornwallis's men back. Furthermore, the allied armies would be ready to cooperate in the capture of New York should de Grasse appear.[13]

For once, Rochambeau could cheerfully and frankly obey Washington's orders; New York was on the way south. However, an argument developed concerning Barras's fleet, which would be left by the departure of Rochambeau's army in an exposed position at Newport. Washington wanted the fleet to move to Boston where the inhabitants could protect it. But what, asked Rochambeau, of the valuable installations the French had built at

Newport and the bulk supplies that were stored nearby on the mainland? Washington's theory was that while New York was so menaced, the British would not be able to attack the French positions with "any considerable body of men." Two hundred French soldiers could guard the mainland depots; five hundred militia would hold Newport—and more militia could always be called out.[14]

Whatever Rochambeau thought of the safety of this scheme, he did not wish to send the fleet north of Cape Cod, which might delay fatally a possible junction with de Grasse in the Chesapeake. However, he was able to agree politely because his acquiescence meant nothing. The decision was really up to the absent Barras.[15]

Washington had hardly returned from the conference to his headquarters when that dashing cavalry commander and lover (he claimed to have been intimate with Marie Antoinette) the Duc de Lauzun came galloping in with a dispatch: a French Council of War had decided that the fleet would stay in Newport. Lauzun's memory that the news put Washington "in such a rage" that he could not bring himself to write a reply for three days is substantiated by the fact that three days actually did pass. Then Washington took "the liberty still to recommend" removal to Boston. In a private letter to his friend Chastellux, he explained that he was afraid that if the fleet stayed at Newport "every mysterious preparation of the enemy" would induce the admiral nervously to call for militia. However, when it became clear that the French had no intention of doing what he urged, Washington kept up the fiction of his top command by agreeing with what had been determined.[16]

Washington now broadcast in his letters that a combined allied force intended to take New York. He used this news in circulars to the states as an argument for rapid recruiting, and sent the word weaving down south to Lafayette. That the letter to Lafayette was captured by the British opened Washington to charges of renewed indiscretion which are to be found in books ranging from Rochambeau's *Memoirs* to Freeman's *Washington*. However, Washington, as he later admitted, was anxious that the information should leak to the enemy. Having no reason really to expect a French fleet and seeing his own levies come in with a dreadful if familiar slowness, he felt that the possibility of an actual attack on New York was very remote. The objective visibly achievable was to take pressure off the south by frightening Clinton. The captured letter served this end to perfection.[17]

In a blue funk, Clinton sent a copy of Washington's words to Cornwallis along with the order that the subordinate abandon all idea of subduing Virginia, send two thousand of his men back to New York, and take up a defensive station at Williamsburg or Yorktown. Thus, by pushing Cornwallis into a besiegable position on the coast, Washington stacked the cards in favor of a move which Rochambeau was going to force him to undertake.

[431]

However, for the time being, neither he nor Rochambeau knew of Clinton's order, or that Cornwallis was destined for Yorktown.[18]

In Washington's New Windsor headquarters, Martha was very ill with "a kind of jaundice." As it was about time for her to return to Virginia and she was too weak to go, she clamored so of anxiety to see her son that Washington wrote the young man to come to headquarters if possible. Jackie did not come. For himself, Washington wrote a dentist to send him "a pair of pincers to fasten the wire of my teeth," and also "one of your scrapers, as my teeth stand in need of cleaning, and I have little prospect of being in Philadelphia soon."[19]

On May 26, Washington received directly from his representative in Paris, John Laurens, his first inkling that the French West Indian fleet had been ordered to send a major detachment to America. The vessels would, Laurens reported, probably arrive in July. The envoy's letter also stated that the Court of Versailles had donated six million livres to the United States, part to purchase supplies for the American troops, and part to be spent at Washington's personal discretion. It was gratifying to receive from his friend the statement that the "only hope of obtaining additional succor is founded on the exalted opinion which the Ministers have of your Excellency and everything which comes from you."[20]

More than two weeks after Washington had received the news from Laurens, Rochambeau (who had now heard that de Grasse approved of his plans) notified Washington that the arrival of the fleet from the Indies was imminent. He went on to say that he had told de Grasse of Washington's preference for New York, but had suggested that on the way there the admiral make a quick stroke at the enemy shipping in Chesapeake Bay.[21]

The disingenuous account of what Rochambeau had written elicited from Washington a reply that must have made the French general smile. Washington was worried lest "you have in your communication to him confined our views to *New York* alone. . . . Your Excellency will be pleased to recollect that *New York* was looked upon by us as the only practical object under present circumstances; but, should we be able to secure a *naval superiority,* we may perhaps find others more practicable and equally advisable."

However, Washington felt that instead of running immediately into the Chesapeake, de Grasse should leave his objective open so that it could be determined what was, at that instant of time, "the most advantageous quarter for him to make his *appearance* in." This would require contact with the fleet in the ocean. Should such contact be impossible, de Grasse should, Washington still believed, appear off Sandy Hook, since "by suddenly coming there, he would certainly *block* up any *fleet* which might be *within;* and he would even have a very good chance of *forcing* the *entrance* before dispositions could be made to *oppose* him. Should the *British fleet* not be there, he could follow them to *Chesapeake,* which is always accessible to a superior force."[22]

Rochambeau continued with his own plan, which precluded any possibility of surprising New York, but enhanced the possibility of surprising any British force that might be garrisoned at that time on the Virginia coast. Not having second sight (or the hindsight often applied to this matter by historians), Rochambeau did not foresee trapping Cornwallis's large army, which was still inland and could (as far as Franco-American intelligence went) very well stay there. Rochambeau urged as de Grasse's objective Portsmouth, where the British kept a garrison of fifteen hundred and the shipping directly attached to the Virginia expedition. After these had been overcome, de Grasse could, if it proved feasible and he had time, fall in with Washington's plan of attacking New York.[23]

Washington kept all possibilities open by ordering that army supplies raised to the southward be held rather than forwarded. He also, in his eternal search for expedients, worked out a scheme by which Barras could improvise so many additional boats that, without awaiting de Grasse, he could perhaps run safely to the Chesapeake and there "take a position with security." This, by neutralizing the British post at Portsmouth, would keep Cornwallis from getting supplies or sailing away. Washington's polite disclaimer—"I barely mention this as an idea which has struck me, not as a matter which I would undertake to advise, unacquainted as I am with naval affairs"—probably did not keep his suggestion from irritating the conservative French admiral.[24]

As the time approached for the French army to join him on the banks of the Hudson, Washington evolved another of his schemes. He reasoned that the British, who knew that the unaided Americans were too weak to attack, would doze in assumed security as long as they were kept in ignorance of the French march. If the French advanced secretly enough to appear by surprise, the allies might, before the British realized what was happening, overrun Harlem Heights, capturing Fort Knyphausen (once Fort Washington). This would be the best possible jumping-off place from which to move on the rest of New York.

Washington urged Rochambeau to come rapidly from Newport by an unexpected route, and to send ahead Lauzun's Legion of cavalry and light infantry. On the night of July 2, Lincoln, with a picked American force of about a thousand, would float down the Hudson under the dark shadow of the Jersey shore and finally tie up under overhanging boughs. Toward morning, when the moon had set, they would start out again, cross the river with muffled oars, tiptoe up the high bank onto Harlem Heights, and overwhelm Fort Knyphausen. As rumors of what was happening created

[433]

confusion among the enemy, Lauzun's Legion would swoop out of the blackness into Morrisania, the strongest outpost on the mainland, which was directly across the Harlem River from Harlem Heights.[25]

Should the surprise be successful, it would take major power to hold what had been gained. Washington, therefore, would be coming down the Hudson, and he hoped that as he advanced he would be joined by Rochambeau's three remaining regiments. All would hurry through Morrisania, pour across Kingsbridge, and hold the Heights.

Lincoln's hopes depended on catching the British off guard. If for any reason he believed that the enemy had been warned, he was to forget about Fort Knyphausen and join with Lauzun in beating up Morrisania.

As it turned out, Lincoln's expedition was seen by a British party that was foraging on the Jersey shore. They rowed for Morrisania and got there before Lauzun, who was late. The result was an indecisive skirmish: the enemy garrison managed to scuttle across the Harlem River into the safety of Manhattan Island. Arriving with the main American army a little after daylight (Rochambeau was still on the way), Washington and his engineer, Duportail, took "the most favorable opportunity" of staring across the Harlem at the British works on the north of the island. This was the closest they had got to Manhattan in five years.[26]

Now Washington laid out contiguous camps for the Americans and the French some twelve miles north of Manhattan near Dobbs Ferry, in an area which had previously been no-man's-land between the two armies. Rochambeau, who was taking his time in the extreme heat, did not bring his army in beside the American until July 6.[27]

When the French staged a grand parade for the American officers, they achieved more complicated maneuvers with more crispness than the Continentals ever achieved, but this did not impress the Americans as much as their spotless uniforms. All were white, the different regiments being distinguished by the colors of their lapels, coat collars, and buttons. The Bourbonnais wore crimson lapels, pink collars, and white buttons; the Soissonnais, rose-colored lapels, sky-blue collars, and yellow buttons. To an intaking of American breaths, Lauzun's Legion pranced by in plumes. The French staff was pleased by the amazed appreciation which appeared on most of their visitors' faces. In noting that Washington seemed less "ecstatic" than the others, Rochambeau's aide, Von Closen, assumed that this was because he had seen the French march before.[28]

The French officers, as they wandered through the American camp, were moved by the poverty everywhere visible and puzzled by a military phenomenon utterly outside their experience. "I admire the American troops tremendously!" wrote Von Closen. "It is incredible that soldiers composed of men of every age, even of children of fifteen, of whites and blacks, almost naked, unpaid, and rather poorly fed, can march so well and withstand fire so steadfastly."• He credited "the calm and calculated measures of General Washington, in whom I daily discover some new and eminent qualities. . . . He is certainly admirable as the leader of his army, in which everyone regards him as his father and friend."[29]

Although Washington had failed to find an adequate steward to take charge, and in his situation found the cost of such entertaining frightening, he kept open house for the high French officers. The Count de Ségur, son of the Minister of War, noted that "at his table thirty people sat every day." The French found the food "pretty abundant," but complained that the coffee was weak and the salad served only with vinegar, and that since each was given only one plate, they had to slosh all the foods together. As Chastellux had been, they were amazed at the length of time Washington sat at table. After the meal had been washed down with beer and rum, ten or fifteen toasts were drunk in Madeira, cheese was munched, and "the reunion went on into the night." Dumas noted that Washington "animated the conversation by unaffected cheerfulness." Ségur commented that, since Washington remained temperate, he had no reason for prolonging the meal except to enjoy conversation and relax his fatigue.[30]

Since the British had, except for outposts that fled any sizable force, abandoned the mainland, Washington and Rochambeau, in company with a cloud of map-drawing engineers, amused and informed themselves by reconnoitering all around the edges of Manhattan and once (if du Bourg is to be believed) made a quick excursion across the Harlem to set foot on the island itself. They were fired at by cannon; on one expedition they rode for twenty-four hours without resting; and in reconnoitering Throg's Neck (where a British force had once landed), they had an adventure which the French found very romantic.[31]

As the engineers performed their "geometrical operations," Rochambeau and Washington went to sleep behind a hedge. On being awakened by peevish firing from some British ships, Rochambeau saw something that alarmed him more than the enemy. He roused Washington: they had forgotten about the tide: they were surrounded with water.

Two American small boats served to get the men off, but what of the horses? The French cavalrymen were busy tying bridle ropes with which they could guide their mounts through the flood, when they heard a vast splashing. The American mounts had been driven into the water and, without any guidance at all, were swimming, ninety strong, to the other shore. An officer explained that American horses were "accustomed to this from birth."[32]

Since he remained convinced that there was no other way to stop the war in its tracks, Washington still dreamed of an attack on New York—he was

[435]

building landing craft—but the Confederation was not backing him up. His army had not been augmented since it emerged from winter quarters, nor had he been notified by the governors whether the states would really send him any more troops. Washington ordered that none of the few soldiers he had be under any circumstances discharged unless they were small boys or bore "visible marks of imbecility."[33]

In mid-July, Rochambeau—who had still not admitted that the matter had been independently decided—called on Washington for "a definitive plan of campaign." Although the American commander "could not but acknowledge" the weakness of his army, something might turn up, and in any case he still hoped that de Grasse would appear off Sandy Hook so that, from "a full view" of the circumstances then existing, plans could be concerted "on the surest grounds." Perhaps the admiral could destroy the British fleet in the harbor even if the city were not taken. Or, if a British army were still operating in Virginia and it seemed most expedient to attack that force, de Grasse could carry the allied armies by water to the Chesapeake.[34]

On August 1, Washington noted in his diary, "I could scarce see a ground upon which to continue my preparations against New York . . . and therefore I turned my views more seriously than I had before done to an operation to the southward." He decided to determine whether the two armies could be transported to Virginia without French naval help. Moving cautiously so as not to unfold "matters too plainly to the enemy," he investigated what shipping would be available on those two inland waterways the Delaware and the Chesapeake. Were there any "deep-waisted sloops and schooners proper to carry horses?"[35]

Yet it would be so much better to go by the ocean! Rochambeau, who knew there was no chance that de Grasse would appear off Sandy Hook, must (if he was notified) have smiled to learn that Washington had drafted a letter to de Grasse which nestled in the pocket of General Forman as that officer scanned the ocean around Sandy Hook from the New Jersey heights. Washington spent more money than the impoverished army could well bear to establish a chain of mounted dragoons between Forman and his headquarters.[36]

On August 14, Washington finally discovered what was in store for him and his army. The letter was from Barras. It stated that the frigate *Concorde* had arrived in Newport bringing news from de Grasse. The admiral would not appear off Sandy Hook either to attack the New York shipping or concert plans with Washington. He had already left Santo Domingo and was sailing directly for the Chesapeake. He expected to arrive on September 3. He would be powerful, bringing "between twenty-five and twenty-nine sail of the line and 3200 land troops," but he could not stay long. Since he had to start back to the Indies by the middle of October, if Washington and Rochambeau were to cooperate with him, they would have to be on the Chesapeake by the time he arrived. Barras gave no indication that he himself would be willing to do any ferrying. Washington, as he recognized at once, was left "no alternative." An inland advance covering the four hundred and fifty miles to the Chesapeake "took place [as he later noted] of necessity."[37]

47

Down Fortune's Mazes

NOW that a march to the Chesapeake was irrevocably ordained, it was most passionately to be hoped that some enemy would be there to be attacked if the allied forces and de Grasse's fleet did successfully converge. The latest word from Lafayette in Virginia was that Cornwallis had withdrawn to the waterside at Portsmouth. He was putting some of his troops on boats, but whether to return to New York or go raiding in Virginia, Lafayette could not determine.[1]

In notifying Lafayette of de Grasse's intended arrival, Washington wrote, "Whether the enemy remain in full force or whether they have only a detachment left," Lafayette should "take such a position as will best enable you to prevent their sudden retreat through North Carolina, which I presume they will attempt the instant they perceive so formidable an armament."[2]

Logic indicated that, since Cornwallis's whole army of seven thousand could easily brush Lafayette aside, the enemy could only be trapped—even if every other aspect of the campaign succeeded—if their force had been so reduced that its capture would not repay the vast effort of marching down on them. That is, unless luck, having first made Cornwallis decide to stay with his whole army, then conspired to keep him in ignorance of his danger.

One thing was sure: if the allies were to get to the Chesapeake in time to achieve anything, "we have not a moment to lose." Having left behind a garrison at West Point and a few other Continental forces to cooperate with the militia in covering "the country contiguous with New York," Washington took the rest of his troops across King's Ferry, moving fast so as to get out of the way of the French who were supposed to be on his heels. He spent that night, August 21–22, 1781, at Robinson's House, that structure embedded among gloomy mountains where he had learned of Arnold's treason and listened to the hysterical screams of Arnold's young wife. He was taking tea when in came Commissary Blanchard, bearing a dispatch. Although the document was not complicated, Washington, as the French officer noted, read it through twice. It explained that the French army had been delayed.[3]

Before the French actually crossed at King's Ferry their engineers built on an overlooking height an ornamental pavilion from which Washington could watch. The Americans had crossed the river in one day, but the French were so lavishly appointed that it took them four. Washington writhed with impatience. The elegantly uniformed officers he saw moving below him with slow and ceremonious efficiency were engaged in an unemotional exercise in military know-how. For them, the expedition was no more than a passing adventure through which they hoped to serve their personal ambitions in a distant land. Those not actually killed would go home to tell fine stories in well-lighted drawing rooms. But Washington and his brave men might soon have no homeland: a peace treaty loomed by which any disaster to the American cause might well be perpetuated in the law of nations.[4]

Washington was by nature a gambler, but this was not his gamble and the negative odds seemed to him wildly unsuited to his situation. Earlier in the war, when the cause had been transfigured by hope and when losses had been easy to repair, he had willingly taken big risks. But for the last two years his army had been shrinking without a defeat. Recruiting was now so difficult that he could no longer be sure when he lost a man that the man would ever be replaced. Not only enemy action, but the attrition caused by the march or even the frustration of having the move to the Chesapeake come to nothing, might sink the cause past remedy.

Washington's memory, like that of lesser men, was sometimes to edit the past to make it seem more reasonable. In 1788, he played down for publication the fact that Rochambeau, although titularly under his command, had forced him to undertake the Yorktown campaign against his better judgment. However, his contention that he had willingly consented forced him to misstate wildly what was the strategic situation when the campaign had started. Since "our affairs were then in the most ruinous train imaginable . . . I never would have consented to embark in any enterprise wherein, from the most rational plan and accurate calculations, the favorable issue should not have appeared as clear to my view as a ray of light."[5]

As Washington watched the French troops cross the river, no ray of light prophesied a favorable issue. Although the whole future of America was being staked on a junction with de Grasse, Washington could have no confidence that the rendezvous would ever be achieved. French promises had so often been unfulfilled. The admiral could have been called back by new developments in the Indies or new dispatches from Versailles—or he might simply have changed his mind. How full of vagaries French sailors could be had just been brought home again to Washington by the behavior of Barras.

Since de Grasse was Barras's junior in the service, recently promoted to a higher rank, he had not felt free to order the commander of the Newport squadron to join him at the Chesapeake. And Barras, who did not like the idea of serving under de Grasse, had announced his intention of sailing in the opposite direction, of (as Washington put it) "enterprising something against New Foundland." Not only would this have weakened the available naval strength, but it would have left no way of transporting to the Chesapeake Rochambeau's heavy cannon, which would be necessary in case of a siege, or the essential salt provisions Washington had been hoarding for an emergency.[6]

Barras had, it is true, been persuaded to cooperate, but would he ever get to the Chesapeake, particularly as he could not accompany de Grasse's superior force but would have to meet it, sailing—as he had always previously refused to do—in the face of the stronger New York squadron? And then there were storms! Again and again Washington had seen how they could scatter fleets of sailing vessels. Even if Barras and de Grasse were all zeal, they might never arrive.

It was, of course, the habit of the British to counter every French naval move with a stronger move of their own. Rumors had reached Washington that, even as he was expecting de Grasse, Clinton was expecting the British West Indian fleet under Admiral Sir George Rodney.[7] Supposing the two fleets met as they approached through the ocean: de Grasse might be defeated and Washington find, when he arrived at the Chesapeake, that the bay was a-crawl with English ships.

If the initial steps all went well, if Rochambeau and Washington and Barras and de Grasse all convened on schedule, would de Grasse, who had stated that the time he could spare for North America was very short, stay long enough to achieve anything? He might, as d'Estaing had done, sail off in the middle of the operation, leaving the rest of the expedition on a limb from which they might be unable to climb down.

On the crucial question of whether there would be any enemy on the Chesapeake to attack, the indications had veered favorably. Washington had half expected that his lookouts would report the appearance of most or all of Cornwallis's force in New York Harbor. But none had appeared, and then word came from Lafayette that the troops Cornwallis had embarked had not sailed off into the ocean but rather moved a short distance up the James River to Yorktown and Gloucester.* The transports returned to

---

* Cornwallis's original embarkation of a detachment had been a direct result of Washington's intercepted letter that had frightened Clinton for the safety of New York: Clinton had ordered Cornwallis to send him the men. But then communications from his

Portsmouth, probably to get the rest of the army. If, as Lafayette believed, Cornwallis intended to fortify the posts he was beginning to occupy, he was making himself into a sitting duck delightfully available for plucking. "York," Lafayette wrote, "is surrounded by the river and a morass. . . . Gloucester is a neck of land projected into the river and opposite to York." Both were vulnerable to amphibious attack: they could be surrounded on the land side while naval supremacy made impossible escape by water.[8]

To keep Cornwallis where he was, secrecy concerning allied intentions was, of course, of the essence. Washington could not, like a latter-day Poseidon, lift a gigantic hand from the sea and pull down any fast sailing vessel that might sight de Grasse's fleet and give alarm. However, he could try to fool the British in New York as to the objective of his own and Rochambeau's completely visible march.

Hoodwinking Clinton for a considerable period of time was made feasible by the fact that more than two-thirds of the march from King's Ferry to the Delaware was the same route the armies would traverse if they intended to meet de Grasse at Sandy Hook and then attack Staten Island. To encourage the enemy into a belief that this was what they intended, Washington dragged along landing craft suited to crossing the isthmus from New Jersey to Staten Island, and the French built ovens at Chatham, New Jersey, as if in preparation for a long stay. However, Washington had no way of knowing whether the British were actually being fooled. He longed for southern mails that would tell him Cornwallis had not budged.[9]

When he had been marching for eight days and was level with the bottom of Manhattan Island, he received in the twilight from his lookout on Sandy Hook a dispatch: "Sir: I am this minute informed that eighteen large ships of war appeared standing in from the southward. . . . Their colors was discovered British. . . . If it should prove to be Admiral Rodney, which at present appears most probable . . . I shall not send any further information."

Washington's information was that Admiral Thomas Graves, who had succeeded Arbuthnot in command of the New York squadron, had eleven ships of war. Eighteen plus eleven equals twenty-nine. De Grasse was supposed to be approaching with between twenty-five and twenty-nine. De Grasse's strength might well be inferior unless Barras succeeded in joining him, but how would Barras succeed when he had somehow to evade so overpowering a British armament?[10]

Further news swung the balance this way and that. The arriving fleet was not under the command of Rodney but his less celebrated subordinate

home government had frightened Clinton the other way: the ministry wished the Chesapeake to be used as a springboard for major military operations that might include the recapture of Philadelphia. Clinton ordered Cornwallis to keep all his men and fortify for future use a strong base on the perimeter of the bay. Cornwallis obeyed by advancing to the cooperating posts of Yorktown and Gloucester.[11]

Admiral Sir Samuel Hood. The boats showed no scars of battle, which meant they had not intercepted de Grasse. And the estimate of the combined British strength went down: it was now reported that Hood had brought fifteen ships and four frigates, while only seven of Graves's ships were ; eaworthy. It seemed that de Grasse—that is, if he arrived and with the numbers promised—would have superiority after all. However, the news in relation to Barras was most alarming. He had actually sailed, and now the combined British fleet took off into the same ocean. They were probably intending pursuit. If they overtook Barras, no reinforcement for de Grasse, no siege guns, no fifteen hundred barrels of salt meat![12]

Washington intended that as much of the advance of the two armies as possible be on boats along inland waterways. From Trenton they would sail down the Delaware to Christiania (near Wilmington), whence it was only a twelve-mile march to the northern tip of the Chesapeake at the Head of Elk. He looked forward to seeing, on his arrival at Trenton, a vast concourse of small vessels pulling at their anchors in the rapid current that would bear them southward. However, he found hardly more bottoms than would hold the heavy baggage. Rochambeau nobly offered to allow American troops to occupy what space was left; all the French would march, with the bulk of the American army, overland via Philadelphia to the Head of Elk.[13]

Washington had encouraged the Continental Army to believe that they were marching to attack Staten Island. When the troops found themselves on the banks of the Delaware and were then ordered to cross it, they realized that they were being carried far from home into a climate which most of them considered lethal. So great was the resulting unrest that Washington felt it essential to do everything in his power to reduce all further reason for discontent. Leaving the direct command of the army to Lincoln, he galloped to Philadelphia to importune governors and legislators and businessmen for food and clothing and equipment,* and also for boats that would allow the men to embark once they reached the Chesapeake. In particular, he bombarded Robert Morris, who had been appointed superintendent of finance, with pleas that he find specie with which to give the troops a month's pay in what they had not seen for years: hard money. Morris replied that he was rounding up what gold he could find, but he warned Washington to foresee disappointments.[14]

Washington's appearance in Philadelphia elicited shouts, acclamations, and amazement. Entertainments were improvised, but Washington was, although "all the foreign wines possible" were somehow made available, in no mood to drink toasts.[15]

Cornwallis was continuing to fortify Yorktown and Gloucester, seemingly

---

* The French had much less difficulty with supply, since they could pay in hard money.

unaware of his danger. However, he could not be kept in ignorance forever. Everything still hung in the balance. To Lafayette, Washington burst out, "I am distressed beyond expression to know what is become of the Count de Grasse and for fear the English fleet by occupying the Chesapeake (towards which my last accounts say they were steering) should frustrate all our flattering prospects in that quarter. I am also not a little solicitous for the Count de Barras, who was to have sailed from Rhode Island on the 23rd ulto. and from whom I have heard nothing since that time."[16]

Leaving the French generals behind in Philadelphia, Washington galloped ahead toward the Head of Elk down the very road he had traversed four years before in an effort to head off the British landing which had led to the loss of Philadelphia. By glancing over his shoulder, he could see the house where he had written his dispatch describing his defeat at Brandywine.[17] A defeat had then been a setback; but what would happen if, after all the effort of the expiring cause, de Grasse failed to appear or did not appear in time?

Eventually, Rochambeau and his staff started drifting down the Delaware in a small boat. It was September 5, 1782. They had "the prettiest trip imaginable. It would," they concluded, "be difficult to have a more beautiful view than that of Philadelphia as one leaves it by water." Military sightseeing carried them to the sites of the three forts—Mud Island, Red Bank, and Billingsport—which had blocked the river in 1777. By then they were fatigued, but "an old militia officer" who commanded at Billingsport gave them "some bread and butter and tea." Then "we continued to sail towards Chester."

On the waterfront at Chester they descried an amazing sight. A tall officer in blue and buff regimentals was jumping up and down, waving in one hand his hat and in the other a white handkerchief. Seen from the approaching boat, the dancing figure seemed to be His Excellency, General Washington, but, of course, that was impossible. The Frenchmen knew that Washington was (in the words of the Duc de Deux-Ponts) "of a natural coldness and of a serious and noble approach."

The boat came closer: the figure was indeed His Excellency, and he was not only jumping and waving but shouting. They heard the words "de Grasse." The admiral and his fleet, Washington yelled, were in the Chesapeake. "A child whose every wish had been gratified," ruled Deux-Ponts, could not have expressed "a sensation more lively. His features, his physiognomy, his deportment" had all changed. According to Lauzun, "I have never seen a man more overcome with great and sincere joy than was General Washington."

When the French boat ground to shore, "MM. Rochambeau and Washington," so Von Closen noted, "embraced *warmly.*" The staff officer, who had previously recorded a coldness between the two generals, was delighted by this sign that Washington had forgiven Rochambeau for forcing the campaign. Everyone, Von Closen added, "spoke of Cornwallis as if they had already captured him—but one must not count his chickens before they are hatched."[18]

De Grasse had brought with him twenty-eight ships of the line, four frigates, some fifteen thousand sailors, eighteen hundred marines, and three thousand troops.[19] Cornwallis had been completely caught by surprise:* he was still in Yorktown and Gloucester, and he seemed to have little chance of fleeing, since de Grasse had landed his troops to help Lafayette hold shut the trap.

However, problems remained. Barras was still unheard from and sailing the same sea-lanes with a much larger British fleet. A letter from de Grasse stated that he feared the time at his disposal would not enable him to give the help he would wish. He was, indeed, in such a hurry that he had impetuously resolved to attack Yorktown without waiting for Washington and Rochambeau. However, he had been dissuaded by Washington's French engineer, Duportail.[20]

A letter from Duportail stated that Cornwallis's fortifications were so strong that they could be forced only with the greatest difficulty. It might be better to starve the British out, but that would take time. How to proceed "requires a very great judgment." Duportail praised Lafayette's judgment, but added, "dear General, come with the greatest expedition."[21]

Speed was more than ever indicated; but when Washington reached the Head of Elk and surveyed the harbor, he saw only a slight prickling of masts where he had hoped a forest of spars would rise from the many boats required to move the combined armies down the Chesapeake.† He knew that the French navy could not help, since de Grasse's ships were too big to navigate the Chesapeake, while Barras, who had transports that could get up the bay at least to Baltimore, was somewhere unknown on the top or the bottom of the ocean.[22]

Washington dreaded the effect on the men of a second disappointment in shipping, a further march. In eloquent general orders, he announced the arrival of de Grasse—"at the same time [as] he felicitates them on this auspicious occasion, he anticipates the glorious events which may be expected"—and promised a month's pay to all except "any infamous charac-

---

* No word had come from the ocean of the approach of the fleet, since de Grasse had met no British shipping which he had been unable to capture. And the British command in New York, still convinced by Washington's intercepted letter that the attack was to be made on Staten Island, did not wake up to the allies' true destination until the armies were passing through Philadelphia. It was then September 2, much too late tò get effective word to Cornwallis.

† British raiders had destroyed almost all the shipping that normally plied the Chesapeake.

ters who may have been so far left to the sense of honor . . . as to desert the standard of freedom at this critically interesting period." He had rushed off to Morris another appeal for the necessary specie. Morris replied that his most deperate efforts had only raised $20,000. This was far short, but Rochambeau came to the rescue, giving Washington what Von Closen stated was a third of the 150,000 livres still in his war chest. For the first time in years, the trousers of the soldiery gave that agreeable tug on the waist that comes from hard money in the pocket.[23]

Having "beseeched" gentlemen of influence on the eastern shore of Maryland to "exert themselves in drawing forth every kind of vessel" that would float, Washington wrote de Grasse that in about two days he should have enough shipping at the Head of Elk to move some two thousand men. The rest of the combined armies would have to march to Baltimore in hope of finding shipping there. Washington galloped ahead, but not so fast that the news failed to precede him. Baltimore received him with "great joy," with "illuminations, addresses, etc." He spent as much time as he could talking shipping with any man who owned a boat.[24]

On September 9, Washington rode out of Baltimore early in pursuit of a dream which had haunted him now for seven years. Probably because of a shortage of fast horses, he left all his staff behind except two aides. He intended, while daylight lasted, to pelt through the countryside for all of sixty miles until he came to familiar gates, saw on a rise a wide white house flanked with pillared arcades, turned left with the road into a little wood every tree of which he could reconstruct from memory, and cantered up at last to the pedimented doorway of his heart's ease and his heart's delight, Mount Vernon.[25]

He found clustered to greet him not only familiar faces but four Lilliputian figures he had never seen. Two little girls curtsied gravely, a smaller one stared only half comprehending, and a male baby gurgled from a cradle or his mother's arms. Surely George was deeply moved by the stepgrandchildren who had been born during his long absence, these new lives that had budded in the gentle sunshine of home as he had fought his way through distant, desperate winter.

After (so we can assume) he had admired and re-admired the children singly and severally, he was finally allowed to ask Martha how she did. Then the parents took the babies away. The fireside became as he remembered it when Martha sat quietly beside him with her sewing, lifting her head sometimes to question him on matters no more grievous than the little business of the countryside.

Probably, before he finally gave way to sleep, the General walked down his central hall and out the far door to stand on the great porch that seemed so high above the world. The Potomac, flowing a mile wide beneath him, could be seen only as dark gleams around reflected stars. The sweep and undulation of the far hills were invisible. Yet, Washington's heart supplied all the details that the brightest daylight could reveal. Here was not the vanishing past or the onrushing future, not danger or striving, but permanence: what he had seen when first brought to this hilltop when a little child; what he hoped would be his last sight as the world faded. How often it had appeared to him that he would never stand again on his beloved earth. And victory, peace, retirement now seemed closer than a few days before he would have dared even to hope.

The next morning, Washington was hard at work arranging for the repair of the roads through Virginia which would probably have to be traversed, due to the continued shortage of shipping, by "the wagons of the French and American armies, the cavalry, and the cattle." Martha was all action preparing to receive the French generals and their suites. Rochambeau arrived that night; Chastellux the next morning. Washington's aide, Colonel Jonathan Trumbull, recorded, "A numerous family now present. All accommodated. An elegant seat and situation: great appearance of opulence and real exhibitions of hospitality and princely entertainment."[26]

Washington spent three nights at Mount Vernon. This gave plenty of time for his impeccably dressed stepson, John Parke Custis, to take him aside. Although much in control of his mother, Jacky was frightened of his stepfather. He surely had pinned on his face, under his soft cheeks and beady eyes, above his vanishing chin, an ingratiating smile.

The young man, who had so far shown no martial ardor whatsoever, now claimed to be infused with it. He burned to save his country by being in on a victory, by accompanying the delightful, highborn Frenchmen he had just met to Yorktown as volunteer aide to that stepfather he so tremendously admired. The General, who had no high opinion of his stepson,* could only

---

* Legend, which invests Washington with every conventionally correct emotion, depicts him as devoted to Jacky Custis. This seems to have been the case when Jacky was a child, but the opposite is indicated by all relevant documents during the Revolutionary years. Surely because Martha had so spoiled him, probably in reaction to the power of his stepfather, perhaps in response to a strangeness in the Custis blood, Jacky had turned into a man as sinister as he was weak. This is made most clear in an autobiographical letter by the oldest of Jacky's daughters written twenty-seven years after she had first curtsied to her stepgrandfather. Elizabeth Parke Custis had by then been married; had separated from her husband; had given a lover (as she put it) "proofs of regard which no other would have *dared* to give"; had been deserted by that lover; and was now writing him a long, pitiful letter that combined cringing with pride, and was basically an appeal that he would comprehend and not blame her strange, tortured nature. She tells how, when she was too young to comprehend their meaning, her father taught her many very improper songs. After his male guests were deep in their wine, he would stand the little girl on the dining room table, and get her to sing the lewd verses. "I was animated to exert myself," she remembered, "to give him delight. The servants in the passage would join their mirth, and I, holding my head erect, would strut about the table to receive the praises of the company. My mother remonstrated in vain." Jacky replied that he had been given no son, and "little Bet . . . must make fun for him until he had."[27]

hope that Martha would react with her usual panic when she visualized her chick running into danger. But, alas, Martha had already been won round: her sweet face glowed with pride that her son was nobly offering to help her husband. George had to comfort himself with the realization that Jacky's elegant manners made a favorable impression on strangers.

However, things were going too well for Washington to feel anything but cheerful as he left Mount Vernon for Williamsburg to supervise the impaling of Cornwallis. It was incredible, but it was true! The English general had waited as if spellbound by a pro-American wizard. The American and French armies were descending upon him without showing any real signs of falling apart. De Grasse was there, and the word was that his fleet was by itself stronger than the combined enemy fleets of Graves and Hood. It seemed almost blasphemy to worry about the remaining difficulties which seemed so secondary to the unforeseeable bounties Providence had showered on the American cause.

Then a rider approaching on the road; a dispatch handed to Washington; the news that de Grasse's fleet had disappeared. French lookouts having seen the sea-lanes to the Chesapeake whitening with British sails, de Grasse had hoisted his own sails and vanished into the ocean. De Grasse was gone. The dice which had fallen so incredibly right had been scooped up and were to be thrown again. Washington's aide Trumbull noted tersely: "Much agitated."[28]

48

War Reduced to Calculation

O N learning that de Grasse had vanished, Washington sent messengers
desperately backtracking to halt all marchers and urge all troop-
laden ships to seek inlets and shallows where they would be as safe
as possible if a British fleet came roaring into the vacuum left by the departure of the French. Then he posted for Williamsburg. As he entered the
town, a horseman galloped at him, reined in, spread out his arms, leaned
out, "and embraced him with an ardor not easily described." Lafayette was
reunited with his adopted father. However, there was no word of de Grasse.[1]

That night the Marquis de Saint Simon, who commanded the French
troops that had come from the Indies with de Grasse, staged a rich supper.
Everyone cheered Washington as "an elegant band of music" played a song
from a French opera (probably *Lucille*) "signifying the happiness of the
family when blessed with the presence of their father." The banquet broke
up "with mutual congratulations and expressions of joy": de Grasse was
back at his anchorage, having in what Washington called "a partial engagement" driven off the British fleet. And during the fracas, Barras had slipped
quietly into the bay, bringing not only siege guns and salt provisions, but
also transports small enough to ferry the allied armies down the Chesapeake.* [2]

In from de Grasse came a letter for Washington which addressed him as
if he were an incompetent subordinate. The admiral was "annoyed" at the

---

* Naval historians state that the British fleet, although numerically inferior, missed a
chance to chew up de Grasse's ships singly as they straggled out of the mouth of the
Chesapeake. Thus, the illness of Rodney, which kept the brilliant admiral (who surely
would have seized the opportunity) from coming to North America and allowed the
command to devolve on the incompetent Graves, may be considered another of the acts
of Providence that helped along the Yorktown campaign. Add that, although Barras had
been sailing parallel with Graves, the British never sighted the much smaller French
squadron.[3]

delay in the arrival of the troops from the northward: "The season is approaching when, against my will, I shall be obliged to forsake the allies for whom I have done my very best and more than could be expected."[4]

To Lincoln, who was up-bay with the army, Washington wrote, "Every day we lose now is comparatively an age. . . . Hurry on then, my dear General, with your troops upon the wing of speed." Barras was sending transports which could hold more than four thousand men.[5]

Washington and Rochambeau agreed to confer with de Grasse at his anchorage in Lynnhaven Bay, which was on the ocean side of the Chesapeake's huge mouth. They would have to sail some thirty miles down the James and another thirty across the bay in almost open water. For the trip, de Grasse supplied an elegantly appointed officer's launch which he had captured from the British. It would "bear you across as comfortably as it is possible to do in this kind of boats."[6]

With Rochambeau, Chastellux, Knox, Duportail, and all their staffs, Washington embarked on September 17 and early the next morning saw hulking against the horizon thirty-two ships of the line. "A grand sight," Trumbull reported. By noon, they were aboard the flagship *Ville de Paris,* which was said to be the largest warship in the world. They were, Trumbull continued, "received with great ceremony and military naval parade and most cordial welcome. The Admiral is a remarkable man for size, appearance, and plainness of address."[7]

According to legend, de Grasse, who was a little taller than Washington and much stouter, dashed up to His Excellency, embraced him heartily, and shouted, "*Mon cher petit général!*" Knox is supposed to have rocked his own fat stomach with laughter, but we may doubt that (if this really happened) Washington was amused. He represented the dignity of the United States, which had taken quite a beating from her ally in the last few months. His final appraisal of de Grasse was that he was a "gallant" officer marred by "impetuosity."* [8]

During the conference on strategy, Washington asked whether the fleet and its military contingent could stay long enough to permit a conventional siege rather than a *coup de main* (assault over largely unbroken walls): "The first may be slow, but sure; the second must be bloody and precarious." De Grasse answered that his instructions had fixed his departure for October 15, but he would stay till the end of that month. So far, so good: six weeks seemed to give plenty of time.

Next, Washington pointed out that as long as the British controlled the York River above their fortifications, they could gather in supplies, hinder American communications, and, indeed, make off into the hinterland of Virginia. Washington wished de Grasse to send some frigates into the upper

---

* Rochambeau agreed, writing Washington in 1788, "By the vivacity of his head, he did take always violent parts."[9]

river. Moving fast with a favorable wind and tide, they should run the gauntlet of the British fortifications. Too dangerous, said de Grasse. Washington's statement that it had been his experience that it was almost impossible for shore batteries to stop rapidly moving boats only made the French professionals smile at the incompetence of American artillery.

Washington failed to persuade de Grasse that the fleet could, if Yorktown were quickly taken, help in attacks on the British garrisons at Wilmington, North Carolina, or Charleston. However, the admiral agreed to lend cannon, powder, and eighteen hundred to two thousand sailors should, despite everything, it become necessary to attempt against Yorktown a *coup de main*.[10]

Once the conference was over, Washington wanted to get back as quickly as possible to Williamsburg so that he could speed the troops that must now be approaching by foot or horse or boat. However, what seemed like all the officers in the French fleet insisted on climbing down the side of the *Ville de Paris* and crowding Washington's launch to say farewell. Finally, the Frenchmen climbed up again, and Washington set sail into the sunset.

Behind him as the small boat advanced slowly, the waning light reddened an amazing spectacle: on every possible perch in the more than a hundred towering square-rigged masts sailors balanced, holding upright on their shoulders muskets which they successively discharged in that running fire known as a *feu de joie*. Below them pink clouds exploded from the vessels' sides as cannon fired.

Washington had always consistently avoided water travel. This visit to de Grasse comprised the first considerable trip over open water he had made since he had accompanied, when in his teens, his dying brother to the tropical Indies. Now the weather gods made everything as unpleasant for the landlubber as possible. For three frustrated, unhappy, sometimes drenched days, his launch was becalmed, aground, beating vainly into a headwind, or cowering from storm anchored under a protecting shore.[11]

When Washington finally got back to Williamsburg about noon on the 22nd, he found that almost all his troops had come in, as well as the first division of the French. The fears he had for more than a year expressed of great losses—a third to half his men—during a march to the south through sickness and desertion had, despite some minor diminution, proved blessedly unfounded.[12] His spirits now bounced so high that he was unperturbed by a report that the British fleet had, after its return to New York Harbor, received a reinforcement variously estimated at three to ten ships of the line.

Confident that de Grasse remained superior, Washington wrote happily, "Everything has hitherto succeeded to our wishes. Nothing could have been more fortunate than the cooperation of the several parts of this great expedition in point of time. . . . The debarkation and movement of the heavy artillery and stores will necessarily occasion some delay, but in a very few days, I hope, the enemy at York will be completely invested. . . . The prospects . . . are as favorable as could possibly have been expected."[13]

Then he heard from de Grasse. The admiral was not taking the British naval reinforcement calmly. He found it "most distressing. . . . Our position," he insisted, "is changed." He intended "to hoist sail and hold out in the offing, so that . . . I can engage them in a less disadvantageous position. But it could happen that the course of the battle may drive us to leeward and put it beyond our power to return." Therefore, he would have to take away with him the troops he had brought. "In this case," he asked Washington, "what would you do?"

On the other hand, so the admiral continued, perhaps he could leave his troops behind and sail for New York to blockade the British there. In any case, "I shall set sail as soon as the weather permits me." He would pause in the middle of the bay to hear from Washington.[14]

With "painful anxiety," Washington replied that if the fleet stayed, victory was certain, but if the fleet withdrew, disaster would ensue. He continued cajolingly but ungrammatically, "The confidence with which I feel myself inspired by the energy of character and the naval talents which so eminently distinguish your Excellency leaves me no doubt that, upon a consideration of the consequences which must follow your departure from the Chesapeake, that your Excellency will determine upon the possible measure which the dearest interests of the common cause would dictate."[15]

De Grasse, having calmed down, changed his mercurial mind. In notifying Washington that he would stay after all, he stated testily, "Your Excellency may be very sure that I have, so to speak, more at heart than yourself that the expedition to York may terminate agreeably to our desires."[16]

On September 28, 1781, Washington and Rochambeau advanced their armies through the some fifteen miles from Williamsburg to the outskirts of Yorktown. Had he been Cornwallis, Washington would have sent out harassing parties of light troops. However, "the enemy gave us no annoyance on the march."[17]

Washington moved across "a beautiful, fertile country," but the fields were uncultivated. Fences lay prostrate; grass was high in the roads and overloaded the dooryards. Washington passed houses where he had often been entertained, but there were no friendly voices. Windows were shattered, doors flapping wide. Washington's homeland festered under the pall of war.

When the British fortifications became visible, Washington saw a body of horse parading in front of them. The French and American field artillery unleashed a few shots, at which the cavalry wheeled and disappeared into the enemy works.[18]

That night, Washington slept under "the small spreading branches of a tree." The next morning, he joined Rochambeau for a reconnoiter. They could not get close to the town, for in front of it stretched a sandy plain— "a rise of five yards," wrote a New England soldier, "is called a hill"—from which all vegetation had been cut. This desert was so swept by English cannon that it would have been suicide to step there. Glasses showed that a marshy ravine cut through the northern half of the plain in a wide arc and then disgorged into the York River above the town. There, and in other places where geography offered encouragement, the enemy had built small redoubts which would have to be possessed before the allies could make any other move.[19]

The main works loomed farther back, a zigzagging of scientifically designed walls, sometimes one and sometimes two tiers deep, that curved and opened out into redoubts in such a manner that stormers approaching any part could be fired at from the side as well as from above. The walls were pierced with numerous embrasures from which peeped the mouths of cannon.

Behind these works, Washington knew, was a town of one main street and four cross streets. Its back overhung the river on a high bluff beneath which (invisible to Washington and protected from his guns) huddled Cornwallis's shipping. At this spot the river, that was normally two miles wide, was reduced to half a mile by a spade-shaped peninsula which protruded from the opposite shore. On the point of the spade was the village of Gloucester, which the British had fortified and had garrisoned with a medium-size detachment of horse and foot. This secondary post was being watched by a mixed American and French detachment under French command.

Washington calculated that Cornwallis had in all five to six thousand men. These were opposed not only by de Grasse's majestic fleet (which was out of sight except for a few frigates that hovered where the James joined the Chesapeake), but by ninety-five hundred American effectives and eighty-eight hundred Frenchmen under Rochambeau and Saint Simon. However, the outnumbered British had their walls.[20]

When Washington had faced scientifically built fortifications in Boston, he had known no way to overcome them except by *coup de main*. Rochambeau, however, was said to have been present at fourteen sieges, and the French engineers, both those in their own and those in the American service, were well trained in such matters. They assured Washington that, considering the "decisive superiority of strength and means," the conquest of Cornwallis "is, in fact, reducible to calculation."[21]

Washington did not doubt that this was the case provided that Cornwallis

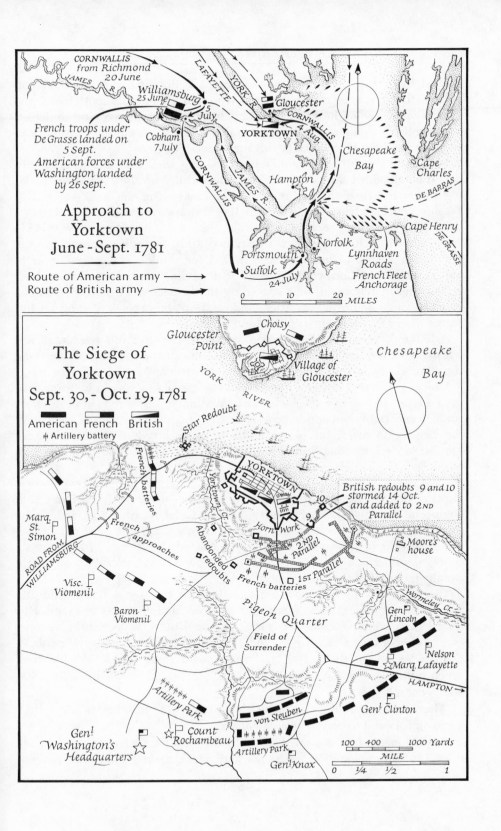

Approach to Yorktown June-Sept. 1781

CORNWALLIS from Richmond 20 June

JAMES R.

Williamsburg 25 June

LAFAYETTE

YORK R.

Gloucester

CORNWALLIS 4 Aug.

YORKTOWN

5 July

Cobham 7 July

French troops under De Grasse landed on 5 Sept. American forces under Washington landed by 26 Sept.

CORNWALLIS

JAMES R.

Hampton

Chesapeake Bay

Cape Charles

DE BARRAS

Portsmouth

Suffolk

24 July

Norfolk

Lynnhaven Roads French Fleet Anchorage

Cape Henry

DE GRASSE

Route of American army ——→
Route of British army ——➤

0   10   20   MILES

The Siege of Yorktown Sept. 30,- Oct. 19, 1781

American French British
⚓ Artillery battery

Choisy

Gloucester Point

Village of Gloucester

YORK RIVER

Chesapeake Bay

Star Redoubt

French batteries

YORKTOWN

British redoubts 9 and 10 stormed 14 Oct. and added to 2ND Parallel

10

9

Horn Work

Moore's house

Marq. St. Simon

French approaches

Abandoned redoubts

2ND Parallel

1ST Parallel

ROAD FROM WILLIAMSBURG

French batteries

Wormeley Cr.

Visc. Viomenil

Pigeon Quarter

Genl Lincoln

Baron Viomenil

Field of Surrender

Marq. Lafayette

Nelson

HAMPTON →

Artillery Park

von Steuben

Genl Clinton

Genl Washington's Headquarters

Count Rochambeau

Artillery Park

Genl Knox

100   400   1000 Yards

MILE

0   ¼   ½   1

obeyed the rules. He himself would not have done so, and he could not believe that the able British general, who had exhibited almost foolhardy aggressiveness when he had burned his baggage and chased Greene across the Carolinas, would not make some violent move to smash the conventional sequence at the end of which lay his surrender.

Surely on a dark night, "embracing a leading wind and tide," Cornwallis would overload his shipping with his army and flee up the York, disembarking where the river divided into the Plamunkey (on the banks of which Washington had been married) and the Mattapony. Having one of these tributaries guarding each of his flanks, he could, Washington reasoned, "push his way with a compact, disciplined army through a country whose population is too scattered to be collected for sudden opposition." Was it not ominous that Cornwallis, instead of defending his outer redoubts, had pulled their garrisons in, thus conceding the first move in the conventional game of siege before it was attempted, and, in the process, getting all his forces where they were invisible behind his walls?[22]

Again and again, Washington implored de Grasse to risk a passage of his frigates past the fortifications so that they could block the York. Sometimes the admiral temporized, but he never gave the order.[23]

Unless the British suddenly reshuffled the cards, this was to be war at its most static and its most mechanical. Washington secured from French sources and published in his general orders "Regulations for the service of the siege." However, this screed, which ran to fifty-five numbered paragraphs, proved too complicated for the Americans and was never referred to again.[24]

Each day's labors were worked out in an early morning conference attended by Washington, Rochambeau, and the heads of the artillery and engineers. Although titularly Commander in Chief, Washington could only listen and agree. As Rochambeau put it condescendingly, "I must render the Americans the justice to say that they conducted themselves with that zeal, courage, and emulation, with which they were never backward," although "totally ignorant of the operations of a siege."[25]

The allies had the first move since at the start the enemy had nothing to fire at—that is, unless some ignoramus allowed himself to get in range. His Excellency, reconnoitering too close to the British walls, did give one enemy gunner target practice. As the ball buried itself in the nearby earth, it sprinkled sand on the hat of a chaplain who stood beside Washington. Much agitated, the Rev. Mr. Evans took off the hat and exclaimed, "See here, general!"

"Mr. Evans," Washington replied solemnly, "you had better carry that home and show it to your wife and children."[26]

The engineers laid out on their maps the first parallels: trenches which started outside enemy cannon range and which came into distant range—

not closer than half a mile—at angles designed to protect the occupants from cannon fire. One trench arced gingerly around the western bastions, while the other aimed obliquely at a star-shaped redoubt. Work on the trenches was undertaken on a dark, rainy night. It proceeded to much barking of British watchdogs and confused firing of British cannon.

The morning dawned clear. To music and with flags flying, American and French troops entered the trenches at the safe end and disappeared below the ground. Surely they were soon jostled by Washington, who could now train his telescope, from closer than he ever had before, on various parts of the British fortifications.[27]

The next step was for diggers to expand the entrenchments at pre-arranged spots into little malls. Then, again at night, there was a mole-like advance of cannon towed by crews of crouching men. Engineers fixed the guns in the malls, and then the schedule called for the first artillery duel.

It was three in the afternoon on October 9, and a pair of French batteries—four sixteen-pounders and six mortars and howitzers—were ready to open. After the artillerymen had aimed their guns, Washington stepped up. His was to be the honor of releasing the first discharge. He did so and stared with delighted amazement to see the fast-traveling black cannonball strike the enemy fortifications exactly where the French artillery commander had said it would.[28]

Three hours later, some American batteries opened fire. The contrast was humiliating. While the French fired with accuracy and "great elegance," the American balls landed at haphazard and the shells often failed to explode. Commissary Blanchard explained that the French cannon were new and the ammunition perfectly suited to their caliber. Furthermore, "the perfection of our gunners . . . were the admiration of General Washington."[29]

On the 10th, both the French and the Americans opened more batteries. Holes appeared in the British walls and one after another the enemy cannon were silenced. "I have more than once," wrote surgeon Thacher, "witnessed fragments of mangled bodies and limbs of British soldiers thrown into the air by the bursting of our shells."[30]

Toward nightfall, the French gunners achieved an angle which enabled them to hit Cornwallis's shipping in the river. Red-hot balls set the vessels on fire. In the thickening darkness, flames roared over dry wood, climbed the tall masts. The half-ruined city appeared as a shaggy silhouette against throbbing, apocalyptic light. Cannon-thunder was incessant, and shells, appearing like fiery meteors, dragged blazing tails across the sky as they majestically rose and then dropped, it seemed gradually, on their bleeding prey.[31]

After this, the British cannon fire greatly slackened. The time was thus ripe for a second parallel which was to approach within a thousand feet of the enemy works. It was dug at night. When daylight revealed the trench, enemy reaction was feeble. The next night, cannon were moved forward to the new position. Washington could not sleep. He found the enemy's passivity "beyond conception. . . . I shall think it strange, indeed, if Lord Cornwallis makes no vigorous exertions in the course of this night, or very soon after."[32]

The second parallel was blocked from going all the way to the river, whence cannon fire could enfilade the British rear, by two strong redoubts on the enemy right. After these had been softened up by artillery fire, they would have to be taken by storm. One was assigned to the French, one to the Americans. In setting up the detachment to carry out his part of the violent assignment, Washington demonstrated that Hamilton's rudeness in breaking with him had not made him forget that the brilliant young man was owed a debt of gratitude for his long, valuable service on the headquarters staff. Washington entrusted Hamilton with the command of the American party of four hundred men.[33]

Visiting the detachment toward nightfall, Washington addressed the soldiers on the importance of being firm and brave. "I thought then," wrote a young officer, "that His Excellency's knees rather shook, but I have since doubted whether it was not mine."

Darkness sank over the battlefield. The signal for the coordinated attacks on the two redoubts was to be six French cannon shots in a peculiar rhythm. As Washington waited on a tiny rise that overlooked the scene of action, an aide pulled on his sleeve. "Sir, you are too much exposed here. Had you not better step a little back?"

His Excellency, who was always bothered thus when he wished to share in the excitement of a battle, answered grumpily: "Colonel Cobb, if you are afraid, you have liberty to step back."[34]

As had been true in every aspect of this siege, the outcome of the attacks had been established before the action started. Although the redoubts were too damaged to hold out for long, the attackers would have to surmount obstacles under enemy fire and then plunge bayonets into flesh. Thus the assaults would, before the inevitable result was achieved, drop to the ground a considerable number of dead and mangled men.

So it happened. The silent darkness into which Washington stared was suddenly broken with shots and tattooed with musket flashes. Then the shooting frayed away and there emerged the incoherent sounds of struggling men and cries of human agony. After fifteen minutes there were cheers: the American action was over. The French action, which was eliciting similar phenomena in another part of the field, lasted a few minutes longer.

Washington could not see what then occurred in the dark, but he knew that, as the wounded were being carried back, engineers and work parties with spades and prefabricated obstructions were dashing from the end of the second parallel across the little strips of no man's land to the captured redoubts. Their task was to fortify instantly the sides which, since they faced the British fortifications, had been left open. Now was the time for the few British guns still active to interfere, but most strangely they had not been prepared. Since they could not be adequately lowered, the shells sailed over the fortifiers' heads. However, another group of diggers, who were passionately extending the second parallel to include the captured redoubts, were hit with moderately heavy losses.* [35]

After the trenches had reached the captured redoubts, two howitzers were placed in each. These cannon were, as Rochambeau wrote, "able to pour in ricochet projectiles [balls that bounded along the surface of the earth destroying everything in a straight line] to the body of the place, which was within such a limited range that the effect must have been tremendous."[36]

That night, Washington was awakened at about 4 A.M. by some cries and a fusillade. The British had at last made a sortie: there was hand-to-hand fighting in the center of the second parallel. But before Washington was well in his saddle,.the noise ceased. Cornwallis had undertaken no more than the minimum gesture required by the honor of his army: he had sent out some three hundred and fifty picked troops who had killed a few Frenchmen and superficially damaged six guns before they rushed back into their own lines.[37]

Cornwallis, so stragglers from the doomed city reported, had "built a kind of grotto . . . where he lives underground." He seems to have lurked there in a stupor of despair and rage, his principal activity being to curse Clinton, who had ordered him to garrison a weak position and had then led him, when he was endangered, to count on being extricated by a British fleet. He was later to explain, in defending his actions, that his expectation of naval relief had made him eschew, in favor of concentrating his force behind his highest walls to await rescue, any such "desperate attempts" as harassing the allied advance, trying to hold the outer redoubts, or making, either before or after the allies had invested the town, any effort to break free for a long, hazardous overland retreat.[38]

However, as the allies opened more and more guns ever closer to his walls; as the whole riverbank shook under their fire, while his own fire dwindled to almost nothing; as, when he emerged from his grotto, he saw the toppling ruins that were his ramparts come every minute more apart; as more and more wounded and dying crawled or lay prone in the streets around him; Cornwallis reached a melancholy resolve. He sent off in code a

---

* Washington gave the total American casualties in the siege so far as 88, the French as 186.[39]

dispatch to Clinton telling him not to come: it would be too late. And then, like a stricken animal, he gave a convulsive jerk.[40]

Sixteen large, oared boats had been preserved from enemy cannon fire. They would not serve to carry his army to the hinterland up the York, but, if several trips were made, they could get his men across the river to Glouces-ter. It would be a midnight adventure. That almost none of his horses had survived the siege—for days the tidal river had been swirling with their shrunken or broken bodies—would make a successful getaway doubly difficult unless he could find new animals. However, now that despair had set fire to his torpor, the wildest schemes seemed feasible. He would so overwhelm Lauzun's cavalry, who were encamped outside Gloucester, that the men would disappear and the horses remain. He would lay the country-side under contribution for more horses, and fight his way to safety, living off the land.[41]

Washington slept as the first British division was ferried across the York. Then he may have been awakened by the sound of storm. "It was," wrote one of his soldiers, "almost as severe a storm" as he had ever experienced. The god of the weather, who had so often interfered in the affairs of this war, had interfered again. The storm passed, and, under a pink dawn that glinted on what foliage had escaped the destruction of warfare, messengers galloped to Washington's tent: British boats were on the river. Cornwallis had evidently tried to ferry his troops to Gloucester and been interrupted by the weather. He was now bringing back those soldiers who had got across.[42]

Washington had just sat down to his morning's correspondence, when in came another messenger, this one very excited. He carried a letter which had come out of Yorktown under a flag of truce. Having read it through, Washington told his aides that it had come "at an earlier period than my most sanguine hopes had induced me to expect." The letter read:

"Sir, I propose a cessation of hostilities for twenty-four hours, and that two officers may be appointed by each side to meet at Mr. Moore's house to settle terms for the surrender of the posts of York and Gloucester.

"I have the honor to be, etc.,
Cornwallis"[43]

49

The World Turned Upside Down

ORNWALLIS'S letter asked for a twenty-four-hour truce in which to discuss terms. His objective could be, Washington realized, a long-drawn-out negotiation during which, unharmed, he awaited succor from New York. Washington demanded "your Lordship's proposals" during a two-hour cease-fire. Cornwallis rushed proposals which indicated "there would be no great difficulty in fixing the terms. Accordingly," Washington noted, "hostilities were suspended for the night."[1]

In contrast with the previous pounding and shrieking, the "solemn stillness" of that night inspired awe. When Washington stepped out of his tent, he stood under ten thousand of stars at their brightest. High up, he saw bursts of celestial artillery, "numberless meteors" traveling like silent bombs through the hushed, translucent heavens.

Dawn was ushered in by wild music: the bagpipes of a Scots regiment wailed from the shattered British walls. Soon sophisticated notes replied from the French encampment: tunes reminiscent of Paris music halls, of gilded cupids at Versailles.

The rising sun revealed that the shell-pocked sandy plain, where for so long no man could stand and live, was now crowded with human beings, civilians and soldiers, who stared from a distance of a few hundred yards at the half-fallen British parapets. Wherever the shattered masonry offered footing, troops and civilians stared back. The houses visible beyond the walls were no longer rectangular—corners were missing; roofs gaped and sagged. Beyond, on the beach, hundreds of people moved to and fro. In the shallows of the York, charred hulks wallowed at crazy angles, while from the deep channel protruded masts, yards, topgallants: a withered aquatic glade.[2]

In his grotto, Cornwallis received a letter from Washington outlining surrender terms. One sentence filled his heart with dismay. To foreseeable propositions, Washington had added: "The same honors will be granted to the surrendering army as were granted to the garrison of Charleston."

When General Lincoln had been forced to surrender at Charleston, Clinton had expressed his disdain for the rebels by refusing to grant the "honors of war" traditionally accorded a defeated army which had fought well. If Washington were to insist on retaliation, the British could not march out of Yorktown with their colors flying—the colors would have to be "cased" as Lincoln's had been. And the garrison, as they advanced to the surrender ceremony, would be further disgraced by being forbidden to pay the victors the compliment of playing a French or an American march. They would be shamefully restricted to march natural to their own army, either English or German. Thus to apply to the professionals in Yorktown what Clinton had thought suitable for American amateurs and barbarians, would disgrace Cornwallis and his officers before all civilized Europe. The British command could only hope that their French opponents would not permit this to happen. Surely, as true soldiers and European gentlemen, the French would realize that equating Cornwallis's sophisticated force with Lincoln's rabble was bizarre.[3]

To reach final terms, two commissioners from each side met during the early afternoon in the Moore house, a half-mile downriver from Yorktown. The allied representatives were Lafayette's brother-in-law, Viscount de Noailles, and John Laurens, who had been part of Lincoln's army that had been refused the honors of war.

All issues except this one of honors were capable of compromise. After (as had been expected) Washington refused to consider allowing the troops to return to Europe, the British agreed that they be ordinary prisoners of war. Recaptured slaves would be returned to their owners.* The Tories who were with the British presented a knottier problem: they needed protection from enraged patriots, but Washington could not give it to them directly, as they were subject not to military but to civil authority. However, the British had found a stratagem which the allied representatives eagerly embraced. Cornwallis should be allowed to send a sloop to New York with dispatches. The British would return the sloop to the captors and credit the crew and accompanying military personnel to the American account in future prisoner exchanges. That the boat was to sail "without examination" and there was no restriction on its use by civilians, was an escape hatch for Tories. That the soldiers that went along would be returned mathematically but not bodily, would enable the British to spirit away deserters from the American army who would, if captured in the British service, have to be hanged.[4]

On the matter of honors, Cornwallis's representatives pointed out that their general had not been responsible for the terms forced on Lincoln.

* Washington regained two house servants who had decamped from Mount Vernon: Lucy, about twenty years old, and Esther, about eighteen.[5]

Laurens replied that it was not individuals who were concerned, but nations. If Noailles secretly sympathized with the anguish of the aristocratic professionals, he nonetheless backed his ally. The debate was so heated that unless Washington instructed Laurens to give in, there was no hope of concluuding the surrender by night.[6]

In the meanwhile, great pressure was put on to get the surrender quickly consummated. Word came in "of immense preparations which were making in New York for the succor of Earl Cornwallis, and that the fleet consisting of twenty-eight or twenty-nine line ships with many frigates, fireships, and transports, having on board Sir Henry Clinton with 5000 rank and file, would sail for the Chesapeake about the 18th instant."[7]

This was the 18th. Although the fastest possible voyage would take several days, the fleet might have set out sooner than Washington's spies expected. Furthermore, Cornwallis might learn of the intended succor and, breaking off the negotiations, hold out until it came.

It was a sad fact that de Grasse had also been notified. To him, Washington wrote soothingly, "I beg leave to assure your Excellency that I have not the least disquiet on the subject, knowing by experience how doubtful such relations generally are. It appears to me above all improbable that an expedition in the Jerseys should be undertaken concomitantly with the pretended one against your Excellency's fleet."[8] However, this must have sounded lame even to Washington. He had no way of making certain that the impetuous admiral would not decide that the safety of his fleet required him to pick up his men and take off into the ocean.

Although the line of caution was to get the surrender instantly signed, Washington felt so strong a need to avenge dishonor that he allowed the stalemated conference to run on until almost midnight, which forced another night of truce.

The next morning, the final terms were agreed on. The matter of honors was slightly compromised by the agreement that since Gloucester was still intact (it had been watched but not besieged), the cavalry there could come out with their swords drawn and to the sound of trumpets. This so little comforted Cornwallis that, although he signed the paper which refused his main army "the usual honors," he could not bear the idea of being himself present at "the humiliating scene." Obeying emotions which his admirer Light Horse Harry Lee considered "his great character ought to have stifled," the British commander decided to pretend that he was ill.[9]

The surrender ceremony was set for two in the afternoon of September 19, 1781. It was a clear autumn day with an exhilarating nip of chill; the trees had hardly started to turn brown. On both sides of a main road out of Yorktown, the allies drew up their armies, each two ranks deep: the

Americans on the right side, the French on the left. The narrow passage between the files was a half-mile long. At the far end, the general officers waited on horseback: Washington and Rochambeau, Chastellux and Lincoln, and many another. De Grasse had stayed with his fleet: the navy was represented by Barras. The sea dog rocked uneasily on a borrowed horse.*

For a while, the bands played: the French "magnificently," the Americans "moderately well." Then a nervous silence sank over the conquering armies. Finally, from a distance, approaching music could be heard. The tune was slow, melancholy: Washington recognized "The World Turned Upside Down."[10]

When the head of the enemy column came in view—officers with swords drawn and the men with shouldered muskets—it glowed in splendor. Behind Yorktown's shattered walls, the chests that contained dress uniforms had been preserved undamaged. The troops had polished and polished, the officers had inspected and inspected, and now the British and Hessians glittered as they moved with the slowness of a death march.

To the enemy right, the French were resplendent in their white uniforms bordered with bright colors, their plumed hats, their black gaiters, the officers bedizened with stars and jeweled badges. But to the left of the British and Hessians was an armed rabble. The Continentals in the front rank wore, at their most consistent, ragged, smock-like hunting jackets of rough white cloth. Theirs was a mean and impoverished look, but they were richly clad compared to the militia who stood behind them in the worn-out work clothes of woodsmen and laborers, many almost barefoot.

The difference between the panoply of two Old World armies and the strangeness of the New was forcibly obvious. The French officers were vaguely perturbed, although none could foresee that the forces being unleashed this day, moving with wilder fury in their own land, would bring many a neck that turned there in its lace collar to the guillotine.[11]

As the Britons and Hessians moved between the contrasting lines, the band still playing its melancholy air, the officers ordered their men to turn their heads to the right, acknowledging their French conquerers, ignoring the American. Lafayette, who had stationed himself proudly beside his tattered division, shouted an order. A fife and drum corps broke into the puckish irreverence of the tune the French called "Janckey-Dudle." The British were startled into looking at the men who were to reap the true advantage from the victory.[12]

As the head of the surrendering column approached closer, Washington stared with puzzlement at the enemy commander. The American could have little idea of what Cornwallis looked like, but surely the Earl was not young and Irish of feature, did not look so much like a buck from the gambling

---

* Of Barras, Von Closen wrote, "It is true that during this ceremony, when his horse stretched to vent himself, he cried, 'Good heavens! I believe my horse is sinking!' "[13]

The Surrender of Cornwallis at Yorktown, sketch by John Trumbull. Courtesy of the Detroit Institute of Arts.

halls. The man, indeed, bore the insignia of only a brigadier general. Coming to the end of the long troop-lined passage, the British leader turned his horse toward the French general officers, rode up, and asked which one was Rochambeau.

Divining the brigadier's intention of offering his sword to the French commander, Dumas, interposed. "You are mistaken. The Commander in Chief of our army is on the right."

The British officer was forced to turn and ride over to Washington. He explained that Earl Cornwallis was indisposed: he was Brigadier General Charles O'Hara. He offered Washington his sword.

Washington refused it. Since the British had chosen to send a subordinate, one of Washington's subordinates would accept the surrender and give orders to the surrendered army. Washington indicated General Lincoln (whose capture at Charleston was being avenged). With the nonchalance of an aristocratic gambler whose chips have been gathered up from the board, O'Hara went through the ceremony with Lincoln.[14]

Lincoln's orders to the surrendered army were that the men should march to a nearby field where they should put down their arms. The field proved to be surrounded with French Hussars, who of all the allied troops most resembled ancient European chivalry. But they were too few to block out the wide view of a wild new world. A wave of anger, of grief, of despair swept over the surrendering troops. Until Lincoln intervened, the men tried to throw down their muskets in such a way as to break them. Tears streamed down the faces of the officers; some bit in anguish the tips of their swords.

Now, shorn of their arms, the enemy troops marched back between the allied columns. The Americans, who had before watched quietly, had by now digested the scorn with which they had been treated. Their officers could not prevent the men from hooting at their fallen adversaries. Hearing the strange, unmilitary noise, the British officers were afraid that, in their defenseless state, they would be attacked, despite all civilized agreements, by these undisciplined ragamuffins. They looked at the French officers with eyes that pleaded for protection, and saw in the Gallic faces brotherly looks of concern.[15]

Washington gave a dinner that night for the general officers of the three armies. Since Cornwallis still claimed sickness, O'Hara led the English group. He affected so much upper-class unconcern that the watching French were touched. They were "profuse" in offering their fellow Europeans "sympathy." According to Commissary Blanchard, the American officers were annoyed to the point of a quarrel by the "civility" their allies showed the enemy and the "attention" the enemy showed the French.[16]

And so, not without misgivings on the part of the European co-conquerors, the curtain fell on the greatest defeat which the European aristocratic way of life had so far ever suffered.

IX

The Nation's Most
Dangerous Hour

50

But the War Goes On

I N all his public statements concerning the victory at Yorktown, Washington praised lavishly the role of the French army and the French
fleet. However, he adhered firmly to his official rank as Commander
in Chief, thanking Rochambeau for "very cheerful and able assistance."[1]

If Washington had admitted that the strategy had been forced upon him
by the French, he would have exploded the still useful fictions of his top
command and a complete harmony between the allies. He would have had,
furthermore, to justify his opposition by stating the reasons why he had
gone along reluctantly. Although he urged on his troops the "gratitude of
heart which the recognition of such reiterated and astonishing interpositions
of Providence demand of us," he engaged in no public strictures on a
strategy that needed for success such "reiterated and astonishing" supernatural aid.* [2]

In accepting the principal credit for a campaign of which he had disapproved, Washington may well have reasoned that he had been forced by
the pretense that he possessed the top command to take the responsibility
for the desperate gamble. Had it ended in disaster, he could under no
circumstances have publicly accused the French. Surely, then, he had an
equivalent right to credit when the gamble succeeded. And in the back of
his mind there may well have glowed the conviction that Providence had
come to the rescue because of the nobility of the American cause, which
made Yorktown, after all, in essence an American triumph. Furthermore,
Washington saw no reason to step blushing into the shade when his own
plans for de Grasse, had they not been sidetracked, could have resulted in
an equal or possibly an even greater victory.

For their part, the French were proud of the campaign, from planning to

---

* He eventually in 1788 admitted that the French had conceived the Yorktown
campaign, but never publicly stated that he had gone along unwillingly.[3]

triumph, and felt they deserved full credit for it. Being ever statesmanlike, Rochambeau showed no public annoyance as Washington received the principal praise. However, he made an eventual effort to get what he considered his own back in the *Memoirs* he wrote after his return to France and ordered to be published after his death. He painted Washington as an indiscreet military primitive, so obsessed with attacking New York that he could see no other alternative.[4]

The size of the victory grew when the allies entered the captured city and counted up their bag. Instead of being 5000 to 6000, the prisoner count came to 7241 soldiers plus 840 seamen. There were also eighteen German and six British regimental standards, 244 pieces of artillery, and thousands of small arms. However, Washington scouted as very dangerous the conclusion then drawn by many of his contemporaries (and subsequently by most historians) that the war was as good as won.[5]

Although the British had lost about a quarter of their North American army, they still had on American soil—in Canada; Halifax; Penobscot, Maine; New York; Wilmington, North Carolina; and Charleston—forces several times as large as Washington's.[6] There was nothing to keep the ministry from sending in more troops. And, at the very moment of surrender, the great armada which was supposed to have sailed from New York to save Yorktown was probably on the ocean. It could be expected any day off the capes. De Grasse was sniffing the southerly breezes and intended, even if no sea battle developed, to return to the Indies, leaving the British again in control of North American waters.

Washington's plans were now aimed at South Carolina, where Greene had been so successful that the occupying British force, some thirty-three hundred men, were confined to Charleston, a post, like Yorktown, open to combined land and sea siege. "Fortune," Washington had written Greene, "must have been coy indeed had she not yielded at last to so persevering a pursuer as you have been. I hope now she is yours, she will change her appellation of fickle to that of constant." He gave an officer he was dispatching to Greene a message to memorize and then destroy: If he could persuade de Grasse to carry troops to South Carolina, "personal regard" for Greene as well as "principles of generosity and justice" would prevent him from going along and thus automatically taking the command, and with it the laurels of victory, away from his subordinate who had deserved both. However, Washington added the proviso that if Rochambeau went, he could not stay away, since only his presence could keep the Frenchman from commanding the Americans.[7]

Although de Grasse had never given Washington the least hope that he would find time for another siege, Washington continued his efforts to sell an attack on Charleston: "A campaign so glorious and so fertile in consequences could be reserved only for the Count de Grasse!" The admiral replied that the best he could do was to ferry and drop off two thousand men at Wilmington to wipe out the small British garrison there. However, while the French fleet was still preparing to sail, the British amphibious force which had been dispatched to save Cornwallis appeared in the offing. The wind being against him, de Grasse decided to sit this one out at his anchorage, and the British, finding that Yorktown had already fallen, turned round and returned to New York.[8]

De Grasse then stated that his timetable had been delayed to a point where he would have to forget about Wilmington and sail directly for the Indies. Washington, as he himself put it, employed "every argument and persuasive," but was in the end forced to "submit." De Grasse with his flotilla and his military detachments vanished from the North American scene.[9]

Washington could not help mourning that the great conjunction of allied force, which might well never happen again, had not somehow resulted in the capture of New York. That would have ended the war. As for Cornwallis's surrender, it was, he wrote, "an interesting event that may be productive of much good if properly improved, but if it should be the means of relaxation and sink us into supineness and [false] security, it had better not have happened."[10]

51

Vacation Without Rest

D E GRASSE'S departure closed the 1781 campaign. Rochambeau, "from the exhausted state of his stores and other considerations," decided that his army would winter in Virginia. Washington ordered the Virginia, Maryland, and Pennsylvania lines to join Greene in South Carolina, while the more northerly regiments returned to their old encampments in New Jersey and on the Hudson. He would join them eventually, but since morale was high with victory and the British were quiescent, he felt he could take his time. For almost seven years his mind had been ever "on the stretch"; he intended to enjoy at Mount Vernon a few weeks of the "domestic felicity" which had soothed so many of his happier hours. The expectation seemed too good to be realized—and so it was to prove.[1]

Jacky Custis had taken so lightly his role as volunteer aide that when Washington had galloped to Williamsburg in an agony of apprehension over the disappearance of de Grasse, the young man had loitered on the road to pay visits. However, he eventually reached his stepfather's headquarters, where he came down with camp fever. Washington hurried him off for nursing to Eltham, the seat near Williamsburg of Martha's brother-in-law, Burwell Bassett.[2]

November 5 dawned fair and warm, the wind from the northwest: just the kind of day that made the Potomac smile and sparkle as it loafed past Mount Vernon. By ten in the morning, Washington had untangled the last of the complications immediately involved in reorganizing after the Yorktown siege. He mounted his horse in high spirits for what was to be his trip home. After attending to some ceremonial chores at Williamsburg, he enjoyed an agreeable light supper with his aides at Bird's Ordinary, and rode on to spend the night at Eltham. What was his amazement to be met at the door by Martha and her daughter-in-law, both in the final extremity of grief. He rushed upstairs to a fetid room where, almost as he crossed the threshold, Jacky Custis died.[3]

In warning aides he had left behind at Bird's Ordinary not to follow him to Eltham, Washington commented wryly, "In spite of Mr. Sterne's observation, the House of Mourning [is] not very agreeable." Since the aides could not be comfortable in "the dirty tavern you are now at," they should go to Mount Vernon and await him there. Expressing no personal grief over Jacky's death (he could never bring himself to do that), Washington explained, "The deep and solemn distress of the mother and affliction of the wife of this amiable young man requires every comfort in my power to afford them. The last rites of the deceased, I must also see performed. These will take me three or four days, when I shall proceed with Mrs. Washington and Mrs. Custis to Mount Vernon."[4]

Washington was held at Eltham for six days. Then he sent the mourners limping to Mount Vernon and (family duties being upon him) rode to Fredericksburg to call on his seventy-four-year-old mother, whom he had not seen since he had gone off to war. He had heard that "she is upon all occasions and in all companies complaining of the hardness of the times, of her wants and distresses," with particular reference to how her children neglected her. "That she can have no *real* wants that may not be supplied," he commented, "I am sure of. *Imaginary* wants are indefinite and oftentimes insatiable, because they are boundless and always changing." Washington was resentful but did not like to upbraid his mother. It did not promise to be an agreeable interview. He was probably not heartbroken to find that his mother was not home.[5]

George eventually received a letter from Mary Washington, the spelling and punctuation of which should be preserved: "My dear Georg I was truly unesy by Not being at hom when you went thru fredirceksburg it was a onlucky thing for me now I am afraid I Never Shall have that pleasure agin I am soe very unwell this trip over the Mountins has almost kill'd me I gott the 2 five ginnes you was soe kind to send me i am greatly obliged to you." She went on to implore, although her son had established her in Fredericksburg in an elegant small house, that she be allowed, on some land he owned over the mountains, "some little hous of my one if it is only twelve foot squar." In sending her love to Martha, she made an appeal for pity which she scratched out: "to her I would have wrote to her but my reason has jis left me." Typically, the conquering hero's mother made no mention of his military achievements or the victory at Yorktown.[6]

Back at what had now become "the House of Mourning," at Mount Vernon, Washington resisted pressure that he accept the executorship of Jacky's estate, which, a cursory examination revealed, had been endlessly confused by the incompetence of the deceased. In urging the task on

Martha's brother, Bartholomew Dandridge, Washington stated that he wanted to do all he could for the children, "especially the boy." However, it would be "injurious to the children and madness in me" to add to the business with which he was already burdened. Not only were his own farming and financial affairs in a ruin, but old courtesy obligations loomed so large that if peace ever came, his personal welfare would have to be "the least of my concern, unfortunately for me."

He had become, much against his inclination, executor for Colonel Thomas Colville, who had left legacies to people in England "not by name but by description and descent almost from Adam." This had given him "infinite trouble" before he had left Virginia for the army, and since then the other executor, after getting everything even more involved, had died. And in another similar trust, the man to whom he had confided the settlement had "died insane, so that that matter stands on a most wretched and ruinous footing." Furthermore, he had accepted a power of attorney for George William Fairfax and Fairfax's wife, his own old love Sally, who were both in England.[7]

Although Washington's military dispatches remained as clear as usual, when he sat down at his peacetime desk to write a letter about purchasing some land contiguous to Mount Vernon, the sentences refused to go down clearly. He had not, since his emotional turmoils decades before during the French and Indian War, expressed himself in a manner so verbose and confused. To fix his mind effectively on his civilian affairs seems to have been too great a leap for that exhausted organ which had been aimed in one direction for so long.[8]

Washington had dreamed for years of getting back to Mount Vernon, but it was almost with relief that after a short stay he set out for the familiar treadmill at headquarters, escorting Martha toward scenes that would not remind her every minute of her loss. His objective was the Hudson, but military affairs were now so obviously in a less grievous state than the civil that Congress held him in Philadelphia. He spent four winter months in America's largest and most sophisticated city. Such an opportunity to find relief from drudgery had often beckoned to him in military camps. Now he summarized to Chastellux that his time "was unusually (for me) divided between parties of pleasure and parties of business: the first, nearly of a sameness at all times and places in this infant country."[9]

His comment was deeply indicative of his own weariness: the social season he shared was full of innovations for the infant country and new experiences for the untraveled Washington.

There was his welcome itself. Many a town had honored him by illuminations achieved with candles placed in every window, but never before had he seen windows acting as frames for large transparent paintings that were

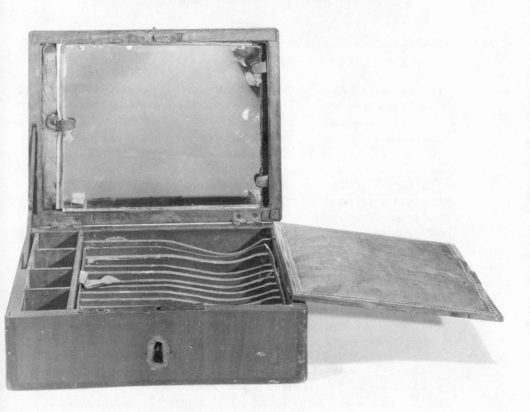

Mahogany shaving case with painted initials; mirror inside lid; interior painted blue. Courtesy of the Mount Vernon Ladies' Association of the Union.

lighted from behind. This conceit had, during the celebration of Cornwallis's surrender, been introduced to Philadelphia by Alexander Quesnay
de Golray, newly arrived from France to become a teacher of the "polite
sciences." The idea was enthusiastically grasped by the city's own ingenious
artist Charles Willson Peale, and so to celebrate Washington's arrival the
façades of both Quesnay's and Peale's houses rose into the night aglow with
tiers of allegorical compositions. Washington saw many versions of his own
laurel-crowned head, and an iridescent full-length of himself brandishing a
spear as he trampled on a golden crown symbolic of British pride.[10]

On January 2, in honor of Washington, Quesnay hired the Southwark
Theatre and showed off his pupils' French in a performance of Beaumar-
chais's comedy *Eugénie*. Unable to understand a word, Washington had
either to laugh like a parrot when the others did, or look embarrassingly
solemn. However, he could enjoy the other play, Garrick's *The Lying Valet*.
The prologue to the entire evening had contained an appeal, spoken directly
to Washington:

> "While arts of peace thy kind protection share,
> Oh, let the muses claim an equal share!"

He was begged to support "a new Athens rising in the west." Why this
should be asked of a general was not clear—or too clear. In any case, Washington was surely moved, as he always was by that ripeness of culture in
which the self-educated hero felt unhappily that he did not share. He confessed to "an ardent passion" for "the promotion of the cause of literature in
general."[11]

The Temple of Minerva, considered the first serious American attempt at
grand opera, was written by Joseph Hopkinson for a party Luzerne gave in
honor of Washington. In one scene, young ladies representing Minerva and
the Genius of France joined with the rest of the cast and the chorus in
focusing their eyes on the tall guest of honor as they sang:

> "Now the dreadful conflict's o'er
> Now the cannons cease to roar.
> Spread the joyful tidings round,
> He comes, he comes, with conquest crowned.
> Hail Columbia's warlike son!
> Hail the glorious Washington!"[12]

For Washington, who suffered in such situations from painful shyness, the
incident was made doubly disturbing by the words with which the congratulatory verse had started. The thing he now feared most in the world
was that Congress and the states would relax their efforts because they
believed that "the dreadful conflict's o'er." To everyone his voice or pen
could reach, he expostulated that there was no peace, no victory, and that

defeat was still very possible. His duty, he felt, was to stimulate all patriots to make possible for 1782 an early and decisive campaign.[13]

Dispatches and newspaper extracts coming in from England indicated that the King was determined to pursue the war. But, since he had made no new foreign alliances, any major British reinforcements were not to be expected. Wilmington, Washington heard, had been evacuated; Charleston probably would be soon. But the enemy would certainly stay in New York unless forcibly expelled. New York was still the key. As long as the enemy remained there, the war would go on.[14]

What France would do by way of sending another navy or more troops or more money could not, of course, be determined. The obvious course, Washington argued, was to make the Continental Army so strong that it could take advantage of any favorable turn. The Congress, although poorly attended and largely shorn of power, did what it could to back Washington. It voted to keep the existing number of regiments and urge the states to fill them; it begged the states for the necessary money. Washington added hortatory letters in which he arrayed "every argument I could invent" to persuade the states to comply. He pointed out that there were continuing rumblings of mutiny—he had once to keep Martha home from a tea party because of disorder on the Philadelphia streets. True, nothing serious had happened yet, but he could not answer for the effect on the army if a failure by the states to raise the eight million dollars Congress had appropriated for the new campaign should result in disappointment of pay, food, clothing.[15]

Congress had at long last set up the rudiments of an executive. Robert Morris had for some time been secretary of finance; Robert R. Livingston held the portfolio of foreign affairs. There had been an effort to have Gates made secretary of war, but his partisans had only proved strong enough to block Washington's preference, Schuyler. The berth went in the end to one of His Excellency's men, General Lincoln. Once a week, Washington met with the three secretaries, as he was later, when President, to meet with his cabinet. He was enchanted to escape from congressional committees, seeing in particular "infinite public advantages" from Morris's activity as financier.[16]

Drastic financial measures were clearly necessary. The states had not levied the taxes that were required of them when Congress had returned to them the responsibility for maintaining the army and creating currencies that would not begin to depreciate the instant the paper was printed. The states had not even made possible the paying of interest on the national debt, which meant, Morris complained, that those "who trusted us in the hour of distress are defrauded." A corollary was that the loans from abroad, which had done so much to keep the cause afloat, would surely cease, since "to expect that foreigners will trust a government which has no credit with its own citizens would be madness."

The Articles of Confederation, Morris continued sourly, while giving

Congress "the privilege of asking everything," gave the states "the prerogative of granting nothing." And Congress did not dare even to suggest that it be given any power to coerce delinquent states.[17]

As a giant step toward a long-range solution, Morris had persuaded Congress to ask the states for the right to raise income of its own by collecting customs duties. The sums that would result would admittedly be inadequate to run the war, yet the principle was, as Washington enthusiastically agreed, all-important. The "impost" would be an entering wedge for the federal taxation absolutely necessary if the Confederation were to meet its obligations, and, indeed, not fall apart. Since the Articles of Confederation would have to be amended, unanimous vote agreement of the states was called for. Such approval involved overriding old fears of outside taxation. Yet Washington hoped for the best, since at a time of crisis, necessity can speak in a persuasive voice to rational men.

In the meanwhile, Morris engaged in various expedients which Washington observed with fascinated admiration. The help the Bank of Philadelphia had been able to give the army promised much from Morris's success in dragooning a reluctant Congress to charter the private institution as a national bank. Furthermore, the financier arranged with a private partnership, Comfort Sands and Company, to agree to supply the army on credit. Very ingenious, it seemed to Washington, were the notes payable in six months given the officers with which to buy their own uniforms. If the officers were already clothed, they could buy other things with the notes which would, in any case, continue to circulate as currency. Washington was particularly pleased that the regiments from the various states were now all on an equal basis for clothing, which would remove former galling contrasts.[18]

With the approach of spring, on April 1, 1782, Washington returned to his headquarters at Newburgh, among those Hudson Highlands that had frowned from their rugged declivities on so many of his disconsolate hours. He soon concluded that he could only expect enough new levies to keep his force at about ten thousand. And the few men that did come in were often of the lowest quality: Lieutenant Colonel Ezra Badlam of the Eighth Massachusetts Regiment was convicted of having enlisted two recent deserters from the enemy and two from the French, four "boys undersized," two immigrants who instantly decamped, "a Negro lame in the ankle," and George West, "an idiot."[19]

As for the levies from Maryland southward, who were supposed to join Greene, Washington notified that general in code (a refinement in secrecy he had picked up from the French) not to expect to be strong enough to attack Charleston. Greene could only hope to prevent the British from breaking out and ravaging South Carolina.[20]

[476]

When warmer weather presaged what would be his eighth campaign as Commander in Chief, Washington began one of those elaborate memoranda to himself—printed, it runs to twenty-two pages—in which he balanced the pros and cons of every conceivable course of action. He estimated the total British force of regulars and established provincial regiments in America at about twenty-six thousand: thirteen thousand in New York, thirty-three hundred in Charleston, five thousand in Canada, thirty-five hundred in Halifax, and five hundred at Penobscot. Having weighed attacks on New York and Charleston, he returned to his old concern with Canada: might not a force of eight thousand marching overland in the autumn, might they not, if the inhabitants proved as friendly as some reports said, capture everything except Quebec before the British could draw their scattered forces together? Quebec would have to be reserved for a second year. He went on to considering actions in conjunction with the French fleet against either Halifax or Bermuda. On the final balance it was completely clear that he had neither the men nor the supplies to make any move at all without greater French aid than Rochambeau's force of four thousand that was still encamped in Virginia.[21]

Washington must have got some grim satisfaction when he learned in May that he had now outlasted three British commanders in chief: Clinton had been recalled. He was replaced by the longtime commander of Canada, Sir Guy Carleton. Carleton brought no significant reinforcements, but made no preparations to take the army in New York away. As Washington wrote Bartholomew Dandridge, he saw little prospect of ending the war during this campaign.[22]

And what prospect there was flew out the window when de Grasse's fleet was decisively defeated and the admiral himself captured by Rodney off Guadeloupe. A squadron under the Marquis de Vaudreuil, which took refuge in Boston Harbor, was instantly pinned there by the appearance of a greater British fleet under Admiral Hood.[23]

Martha having returned to Mount Vernon, Washington was in his enforced inactivity very lonely. His favorite military disciples were far away: Greene and Laurens outside Charleston, Lafayette in France. He wrote them affectionate, praising letters, adding to Greene, "To participate and divide our feelings, hopes, fears, and expectations with a friend is almost the only source of pleasure and consolation left us, in the present languid and unpromising state of our affairs." Hope that Chastellux might soon appear at his headquarters made him write the French soldier-philosopher, "I love you. . . . I shall embrace you when it happens with the warmth of perfect friendship."[24]

CHAPTER

52

The Brink of the Abyss

W E are now advanced," Washington wrote during August 1782, "to the critical and awful period when our hands are to be tried at the arts of negotiation." The British command in New York had notified him "by authority, that negotiations for a general peace have already commenced at Paris," and that "His Majesty, in order to remove all obstacles to that peace, which he so ardently wishes to restore" had ordered his ministers not only to accept but to propose "the independency of the thirteen provinces."[1]

On this and other similar reports, Washington commented, "We wanted no fresh opiate to increase that stupor into which we had fallen." He wondered whether the British were not trying to lull the Americans while the villains made peace with their European adversaries, after which they would turn their full force on their former colonies. Or if they actually offered independence, it might prove limited, as in Ireland. Or they might be "trying the chapter of accidents," delaying in the hope that something favorable would turn up. "From the former infatuation, duplicity, and perverse system of British policy, I confess I am induced to doubt everything, to suspect everything."[2]

One thing, however, was certain: the news from Europe had spread "universal consternation" among the Tory refugees in New York. "Actuated by different passions," Washington continued, "or rather by the same passion in different degrees, [they] are little better than a medley of confused, enraged, and dejected people. Some are swearing, and some crying, while the greater part of them are almost speechless."[3]

They were also insanely violent. As the British regulars remained quiescent, almost the only enemy military activity consisted of raids, often from Staten Island into New Jersey, staged by Tory corps against their former neighbors who had exiled them. Such forays and the inevitable retaliations had been, throughout the Revolution, a continuous tragic undercurrent. Civil conflicts engender more hate than foreign wars; the confrontations were always bloody far beyond military necessity. And now at this time of passionate Tory despair, Washington became unhappily involved as the fraticidal brutality exploded into an even more monstrous form.

A Tory irregular named Philip White had been killed while a captive. The patriots claimed that he had grabbed a gun and shot a sentry and been in turn shot. The Tories insisted that he had been wantonly tortured to death. As a reprisal, a company of Jersey loyalists, led by Captain Richard Lippincott, took from a British prison ship one Captain Joseph Huddy. Carrying Huddy to the Jersey shore, they hanged him from a tree and left the body swinging there with a placard on its back: "We, the Refugees . . . taking vengeance for the numerous cruelties . . . have made use of Captain Huddy as the first object to present to your view, and further determine to hang man for man while there is a refugee in existence. *Up goes Huddy for Philip White.*"[4]

Onto Washington's desk poured New Jersey protests which included threats of counterassassination. Himself angry at what he called "the most wanton, unprecedented, and inhuman murder that ever disgraced the arms of a civilized people," recognizing a situation which could easily explode into spasms of senseless bloodshed, Washington, after consulting Congress and his own officers, decided on a firm line with the British command. As "the only means left to put a stop to such inhuman proceedings," he would select by lot a captain from among the British prisoners in his hands and hang that captain if Lippincott were not delivered to him for trial. At the same time as he sent this ultimatum across the lines, Washington notified the Jersey patriots that he intended to "deliver up to the enemy or otherwise to punish" any of them who committed "any act which is in the least contrary to the laws of war."[5]

The lot was drawn and fell on "Captain Charles Asgill of the Guards, a young gentleman seventeen years of age,* a most amiable character, the only son of Sir Charles Asgill, baronet; heir to an extensive fortune, an honorable title." The officer who sent Washington this news added happily that the hostage had "great interest in the British Court and armies." Washington, however, felt regret that fate had presented him not with some hardened professional warrior but, as in the case of Major André, with a most attractive potential sacrifice. Although he wrote on one occasion, "While retaliation was apparently necessary, however disagreeable in itself, I had no repugnance to the measure," he also stated that Asgill's plight "often filled me with the keenest anguish. I felt for him on many accounts, and not the least when, viewing him as a man of honor and sentiment, I

---

* He was actually nineteen.

considered how unfortunate it was for him that a wretch who possessed neither should be the means of causing in him a single pang." For publication and to the British he wrote firmly that whatever were his personal feelings, "no gleam of hope can arise to him but from the conduct of the enemy themselves."[6]

The British themselves brought Lippincott to trial with results that, so Washington wrote Congress, "changed the ground I was proceeding upon and placed the matter upon an extremely delicate footing." Lippincott was freed because he had been merely obeying orders. The orders had come from the central Tory organization in the British camp, the Board of the Associated Loyalists, which was presided over by no less a figure than William Franklin, Benjamin's illegitimate son and the former royal governor of New Jersey.* In reporting this, Carleton had assured Washington that the murder had been contrary to British policy. To make sure that it would not be repeated, the British had dissolved the Loyalist Board and was investigating further to unearth and punish the individuals directly responsible.[7]

Washington felt that the object of the threatened reprisal, which was to make sure that the wanton bloodshed would cease, had been achieved and that, as Carleton requested, Asgill should now be freed. However, he referred the decision to Congress as a matter of "great national concern upon which an individual ought not to decide." He was soon sorry he had done so, for Congress did nothing, leaving the young man under terror of death and Washington himself in a "cruel situation." From the first, he had ordered that the hostage be treated with "every possible tenderness that is consistent with the security of him." Now he loosened the security, allowing Asgill, "for the benefit of his health and the recreation of his mind, to ride not only about the cantonment [Morristown] but into the surrounding country," accompanied only by a friend he had made among his captors.[8]

Finally, Washington broke out to Congressman James Duane that this was not the first time Congress had left him in the lurch "in matters of high importance, and which the good of the service and my official duty has obliged me to call upon them (as the sovereign power of these United States) to decide. It is only in intricate and perplexing cases I have requested their orders; being always willing to bear my proportion of public embarrassments, and take a full share of responsibility. Conscious that I have treated that honorable body and all their measures, with as much

---

* Five years before when Governor Franklin had been in a Connecticut jail for breaking his parole, he had sent Washington a piteous letter stating that his wife was sick and he wished to visit her. The ever softhearted and ever uxorious Washington had written Congress, "His situation is distressing and must interest all our feelings. . . . Humanity and generosity plead powerfully in favor of his application." Congress refused. Franklin later escaped to New York where he became one of the most inexorable of the refugees.[9]

deference and respect as any officer in the United States, I expected this aid." Why, if policy forbade a decision, "I am not to be informed of it is beyond my conception, unless I was to ascribe it to causes which I flatter myself do not exist."[10]

Across the lines from the British in New York came a most annoying and humiliating packet. It contained a copy of a letter which the hostage's mother had written to the French minister of war, Vergennes, and also a letter, addressed to Washington, which Vergennes had sent not directly to his ally but to the mother for forwarding.

Lady Asgill wrote a most lush prose style (which would in the twentieth century have made her the queen of soap operas). She had begged Vergennes to interpose, "like a voice from heaven," to save "my son, my only son, as dear to me as he is brave, amiable as he is beloved, only nineteen years of age." She went on: "Surrounded as I am with objects of distress, bowed down with fear and grief, words are wanting to express what I feel and to paint such a scene of misery: my husband, given over by his physicians some hours before the arrival of this news, not in a condition to be informed of it; my daughter, attacked by fever accompanied with delirium, speaking of her brother in tones of wildness, and without an interval of reason unless it be to listen to some circumstance which may console her heart. . . . I feel the whole weight of the liberty taken in presenting this request, but I feel confident, whether granted or not, that you will pity the distress by which it is suggested; your humanity will drop a tear on my fault, and blot it out forever."[11]

This epistle, so Vergennes's letter to Washington revealed, had sent the French Court into a happy paroxysm of sentimentality. The minister stated that he was not writing in his official capacity, "but as a man of sensibility and a tender father, who feels all the force of paternal love." Surely Washington could not read Lady Asgill's description "of a mother and family in tears . . . without being extremely affected: it had that effect on the King and upon the Queen. . . . The goodness of their Majesties' hearts induced them to desire that the inquietudes of an unfortunate mother may be calmed and her tenderness reassured." Having struck this lofty, lachrymose vein, Vergennes was loath to leave it. He went on, repeating himself, admonishing Washington that "it is rendering homage to your virtue to implore it," and pointed out that, as Asgill had been captured at Yorktown, the French had, so to speak, placed him in Washington's hands. He added that it was not France's intention that Washington "seek another victim. The pardon, to be perfectly satisfactory, must be entire."[12]

When referred to Congress, these documents achieved what Washington's own appeals had failed to do; they procured the release of Asgill. Washington was happy so to notify the young man. However, the unbuttoned emotion springing from the letters of the mother and the minister, plus the

[481]

report of the surges in royal hearts, irritated Washington into taking, in his reply to Vergennes, the stoniest possible stance. Instead of emphasizing (as he was to do four years later when he heard that European criticisms of his supposed heartlessness were still high) his kindness to Asgill* and his true eagerness to get him off once Carleton had acted, he told the French minister that "the very unsatisfactory measures which had been taken by the British commander in chief to atone for a crime of the blackest dye" had not justified the release Asgill had been granted by Congress. "I have no right to assume any particular merit from the lenient manner in which this disagreeable affair has terminated." However, he was rejoiced to see "your humane intentions" and those of the King and Queen satisfied.[13]

Although Carleton never carried out his promise of prosecuting further in the Huddy murder, he signalized a determination to bring an end to all Tory raiding by returning to Washington two patriot dragoons whom a loyalist band had captured. Again and again he sent Washington assurances that no belligerency of any sort would be initiated from his headquarters. Washington, who could officially countenance no peace as long as British soldiers were on American soil, made no similar pacific promises. He continued to dream of capturing New York or Canada, or at least punishing the Indians who had devastated the New York frontier. But the first two objectives far exceeded his foreseeable possibilities, and he decided not to stir up the Iroquois, whom the British really seemed to be trying to calm down.[14]

Late in August, the army made its first move of the 1782 campaign: down the Hudson to the region around Verplanck's Point. Significantly, the object was not military but to help, by entering a fresh region, the tottering services of supply.[15]

Since the army had a grievance to accompany every one of its needs, and boredom is under the best of circumstances a potent enemy of morale, Washington labored to keep his soldiers amused. He granted officers extensive furloughs—thus increasing his own burdens—and urged everyone in camp to bring "a degree of elegance" to their temporary habitations. A civilian visitor thus described the decorative arbors the men wove to achieve autumn shade: "In front of the tents was a regular, continued portico formed by the boughs of trees in verdure, decorated with much taste and fancy. Each officer's tent was distinguished by superior ornament." Washington smiled to see the men lounging in their outdoor living rooms, but was worried, as the branches dried, by danger of fire.[16]

Himself highly susceptible to the pleasures of dressing up, Washington

---

* Washington was, indeed, hurt that, after being freed, Asgill did not thank him for so much kindness: "The treatment he met with, in my conception, merited an acknowledgment."[17]

urged the men, when he issued new hats, to be "extremely attentive to give them a military and uniform appearance by cutting, cocking, or adding such other decorations as they think proper." For Sundays, he advised attendance at religious services, which "tend to improve the morals and at the same time to increase the happiness of the soldiery, and must afford the most pure and rational entertainment for every serious and well-disposed mind." And then, of course, there was drill, that pleasurable military exercise that in its synchronized movements to music considerably resembled the social dances of the time.[18]

To honor enlisted men, Washington established chevrons to be worn on sleeves denoting length of service. He also decreed that in reward for singular merit—"not only instances of unusual gallantry but also of extraordinary fidelity and essential services in any way"—a common soldier should be entitled to wear on his left breast "the figure of a heart in purple cloth or silk." This would empower him "to pass all guards and sentinels which officers are permitted to do." What Washington called the "Badge of Military Merit" was the first general decoration established in the American army. Being limited to privates and noncommissioned officers, it revealed, Washington wrote, that "the road to glory in a patriot army and a free country is thus open to all."* [19]

"When the annals of the army shall exist," Washington announced on another occasion, "it is the General's intention it shall be known that he had great reasons to be satisfied at this period of the war with the troops under his command." Yet he did not hide from his own nerves and his masters in Philadelphia that the situation was becoming daily more dangerous. The states were continuing to ignore the financial quotas that were necessary to support the federal structure and its military arm. By May, not a single quarterly installment called for in the preceding autumn had been paid. The financier had indeed received from all the thirteen states the princely sum of $5500, less than a day's expenses. That same month a near-mutiny in the Connecticut line had to be stopped by the summary execution of the ringleaders. This was not an altogether new phenomenon, but, as bankruptcy in Philadelphia continued to cast its baleful shadow over the unpaid and perilously supplied army, Washington observed something new that chilled his blood: "Hitherto the officers have stood between the lower order of the soldiery and the public, and in more instances than one, at the hazard of their lives, have quelled very dangerous mutinies." But now the officers were expressing as much angry dissatisfaction as the men.[20]

A major inciting cause seemed on the surface mild, but, as Washington wrote, "minds soured by distresses are easily rankled." Sands and Company, the contractors for feeding the army, were allowing the officers no credit for

---

* After having been allowed to lapse, the decoration was revived in 1933 as the Purple Heart. It was then made available to officers as well as enlisted men.

rations not instantly eaten from the common pot. Thus, individuals who dined with friends or themselves corned a little beef or bought a little poultry were penalized. Since lack of funds prevented giving the officers any pay, the subsistence which had been promised seemed their only means of support—and now to have that meager dole curtailed by bureaucratic suppliers! The officers were "extremely hurt and alarmed at their situation," even before it was given an added twist by the appearance of the French army.[21]

After wintering in Virginia, Rochambeau's force had moved to Baltimore to be in touch with the northern as well as the southern theater. Eventually, they received orders to proceed in a leisurely manner to Boston for shipping, when the sea-lanes opened, to the Indies. From mid-September to mid-October, they settled down in the Hudson Valley next to their American allies.

Together again after a victory and ten months' separation, the armies viewed each other with great affection. "It was," wrote Dumas, "a real family fete." Family fetes involve mutual entertaining. The French officers mounted excellent tables, but when the Americans invited their allies back, they could not, having been refused the privilege of amassing or selling their rations, serve anything (as Washington put it) but "stinking whiskey—and not always that—and a bit of beef without vegetables." The embarrassed Americans could not excuse their Spartan fare on the grounds of a general scarcity of provisions, since the country was "surcharged" with eatables and potables which they lacked any means to secure.

After his repeated protests had still failed to stir Congress into restoring the officers' rations, Washington asked angrily, "Is it policy, is it justice to keep a sore constantly gangrened? . . . Would to God false policy, inattention, or something else may not be productive of disagreement which will prove irreconcilable!"[22]

To the Secretary of War, Washington described "a persuasion which somehow has taken deep root in their minds that they are the most neglected and injured part of the community." But Washington did not mean the "somehow." He knew exactly how. Rumor had it that when the central government got a little money they used it to pay not the army but civilian officials.[23]

At the bottom of everything, of course, lay the vast inadequacy of funds. Sands and Company could not be pressed because they could not be paid. They were, indeed, finally forced to give up, when, so Washington wrote, "fortunately for us we met with gentlemen who, for an advanced price per ration, have saved us from starvation or disbandment by giving a credit."[24]

Desperate credit built on slippery credit: the higher such a crazy structure was built, the greater would be the fall in the end. But the one hope that the crisis would be solved rationally seemed to be getting stronger.

Although at slow intervals, the states were ratifying the change in the Articles of Confederation that would enable the Congress itself to collect customs duties. True, the necessary unanimity had not yet been reached. Washington shuddered away from thinking what would happen if some state took an unreversible negative vote which would make clear to the army that it could not expect to be paid, and would frighten capitalists, here and abroad, by revealing that Congress had no means of raising funds, even to meet the interest of its debts.[25]

Shoring up the federal credit was made the more urgent by Congress's resolve to save money and increase efficiency through combining regiments until each numbered at least five hundred rank and file. The Massachusetts regiments would, on January 1, 1783, be reduced from ten to eight, the five Connecticut to three, and so forth. This would release many officers. Unless effective steps were taken to find them some back pay, they would depart bankrupt; nor did the future promise them anything as long as the Congress had no visible way of implementing its promises of pensions—half pay—for veterans.[26]

To Secretary of War Lincoln, Washington wrote, "I cannot help fearing the result . . . when I see such a number of men, goaded by a thousand stings of reflection on the past and of anticipation on the future, about to be turned into the world, soured by penury and what they call the ingratitude of the public, involved in debts, without one farthing of money to carry them home, after having spent the flower of their days, and many of them their patrimonies, in establishing the freedom and independence of their country, and suffered everything human nature is capable of enduring on this side of death. I repeat it: these irritable circumstances, without one thing to soothe their feelings or frighten the gloomy prospects—I cannot avoid apprehending that a train of evils will follow of a very serious and distressing nature. . . .

"You may rely upon it, the patience and long sufferance of this army are almost exhausted, and that there never was so great a spirit of discontent as at this instant. While in the field, I think it may be kept from breaking out into acts of outrage, but when we retire into winter quarters (unless the storm is previously dissipated) I cannot be at ease respecting the consequences. It is high time for a peace."[27]

The peace negotiations that were going on in Paris were, as far as Washington could learn, lagging. And Lincoln wrote that Congress could supply no pay in cash and would not even be willing to give disbanded officers certificates of indebtedness for the back pay owed them and the pensions promised.[28]

Washington had been planning to spend the winter at Mount Vernon, attending to "my long-neglected private concerns." But he reluctantly decided that "the temper of the army" was so "soured" that he would have to stay. In December, he wrote Congressman Jones, "The dissatisfactions of the army had arisen to a great and alarming height, and combinations among the officers to resign, at given periods, in a body were beginning to take place, when, by some address and management, their resolutions have been converted into the form in which they will now appear before Congress."[29]

The form was a petition which Washington boasted was "couched in very respectful terms." It presented the officers' minimum demands: advance of part of the pay due, security for the rest, and commutation of the half pay for life which had been voted the officers into either a lump sum or full pay for a reasonable number of years. This was replaying old tunes, but a new ominous note of urgency was added. The petition was not sent to Congress by a messenger but carried by a committee of high officers, which had instructions to stay in Philadelphia until Congress acted and then report back to the army.

When the committee arrived, modified optimism reigned in Philadelphia: twelve states had ratified the impost which would provide federal funds. Only the smallest, Rhode Island, had not ratified. Then the word came in: Rhode Island had refused. As Congress prepared a high-powered delegation to reason with the midget, more news: Virginia, the largest state, had reconsidered and changed its vote from yes to no. The measure was dead. Congress was bankrupt.

The committee of officers did not go quietly away. They waited grimly in the town. On the evening of January 13, 1783, they were given an audience. The chairman, crusty, Scotch-born General Alexander McDougall described the sufferings and disappointments of the officers, so James Madison noted, "in very high-colored expressions." He declared that the army "were verging to that state which we are told will make a wise man mad." The other members of the committee were equally violent. Colonel John Brooks asserted that "the temper of the army was such that they did not reason or deliberate coolly on consequences, and therefore a disappointment might throw them blindly into extremities." Colonel Mathias Ogden declared that "if he was to be the messenger of disappointment to them," he did not wish to return to the army.[30]

Most of the members of Congress sat there aghast, not knowing what to do. But there were others, including men of great influence, who agreed with Alexander Hamilton that, if handled properly, the desperate situation "may be turned to good account." Perhaps the army could be induced to rise against the civilian authorities; perhaps George Washington could be persuaded to lead what would be put forward as a salutary insurrection.[31]

53

The Road to Dictatorship

Y ORKTOWN had been a pivot on which the American scene had
swung, reversing foreground and background. Before Cornwallis had
surrendered, war had been reality, peace had been vision. Now, although the war had not officially ended, the people and the army expected it
to fade away behind them, while they looked ahead at a new day.

The dawn they saw was murky, and every accession of light made clear a
web of problems stretching from one central issue: To what extent was the
United States a nation, to what extent a regional alliance of sovereign states?

The issue was old and traditions were on the side of disunity. Not until
the injustices that had kindled the Revolutionary War had become burning,
not until some one hundred and sixty years after the first permanent
settlement in North America, had the thirteen states ever sat down together
to achieve cooperation. If that cooperation had continued, however imperfectly, for eight years, it had always been on the basis of critical necessity.
And now that the crisis was fading, the old behavior patterns increasingly
asserted themselves.

But the exceptional eight years had nurtured phenomena that carried
with them the momentum of permanence. Paradoxically, the most obvious
was among the less formidable. Although titularly a central government, the
Continental Congress, its members delegated by the state legislatures, had
veered with the political winds. During the early years of the war it had
been in fact a national legislature commanding the best minds on the
continent. But little by little, the best minds had gone home to help draw up
constitutions for their states and occupy the offices thus created. They had
watched the Continental Congress become feebler and feebler until, as
peace loomed, it was financially bankrupt and often lacked the representation of nine states necessary to get any major business done. No new
departure would be required to solidify the Congress into a regional

debating society, since, in the Articles of Confederation, the states had preserved sovereign powers.

The army had been conspicuously less amenable to state sovereignty. It had from the first been considered necessary to have one commander in chief rather than thirteen. Although the results of Washington's most daring political act, his creation by his own authority of the "Additional Regiments" on a continental basis, had in the end been torn apart, the army had as a whole turned in the opposite direction from the drift of Congress. Despite political theory, the militia and also men separated from their states for only one year had proved militarily inadequate. The states had been forced to accept enlistments for three years or even the duration of the war. They had done their best to blunt the continental impact by insisting that each regiment be made up of the citizens of a single state and by keeping as much local authority over each officer corps as possible. However, a general who commanded many regiments could not be put together of a head giving allegiance to, let us say, Massachusetts, a stomach to New York, and legs to the Carolinas—and as men from various areas served together year after year, facing the same death as men from other states on whose actions their own lives often depended, they ceased to think in state terms. Washington was to point out that, more than any other single phenomenon, service in the army had fostered a federal turn of mind.

Recognizing, as they saw peace approaching, that the army was a force dangerous to states' rights, the states wished to see it disbanded as soon as possible, the men being returned home to be re-educated in their several "countries." However, as divisive sentiment had mounted, the states had allowed federal debts to the army to remain unpaid. The army was owed, as Washington stated, back pay for "four, five, perhaps six years."[1] The officers had been promised, when the civilians wanted them to stay in service, pensions if they served till the end of the war. Now retribution loomed. It was common talk that the soldiers were angry, would refuse to go home until governmental obligations to them were met, and a committee of three high officers was waiting grimly in Philadelphia for the politicians to take steps.

The state governments were thus put on the spot. The various regiments could not be directly paid by the states of their origin unless the local politicians were willing and able to levy taxes which their constituents would be the less willing to pay because they believed the war was almost won. And, in any case, it was doubtful whether the federally minded army, led by generals who were attached to no specific state lines, would break up on promises of local payment after they got home. The army saw its salvation in payments from the federal authorities. And to enable the federal authorities to make such payments would involve the acceptance of measures that would dilute local sovereignty. On the horns of this dilemma, the states procrastinated, hoping that the problem would somehow go away.

[488]

Even more basically dependent on federal funds than the soldiers in state lines, were the holders of paper representing Congressional obligations. These included some simple citizens who had received certificates in return for impressed farm produce, but, on the whole, such citizens had sold the certificates, for what they would bring, to speculators. Other members of the financial community had lent money to the government or had used their own credit to procure military supplies. If states' rights were allowed to flourish to a point where federal obligations languished unpaid, many a rich man might end up bankrupt. The business community and the well-to-do, from the solidest merchant to the slipperiest shyster blown high by the storms of war, had a heavy stake in federalism and thus, it seemed, common cause with the angry army.

The weakness of the Articles of Confederation was pointed up by the way its provisions frustrated all honest efforts to meet the obligations of Congress. Before a state would heroically tax itself to pay its share, it wanted to be sure that its neighbors would not take advantage of its virtue by smugly sitting back and letting it carry all the burden. There was no way to be sure, and, indeed, no way that even twelve of the states could force a delinquent thirteenth to do anything contrary to its will.[2]

The case for a stronger central government could, of course, be backed by many other trenchant arguments. Although foreign affairs had been entrusted in the Articles of Confederation to Congress, this could not carry much weight as long as Congress had no funds, was so often without a quorum, and had no way to enforce its decrees. Once the common cause was won, European powers would surely fish in American political waters, taking advantage of the different interests of different regions to create spheres of influence and perhaps break up America into another Europe full of warring powers.[3]

Then there was western land to be administered and new states to be admitted, a matter already in a desperate tangle as Massachusetts and New York argued about boundaries with the settlers of Vermont, who had declared themselves what was in effect a separate republic and were treating with the British for support and with Congress for admission to statehood on their own terms.

Solving this political puzzle was, of course, not the responsibility of the Commander in Chief, but there were disturbing military implications. On one hand, Vermont might give actual aid to the enemy; on the other, Washington might be asked to do what he greatly dreaded: use his army not against the enemy but to settle squabbles between states and near-states. He thus gave in to urging by leading members of Congress that he bring his unique prestige to bear in what was delicately described as his "private character."

Washington pointed out to Thomas Chittenden, Vermont's so-called "governor," that it would be an impossible precedent to allow the first new state to make a condition of its admission to the union be encroachment on its neighbors. And he warned Chittenden, "A necessary coercion on the part of Congress . . . must involve the ruin of that state against which the resentment of the others is pointed." However, he warned Congress that every possible concession should be made to avoid the necessity of coercion. Had not the British, in embarking on force against the Americans, "thought it was only to hold up the rod, and all would be hush?"[4]

Washington was finding himself increasingly involved in matters outside his military province. He had kept out of the controversy over federal customs taxes as long as everything had seemed to be going well, but when Rhode Island and then Virginia blocked the measure, he expressed dismay. He wrote Virginia's governor that he was "decided in my opinion that, if the powers of Congress are not enlarged and made competent to all *general purposes* that the blood which has been spilt, the expense that has been incurred, and the distresses which have been felt, will avail us nothing; and that the band, already too weak, which holds us together, will soon be broken; when anarchy and confusion must prevail."[5]

How should this anarchy and confusion be repelled? England, whose traditions America had inherited, had always been ruled by a succession of sovereigns except for one "protector" who was the same thing under a different name. At the time of the American Revolution, every major European nation was presided over by a king. It thus seems remarkable that, despite the hardly applicable Roman example and the quickly doomed example of Holland, Americans had assumed from the first that their government would take a republican form.

Republicanism had, of course, a deep history on the American continent— but only on a local level. The legislatures of the various states were elected bodies who had traditionally tilted with the representatives of distant British royal power, and against that power the Revolution was eventually fought. Yet, in the colonial experience, the only adhesion between the colonies, the only central governmental force, had been the Crown. And the Revolutionary experience was demonstrating, every day more clearly, that the American statesmen had failed to forge any republican form that would create the unity traditionally imposed by a royal court and royal ministers.

Baroness Riedesel, the wife of a captured Hessian general, complained that she was kept awake all night by Americans singing "God save great Washington: God damn the King."[6] The substitution of one for the other had already taken place on many levels, both emotional and practical. To appreciate Washington's personal magnetism, his ability to strike in the hearts of strangers a chord made up of love and trust and awe, we need only to compare him with the man who was during the Revolution certainly the most important purely political leader, John Adams. In the arenas of public trust, Adams was to Washington what a dumpy lady intellectual is on the dance floor to a great belle. This annoyed John Adams; it seemed to him most unreasonable; yet it was as much a fact of nature as the rising sun.

When the main activity of the union had been military, Washington had filled in for the inefficiency and the purely legislative organization of Congress, to become the only effective central executive officer. Should he, while the alliance fell apart, be allowed to step down merely because the problems had changed from those of war to those of peace?

No machinery existed for electing George Washington, or indeed anyone, as President, and the establishment of such machinery by orderly, democratic processes would have involved a greater acceptance of federal power than the states would voluntarily accept. If an effective national government were to be established in time to deal with the existing crisis, it would have to be created out of hand by those most immediately concerned: federally minded politicians, the creditor class to which those politicians usually belonged, and, above all, the army. Above all the army, because it was clear that the reform could not immediately triumph over states' rights sentiment without at least the threat of force.

In May 1782, Washington had received a letter from one of his colonels, Lewis Nicola. An Irish-born Huguenot, Nicola had been particularly useful to the cause in drawing up and publishing military manuals. Now he enclosed a seven-page screed in which he argued that the experience of "the war must have shown to all, but to military men in particular, the weakness of republics." The general who had led the army to victory "through difficulties apparently unsurmountable by human power," must lead in peace. Since "some people have so connected the ideas of tyranny and monarchy as to find it very difficult to separate them," it might be necessary to give Washington "some title apparently more moderate," but Nicola personally was in favor of designating George I of the United States what he would actually be: the king.[7]

"Be assured, sir," Washington replied, "no occurrence in the course of the war has given me more painful sensations than your information of there being such ideas existing in the army as you have expressed and [as] I must view with abhorrence and reprehend with severity. . . . I am much at a loss to conceive what part of my conduct could have given encouragement to an address which to me seems big with the greatest mischiefs that can befall my country. If I am not deceived in the knowledge of myself, you could not have found a person to whom your schemes are more disagreeable." How seriously Washington took the matter is revealed by his securing—it was the only time during the whole Revolution—a written statement from his aides that his letter had been sealed and sent off.[8]

Nicola's arguments were not the true voice of the devil. The devil operates more subtly. This was brash interference by a semi-outsider, and a foreigner at that. If Washington had been susceptible to so crude an appeal, he would never have reached the position to receive it.

Strangely enough, fears that Washington would overthrow republican government, so loudly enunciated at the start of the war, were less often expressed as the vacuum to be filled grew. Everyone had got used to Washington's eminence, which had not been seriously challenged since defeat of the Conway Cabal. The ever-suspicious John Adams was off negotiating in Europe, and those other leaders who sniffed every breeze for tyranny were state-sovereignty men, most of whom had withdrawn from the federal scene to enjoy the sweet savor given off in their praise by their local governments. Some, like Lee, had actually been frightened into wishing Washington would play a larger role. As for the federal men, they did not cry danger, since their fear was that Washington would not be too eager but too reluctant to exert power.

In Philadelphia the situation seemed desperate. Congress, having been refused the right to collect customs duties, was as helpless as a turtle that had been turned over on its back. Waving little legs in the air, the legislature ordered the financier, despite his insistence that all foreign loans were already overdrawn, to draw on them further to meet current expenses. Off went more letters to the states begging for the thousandth time that already voted requisitions be met. Then Congress got down to debating long-range schemes for raising revenue that could not be realized for months and years, if at all.[9]

The committee from the army waited angrily, but no way could be foreseen to meet the officers' just demands. As federal obligations wilted in strongboxes, the business community foresaw intolerable losses. All the forces that made for federal union seemed to be coming unstuck. Out of this seemingly desperate situation there hatched a desperate expedient, which was spread from one mind to another by letter and conversation and semi-public toast. It appealed to the federal creditors, who were already organizing a national association, to outraged soldiers, to congressmen and ordinary citizens who dreaded disunion. Prime movers included the two financial Morrises—Robert and Gouverneur—and the three officers—McDougall, Brooks, and Ogden—who constituted the army's official committee to Congress. Among the correspondents in Washington's camp on the Hudson were two top generals—Gates and Knox—with their staffs. Alexander Hamilton gladly cast himself as spokesman and prime agitator.

This promising coalition wished the army and the creditors to make common cause, each group swearing to stand by the other. The army would fire the opening gun by announcing that it would refuse to disband even if peace were declared, living if necessary off the land, until the states took the necessary steps to put the federal government on a sound financial basis that would enable Congress to pay its debts.

Such an alliance between the business community and an angry army in a cause that could be described in terms of patriotism, and rights for the poor soldier, and the establishment of order will be recognized by the modern reader as a perfect springboard for fascism. The eighteenth century did not know of fascism, but it was familiar with Roman precedent. Gouverneur Morris wrote John Jay: "The army have swords in their hands. You know enough of the history of mankind to know much more than I have said and possibly much more than they themselves think of."[10]

The publicized contention was that it would only be necessary for the army to threaten: fear would then join with reason to establish federal taxation, and the army, having saved the nation from inner as it formerly had from outer foes, would finally dissolve into the utopia it had created. No one could, however, deny that the battle might not so easily be won. By what means force would be brought to bear on the state legislatures if they did not instantly knuckle under, how far reforms would have to go before civil institutions were restored to complete authority, were matters impossible to foresee. Much would depend on circumstances, and each adherent had his own desires and prophetic visions. The odor of violence was definitely in the air. Knox and McDougall, for instance, agreed that the illiberal and injust men who were engaged in driving the army to the brink of destruction should be punished with severity.

That the movement was in essence anti-republican was not openly insisted on, but was clear to many minds, including those who regretted what they foresaw as an unfortunate necessity. To Greene, Gouverneur Morris expressed a wish that the war would keep going, since, should it come to a rapid end, "I have no hope that our union can subsist except in the form of an absolute monarchy." General David Cobb noted that it was common talk among certain Philadelphia circles that an effort was being made to force a crown on Washington.[11]

Washington bestrode the scene like a colossus. If he agreed to lead, an armed protest by the army would certainly take place. However, he had previously blocked all efforts at direct political intervention by the military. Might he not, despite the deepening of crisis, stubbornly do so again?

There was much talk among the agitators as to whom they could set up if Washington refused. Where could they find someone His Excellency did not completely overshadow? So hard was it to find another leader that gossip tended toward Washington's old and half-discredited opponent, Gates. That general's projected trial after the defeat at Camden had never been held. He had eventually been restored to active service and was now at the camp on the Hudson, ranking, because of his seniority, as second in command.

Gates, himself, was feeling too battered for great ambitions, and he did not favor any movement which might increase Washington's power—he did not want, as he put it, "to offer the crown to Caesar"—but he allowed his headquarters to be the citadel of the movement in the military camp. What hotheads flourished there is revealed by a letter to Gates from his aide, Major John Armstrong, the very man who was soon to fire in public the opening gun of the agitation. Armstrong wrote that, with "Mad Anthony [Wayne] at their head, I know not where they [the troops] would stop. They feel like men and, could they be taught to think like politicians, they might do good."[12]

The young Virginia congressman James Madison noted in his journal that Hamilton and Richard Peters, the former secretary of the Board of War, had told a group of their fellow congressmen gathered in Philadelphia that the army had secretly determined not to lay down their arms until they had a satisfactory prospect of being paid; that a public declaration was soon to be expected; that the Commander in Chief was extremely unpopular with all ranks because of his known dislike of every unlawful proceeding; and that this unpopularity was being industriously promoted by many leading characters. Washington's choice of unfit advisers was the pretext, but the real motive was to substitute General (erased) as leader.

"Mr. Hamilton said that he knew General Washington intimately and perfectly. That his extreme reserve, mixed sometimes with a degree of asperity of temper, both of which were said to have increased of late, had contributed to the decline of his popularity." Yet Hamilton felt that Washington should somehow be persuaded to lead the protest, since he would "never yield to any dishonorable or disloyal plans," while others "may foment and misguide their councils."[13]

Despite gossip and dreams like Armstrong's of Mad Anthony Wayne, the soberer agitators did not wish to function without Washington except in the very last extremity. If some believed that Washington would have to be pushed much further than anyone had any intention of publicly admitting— or might even in the end have to be superseded by a man more resolute—no one could deny that Washington's participation implied safety, would quiet consciences in the army, and would go far toward winning public acceptance. Furthermore, there was the worrisome and incontrovertible fact that if subjected to Washington's expressed opposition, the scheme might quickly expire.

Hamilton, who had already seen the vision of using Washington as a shield behind which he achieved his own ends, felt that he knew the way to appeal to His Excellency. It would be vain to try to stimulate his ambition, to try to wake in him a greed for power. The line was to convince the tired soldier that commanding the insurrection was another of the onerous responsibilities required of him by his loyalty to the United States. No more than the agitators did Washington want to see the army defrauded; no more than they did he want the continent to become a cockpit of bickering small nations. Thus it would be unnecessary to persuade him of objectives; he needed to be persuaded only of methods. His natural tendency, Hamilton knew, would be to hold the army on the leash, continue to argue with the civilian authorities, and hope for the best. He must be shown that such temporizing was evasion of his duty.

The agitators were trying to keep Washington ignorant of what was going on. They hoped that when at last he made the discovery, the current would be flowing so strongly that no one could be sure it could be stopped. They could then argue that if Washington were unwilling to take the lead in the name of justice and moderation, someone else would take over with results that would be disastrous to all the noble aspirations for which he had fought. That Gates, whom Washington so distrusted, could be put forward as the alternate leader seemed a masterstroke.

His Excellency would be assured that no more than a threat from the army would be necessary. In a few weeks or months, the planter could return to Mount Vernon in the happy consciousness that he had not shirked his final task. Tact would exclude any hints that Washington might in the end be forced by duty to accept the burden of a crown.

There remained, of course, the possibility that Washington could not be lured into going along—a grim possibility, but it had to be faced. In that case, perhaps the actual injustices being heaped on the army, as they were being inflamed by the propaganda of the agitators, would make it possible to sweep George Washington aside. Perhaps it might be necessary after all to conjure up some younger and more determined man on horseback.

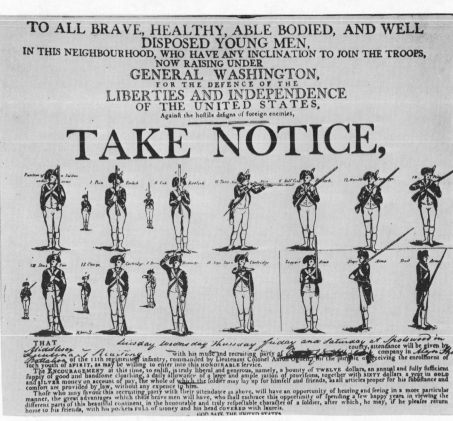

Recruiting poster. Courtesy of the Museum of the City of New York.

Washington's Headquarters at Newburgh, from a steel engraving after a painting by Robert W. Weir. Courtesy of Washington's Headquarters, Newburgh, New York.

CHAPTER

54

The Devil's Web

WASHINGTON was sticking close to his army, trying, as he put it, "like a careful physician to prevent, if possible, the disorders getting to an incurable height." Time, he added, passed "heavily on in this dreary mansion in which we are fast locked by frost and snow."[1]

The French had marched away to sail from Boston for the Indies, but a few days of diversion were promised by a last visit from Chastellux and Rochambeau, who, having seen their troops off, were riding south to make a separate departure from Baltimore. Chastellux came first. He was impressed by the tiny size and crowding of the headquarters at Newburgh, New York: only one room was "tolerably spacious," and its walls were broken by seven doors and one window. His visit was spent in conversation, much of it at the dinner table. At bedtime, a camp cot was set up for him in the parlor where the family assembled when not eating. He was amused by the speed with which the cot was folded and carried off in the morning. Another winter having come, Martha was in residence, and American manners, the Frenchman noted smilingly, would not permit a bed in a room where women were received.[2]

Concerning the whole adventure with the French troops, Washington wrote that he doubted if ever before the armies of two nations had parted "with such sentiments of sincere affection and mutual regret." The historian can rule that the amity was due more to Rochambeau than to Washington: the French professional soldier, long experienced in serving under capricious princes whose abuse he had to bear and whose elbows he had to jog, had kept his temper more successfully than the American who was in legend to epitomize self-control. But it did not follow that Washington felt any affection for Rochambeau. His final letter of farewell to the French com-

[497]

mander in chief was formal and stilted.* His feeling for Chastellux was another matter.[3]

Chastellux was moved by the "real tenderness" Washington expressed at their parting. Washington, however, feared that he had not given adequate expression to his admiration for this exciting and charming European intellectual. "I felt too much," he wrote Chastellux, "to express anything. . . . A sense of your public services to this continent and gratitude for your private friendship quite overcame me at the moment of our separation. . . . I can truly say that never in my life did I part with a man to whom my soul clave more sincerely." Nothing could give him more pleasure than, when the war was over, to accompany Chastellux on a tour of the American continent "in search of the natural curiosities with which it abounds, and to view the foundations of a rising empire."[4]

Devotees of puzzles may be interested in trying to extract the meaning from a letter Washington wrote at this time to his aide McHenry, then on leave in Baltimore. Washington destroyed all other letters—both McHenry's and his own—which might give the secret away.

"Let me congratulate you," Washington wrote, "and I do it very sincerely, on your restoration to health. I was in pain for *you*. I was in some for *myself* and wished for my PS of M——; and both my P——e L——s. in J——, resolving (like a man in the last agony) not to follow the trade and occupation of a G——. and more.

"I attribute all the delays, and my disappointments in this business, to your sickness; for otherwise, I should denominate you an unfeeling, teasing mortal. In proof of it, I would assert that in March last, I committed a matter to your care of which you took no notice till July following, and then *in such a way* as to set afloat a thousand ideas; which resolved themselves into almost as many anxious questions. These, again, you acknowledged the receipt of on the 26th of July, and on the 3d of August promise an answer, when? When: three or four weeks from that date. During this time my imagination is left on the rack. I remain in the field of conjecture, unable to account for the causes of somethings, or to judge of their effect. In a word, I cannot develop some mysteries; the appearance of which gave rise to those queries which were made the contents of a letter.

"Do not, my dear doctor, tease your mistress in this manner; much less your wife, when you get one. The first will pout, and the other may scold. A friend will bear with it, especially one who assures you, with as much truth as I do, that he is sincere. Adieu."[5]

---

* Washington and Rochambeau were in later years to exchange the complimentary letters of victorious fellow veterans. In preparing the manuscript of his *Memoirs*, Rochambeau wrote that, although "politics [the French Revolution] brought an end to our correspondence, our hearts will remain united in life and in death." Then, for whatever reason, he scratched the phrase out.[6]

McHenry was only one of Washington's aides who was off elsewhere. Considering it heartless to deny the young men the time off he had to deny himself, Washington was kept indoors "more than I wish or ought to be." When the tired, fifty-one-year-old soldier labored over documents, he was often impeded because the lines of letters appeared "like a mist, blended together and confused." He experimented with the eyeglasses of various officers, and, having found a pair that seemed to suit his sight, sent them as models to the ingenious David Rittenhouse in Philadelphia. "The spectacles," he eventually wrote, "suit my eyes extremely well, and I am persuaded the reading glasses also will when I get more accustomed to the use of them. At present, I find some difficulty in coming at the proper focus." These reading glasses were soon to become major instruments in molding the United States.[7]

Less significant to history but more to American legend was Washington's preparation to have some of his own teeth, long previously pulled, fixed in a bridge that would fill the gaps in his mouth. He wrote Lund to find at Mount Vernon and send him "two small foreteeth" which might be in the secret drawer of his desk.[8]

Washington's next step was to write Dr. John Baker, a dentist in Philadelphia, "I shall be obliged to you for some of the plaster of Paris or that white powder with which you take in wax a model of the mouth for your false teeth, and directions how to mix and make use of it. When you have done this," so the optimistic improviser continued, "I can then give you such a model as will enable you to furnish me with what I want."

The Commander in Chief's skill at making a model of his own mouth was never tested, as the letter to Dr. Baker was captured and contributed to amusement at British headquarters.[9] Washington thus had to try again.

He was electrified to learn that a Frenchman, whose application to come through the lines from New York he had shunted aside as a routine matter, was in fact "the dentist of whose skill much has been said." Off to Lieutenant Colonel William Stevens Smith, who commanded on the lines, he rushed a letter urging inquiries as to whether the man was really competent. If he was, he should be encouraged to enter patriot-held territory at "whatever post or place." Washington explained that he had "some teeth which are very troublesome to me at times, and of which I wish to be eased, provided I could substitute others (not by transplantation, for this I have no idea, even with young people, and sure I am it cannot succeed with old) and gums which might be relieved by a man of skill." As if with a foreknowledge of how his dental problems would fascinate future generations, Washington admonished, "I would not wish this matter should be made a parade of."

The dentist, Jean Pierre Le Mayeur, proved to have practiced successfully in London and to be "considered particularly eminent." He visited Washington's headquarters in June 1783, conducting behind closed doors what operations we know not. After his return to New York, Washington wrote him in language designed to frustrate prying eyes, "The valise arrived safe, as did the three articles which accompanied your card. . . . I can only repeat my thanks to you for your great and constant attention to me, and wish for opportunities to show my sense of them. The small matters [his own foreteeth?] which were expected from Virginia are not yet received, and it is to be feared will never be found. . . . You will be pleased to receive further assurances of the pleasure I will have in entertaining you [after the peace] in my house in Virginia, and in showing you every civility in my power in that state."* 10

Like humbler soldiers, Washington worried over what would be his situation when he was let go. He reminded Lund, "I shall come home with empty pockets whenever peace shall take place." He wanted his manager to send him figures on the state of his affairs, but Lund, who had an aversion to account books, procrastinated until Washington burst out that it was unreasonable to expect that he could be "totally insensible to the *only means* by which myself and family, and the character I am to maintain in life hereafter, is to be supported."11

In early January, Washington received certain news that George III had agreed to treat with the Americans as representatives of an independent nation. "I dare say," Washington commented, "[he] felt some severe pangs at the time he put his hand to the letters patent." However, the concession might have been made simply to achieve a parley, and the subsequent rumors coming in from Europe were "so equivocal that the best informed were much at a loss whether we must expect peace or a war." Being deprived of all "amusements or avocations," Washington looked "wistfully to the east and to the south" (toward the seacoast), awaiting some message that might speed his return to "domestic life."12

The crucial dispatch of the winter, perhaps the most crucial in Washington's entire career, came in mid-February directly from Philadelphia and bore Hamilton's signature. The New York congressman reported that "the state of our finances was perhaps never more critical," and that Congress, "not governed by reason or foresight but by circumstances," would probably be unable to take "the proper measures." Considering "the temper and situation of the army," this promised "an embarrassing scene."

Hamilton stated that the possibilities for supply were so bad that if the

---

* How British aristocrats would have sneered at such courtesy shown by any gentleman—all the more a great national leader—to a man whose trade was then considered so lowly. Mayeur himself expressed wonder, after he did visit Mount Vernon, at the "civility and attention that His Excellency and Mrs. Washington pays to a poor dentist."

war continued, the army would by June have to live completely off the land *"to defend the* country." Hamilton added that should peace take place, the army would do the same *"to procure justice to itself.* It appears to be a prevailing opinion in the army that the disposition to recompense their services will cease with the necessity for them, and that, if they once lay down their arms, they will part with the means of obtaining justice. It is to be lamented that appearances afford too much ground for their distrust."

Should the army urge its claims "with moderation but with firmness," Hamilton continued, that might "operate on those weak minds which are influenced by their apprehensions more than their judgments, so as to produce a concurrence in the measures which the exigencies of affairs demand. They may add weight to the applications of Congress to the several states." However, "the difficulty will be to keep a *complaining* and *suffering army* within the bounds of moderation. This your Excellency's influence must effect."

Instead of discountenancing the army's endeavors to procure redress, Washington's effort should be *"to take the direction of them."* He should do this not publicly, but "by the intervention of confidential and prudent persons," in such a way as to preserve the confidence of the army without losing that of the people. He would thus be enabled "in case of extremity to guide the torrent and bring order, perhaps even good, out of confusion. 'Tis a part that requires address, but 'tis one which your own situation as well as the welfare of the community points out.

"I will not conceal from your Excellency a truth which it is necessary you should know": the army felt that "delicacy carried to an extreme" prevented him from giving them adequate support, a situation which would damage the influence toward moderation he could exert, "should any commotions unhappily ensue."

Hamilton then defined the army's role: it was to cooperate with "all men of sense" in the establishment of the federal taxation "which alone can do justice to the creditors of the United States . . . and supply the future wants of government." He tactfully threw in that, of the creditors, "the army forms the most meritorious class." General Knox, Hamilton continued, "may be safely made use of" as Washington's representative to the creditors and the politicians. "Situated as I am," he concluded, "Your Excellency will feel the confidential nature of these observations."[13]

In came another letter, this one from Washington's confidential correspondent in Congress, Joseph Jones. "Reports are freely circulated here," Jones wrote, "that there are dangerous combinations in the army, and within a few days past it has been said, they are about to declare they will not disband until their demands are complied with." Jones warned that "sinister practices" were being used by conspirators to hurt Washington's "reputation"—as he read, Washington underlined the word "reputation"—so that "the weight of your opposition will prove no obstacle to their ambitious designs." Jones did not deny the possibility that "they are likely to succeed. . . . Whether to temporize or oppose with steady, unremitting firmness . . . must be left to your own sense of propriety and better judgment."[14]

The adjutant general, Colonel Walter Stewart, appeared from Philadelphia to tell Washington that the public creditors would join the army in the field, if necessary. Stewart asked oblique questions aimed at determining whether Washington would come along.[15]

Then Colonel Brooks, member of the committee the officers had sent to Congress, walked into headquarters where, so his fellow committeeman Ogden complained, "the timid wretch discovered it to the only man from whom it was to be kept." The "it" was that Brooks had been sent to camp to prepare minds "for some manly, vigorous association with the other public creditors."[16]

The continuing direction from which the news came—from Philadelphia—suggested to Washington that the center of the agitation was the city rather than the military camp. However, he started his own investigation, which turned up information he found very disturbing. The agitation among his soldiers might be more extensive than he was inclined to believe; and it rose from "the old leaven"—i.e., Gates and his supporters—"beginning to work under a mask of the most perfect dissimulation and apparent cordiality."[17]

During "many contemplative hours," as he put it, Washington puzzled over "the predicament in which I stand as Citizen and Soldier." His situation was "as critical and delicate as can well be conceived. The sufferings of a complaining army on one hand, and the inability of Congress and tardiness of the states on the other, are," he could not deny, "the forebodings of evil and may be productive of events which are more to be deprecated than prevented." Since the army was truly suffering, could it be his duty willingly to lead his faithful followers in whatever measures were necessary to win them justice? Or should he unwillingly take the lead in a movement of which he still disapproved, in order to keep it from getting out of hand? Of one thing he could be certain: there were great abuses that needed remedy. And, as if to point up the gravity of the financial situation, Morris, in whom Washington had such faith, resigned as financier with an angry public blast: "I will never be the minister of injustice."[18]

Washington did not act quickly. It was March 4 before he answered Hamilton's letter. He had often thought, he wrote, "that the public interest might be benefited if the commander in chief of the army was let more into the political and pecuniary state of our affairs. . . . A man may be upon the brink of a precipice before he is aware of his danger. . . . So far was I from conceiving that our finances was in so deplorable a state *at this time* that I had imbibed ideas from some source or another that, with the prospect of a loan from Holland, we should be able to rub along."

He was amazed that Hamilton, having observed the occasions when the army had subsisted itself, would not recognize "the fatal tendency of such a measure; but I shall give it as my opinion that it would at this day be productive of civil commotions and end in blood. Unhappy situation this! God forbid we should be involved in it."

Under so serious a threat, Congress might be wise to adjourn for a few months so that the members could go home and explain matters to the state legislatures. Surely, the just claims of the army would "have their weight with every sensible legislature in the Union." He was "not without hope" that, if "prudence and policy" were listened to, Hamilton's "apprehensions in case of peace are greater than there is cause for. In this, however, I may be mistaken, if those ideas which you have been informed are propagated in the army should be extensive. . . .

"Be these things as they may, I shall pursue the same steady line of conduct which has governed me hitherto, fully convinced that the sensible and discerning part of the army cannot be unacquainted (although I never took pains to inform them) of the services I have rendered it on more occasions than one." He would continue to steer the army into peaceful petitions and was "under no *great* apprehension of its exceeding the bounds of reason and moderation."[19]

Washington had now made it completely clear that he would not willingly support armed intimidation of the recalcitrant legislatures. The agitators would now have to move to the next step. They would have to try to force Washington's hand.

On March 10, there circulated in camp at Newburgh an unsigned call to a mass meeting of officers on the next day. The meeting would consider measures to achieve that redress of grievances which the army's representatives in Philadelphia "seem to have solicited in vain." Since it was not authorized by Washington and was thus contrary to regulations, the call was something altogether new and implied revolutionary action.[20]

Washington was pondering the mutinous call when he was handed a copy of a more extensive paper. Despite a "dreadful alternative" they presented, he was moved by the words into considering that the appeal "in point of composition, in elegance and force of expression, has rarely been equaled in the English language."* [21]

"Gentlemen," Washington read, "A fellow soldier, whose interest and affections bind him strongly to you, whose past sufferings have been as great

---

* Gates's aide Armstrong is generally accepted as having been the author of what came to be known as the "Newburgh Addresses."

and whose future fortune may be as desperate as yours—would beg leave to address you. . . .

"Like many of you, he loved private life and left it with regret. . . . He has long shared in your toils and mingled in your dangers. He has felt the cold hand of poverty without a murmur, and has seen the insolence of wealth without a sigh. . . . He has till lately—very lately—believed in the justice of his country. . . . But faith has its limits, as well as temper."

Did his fellow soldiers see, the author asked, "a country courting your return to private life with tears of gratitude and smiles of admiration, longing to divide with you that independency which your gallantry has given, and those riches which your wounds have preserved? Is this the case? Or is it rather a country that tramples upon your rights, disdains your cries, and insults your distresses? . . .

"If this, then, be your treatment while the swords you wear are necessary for the defense of America, what have you to expect from peace, when your voice shall sink and your strength dissipate by division? When those very swords, the instruments and companions of your glory, shall be taken from your sides, and no remaining mark of military distinction left but your wants, infirmities, and scars? . . . Can you consent to wade through the vile mire of despondency and owe the miserable remnant of that life to charity, which has hitherto been spent in honor? If you can—GO—and carry with you the jest of Tories and scorn of Whigs—the ridicule and, what is worse, the pity of the world. Go starve and be forgotten."

Otherwise, the army should "suspect the man who would advise to more moderation and longer forbearance." They should draw up a remonstrance which stated "that the slightest mark of indignity from Congress now must operate like the grave and part you forever; that in any political event, the army has its alternative. If peace, that nothing shall separate them from your arms of death. If war, that, courting the auspices and inviting the direction of your illustrious leader, you will retire to some unsettled country, smile in your turn, and 'mock when their fear cometh on.' "[22]

The manner in which his own emotions were stirred by these words filled Washington with "inexpressible concern." He had been prepared for nothing like this. He considered it a "storm which had gathered so suddenly and unexpectedly." Was he tempted to let the storm continue to swirl away with his emotions?[23]

Washington could not credit what Hamilton and others told him: that the intervention of the army into civilian affairs was an expedient that need not go beyond a threat, that would quickly succeed and be as quickly forgotten. He saw that the most important matter of all was the direction of the deep historical flow on which momentary events are but ripples. He saw that if the army were allowed to terrorize civilians for political ends, the whole future of the United States would have been turned into a new course. That course offered to him personally great rank and glory. Was he tempted?

"If I have been led to detest the folly and madness of unbounded ambition," Washington was later to state, "if I have been induced from other motives to draw my sword and regulate my public behavior, let me not arrogate the merit to human imbecility, but rather ascribe whatever glory may result . . . to a higher and more efficient cause: . . . the Greatest and Best of Beings."[24] Did Washington actually feel a need for the hand of Providence to dash from his lips the cup of ambition?

As far as the world could see, his determination was firm and clear. It was his duty, he wrote Hamilton and Jones, "to arrest on the spot the foot that stood wavering on a tremendous precipice, to prevent the officers from being taken by surprise while the passions were all inflamed, and to rescue them from plunging themselves into a gulf of civil horror from which there might be no receding. . . . It is easier," he explained, "to divert from a wrong to a right path than to recall the hasty and fatal steps which have already been taken."[25]

But could the foot be arrested or was it already so far out over the precipice that the rest of the plunge inevitably followed? Washington issued an order expressing "disapprobation of such disorderly proceedings" as the illegally called meeting, and summoned a meeting of his own for the following Saturday. The anonymous pamphleteer then produced another paper approving the change, stating that the new meeting could be used for the purposes of the old, and hinting that Washington's action implied sympathy with the revolutionary plans.[26]

The meeting was held on March 15, 1783, in the Temple, a spacious hall with a vaulted roof which the troops had built from green timber to serve as a church on Sunday and at other times as a dancing academy. It was large enough for a brigade, and on that Saturday noon it was crowded to the walls. In calling the meeting, Washington had stated, "The senior officer in rank present will be pleased to preside and report the result of the deliberations to the Commander in Chief." Surveying the general officers who were sitting on a little dais, the conspirators were pleased to see that Washington had adhered to his resolution: he was not present. As the second in seniority, Gates would preside—and Gates was their creature.[27]

A door giving onto the dais opened. Everyone turned their heads, and then His Excellency strode out into general view. A murmur of excitement went up from the crowd. As he looked out at his command, Washington appeared "sensibly agitated." For the first time since he had won the heart of the army in Cambridge, Washington saw in the faces of his officers not affection, not pleasure in his being present, but resentment, embarrassment, and in some cases anger.[28]

"If my conduct," Washington said, "heretofore has not evinced to you that I have been a faithful friend to the army, my declaration of it at this time would be equally unavailing and improper. But as I was among the first who embarked in the cause of our common country; as I have never left your side one moment but when called from you on public duty; as I have been the common companion and witness of your distresses, and not among the last to feel and acknowledge your merits; as I have ever considered my own military reputation as inseparably connected with that of the army; as my heart has ever expanded with joy when I have heard its praises, and my indignation has arisen when the mouth of detraction has been opened against it, it can *scarcely be supposed,* at this late stage of the war, that I am indifferent to its interests." Washington paused to examine the faces before him: they were not moved.

He asked how the interests of the army were to be promoted. "The way is plain, says the anonymous addresser. If war continues, remove into the unsettled country; there establish yourselves, and leave an ungrateful country to defend itself. But who are they to defend? Our wives, our children, our farms and other property which we leave behind us? Or, in this state of hostile separation, are we to take the two first (the latter cannot be removed) to perish in a wilderness with hunger, cold, and nakedness? If peace takes place, never sheath your swords, says he, until you have obtained full and ample justice. This dreadful alternative, of either deserting our country in the extremest hour of her distress or turning our arms against it (which is the apparent object, unless Congress can be compelled into instant compliance) has something so shocking in it, that humanity revolts at the idea. My God! what can this writer have in view by recommending such measures? Can he be a friend to the army? Can he be a friend to this country? Rather, is he not an insidious foe? Some emissary perhaps from [British-held] New York, plotting the ruin of both by sowing the seeds of discord and separation between the civil and military powers of the continent?" The faces in front of Washington appeared uneasy—many stared away from him—but he still saw frowns.

. "There might, gentlemen, be an impropriety in my taking notice, in this address to you, of an anonymous production. . . . With respect to the advice given by the author, to suspect the man who shall recommend moderate measures and longer forbearance, I spurn it. . . . If men are to be precluded from offering their sentiments on a matter which may involve the most serious and alarming consequences that can invite the consideration of mankind, reason is of no use to us. The freedom of speech may be taken away, and, dumb and silent, we may be led, like sheep, to the slaughter."

Washington then assured his hearers that it was "My decided opinion" that Congress entertained "exalted sentiments of the services of the army" and would, despite the slowness inherent in deliberative bodies, act justly. He declared "in this public and solemn manner that, in the attainment of complete justice for all your toils and dangers, and in the gratification of every wish, so far as may be done consistently with the great duty I owe my country and those powers we are bound to respect, you may freely command my services to the utmost of my abilities. . . .

"And let me conjure you, in the name of our common country, as you value your own sacred honor, as you respect the rights of humanity, and as you regard the military and national character of America, to express your utmost horror and detestation of the man who wishes, under any specious pretenses, to overturn the liberties of our country, and who wickedly attempts to open the flood gates of civil discord and deluge our rising empire in blood. By thus determining and thus acting, you will pursue the plain and direct road to the attainment of your wishes. . . . And you will, by the dignity of your conduct, afford occasion for posterity to say, when speaking of the glorious example you have exhibited to mankind, 'had this day been wanting, the world had never seen the last stage of perfection to which human nature is capable of attaining.' "[29]

Washington had finished his prepared speech, but the chill in the Temple had not thawed. The familiar faces looking up at him were uneasy, perplexed, sullen. Washington reached in his pocket and pulled out a piece of paper. This, he stated, was a letter from a member of Congress that would show the officers what that body was trying to do and what the problems were. He would read it.

The officers stirred impatiently in their seats, and then suddenly every heart missed a beat. Something was the matter with His Excellency. He seemed unable to read the paper. He paused in bewilderment. He fumbled in his waistcoat pocket. And then he pulled out something that only his intimates had seen him wear. A pair of glasses. With infinite sweetness and melancholy, he explained, "Gentlemen, you will permit me to put on my spectacles, for I have not only grown gray but almost blind in the service of my country."

This simple statement achieved what all Washington's rhetoric and all his arguments had been unable to achieve. The officers were instantly in tears, and, from behind the shining drops, their eyes looked with love at the commander who had led them all so far and long.[30]

Washington quietly finished reading the congressman's letter. He knew the battle was won, and avoiding, with his instinctive sense of the dramatic, any anticlimax, he walked out of the hall, mounted his horse, and disappeared from the view of those who were staring from the windows.

Washington's departure had been a daring move, since it left Gates to preside. Pickering rose to his feet and tried to sweep the army back toward violent action. There were those who thought that had a second orator followed Pickering, the conspiracy might still have been saved; but a motion was put to thank Washington for his counsel, and no other speaker opposed the motion. A committee drew up a new address to Congress, which was "unanimously" approved.[31]

The paper stated that since the officers had from the start of the war served their country "from the purest love and attachment to the rights and liberties of human nature," no distresses or dangers could make them sully the reputation they had earned during eight years. Continuing their unshaken confidence in the justice of Congress and their country, they abided in the conviction that the army would not be disbanded until accounts were settled and adequate funds foreseen for the eventual payment of pensions and back pay. Indeed, the officers "view with abhorrence and reject with disdain the infamous propositions" contained in the anonymous addresses, and they requested Washington to forward to the President of Congress their present petition, the granting of which would "prevent any further machinations of designing men."[32]

After the meeting had dissolved, all the officers, except the most determined of the conspirators, returned to their quarters with a sense of happiness at their own noble behavior and with gratitude to their leader who had led them into virtuous paths.

The historian may well ask what would have happened had Washington been persuaded to lead the insurrection or proved unable to suppress it. The result would certainly have been what he foresaw: bloodshed. It is hardly conceivable that all the state governments would have instantly capitulated. Washington (or whatever other man was in the saddle) would then have been frustrated, as the British had been, by the lack of any few centers the control of which meant the control of the nation. Had expeditionary forces captured all thirteen capitals, even that would not necessarily have pacified the countryside.

Since the cleavage between federalism and states' rights followed roughly the political cleavage between conservative and radical, those civil aspects of the conflict which Washington had always labored to minimize would have burst into flame. Even if England had not taken advantage of the resulting chaos, when the fire burnt out it would probably have left behind several nations, the largest (if you please) under the kingship of George I, the others practicing various types of government. Deep-seated ideological hatred would have prevented reunion, fomented border wars.

Americans can never be adequately grateful that George Washington possessed the power and the will to intervene effectively in what may well have been the most dangerous hour the United States has ever known.

X

The Curtain of Separation

CHAPTER

55

A Clouded Parting

A S winter gales abated and the white, turbulent ocean sank to a smoother blue, straining sails brought in quick succession word of successive treaties signed. There had been an armistice; England had acknowledged the independence of the thirteen United States; France and Spain had joined England and America in the provisional peace. Although English troops were still on American soil, saving the most unexpected the war was over. On April 18, 1783, Washington formally congratulated his troops on having "assisted in protecting the rights of humane nature and establishing an asylum for the poor and oppressed of all nations and religions."[1]

In keeping his promise to the mass meeting that he would again argue with Congress about the plight of the army, Washington penned a personal appeal to the emotions of the nation: If the officers were forced, after their great services, "to wade through the vile mire of despondency and owe 'the miserable remnant of that life to charity which has hitherto been spent in honor,' then shall I have learned what ingratitude is; then shall I have realized a tale which will embitter every moment of my future life. But I am under no such apprehensions. A country rescued by their arms from impending ruin, will never leave unpaid the debt of gratitude."

Washington urged that Congress grant "everything requested" by the army "in the late memorial to Congress." He added his "decided opinion" that the establishment of federal funds "will be the most certain means of preserving the national faith and future tranquillity of this extensive continent."[2]

In a private letter to Congressman Jones, Washington stated that the army did not expect what was "impractical." They wished that before they were discharged the balances owed them be ascertained, but would accept for most of the debt certificates entitling them to future payment. This, Washington mourned, would make them "considerable sufferers," because

[511]

"necessity will compel them to part with their certificates for what they will fetch" to "unfeeling, avaricious speculators."[3]

Washington had both personal and public reasons for being angry with the financial community. When the opportunity finally opened to buy land contiguous to Mount Vernon which he had wanted for twenty years, none of the Philadelphia businessmen would lend him a cent: he had to borrow from a fellow agrarian, Governor Clinton of New York.[4] And as he investigated the causes of the dangers he had just successfully breasted, he concluded that the army had been cast by Hamilton, the Morrises, and others as "mere puppets to establish continental funds" which, if secured, would have gone into the pockets of the private creditors.

To Hamilton, Washington wrote one of his most eloquently angry passages to demonstrate that the army deserved much more gratitude from the nation than did the moneymen. He warned Hamilton in general terms—"the army . . . is a dangerous instrument to play with"—and added a specific threat which must have sent a chill through the agitators' hearts: If the soldiers could not get justice any other way, they would ignore the federal funds on which the civilian creditors were forced to rely, and seek, as they were in a position to do, payment directly from the states. This, Washington added, "might *tend* to defeat the end" which the Morrises and their allies "had in view by endeavoring to involve the army."[5]

Historians, after long accepting the federalist line that the central government had actually been in extremis, have recently suspected that the rat Washington smelled was actually there. It is now being argued that the moneymen intentionally deepened the financial crisis in order to entrap the army. The financier, it is stated, had resources left that he did not use, and certainly his resignation at the crucial moment (he soon took it back) was a propaganda gesture. Hamilton, so his biographer John C. Miller points out, put forward a theoretical reason for paying the businessmen in preference to soldiers. By expending for food and clothing what pittances they received, the soldiers would trickle the money out across the countryside where it would disappear, while large creditors would, by investing impressive sums, augment the national credit.[6]

Congress obediently voted to determine the debts owed all individual soldiers, and award the officers, instead of half pay for life, certificates for five years' extra pay drawing six per cent interest. This gave the army "the highest satisfaction," Washington wrote, but all should also receive some cash—three months' pay at least—so that they would not return home as paupers. However, Congress had exhausted itself. Without actually drawing up the accounts,* without producing any cash, it voted to send most of the

---

* Actually, the federal records, kept by no single agency throughout the war, were in such confusion that the god of wisdom turned accountant would have been unable rapidly to straighten out the archives.

army home on furloughs that would become permanent when the final peace was signed.[7]

What was Washington to do? Should he, in loyalty to his loyal troops, at long last countenance disobedience to the civil authorities? The rumor may well have reached him that (as Armstrong wrote Gates) many officers looked back on the meeting he had quieted with "horror and regret," wishing that they had not given in to His Excellency's blandishments. Heath appeared at headquarters bearing an "Address of the Generals and Officers Commanding the Regiments" which requested that no men be sent home until Congress could be informed of the wretched condition into which the troops would be flung. However sadly, Washington replied that the troops must trust to the eventual justice of the Congress and the states. Furthermore, by accepting the furlough, the army would help the financier to raise the credit that would enable him to give them some pay in notes redeemable in four or six months.[8]

When Heath, accompanied by Knox and Steuben, appeared with another document to show Washington, the commander's heart must have sunk. What was his delight to discover that his old companions had now brought him a paper he felt he could sign! He accepted the presidency of a new club, the Society of the Cincinnati.

Not having been present at the organizational meetings, he did not know that there had been stormy scenes as the more radical officers objected to the provision, finally adopted, that membership in the Cincinnati pass to the descendants of the original holders according to the aristocratic principle of primogeniture. Nor did he reason that the provision for the admission to the society of honorary members, elected for life, opened the ranks to politicians and businessmen, raising the possibility that the Cincinnati would become what Washington greatly distrusted: a pressure group in the service of "faction." The statement that one of the objectives was "to promote and cherish between the respective states that national honor so necessary to their [the officers'] future happiness and the dignity of the American empire" failed to make Washington fear that this was a renewal of the effort to bring the military into politics on the federalist side. It seemed to him that the principal object of the Cincinnati was to establish a charitable fund for impoverished officers, since the government had made no provision for them. After the establishment of the society had created a national storm, Washington stated that not a member had, at its inception, realized that it would cause "the least uneasiness."[9] *

Although Washington was later to be "most amazingly embarrassed" by

---

* As an old man, Jefferson remembered that it had "always been believed" that officers of the army, led by Steuben and Knox, had offered Washington a crown. When Washington had indignantly refused, as their next effort to the same end, the officers had established "an hereditary order . . . to be engrafted into the future frame of govern-

the Cincinnati, for the moment he was delighted with this symbol of the continued mutual affection of his officers. He used his influence to persuade Louis XVI to relax a ban on foreign decorations so that membership could be extended to the French officers who had served in America. He offered to help finance the society with a gift of five hundred dollars, and ordered eight of its badges, wishing, if such a luxury were not against the rules, to have one "finished in a masterly manner" for "extra occasions."[10]

As the moment neared for the bulk of the army to disband, Robert Morris announced that, far from coming up with cash, he could not finance certificates payable in any finite time for three months' pay, and that he could not produce certificates for one month's pay as he lacked the cash to buy paper to print them on. A great resentment against the Commander in Chief, who had placed them in this vile position, surged upward in the breasts of his fellow veterans. History has preferred to dwell on a later farewell between Washington and the remnant of officers then still in service, forgetting that when most of the Continental officers went home, they canceled—"to the chagrin," as Colonel Stewart wrote, of "certain characters"—a final dinner together at which the Commander in Chief would have occupied a place of honor. "The sensibility," Washington confided to Congress, "occasioned by a parting scene under such peculiar circumstances, will not admit of description."[11]

He decided to put every ounce of his prestige behind another circular letter to the states, which he would give double impact by stating that it was the last official communication he would ever write, as he was about to retire forever. The document, indeed, came to be known as "Washington's Legacy," and was to enjoy for a time the celebrity that was later achieved by "Washington's Farewell Address."

Washington wrote that, since he would never again take "any share in public business," this interference in political matters could not be attributed to personal ambition. But even after this disclaimer, he did not fully state his mind. His private belief was that "a convention of the people" should be called to establish "a federal constitution," which would reduce the states to the position of counties. Local problems would go to local legislatures, but "when superior considerations predominate in favor of the whole," local "voices should be heard no more."

However, the Constitutional Convention lay years in the future, and in his

ment, and placing Washington still at the head." At the time, John Adams and Jefferson agreed with many other leaders that the Cincinnati was a subversive organization; the Massachusetts legislature denounced the society, and Rhode Island threatened to disfranchise the members. The organization, a flaming pamphleteer argued, "ere long must strip the posterity of the middling and lower classes of every influence or authority, and leave them nothing but insignificance, contempt, and the wretched privilege of murmuring when it is too late."[12]

"Legacy" Washington only argued for what he thought might be immediately attained. He urged that the existing Articles of Confederation be interpreted and extended to create a central government adequate to the obvious needs. "Whatever measures have a tendency to dissolve the union . . . ought to be considered as hostile to the liberty and independency of America." Americans were facing a choice "whether they will be respectable and prosperous, or contemptible and miserable as a nation . . . whether the Revolution must ultimately be considered as a blessing or a curse: a blessing or a curse not to the present age alone, for with our fate will the destiny of unborn millions be involved." He warned that, if the central government were allowed to fall apart, "we may find by our own unhappy experience that there is a natural and necessary progression from the extreme of anarchy to the extreme of tyranny."

In addition to "an indissoluble union," Washington pressed three points: the establishment of an adequate peacetime army and navy, "a sacred regard for public justice," which included paying what was owed to both civilians and soldiers; and the forgetting of the "local prejudices" which divided the nation.[13]

56

The Emptying Stage

I NCREASINGLY the world of great events appeared to Washington as a theater putting on shows less real than the humdrum of everyday life. Before sending most of his army home on furlough, he had written, "Nothing now remains but for the actors of this mighty scene to preserve a perfect, unvarying constancy of character through the very last act, to close the drama with applause, and to retire from the military theater with the same approbation of angels and men which have crowned all their former virtuous actions."[1]

Of course, as the old play ended a new one began. He feared that, being "placed among the nations of the earth," having "a character to establish . . . we shall be guilty of many blunders in treading this boundless theater before we shall have arrived at any perfection in this art." Be that as it may, he felt that "relaxation and repose" were "absolutely necessary for me."[2]

However, he felt that his duty still required him to remain in command of the skeleton force that waited at the lower Hudson until the final peace treaty was signed and until the British (who had already evacuated Charleston) disappeared from their last foothold in the populated part of the United States: New York. As it turned out, he had to "wear away" seven months of "this distressing tedium," during which Martha, who had again joined him, suffered from "an incompetent share of health: bilious fevers and colics attack her often, and reduce her low."[3]

As an impoverished boy associating with richer companions, Washington had kept careful accounts of his expenditures. After he had grown up and achieved prosperity, the habit had not shrunk from him. He seemed, indeed, to enjoy the clean world of interlocking numbers where he could occupy his attention in times of anxiety. And during the war, since he had insisted that he should not be paid but only have his expenses reimbursed, keeping track of his expenses had been essential to his future prosperity. Year after year, he had joined in interminable bookkeeping with the succession of aides who had handled his privy purse. Now, as he waited in depressing doldrums for the war actually to end, he pulled the accounts together into page after page of chronological summary. The task was made infinitely more complicated by the way money had changed in value from month to month. Every sum had to be adjusted according to a table, sanctioned by Congress, which ruled (to take a few examples) that a thousand pounds in paper had been worth three hundred in "lawful money" during April 1777; seventy-five pounds in September 1778; ten pounds, four shillings in January 1780; and again seventy-five in May 1781.

Washington interpreted his agreement with Congress to mean that, while his renunciation of a salary would preclude his earning anything from his service in the war, his grant of expenses would be so inclusive that his personal activities would involve him in no cost. He was thus disturbed to find, on totaling his recorded expenses, that what Congress still owed him would only partially reimburse cash that he had spent from his own pocket. "Through hurry, I suppose, and the perplexity of business (for I know not how else to account for the deficiency)," he mourned, there must have been many items "I have omitted to charge."

That he stood thus unfairly to be "a considerable loser" nudged Washington on a question which he had long been arguing out with his conscience: who should pay the expenses Martha had incurred when she had traveled back and forth between Mount Vernon and the army? She had made six round trips and one leg of a seventh. The total cost had been £1064.1.0 lawful money.

Finally, Washington included Martha's expenses in his bill to Congress, noting that he had not entered them "into my public accounts as they occurred" because they appeared "in the commencement of them to have the complexion of a private charge." However, since "the embarrassed situation of our public affairs" obliged him "to postpone the visit I every year contemplated to make my family between the close of one campaign and the opening of another, and, as this expense was incidental thereto, and consequent of my self-denial" he "adjudged the charge as just with respect to myself."

Under the date of July 1, 1783, Washington submitted accounts totaling £8422.16.4 in "lawful." Of this, he noted £3387.4.4 had gone for the household expenses of eight years, and £1982.10.0 for "secret intelligence." Congress owed him above what he had already received the sum of £1972.9.0.* [4]

---

* July did not, of course, mark the completion of Washington's service. After his final return to Mount Vernon, he sent in a second accounting. All his charges were approved. Indeed, when his books were audited by professionals, Washington's balances were found to be out by less than a dollar.[5]

Having completed and sent off his accounts, Washington was again at loose ends. For nineteen days in July and August, he sought surcease in such a wilderness as he had wandered and fought over when a young man. He explored the New York frontier, covering seven hundred and fifty miles on horseback, by canoe, or by breaking through the forest on foot. Although he examined the battlefields where the lakes had been defended, where Burgoyne had been defeated, and where Indian raids had disgorged, he found his mind turning irresistibly to his former fascination with land speculation and canals. Remembering how he had taken dying relatives and also his own aching body to the Virginia hot springs, he was impressed by the hot springs at Saratoga; he made, in partnership with Governor Clinton, an unsuccessful offer for the wild land that was eventually to groan under luxury hotels. The man who had promoted a canal up the steeps and rapids of the Potomac, which he hoped would bring the goods of the west to his own part of Virginia, eyed with envy the New York's almost flat waterway (later the route of the Erie Canal) from the Hudson to the Great Lakes. Again with Clinton, he tried to buy the land around Fort Schuyler which dominated the vital crossing from the west-flowing Mohawk to north-flowing Wood Creek. Failing in this, he secured other land on the Mohawk that proved one of the most rewarding of his speculations.[6]

Now that the war was almost done, Washington was swinging back to his old stance, looking west. He wrote Chastellux not of any plan to visit that friend in France, but that he intended "taking a more contemplative and extensive view of the vast inland navigation of these United States. . . . I shall not rest contented till I have explored the western country, and traversed those lines (or a great part of them) which have given bounds to a New Empire."[7]

While Washington's regulars were sadly accepting injustice, a few raw recruits had rioted for the little pay owed them and frightened Congress out of Philadelphia.* Congress raised their shaky banner at Princeton, New Jersey, and summoned Washington there to discuss with them a peacetime military establishment.[8] On his way from the Hudson Highlands, His Excellency and officers who were seeing him off, weighed themselves at West Point, with results that must have elicited hilarity when Knox jumped ponderously onto the scales: Washington, 209 pounds; Lincoln, 244; Knox, 280.[9]

Lodgings were supplied the Washingtons in a "rustic mansion"—i.e., farmhouse—a few miles from Princeton on Rocky Hill. Public matters pro-

---

* That the federal government could be set to flight by the fleabite insurrection of a few amateurish companies further demonstrates how dangerous it would have been to civil institutions had Washington consented to lead in armed protest the strong and well-organized Continental Army.

ceeded languorously, as Congress rarely boasted a quorum. Despite his impatience to get things done, to get home, tension flowed away from Washington. A friend noted, "The General's front is uncommonly open and pleasant. The contracted, pensive phiz, betokening deep thought and much care . . . is done away, and a pleasant smile and sparkling vivacity of wit and humor succeeds."[10]

The handsome widow Annis Boudinot Stockton sent Washington an ode in his praise with a coy request that he give her absolution for writing poetry. He replied, "I find myself strangely disposed to be a very indulgent ghostly adviser on this occasion; and, notwithstanding 'you are the most offending soul alive' (that is, if it is a crime to write elegant poetry), yet if you will come and dine with me on Thursday, and go through the proper course of penitence, which shall be prescribed, I will strive hard to assist you in expiating these poetical trespasses on this side of purgatory." He would certainly urge her to write more poetry. "You see, Madam, when once the Woman has tempted us and we have tasted the forbidden fruit, there is no such thing as checking our appetites, whatever the consequences may be." Then, perhaps thinking that he had gone too far, he stated that he was not "conscious of deserving anything more at your hands than the most disinterested friendship has a right to claim," and thanked her for sending kind wishes not only to him but to "the partner of all my domestic enjoyments."[11]

A joke Washington made at this juncture has survived for posterity. Shaking his head sadly, the President of Congress croaked that the financier had his hands full.

"I wish," Washington replied, "he had his pockets full."[12]

Every day, when he was not in attendance on Congress, Washington rode through the countryside. As he was returning to his lodging one evening, he heard an awe-inspiring uproar. Coming nearer, he saw the farmer who was his host—"a man of uncommon size and strength and bulky withal"—standing over a colored boy as sweat poured from his brow and he held high in one hand a squealing and wiggling pig. "I'll show you," roared the farmer, "how to run down a pig!" Glimpsing His Excellency, the farmer, still holding the pig, tried to change his angry expression into a courtly smile, essayed a bow, and undertook a ceremonious apology which the pig, who was redoubling his kicks and squeals, completely drowned out. His Excellency "shook his sides" with "unrestrained laughter."[13]

Yet the days passed slowly. Some diversion was supplied by Thomas Paine, who stayed for a while with Washington while the General tried to persuade Congress to reward the services, to the American cause, of the man whom they were now shying away from as an arch-radical. Paine took Washington out hunting marsh gas. Because of his speculations on the causes of yellow fever, Paine was concerned with such "effluvia," and

Washington had heard of a nearby creek that could be set on fire. At night, Washington, Paine, and a whole party from headquarters set out in a scow from a milldam; soldiers stirred with poles the mud at the bottom of the creek, and, as the bubbles rose, Washington leaned down to hold within a few inches of the water a roll of lighted cartridge paper. Lo and behold, the flame spread across the surface of the water![14]

When Washington rode to Princeton, the old sense of urgency came upon him. He wished to have the peacetime military establishment settled soon enough to include the remnant of the Continental Army that was still serving. His plan, however, urged the greatest expenditure on a navy to turn back invaders and also to ferry troops from one part of the continent to another. Since America should not again enter a war weakened by ignorance, military academies should be set up, particularly for engineers and artillerymen. Agreeing that a large professional army might be dangerous to liberties, Washington, in the favorite of the several plans he proposed, urged that the "bulwark" of independence should be a "national militia" raised by the individual states, but uniformly organized and equipped. It should comprise most males between eighteen and fifty.* Included would be bodies of "minutemen" who could contain a sudden attack until the larger force could mobilize. To garrison West Point, frontier forts, and those magazines of arms as would have to be established, a permanent force of 2631 men would be needed. Two thousand, six hundred and thirty-one men! Congress, shuddering at the thought of so powerful a potential instrument of tyranny, procrastinated.[15]

Washington argued continually that what was due them be paid the soldiers, not only in cash but in the bounties of western land which had at one time or another been promised.[16] This line of argument got him into discussions on how best to move the frontier westward while avoiding Indian wars, which in turn produced recommendations on how the frontier should be governed and where new states should be established. Washington could not help recognizing the drift of his thoughts toward civilian administration, but he did not intend that to be a portent.[17]

To those who came to him crying crisis, shouting that it was his duty to save the peace as he had saved the war, he replied soothingly. His compatriots seemed to him "like young heirs, come, a little prematurely

---

* Washington, who had been for so long tied to the practicalities of mean military possibility, seems to have allowed himself to daydream when he suggested that almost the entire male population be enrolled in such a militia. Even if American economic and manufacturing possibilities had served to equip so large a force with that minimum Americans needed for warfare, the uniformity of organization which Washington urged would have involved, despite the proviso that the regiments stay under the titular command of the state governments, federal intervention far beyond what most of Washington's compatriots would at that juncture conceivably have accepted.[18]

perhaps, to a large inheritance. It is more than probable they will riot for a while." However, the situation "will work its own cure, as there is virtue at the bottom."[19]

He had done his part. As he wrote Lafayette, "To form a constitution that will give consistency, stability, and dignity to the Union, and sufficient powers to the great council of the nation for general purposes is a duty which is incumbent upon every man who wishes well to his country, and will meet with my aid as far as it can be rendered in the private walks of life: for henceforward my mind shall be unbent."[20]

Despite his yearnings, Washington's complicated nature wondered sometimes whether he would not, after all, be bored by the quiet he so desired. While writing to Robert Stewart, the man who had been his most intimate companion during his adventures in the French and Indian War, he found himself blaming "an impaired fortune (much injured by this contest)" for forcing him into "those walks of retirement where perhaps the consciousness" of having done his best to discharge "the duty I owed my country must supply the place of other gratifications, and may perhaps afford as rational and substantial entertainment as the gayer scenes of a more enlarged theater."* [21]

In inviting his habitual correspondents to visit him at Mount Vernon after the peace, Washington expressed the hope that the friendships "which have been planted and fostered in the tumult of public life may not wither and die in the serenity of retirement."[22] He wrote to New York asking whether some Hessian officer would not leave behind "a *good* cook." He needed at Mount Vernon a man "who can order, as well as get, a dinner; who can make dishes as well as proportion them *properly* to any company which shall be named to him to the amount of thirty." Having been assured from Philadelphia that French plated silver was "fashionable and much used in genteel houses in France and England," Washington wrote Lafayette that, as he was disinclined to import from England anything "I can get on tolerable terms elsewhere," he would like to purchase a quantity of French plate, including two salvers each large enough to hold twelve glasses of wine.[23]

At the very opening of November, news came that in Paris the definitive peace treaty had been signed: the war was over! Congress reacted, as Washington wrote, "equally unexpectedly and surprisingly to me." They adjourned without bringing the peace establishment, payment for the army, or any other pressing matter to decision. Washington sent his baggage to Mount Vernon and rode himself to the little army camp on the Hudson.[24]

---

* Stewart had written from abroad to ask for an appointment in the American government. Washington answered that he had been afraid that his old friend was dead—"how else could I account for a silence of fully fifteen years?"—and that the governmental posts would have to go to men who had earned them "with halters about their necks."

[521]

CHAPTER

57

An End and a Beginning

EVEN before word came in of the definitive peace. Congress, on hearing that the British were making active preparations to leave New York, decided officially to release that lion's share of the army which had gone home supposedly on furlough. In farewell orders sent from Rocky Hill, Washington wrote, "It only remains for the Commander in Chief to address himself once more and that for the last time to the armies of the United States (however widely dispersed the individuals who compose them may be) and to bid them an affectionate, a long farewell." He exhorted his former soldiers to become absorbed in civilian life, confident that their just grievances as soldiers would in the end be attended to.[1]

After Washington had arrived at the military camp on the Hudson, the officers there decided to reply formally to his farewell orders. Their unhappy mood was revealed by their confiding to Pickering, the one man who had publicly opposed Washington at the meeting where the army had withdrawn its threats, with the drafting of the document. Pickering took care, as he put it, to see that the paper was not "fulsome." It was mostly a reiteration of the army's grievances, the best said of Washington being the admission that his acts had been "urged by patriot virtues and magnanimity." The officers did not carry this document to Washington personally, but dispatched it with a covering letter.[2]

Washington was notified that the British would finally leave New York City on November 25. The day dawned crisp and sparkling, the wind from the northwest. But Washington and his little army saw no remains of autumn foliage as they advanced down Manhattan Island, for no trees still stood. Everything that could be used for fuel—forests, fences, outhouses, even ornamental shrubs—had vanished. Mansions, which had been preserved as officers' quarters, rose solitary from seas of weeds, clapboards fallen, gray from lack of paint. Washington moved through a countryside once familiar, but now, because it was naked, revealing strange gullies and outcroppings and vistas.[3]

The advance came to a halt at a barrier (the Bowery and Third Avenue) closing the entrance to the inner city. After a short wait, a discharge of cannon indicated that the British had embarked. Washington passed the barrier and rode to Bull's Head Tavern, where he would wait until his troops had taken over the city and established order. The wait stretched unaccountably long, and then an angry aide appeared to report that, in order to keep the American flag from rising on the high pole above Fort George, the British had cut the halyards, knocked off the cleats, and greased the pole. As some of the retiring enemy rested on their oars in the harbor and watched sarcastically, sailors were trying to get up the pole. Each one invariably slipped down.

Another messenger reported that Yankee ingenuity was about to triumph. Someone had rummaged through an ironmonger's and found new cleats. A sailor, with the halyards tied around his waist, was ascending step by step, driving in the cleats as he mounted. Sure enough: there came through the window the roar of thirteen cannon shots which marked the rising of the flag over the last bit of territory in the United States (except for frontier forts) that had been held by George III.

Now, for the first time in the war, Washington accepted his rightful role in a triumphal procession.[4] After some Westchester horse had clattered by, the Commander in Chief appeared, mounted on a magnificent gray, with beside him Governor Clinton on a fine bay gelding. Then aides and officers and prominent civilians. Citizens came out to cheer, but they were few and haggard. Overhead, broken windows gaped and roof lines sagged. Soon Washington saw an extensive wilderness of charred timber and black, free-standing chimneys: the unrebuilt ruins left by the fire that had destroyed a third of the city in 1776. Although the imagination leapt at what it symbolized, this homecoming was from moment to moment a sad one—all the more so for Washington because of the cloud that hung between him and his justly dissatisfied officers.

The next few days were full of celebrations—congratulatory addresses ceremoniously delivered to Washington, dinners at which many toasts were drunk, the upward darting of fireworks—and then the moment approached when the British fleet, which was still anchored in the outer harbor, would actually vanish, when Washington's military tasks would be accomplished to the last detail. He arranged that a barge should await at Whitehall to carry him to New Jersey on the start of his trip to resignation and home. But first he would say a personal farewell to the officers still in the service or residing near enough to be summoned. The time, noon on December 4; the place, Fraunces Tavern.[5]

It was a small group—of the twenty-nine major generals who had served, only three; of the forty-four brigadiers, only one; a smattering of lower officers. But the group was nonetheless typical—dear friends, acquaintances, men Washington did not recognize—of the soldiers who had fought and suffered, had frolicked and died throughout the long, now triumphant war. That they were so few, the raveling end of a glorious endeavor, may well have induced Washington to find this final meeting even more poignant. In any case, he came among them already under the influence of strong emotion.

A collation had been laid out on a table. Laboring to control himself, Washington tried to eat but failed. With a shaking hand, he filled a glass of wine and motioned for the decanters to go round. Every eye was fixed on His Excellency, and, as he stood there with a trembling lip, all the bitterness that lurked in the hearts of his officers was washed over by a rising flood of love.

Washington waited politely for all the glasses to be filled. Then, though his hand still shook, he lifted his glass in a gesture familiar to his aides, and spoke in a choked voice. "With a heart full of love and gratitude, I now take leave of you. I most devoutly wish that your latter days may be as prosperous and happy as your former ones have been glorious and honorable."

He drank "in almost breathless silence," and then they all drank.

In an even more choked voice, Washington said, "I cannot come to each of you, but shall feel obliged if each of you will come and take me by the hand."

General Knox was nearest. He "turned to the Commander in Chief, who suffused in tears, was incapable of utterance, but grasped his hand; when they embraced each other in silence. In the same affectionate manner," so continued the reminiscences of Major Benjamin Tallmadge, "every officer in the room marched up to, kissed, and parted with his general in chief. Such a scene of sorrow and weeping I had never before witnessed. . . . The *simple thought* . . . that we should see his face no more in this world seemed to me utterly insupportable."

The occasion was "too affecting to be of long continuance." Having embraced every officer in complete silence, Washington walked out of the room.[6]

After the General and his officers had composed themselves, they assisted in further ceremonies: "Governor Clinton, the honorable councils, and citizens of the first distinction" waited on His Excellency. Then, accompanied by Steuben and several aides, Washington walked through sparse lines of infantry to the waterfront. He descended into his barge. As the boat took off and diminished with distance, the watching civilians waved and

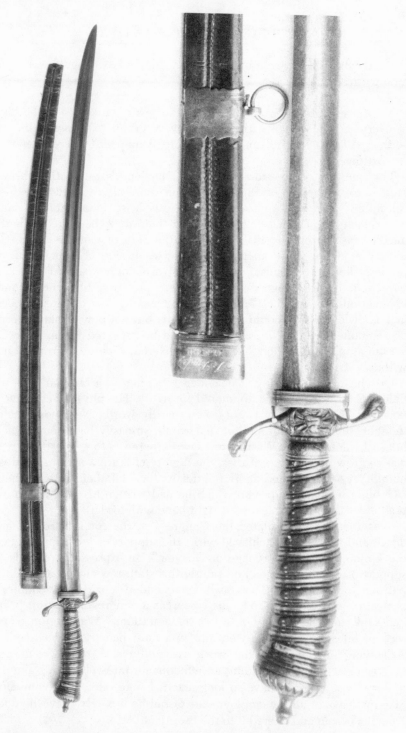

Washington's "service sword" and scabbard. Length of sword, 36 inches, with 30-inch blade. The hilt, shown in detail, is silver and green-stained ivory wound with silver wire, quillons terminating on serpents' heads. Scabbard is russet leather with two silver bands. Courtesy of the Smithsonian Institution.

cheered. But the tearful officers stood motionless, engulfed in "silence, military grief."[7]

His movements clogged by the desire of every citizen to shake his hand, of every lady to dance with him, of every group to present him with an address, Washington advanced slowly to Annapolis, where Congress was now sitting.

The question of how to receive His Excellency's resignation threw Congress into an agony of dignity, all the more fierce because (due to a continuing lack of a quorum) it was otherwise impotent. A committee, which included Thomas Jefferson, ruled that, after the secretary had introduced Washington and his aides into "the Hall of Congress," the General should sit down while an aide stood on each side of him. Then, after a properly impressive pause, the President of Congress should say, "Sir, The United States in Congress assembled are prepared to receive your communications." When the General rose, he should bow to his superiors who, in acknowledgment, should raise their hats but not bow. A similar exchange of a genuflection for "uncovering" should be repeated when, after General Washington's resignation had been delivered, George Washington, Esq., withdrew.[8]

On the appointed day, December 23, 1783, Washington was ushered before Congress with the appointed formality. His physical eye saw a tiny, powerless body of some twenty men, hardly worth, Napoleon would have thought, the whiff of grapeshot that would so easily have sent them flying; but in his mind's eye, Washington saw gathered before him the power that was to grow down the centuries, the dignity of a great nation. Bowing in all humility as the tall and short politicians took off their hats, he held in a trembling hand the paper on which he had written his address. In order to read, he was forced to steady his right hand with his left.

Washington congratulated the Congress on the confirmation of independence and sovereignty achieved with "the support of the Supreme Power of the Union, and the patronage of Heaven." He expressed gratitude for the support of his countrymen and praised his staff, recommending them to the patronage of Congress. Then, as he commended "our dearest country to the protection of Almighty God," his voice (as a congressman wrote) "faltered and sank and the whole house felt his agitations." Washington paused "to recover himself," and then went on "in a most penetrating manner":

"Having now finished the work assigned me, I retire from the great theater of action, and, bidding an affectionate farewell to this august body under whose orders I have so long acted, I here offer my commission, and take my leave of all the employments of public life." He drew the document from his bosom and offered it to the President.

Again he had engendered tears. The President, who was none other than the former leader of the Conway Cabal, the famed orator Thomas Mifflin, could not in his reply vie with the simple three-and-a-half minute message. His orotund periods fell on the assembled ears as dignified but "without any show of feelings."[9]

Now Washington had said good-by to the various congressmen, bowed over the hands of still lachrymose ladies, and he was on his horse, with two of his closest aides galloping beside him, free, free for the first time in almost nine years! The winds whistled and the horses' shoulders rose and fell, and it was hard to rein in and be courteous to the well-wishers who perpetually stopped him on the road, who gathered in every village square. Little by little, the faces became more familiar until they were all old friends and neighbors, and then the familiar driveway, the trees he had himself planted. Martha stood in the doorway. This was Mount Vernon and it was Christmas Eve.

For four days, Washington enjoyed the luxury of not writing a single letter. Then he wrote Governor Clinton, "The scene is at last closed. I feel myself eased of a load of public care."[10]

After so long, it was hard to believe. Two months later, he wrote Knox that he was just beginning to "get the better of my usual custom" of waking in the morning with the wheels in his mind already spinning in preparation for the business of the day. After revolving "many things in my mind," he was surprised, "to find that I was no longer a public man, or had anything to do with public transactions."[11]

Sometimes he found it hard to keep his attention on the winter chores of his plantations, or selecting gilded papier-mâché borders to go with the new stucco work on his ceilings. "If you have any news that you are at liberty to impart," he wrote Jefferson, "it would be charity to communicate a little of it to a body."[12]

However, happiness was descending. "At length, my dear Marquis," he wrote Lafayette, "I am become a private citizen on the banks of the Potomac, and under the shadow of my own vine and my own fig tree. Free from the bustle of a camp and the busy scenes of public life, I am solacing myself with those tranquil enjoyments of which the soldier who is ever in pursuit of fame; the statesman whose watchful days and sleepless nights are spent in devising schemes to promote the welfare of his own, perhaps the ruin of other countries (as if this globe was insufficient for us all); and the courtier who is always watching the countenance of his prince, in hopes of catching a gracious smile, can have very little conception. I am not only retired from all public employments, but I am retiring within myself, and shall be able to view the solitary walk and tread the paths of private life with heartfelt satisfaction. Envious of none, I am determined to be pleased

[527]

with all, and this, my dear friend, being the order for my march, I will move gently down the stream of life until I sleep with my fathers."[13]

Washington hoped "to spend the remainder of my days in cultivating the affections of good men and in the practice of the domestic virtues." Did he really believe that his countrymen would not summon him again, that he would not obey their call?[14]

XI

Conclusion

Cincinnatus Assayed

RGUMENTS on Washington's skill as a soldier are as old as the history of the United States, and extreme positions have been taken. A school which insists that he would have been ignominiously defeated by any general except the dullards the incompetent English ministry sent against him has a fantastic fringe which believes that what happened can only be explained by assuming that General Howe (as a British Whig) purposely avoided crushing Washington's army. However, two distinguished military historians have recently stated that by 1781 Washington had "developed a competence worthy of favorable comparison beside Alexander at Granicus, Caesar at the Rubicon, Hannibal at the Alps, Genghis Khan at the Great Wall, Frederick the Great at Prague, or Napoleon at Montenotte."[1]

An intelligent comparison between Washington and the celebrated soldiers of the past is greatly impeded by a fact too often overlooked: Washington was never truly a military man. He remained to the end of the war a civilian serving half-reluctantly in uniform.

If we read Washington's writings beside those of any dedicated warrior—say, Light Horse Harry Lee—it is instantly clear how little the basic bent of his mind was military. The numerous metaphors he wrote down in armed camps are almost never drawn from warfare: they recall the fields and forests, the mounting and sinking suns of a peaceful home. He never wrote of a Revolutionary battle in terms of sanguinary exultation; he never, in all his exhortations to his troops, appealed to bloodlust or glorified carnage. Such happy visions of military adventure as he had enjoyed as a younger man and in an earlier war had faded from him. "It is time," he admonished Chastellux, "for the age of knight-errantry and mad heroism to be at an end." The French staff officer Barbé-Marbois wrote, "I have been told that he preserves in battle the character of humanity which makes him so dear to his soldiers in camp."[2]

Washington at the Battle of Princeton, by Charles Willson Peale. Courtesy of
The Art Museum, Princeton University.

Washington would take military risks to protect what he referred to as "the essential interests of any individual." He wrote, "The misfortunes of war, and the unhappy circumstances frequently attendant thereon to individuals, are more to be lamented than avoided: but it is the duty of everyone to alleviate these as much as possible." Although recognizing the military genius of Harry Lee, he was horrified by the cruelties that dedicated soldier perpetrated. Congressman Charles Carroll of Carrollton complained of Washington, "He is so humane and delicate that I fear the common cause will suffer. . . . The man cannot be too much admired and lamented."[3]

While the true military mind is most concerned with the exertion of force, Washington considered force secondary in winning the war to gentleness, justice, forbearance. This was because the unreconstructed civilian was, as he stated again and again, infinitely less afraid of military defeat than of doubt and disunity within the patriot cause.

Although he never abandoned the hope of a sledgehammer blow that would end the war overnight, from week to week and year to year such a quick solution remained a seductive will-o'-the-wisp. In the long reaches, Washington used the army as a propaganda instrument. "Popular expectations," he wrote, "should always be complied with where injury in the execution is not too apparent, especially in such a contest as the one we are engaged in, where the spirit and willingness of the people must in a great measure take place of coercion."[4]

What the public believed had happened, Washington wrote, "might almost as well be so."[5] This opened a way to retrieve defeats: claim at the very least that the enemy casualties had been greater than your own. He also created on paper, for the consumption of the home front as well as the enemy, imaginary legions.

Washington's propaganda activities did not involve infringement of the freedom of the press, a principle which he often stated was essential to a free nation. Since no war correspondents existed, the newspapers relied on letters written from the front by private or public individuals. There is no evidence that Washington ever tried to influence the writers except by controlling the information they in the first place received. He on one occasion asked Congress for "a small traveling press to follow headquarters" and "an ingenious man to accompany this press and be employed wholly in writing for it. . . . If the people had a channel of intelligence that from its usual authenticity they could look up to with confidence," that would frustrate false rumors, undermine despondency and the propaganda of the enemy.[6] Congress did not fall in with this suggestion, and Washington remained his own principal disseminator of information, broadcasting in personal letters to officials his approved version of events.

[533]

The hindsight of the historian can only reinforce Washington's conviction that the crucial battles of the war were in the arenas of public opinion. Had the British been able to bring even a large minority of the Americans back into active support of the Crown, all opposing military efforts would have been unavailing. Their intelligence would have sprung up like the grass of midsummer, hampering Washington's every move. Guerrillas would have met guerrillas in the glades and under the rocks until everyone would have cried for peace. And the British, as they marched at will from state to state, would have needed to leave behind no more than small detachments to help the local Tories keep the captured communities loyal. They could thus have pinned down the rebellion bit by bit.

Convinced that the uprising had been forced on the population by a small group of agitators and terrorists, the British alternated a withering carrot with an unwieldy stick. Their propaganda opportunities were, indeed, great. Not only had the Revolution started with no unanimity of opinion even among its supporters, but the cause had moved so rapidly that a patriot who moored his boat to any fixed political doctrine was soon left behind. It was not enough to persuade a man once: he had to be persuaded again and again. And the war seemed endlessly long. Mounting discouragement, confusion, and apathy caused serious shrinkage in Washington's army. But whenever a British advance forced the inhabitants of a neighborhood to take sides, it became clear that all the unhappiness had not created renewed allegiance to the Crown. Although some males did join loyalist corps, more became American guerrillas; and when stay-at-homes saw columns moving in the night, they sent word not to the British marchers but the patriot skulkers. There can be no doubt that the British were totally outclassed in the warfare for the minds of men.

It was in those mental arenas that the civilian-soldier George Washington shone the brightest. He kept forever in mind, as more radical statesmen of either the right or the left could not do, that the fundamental objective was not to foster division but to increase unity.

Every man imprisoned or driven to the British was a loss; every man who hesitated in a way not immediately and actively dangerous to the cause should be regarded not as an enemy but as a potential convert. And conversion was best achieved not by political arguments—Washington was never much of a political arguer—but by visible virtue: an army less destructive than that of the enemy; broad tolerance which promised happiness to the widest possible segment of humanity. Washington reversed the usual role of a commander in chief by urging on rampant civilian authorities greater respect for civilian rights.

Although Washington often phrased his arguments for tolerance in terms of expediency, his sentiments stemmed from deep moral principles. While sadly recognizing the necessity for curbing inimical behavior that was a danger to the cause, he did not believe that a man should be persecuted as a result of any opinions he held that had not exploded into action. As he put it in explaining a conception that has been echoed down the years by Jefferson and other liberals, "Our actions, depending upon ourselves, may be controlled, whilst the powers of thinking, originating in higher causes, cannot always be molded to our wishes."[7]

In military matters, Washington was much less sure of himself. His previous experience had been limited to leading untrained and unconventional Indian-fighters mostly against savages and always in the wilderness. His contact with professional soldiers had only been close enough to make it clear to him how much he had to learn. Even on his own wild terrain, the regulars had captured Fort Duquesne in a manner that he did not comprehend. As he rode to Cambridge to assume his new command, George Washington knew he was as green as grass.

His British opponents sailed across the ocean with an exactly opposite attitude: they intended to exert proven skills on comical amateurs. However, the doctrines of the great European commanders like Frederick the Great were in reality no more applicable to the American war than were the naïvetés of a wilderness fighter. The crucial military difference (apart from levels of innate ability) between Washington and the commanders who opposed him was that they were sure they knew all the answers, while Washington tried every day and every hour to learn.

The objective of the type of warfare to which the British had been trained was to drive the enemy backward from position to position with as little loss as possible to your side. But, however successfully this was carried through, it failed to achieve victory on the vast and disorganized American continent, where there were no crucial cities to capture and the unworthy rebels, living like beetles off a leaf, depended on no magazines that could be destroyed, no supply lines that could be cut. A more daring British strategy was needed—but everything in their situation inhibited British daring. The normal pressure on the commanders of expensive professional armies not to endanger them rashly was redoubled by the fact that this one would have to be resupplied and reinforced across three thousand miles of ocean. Furthermore, it is axiomatic that the convinced practitioners of accepted skills are inclined, when their rules fail to work, not to question the rules but to become more and more cautious in situations which seem to them inexplicable.

A recognition, it is true, that this strange war could not be won until Washington's force was destroyed rather than just pushed back, had, as the 1776 campaign unrolled, entered the minds of Howe and his officers. However, this consideration was so far from the established doctrines of the war of position that it was hard to take seriously. And insofar as they did take it seriously, the British lacked the means. Not only were techniques of destructive pursuit lacking in the military copybooks of that time (they were to be worked out later), but the American situation presented particular obstacles. Cavalry could not mop up effectively where walls and trees interposed, and European infantrymen could not hope to catch up with the Americans, who, with their strong legs and shoulders unburdened by equipment, got off as fast as rabbits. And so much of the country over which the regulars had to fight was seamed with stone walls, bumpy with hills, obscured with vegetation: untidily suited to the guerrilla activity of a peasantry familiar with firearms. Guerrilla reprisal was almost impossible to a force in which individual soldiers had been trained not to think for themselves, and from which the men—cavalry, as well as infantry—might desert if they got out of sight of their officers.

The British made various sporadic efforts to break out of the established molds. Despite flocks of difficulties which occurred to well-trained minds, they did make some use of Tory irregulars to counteract the patriot guerrillas. Although it was an established principle that troops in mercenary armies, who were fighting only to earn their livelihoods, would desert if made too uncomfortable, the British command sometimes took the risk of leaving some baggage behind in order to achieve speed. They flirted, albeit in a most gingerly manner, with a scorched-earth policy which (despite its unfortunate propaganda effect) would have enabled their army to leave an impression on the countryside through which they marched. However, the British generals never carried any innovations far enough to achieve solid results.

Although he was at first pushed around like the most ignorant beginner, Washington finally stymied the well-trained and able regulars opposing him. This does not mean that what he taught himself would have been effective against Frederick at Prague or Napoleon at Montenotte. His strategy was a Darwinian achievement of adaptation to environment; it was evolved to overcome the specific problems with which he was faced. It was the triumph of a man who knows how to learn, not in the narrow sense of studying other people's conceptions, but in the transcendent sense of making a synthesis out of the totality of experience.

Poised at the break between the age of reason and the age of empirical knowledge, Washington drew strength from both outlooks. He discarded outworn paraphernalia left over from the past without abandoning himself to the pure expediency of the experimental method. His doctrine was "Good judgment and experimental knowledge properly exerted, never can, when accompanied with integrity and zeal, go wrong."[8]

As a young man, Washington had been interested in his ancestry and had ordered the coat of arms he claimed emblazoned on all amenable articles.

After the Revolution, he no longer exhibited any interest in his forebears, answering the queries of genealogists with bored courtesy. He stated that precedents are dangerous things, as they impose on the present the dead hand of the past. In thanking an admirer for his "politeness" in sending him a "piece of antiquity," Washington wrote wryly that its age "and having once been the property of so remarkable a character as Oliver Cromwell, would undoubtedly render it pleasant to almost anyone, and to an antiquary perhaps invaluable."[9]

The Virginian who had found his manhood in a wilderness unknown to literature and had achieved economic independence by discarding the established trade patterns of his neighbors, who was fighting his king and advancing into uncharted political seas, preferred to find things out for himself. As an old man, he was to write sadly, "I must now benefit from the studies and experience of others, but a remnant of it [his life] being left to essay either myself."[10]

But experience is not an instantaneous teacher. To escape from what he considered the "infant state" of his knowledge, he read, on his assuming the Revolutionary command, military manuals imported from abroad and questioned men he considered knowing. In particular, he sat at the feet of the former British regulars Gates and Lee.[11]

Congress had instructed Washington to consult with his officers, and this he gladly did in Councils of War which he ran like miniature legislative assemblies. He took votes. If he were in the minority, he might complain but he gave in. This was not the soul of forceful generalship, but certainly the councils he held in Cambridge were useful as brakes on the Commander in Chief's impetuosity. For Washington, despite the reputation for caution which later experience taught him to earn, was by natural inclination both a rash and overoptimistic fighter.

As Washington, mounting from grade to grade in his college of experience, became surer of himself, he less and less often called his officers together in conferences. Instead (as he was to do when President), he asked for written advice on specific questions. The answers became part of the evidence he weighed. "In all matters of great national moment," he wrote, "the only true line of conduct in my opinion is dispassionately to compare the advantages and disadvantages of the measure proposed, and decide from the balance. The lesser evil, where there is a choice of them, should yield to the greater."

His method of classifying, in his mind and also sometimes on paper, the facts of a situation as opposites, of "collecting" (as he put it) his decision, forced emphasis not on the "speculative" but on the "practical"—i.e., the problem exactly as it existed. However, although he became increasingly uninterested in military theory, he kept always before him general philosophic considerations: "that great line of duty which, though hid under a cloud for some time from a peculiarity of circumstances, may nevertheless bear scrutiny." Because he conceived of men as moral beings and recognized that the major function of his efforts was to sway the minds of men, he labored to merge the moral and the practical. "Nothing in life," he wrote, "can afford a liberal mind more rational and exquisite satisfaction than the approbation of those both wise and virtuous."[12]

Washington's method of weighing evidence blocked his tendency toward rashness, but the method took time, especially when the balance refused to tip one way or the other. Resulting delays sometimes proved unfortunate— obviously at Fort Washington, perhaps in the hesitations that led up to Monmouth—and were the basis of the charges of "indecision" made by Reed and others. However, another possible disadvantage of the method did not develop.

To examine all alternatives and accept the one which seemed, however slightly, the least objectionable, would in ordinary minds induce continuing doubts and halfhearted execution. Once Washington had reached a decision, his hesitations were—as Gouverneur Morris wrote—over: "He could, at the dictate of reason, control his will and command himself to act. Others may have acquired a portion of the same authority. But who could, like Washington, command the energies of his mind to cheerful execution?"[13]

When irritated, his intimates could attribute this, as Lafayette once did, to "his invincible repugnance to retract." However, that combination described by Brissot de Warville of "great diffidence in himself" with "an unshakable firmness of character once he had made a decision" was a major secret of Washington's effectiveness.[14]

It also tinged much of Washington's behavior with the appearance of inconsistency. Only in situations which deeply involved what he recognized as his "great line of duty"[15] can one foresee how he is going to act. He was no Byronic hero whose emotional obsessions always thrust him down dictated paths. Operating in a more classical manner, his mind seemed to swing like a pendulum from a stable center. He could move out, as pushed by the momentary summation of forces, in any direction, even if it were opposite to that which had been made expedient by other circumstances the day before. Add to the resulting variety those occasions when his passions overwhelmed his judgment, and others when he hid his true opinions in order to present persuasive arguments to men whose differences of prejudice he recognized, and you get that appearance of random multiplicity which often seems to characterize his day-to-day routine.

As Washington's self-education carried him ever further away from accepted military ideas, he turned from imported books and his original advisers to discussions with new men whom he had personally guided through the same school of experience where he himself still studied. One

[538]

reason for the successes of the French Revolutionary armies was that, the old hierarchical officer corps having been shattered, naturally brilliant soldiers were able to rise to leadership apart from birth, wealth, and precedent.* The same was true in Washington's army. Of the leading generals who opened the war, none except Washington remained till the end influential. Indeed, only Gates and Washington were still in active service.

Washington encouraged to rise around him Arnold, a disreputable apothecary and trader who (before he turned traitor) became the greatest combat general of the war; Knox, the overweight bookseller who taught himself the fine art of artillery; Greene, the ironmonger with a stiff knee whom those who deny the honor to Washington consider the conflict's ablest all-round general; Lafayette, the twenty-year-old spoiled darling of the French Court who, for all his wildly romantic and egotistical talk, became a cautiously effective general; Hamilton, another twenty-year-old, this one a bastard from the Indies, in whom Washington found the ideal staff officer; the brilliant John Laurens, who might, had it not been for his untimely death, have been one of the greatest of the younger Founding Fathers.† Of Washington's final inner team only Steuben had come to the army with accepted military knowledge, and the bogus baron was in European terms a fraud: his contribution was to make drill over again, under American advice, in a manner that suited the American army.

When Washington went increasingly his own way, he was plagued by his former dependences. Reed and Mifflin could not believe that the man whose early palpitations they had witnessed could ever become a brilliant commander. Gates and Lee became convinced that Washington had fallen into the hands of incompetent sycophants, all the more because, after consulting with new men, he was heretical to his old advisers' teachings. The idea that Washington was sinking into military ineptitude was further encouraged by high-ranking European volunteers, men like Conway who had come from abroad as convinced as were the British regulars that they were bringing with them the ultimate answers. All this contributed, during 1777 and 1778, to fracases.

Washington, the usually mild, struck out with his gigantic limbs, and the older order went down. Since the new order remained on the whole loyal to the man who had created and trained them, Washington became, in his control of the American military, unrivaled. This unique position contrib-

---

* In aristocratic armies, only a tiny proportion of the population was eligible for the officer corps, and within this group promotion was less based on ability than family position.

† Characterized by "intrepidity bordering on rashness," Laurens was killed in August 1782, after all serious fighting was over, in what Washington called bitterly "a trifling skirmish." He was the only member of Washington's inner military circle to succumb, during the entire war, either to bullets or to sickness.[16]

uted, in itself, toward the eventual victory. Throughout the war, the British high command had been weakened by perpetual inner feuds: Clinton against Howe; Cornwallis against Clinton; the generals against the admirals; etc., etc. Cornwallis's plight at Yorktown was due as much to his disagreements with Clinton as to anything else.

However, Washington often asked of his men more than ordinary persons could achieve: desertions were high and many short-term recruits refused to re-enlist. By their hearths, the returned soldiers told tales that frightened their neighbors from enlisting. Although this contributed to the progressive shrinking of the Continental Army, it did not—most amazingly—have a negative effect on the support for the cause or the national image of Washington. He remained so widely revered that one of the major problems of the party which arose after the war under the leadership of Jefferson was that Washington, whom they considered a political mossback, was more popular with the common people than the Jeffersonians themselves.

As he had felt when a leading landowner in Fairfax County, Virginia, Washington did not regard his military eminence as an excuse for self-indulgence, but rather as the opposite. In this, he was very different from the highborn British generals with their mistresses, their hangovers and gaming tables.* Washington asked nothing of his men that he was unwilling to do himself. Probably not another soldier in the entire army served so unrelentingly as did the Commander in Chief, who year after year did not allow himself a single day's furlough. And, although he kept up enough dignity at headquarters so that the men did not have to be ashamed of meanness, he shared their shortages and physical hardships whenever crisis made that reasonable.

That Washington was seeking no direct personal gain from his service had been dramatized at the start of his command by his refusal of any salary. Although (as we have seen) he did try to buy in for his plantation some depleted cavalry horses, he never took the least personal advantage of his great powers in the control of supply. This made him a paragon in the eighteenth century, when it was standard practice for military officers (like government officials) to further their personal fortunes by collecting what was then considered not dishonest graft but the rightful perquisites of place and rank. Very revolutionary too, because contrary to the whole system of aristocratic preferment by which great families took care of their own, was Washington's utter refusal to practice or countenance nepotism in the

---

* Washington could handle sex and liquor like a well-adjusted man: he seems never to have suffered from great temptations to overindulgence in either. But gambling was another matter: it had been so greatly the favorite sport of his young manhood that his encouragement of it in his regiment during the French and Indian War had got him into trouble. Now he denounced gambling in his general orders with a vehemence that seemed to reflect a continued personal yearning for his old, exciting vice.[17]

appointment of officers. As far as the Continental Congress and the state governments would permit, he followed seniority or rewarded merit.

Men in danger, men conscious of their own inadequacy, do not want a general who might be their equal, who could easily be as bewildered and frightened as they. Yet they do not wish to feel that the commander moves in another orbit, indifferent to their affairs. Washington, so Abigail Adams noticed, "has a dignity which forbids familiarity, mixed with an easy affability which creates love and reverence." A French officer found Washington's face "something grave and serious, but it is never stern, and, on the contrary, becomes softened by the most gracious and amiable smile. He is affable and converses with his officers familiarly and gaily." He could play a wicket with the young men of his staff without having them feel that he was cheapening himself. He would chat with a lonely sentry.[18]

Washington's quality that has been most rubbed away by the fingers of the years and the historians is the charm he exerted on his contemporaries and which contributed much to his riding the wild horses of the times. This was grounded on characteristics which legend no longer allows him: on vulnerability, on the sensitivity of his own feelings which enabled him to be exquisitely responsive to the feelings of others. If he sometimes did wear the cold face of a marble bust, it was because he had to protect his sensibilities from an ever-present prying, tearing, demanding world.

Although Washington was by no means an equalitarian who slapped his social inferiors on the back, he responded to all men who came into his focus—however lowly their rank—as individuals whose personal interests should be considered, who had rights as well as duties. In the conventional sense Washington was not a reformer, because when intolerance of human weakness emerged among his emotions, he did not make it a basis of action but did his best to suppress it. He expected men to be weak and fallible, regarding this condition, like the infertile soil at Mount Vernon, as the essential ground on which fine effects would have to be achieved.

He could be corrosive in irritation and terrible in rage, yet he twice allowed himself to be walked over by younger men he admired—first by Reed and then by Hamilton. In each case, not only did he forgive, but he pled humbly for the continued assistance of the friend who had turned on him. When he finally accepted suspicion he reacted with passion, but Washington hated to distrust any man.

"I might," he wrote good-humoredly in answering a gossipy letter from an old friend, "entrench myself behind the parade of great business with as much propriety as most men"[19]—but this was contrary to his nature. Some historians have accused him of being a poor executive who wasted his time on small details. But very often those small details would be lack of food, of supplies, of medicines in a regiment; and then he would ride there, at full speed as always,[20] to see what could be done. Even if he could do nothing, that he had come was a poultice to hurt minds and even added warmth to a dying fire. His face would darken to see his men suffer. That he suffered too, the cast of his features revealed.

It was well known in the army that His Excellency hankered as much as any man of them to get back to his farm which he had not seen at all for a lengthening number of years. And yet the glory and excitement of what the army was achieving found eloquent expression from his tongue and pen. He might sometimes ride past his troops with an iron countenance, but when he spoke, color came to his blue-gray eyes and his words tended to flow in metaphor. Farmers recognized his images, since so many came from the fields and the sky. Often his speech was far from tempered: he enjoyed wild exaggerations. His soldiers at Valley Forge "suffered greater inconveniences and distresses than soldiers ever did before for want of clothing." From 1776 to 1778, the army had undergone "the strangest vicissitudes that perhaps ever attended any one contest since the Creation." Concerning a frustrated British envoy, Washington wrote, "He tries to convince you . . . that he is not in a passion, while he exhibits a striking proof of his being cut to the quick and actually biting his fingers in an agony of passion."[21] Not only in battle but in the events of every day, His Excellency showed fire as well as judgment and compassion.

Washington's optimism was the kind that inspires desperate men, for he never pretended that situations were not grave. He saw darkness, indeed, where the less well-informed never glimpsed it; he complained as loudly as any hungry private bitching by a cold fire; and yet he was the bravest of the brave—the way he took risks in battle may have horrified his aides but it delighted his men. And he never despaired: he was always sure that the virtue of the men and the nobility of the cause would inspire beneficent and rewarding Providence to carry them all to victory and an Elysium where, as civilians, they could enjoy in tranquillity the fruits of their past agonies.

In those years when soldiers were supposed to practice their profession as ordered, without personal concern for the matters about which they were fighting, the greatest innovation of the Continental Army was the conception that men could be successfully called on to make great sacrifices if they believed that they were serving their own welfare as civilians and also the truth. This military invention, as it came to be practiced in Europe by the armies of the French Revolution and moved onward to sweep the world, was entirely to recast warfare. It was an outgrowth of the rise of nationalism, unusable by international aristocracies, since a man taught to fight for himself might end up fighting an alien (or an unpopular) king. However, a sense of dedication to freedom was natural to the American air. Washington believed with all his heart in its military importance, and worked out how to harness by strategy this strange new force of popular enthusiasm.

Washington labored to inspire his soldiery with confidence in the value and the nobility of the cause. He could in the deepest sincerity make his orders receptacles for patriot propaganda, since every high sentiment he expressed was grounded in personal conviction. Patriotism was for him the basic political virtue.

In the 1770's and 1780's, the dark side of nationalism had not yet come in view. The lessons then presented by history backed Washington in blaming aggressive war not on the desire of one national folk to dominate another but on the ambitions of princes. Nor could he see that embattling whole populations* rather than just professional mercenary armies would increase many times over the destructiveness of war.

The best check on the aggression of kings was, as Washington saw it, the self-determination of peoples. This principle, if adequately disseminated and enforced, would give the inhabitants of every region an indisputable right to their own territory and encourage every man to join with his neighbors for the protection of the liberty and property of all. Since (so Washington believed) man was naturally good, a release from aristocratic restraints would permit the emergence of virtue: the result would be the creation of free, democratic, and peaceful states. As Washington put it when the forming United States seemed to be foundering in a sea of confusion and selfishness, everything would eventually work out for the best as there was "virtue at the bottom."22

Since Washington foresaw that the establishment of political liberty would create a better world, the cause of American freedom became, by extension, the cause of all mankind. It also took on religious significance.

Long before the conflict with England exploded, Washington had felt that some supernatural force—he liked to call it, in the manner of Stoic philosophers, "Providence"—moved actively in the affairs of men. He was sure that it was a virtuous force, furthering the welfare of mankind. Lacking the specific contexts supplied by dogma or (despite his polite adherence to his ancestral Church of England) sectarianism, his religious convictions merged naturally and completely with his philosophical and political conceptions. He could not doubt that, since national political liberty would establish international peace and happiness, fighting the American Revolution was worship to the "Great Governor of the Universe," who would protect and reward his servants.23

This confidence in celestial assistance seemed doubly important to him when he first assumed the command because he was very conscious of his

---

* Napoleon, the first great user of mass armies, is supposed to have commented to Lafayette that during the American Revolution the future of the world was decided by forces no larger than corporals' guards. In 1812, Napoleon's army was almost twenty times the Continental Army at its very largest. This was because American nationalism had not so far overcome individualism as to make feasible a general draft. The *levée en masse* was first enacted by the French in 1793.24

own inadequacy for the task ahead, and also of the imperfections of his army. He was inclined to conclude that faith by itself must and would do wonders. Believing that soldiers adequately inspired could overcome any inferiority in numbers, equipment, military know-how, he several times during 1776—at Kip's Bay, Fort Washington and elsewhere—put his men in impossible positions.

Indeed, 1776 was Washington's most educational year. Sir William Howe, proving himself the very model of a British major general, triumphed again and again in the struggle for positions to which he had been trained: the Americans were driven from Long Island, from New York City, from Manhattan, up the Hudson to White Plains, and across the Hudson and out of New Jersey. But in the process Washington came to appreciate a great advantage his army had over the enemy: superior mobility. On one aspect of this, the ability of his troops to think for themselves and take off without waiting for orders when in impossible positions, Washington never commented upon favorably—he could not do so and keep an army capable of obeying orders—but he may well have learned to include it in his calculations as a safety hatch. The more unequivocally favorable aspects of the American mobility were based not only on self-reliance but also on morale.

Because the men were willing to suffer great hardships for a cause which they believed involved all that made life worth living, they did not need to drag behind them slow trains of wagons, were not encumbered by quantities of equipment, were willing to march in any weather for any number of hours that the human frame, strained to its utmost, could stand. This opened to Washington the possibility of the kind of action which he had seen the Indians carry off in the wilderness: raiding parties that struck the enemy unexpectedly, completed their victory in a few hours, and vanished before any superior force could reach them. The first fruits of this strategy were the battles of Trenton and Princeton, which were, in turn, triumphant proofs of how effective a hit-and-run technique could be in this war. Not only was the propaganda impact sensational, but the British were frightened into abandoning their effort to hold New Jersey down with a network of small garrisons. Sudden raids—or the threat of them—would keep the enemy from setting up and protecting Tory enclaves with anything short of major power.

European strategy involved face-to-face confrontations of the opposing armies as each tried to push the other back. Since both armies moved ponderously, battles were foreseeable: this had been the situation in most of the American action during 1776. After that, Washington tried to function differently. Although he was in 1777 maneuvered into a battle of positions at Brandywine, and he tried in 1778 to take advantage of obvious strategic possibilities at Monmouth, he had become convinced that formal battles did not suit the American genius. His first military mentor, the Iroquois chief known as the Half-King, would have been pleased to see how greatly Washington came to rely on the conception of surprise.

However, if the British were not to march at will wherever they pleased, Washington needed to find some method of stopping them that did not involve drawing up his army in their path. He discovered how to keep the British in New York with completely conventional strategy which was geared to the conventional organization of their army. Since they could not advance if their supply lines were seriously menaced, he could prevent their marching overland to Philadelphia by merely sitting on the heights near Morristown that overhung the road. A similar strategic post in the hills behind White Plains could be used to block any overland incursion into New England. Moving past unconquered forts (as the Indians did) seemed to Washington a reasonable maneuver,[25] but he knew that the British would never go up the Hudson Valley leaving West Point in their rear, all the more because they were dependent for supply on shipping that could not circumnavigate the fort. The British were thus, as far as overland movement was concerned, trapped in New York unless they were willing to attack one of his strongpoints at great disadvantage.

Although not averse to a plum that could easily be shaken off a bough, the British were not, as a matter of policy, perpetually probing the American position for small advantages. They thought primarily in terms of operating with large units and when superiority of force tended largely to their side. Washington, on the other hand, was forever alert. He forever sought to make a strike, large or small, if only for the propaganda effect. Increasingly, he aimed his spy network at searching out any place where any group of the enemy had got off base—and he seemed Argus-eyed, since the inhabitants who watched the British from their windows were usually patriot sympathizers. The skillful enemy commanders did not give Washington many opportunities, but the ever-present danger urged them to keep their forces concentrated and contributed to the conservatism to which they had, in any case, been trained.

Washington developed what were, in effect, three striking forces graduated in strength. Although the continual threat that hordes of militia would arise like mists from the fields was a deterrent to enemy enterprise—the British could never confidently foresee what numbers a thrust would have to overcome—Washington had little faith in the militia as a mass force. He did his best to keep those spreaders of confusion quarantined from his main army. Taking advantage of the special gifts of the individual American farmer, he kept the militia, in units that could be as small as a single soldier, forever on the prowl. They were particularly useful as lookouts, in harassing small British foraging parties, and in turning back incursions by Tory irregulars.*

---

* The militia operated in larger units and on a more important scale where Washington and the Continental Army were not, particularly in South Carolina.

Next in impact after the militia were small, elite units of the Continental Army—the riflemen earlier in the war, light infantry detachments at a later date—who could retard, although not stop, a major British march and could be sent out secretly at night (as in the action against Stony Point) to beat up important British outposts. And then there was the Continental Army in its entirety, which Washington was perpetually trying to enlarge and train so that it could deliver the knockout punch which would be necessary if the war were to be ended by military action.

In the war's earlier campaigns, the British only needed to fear the fighting power of the Continental Army under special circumstances: when Washington was defending some extremely strong terrain or when he could (as at Trenton and Princeton) surprise an outpost. However, Germantown presaged a new era, since the main encampment of the British force was, if only temporarily, overrun. Then came the reorganization of the Continental Army at Valley Forge. How effective this had been was demonstrated at Monmouth, which was not by any means a surprise attack, as Germantown had been, but such a foreseeable engagement on a conventional battlefield as had formerly brought easy British triumphs. Monmouth demonstrated to the enemy command the frightening fact that the Continental Army was now so improved that it was capable of meeting the British and German regulars on their own terms.

The British high command never dared challenge Washington again in any major way. Rather than come out from behind his fortifications in New York, Clinton sent detachments to the south, where the population was less concentrated and there was the possibility of a slave revolt; where there was no Continental Army and no Washington. Since the British held on to their New York base, their southern operations forced them to divide their army in a way which Washington recognized at once offered the chance of subduing them piecemeal.[26] Although the march to Yorktown was not specifically his idea, his strategy had set the stage.*

However, the years in military service which trained Washington to be an expert soldier did not in the least incline him to visualize his role in the future as that of a veteran looking backward. This was dramatically demonstrated by his decision, at the moment of parting, to accept injustice to the

---

* The arrival of the French had, until the inauguration of the Yorktown Campaign, amazingly little effect on the strategic situation. The admirals, like their British counterparts, totaled up the relative weights of armament and, usually finding themselves outclassed, made no effort to meet the enemy. And compared to Rochambeau's usual stance, Howe and Cornwallis were wild radicals. From Rochambeau's arrival in July 1780 to June 1781, the French lent hardly any further assistance to Washington than that supplied by the menace to the British army and navy of their mere presence at Newport. (They did not even assign to Washington an artillaryman or an engineer.) Then, as cautious men can suddenly be goaded into throwing discretion to the winds, Rochambeau forced the Virginia campaign which even Washington considered foolhardy.

demobilizing soldiers in preference to action that would endanger the development of the free civilian institutions to which they would now return. And the fact that his opposition stopped the anti-democratic movement not only in the army but among the financiers and politicians makes it plain that he was playing a role much wider than that of Commander in Chief.

Even as during the war all the generals who were Washington's rivals faded away, he increasingly overtopped all civilian leaders active on the continent. John Adams, having beaten somewhat vainly against the great Virginian rock, went off to France. Franklin was coming to the end of his great career and also labored abroad. Jefferson, after writing the Declaration of Independence, went back to Virginia where he proved not very effective as the governor of a war-torn state. Robert Morris, who for a time wielded great power, continued to be distrusted outside the financial community; Thomas Paine was distrusted by almost everyone. John Hancock was a windbag with a large signature, and Patrick Henry was a windbag with a large voice. Samuel Adams was shrinking. Hamilton and Madison were too young to show their full stature.

Historians have not adequately stressed the all-important fact that Washington did not (like Grant and Eisenhower) pass through two semi-independent careers, one as soldier and the other as President. In many and in continually augmenting respects, he became in 1775, twelve years before his official inauguration as President of the United States, the chief executive of the emerging nation. Except for the loop created by his temporary return to Mount Vernon, Washington moved, from his acceptance of the Revolutionary command to his Farewell Address, in one single straight line.

From the first, Washington could have put on the portable desk he carried around with the army, the sign sported in the White House by Harry Truman: "The buck stops here." This was a situation far from pleasant to Washington. The hard matters, the issues that courted unpopularity, moved with the most alacrity to his door. Whenever possible, he would send them scurrying back to Congress, accompanied by impassioned missives saying that if the matters were not instantly solved, the war effort would surely collapse. The executiveless Congress would refer the matter to a standing committee, debate the committee's report, and then, perhaps, appoint a special committee. As inaction followed inaction, the issue would appear in a more urgent form at headquarters. If he could see no other way out, Washington would make the necessary decision. Otherwise, he would send the orphaned issue back again to Congress with an even more emotional letter in which he might point out that he was always willing to take his share of responsibility, but this time it was too much: this was altogether Congress's problem. The legislators, who were capable of criticizing their general for presumption when he settled matters, might now formally censure him for irresolution. Or they might let the matter sink, as far as Washington could see, into utter obscurity. Then he would ask how he was expected to lead the army when no one would tell him what was happening.

This continuing activity forced Washington to face almost every type of problem he would eventually have to face as President. He found himself involved in naval matters, in foreign affairs, in the use of rivers and highways, in politics, in commerce, in manufacturing. The Virginia agrarian was even driven into racking his planter's brain in searches for the solutions to problems of currency and finance. His wartime experiences, which demonstrated that a nation could not be powerful without a strong and fluid economy, undoubtedly made Washington, when President, so much more receptive than was his fellow agrarian Jefferson to Hamilton's advanced, non-agrarian economic conceptions.

Writers who equate the Continental Congress with the long-established governments of stable nations, and who assume that Washington penned on all occasions everything he thought, have deduced from his endlessly iterated complaints that the Congress frustrated their Commander in Chief out of incompetence both willful and malignant. Actually, although he often tried, by ignoring excuses, to stir the legislature into overriding difficulties, Washington realized that the congressmen struggled, even as he himself did, with woefully inadequate means. Despite his verbal protests, he was in action extremely tolerant of such confusion and inefficiency as could be remedied—if at all—only by revolutionary changes within the cause. Having been wildly insubordinate in fighting his king, he was respectful and subordinate to Congress in a way that seemed pusillanimous to radicals like Charles Lee.

As a farmer, as a tamer of wildernesses, as a plantation owner rebuilding his estate, Washington had learned that the best results cannot be achieved overnight. And he had served long enough in the Virginia Burgesses to realize that slow maturing also characterizes legislatures. He did not expect matters to proceed in an orderly manner, nor, though he often expressed despair, did he ever really repine. However black were his military prospects during the Revolution, he was never as helpless as he had been when entrusted with turning back savage raids during the French and Indian War. Improvisation had always been his way of life. Having needed to import so many of his plantation tools from across the ocean through the lame cooperation of venal and indifferent factors, he was used to not receiving what he expected and was entitled to receive. Yet he had always got by somehow. He was not one of those forceful executives who argue that you invite worse trouble by postponing problems. He believed that if you could by temporary expedients keep a leaky ship afloat and on the right course for long enough, some unforeseeable dawn would reveal opening before you the friendly harbor of your dreams.

Had Washington been less accommodating at the start of his command, he would surely never have been allowed to reach the unrivaled power he eventually attained. Yet men have come up modestly before in history only to have modesty vanish: it is an axiom that power corrupts. Surely a man endowed with such gifts for leadership as Washington possessed must have desired, in some part of his complicated nature, to indulge his genius to the hilt. As we have seen, he thanked "the Greatest and Best of Beings" for leading him to "detest the folly and madness of unbounded ambition."[27]

But he felt temptations in the opposite direction too. The American farmer often dreamed of resigning so that he could go home: homesickness was a continuing aspect of Washington's military moods. How he longed for the mail that would bring him news of Mount Vernon: how he repined when the letters were lost or delayed! The arrival in camp every winter of that living symbol of a peaceful hearth, his wife, helped to keep him from being overwhelmed by that despair which on her arrival he poured into her ears, filling her with sorrow for his unhappiness.

Although he carried it out so well, Washington found his military task in many ways a painful one. He was by nature not a destroyer but a builder: he was an appreciater not a hater. There were, of course, chained in his nature, wolves of violence which could be released to make him an effective fighter, yet this fierceness, too closely allied to the other passions which he made it a lifetime effort to control, was not among the aspects of his personality with which his intellect was most congenial. In practicing cruelty and inducing pain, he tore himself as well as the enemy.

And, although he was a transcendent improviser, the labor of carrying on the war was almost more than his strength could bear. He could not, like an English general, rise from his wine, give an order, and return to his bottle, sure that the order would be carried out. As commander of a hand-to-mouth army, he was, so he complained, "a perfect slave." How he yearned for "that ease and tranquillity to which, for more than eight years, I have been an entire stranger, and for which a mind, which has been constantly on the stretch during that period and perplexed with a thousand embarrassing circumstances, oftentimes without a ray of light to guide it, stands much in need." Oh, to be a man "free from the load of public cares and subject to no other control than that of his own judgment and a proper conduct for the walk of private life!"[28]

Many another man would have thought that the way to escape from outside control was to make his word a law through the land which no one would dare contravene. This conception was utterly foreign to Washington.

To take responsibility, he wrote, "must make me responsible to the public" for any failure.[29]

Washington welcomed criticism from people he trusted if it were given directly to him and in private. As he wrote Reed, "I can bear to hear of imputed or real errors. The man who wishes to stand well in the opinion of others must do this, because he is thereby enabled to correct his faults or remove prejudices which are imbibed against him." As he explained to Rochambeau, "Our popular government imposes a necessity of great circumspection." This was because the voice of criticism could not be silenced. "Error is the portion of humanity, and to censure it, whether committed by this or that public character, is the prerogative of freemen."[30]

However, Washington resented and feared public criticism which might alienate from him the affections of the people. This dread of censure lay behind many of his most obvious faults. We have seen him shove blame off on others which his own shoulders should have more largely borne, and it is reasonable to suspect that his tendency to muddy the record in order to present his defeats as victories was motivated by personal reasons in addition to a desire to keep up the national morale. And, as he defended himself from even the implication of error, Washington could assume a disturbingly self-righteous tone. Yet his uneasiness under public criticism was more than a meanness: It was the reverse side of his great political virtue.

He sought power not for its own sake but in order to earn love and praise. Washington still subscribed to the principle of Stoic philosophy he had embraced as a young man: the conviction that "the approbation and affections of a free people" was "the greatest of earthly rewards." Power imposed by fear, inspiring hate, could have brought him nothing but acute unhappiness. "How pitiful in the eyes of reason and ambition," he wrote, "is that false ambition which desolates the world with fire and sword for the purposes of conquest and fame, when compared to the milder virtues of making our neighbors and our fellow men as happy as their frail conditions and perishable natures permit *them to be.*"[31]

Washington wished to act in a manner satisfactory to his fellow citizens, but his yearning to be loved did not urge him to cater to popular whim. "The wishes of the people," he wrote, "seldom founded in deep disquisitions or resulting from other reasonings than their present feeling, may not entirely accord with our true policy and interest." And again: "It is on *great* occasions *only,* and after time has been given for cool and deliberate reflection, that the *real* voice of the people can be known."[32]

Washington's formative years had been spent among those patriarchal leaders of a semi-aristocratic agrarian society whose ranks he had eventually joined. Although Virginia voters had a right to get drunk at the expense of the candidates on election day, the leaders did not normally kowtow to the electorate. They did not wander the fields taking public opinion polls. They gained ascendancy by being willing and able to bring their intelligence and property to bear in effectively helping their less powerful and less informed neighbors to achieve ends which they persuaded their followers were for the common good. Nothing in Washington's Virginia training urged him to seek popularity by shaking hands and grinning. And his elevation to leadership in the Revolution had not resulted from electioneering—quite the reverse. He had sought to evade the responsibility which had been forced upon him.

Rising as if in answer to some scientific law, Washington took to leadership like a balloon taking to the air. When, as in the case of the Conway Cabal, rivals tried to shoot him down, he defended himself with both rancor and brilliant skill; but from day to day he accepted his preeminence as naturally as a man accepts his right hand. He did not even seem conscious of how powerful he was, how grievously he outdazzled those around him. All the more because it was so effortless, this dominance made enemies of men who considered themselves as good as he was, or better—or who disapproved of his opinions. And some historians, more used to contemporary patterns, have assumed that because he did not struggle for office, Washington was a clod-like puppet lifted by brute chance.

Since he did not have to stoop to conquer, no important outside pressure impeded Washington's efforts to steer by the highest stars. He could wholeheartedly pursue his conviction that he could serve his fellowmen best by serving the great principles.

It was in his ability to recognize the great principles that Washington's most fundamental greatness lay. He was not an effervescent thinker throwing off those plumes of inspiration which delight the inventive intellectual mind. His mind, indeed, was not inventive in the sense of defining conceptions for the first time. He selected rather among the alternatives that were presented to him by the possibilities of his place and generation.

Washington undertook his lifelong course in self-education and self-discipline at a time of major transition, when the old order, having not yet been conquered by the new, existed simultaneously with it. Although he took a leading part in the warfare that arose between the two systems, he was far from being, on a philosophical plane, a blind partisan. He had, indeed, a foot planted firmly on both sides of the divide. In a lesser man, this would have made for shilly-shally. In Washington, it made for double strength. He blended the romantic and the republican with the classical and the aristocratic into a synthesis that embraced much of the best in both orders.

As a leader, Washington brought to elective office the highest aristocratic ideals. His creativity was in the classical manner: the gift of seeing clearly, judging comprehensively and deeply. Yet he belonged to the romantic era in his disdain for precedent, his eagerness to think all matters out anew. He

[551]

was no more inclined to travel history's long-built highways than to cut his way along lightly blazed trails into that blind wilderness the future.

Again and again to discover, when immersed in the welter of troubled times, the best routes ahead is a towering intellectual achievement. Gathering up complexity, he transmuted it into simplicity. His gift was to grasp so profoundly the heart of the matter that he could resolve what others endlessly argued about in a few clear sentences which, however radical their substance, carried the conviction of the obvious.

And typically, the obvious that he discovered was inspiring. "It should be the highest ambition of every American," Washington wrote, "to extend his views beyond himself, and to bear in mind that his conduct will not only affect himself, his country, and his immediate posterity; but that its influence may be co-extensive with the world, and stamp political happiness or misery on ages yet unborn."[33]

Acknowledgments
Bibliography
Source References

Acknowledgments

T WO of the great libraries in New York City have given me, during my labors on this volume, not only assistance but hospitality. I have had the pleasure of working both at the New-York Historical Society and in the Frederick Lewis Allen Room in the New York Public Library.

The Mount Vernon Ladies' Association of the Union, who have so graciously preserved Washington's home, have continued their great courtesy to me. Among other institutions that have been helpful to me are the library of the Century Association, the Free Library of Cornwall, Connecticut, the Clements Library, the Frick Art Reference Library, and the Library of Congress. The editors of *American Heritage* have kindly permitted me to consult their picture files.

My wife, Beatrice Hudson Flexner, and my daughter, Helen Hudson Flexner, have helped in many ways, as have my editors at Little, Brown and Company, Arthur Thornhill, Jr., and Llewellyn Howland III. Patricia J. Billfaldt has continued to rationalize my manuscripts as they pass through her typewriter.

I am also grateful to Frederick B. Adams, Jr., Harry W. Baehr, Shirley Beresford, Julian P. Boyd, Edward Di Roma, James Gregory, James J. Heslin, Oliver Jensen, Mr. and Mrs. Louis C. Jones, Richard M. Ketchum, Barbara Klaw, Mary-Jo Kline, Dumas Malone, Christine Meadows, George Wall Merck, Walter Millis, Henry Allen Moe, Frank E. Morse, Sanford L. Silverman, Douglas Turnstell, Charles C. Wall, and Arnold Whitridge.

Bibliography

ALTHOUGH designed to stand on its own feet, this book is the second in a projected three-volume life of George Washington. The first volume was published in 1965 under the title *George Washington: The Forge of Experience* (*1732–1775*), and dealt with his life from his birth to the event with which this book begins: Washington's acceptance of the command of the Continental Army.

The object of the series is to rescue the Washington who actually lived from the mass of legend and special pleading that has obscured his true image. Toward this end, I have concentrated my research not on those later writings which have too often been the creators and carriers of error, but on the original sources. As in the previous volume, my main reliance has been on Washington's own words. For his relations with his close associates, I have consulted what they themselves wrote. However, as my protagonist stepped from his Virginia years onto a stage as wide as settled North America, connected by boats and men with Europe and the Indies, I have been unable to do original research on the more far-flung aspect of my tale. While in my first volume, I had no need for an extensive list of books consulted, such a list has seemed called for here.

The purpose of the bibliography is specific and pragmatic: to interlock with the source references in making clear the foundations on which individual passages of my book were built. My previous volume contained an essay on biographies of Washington in general, which need not be repeated. As before, the only secondary source upon which I have placed major reliance has been Douglas Southall Freeman's massive *George Washington,* where the time span here covered is discussed in about 1500 closely printed pages. Assisted by a foundation-supported research team, primarily a documentary writer, Freeman, even if he rarely lifted his eyes to see the larger landscape, was a major pathfinder through the jungle of Washingtoniana. I have often followed in his footsteps.

My debt is great to the scholars who have searched out and put in print the manuscripts of our forefathers, particularly to the great editor of Washington papers, John C. Fitzpatrick.

Fitzpatrick completed his compilation in 1940. Since then, a considerable number of Washington documents have come to light, although few are of first importance. Since ownership is widely scattered and the location of those from which I have quoted are specified in the source references, along with citations of various other manuscripts, I have not in the following list attempted to include manuscript collections. The most important collections I consulted are in the Library of Congress, Mount Vernon, the New-York Historical Society, and the Morristown (N.J.) Historical Library.

Perhaps I should add that my objectives have prevented me from placing primary emphasis on documents that I can claim to have used for the first time. Since the importance of a fact in the total picture has no inherent correlation with whether it is familiar or unfamiliar, a biographer seeking the profoundest image of which he is capable must weigh his own findings on an equal scale with truths that have been long known. In such a book as this, originality must be sought through synthesis without bias, through fresh interpretation based on both fact and insight, through a happy marriage of scholarship and art.

Abbott, William, *The Crisis of the Revolution* (New York, 1899).

Adams, Abigail, *New Letters, 1788–1801* (Boston, 1947).

Adams, John, *Familiar Letters of . . . and his wife Abigail Adams* (New York, 1876).

———, *Papers*, ed. Lyman H. Butterfield, vols. I–IV (Cambridge, Mass., 1961).

Adams, Randolph G., *The Burned Letter of Chastellux* (New York, 1935).

Alden, John Richard, *General Charles Lee* (Baton Rouge, La., [1951]).

Anderson, Troyer Steele, *The Command of the Howe Brothers during the American Revolution* (New York and London, 1936).

André, John, *André's Journal*, 2 vols. (Boston, 1903).

———, *The Case of Major John André* (New York, 1780); original in John Carter Brown Library; manuscript copy in New-York Historical Society.

———, *Minutes of a Court of Inquiry upon the Case of Major John André* (Albany, N.Y., 1865).

Armstrong, John, "Review of Sketches of the Life and Correspondence of Nathanael Greene . . . by William Johnson," *United States Magazine*, I (1823), 3–44.

[Arnold, Benedict], *Proceedings of a General Court Martial . . . of Major General Arnold* (Philadelphia, 1780).

Bakeless, John, *Turncoats, Traitors, and Heroes* (Philadelphia and New York, [1959]).

Baker, William S., *Early Sketches of George Washington* (Philadelphia, 1894).

———, *Itinerary of George Washington* (Philadelphia, 1892).

Bancroft, George, *History of the Formation of the Constitution*, 2 vols. (New York, 1882).

Bangs, Isaac, *Journal, April 1 to July 29, 1776* (Cambridge, Mass., 1890).

Baurmeister, Carl Leopold, *Confidential Letters and Journals* (New Brunswick, N.J., 1957).

Belcher, Henry, *The First American Civil War, 1775–1778*, 2 vols. (London, 1911).

Bemis, Samuel Flagg, *The Diplomacy of the American Revolution* (Bloomington, Ind., 1965).

Bill, Alfred Hoyt, *The Campaign of Princeton* (Princeton, N.J., 1948).

Billias, George Athan, ed., *George Washington's Generals* (New York, 1964).

Biron, Armand Louis de Contaut, Duc de, *Memoirs of the Duc de Lauzun* (New York, 1912).

Blanchard, Claude, *Journal* (Albany, N.Y., 1876).

Bliven, Bruce, *The Battle for Manhattan* (New York, 1956).

Boudinot, Elias, *Journal or Historical Recollections of American Events during the Revolutionary War* (Philadelphia, 1894).

Bourg, Cromot du (attributed to), "Diary," *Magazine of American History*, IV (1880), see index.

Brissot de Warville, Jacques Pierre, *New Travels* (London, 1797).

Burke, Aedanus, *Considerations on the Society or Order of Cincinnati* (Philadelphia, 1783).

Burnett, Edmund C., *The Continental Congress* (New York, 1941).

——, ed., *Letters of Members of the Continental Congress*, 8 vols. (Washington, D.C., 1921–1926); referred to in Source References as "B."

Butler, Richard, "Journal of the Siege of Yorktown," *Historical Magazine*, VIII (1864), 102–112.

Callahan, North, *Henry Knox* (New York, 1958).

Chadwick, Mrs. French E., "The Visit of General Washington to Newport," *Bulletin Newport Historical Society*, No. 6 (1913).

Chase, Eugene Parker, *Our Revolutionary Forefathers: The Letters of François Marquis de Barbe-Marbois* (New York, 1929).

Chastellux, Marquis de, *Travels in North America*, trans. and ed. Howard C. Rice, Jr., 2 vols. (Chapel Hill, N.C., 1963).

Chinard, Gilbert, *George Washington as the French Knew Him* (Princeton, N.J., 1940).

Clap, Caleb, "Diary . . . March 29 until October 23, 1776," *Historical Magazine*, 3d Ser., III (1874), 133–138, 247–251, and ff.

Clinton, Sir Henry, *The American Rebellion*, ed. William B. Willcox (New Haven, Conn., 1954).

——, *Narrative* (London, 1783).

Closen, Baron Ludwig Von, *Revolutionary Journal*, trans. and ed. Evelyn A. Acomb (Chapel Hill, N.C., [1958]).

Cobb, David, "Diary," *Massachusetts Historical Society Proceedings*, XIX (1881), 69 ff.

Coleman, Mary Haldane, *St. George Tucker* (Richmond, Va., 1938).

Continental Congress, *Journals, 1774–1789*, 8 vols. (Washington, D.C., 1921–1926); referred to in Source References as "JCC."

Cornwallis, Charles, *An Answer to . . . the Narrative of Lieutenant-General Sir Henry Clinton* (London, 1783).

Cunliffe, Marcus, *George Washington, Man and Monument* (Boston, 1958).

Custis, Eliza, "Self-portrait," *Virginia Magazine*, LIII (1945), 89–100.

Custis, George Washington Parke, *Recollections of Washington* (New York, 1860).

Doniol, Henri, *Histoire de la Participation de la France à l'Établissement des États-Unis D'Amérique*, vols. IV and V (Paris, 1890, 1892).

Drake, Francis S., *Life and Correspondence of Henry Knox* (Boston, 1873).

Drake, Samuel Adams, *Historic Fields and Mansions of Middlesex* (Boston, 1874).

Dumas, Mathieu, *Memoirs of his Own Time*, vol. I (Philadelphia, 1839).

Dunlap, William, *Rise and Progress of the Arts of Design*, vol. I (New York, 1834).

Du Ponceau, Pierre Étienne, "Autobiography," *Pennsylvania Magazine of History and Biography*, LXIII (1939), 189–227, 311–343, 432–461.

Dupuy, R. Ernest, and Trevor N. Dupuy, *The Compact History of the Revolution* (New York, [1963]).

Du Roi, the Elder, "Journal," *American-German Annals*, N.S. IX (1911), 40 ff., 77 ff., 131 ff.

Earle, Edward Meade, *Makers of Modern Strategy* (Princeton, N.J., 1943).

Ewing, George, *Military Journal* (Yonkers, N.Y., 1928).

Ferguson, Elmer James, *The Power of the Purse* (Chapel Hill, N.C., 1961).

Field, Thomas Warren, *The Battle of Long Island* (Brooklyn, N.Y., 1869).

Fitzpatrick, John C., *George Washington Himself* (Indianapolis, Ind., 1933).

Fleming, Thomas J., *Beat the Last Drum* (New York, [1963]).

Flexner, James Thomas, *America's Old Masters* (New York, 1939).

———, *Doctors on Horseback* (New York, 1937).

———, *George Washington: The Forge of Experience, 1732–1775* (Boston, 1965); referred to in Source References as "F, F."

———, *Gilbert Stuart* (New York, 1955).

———, *The Traitor and the Spy: Benedict Arnold and John André* (New York, 1962).

Foner, Philip S., *The Complete Writings of Thomas Paine*, 2 vols. (New York, [1945]).

Force, Peter, compiler, *American Archives*, 9 vols. (Washington, D.C., 1837–1853); referred to in Source References as "F, A."

Ford, Paul Leicester, *The True George Washington* (Philadelphia, 1898).

Ford, Worthington Chauncey, *The Spurious Letters Attributed to Washington* (Brooklyn, N.Y., 1889).

Franklin, Benjamin, *Letters to Benjamin Franklin from his Family and Friends* (New York, 1859).

Freeman, Douglas Southall, *George Washington: A Biography*, completed by J. A. Carroll and M. W. Ashworth, 7 vols. (New York, 1948–1957); referred to in Source References as "F."

Godfrey, Carlos E., *The Commander-in-Chief's Guard* (Washington, D.C., 1904).

Gordon, William, *History of the Rise, Progress, and Establishment of the Independence of the United States of America*, 4 vols. (London, 1788).

Gottschalk, Louis R., *Lafayette Joins the American Army* (Chicago, 1937).

[Grasse, Comte de], *Correspondence of General Washington and Comte de Grasse*, ed. François J. P. Grasse-Tilly (Washington, D.C., 1931).

Graydon, Alexander, *Memoirs of His Own Time* (Philadelphia, 1846).

Greene, George Washington, *The Life of Nathanael Greene*, 3 vols. (New York, 1867–1871).

Hamilton, Alexander, *Papers*, vols. I–III, ed. Harold C. Syrett (New York and London, 1961–1962).

Hamilton, Stanislaus Murray, *Letters to Washington and Accompanying Papers*, 5 vols. (Boston and New York, 1898–1902).

Haven, C. C., *30 Days in New Jersey* (Trenton, N.J., 1867).

Heath, William, *Heath's Memoirs of the American War* (New York, 1904).

Heitman, Francis B., *Historical Register of the Officers of Continental Army* (Washington, D.C., 1914).

Howe, William, *Narrative* (London, 1780).

———, *Orderly Book . . . June 17, 1775 to May 26, 1776 . . . to Which Is Added an Abridgement of General Howe's Correspondence with the English Government During the Siege of Boston* (London, 1890).

Hoyt, E., *Rules and Regulations for Drill, Saber Exercise, Equitation, Formation and Field Movements of Cavalry* (Greenfield, Mass., 1816).

Hughes, Rupert, *George Washington*, 3 vols. (New York, 1926–1930).

Humphreys, David, *The Conduct of General Washington Respecting the Confinement of Captain Asgill* (New York, 1859); reprinted from the *New Haven Gazette*, 1786.

[Hunt, Louise Livingston], *Biographical Notes Concerning General Richard Montgomery* (n.p., 1876).

Hunter, Robert, *Quebec to Carolina in 1785–1786*, ed. Louis B. Wright and Marion Tinling (San Marino, Cal., 1943).

Ives, Mabel Lorenz, *Washington's Headquarters* (Upper Montclair, N.J., [1932]).

Jefferson, Thomas, *Papers*, ed. Julian Boyd, vols. I–VI (Princeton, N.J., 1950–1952).

———, *Writings*, ed. Paul Leicester Ford, vols. I–III (New York, 1892–1894).

Jensen, Merrill, *The New Nation* (New York, 1950).

Johnston, Henry P., *The Campaign of 1776 Around New York and Brooklyn*, with documents appended and separately paginated (Brooklyn, N.Y., 1878).

Jones, Thomas, *History of New York During the Revolutionary War*, 2 vols. (New York, 1879).

Kapp, Friedrich, *Life of Frederick William von Steuben* (New York, 1859).

Kemble, Stephen, *Journals, 1773–1789*, 2 vols. (New York, 1884–1885).

King, Rufus, *Life and Correspondence*, ed. Charles R. King, vol. I (New York, 1894).

Knollenberg, Bernhard, *Washington and the Revolution* (New York, 1940).

Konkle, Burton Alva, *Thomas Willing* (Philadelphia, 1937).

Lafayette, Marquis de, *The Letters of Lafayette to Washington*, ed. Louis Gottschalk (New York, 1944).

————, *Memoirs . . . Published by his Family*, vol. I (New York, 1837).

Larrabee, Harold Atkins, *Decision at the Chesapeake* (New York, 1964).

Lassernay, André, *Les Français sous les Treize Étoiles*, 2 vols. (Paris, 1935).

Laurens, John, *Army Correspondence* (New York, 1867).

Lee, Charles, *The Lee Papers*, 4 vols. (New York, 1872–1875); referred to in Source References as "L."

Lee, Henry, *Memoirs of the War in the Southern Department of the United States* (Washington D.C., 1827).

Lee, Richard Henry, *Letters*, ed. James Curtis Ballagh, 2 vols. (New York, 1914).

Little, Shelby, *George Washington* (New York, 1929).

Lossing, Benson J., *Mary and Martha Washington* (New York, 1886).

————, *The Pictorial Field Book of the Revolution*, 2 vols. (New York, 1852).

MacElree, Wilmer W., *Along the Western Brandywine* (Chester, Pa., 1912).

Mackenzie, Frederick, *Diary*, 2 vols. (Cambridge, Mass., 1930).

Mackesy, Piers, *The War for America, 1775–1783* (Cambridge, Mass., 1964).

Malone, Dumas, *Jefferson the Virginian* (Boston, 1948).

Marshall, Christopher, *Extracts from the Diary of . . .*, ed. William Duane (Albany, N.Y., 1877).

Marshall, John, *George Washington*, 5 vols. (Fredericksburg, Va., 1926).

Martyn, Charles, *The Life of Artemas Ward* (New York, 1921).

McCurtin, Daniel, "Journal," in *Papers Relating Chiefly to the Maryland Line*, by Thomas Balch (Philadelphia, 1857).

[Michener, John H.], *Bank of North America* (New York, 1906).

Miller, John C., *Alexander Hamilton* (New York, 1959).

Millis, Walter, *Arms and Men* (New York, 1956).

Montresor, Captain John, "Journals," *New-York Historical Society Collections for 1881* (New York, 1882).

Moore, Frank, *Diary of the American Revolution*, 2 vols. (New York, 1865).

Morison, Samuel Eliot, *The Young Man Washington* (Cambridge, Mass., 1932).

Mount Vernon Ladies' Association, *Annual Report, 1944–1966* (Mount Vernon, Va., 1945–1967).

North, William, "Baron Steuben," *Magazine of American History*, VIII (1882), 187–199.

Ogden, Colonel Aaron, "Autobiography," *Proceedings of the New Jersey Historical Society*, 2d Ser., XII (1892–1893), 15–31.

Palmer, John McAuley, *General von Steuben* (New Haven, Conn., 1937).

Paullin, Charles Oscar, *The Navy of the American Revolution* (Cleveland, Ohio, 1906).

Pennsylvania Magazine of History and Biography, vols. I–XCI (1877–1967).

Pickering, Octavius, *The Life of Timothy Pickering*, vol. I (Boston, 1867).

Reed, William B., *Life and Correspondence of Joseph Reed*, 2 vols. (Philadelphia, 1847).

Robertson, Archibald, *Diaries and Sketches* (New York, 1930).

Rochambeau, Marshal Count de, *Memoirs . . . relative to the War of Independence* (Paris, 1838).

Rösch, John, *Historic White Plains* ([White Plains, N.Y., 1939]).

Rossman, Kenneth R., *Thomas Mifflin* (Chapel Hill, N.C., 1952).

Rowe, John, *Letters and Diaries* (Boston, 1903).

Rush, Benjamin, *Autobiography*, ed. George W. Corner (Princeton, N.J., 1948).
——, *Letters*, ed. L. H. Butterfield, 2 vols. (Princeton, N.J., 1951).
Rush, Richard, *Occasional Productions* (Philadelphia, 1860).
Scheer, George F., and Hugh F. Rankin, *Rebels and Redcoats* (Cleveland, Ohio, 1957).
Scott, James Brown, *De Grasse at Yorktown* (Baltimore, Md., 1931).
Sellers, Charles Coleman, *The Artist of the Revolution: the Early Life of Charles Willson Peale* (Hebron, Conn., 1939).
Shaw, Samuel, *Journals* (Boston, 1847).
Smith, Page, *John Adams*, 2 vols. (New York, 1962).
Sonneck, Oscar G., *Francis Hopkinson . . . and James Lyons* (Washington, D.C., 1905).
Sparks, Jared, ed., *Correspondence of the American Revolution; Being Letters of Eminent Men to George Washington*, 4 vols. (Boston, 1853); referred to in Source References as "S, C."
——, *Life of Gouverneur Morris*, 3 vols. (Boston, 1832).
Steiner, Bernard C., *The Life and Correspondence of James McHenry* (Cleveland, Ohio, 1907).
Stevens, Benjamin F., *The Clinton-Cornwallis Controversy* (London, 1888).
——, *Facsimiles of Manuscripts in European Archives Relating to America, 1773–1783* (London, 1891).
Stevens, John Austin, *The French in Rhode Island* (n.p., 1928).
Stiles, Ezra, *Literary Diary*, 3 vols. (New York, 1901).
Stokes, I. N. Phelps, *The Iconography of Manhattan Island*, vol. IV (New York, 1922).
Stryker, William S., *The Battle of Monmouth* (Princeton, N.J., 1917).
——, *The Battles of Trenton and Princeton* (Boston and New York, 1898).
Sullivan, John, *Letters and Papers*, ed. Otis G. Hamilton, 3 vols. (Concord, N.H., 1930–1939).
Tallmadge, Benjamin, *Memoir* (New York, 1904).
Thacher, James, *Military Journal of the American Revolution* (Hartford, Conn., 1862).
Thane, Elswyth, *Potomac Squire* (New York, 1963).
Tower, Charlemagne, *The Marquis de Lafayette*, 2 vols. (Philadelphia, 1895).
Townsend, Joseph, *Some Account of the British Army . . . and of the Battle of Brandywine* (Philadelphia, 1846).
Trevelyan, Sir George Otto, *The American Revolution*, 4 vols. (New York, 1899–1907).
Trumbull, Jonathan, "Minutes of Occurrences Respecting the Siege and Capture of Yorktown," *Massachusetts Historical Society Proceedings*, XIV (1875–1876), 331–338.
Tuckerman, Arthur, *When Rochambeau Stepped Ashore* (Newport, R.I., [1955]).
Van Doren, Carl, *Mutiny in January* (New York, 1943).
[Varick, Richard], *The Varick Court of Inquiry* (Boston, 1907).
Waldo, Albigence, "Diary, Valley Forge, 1777–1778," *Pennsylvania Magazine of History and Biography*, XXI (1897), 299–323.
Ward, Christopher, *The War of the Revolution*, 2 vols. (New York, 1952).
Warren-Adams Letters; Being Chiefly a Correspondence among John Adams, Samuel Adams, and James Warren, ed. W. C. Ford, 2 vols. (Massachusetts Historical Society Collections, 1917, 1925).
Washington, George, *Account of Expenses while Commander in Chief*, with annotations by John C. Fitzpatrick (Boston and New York, 1917).
——, *Calendar of the Correspondence of George Washington . . . with the Continental Congress*, ed. John C. Fitzpatrick (Washington, D.C., 1906).
——, *Calendar of the Correspondence of George Washington . . . with the Officers*, ed. John C. Fitzpatrick, 4 vols. (Washington, D.C., 1915).
——, *Calendar of the Washington Manuscripts in the Library of Congress*, ed. Herbert Friedenwald (Washington, D.C., 1901).
——, *Diaries*, ed. John C. Fitzpatrick, 4 vols. (Boston and New York, 1925); referred to in Source References as "GW, D."
——, *The George Washington Atlas*, ed. Lawrence Martin (Washington, D.C., 1932).

————, *Presidential Papers Microfilm, George Washington Papers* (Washington, D. C., 1965).

————, *Writings,* ed. Jared Sparks, 12 vols. (Boston, 1834–1837); referred to in Source References as "S, W."

————, *Writings,* ed. Worthington Chauncey Ford, 14 vols. (New York and London, 1889–1893).

————, *Writings,* ed. John C. Fitzpatrick, 39 vols. (Washington, D.C., 1931–1944); referred to in Source References as "GW."

Watson, John F., *Annals of Philadelphia,* 3 vols. (Philadelphia, 1907).

Webb, Samuel Blachley, *Correspondence and Journals,* ed. Worthington Chauncey Ford, 2 vols. (New York, 1893–1894).

Weedon, George, *Valley Forge Orderly Book* (New York, 1902).

Wheatley, Phillis, *Poems and Letters* (n.p., 1915).

Whitridge, Arnold, *Rochambeau* (New York, 1965).

Wilkinson, James, *Memoirs of My Own Time,* 3 vols. (Philadelphia, 1816).

Willard, Margaret Wheeler, *Letters of the American Revolution, 1774–1776* (Boston and New York, 1925).

Willcox, William B., *Portrait of a General: Sir Henry Clinton* (New York, 1964).

Williams, Mrs. [Catherine], *Biography of Revolutionary Heroes* (Providence, R.I., 1839).

Source References

THE effort has been made in these source references to be as succinct as utility allows. Had I noted all the passages in which Washington or his contemporaries mentioned matters summarized in my text, I would have created an underpinning perhaps more extensive than the super-structure. References are commonly to the passages from which specific quotations have been taken.

Since the *Bibliography* gives fuller citations, the source references have been kept as brief as seems clear. When a title is repeated in the notes to one chapter, I have in the later references omitted, as superfluous, the form *"op. cit."* Manuscript dates are eighteenth century unless otherwise specified. The sources most often repeated are referred to by the following abbreviations:

B: Burnett, Edmund C., ed., *Letters of Members of the Continental Congress*, 8 vols. (Washington, D.C., 1921–1926).

F: Freeman, Douglas Southall, *George Washington: A Biography*, completed by J. A. Carroll and M. W. Ashworth, 7 vols. (New York, 1948–1957).

F, A: Force, Peter, compiler, *American Archives*, 9 vols. (Washington, D.C., 1837–1853).

F, F: Flexner, James Thomas, *George Washington: The Forge of Experience, 1732–1775* (Boston, 1965).

GW: Washington, George, *Writings*, ed. John C. Fitzpatrick, 39 vols. (Washington, D.C., 1931–1944).

GW, D: Washington, George, *Diaries*, ed. John C. Fitzpatrick, 4 vols. (Boston and New York, 1925).

JCC: Continental Congress, *Journals, 1774–1789*, 8 vols (Washington, D.C., 1921–1926).

L: Lee, Charles, *The Lee Papers*, 4 vols. (New York, 1872–1875).

S, *C:* Sparks, Jared, ed., *Correspondence of the American Revolution; Being Letters of Eminent Men to George Washington,* 4 vols. (Boston, 1853).

S, *W:* Washington, George, *Writings,* ed., Jared Sparks, 12 vols. (Boston, 1834–1837).

INTRODUCTION

1. Chase, *Forefathers,* 116; Gouverneur Morris to John Marshall (6/26 1807), Library of Congress; Martha Washington to Burwell Bassett (7/13/80), Morristown.
2. GW, XXVII, 269.

1: DARK DAWN OF ADVENTURE

1. JCC, II, 91.
2. Rush, *Autobiography,* 112–113.
3. Rush, 113; GW, III, 297; JCC, II, 92.
4. GW, III, 294.
5. GW, III, 242.
6. F, *F,* 311; GW, III, 231, 241.
7. GW, III, 291–292.
8. F, *F,* 309–323.
9. Baker, *Sketches,* 77; Flexner, *Stuart,* 127.
10. Ford, *True,* 195.
11. F, *F,* 327.
12. Flexner, 127; Ford, 44–45.
13. F, *F,* 334–335.
14. GW, III, 298.
15. Adams, *Papers,* III, 321 ff.
16. JCC, II, 97.
17. Ford, *Spurious,* 32; JCC, II, 91, 97.
18. GW, III, 452–454.
19. Hughes, *Washington,* III, 61.
20. GW, XXVII, 88–89; Little, *Washington,* 127.
21. JCC, II, 92.
22. GW, XXX, 297.
23. JCC, II, 96.
24. GW, III, 297.

2: A DESPERATE SEARCH FOR ADVISERS

1. JCC, II, 96.
2. F, *F,* 334.
3. F, *F,* 328–329.
4. B, I, 136; F. III, 501; JCC, II, 98.
5. Samuel Washington to Gates (6/22/75), New-York Hist. Soc.
6. JCC, II, 100.
7. GW, XXVIII, 472–473.
8. Reed, *Reed,* I, 105–107.
9. F, III, 459.
10. Adams, *Familiar,* 70.
11. GW, III, 295, XXIX, 22.

3: TRAVELER'S DUST

1. B, I, 141; F, III, 461.
2. Washington, *Account,* 3.
3. GW, III, 320.
4. American Scenic and Hist. Preservation Soc., *Nineteenth Annual Report* (1914), 257.
5. F, *A* (4th Ser.), II, 1039–1040.
6. Jones, *History,* I, 55–56.
7. Stokes, *Iconography,* IV, 894.
8. F, *A* (4th Ser.), II, 1321.
9. GW, III, 305.
10. GW, III, 302–305.
11. GW, III, 371, XXVIII, 291.
12. F, *A* (4th Ser.), II, 1472–1473.
13. Martyn, *Ward,* 151.
14. Drake, *Knox,* 262–263; Hughes, *Washington,* III, 270–271.

4: A VIRGINIAN AMONG NEW ENGLANDERS

1. GW, III, 326.
2. GW, III, 325–326.
3. GW, III, 326, 358–361.
4. Trevelyan, *Revolution,* I, 345.
5. GW, III, 450.
6. Fitzpatrick, *Himself,* 176; Hughes, *Washington,* II, 303.
7. GW, III, 511.
8. GW, III, 371–372.
9. GW, III, 325; Webb, *Correspondence,* 84.
10. GW, III, 347, XXI, 8.
11. GW, III, 394.
12. GW, III, 319, 329–330.
13. GW, III, 320n, 331.
14. GW, III, 349.
15. B, I, 136; GW, III, 508, VI, 167, 386; *Warren-Adams,* I, 189, 194.
16. GW, III, 451.
17. S, W, III, 491.
18. F, *A* (4th Ser.), III, 1159; *Warren-Adams,* I, 180.
19. GW, III, 394; Little, *Washington,* 123.
20. F, III, 517; GW, III, 384, 395.
21. GW, III, 385–387, 495.
22. GW, III, 357.
23. GW, III, 434, 442n.
24. GW, III, 454.
25. GW, III, 309, 433, IV, 320.

26. B, I, 174; GW, III, 450.
27. Smith, *Adams*, I, 202.
28. Hamilton, S. M., *Letters*, I, 254.
29. GW, III, 378–399.
30. GW, IV, 165, 240–241.
31. Thacher, *Journal*, 30.
32. Willard, *Letters*, 228.
33. Smith, I, 201.
34. Thacher, 30, 37.
35. JCC, II, 92.
36. GW, IV, 247n.
37. F, *F*, 166.
38. *Warren-Adams*, I, 189.
39. GW, III, 325, 357, 511, IV, 180, XIII, 480–481.
40. Drake, *Knox*, 18; *Warren-Adams*, I, 186.

5: THE WAR OF POSITIONS
1. GW, III, 407n.
2. GW, III, 372–373.
3. Webb, *Correspondence*, 84.
4. Thacher, *Journal*, 36.
5. F, *A* (4th Ser.), III, 1672; GW, III, 485n.
6. Earle, *Strategy*; Mackesy, *War*; Millis, *Arms*.
7. Earle, 54.
8. Chastellux, *Travels*, I, 190; Fitzpatrick, *Himself*, 206.
9. Fitzpatrick, 205; GW, IV, 300, 315–316.

6: THE SPREADING BLAZE
1. GW, III, 435, 488.
2. F, *A* (4th Ser.), III, 768, 1153; GW, III, 485n, 511, IV, 243.
3. GW, IV, 243, XVI, 8.
4. F, III, 529; GW, III, 485n.
5. Flexner, *Traitor*, 60–61.
6. S, *C*, I, 54; GW, III, 374.
7. GW, III, 436, 473, 491–499.
8. GW, IV, 45, 47.
9. F, III, 561; GW, IV, 65, 74, 77, 106.
10. GW, IV, 147.
11. Flexner, 65–71.
12. GW, III, 467–469.
13. GW, XXXVII, 517.
14. Flexner, *Doctors*, 4–5; GW, IV, 128n.
15. GW, IV, 77, 144.
16. GW, IX, 117.
17. Howe, *Orderly*, 311.
18. GW, IV, 44.
19. GW, III, 391, IV, 77, 83.
20. GW, IV, 126, VI, 154, VII, 153.
21. GW, IV, 57, 124.
22. GW, IV, 185.

23. GW, IV, 243.
24. GW, IV, 104, 268–269.
25. Fitzpatrick, *Himself*, 215; GW, IV, 202, 210–211.

7: FOREIGN WAR OR SOCIAL REVOLUTION
1. Lund Washington to GW (10/29 & 11/5/75), Mount Vernon; F. *F*, 261; GW, IV, 28.
2. Martha Washington to Miss Ramsay (12/30/75), Morgan Library.
3. Marshall, *Diary*, 51–53.
4. Webb, *Correspondence*, I, 121.
5. *American Hist. Rev.*, VI (1900–1901), 328; *Warren-Adams*, I, 200.
6. *Warren-Adams*, I, 228.
7. Martha Washington to Miss Ramsay 12/30/75).
8. Washington, *Account*, 6–7, 11, 35–36.
9. GW, XXVII, 451; Thane, *Potomac*, 93.
10. GW, XIII, 248; Washington, *Account*, 14–15, 18–19.
11. GW, XXVIII, 15.
12. Ives, *Headquarters*, 38.
13. GW, XXIV, 261; Morison, *Young*, 8–9.
14. *Warren-Adams*, I, 167, 201–202.
15. GW, IV, 323; Wheatley, *Poems*, 53.
16. GW, III, 379–380, 503–505; S, *C*, I, 31, 37.
17. GW, IV, 483.
18. GW, XI, 2–3.
19. GW, IV, 67, 70, 90.
20. GW, IV, 197.
21. GW, IV, 321.
22. S, *C*, I, 106–107.
23. F, *A* (4th Ser.), IV, 604; GW, IV, 209, 218–219; S, *C*, I, 112–114.
24. F, IV, 13.
25. GW, IV, 266, 367.
26. GW, IV, 352n.
27. GW, IV, 187; S, *C*, I, 165.
28. GW, IV, 259.
29. GW, IV, 121, 300, 315–316.
30. *Warren-Adams*, I, 197–198.
31. GW, XVII, 127.
32. Lund Washington to GW (1/31 & 2/22/76), Mount Vernon; GW, IV, 167, 172, 186, VI, 107–109.
33. GW, IV, 297, 321.

8: PROVIDENCE RIDES A STORM
1. GW, IV, 321, 336.
2. F, *A* (4th Ser.), IV, 1193.
3. GW, IV, 336.
4. Chastellux, *Travels*, I, 112.
5. Billias, *Generals*, 241.
6. GW, IV, 349.

7. F, *A* (4th Ser.), V, 458.
8. GW, IV, 349, 351.
9. GW, IV, 373–374.
10. GW, IV, 359.
11. GW, IV, 355.
12. Adams, *Familiar*, 137; F, IV, 23; GW, IV, 370; Webb, *Correspondence*, I, 133.
13. GW, IV, 370–371.
14. Webb, I, 134.
15. GW, IV, 380.
16. F, *A* (4th Ser.), V, 425; Robertson, *Diaries*, 74.
17. *Mass. Hist. Soc. Proc.* XIV (1875–1876), 281–282.
18. Bangs, *Journal*, 12; F, *A* (4th Ser.), V, 426; McCurtin, *Journal*, 33.
19. GW, IV, 433–434.
20. Howe, *Orderly*, 319; Robertson, 74.

9: THE TASTE OF VICTORY

1. GW, IV, 375–376; Howe, *Orderly*, 319.
2. F, *A* (4th Ser.), V, 459; GW, IV, 378, 395.
3. GW, IV, 367–368.
4. GW, IV, 401.
5. GW, IV, 403n.
6. F, IV, 53; GW, IV, 389, 404; Rowe, *Letters*, 304.
7. GW, IV, 395, 431, 437.
8. Rowe, 304.
9. GW, IV, 405–406, V, 2.
10. Lund Washington to GW (1/31 & 2/15, 22, 29/76), GW to Lund Washington (10/26/75), Mount Vernon; GW, IV, 404, 446n.
11. GW, IV, 404, 407, 449, 456; S, *W*, III, 325–326.
12. GW, IV, 415, 417, 420, 422, 431.
13. GW, IV, 436.
14. GW, IV, 446–450.

10: AWAITING THE BLOW

1. GW, IV, 387–388
2. *New Jersey Hist. Soc. Proc.*, LI (1933), 250–253 (misnumbered 150–153).
3. F, IV, 89–90; GW, IV, 241n; Washington, *Account*, 31.
4. JCC, IV, 201–204; Kemble, *Journals*, I, 89.
5. GW, VI, 170.
6. F, IV, 88; GW, IV, 512, 520, 530.
7. GW, IV, 530.
8. GW, IV, 486–488, 521.
9. GW, V, 121; McCurtin, *Journal*, 38.

10. Bangs, *Journal*, 43.
11. Bakeless, *Turncoats*, 93–109; GW, V, 182, 193–195.
12. GW. IV, 522, 528, V, 3.
13. GW, V, 2.
14. GW, V, 361–362.
15. Flexner, *Doctors*, 28; GW, IV, 531.
16. F, *A* (4th Ser.), VI, 472–473; GW, V, 87, 93.
17. GW, V, 92.
18. GW, V, 92.
19. GW, V, 16–17; JCC, IV, 383 ff, 399–400, 412.
20. GW, IV, 355, V, 93.
21. Bangs, 40.
22. B, I, 512; GW, V, 112, 190.
23. McCurtin, 40.
24. GW, V, 207, 498.
25. F, IV, 131.
26. GW, IV, 220–221, 225–226, 250.
27. GW, V, 227, 412–413.
28. GW, V, 379, 395.
29. GW, V, 92, 239, 247; S, *C*, I, 256.
30. F, IV, 134–135; GW, V, 245–247.

11: THE CARROT AND THE BIG STICK

1. GW, V, 264, 269, 444.
2. GW, V, 275, 446, 458.
3. S, W, III, 535–538.
4. GW, V, 66, 223, 290.
5. GW, V, 173n, 349, XIV, 385.
6. S, *C*, I, 267.
7. F, IV, 143; GW, V, 289–290, 302, 430–431, 434.
8. GW, V, 433.
9. F, IV, 138–139; GW, V, 273, 279, 304.
10. GW, V, 297; Webb, *Correspondence*, I, 156.
11. Clap, *Diary*, 248; GW, V, 321n–323n.
12. Willcox, *Portrait*, 95, 99.
13. F, *A* (5th Ser.), I, 967; GW, V, 387, 454, 457–458.
14. Reed, *Reed*, I, 209.
15. F, IV, 152; GW, V, 152, 469.
16. GW, V, 459.
17. F, *A* (5th Ser.), I, 1111–1112.
18. Fitzpatrick, *Himself*, 242; GW, V, 250.

12: THE ENEMY STRIKES

1. GW, V, 494, 508.
2. GW, V, 485.
3. GW, IV, 290, VIII, 68.
4. GW, V, 485, 491.
5. GW, V, 488.
6. Field, *Battle*, 169; Johnston, *Campaign*, 152–154.

7. Chastellux, *Travels*, I, 106–107; Waldo, *Diary*, 320.
8. Johnston, 176–180, 193, documents, 61, 63.
9. Field, 333.
10. F, IV, 163–164; Field, 502.
11. F, IV, 165; Field, 183.
12. F, *F*, 133; GW, VI, 75–76.
13. Field, 202; GW, VI, 75–76.
14. Johnston, 189.
15. Field, 381.
16. Baurmeister, *Confidential*, 39; Field, 380; Howe, *Narrative*, 5.
17. F, IV, 168.
18. Baurmeister, 40; Field, 380.
19. Johnston, 210.
20. GW, V, 194–195, 496–497.
21. F, IV, 170.
22. GW, V, 508–509.
23. F, *A* (5th Ser.), I, 1246; GW, V, 508–509.
24. Field, *passim;* Johnston, *passim.*
25. Field, 275–276.
26. Field, 280–282.
27. GW, V, 506.

13:   IF ONLY THE TROOPS WILL STAND BY ME

1. GW, VI, 5–6.
2. F, IV, 179.
3. GW, VI, 10–11, 21.
4. Johnston, *Campaign*, 227; Rossman, *Mifflin*, 63.
5. F, IV, 167n; Field, *Battle*, 204–205.
6. Bliven, *Manhattan*, 16; GW, VI, 5, 16, 32.
7. Fitzpatrick, *Himself*, 251–252; GW, VI, 28–29.
8. GW, VI, 6–7; XXXVII, 532.
9. GW, VI, 29–30.
10. GW, VI, 27–33.
11. GW, VI, 18–19.
12. GW, XXXVII, 533.
13. GW, VI, 53–54.
14. GW, VI, 52–53, XIV, 399; Johnston, 227.
15. GW, VI, 49, 51, 55.
16. GW, XXVI, 78–79.
17. Baurmeister, *Confidential*, 47.
18. F, *A* (5th Ser.), II, 378; GW, VI, 57–58.
19. Bliven, 26; GW, VI, 58.
20. Johnston, documents, 81–82.
21. GW, VI, 58.
22. F, *A* (5th Ser.), II, 1013, 1251–1252.
23. GW, VI, 58, 95; Johnston, documents, 83.

24. F, IV, 194n; Heath, *Memoirs*, 70.
25. GW, VI, 170; Reed, *Reed*, I, 236.
26. Bliven, 61–65; GW, VI, 94, 117.
27. Gordon, *History*, II, 328–329.
28. F, IV, 194–195.
29. Bliven, 40; Clinton, *Rebellion*, 46–47.
30. Bliven, 61.
31. F, *A* (5th Ser.), II, 378.

14:   BLOOD ON THE BUSHES

1. GW, VI, 57–59.
2. Reed, *Reed*, I, 237.
3. GW, VI, 68, 164.
4. GW, VI, 68.
5. GW, VI, 68, 165; Johnston, *Campaign*, 257n.
6. GW, VI, 83.
7. F, IV, 202; F, *A* (5th Ser.), II, 379; GW, VI, 69, 170; Mackenzie, *Diary*, I, 51.

15:   A HEAVY HEART

1. GW, VI, 106n, 116, 138.
2. GW, VI, 92, 99, XXXVII, 533.
3. GW, VI, 138, 169.
4. GW, VI, 116n.
5. GW, VI, 106–107.
6. GW, VI, 91, 115–116.
7. GW, VI, 114; JCC, V, 788 ff.
8. GW, VI, 90–91, 103; Reed, *Reed*, I, 238.
9. GW, VI, 107–108.
10. GW, VI, 110–112.
11. Flexner, *Doctors*, 23–24; GW, VI, 113.
12. F, IV, 206 ff.
13. JCC, VI, 762–763.
14. GW, VI, 155.
15. GW, VI, 186.
16. GW, VI, 136, 149, 154, 156.
17. GW, XI, 212.
18. F, IV, 216; JCC, V, 850–851; L, III, 343.

16:   BRITISH MIGHT DISPLAYED

1. GW, VI, 137.
2. GW, VI, 197, XXXVII, 534.
3. Robertson, *Diaries*, 102.
4. F, IV, 219; F, *A* (5th Ser.), II, 1178; JCC, VI, 866.
5. GW, VI, 218.
6. GW, VI, 219.
7. Robertson, 103.
8. Heath, *Memoirs*, 76–77.
9. Chastellux, *Travels*, I, 48, 92, 269.
10. F, *A* (5th Ser.), III, 923, 1282; Heath, 78; Moore, *Diary*, I, 335–336.

11. Heath, 78; Moore, I, 336; GW, VI, 243.
12. Heath, 79; GW, VI, 243; S, W, IV, 526–527.
13. F, *A* (5th Ser.), III, 921, 923; Howe, *Narrative*, 6–7.
14. F, *A* (5th Ser.), III, 923.
15. F, *A* (5th Ser.), III, 923.
16. F, *A* (5th Ser.), III, 923.
17. Heath, 81–82.
18. F, *A* (5th Ser.), III, 923; GW, VI, 243.
19. GW, VI, 243–244.
20. GW, VI, 255.

17: THE BLACKEST DEFEAT

1. GW, VI, 228n, 249–250, 253–254.
2. F, IV, 241; GW, VI, 244.
3. Dupuy, *Compact*, 154.
4. GW, VI, 244; L, III, 343.
5. GW, VI, 263–266.
6. F, *A* (5th Ser.), III, 484.
7. F, *A* (5th Ser.), II, 312, III, 523.
8. GW, VI, 257–258.
9. F, *A* (5th Ser.), III, 618–619.
10. GW, VI, 223, 273.
11. F, IV, 247; GW, XVI, 151; Heath, *Memoirs*, 95.
12. F, IV, 241–242; GW, VI, 397.
13. Reed, *Reed*, I, 262.
14. GW, XVI, 151–152.
15. GW, VI, 244–245.
16. F, *A* (5th Ser.), III, 699–700; GW, VI, 286.
17. GW, IV, 286.
18. Dupuy, 153; F, IV, 243–244; F, *A* (5th Ser.), III, 924–925; Graydon, *Memoirs*, 200; Johnston, documents, 100.
19. GW, VI, 245.
20. GW, VI, 286; Heath, 86.
21. GW, VI, 286–287.
22. GW, VI, 244, 287.
23. GW, VI, 287n.
24. L, II, 288–289.
25. GW, VI, 243; Reed, *Reed*, I, 256.
26. GW, VI, 257–258, XXVII, 97–98; Knollenberg, *Revolution*, 138.
27. GW, VI, 246.
28. GW, VI, 245, 293–295.

18: THE MUTINY OF GENERAL LEE

1. F, IV, 257; GW, VI, 295–296.
2. F, *A* (5th Ser.), III, 1291; GW, VI, 298.
3. F, *A* (5th Ser.), III, 1071, 1291; GW, VI, 295–296; *N.Y. Public Library Bull.*, VIII (1904), 549.

4. Heath, *Memoirs*, 88.
5. GW, VI, 298–299.
6. Robertson, *Diaries*, 112–113.
7. GW, VI, 300–301n; Reed, *Reed*, I, 255–256.
8. GW, VI, 306; Heath, 88 ff; L, II, 290–291, 299, 303–305, 313–314.
9. GW, VI, 309; L, II, 307.
10. GW, VI, 303, 304–307; Rossman, *Mifflin*, 70.
11. GW, VI, 281.
12. Reed, *Reed*, I, 257.
13. GW, VIII, 247.
14. GW, VI, 313.
15. F, IV, 272–273, 318–319; F, *A* (5th Ser.), III, 1316; GW, VI, 321–322.
16. Reed, *Reed*, I, 268.
17. GW, VI, 319–320, 330–331.
18. GW, VI, 336.
19. GW, VI, 339.
20. F, *A* (5th Ser.), III, 1316–1317; Willcox, *Portrait*, 150.
21. Flexner, *Old Masters*, 195–196.
22. Reed, *Reed*, I, 259, 268.
23. GW, VI, 339, 346, 358.
24. GW, VI, 336.
25. B, II, 198, 202; JCC, VI, 1027.
26. L, II, 289.
27. GW, VI, 402–403.
28. GW, VI, 403.
29. GW, VI, 401.
30. GW, VI, 400–409.
31. GW, VII, 53, 57.
32. Hughes, *Washington*, III, 9.
33. GW, VI, 366.
34. L, II, 322, 329–330.
35. GW, VI, 340–341.
36. GW, VI, 367–368.
37. GW, IV, 451; L, II, 348.
38. Alden, *Lee*, 159.
39. Alden, 160; F, V, 316n; Moore, *Diary*, I, 360–361.
40. GW, VI, 375–376, 378, 398; L, II, 356.

19: AN ICY RIVER

1. F, *A* (5th Ser.), III, 1292.
2. GW, XXXVII, 536–537.
3. GW, VI, 417, 420, 431.
4. GW, VI, 374–379.
5. GW, VI, 401, 420–421.
6. F, *A* (5th Ser.), III, 1317.
7. Stryker, *Trenton*, 49, 84.
8. Stryker, 371.
9. F, IV, 307–308; GW, VI, 442; Stryker, 113–115.
10. Billias, *Generals*, 29; Stryker, 129.

11. GW, VI, 442, 446; Stryker, 371; Wilkinson, *Memoirs*, I, 128.
12. GW, VI, 444; Stryker, 473.
13. Wilkinson, I, 129.
14. Stryker, 374.
15. F, IV, 315.
16. GW, VI, 442.
17. GW, VI, 442; Stryker, 371.
18. F, IV, 316; GW, VI, 446; Stryker, 409 ff, 420.
19. F, IV, 317; GW, VI, 443.
20. Stryker, 372; Wilkinson, I, 130n, 131.
21. GW, VI, 441.
22. F, IV, 32; GW, VI, 443.
23. F, *A* (5th Ser.), III, 1443; GW, VI, 441, 444, 446; Stryker, 206–207.
24. F, IV, 324; GW, VI, 450.
25. GW, VI, 444.

20: WHERE NO SENSIBLE GENERAL WOULD GO

1. Dupuy, *Compact*, 174–175.
2. GW, VI, 452.
3. GW, VI, 447, 451–452.
4. Dupuy, 175; F, IV, 374–375; GW, VI, 447–448, VII, 60, XXXVII, 548.
5. F, IV, 325; *Pa. Mag. of Hist. and Biog.*, XX (1896), 515–516.
6. GW, VI, 455, 461, VII, 29, 53.
7. Bakeless, *Turncoats*, 170; GW, VI, 457–458; Stryker, *Trenton*, 256.
8. GW, VI, 434, 462, 467; Stryker, 434.
9. GW, VI, 467.
10. Haven, *Thirty*, 38; GW, VI, 467–468; Wilkinson, *Memoirs*, I, 138.
11. *Gentleman's Mag.*, XLVII (1777), 90; Hughes, *Washington*, II, 538; Robertson, *Diaries*, 119.
12. GW, VI, 468.
13. F, IV, 345–346; Hughes, III, 23; Williams, *Biography*, 143.
14. GW, VI, 468–469.
15. F, IV, 349; GW, VI, 468; Wilkinson, I, 140.
16. F, IV, 350–353; GW, VI, 469; *Pa. Mag. of Hist. and Biog.*, XX (1896), 517.
17. Custis, *Recollections*, 190–192.
18. F, *F*, 216–217.
19. F, IV, 355, Wilkinson, I, 145.
20. GW, VII, 15, 108, 152; Hughes, III, 33–34; *Pennsylvania Packet*, 2/22/77; Stryker, 440.
21. F, IV, 357.
22. GW, VI, 469; Stryker, 458.
23. F, IV, 356; GW, VI, 469–470; Wilkinson, I, 148.

24. Dupuy, 174.
25. GW, VI, 486n; Moore, *Diary*, I, 397.
26. F, IV, 365–366; GW, VII, 44.
27. Stryker, 464.
28. GW, VII, 74.

21: A HOPEFUL PESSIMIST

1. GW, VI, 481.
2. GW, VI, 478–489; Wilkinson, *Memoirs*, I, 149.
3. GW, VII, 175.
4. GW, VII, 61–62, 165–166, 198; JCC, VII, 165–166.
5. GW, VII, 109, 142, 144, 175.
6. GW, VII, 95, 198.
7. Lund Washington to GW (4/1/78), Mount Vernon.
8. GW, VII, 8, 89, 111–112, 139n, 257, 439, VIII, 81n.
9. GW, VII, 398.
10. GW, VII, 67, VIII, 114–115, 130.
11. F, IV, 438–441; GW, VIII, 130, 325.
12. GW, VII, 215, 328, 463, IX, 9, XI, 289.
13. GW, VII, 170, 177–178.
14. GW, VIII, 75; Rachel Stille and Thomas Houton, tavern bill to GW (12/7/76), Morristown.
15. B, II, 405–406; GW, VII, 100n, 133, VIII, 160n.
16. GW, VII, 308, XIII, 262, XVII, 339.
17. GW, VIII, 30–31.
18. GW, VI, 230; Hoyt, *Rules.*
19. Hughes, *Washington*, II, 447–449.
20. GW, VI, 256, 258.
21. GW, XX, 249.
22. Ford, *Jefferson*, I, 182; GW, VI, 350, VIII, 294.
23. GW, VII, 1, 323, VIII, 158, XXXVII, 539.
24. GW, VII, 181.
25. Flexner, *Doctors*, 40–45, 75.
26. GW, VI, 105, VII, 111, 168, 176.
27. Boudinot, *Journal*, 54–55.
28. GW, VII, 192, XI, 182–183.
29. B, II, 274–275; GW, VII, 168, 185.
30. GW, VII, 222n.
31. GW, VII, 224.
32. GW, VII, 225.
33. F, IV, 382n.
34. GW, XXII, 176.
35. GW, VII, 204, 395.
36. GW, XIV, 299–300, XXI, 378.

22: RECAPTURE OF A STATE

1. F, IV, 396–397; GW, VII, 268n.
2. GW, XI, 268.

3. *New Jersey Hist. Soc. Proc.*, LI (1933), 250–253 (misnumbered 150–153).
4. GW, VII, 218.
5. GW, VIII, 181–182, 199.
6. GW, VII, 368 ff, VIII, 139, 157, 198.
7. GW, VII, 272–274, 437, VIII, 43.
8. GW, VII, 411, VIII, 450.
9. Mackesy, *War*, 124.
10. GW, VIII, 260–261.
11. GW, VIII, 244, 295.
12. André, *Journal*, I, 40; GW, VIII, 261.
13. GW, VIII, 267, 294; Howe, *Narrative*, 15–16; *New Jersey Archives* (2nd Ser.), I, 476–478.
14. André, I, 47; Pickering, *Pickering*, I, 144.
15. F, IV, 434; GW, VIII, 315; *Warren-Adams*, I, 334.

23: THE ENEMY VANISHES

1. GW, VIII, 277, 333, 366.
2. GW, VIII, 376, 407.
3. GW, VIII, 495.
4. Flexner, *Traitor*, 120, GW, VII, 233–234, 251–252.
5. GW, VII, 352.
6. Flexner, 125–128; GW, VIII, 42.
7. Flexner, 128; GW, VIII, 16.
8. GW, VIII, 377, 427.
9. Chastellux, *Travels*, I, 189, 338.
10. GW, VIII, 410, 445n.
11. GW, VIII, 445, 449, 468, 484.
12. GW, VIII, 461, 499.
13. GW, VIII, 491, 499.
14. GW, VIII, 503–505, 507.
15. GW, IX, 10.
16. F, IV, 459; GW, VIII, 87n, 237, IX, 8–9.
17. Gottschalk, *Joins*, 27–30; GW, VIII, 483.
18. Lafayette, *Memoirs*, I, 19; *Pa. Mag. of Hist. and Biog.*, XVI (1892), 146.
19. GW, IX, 95.
20. GW, XXIII, 431; Knollenberg, *Revolution*, 92.
21. GW, IX, 40.
22. GW, IX, 54n, 55, 106–107, 114–115; *Pa. Mag. of Hist. and Biog.*, I (1877), 275 ff.
23. GW, IX, 115.
24. Howe, *Narrative*, 19–24.
25. Hughes, *Washington*, III, 139–140.

24: A FAILURE OF INTELLIGENCE

1. GW, IX, 124–127; Lafayette, *Memoirs*, I, 20.

2. Adams, *Familiar*, 298; GW, IX, 128n; Hist. Soc. of Del., *Papers*, XIV (1896), 40.
3. GW, IX, 136–137.
4. Lafayette, I, 20.
5. GW, IX, 451–452.
6. André, *Journal*, I, 72; Greene, *Greene*, I, 446; GW, IX, 148, 160, 195.
7. GW, IX, 197.
8. GW, IX, 197; Montresor, *Journal*, 448.
9. Adams, 303–304; GW, IX, 73, 199.
10. GW, IX, 426.
11. F, *F*, see index; GW, VII, 472, VIII, 53.
12. GW, IX, 426; S, W, V, 458.
13. GW, IX, 206; Lafayette, I, 22, 24.
14. F, IV, 475; GW, IX, 205–206.
15. Sullivan, *Letters*, I, 475–476.
16. F, IV, 476.
17. GW, IX, 207.
18. McElree, *Brandywine*, 140–141; Townsend, *Account*, 30–33.
19. F, IV, 478–479.
20. GW, IX, 207; Sullivan, I, 463 ff.
21. F, IV, 480–482; GW, IX, 426; Sullivan, I, 473.
22. GW, IX, 241–242; Lafayette, I, 64.
23. GW, IX, 241–242; Montresor, 450.
24. Howe, *Narrative*, 26.
25. Townsend, 58.
26. F, IV, 483; Greene, *Greene*, I, 454; GW, IX, 207–208; Pickering, *Pickering*, I, 156–157.
27. F, IV, 492; GW, IX, 216, 227–229.
28. F, IV, 485–488.
29. GW, IX, 425; Washington, *Atlas*, pl. 15.
30. *Pa. Mag. of Hist. and Biog.*, LXII (1938), 499.
31. Flexner, *Doctors*, 80; Rush, *Autobiography*, 132–133.

25: THE PRIZE: PHILADELPHIA

1. GW, IX, 212, 220.
2. GW, IX, 248–250, 275; Hamilton, *Papers*, I, 330 ff.
3. Pickering, *Pickering*, I, 158.
4. GW, IX, 247; Weedon, *Orderly*, 46.
5. F, IV, 493; GW, IX, 262; Howe, *Narrative*, 26.
6. GW, IX, 235.
7. GW, IX, 257.
8. Greene, *Greene*, I, 468; GW, IX, 238n.
9. GW, IX, 235–236.
10. Adams, *Papers*, II, 265; B, II, 504; Hughes, *Washington*, III, 183.

11. GW, IX, 248–249, 263, 397.
12. GW, IX, 276–277, 305.

26: TO BRING THE MEN TO THIS

1. John Armstrong to Thomas Wharton (10/2/77), New-York Hist. Soc.; Howe, *Narrative*, 27.
2. GW, IX, 278, 305.
3. Belcher, *First*, II, 274.
4. GW, IX, 307–308.
5. Belcher, II, 274.
6. GW, IX, 309, 331, 336, 397.
7. GW, IX, 309n.
8. GW, IX, 398; *North American Rev.*, XXIII (1826), 427.
9. Flexner, *Traitor*, 158; *North American Rev.*, XXIII (1826), 428; GW, IX, 397.
10. Belcher, II, 263; GW, IX, 311–312; Pickering, *Pickering*, I, 170–171.
11. Foner, *Paine*, II, 1147; GW, IX, 320, 397; Sullivan, *Letters*, I, 547.
12. GW, IX, 310, 312.
13. Belcher, II, 274.
14. *Pa. Mag. of Hist. and Biog.*, XVI (1892), 152.
15. GW, IX, 310, 398.
16. F, IV, 508; GW, IX, 309.
17. GW, IX, 320.
18. Closen, *Journal*, 119.
19. Belcher, II, 275; F, IV, 515; Howe, *Narrative*, 27–28.
20. GW, IX, 310, 337, 374.
21. Knollenberg, *Revolution*, 190; S, W, V, 470.
22. F, IV, 490.
23. GW, IX, 371.
24. GW, IX, 378.
25. Adams, *Familiar*, 322–323.
26. Rush, *Letters*, I, 159–160.

27: GEORGE WASHINGTON ECLIPSED

1. Rush, *Letters*, I, 158.
2. F, IV, 547; Lafayette, *Memoirs*, I, 28; Laurens, *Correspondence*, 102–103.
3. Knollenberg, *Revolution*, 184–185; Sullivan, *Letters*, II, 2–3.
4. Conway to Gates (4/2/78) and to Mifflin (10/11/77), New-York Hist. Soc.
5. Graydon, *Memoirs*, 299–300; GW, IX, 388–389, X, 236–237, 441; *South Carolina Hist. and Geneal. Mag.*, VII (1906), 127.
6. F, IV, 547–548; GW, IX, 387.
7. GW, IX, 387; S, C, II, 6.
8. GW, IX, 387–389.

9. GW, IX, 389n.
10. GW, IX, 391.
11. GW, X, 52–54.
12. Wayne to Mifflin (11/10/77), New-York Hist. Soc.
13. GW, X, 10 ff, XXXVII, 544; Knollenberg, 141–149.
14. GW, IX, 422, 440, XXXVII, 543–544.
15. GW, IX, 465–468.
16. Hamilton, *Papers*, I, 349–358, 362.
17. Gates to wife (10/20/77), New-York Hist. Soc.; Rossman, *Mifflin*, 109.
18. Wilkinson to Gates (10/4/77), New-York Hist. Soc.
19. Wilkinson to Stirling (2/4/78), New-York Hist. Soc.; Graydon, 298–299; Wilkinson, *Memoirs*, I, 370–373.
20. Wilkinson to Stirling (n.d. [1–2/?/78]), New-York Hist. Soc.
21. GW, X, 19; Laurens, 62, 69.
22. F, IV, 550.
23. GW, X, 264.
24. GW, X, 29.
25. F, IV, 556–557.
26. Gates to Washington (10/2 & 7/77), New-York Hist. Soc.
27. GW, IX, 429, X, 74.
28. GW, IX, 48–49; Marshall, *Washington*, II, 340–341.
29. GW, X, 76.
30. GW, X, 104, 106–108; Laurens, 81.
31. B, III, 42; GW, X, 253; JCC, IX, 1013–1014.
32. GW, X, 37, 159–160.
33. GW, X, 142 ff.
34. GW, X, 167–168; Laurens, 93.
35. GW, X, 94, 175.

28: MAKE WASHINGTON RESIGN

1. Rush, *Autobiography*, 113.
2. F, *A* (5th Ser.), II, 840.
3. Rossman, *Mifflin*, 65, 70.
4. Rossman, 40, 52, 56, 79.
5. Rossman, 68, 81, 96.
6. GW, IV, 432, VII, 301–302.
7. Greene, *Greene*, II, 30; Rossman, 97.
8. Rossman, 94–95.
9. GW, IX, 389n.
10. F, IV, 609; *Pa. Mag. of Hist. and Biog.*, XX (1896), 93–94; Lee, R. H., *Letters*, I, 358.
11. Rossman, 113.
12. GW, X, 286, XI, 389, 501.
13. GW, X, 29.
14. GW, X, 263–264.
15. Mifflin to Gates (10/28/77), New-York Hist. Soc.

16. Gates to Mifflin (12/4/77), New-York Hist. Soc.; S, W, V, 486–488, 501; Wilkinson, *Memoirs*, I, 373.
17. GW, X, 227n.
18. GW, IX, 441–442; S, W, V, 249–250, 494.
19. Hamilton, *Papers*, I, 498–499; JCC, IX, 818–819; Palmer, *Steuben*, 132.
20. Knollenberg, *Revolution*, 85; Rossman, 120.

29: THE BATTERIES OF INTRIGUE

1. F, IV, 563–564; GW, X, 436–437.
2. GW, X, 170–171, XIII, 395, XXVII, 411.
3. Foner, *Paine*, II, 1150.
4. Hughes, *Washington*, III, 232; Waldo, *Diary*, 306–307, 309.
5. GW, X, 311, 345.
6. GW, X, 196, 343, XI, 291–292.
7. GW, X, 192; Waldo, 309.
8. F, IV, 590–591; GW, X, 226–227.
9. GW, XI, 35, XIII, 37.
10. S, W, V, 495.
11. Lafayette, *Letters*, 12–16.
12. GW, X, 236–237.
13. Rossman, *Mifflin*, 120.
14. F, IV, 590–591.
15. S, W, V, 494–495.
16. GW, X, 249–250; Laurens, *Correspondence*, 103–104.
17. Laurens, 103.
18. GW, X, 263–265.
19. B, III, 20–21.
20. S, W, V, 493–494.
21. GW, X, 410–411; S, W, V, 497–499.
22. GW, X, 337–338.
23. GW, X, 416n, XI, 159–160; Hughes, III, 260; S, W, V, 495–496.
24. Hughes, III, 260.
25. GW, X, 356; Knollenberg, *Revolution*, 79–80, 202, 213; Lafayette, *Memoirs*, I, 75.
26. GW, X, 432–433.
27. Conway to Gates (2/25/78), New-York Hist. Soc.; Knollenberg, 86–87; Lafayette, I, 75.
28. Robert Troup to Gates (2/23/78), New-York Hist. Soc.
29. Conway to Gates (7/9/78), New-York Hist. Soc.; S, W, V, 372n, 516.
30. GW, X, 440–441.
31. GW, X, 509; S, W, V, 511–512.
32. Greene, *Greene*, II, 37.
33. Wilkinson to Gates (2/3, 22, 24/78), New-York Hist. Soc.; S, W, V, 516.
34. Knollenberg, 70, 208.
35. S, W, V, 517.

30: WHAT WAS THE CONWAY CABAL?

1. Knollenberg, *Revolution*.
2. B, III, 20–21, 29.
3. GW, XI, 164–165, 493–494, XXXVII, 245.
4. S, W, V, 509.
5. GW, XI, 290–291.
6. GW, XXXV, 199–200.
7. GW, XXI, 413.
8. Chastellux, *Travels*, I, 92.
9. B, III, 21; GW, XI, 493.
10. GW, X, 463.
11. Greene to McDougall (2/5/78), New-York Hist. Soc.
12. GW, XIV, 163.
13. GW, X, 412, 474; Pickering, *Pickering*, I, 205.
14. Du Ponceau, *Autobiography*, 208; GW, X, 427.
15. Greene, *Greene*, II, 46; GW, X, 469, XI, 9.

31: THE OTHER VALLEY FORGE

1. GW, XI, 68.
2. Du Ponceau, *Autobiography*, 208.
3. GW, X, 366; Waldo, *Diary*, 306.
4. Ewing, *Journal*, 38; GW, II, 292–294.
5. GW, X, 290, 414, XII, 92.
6. Martha Washington to Burwell Bassett (12/22/77), Mount Vernon.
7. GW, X, 414n, XI, 270; Pickering, *Pickering*, I, 189, 199.
8. Blanchard, *Journal*, 166; Chastellux, *Travels*, I, 298; *New-York Hist. Soc. Quart.*, XXXI (1947), 74.
9. Hunter, *Quebec*, 197.
10. Du Ponceau, 209, 313.
11. Watson, *Annals*, II, 61.
12. Greene, *Greene*, II, 44–49; GW, XIX, 381.
13. GW, XI, 137–140, 235–241.
14. F, IV, 497–498; GW, IX, 143–144, 244, X, 368.
15. GW, IX, 7.
16. GW, XI, 20.
17. GW, X, 182, XI, 179; Howe, *Narrative*, 42–43.
18. GW, XI, 223–224; *Pa. Mag. of Hist. and Biog.*, LX (1936), 171.
19. Howe, 52–55.
20. GW, XI, 3–4, 277.
21. Palmer, *Steuben*, 96–97, 115, 133.
22. Du Ponceau, 201–202; GW, X, 519; Palmer, 129, 136n.

23. Laurens, *Correspondence,* 137.
24. GW, XI, 329, 331; North, *Steuben,* 189; Palmer, 157.
25. Du Ponceau, 208.
26. Kapp, *Steuben,* 114–128.
27. GW, XI, 163; Palmer, 154–155.
28. Du Ponceau, 219; Palmer, 140.
29. GW, XI, 341; Palmer, 144–146.
30. North, 197.
31. Ewing, 37; Scheer, *Rebels,* 312.
32. GW, XI, 289–290, XVI, 10; Laurens, 170.
33. GW, XI, 324, 332–333, 354.
34. Stevens, *Facsimiles,* 821.
35. GW, XI, 354–355; Laurens, 169; Moore, *Diary,* II, 49–52.
36. Ewing, 51; Laurens, 169–170; Moore, II, 51; S, W, V, 356–357; Stevens, 821.
37. GW, XI, 390, 392, 453.
38. GW, XI, 457.

32: GENERAL LEE RIDES AGAIN

1. GW, XI, 397, 471–472.
2. GW, XI, 363–366.
3. GW, XI, 306n, 459–460, XII, 18–19.
4. GW, XI, 413–414.
5. Boudinot, *Journal,* 77.
6. L, II, 361–366.
7. Boudinot, 78–79; Godfrey, *Guard,* 275; L, II, 390; Rossman, *Mifflin,* 152.
8. GW, XI, 295.
9. L, II, 383–389.
10. GW, XI, 445, XII, 62–63.
11. GW, XI, 397, 471–472, XII, 2; Laurens, *Correspondence,* 176.
12. GW, XI, 476–477, 495, XII, 2.
13. GW, XII, 82–83; Laurens, 191.
14. GW, XI, 485–486.
15. GW, XI, 489–490, XII, 85.
16. GW, XI, 140.
17. GW, XII, 115–117.
18. F, V, 16, 38; Hamilton, *Papers,* I, 510; Lafayette, *Memoirs,* I, 50.
19. L, II, 461–462.
20. F, V, 17; GW, XII, 141; Lafayette, *Letters,* 46–47; L, II, 461–462.
21. GW, XII, 117, 140–141.
22. Hamilton, I, 511.
23. F, V, 18 ff; GW, XII, 141.
24. GW, XII, 119n.
25. GW, XII, 119.

33: THE BATTLE OF MONMOUTH

1. Steiner, *McHenry,* 24.
2. GW, XII, 127, 142.
3. GW, XII, 128; L, III, 5, 203.

4. GW, XII, 142.
5. GW, XII, 145.
6. L, III, 52–53, 78, 431.
7. L, III, 231.
8. L, III, 72, 79–80.
9. L, III, 72.
10. L, III, 72, 82.
11. L, III, 80.
12. L, III, 80.
13. L, II, 432, 458, 463, III, 78, 81, 112, 147, 191.
14. GW, XIII, 119; Stryker, *Monmouth,* 180–181.
15. GW, XII, 157; L, III, 81.
16. L, III, 81.
17. GW, XII, 157; L, III, 75.
18. L, III, 81.
19. Lafayette, *Memoirs,* I, 54; L, II, 469–470.
20. GW, XII, 157; L, III, 69, 75, 81–82.
21. L, III, 22.
22. L, III, 69.
23. L, III, 75, 78, 147–148, 157.
24. GW, XII, 143; L, II, 470.
25. GW, XII, 143–145; L, II, 433.
26. GW, XII, 144.
27. GW, XII, 144; Lafayette, I, 54.
28. GW, II, 145.
29. F, V, 43n; GW, XII, 145–146, 157, 163.
30. GW, XII, 131.

34: MONMOUTH'S AFTERMATH

1. L, II, 430, 457–459, III, 206.
2. L, II, 435–436, III, 206.
3. L, II, 438–440.
4. GW, XII, 132–133.
5. L, III, 206.
6. L, II, 437–438.
7. GW, XII, 133; L, II, 438.
8. L, III, 2.
9. L, III, 1–208.
10. GW, XII, 487, XIII, 335.
11. L, III, 228–229, 237, 255, 270, 276–277.
12. GW, XIII, 383–384.
13. L, III, 283–285.
14. Willcox, *Portrait,* 236–237.

35: THE WHEEL TURNS FULL CIRCLE

1. GW, XII, 147, 150, 166.
2. Godfrey, *Guard,* 280.
3. Steiner, *McHenry,* 21–22.
4. Steiner, 22–23.
5. F, V, 45.
6. F, V, 45.

7. GW, III, 305; Steiner, 23.
8. GW, XII, 343.

36: NEW CARDS IN AN OLD GAME

1. GW, XIII, 231.
2. Willcox, *Portrait,* 211–218.
3. GW, XII, 211; Whitridge, *Rochambeau,* 137.
4. F, V, 64; GW, XII, 184, 211, 487.
5. GW, V, 152, VII, 290–291, XII, 516; S, C, II, 155–156.
6. GW, XII, 186n, 477; S, C, II, 156.
7. GW, XII, 488.
8. GW, XII, 281.
9. F, V, 60; GW, XII, 329.
10. F, V, 67–68.
11. GW, XII, 227, 233–234, 438 ff.
12. F, V, 65n, 69n, 76; Mackenzie, *Diary,* I, 39.
13. F, V, 70–71; Lafayette, *Letters,* 59.
14. GW, XII, 364, 382–383, 385.
15. GW, XII, 516.
16. GW, XIII, 12, 20, 142.
17. GW, XII, 424, 428.
18. GW, XIII, 12.
19. GW, XIV, 387.
20. GW, XIII, 11, 47.
21. F, *F,* 151; GW, XII, 214, 496–497, XIII, 264.
22. GW, XII, 501–502.
23. Gottschalk, *Joins,* 281 ff; GW, XIII, 232; JCC, XII, 1042–1052.
24. Lafayette, *Memoirs,* I, 63.
25. GW, XIII, 257.
26. GW, XIII, 223–244.
27. GW, XIII, 254–257.
28. GW, XII, 366, XIII, 156–157, 190.
29. GW, XII, 471.
30. GW, XIII, 15–16.
31. GW, XIII, 266
32. Du Roi, *Journal,* 192–193; Ernest J. F. S. von Senden, Journal (11/29/78), Morristown.
33. GW, XIII, 389–390, 443, 459–460.
34. GW, XIII, 461, XIV, 221.

37: THE MEASURE OF INIQUITY

1. GW, XIII, 385.
2. GW, XIII, 466–467, 478.
3. GW, XIII, 21, 467–468.
4. Martha Washington to Bartholomew Dandridge (10/2/78), Mount Vernon.
5. Franklin, *Letters,* 92; Greene to McDougall (2/11/79), New-York Hist. Soc.
6. GW, XII, 227.

7. Greene, *Greene,* II, 161–162.
8. GW, XIII, 424–428, XIV, 432, XVI, 124.
9. GW, XVI, 123–125, 289–291.
10. Mary Washington to Lund Washington (12/19/78), Hist. Soc. of Pa.
11. GW, XIII, 428–429.
12. Lund Washington to GW (12/24/77, 9/2/78), Mount Vernon; GW, XIII, 327–328.
13. GW, XIII, 335, 383.
14. GW, XIII, 348, 464–467.
15. GW, XV, 61.
16. Chastellux, *Travels,* I, 136, 301.
17. GW, XV, 161.
18. GW, XIV, 313.
19. GW, XXII, 283.
20. GW, XIX, 135.
21. GW, XXI, 341.
22. GW, XII, 327.
23. Laurens, *Correspondence,* 117–118.
24. GW, XIV, 267, XIX, 93, XXIV, 88n.
25. GW, XIV, 147–148, XXIX, 165.
26. GW, X, 197, XIV, 27, 29, 31, 71, 348, XV, 404, XVI, 203.
27. GW, XIII, 145, 488, XIV, 9–11, 381.
28. GW, XII, 274.
29. GW, XXIII, 30.
30. GW, XIII, 488–491, XIV, 36, 65–66.
31. GW, XIV, 12, 53, 300, 312.

38: THE FLEET THAT NEVER CAME

1. GW, XIII, 395, XIV, 221, XVI, 91.
2. GW, XIII, 233, XIV, 170.
3. Lossing, *Mary and Martha,* 185.
4. GW, XIV, 470–473, XV, 400, XVI, 470.
5. GW, XV, 148.
6. F, V, 107; GW, XV, 233–235, 291–292, 313.
7. GW, XV, 292, 386, 448.
8. GW, XXXI, 510, XXXII, 78.
9. GW, XV, 396–399.
10. GW, XV, 427n.
11. GW, XV, 430–436, 439, 447–453.
12. F, V, 57; GW, XV, 139 ff, 189 ff.
13. GW, XV, 348–349, 478–479.
14. Flexner, *Traitor,* 299; GW, XVI, 167, 373.
15. GW, XVI, 116–117.
16. Lafayette, *Letters,* 77.
17. GW, XVI, 370, 372, 375–376.
18. GW, XVI, 272–275, 277, 279.
19. GW, XVI, 340.
20. F, V, 136; GW, XVI, 377–378, 395–396, 399, 406–407, 464.

21. GW, XVI, 492.
22. GW, XVII, 91.
23. GW, XVII, 108.

39: RATTLESNAKE ROAD

1. GW, XVIII, 125; Thacher, *Journal,* 185.
2. Shaw, *Journal,* 71.
3. GW, XVII, 272–273, 360–365; Webb, *Correspondence,* II, 241.
4. F, V, 144; Hughes, *Washington,* III, 497; Webb, II, 232.
5. GW, XVII, 400, XVIII, 330, 413.
6. Ferguson, *Purse,* 46 ff.
7. GW, XIX, 132.
8. GW, XV, 330, XX, 277–278.
9. GW, XVIII, 207–210.
10. GW, XIV, 20, XVIII, 425–431.
11. GW, XVIII, 204; Reed, *Reed,* II, 191.
12. GW, XVII, 486.
13. GW, XVIII, 434–439.
14. GW, XVII, 423–424, XIX, 262.
15. GW, XVI, 393–394.
16. GW, XVII, 90–91, 413–414.
17. GW, XVI, 291–292, XVII, 267–268.
18. GW, XIX, 164 ff, 195–198, XX, 146.
19. GW, XVII, 309, XVIII, 300; S. *C,* II, 386, 402.
20. GW, XVIII, 203, 264–265, 299, 307.
21. GW, XVIII, 331, 341; Lafayette, *Letters,* 82.
22. GW, XVIII, 483.

40: ENTER A GALLIC ARMY

1. S, *W,* VII, 493.
2. GW, XVIII, 369–373.
3. GW, XVIII, 360, 387, 460, 476.
4. GW, XIX, 21–22, 36.
5. GW, XVIII, 416–417, 456–457, 483.
6. GW, XVIII, 454, 509–510.
7. GW, XVIII, 510–511, XIX, 23 ff, 135.
8. GW, XIX, 27, 31–32, 134–137.
9. Flexner, *Traitor,* 310; GW, XIX, 64n–65n.
10. GW, XIX, 116, 168.
11. GW, XIX, 180, 184–185.
12. Doniol, *Histoire,* V, 348; GW, XIX, 185–188.
13. Whitridge, *Rochambeau,* 95 ff.
14. GW, XIX, 174–176.
15. GW, XIX, 205n, 211, 234–235.
16. GW, XXX, 26.
17. Rochambeau, *Memoirs,* 12–16; S, *W,* VII, 504–506.
18. Doniol, V, 350; GW, XIX, 237; Whitridge, 97.
19. GW, XIX, 281.

20. GW, XIX, 329, 392–393.
21. Billias, *Generals,* 119; Ferguson, *Purse,* 96; Greene, *Greene,* II, 241–342; GW, XII, 277, XIX, 381; JCC, XVII, 615 ff.
22. GW, XVIII, 185n.
23. GW, XIX, 366–368.
24. F, V, 185n.
25. GW, XIX, 224.
26. GW, XX, 49, 136–137.
27. F, V, 226–227; GW, XX, 181, 189.
28. GW, XX, 238–240, 242, 248–249.
29. GW, XX, 39–42.
30. GW, XX, 15, 137, 374; Rochambeau, 15.
31. F, V, 190; GW, XX, 45, 49n.
32. Chastellux, *Travels,* I, 76, 83; GW, XX, 48.
33. Closen, *Journal,* 241; Dumas, *Memoirs,* I, 29; Whitridge, 101.
34. Doniol, IV, 404–407; GW, XX, 76–81.
35. GW, XX, 76–81, XXI, 209, Rochambeau, 17–18, 25.
36. F, V, 193; GW, XX, 80, 374.
37. GW, XX, 118, 474.

41: TRIBULATIONS OF AN OLD FRIEND

1. GW, XVII, 120, 323.
2. GW, XX, 121–122.
3. Flexner, *Traitor,* 221–222.
4. Flexner, 224, 228.
5. Flexner, 244–246; GW, XIV, 80, XX, 370.
6. Flexner, 248–249.
7. Flexner, 258; GW, XIV, 418, 450.
8. Flexner, 277.
9. GW, XV, 85–87.
10. Flexner, 278–279, 289.
11. Flexner, 252–259, 275–276, 279–280.
12. Arnold, *Proceedings.*
13. GW, XVIII, 127–128, 225.
14. Flexner, 308.
15. Flexner, 313.
16. Flexner, 308–309.
17. GW, XX, 213–214.
18. Rush, *Occasional,* 80 ff.
19. Flexner, 317; GW, XIX, 302.
20. GW, XIX, 313.
21. Flexner, 333; GW, XX, 48.
22. Flexner, 339 ff.
23. Flexner, 363.

42: TREASON MOST FOUL

1. Flexner, *Traitor,* 366; Lossing, *Pictorial,* II, 158.
2. Thacher, *Journal,* 133.

3. Abbott, *Crisis,* 52; Flexner, 362, 367, 369; Rush, *Occasional,* 83.
4. Chase, *Forefathers,* 117; Chastellux, *Travels,* I, 93.
5. Flexner, 370; Rush, 83.
6. GW, XX, 94.
7. F, V, 199; Flexner, 371.
8. Abbott, 16–18; S, W, VII, 531–532.
9. Flexner, 372–373; GW, XX, 91; Hamilton, *Papers,* II, 441.
10. Hamilton, II, 441; Varick, *Inquiry,* 181–182, 191–192.
11. Flexner, 372; Varick, 192–193.
12. Hamilton, II, 441.
13. Flexner, 372; Hamilton, II, 438–439; S, W, VII, 533.
14. Knox to Bauman, 2 letters (9/25/80), New-York Hist. Soc.; GW, XX, 84–87.
15. F, V, 204.
16. F, V, 202.
17. Flexner, 376–379; Hamilton, II, 441–442; Tower, *Lafayette,* II, 168.
18. Flexner, 383; GW, XX, 86–87, 173; S, W, VII, 531–532.
19. André, *Minutes;* Flexner, 294; GW, XX, 150.
20. Flexner, 386–387.
21. Hamilton, II, 448–449.
22. Flexner, 381, 387; GW, XX, 151.
23. Ogden, *Autobiography,* 23–25.
24. Flexner, 389–390.
25. Flexner, 395; GW, XX, 173, 178, 213, 223; S, W, VII, 540–541.
26. Flexner, 395–396; GW, XX, 213–215, 370.
27. GW, XX, 256.
28. GW, XX, 173.

43: MORE EDUCATION FOR GEORGE WASHINGTON

1. GW, XX, 459, 482.
2. GW, XX, 351, 380–395, 425–426, 459.
3. GW, XX, 312–313.
4. GW, XX, 447.
5. F, V, 232; GW, XX, 357, 458, 475.
6. GW, XIX, 114–115, 216.
7. GW, XIX, 376n; Michener, *Bank,* 2–3.
8. GW, XIX, 150, 212, 376–377, XX, 458–459.
9. GW, XX, 371–374, XXI, 14.
10. GW, XX, 143, 209, 507–508.
11. Chastellux, *Travels,* I, 106.
12. Chastellux, I, 106, 113–114.
13. Chastellux, I, 109, 111.
14. Chastellux, I, 114.
15. Chastellux, I, 109–110.

16. Chastellux, I, 106.
17. GW, XXI, 150.
18. GW, XX, 357, 397, 403, 415, 477.
19. GW, XXIX, 483–486.
20. Chastellux, I, 8–9, 350.
21. GW, XXVI, 484–485.
22. GW, XXVII, 270.

44: THE END OF OUR TETHER

1. GW, XXI, 6–7; *Mag. of American Hist.,* X (1883), 410–413.
2. GW, XX, 317.
3. GW, XXI, 56n; S, C, III, 193.
4. GW, XXI, 55–57.
5. GW, XXI, 58.
6. GW, XXI, 58–59, 62.
7. GW, XXI, 61–63, 67.
8. GW, XXI, 79–81, 88n.
9. GW, XXI, 92, 207.
10. GW, XXI, 193.
11. GW, XXI, 124n; Van Doren, *Mutiny,* 204 ff.
12. GW, XXI, 124–128, 136.
13. GW, XXI, 141–142.
14. GW, XXI, 150–151; Van Doren, 219–220.
15. GW, XXI, 125, 148–149, 172, 208.
16. Rochambeau, *Memoirs,* 30–31.
17. GW, XXI, 100–101.
18. GW, XXI, 105–110, 438–439.

45: NEVER GO HOME AGAIN

1. Greene, *Greene,* III, 53; GW, XXI, 330.
2. GW, XXI, 386.
3. GW, XXI, 229–232.
4. F, V, 255–257.
5. Hamilton, *Papers,* II, 563–564.
6. Hamilton, II, 565n–566n, 569.
7. GW, XX, 470–471, XXI, 181; S, C, III, 152.
8. GW, I, xlii–xliv, XXVIII, 177; Steiner, *McHenry,* 27n.
9. *New Eng. Hist. and Geneal. Reg.,* III (1876), 390.
10. GW, IV, 506–507.
11. GW, XXI, 491, XXII, 438, XXXVI, 460.
12. F, V, 257; GW, XXI, 279n, 322.
13. F, V, 263–264.
14. Biron, *Memoirs,* 193–194; GW, XXI, 488; Whitridge, *Rochambeau,* 95.
15. Chadwick, *Visit,* 2; Closen, *Journal,* 62; GW, XXI, 322.
16. Blanchard, *Journal,* 93.
17. Closen, *Journal,* 63.
18. Stevens, *French,* 22.

19. Closen, 63; Stevens, 23.
20. GW, XXI, 361; Stevens, 23.
21. Baker, *Itinerary*, 209; Tuckerman, *Rochambeau*, 20.
22. Blanchard, 93–94; GW, XXI, 331.
23. GW, XXI, 455; Rochambeau, *Memoirs*, 38.
24. GW, XXI, 333–334, 345, 363.
25. GW, XXI, 341n.
26. GW, XXI, 340–342.
27. GW, XXI, 318.
28. GW, XXI, 378.
29. GW, XXI, 361, 373, 376, 378, 386.
30. GW, XXI, 396–397.
31. F, V, 279–280.
32. GW, XXII, 16–17.
33. GW, XXI, 438.
34. GW, XXI, 304, 312.
35. GW, XX, 321, 361, XXI, 345, 378.
36. Jefferson, *Papers*, VI, 32.
37. GW, XXII, 14–15.
38. Jefferson, VI, 32–33.
39. GW, XXII, 178–179, 189–190.
40. GW, XXII, 179; Malone, *Jefferson*, 352 ff.
41. Lee, R. H., *Letters*, II, 233–238.
42. GW, XXII, 382–384.
43. Burnett, *Continental*, 460.
44. GW, XXI, 182, 227, 261.
45. GW, XVII, 22–23, XXII, 194.
46. GW, XXII, 189.

46: FORCING WASHINGTON'S HAND

1. GW, XXI, 429.
2. GW, XXI, 411, XXII, 113–115; GW, D, II, 207; Washington, *Microfilm*, V–VI.
3. Chastellux, *Travels*, I, 153, 193, II, 367–368.
4. Rochambeau, *Memoirs*, 42–45.
5. GW, XXII, 155; Rochambeau, 45.
6. Doniol, *Histoire*, V, 369, 387; GW, XXII, 103; Rochambeau, 42–43, 52.
7. Grasse, *Correspondence*, 2.
8. Rochambeau, 42–43, 45.
9. F, V, 288; GW, D, II, 218; Rochambeau, 52.
10. GW, XXII, 102–104, 107, 154; Rochambeau, 45.
11. Adams, *Burned Letter*, 7; Biron, *Memoirs*, 198–199; Rochambeau, 44; Whitridge, *Rochambeau*, 142, 145.
12. GW, XXII, 105–107; Rochambeau, 50–51.
13. GW, D, II, 217–218.
14. GW, XXII, 105–106; Rochambeau, 45–46.

15. Rochambeau, 48.
16. Biron, 199–200; Closen, *Journal*, 80–81; GW, XXII, 205; GW, D, II, 244.
17. F, V, 291; GW, XXII, 143–144, 384; GW, D, II, 218–219; Rochambeau, 46.
18. Whitridge, 176–177.
19. GW, XXII, 129, 142.
20. GW, XXII, 116n; GW, D, II, 220.
21. Doniol, V, 487–488; GW, XXII, 205–206.
22. GW, XXII, 208–209.
23. Doniol, V, 489.
24. GW, XXII, 230, 272–273.
25. GW, XXII, 287, 289, 303, 306–307, 321–331, 341; GW, D, II, 231–233; Rochambeau, 55.
26. GW, XXII, 330–331.
27. GW, D, II, 233.
28. Closen, 91; Rochambeau, 55; Whitridge, 146.
29. Closen, 102.
30. Blanchard, *Journal*, 115–118; Chinard, *Washington*, 38; Dumas, *Memoirs*, I, 35; GW, XXII, 388; XXIII, 107n–108n.
31. Bourg, *Diary*, 302; GW, D, II, 237–239, 241–245.
32. Closen, 101; Rochambeau, 58–59.
33. GW, XXII, 186, 445; GW, D, II, 240, 248.
34. GW, XXII, 397; GW, D, II, 240.
35. GW, XXII, 450; GW, D, II, 249.
36. GW, XXII, 401; GW, D, II, 241.
37. Doniol, V, 522–523; F, V, 309; GW, XXIII, 193; GW, D, II, 253–254.

47: DOWN FORTUNE'S MAZES

1. GW, D, II, 252–253; Lafayette, *Letters*, 211.
2. GW, XXII, 501–502.
3. Blanchard, *Journal*, 127–128; GW, XXII, 396, XXIII, 6–7; GW, D, II, 256.
4. Blanchard, 129–130; GW, XXIII, 25; Whitridge, *Rochambeau*, 149.
5. GW, XXX, 26–27.
6. GW, XXII, 499–500.
7. GW, XXII, 474, 488.
8. Lafayette, 215.
9. GW, D, II, 256; Rochambeau, *Memoirs*, 62.
10. F, V, 316; Fleming, *Beat*, 100.
11. Whitridge, 208.
12. F, V, 316; GW, XXIII, 68, 72, 77, 85.
13. GW, XXIII, 71; GW, D, II, 258.
14. GW, XXIII, 12, 75 ff, XXX, 28.

15. Closen, *Journal,* 117; Trumbull, *Minutes,* 332.
16. GW, XXIII, 77; Lafayette, 221, 224.
17. F, V, 321.
18. Biron, *Memoirs,* 204; Closen, 121–123; F, V, 322; Grasse, *Correspondence,* 14; GW, XXIII, 87–88; Trumbull, 335.
19. F, V, 513.
20. Grasse, 9–14; GW, XXIII, 101.
21. GW, XXIII, 101–102; Grasse, 13.
22. Grasse, 10, 14.
23. Closen, 124; GW, XXIII, 89, 94–95.
24. GW, XXIII, 105; GW, *D,* II, 259; Trumbull, 333.
25. Trumbull, 333.
26. GW, XXIII, 109–110; Trumbull, 333.
27. *Va. Mag.,* LIII (1945), 89 ff.
28. Trumbull, 333.

48: WAR REDUCED TO CALCULATION
1. Coleman, *Tucker,* 70; F, V, 328.
2. Butler, *Journal,* 106; GW, XXIII, 115; GW, *D,* II, 260.
3. Larrabee, *Decision.*
4. Grasse, *Correspondence,* 33–34.
5. Grasse, 33; GW, XXIII, 119.
6. Grasse, 33.
7. Trumbull, *Minutes,* 333–334; Ward, *Revolution,* II, 884–885.
8. Custis, *Recollections,* 236; GW, XXIX, 474.
9. Bancroft, *Constitution,* II, 456.
10. GW, XXIII, 122–124, 162.
11. Trumbull, 334.
12. GW, XXII, 284, XXIII, 113.
13. GW, XXIII, 129, 132–133, 150.
14. Grasse, 44–47.
15. GW, XXIII, 136–139.
16. Grasse, 51–53.
17. GW, XXIII, 157.
18. GW, XXIII, 157; Thacher, *Journal,* 278.
19. F, V, 347; Trumbull, 334.
20. F, V, 513–514.
21. Closen, *Journal,* 156; GW, XXIII, 136.
22. F, V, 351; GW, XXIII, 161, 210, 213; GW, *D,* II, 262.
23. GW, XXIII, 162, 169, 187, 208, etc.
24. GW, XXIII, 179–187.
25. Closen, 156; Rochambeau, *Memoirs,* 69.
26. Thacher, 280.
27. F, V, 358–360; GW, *D,* II, 263.
28. Butler, 108; GW, *D,* II, 264; Thacher, 283.
29. Blanchard, *Journal,* 148.

30. Thacher, 284.
31. GW, XXIII, 210; Thacher, 283–284.
32. GW, XXIII, 210, 213; GW, *D,* II, 264.
33. F, V, 369; GW, XXIII, 228.
34. Thacher, 285; Williams, *Revolutionary,* 276.
35. F, V, 371–372; GW, XXIII, 228; GW, *D,* II, 266–267; Trumbull, 336–337.
36. Rochambeau, 71.
37. GW, XXII, 228; GW, *D,* II, 267–268.
38. Coleman, 74; Cornwallis, *Answer,* 197 ff, 206–208.
39. GW, *D,* II, 267.
40. Cornwallis, 205.
41. Cornwallis, 210.
42. F, V, 374–375.
43. Cornwallis, 214; GW, XXIII, 241.

49: THE WORLD TURNED UPSIDE DOWN
1. Cornwallis, *Answer,* 214–216; GW, XXIII, 236–237; GW, *D,* II, 268–269.
2. Coleman, *Tucker,* 76–77.
3. Cornwallis, 217, 221.
4. Cornwallis, 219, 223–224; GW, *D,* II, 218–219, 269; Kapp, *Steuben,* 461.
5. GW, XII, 14n.
6. Fleming, *Beat,* 321–322.
7. GW, XXIII, 311–312.
8. GW, XXIII, 239–240.
9. Cornwallis, 220–229; Lee, H., *Memoirs,* 371.
10. F, V, 386–389.
11. Closen, 153; Kapp, 462.
12. Blanchard, *Journal,* 152; Closen, 153; Fleming, 328–329.
13. Closen, *Journal,* 156.
14. Blanchard, 152; Dumas, *Memoirs,* I, 52–53; Rochambeau, *Memoirs,* 73.
15. Kapp, 462–463.
16. Blanchard, 152, 154; Bourg, *Diary,* 393; Scheer, *Rebels,* 495; Trumbull, *Minutes,* 337.

50: BUT THE WAR GOES ON
1. GW, XXIII, 242, 245.
2. GW, XXIII, 247.
3. GW, XXX, 26–27.
4. Rochambeau, *Memoirs.*
5. F, V, 515.
6. F, V, 513; GW, XXIV, 144 ff.
7. GW, XXIII, 190, 193–194.
8. GW, XXIII, 248–249, 250n; GW, *D,* II, 270–272.
9. GW, XXIII, 298n, 310.
10. GW, XXIII, 352.

51: VACATION WITHOUT REST

1. GW, XXIII, 286–287, 291, 295–297.
2. Custis to Martha Washington (10/12/81), Mount Vernon; GW, XXVII, 59.
3. GW, XXIII, 338, 340.
4. GW, XXXVII, 554–555.
5. F, V, 402; GW, XXVI, 42–44.
6. F, V, 409.
7. GW, XXIII, 352–353, XXIV, 139–144.
8. GW, XXIII, 348–350.
9. GW, XXIV, 495.
10. Sellers, *Peale*, 218–219.
11. *Freeman's Jour.*, Philadelphia, 1/9/82; GW, XXIV, 97; *Pa. Mag. of Hist. and Biog.*, LVI (1932), 135–136.
12. *Columbian Mag.*, I (1787), 391–392; Sonneck, *Hopkinson*, 106–110.
13. GW, XXIII, 347.
14. GW, XXIV, 2, 4.
15. B, VI, 273; GW, XXIII, 429, 458–461, XXIV, 2, 76.
16. GW, XXI, 262, 360n, XXIV, 71–73.
17. Burnett, *Continental*, 526–527.
18. GW, XXIV, 26, 39.
19. GW, XXIV, 180, 452.
20. GW, XXIV, 153.
21. GW, XXIV, 194 ff.
22. GW, XXIV, 139, 200.
23. Rochambeau, *Memoirs*, 86.
24. GW, XXIV, 408, 495.

52: THE BRINK OF THE ABYSS

1. GW, XXIV, 472, XXV, 21.
2. GW, XXIV, 471, XXV, 267–268.
3. GW, XXV, 17.
4. Humphreys, *Asgill*, v; Thacher, *Journal*, 313.
5. GW, XXIV, 145n, 146–147, 217, 220–221, 226, 364.
6. GW, XXIV, 219, 223, 306n; Humphreys, 13.
7. GW, XXV, 40, 112.
8. GW, XXIV, 218, XXV, 41, 222; Humphreys, 14, 28.
9. GW, VIII, 474.
10. GW, XXV, 222.
11. Humphreys, 29–30; Thacher, 319.
12. Humphreys, 31–32.
13. GW, XXV, 359–360; Humphreys, 13–15.
14. GW, XXV, 137–138, 198–199, 389, 420, 448.
15. GW, XXV, 121.
16. Chastellux, *Travels*, I, 281; GW, XXV, 101, 184, 247.
17. Humphreys, 15.

18. GW, XXVI, 250.
19. GW, XXIV, 488.
20. Burnett, *Continental*, 527–529; GW, XXV, 289, 431.
21. GW, XXIV, 285–286, 295.
22. Dumas, *Memoirs*, I, 58; GW, XXV, 50, 227, 349.
23. GW, XXIV, 289–290, 295–296.
24. GW, XXV, 269.
25. GW, XXVI, 184.
26. GW, XXV, 286, 461.
27. GW, XXV, 227–228.
28. GW, XXV, 229n.
29. GW, XXV, 430.
30. Burnett, 554–556.
31. Hamilton, *Papers*, III, 240.

53: THE ROAD TO DICTATORSHIP

1. GW, XXVI, 289.
2. GW, XIX, 132.
3. GW, XXVI, 276.
4. GW, XXIII, 419–421, 432, XXVI, 123.
5. GW, XXVI, 184.
6. Chastellux, *Travels*, I, 287.
7. GW, XXIV, 273n.
8. Fitzpatrick, *Himself*, 418; GW, XXIV, 272–273.
9. Burnett, *Continental*, 555.
10. Ferguson, *Purse*, 158.
11. Armstrong, *Review*, 29; Knox to McDougall (3/12/83), New-York Historical Society; Sparks, *Morris*, 240; Pickering, *Pickering*, I, 431–432.
12. Armstrong, 40n; Armstrong to Gates (5/30/83), New-York Hist. Soc.
13. GW, XXVI, 188n.

54: THE DEVIL'S WEB

1. GW, XXV, 269–270, XXVI, 29.
2. Chastellux, *Travels*, II, 513–514; GW, XV, 447.
3. GW, XXV, 279, XXVI, 7, 427–428.
4. Chastellux, II, 514; GW, XXV, 428–429.
5. GW, XXV, 20–21.
6. Whitridge, *Rochambeau*, 101.
7. GW, XXVI, 22, 27, 29, 137.
8. GW, XXV, 472.
9. *Journal Amer. Dental Assn.*, LIX (Sept. 1959).
10. GW, XXVI, 434, XXVII, 67–68; Bernhard Wolf Weinberger, "John Pierre Le Mayeur in America," *Dental Cosmos* (1934), 569–578.
11. GW, XXVI, 126–127.
12. GW, XXVI, 7, 18, 20, 29, 97, 99.
13. Hamilton, *Papers*, III, 253–255.

14. GW, XXV, 431n–432n.
15. GW, XXVI, 213–214; Pickering, *Pickering*, I, 409.
16. Armstrong to Gates (4/29/83), New-York Hist. Soc.
17. GW, XXVI, 186.
18. Ferguson, *Purse*, 160; GW, XXVI, 186, 188.
19. GW, XXVI, 185–188.
20. JCC, XXIV, 294–295.
21. GW, XXVI, 240.
22. JCC, XXIV, 295–297.
23. GW, XXVI, 211.
24. GW, XXVII, 269.
25. GW, XXVI, 213–218.
26. JCC, XXIV, 298–299; GW, XXVI, 213–218.
27. GW, XXVI, 208; Heath, *Memoirs*, 374.
28. GW, XXVI, 229n.
29. GW, XXVI, 222–229.
30. F, V, 435n; GW, XXVI, 222n; Shaw, *Journals*, 104.
31. Armstrong, *Review*, 43n; King, *Life*, I, 622.
32. Gates, Report (3/15/83), New-York Hist. Soc.; Pickering, I, 439.

55: A CLOUDED PARTING

1. GW, XXVI, 336.
2. GW, XXVI, 229–232.
3. GW, XXVI, 232–234.
4. GW, XXV, 361.
5. GW, XXVI, 293, 324.
6. Ferguson, *Purse*, 146 ff; Miller, *Hamilton*, 93.
7. GW, XXVI, 275; JCC, XXIV, 253, 269–270, 364–365.
8. Armstrong to Gates (4/29, 4/30/83), New-York Hist. Soc.; GW, XXVI, 472–478.
9. Drake, *Memorials*, 15–16; GW, XXIX, 113.
10. GW, XXVII, 196, 213–217, 400.
11. GW, XXVI, 78; Walter Stewart to Gates (6/20/83), New York Public Library.
12. Burke, *Cincinnati*, 3; Jefferson, *Writings*, I, 157.
13. GW, XXVI, 482–496; XXVII, 49–50.

56: THE EMPTYING STAGE

1. GW, XXVI, 336.
2. GW, XXVI, 298, 369.
3. GW, XXVII, 60, 70, 269.
4. Mount Vernon Ladies' Assn., *Report*, 1952, 29–32; Washington, *Account*.

5. Fitzpatrick, *Himself*, 528; Washington, *Account*, 122 ff.
6. F, V, 450; GW, XXVII, 66, 70, 99, 377, 501.
7. GW, XXVII, 188–190.
8. B, VII, 193 ff; GW, XXVII, 32 ff, 375.
9. *Pa. Mag. of Hist. and Biog.*, XXXVI (1912), 508.
10. B, VII, 292.
11. GW, XXVII, 127–129
12. B, VII, 292.
13. Dunlap, *Rise*, I, 253.
14. GW, XXVII, 146–147; *Republican Watchtower*, New York, 7/1/1806.
15. GW, XXVI, 374–398.
16. GW, XXVII, 16–18, 163, 411.
17. GW, XXVI, 419; XXVII, 138–140.
18. Millis, *Arms*, 42–45.
19. GW, XXVII, 58.
20. GW, XXVI, 297–298.
21. GW, XXVII, 89–90.
22. GW, XXVII, 294.
23. GW, XXVII, 155, 160–161, 215–219.
24. GW, XXVII, 232.

57: AN END AND A BEGINNING

1. GW, XXVII, 222–227.
2. F, V, 456; Pickering, *Pickering*, I, 488–491.
3. F, V, 459–461.
4. *New York Gazette*, 11/26/83.
5. *New York Gazette*, 12/3/83.
6. F, V, 466; Tallmadge, *Memoir*, 96–98.
7. *New York Gazette*, 12/6/83; Stiles, *Diary*, III, 101.
8. GW, XXVII, 285n.
9. B, VII, 399; GW, XXVII, 284–285; JCC, XXV, 820 ff; Steiner, *McHenry*, 69–70.
10. GW, XXVII, 288.
11. GW, XXVII, 340.
12. GW, XXVII, 347.
13. GW, XXVII, 317.
14. GW, XXVII, 288.

58: CINCINNATUS ASSAYED

1. Dupuy, *Compact*, 474–475; Thomas J. Fleming, "The Enigma of General Howe," *American Heritage*, XV (1964), 6–11, 96–103.
2. Chase, *Forefathers*, 113; GW, XXIX, 485.
3. Charles Carroll of Carrollton to Charles Carroll (10/23/77); GW, VI, 222, XV, 388, 399.
4. GW, XI, 194.
5. GW, XIII, 465.

6. GW, VIII, 443, XXIV, 225.
7. GW, XI, 3.
8. GW, XXXIII, 429–430.
9. GW, XXIX, 34–35, 148; Hughes, *Washington*, I, 6–7.
10. GW, XXXIV, 406.
11. GW, IX, 163.
12. GW, XI, 476, XXIX, 35.
13. Gouverneur Morris to John Marshall (6/26/1807), Library of Congress.
14. Lafayette, *Memoirs*, I, 20; Brissot de Warville, *Travels*, I, 370.
15. GW, IV, 240.
16. GW, XXV, 281, XXVIII, 97.
17. GW, XI, 431–432.
18. Abigail Adams, *Letters*, 15; Blanchard, *Journal*, 117; Ewing, *Journal*, 47.
19. GW, IV, 432.
20. Chastellux, *Travels*, I, 111.
21. GW, XII, 278, 343, 431.
22. GW, XXVII, 58.
23. F, F, 243–245; GW, XXVIII, 66, XXX, 11.
24. Earle, *Strategy*, 77; Whitridge, *Rochambeau*, 145.
25. GW, IV, 47.
26. GW, XIII, 15–16, XVIII, 510–511.
27. GW, XXVII, 269.
28. GW, XXVII, 12, 89.
29. GW, III, 422, 466.
30. GW, IV, 240, XI, 160, XIX, 422.
31. GW, XXX, 5.
32. GW, XI, 289, XXXV, 32.
33. GW, XXX, 395n.

Index

Clove, 211–212, 255, 348, 397
Cobb, David, 456, 493
Cochran, Dr. and Mrs. John, 351
Coit, Captain, 54
Colfax, William, 358
Colville, Thomas, 472
Comfort Sands & Co., 476, 483–484
Common Sense (Paine), 67–68
Concord, Battle of, 10–11
Concorde (ship), 436
Coney Island, 106
Connecticut, 11, 18, 29–30, 35, 51, 66, 96, 99, 118, 138, 261, 355–356
Confederation, Articles of, 273, 318, 475–476, 485, 488–489, 515
Constitution, Fort, 119
Continental Army: additional regiments, 163–164, 273, 356, 488; Adjutant General, 18, 102, 104, 194; artillery, 70, 73–74, 95, 98–99, 120, 164, 174, 177, 183, 185, 195, 203, 223, 293, 306, 449, 451 ff, 546n; bounties, 50, 67, 95, 134, 193–194, 272, 343, 520; cavalry, 140, 196–197, 219, 221, 224, 237, 284–285, 309, 369, 536; clothing and uniforms, 41, 49, 55, 134, 164, 214, 342, 344–345, 362, 434, 482–483; discipline, 34–35, 41, 61, 117–118, 132, 193; draft, 46, 56, 543n; drill, 214, 286–291, 294, 483, 539; engineers, 33, 45, 69, 92, 151, 164, 195, 246, 260, 434–435, 454 ff., 546n; enlistments, 46n, 54–56, 67, 83, 95, 133, 135, 145, 163–164, 173–174, 181, 296, 362, 396, 436, 439, long vs. short, 67, 94–95, 133–135, 193, 272, 309, 343; foreign volunteers, 194–196, 263, 268, 281, 283–285, 539; Flying Camp, 94, 103–104, 114, 144, 148; gunpowder, 33, 35–36, 69–70, 79, 83; Inspector General, 259, 262, 267, 280; Judge Advocate, 37; light infantry, 546; maps, 225; medical corps, 42, 81, 92–93, 99, 120, 133–134, 198–199; mobility, 116–117, 544; music, 203, 217, 283; mutinies, 356–357, 405–409, 518; officer corps, 34–35, 45, 55, 66, 133, 135, 145, 163–164, 194, 244, 342–344, 401, 539; pensions or half pay, 342–343, 405, 488, 512; plundering, 132, 354; quartermaster, 37, 120, 253, 256, 284, 293, 297, 367–369; requisitioning supplies, 227,

251, 262, 276, 355–356, 476; riflemen, 35, 45, 64, 76, 81, 95, 108, 160, 185, 197, 214, 247, 546; sanitation, 28, 30, 41; shoes and lack of, 227, 230, 252, 261–262, 281, 345; spears, 36, 197; women, 120–121, 217
Continental Congress, 20, 25, 35, 37, 42, 51, 55, 92–93, 99–100, 120, 162, 181, 199, 210, 212, 220n, 227, 229–230, 238, 248, 255–256, 327, 329, 339–340, 355, 368, 375, 378, 380, 405–406, 475–476; Washington as member, 10–13, 51; commissions Washington, 9, 12–15; relations with Washington, 14–16, 27, 29–30, 34, 54, 56, 63, 65–70, 80, 90–97, 100, 113, 116–117, 119–120, 128, 132, 134–136, 145, 148–149, 159, 161–164, 166, 178, 184, 192, 194–197, 199–201, 210, 215, 236, 241, 243–245, 251, 262, 272–276, 284, 292–293, 309, 313–314, 323, 330, 333, 335–344, 346, 352–353, 355–357, 362, 365–366, 369, 398, 472, 475, 479–481, 490, 511–514, 518 ff., 521, 540; Conway Cabal, 257, 262, 264–266, 271–276, 288; Newburgh Addresses, 475, 486–495, 500 ff.; Washington returns commission, 525–527; role summarized, 487–488, 547–548
Conway Cabal, 241–245, 247–251, 253–259, 262–281, 294, 314, 375, 492, 527, 539, 551
Conway, Thomas, 195–196, 233, 241–245, 257–259, 262–276, 286–287, 314, 539
Cornell, Ezekiel, 422
Cornwallis, Lord, 159–160, 180, 182, 184, 187, 211, 224, 231, 236–237, 250, 264n, 359, 369–371, 419–420, 428, 431–433, 438, 440–441, 444, 451 ff, 540
Coudray, Philip du, 195
Cowpens, Battle of, 420
Craik, James, 265–266
Crawford, William, 198
Creditors, federal, 489, 492–493, 501, 512, 547
Cromwell, Oliver, 537
Croton River, 386
Crown Point, 100
Custis, Eleanor Parke, 446n
Custis, George W. P., 185n
Custis grandchildren, 445, 472

Canada, 267, 329–334; Washington's envoy to French officers, 325, 327–330, 365–367, 370, 373, 427; and Arnold's treason, 384, 386–389, 391, 394; southern command, 410, 414–415, 420, 431, 438, 440–441, 443–444, 448, 462
Lafayette, Marquise de, 351–352
Lamb, John, 386, 390n
Lancaster, Pa., 266
Langdon, John, 9
Langdon, Samuel, 28
Laurens, Henry, 257, 264–266, 271, 275, 314, 319, 330–332, 341n
Laurens, John, 252, 257, 264–265, 287, 291, 341, 359–360, 409, 412, 419, 432, 460–461, 477, 539
Lauzun, Duc de, 431, 433–434, 443
League of Armed Neutrality, 374n
Lee, Arthur, 338
Lee, Billy, 60
Lee, Charles, 44–45, 191, 241, 266–267, 548; character, 18, 23, 166–167; before Revolution, 17: career before White Plains, 17–18, 22–23, 29, 33, 35, 62, 65–66, 90, 94, 99, 104, 117, 136, 138–139, 537; insubordination, 144–145, 152, 157, 159–160, 163, 165–167, 171–172, 273, 293; captured, 167, 293–294, 314; in Monmouth campaign, 293–294, 296–316, 539
Lee, Henry (Light Horse Harry), 197, 229, 350, 352, 369, 461, 531, 533
Lee, Richard Henry, 34, 36–38, 100, 244–247, 255–259, 266, 268, 275, 292, 422, 492
Lee, Robert E., 197
Lee (ship), 53–54
Lee, Fort, 119, 136, 138, 144, 147–154, 159, 161n, 212; captured, 156, 204
Lewis, George, 58
Liffenwell, Ebenezer, 132–133
Lincoln, Benjamin, 223, 225, 352, 359–360, 433–434, 449, 460–461, 464, 475, 485, 518
Lippincott, Richard, 478
Lisle, Romand de, 195
Lispenard, Leonard, 25
Livingston, Henry Beekman, 306
Livingston, Robert R., 381, 475
Livingston, Mrs., 351
Locke, John, 402
Long Island, 65, 90, 96, 103, 106–118, 122, 150, 192, 317
Long Island Sound, 137–138, 211
Louis XVI, 290, 360, 481–482, 514
Lovell, John, 247–248, 251, 274–275, 422
Luzerne, Chevalier de la, 370, 383, 390, 428
Lynch, Thomas, 55n
Lynnhaven Bay, 449

McCurtin, Daniel, 76
McDougall, Alexander, 275n, 486, 492–493
McHenry, James, 302, 318, 384, 387, 412, 498–499
McKonkey's Ferry, Pa., 173–174, 178
McWilliams, William, 248
Madison, James, 486, 494, 547
Magaw, Robert, 149–151, 153
Maguire, Patrick, 202
Maine, 51
Manley, John, 53–54
Marblehead, Mass., 53, 114, 174
Marie Antoinette, 371, 431
Martha's Vineyard, 328
Martin's Tavern, 222
Maryland, 19, 94, 111, 130, 225, 265, 277, 423, 445
Massachusetts Committee of Safety, 25, 158
Massachusetts Congress, 27–28, 36, 41, 43
Massachusetts General Court, 83
Massachusetts Legislature, 82, 514n
Mattapony, 454
Matthews, David, 92
Maxwell, William, 221–222, 225
Mayeur, Jean Pierre Le, 499–500
Mazarin, Jules, 314
Mediterranean Sea, 324
Mercer, Fort, 246, 249–250
Mercer, Hugh, 149, 184–185, 187
Middlebrook, N.J., 204, 302, 306, 335
Mifflin, Thomas, 20, 22, 37, 122, 159, 248, 253–259, 264, 266, 271, 273–275, 284, 292–294, 367–368, 526–527, 539
Mifflin, Fort, 246, 250
Miles, Samuel, 109, 112
Militia, 14, 28, 30, 34, 63, 91, 94–95, 117–118, 133–135, 145, 147, 159, 162, 165, 172–173, 180–181, 185, 205, 209–210,

Ogden, Aaron, 392–393
Ogden, Mathias, 486, 492, 502
O'Hara, Charles, 464
Ohio River, 423
Oswald, Eleazer, 306
Overpeck Creek, 157n

Paine, Thomas, 67–68, 171, 256, 261, 519–520, 547
Paoli Massacre, 229
Paramus, N.J., 318
Paris, 485–521
Parliament, 10, 141, 286, 374n
Parsons, Samuel Holden, 123
Passaic, Falls of, 318
Patterson, James, 102–103
Patterson, N.J., 318n
Paulus Hook, N.J., 350
Peace negotiations, 398, 423, 500, 511, 516, 521–522
Peale, Charles Willson, 161–162, 474
Peale, James, 162
Peekskill, N.Y., 204, 383
Peg Mullen's Beefsteak House, 9
Pennsylvania Assembly, 56
Pennsylvania Constitution, 378
Pennsylvania Council of Safety, 191
Pennsylvania Gazette, 289
Pennsylvania Journal, 189
Pennsylvania Legislature, 261
Pennsylvania line, mutiny, 397, 405–407
Pennsylvania Provincial Congress, 20
Pennsylvania Supreme Executive Council, 357, 377–378
Pennypacker's Mills, Pa., 237–238
Penobscot, Me., 468, 477
Perth Amboy, *see* Amboy
Peter, Richard, 269, 494
Philadelphia, Pa., 37–38, 58–60, 106, 159, 198, 319, 329, 395, 441; Washington at, 9–22, 93–94, 212–214, 217–218, 333–334, 377, 442, 472; menaced by British, 143–144, 149, 154, 157–189, 199, 204–230, 253, 255–256; captured and occupied, 230–231, 237, 246, 250–251, 256, 261, 285, 292, 295–297
Phoenix (ship), 98–99, 244n
Pickering, Timothy, 194, 211, 225–226, 229, 233–234, 277, 283, 368–369, 408, 507, 522

Piscataway, 220n
Pittstown, N.J., 165–166
Plamunkey River, 454
Poland, 284
Pomeroy, Seth, 30
Pompton, N.J., 408
Poor, Enoch, 310–311
Port Tobacco, Md., 265
Portland, Me., 54
Portsmouth, N.H., 65
Portsmouth, Va., 410, 414, 420, 433, 438, 441
Powel, Mrs. Samuel, 336
Prevost, Mrs. Theodosia, 318
Princeton, Battle of, 166, 183–189, 261, 263
Princeton, N.J., 161, 165, 173, 181, 253, 407; Continental Congress at, 518
Prisoners of war, 47n, 103, 136, 164, 293
Privateers, 52–54, 193n
Providence, R.I., 172
Pulaski, Casimir, 284–285
Purple Heart, 483
Putnam, Israel, 18, 29, 76, 107–108, 121, 129, 149, 173, 237–238, 243, 247, 249n
Putnam, Fort, 113

Quakers, 20, 228, 245, 251, 285
Quebec, 51–53, 66–67, 92, 329, 375, 477
Quibbletown, N.J., 206
Quincy, Josiah, 92

Rall, Johann Gottlieb, 176n
Randall's Island, 121
Raritan River, 159–161, 317
Reading, Pa., 230, 248, 256, 259
Reed, Joseph, 19–20, 22, 36–37, 56, 59, 102, 129, 148, 157–160, 162, 166, 194, 197, 203, 215, 253, 357, 377–379, 395, 397, 538–539, 541, 550
Reed, Mrs. Joseph, 160, 397
Rhea, David, 304, 306, 308
Rhode Island, 11, 35, 172, 292, 324–327, 330, 333, 341n, 381–382, 486, 490, 514
Richelieu, Cardinal, 314
Richmond, Va., 421
Riedesel, Baroness, 490
Ringwood, N.J., 408
Rittenhouse, David, 499
Robertson, Archibald, 75, 183

POLITICAL: and American Monarchy, 63, 490–492; and civil war, 64–65, 93, 100, 163, 166–167, 171, 276, 294–296, 338, 378; and confederation, 273, 318, 475–476, 486, 488–489, 503, 514–515, 520–521; on constitutions, 94, 514, 521; and continental vs. local thinking, 37, 135, 163–164, 192, 272–273, 294–295, 355–356, 422–423, 487–489, 514–515; financial education, 339–342, 357–358, 397, 476, 548; and foreign affairs, 289, 292, 329–334, 432; immigrants, recent, 333n; independence, 67–68, 96–97, 276; preparation for presidency, 331–332, 338, 342, 355–356, 370, 397, 409, 475, 491, 520, 537, 540, 546–552; as symbol of cause, 14, 42, 274–277; and taxation, 340–341, 375, 476, 490; and Tories, 63–66, 79, 82, 91–92, 95–96, 136, 191–192, 276, 284–288, 295, 377, 460, 478, 534–535; and western territories, 422–423, 520

Washington, John Augustine, 83, 94, 149, 153, 313, 332, 338

Washington, Lawrence, 418

Washington, Lund, 37, 58, 81–82, 119, 131–132, 171, 336–337, 341–342, 418, 420–421, 499–500

Washington, Martha, 4, 9, 14, 20, 58–60, 87, 93, 95, 197, 202, 282–283, 285, 291, 336–337, 344, 346, 348, 358–359, 432, 445–447, 471–472, 475, 477, 497, 500n, 516–517, 549; character, 58–60, 282–283

Washington, Mary, 337, 417, 471

Washington, Samuel, 90–91

Washington Elm, 28

Washington, Fort, 76, 119, 138–139, 141, 143–145, 147–149; captured, 149–153, 195, 204, 255, 538, 544

Washington's Testament, 403–404, 514–515

Watertown, Mass., 27, 41

Watkins, Mrs., 318

Wayne, Anthony, 222, 229, 236, 245, 275, 298, 308–309, 311–312, 315, 348–349, 405–407, 494

Webb, Samuel B., 73–74, 355

Weedon, George, 223

Welch Mountains, 34

Welches Tavern, 222

West Florida, 333n

West Indies, 295, 324, 328, 331, 333n, 346, 351, 365, 428, 484

West Point, 90, 141, 301, 348, 354, 364, 408, 438, 520, 545; Arnolds betray, 381–390; described, 384

Westchester County, N.Y., 192

Wethersfield, Conn., 428–430

Wharton, Thomas, 243–244

Wheatley, Phillis, 63

White, Philip, 479

White Plains, N.Y., 138–142, 158, 160, 165, 544–545; Battle of, 139–142

Wilkinson, James, 248, 259, 265, 269, 274

Williamsburg, Va., 19, 431, 447–448, 450, 470

Wilmington, Del., 216, 218, 224, 292

Wilmington, N.C., 450, 468–469, 475

Woodford, William, 310

Worcester Township, Pa., 232

Wyoming Valley, 329

Yagers, 160

Yellow fever, 519–520

York, Pa., 248, 267, 294

York River, 449–450, 452, 454, 459

Yorktown: campaign planned, 428–432, 436–437; march, 436–451, 546; siege, 451–458, 540; surrender, 458–464, 481, 487; credit, 467–468